FROM COMMONWEALTH TO POST-COLONIAL

FROM COMMONWEALTH TO POST-COLONIAL

edited by
Anna Rutherford

Dangaroo Press

ACKNOWLEDGEMENTS

I would like to thank all the organizations that provided grants so that the conference could take place, the University of Kent at Canterbury for providing a venue, and the organizers of the conference, in particular Lyn Innes, for making the event such a success.

For their help towards the preparation of this book I would like to thank Tim Caudery, Signe Frits and Kirsten Holst Petersen.

I would also like to thank Ratna Raghya Dhulsada for granting permission to use his painting on the cover. In this connection I would like to thank Shubhangi Raykar who kindly presented me with the painting and first introduced me to the work of the artist and provided me with the information about it and the Tarpa Dance.

Finally I would like to thank The Commonwealth Foundation which provided a subsidy towards the publication of this volume.

COVER: 'Tarpa Dance' by Ratna Raghya Dhulsada.

© Dangaroo Press 1992

First published in 1992 by Dangaroo Press
Australia: G.P.O. Box 1209, Sydney, New South Wales, 2001
Denmark: Geding Søvej 21, 8381 Mundelstrup
UK: 80 Kensington Road, Earlsdon, Coventry

ISBN 1-87-1049-42-3

For 'Inoke Falatau
who has done so much to promote
the literatures of the Commonwealth countries.

Never again will a single story be told as
though it were the only one.

John Berger

Foreword

This volume contains papers given at the Silver Jubilee conference of the Association for Commonwealth Literature and Language Studies, which was held at the University of Kent, Canterbury, in 1989. Choosing these thirty-seven papers out of the almost two hundred papers presented was not an easy task. In the finish the decision was made to include papers which dealt specifically with the over-all theme: 'Trans – Formations: Cross Cultural Communities, New Forms and Functions of Commonwealth Literature'. There were several papers which would have been included if they had not already been published or promised to another journal for publication. And there were many more which we would have included if there had been space.

I had also hoped to to include work by the creative writers, but again space did not permit this. One of the outstanding features of the conference was the writers' sessions. Very often the creative reading sessions are placed at the end of the day as though they were peripheral to the conference. Lyn Innes counteracted this by placing the writers' reading and discussion sessions at key times during the day, and these sessions were amongst the highlights of the conference.

To comment on each of the papers would be to make the book almost twice as long again. Hence my decision to concentrate in my introduction on the major issues raised by the keynote speakers, issues which are taken up in the papers included. These papers have been split into sections under different sub-headings. That does not mean that they are separate sections, complete in themselves. I believe it is, however, appropriate that in a volume dealing with post-colonial literature and criticism, there should be an overlapping of sections and themes – of borders.

ANNA RUTHERFORD

Introduction: The Essential Heterogeneity of Being

In his opening address, Edward Said chose to concentrate on the overall theme of the conference, 'Transformations, Cross-cultural Communities and New Forms of Commonwealth Literature', and he pointed first of all to the crucial role played by literature in the re-establishment of a national, cultural heritage, in the re-instatement of native idioms and in the re-imagining and re-figuring of local histories, geographies and communities. 'Literature', he said, 'not only mobilized active resistance to incursions from the outside, but also created massively as the shaper, creator, agent of illumination within the realm of the colonized'. Those listening could sit back with a degree of confidence and congratulate themselves on what had been achieved. But Said brought us back from our complacency by going on to discuss much more disturbing matters, the problems with which we are now faced, and with which many of the papers in this volume are concerned.

The Nation as Imagined Community: Negative Nationalism

> 'Where will the unemployed go? They march to the sound of a patriotic drum'
> Wilson Harris: *The Infinite Rehearsal*

The central issue that both Edward Said and Wilson Harris take up is the question of nationalism and the dangers inherent in it. 'Few people', remarks Said, 'during the exhilarating heyday of decolonization and early Third World Nationalism were watching or paying close attention to what would later happen to the presence of a carefully nurtured nativism in the anti-colonial ranks'. In the early days of decolonization there was an understandable euphoria, and a writer such as Chinua Achebe saw his role as that of a teacher whose task it was to help his society gain belief in itself. An easy way of achieving self confidence is to indulge in a certain degree of self-glorification. Achebe was not overly worried about this, as he saw it as a necessary step towards psychological and cultural emancipation.

> You have all heard of the 'African personality'; of African democracy, of the African way to socialism, of negritude, and so on. They are all props we have fashioned at different times to help us get on our feet again. Once we are up, we shan't need any of them any more. But for the moment it is in the nature of things that we may

need to counter racism with what Jean-Paul Sartre has called an anti-racist racism, to announce not just that we are as good as the next man but that we are much better.[1]

Achebe himself never made use of these props; in fact, his fame rests to a large extent on his courage in giving a balanced view of traditional Igbo society in *Things Fall Apart*. By 1966 he was already being overtly critical of nationalist politics in *A Man of the People*. However, like so many others, he failed at that time to see what Fanon saw, namely the dangers posed by an untutored national consciousness to a great socio-political movement like decolonization. One writer who did see this danger was Soyinka, who made it the main theme in the play *A Dance of the Forests*, which he was commissioned to write for the official celebration of Nigeria's independence in 1960. In the play there is a celebration similar to the Independence celebration, and the historian Adenebi sums up the point of both celebrations and at the same time sounds a warning: 'The accumulated heritage — that is what we are celebrating. Mali. Chaka. Songhai. Glory. Empires'.[2]

The concepts of national identity and the relations of power in the postcolonial state, with special reference to Africa, are discussed in detail in Simon Gikandi's paper. The first section of his paper deals with writers like Achebe and Ngugi who, though they were aware that the nation in Africa was an invented community, also believed that it was a concept which could be discarded when the time was ripe. As already mentioned, it did not take long for the period of disillusionment to set in, and with it came the recognition that 'the nation is not the manifestation of a common interest but a repressor of desires'. The second section of Gikandi's paper explores this idea in a detailed analysis of Nuruddin Farah's *Maps*, a work in which Farah foregrounds the textuality of Somalia and challenges the artificial constructions of the official versions of history and the identities fabricated by the oppressors. 'Somalia,' said Farah, 'was a badly written play.... Siad Barre was its author.'

Simon Gikandi noted in his paper that international capital continues to oppress many people in the 'third world', but, from the perspective of the governing classes in those countries, this is considered development. Said and Gikandi deal specifically with the 'third world' countries, but the phenomena they speak about is not restricted to these countries.

Just as the old imperialism was intent on repressing other discourses, so too is the new nationalism, not only in Africa, but in the settler colonies as well. I am referring in particular to the Anglophone nationalism in the white settler countries where elected leaders raise the flag of nationalism to what Leslie Monkman calls 'the comfortable mythologies of WASP possession'.[3] Monkman is referring to Canada and in particular to Michael Ondaatje's rejections of these mythologies in his novel *In the Skin of the Lion*. But such mythologies are not confined to Canada. In Australia and

New Zealand the prior right of the indigenous dispossessed peoples to their land and the role played by the migrant population in the creation of the wealth of the country (little of which is returned to them) is generally unacknowledged.

A similar situation exists in the literature of these countries, where until recently there has been little recognition of the voices of the indigenous, the migrant or the woman. It is not an accident that post-colonialism and feminism often join forces. The power politics of gender and patriarchy (both Colonialist and neo-Colonialist) are discussed in particular by Boehmer and Dodgson.

Those familiar with Australian literature will be aware of Russel Ward's construction of the 'true' Australian, presented in his book *The Australian Legend*.[4] This led not only to the idea of what a true Australian was, but also to the idea of what was authentic Australian literature. Cultural nationalism becomes an ally to political nationalism, and both act in the same way. First one distinguishes, creates, fabricates a pattern, and then one goes on to exclude all those who do not fit it. What we have is the replacement of one monocentric order with another. These new canons can be as destructive as the old (for a detailed discussion of this subject see the section 'Powerful Canons'). One of the consequences in Australia was a rejection of Patrick White's work by the Australian nationalist critics on the grounds that it was un-Australian.[5] Stan Parker and the bush in *Tree of Man* are condemned. Why? Stan because he had no mate. I am not sure of what crime the bush was guilty.

But the more sinister political aspect of negative nationalism has manifested itself on two recent occasions in Australia. During the bi-centennial John Williamson's country and western song 'True Blue' was adopted by the Labor government and given multi-media exposure to promote a sense of national pride, a unity and the idea that the real Australian is the Australian 'hero' of the period of the 1890s, Russel Ward's Australian, the 'true blue' Australian who is Anglo/Celt, male, enjoying male corporate life in the outback, an image which excludes Aborigines, women and people of other ethnic origins. I asked Aboriginal country and western singer Roger Knox what he thought of 'True Blue'. His reply: 'Shit, I don't go along with that. Who's blue? I'm black.We don't want to be blue. I'm true but they can't accept that fact, that I'm true. "True Blue", that doesn't do anything for me. Dundee and all that shit [*Crocodile Dundee*].'[6]

Even more recent is Australia's Prime Minister Paul Keating's rejection of the country's Imperial ties and the call for Australia to be a republic, demands with which I am in full accord. I am not questioning that Keating's desire for a republic is genuine. But behind his promotion of nationalism is also his desire for increased ratings in the polls – here he has been successful. It is also designed to hide the fact that Australia is in its worst economic recession since the 'twenties and 'thirties and that he,

Paul Keating, is one of the major architects of it. In a recent article, Martin Woollacot pointed out that:

> Keating is a founder member of what John Pilger called 'The Order of Mates', the eighties coalition of Labour [sic] political fixers and the Australian new rich. That was in the days when Keating seemed to have unlocked the doors to unprecedented growth, before his boom became a burst. The price paid was to open the country to unprecedented foreign economic penetration and control, something which the Australian Labour [sic] Party had once set itself not only to limit but to reverse. The man so concerned that Australian sovereignty not be hindered by residual British links is actually the architect not only of recession but of a probable irretrievable loss of Australian economic sovereignty to foreign banks, firms, and deracinated Australian magnates, of whom the most typical is Rupert Murdoch.[7]

Whilst I am aware that the Australian and African situations are not parallel, I have placed stress on this negative aspect of nationalism in the white settler dominions in order to correct the idea, too often presented in the media and held in the Western world, that it is only in the 'Third' world that one finds politicians ready to sell their countries' wealth in order to maintain their own privileges.

The Writer as Witness

As the state threw up borders, the smugglers, Said said, found a way to cross these borders and subvert. He drew a parallel between these smugglers and the writers in exile, like Salman Rushdie, Timothy Mo, Michael Ondaatje and Nuruddin Farah, to name but a few, who challenge the borders and images controlled by a few multi-nationals. It is of course not only the writers in exile who challenge the accepted histories and canons, there are many writers in their own communities who do the same (Erna Brodber, Margaret Atwood, Thea Astley, Timothy Findlay), but for the moment I would like to concentrate on the role of the writer in exile.

There are conflicting opinions about what the role of such a writer should be. Some demand that they write about the plight of their own people and present them always in a positive light. To do otherwise is to be a traitor to the cause, in much the same way that male society in Africa regarded the protests of the women writers as betrayals of African nationalism. Most writers have, however, resisted the pressure put on them by their own communities and certain critics to compromise their work in such a way.

In an essay entitled 'Minority Literatures in a Multi-Cultural Society', Salman Rushdie states: 'I can't imagine myself as being in any way prescriptive about how a writer in a multi-cultural, not to say multi-racial environment ought to respond to that environment.[8]

Under pressure from the homogeneous majority he sees the danger of new borders being erected by the minorities. Rushdie goes on to justify his defence of Hanif Kureishi's *My Beautiful Launderette*, which had been attacked by the Asian community for presenting a negative view of Asians and providing food for white racist propaganda.

> The reason for my defence is that there is nothing in it that is imaginatively false, and because it seems to me that the real gift which we can offer our communities is not the creation of a set of stereotyped positive images to counteract the stereotyped negative ones, but simply the gift of treating black and Asian characters in a way that white writers seem very rarely able to do, that is to say as fully realized human beings, as complex creatures, good, bad, bad, good. To do anything less is to be kept captive by the racist prejudices of the majority, and that complexity is what Kureishi's script strives for.[9]

A Dual Agenda

In an article entitled 'Modernism's Last Post', Stephen Slemon states that the post-colonial writer and critic has a 'dual agenda to continue the resistance to (neo) colonialism through a deconstructive reading of its rhetoric *and* to achieve and reinscribe those post-colonial social traditions that in literature issue forth on a thematic level, and within a "realist problematic", as principles of cultural identity and survival'.[10]

To have confidence in one's culture is a privilege. Nayantara Sahgal knew that 'Gunga Din' was a white man's fable and had nothing to do with India. But there were many in the position of the fictional Ella O'Grady, in Erna Brodber's novel *Myal*, a half black, half white child who could present a perfect recitation of Kipling's 'Take up the White Man's Burden' and for whom the literary text was more real than her everyday world. In his discussion of the dual agenda Slemon mentions that one role of the writer is to challenge and interrogate the discourses of power and to explain and show how that 'little scrap [England] filled the text books and ruled the world'.[11] But there is also the recuperative, reinscribing agenda. It is with this dual agenda that Wilson Harris, the most important critic in the field of post-colonial studies, is concerned.

The theme of closure, the dangers posed by the demand for heterogeneity and the hegemonic idea of national purity, has from the beginning been a constant in the work of Wilson Harris. 'Concepts of invariant identity', argues Harris, 'function in the modern world as a block imperative at the heart of cultural politics. The oppressor makes this his or her banner. The oppressed follow suit. *Such is the tautology of power*'. Instead of these 'invariant identities' he proposes a syncretic identity, made up of all the cultures and races which have taken part in the history of a particular place. Along with Abel Martin he believes in 'the essential heterogeneity of being' and rejoices in 'the ecstasy of complex counterpoint between partial origins' (compare Said's statement that he did not believe 'that global and contrapuntal analysis' could be modelled on the notion of a symphony; 'rather we have to do with atonal ensembles'.)

Harris is one of the very few post-war novelists who has offered a third, genuinely original alternative to the contemporary fictional output which arranges itself around the two poles of social realism and the playful experimentation of post-modernism. In the novels he has written over the past thirty years he has repeatedly explored the capacity of the creative imagination to meet the present-day crisis of civilization, and he has always proclaimed his belief in the 'revisionary potential of the imagination'. It is this belief that has led him to criticize post-modernism and de-construction. 'My approach differs rather from de-construction theory that is so fashionable though I find it inadequate and something of a game that masks nihilism and difference between cultures for the sake of difference.'[12] He also compares it to a game for a dictatorship of technologies aligned to sophistry and nihilism. In his opinion, 'cross culturalism needs to break nihilism'.

The final section of this volume, New Synthesis: Transformative Images, explores the debate between post-modernism and post-colonialism and deals with writers and critics who, as Gareth Griffith says, 'embrace the complex and syncretic nature of the post-colonial world and recognize that syncreticity is neither a threat to identity nor a denial of the uniqueness of post-colonial reality'.

My choice of title for the volume is my indication that we have come a long way since that first meeting in Leeds, with its demands that the Commonwealth writer be an internationalist who, though he might come from Wagga Wagga or Enugu, must also be comprehensible in Heckmondwike and Helmsby. I have often wondered how the writer in London or New York would react to the demand that s/he must also be comprehensible to readers in Murrurundi or Kumasi. The internationalist myth has long since been challenged and shown up for what it is, as has the Great Tradition, though anyone listening to Frank Kermode's keynote address at the first ESSE conference, held at the University of East Anglia in 1991, would have felt some shivers running down their spines.

There is reason for celebration, but we must not become complacent. My choice of cover is there to remind us all of the need for constant renewal.

ANNA RUTHERFORD

NOTES

1. Chinua Achebe, 'The Novelist as Teacher', in *Hopes and Impediments: Selected Essays* (London: Heinemann, 1988), p. 30. One can perhaps also note that the theme for the first ACLALS conference held in Brisbane in 1968 was 'National Identity'.
2. Wole Soyinka, *A Dance of the Forests* (Oxford: Oxford University Press, 1963), p. 8.
3. Leslie Monkman, 'Canada', in Bruce King, ed., *The Commonwealth Novel Since 1960* (London: Macmillan, 1991), pp. 33-49.
4. Russel Ward, *The Australian Legend* (Melbourne: Oxford University Press, 1958).
5. T. Inglis Moore, *Social Patterns in Australian Literature* (Sydney: Angus and Robertson, 1971), pp. 222-23. See in particular Chapter 9, 'The Creed of Mateship', and Chapter 10, 'Radical Democracy', pp. 256-57.
6. Roger Knox in Anna Rutherford, ed., *Aboriginal Culture Today* (Sydney: Dangaroo Press, 1988), p. 240.
7. Martin Woollacott, 'The Empire Strikes Back', *Guardian Weekly*, 10 May 1992, p. 12. I am grateful to my colleague Dale Carter for drawing my attention to this article.
8. Salman Rushdie, 'Minority Literatures in a Multi-Cultural Society', in Kirsten Holst Petersen and Anna Rutherford, eds., *Displaced Persons* (Aarhus: Dangaroo Press, 1988), p. 33.
9. Ibid., p. 44.
10. Stephen Slemon, 'Modernism's Last Post', *Ariel*, Vol. 20, No. 4, 1989, p. 3. For further and recent discussions of post-colonialism and post-modernism, see, in particular, Stephen Slemon and Helen Tiffin, eds., *After Europe* (Coventry: Dangaroo Press, 1989), also published as a special issue of *Kunapipi*, Vol. XI, No. 1, 1989, and Ian Adam and Helen Tiffin, eds., *Past the Last Post* (Calgary: University of Calgary Press, 1990). This is an extended version of the issue of *Ariel* mentioned in this note.
11. Nayantara Sahgal, 'The Schizophrenic Imagination', in this volume, p. 33.
12. Letter from Wilson Harris to Anna Rutherford, dated 12 July 1990, in reference to his article on *Myal* in *Kunapipi*.

A note on the cover, 'Tarpa Dance':

The tarpa dance is a distinct feature of the Warlis, an aboriginal tribe inhabiting the west coast region, mainly of Maharashtra but partly also of Gurjarat. The tarpa is a wind instrument played only by the Warlis. On the full-moon night during the harvest the Warlis come together, form a ring with the tarpa player in the centre, and dance until the small hours of the morning. At this dance the young men and women choose their life partners and start living together. They can marry whenever they have money and the inclination, but they have to marry before their first child gets engaged in the same manner and starts living with his or her life partner.

Contents

POLITICS AND LITERATURE:

POWERFUL CANONS:

NEW STRATEGIES/TRANSFORMATIVE IMAGES:

KEYNOTE ADDRESSES

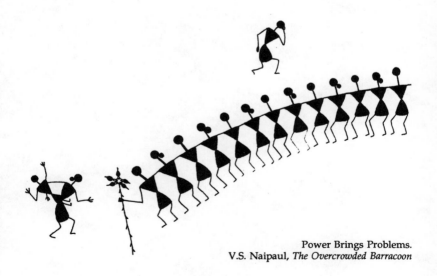

Power Brings Problems.
V.S. Naipaul, *The Overcrowded Barracoon*

EDWARD W. SAID

Figures, Configurations, Transfigurations

It is possible to discern a salutary and invigorating quality in the very notion of Commonwealth Literature today (now that Britannia no longer rules the waves) that is most pleasant to note. Yet this isn't either to mock or patronize the utopian lilt in the idea sustaining the theme of these meetings as it is given in their overall title: 'transformations, cross-cultural communities and new forms of commonwealth literature.' For in fact the most powerful aspect of all these new communities and forms that we both celebrate and study is that they are for the most part post-colonial and in a few instances actively anti-imperial. None of us would disagree, I think, if in the first instance we were to interpret the great mass of recent non-European literature as expressing ideas, values, emotions formerly suppressed, ignored, or denigrated by, and of course in, the well-known metropolitan centres. For in the decades-long struggle to achieve decolonization and independence from European control, literature has played a crucial role in the re-establishment of a national cultural heritage, in the re-instatement of native idioms, in the re-imagining and re-figuring of local histories, geographies, communities. As such then literature not only mobilized active resistance to incursions from the outside but also contributed massively as the shaper, creator, agent of illumination within the realm of the colonized.

What gives the actuality of Commonwealth literature its special force is that of all languages today English is, properly speaking, *the* world language. I say this as someone who grew up outside the Commonwealth orbit and, still outside the Commonwealth, who now lives at the centre of what has become the new English-speaking empire. This gives a particular and perhaps even eccentric perspective on what to an outsider like myself appears as the privileged historical centrality of English within the Commonwealth grouping. I do not for a moment wish to minimize the hardships, violence, or horrors endured by enormous numbers of people on whom the rule of English was impressed with sometimes catastrophic force, even as English also brought the many advantages of a prosperous culture. But I do think that it might serve a purpose here to begin by talking about the relationship between the dominance of English on the one hand and, on the other, resistances to it that come from cultural spheres and practices where English is either adjacent to the main English speaking dominions, or is still confined to specialized status. This will enable us the better to understand the place of English in the global environment. Let me impose a little more autobiography on you. I grew up in what in effect were two British colonies, Palestine and Egypt, but which remained principally non-British culturally as well as politically. In addition to interests requiring a commanding British presence there, Egypt and Palestine were of importance to the French, were technically within the Ottoman Empire until the end of World War One, and of course went their own ways after World War Two. One can get some sense of the dynamics of that now almost forgotten pre-war world from Olivia Manning's *Levant Trilogy*, a somewhat more lurid version of which (mainly concentrated in Alexandria, for whom better guides are E.M. Forster, Cavafy and Ungaretti) turns up in Durrell's *Alexandria Quartet*. Very recently, a young English writer Anthony Sattin in his book *Lifting the Veil* produced an elegant history of British society in Egypt from the middle of the eighteenth through the middle of the twentieth centuries.

From such works one concludes that the kind of culture embodied in the notion of a British Commonwealth surrounded, but remained confined to minority status within, the Arab world. One result of this is that unlike the Caribbean, India, or Anglophone Africa, the Arab world that fell under British control for at least a century and a half never produced any literature to speak of in English. This is strikingly different from the experience of the French Muslim-Arabic imperial realm, where a thriving Francophone literature continues until this day, with eminent writers and critics in it like Ben Jalloun, Kateb Yacine, Mohammed Dib, and el Khatibi who are true cultural amphibians at home both in metropolitan France and in their own societies. In the world in which I was a boy, English was either the language of the ruler, of tiny administrative elites, or of even smaller Christian minorities. Thanks to the researches of a number of historians, we have come to understand the dynamics of national and Islamic resistance by which British institutions (which were unlike their French counterparts and not designed for the assimilation of natives) made their selective incursions on native society, and yet were kept at bay while schools of native reformers harnessed tribes, guilds, fraternities and schools to the mobilizing cause of what would later become full-fledged independence.

Jump now to the middle 1980s. Asked a few years ago by a national university in one of the Gulf States to visit there for a week I found that my mission was to evaluate the English program at the university and perhaps offer some recommendations for its improvement. I was flabbergasted to discover that in sheer numerical terms English attracted the largest number of young people of any department in the university. I was disheartened to find, however, that the curriculum was divided about equally between what was called linguistics (that is, grammar and phonetic structure) and literature. The literary courses were, I thought, rigorously orthodox, a pattern followed pretty much, I think, even in older and more distinguished Arab universities like those of Cairo and Ain Shams. Young Arabs read up dutifully on Milton, Shakespeare, Wordsworth, Austen and Dickens as they might have studied Sanskrit or medieval heraldry; no emphasis at all was placed on the relationship between English and the colonial processes that brought the language and its literature to the Arab world. I could not detect much interest, except in private discussions with a few faculty members, in the new literatures of the Caribbean, Africa or Asia. The result seemed to me an anachronistic and odd confluence of rote learning, uncritical teaching, and (to put it kindly) very haphazard results.

On the other hand I found out two additional things of some concern to me as a secular intellectual and critic. The reason for the large numbers of students taking English was given to me quite frankly by a somewhat disaffected instructor: they take English in droves, he said, because many of them proposed to end up working for the airlines, or for banks, in which English was the worldwide *lingua franca*. This all but terminally consigned English to the level of a technical language almost totally stripped not only of expressive and aesthetic characteristics but also denuded of any critical or self-conscious dimension. You learned English to use computers, respond to orders, transmit telexes, decipher manifests and so forth. That was all. The other (to me alarming) thing I discovered is that English such as it was existed in what seemed to be a seething cauldron of Islamic revivalism. While I was there, for instance, elections to the university senate were being contested; everywhere I turned, Islamic slogans were plastered all over the wall and, I later found out, the various Islamic candidates won a handsome, if not ultimately decisive, plurality. In Egypt where I observed much the same thing earlier this year, it is amusing to mention that at a lecture to the English Faculty at Cairo University, after having spoken for an hour about nationalism, independence and liberation as alternative cultural practices to imperialism, I was asked about 'the theocratic alternative'. (I had mistakenly supposed she was asking about 'the Socratic alternative', and was put right very quickly.) The question came to me from a well-spoken young woman whose head was covered by a veil and who obviously was asking the question because religion constituted the main alternative concern to her as a citizen in a largely secular society. I had simply overlooked *that* in my heedless anti-clerical and secular zeal. I nevertheless proceeded boldly to my attack!

Thus the very same English whose users in the Commonwealth can aspire to literary accomplishments of a very high order and for whom, in the notion of Ngugi wa Thiong'o, a critical use of the language might permit a decolonizing of the mind, coexists with very different new communities in a less appealing new configuration. On the one hand in places where English was once present as the language of ruler and

administrator its residue today is a much diminished presence. Either it
is a technical language with wholly instrumental characteristics and features; or it is a foreign language with various implicit connections to the
larger English-speaking world, but where its presence abuts on the much
more impressive, much more formidable emergent reality of organized religious fervour. And since the language of Islam is Arabic, a language
with considerable literary community and hieratic force, English seems to
me to have sunk quite low, and to a quite uninteresting and attenuated
level.

To gauge this new subordination in an era where in other contexts English has acquired remarkable prominence and many interesting new communities of literary, critical and philosophical practice, we need only
briefly recall the quite stunning acquiescence of the Islamic world to the
over-all prohibitions and proscriptions as well as threats pronounced
against Salman Rushdie because of *The Satanic Verses*. That the novel dealt
with Islam in English and for what was believed to be a largely Western
audience was its main offense. I certainly do not mean that the entire
Islamic world acquiesced, but that its official agencies, spokespeople,
secular as well as religious, took what appeared to be a united stand
either blindly rejecting or vehemently refusing to engage with a book
which the enormous majority had never read. (The Khomeini threat of
course went a good deal further than mere rejection but the Iranian position was a very isolated one.) On the other hand it is equally important
to note two things about the English-speaking world's reaction to *The
Satanic Verses*. One was the relative (although with the usual caution and
squeamishness) unanimity of condemnations of Islam marshalled in a
cause that appeared to most of the writers and intellectuals at the time
both safe and fashionable. As for the many writers either murdered, imprisoned, or banned in places where either American allies like Israel or
irremediably anti-American 'terrorists' like Libya, Iran, and Syria *could*
have been condemned for such reprehensible practices, nothing was said.
And second of all, there seemed to be little further interest either in the
Islamic world as a whole or in the conditions of authorship there once the
ritual phrases in support of Rushdie and denunciatory of Islam were pronounced. Whereas in fact I had hoped that some greater enthusiasm and
energy be expended in dialogue with those considerable literary and intellectual figures from the Islamic world (Mahfouz, Darwish, among others)
who occasionally defended (and occasionally attacked) Rushdie in much
more trying circumstances than those obtaining where writers protested
Rushdie's fate in Greenwich Village or Hampstead.

None of this, however, takes very much away from my main point here,
which is that there are highly significant *deformations* within the new communities that now exist alongside and partially inside the recently coherent outlines of the world-English group, a group that includes the heterogeneous voices, various languages, hybrid forms that give the Common-

wealth its distinctive and still problematic identity. Thus the emergence since the late '70s of a startlingly sharp construction called 'Islam' is, I think, one such deformation; others are 'Communism', 'Japan', and the 'West', (there are still others) each of them possessing styles of polemic, a whole battery of discourses, and an unsettling profusion of opportunities for dissemination. Only if we try to map and register the vast domains commanded by these gigantic caricatural essentializations can we more fully appreciate and interpret the relatively modest gains made by smaller literate groups that are bound together not by insensate polemic but by affinities, sympathies, and compassion.

Few people during the exhilarating heyday of decolonization and early Third World nationalism were watching or paying close attention to what would later happen to the presence of a carefully nurtured nativism in the anti-colonial ranks, how it would grow and grow to inordinately large proportions. I will concede that it is quite easy now to play the role of a retrospective Cassandra, but one still ought to be a little surprised that all those nationalist appeals to pure or authentic Islam, or to Africanism, negritude, or Arabism, were joined by so many without sufficient consciousness that precisely those ethnicities and spiritual essences would come back to exact a very high price from their successful adherents. To his credit Fanon was one of the few to remark on the dangers posed by an untutored national consciousness to a great socio-political movement like decolonization. Much the same could be said about the dangers of an untutored religious consciousness. And so the appearance of various mullahs, colonels, and one-party regimes who pleaded national security risks and the need to protect the foundling revolutionary state as their platform, foisted a new set of problems onto the already considerably onerous heritage of imperialism.

In intellectual and historical terms I do not think it is possible to name many states or regimes that are exempt from active participation in the new post-colonial international configuration. National security and identity are the watchwords. Along with the authorized figures of the ruler, the pantheon of national heroes and martyrs, the established religious authorities, the newly triumphant politicians seemed to require borders and passports first of all. What had once been the imaginative liberation of a people – Aime Cesaire's 'inventions of new souls' – and the audacious metaphoric charting of spiritual territory usurped by colonial masters, were quickly translated into and accommodated by the world system of barriers, maps, frontiers, police forces, customs and exchange controls. The finest, most elegiac commentary on a dismal state of affairs was provided by Basil Davidson in the course of a memorial reflection on the legacy of Amilcar Cabral (published in the Winter 1986 issue of *Race and Class*). Rehearsing the questions that were never asked about what would happen after liberation, Davidson concludes that a deepening crisis brought on neo-imperialism and put petty-bourgeois rulers firmly in command. But,

Davidson continues, this brand of 'reformist nationalism continues to dig its own grave. As the grave deepens fewer and fewer persons in command are able to get their own heads above the edge of it. To the tune of requiems sung in solemn chorus by hosts of foreign experts or would be *fundi* of one profession or another, often on very comfortable (and comforting) salaries, the funeral proceeds. The frontiers are there, the frontiers are sacred. What else, after all, could guarantee privilege and power to ruling elites?' (p. 43). Chinua Achebe's most recent novel *Anthills of the Savannah* is a compelling survey of this enervating and dispiriting landscape.

Davidson goes on to rectify the gloom of his own description by pointing to what he calls the people's 'own solution to this carapace accepted from the colonial period'.

> What the peoples think upon this subject is shown by their incessant emigration across these lines on the map, as well as by their smuggling enterprises. So that even while a 'bourgeois Africa' hardens its frontiers, multiplies its border controls, and thunders against the smuggling of persons and goods, a 'peoples' Africa works in quite another way. (p. 44)

The cultural correlative of that audacious but often extremely costly combination of smuggling and emigration is, of course, familiar to us as exemplified by that new group of writers referred to as cosmopolitan in a perceptive analysis by Tim Brennan (*Race and Class*, Summer, 1989). And the subject of crossing borders as well as the representative deprivations and exhilarations of migration have become a major theme in the art of the post-colonial era.

Although it is possible to characterize these writers and themes as comprising a new cultural configuration and to point with considerable admiration to regional achievements not only in Europe but also in the Caribbean, in Africa, North and South America and the subcontinent I believe the configuration ought to be looked at from a somewhat less attractive but, in my opinion, more realistic and political point of view. While we should quite correctly admire both the material as well as the achievements of, say, Rushdie's work, as part of a significant formation within the general field of Commonwealth Literature, we should be just as willing at the same time to note with what it is encumbered or, to put it more precisely, how the particularly aesthetically valuable work of our time is strikingly also a part of threatening, or coercive, or deeply anti-literary, anti-intellectual formations. 'There is no document of civilization which is not at the same time a document of barbarism.' Those other darker connections, those sinister relationships and partnerships alluded to by Benjamin are where in political and cultural terms today's interesting conjunctures are to be found. They beseech our individual and collective critical work no less than the hermeneutic and utopian work we feel better about doing when we read, discuss and reflect on valuable literary texts.

Let me be more concrete. It is not only tired, harassed, and dispossessed refugees who cross borders and attempt acculturation in new environments, it is also the whole gigantic system of the mass media that is ubiquitous, slipping by most barriers and settling in nearly everywhere. Anyone who has read the work of Herbert Schiller and Armand Mattelart is aware of the practically total encroachment of a handful of multi-nationals on the production as well as the distribution of journalistic representations; Schiller's most recent study attempts to describe how it is that all departments of culture, not just those having to do with news, have been invaded by or enclosed within the ever-expanding circle of this relatively small number of privately held corporations.

There are too many consequences of this for me to list and discuss here, so I shall limit myself to two or three things. First is that the international media system has in actuality done what idealistic or ideologically inspired notions of collectivity or totality aspire to do. I mean by this that when, for instance, we speak about and research a theoretical entity called Commonwealth or world literature in English, our efforts remain pretty much at the level of (in Lukacian terms) a putative wholeness; for example, discussions of magic realism in the Caribbean and African novel allude to and in the most successful cases sketch the possible contours of a post-modern field that binds these works together. Yet we know at the same time that the works and their authors and readers remain concretely specific to and articulated in their own local circumstances, circumstances that are usefully kept separate when we analyze the contrasting conditions of reception in the metropolitan centre (London or New York) on the one hand, the peripheries on the other. Yet compared to the way in which the four major Western news agencies operate, or the mode by which television journalists from CNN or NBC select, gather and re-broadcast pictorial images from India or Ethiopia, or the way programs like *Dallas* and *Dynasty* work their way through even the Lebanese civil war, we not only have in the media system a fully integrated practical network, but there also exists within it a very efficient *mode of articulation* knitting the world together.

I know of no detailed theoretical balance sheet that lays out what the power of this gradually universal system of articulation truly is. I do know, however, that a monument to an attempt by the less developed world to regulate and in other ways to influence it can be found in the McBride Report on the New World Information Order. But that was in the days before UNESCO was first attacked and then re-structured to suit the interests of the major Western powers. Thus the NWIO has ended and market forces rule unchecked. Reinforcing this system is the map of patronage and monetary power elucidated in the North-South Report (the so-called Brandt Commission) in which the old imperial demarcations have reappeared both in the form of the predictable economic discrepancies as well as in the lamentably skewed interrelationships between the debtor nations of the peripheries and the creditor nations of the metropolis.

Lastly, the world system map articulating and producing culture, economics and political power along with their military and demographic coefficients, has also developed an institutionalized tendency to produce out-of-scale transnational images that are now in the process of re-orienting international social discourses and processes. Take as a case in point the emergence of terrorism and fundamentalism during the 1980s. For one, you can hardly begin (in the public space provided by international discourse) to analyze political conflicts involving Kurds and Iraqis, or Tamils and Sinhalese, or Sikhs and Hindus – the list is infinitely extendable – without having resort to categories and images of terrorism and fundamentalism. For another, these images derive entirely from the concerns and from the intellectual factories in metropolitan centres like Washington and London. Moreover, they are fearful images that seem to lack discriminate contents or definitions, and they signify moral power and approval for whomever uses them, moral defensiveness and criminalization for whomever they designate.

During the past decade these two gigantic reductions have mobilized armies as well as dispersed communities. Neither the official Iranian reaction to Rushdie's novel, nor the unofficial or semi-official enthusiasm of expatriate Islamic communities in the West, nor the public and private expressions of Western outrage are intelligible, in my opinion, without reference to the minute logic of articulations, reactions and large-scale movements enabled by the overbearing system I am trying to identify. For in the relatively open environment postulated by communities of readers interested in emergent post-colonial Commonwealth or Francophone literature, the underlying configurations on the ground are directed and controlled not by processes of hermeneutic investigation, nor by sympathetic and literate intuition, nor by informed reading, but by much coarser and instrumental processes whose goal is the mobilization of consent, the eradication of dissent, the promotion of an almost literally blind patriotism. By such means is the governability assured of large numbers of people whose potentially disruptive ambitions for democracy and expression are held down (or narcotized) in mass societies.

The fear and terror induced by the over-scale images of terrorism and fundamentalism – call them the figures of an international or transnational imaginary made up of foreign devils – contribute to hastening the individual's subordination to the dominant norms of the moment. This is as true in the new post-colonial societies as it is in the West. Thus to oppose the abnormality and extremism embedded in terrorism and fundamentalism – I provide what is only a small degree of parody with my example – is also to uphold the moderation, rationality, executive centrality of a vaguely designated 'Western' (or otherwise local and patriotically assumed) ethos. The irony is that far from simply endowing the Western ethos with the confidence and secure 'normality' we tend to associate with privilege and rectitude, this dynamic imbues 'us' with a righteous anger and defensiveness in which all 'others' are seen as enemies, bent on destroying our civilization and way of life. A perhaps exaggerated instance of what I mean is to be found in a *Wall Street Journal* editorial in May 28, 1988 by the eminent Orientalist Bernard Lewis. Addressing the simmering controversy at Stanford University and elsewhere concerning changes in the reading list of courses on Western civilization, Lewis notes that to tamper with these venerable canons of great books is in fact to threaten 'the West' with a good deal more than a modified reading list containing black or female writers. It is, he says portentously, no less than to threaten us with the return of the harem and polygamy, with child marriages, with slavery and the end of political freedom, self-consciousness, and the disinterested pursuit of truth. Only the West, according to Lewis, abolished slavery on its own – one would have thought that slave revolts added some measure of persuasion – abolished polygamy on its own, studied itself and other societies for no other reason than the purest scientific curiosity untainted by profit or the exercise of power.

What I have rapidly sketched here furnishes, I think accurately, a sense of how these patterns of coercive orthodoxy and self-aggrandizement further strengthen the hold of unthinking assent and unchallengeable doctrine. Their slow perfection over time and after much repetition is answered, alas, with corresponding finality by the designated enemies. Thus Muslims or Africans or Indians or Japanese, in their idioms and within their own, constantly threatened local enclosures, attack the West, or Americanization, or imperialism with little more attention to detail or to critical differentiation, discrimination and distinction than is lavished on them by the West. This cannot unfortunately stop or inhibit an ultimately senseless dynamic. For to the extent that what we might call the border wars have aims, those aims are wholly impoverishing. One must either join the primordial or constituted group; or one must as a subaltern Other accept inferior status; or one must fight to the death.

To characterize what I have been calling border wars as a regime of essentializations – Africanizing the African, Orientalizing the Oriental, Westernizing the Western, for an indefinite time and with no alternative because African, Oriental, Western essences can only remain essences – immediately raises the question of what resists this pattern, and the systems that serve it. One obvious instance is identified by Immanuel Wallerstein as what he calls anti-systemic movements whose emergence is a consequence of historical capitalism. There have been enough cases of these late-coming movements in recent times to hearten even the most intransigent pessimism: the democracy movements on all sides of the socialist divide, the Palestinian *intifada*, various social, ecological and cultural movements throughout North and South America. Yet few of these movements seem (to me at least) to be interested in, or have the capacity and freedom to generalize beyond their own regionally local circumstances. If you are part of a Philippine, or Palestinian, or Brazilian oppositional movement you are necessarily circumscribed by the tactical and logistical requirements of the daily struggle. But, on the other hand, I do think that there is developing here, if not a general theory, then a common discursive readiness or, to put it in territorial terms, an underlying world map for efforts of this kind. Perhaps we can start to speak of a common counter-articulation, a phrase which best catches this somewhat elusive oppositional mood and its emerging strategies.

But what new or newer kind of intellectual and cultural politics does this call for, what important transformations and transfigurations are there in our ideas of such traditionally and eurocentrically defined identities as the writer, the intellectual, the critic and so forth? Because English is a world language and because the logics of borders and of warring essences are so totalizing, we should begin with acknowledgments of a world map without divinely or dogmatically sanctioned spaces, essences, or privileges. It is necessary therefore to speak of our element as secular space and humanly constructed and interdependent histories that are fundamentally knowable, but not through grand theory or systematic totalization. These formulations sound much more impressive and ponderous than they really are. I am trying to say that human experience is finely textured, dense, as well as accessible enough *not* to need the assistance of extra-historical or extra-worldly agencies to illuminate or explain it. What I am talking about is thus a way of regarding the whole world we live in as amenable to our investigation and interrogation quite without appeals to magic keys, or to special jargons and instruments, or to curtained-off practices. As one example of how we would proceed having acknowledged these things, there is the pattern implicit in Hobsbawm and Ranger, *The Invention of Tradition*, which suggests that it is a coherent intellectual undertaking to consider that all parts of human history are available to understanding and elucidation because they are humanly constructed and designed to accomplish real talks in the real world. History and geography are susceptible of inventories in other words.

What this and, to mention other examples, Martin Bernal's *Black Athena*, or *Subaltern Studies*, or Coll's and Dodd's anthology *Englishness*, or Paulin Hountoudji's *Sur la 'Philosophie Africaine'* all suggest is a different paradigm for humanistic research than those that have reigned for about a century now. The scholar in these innovative works is frankly engaged in the politics and interests of the present, engaged with open eyes, rigorous analytic energies and with the decently social values of someone whose main concern is not the survival of a disciplinary fiefdom or guild but the improvement and non-coercive enhancement of life in a community struggling among other communities. One must not, however, minimize the inventive excavations that constitute the centre of such work. No-one here looks for uniquely original essences, either to restore them or to set them in a place of unimpeachable honour. The study of Indian history is viewed by *Subaltern Studies* as an ongoing contest between classes and their disputed epistemologies; similarly Englishness for the contributors to the Coll and Dodd volume is not given before history, any more than Attic civilization in Bernal's important study can be extracted from history and made easily and simply to serve as an ahistorical model for superior civilizations.

Nor is this all. The conception of history enabling such work is that official, orthodox, authoritatively national and institutional versions of history tend principally to designate provisional and highly contestable attempts to freeze these versions of history into identities for use. Thus the official version of British history embedded, say, in the durbars arranged for Queen Victoria's visit to India in 1872 pretend that there is an almost mythical longevity to British rule over India; traditions of Indian service, obeisance and subordination are implicated in these ceremonies so as to create the image of an entire continent's trans-historical identity pressed into compliance before the image of a Britain whose own constructed identity is that it has and must always rule both the waves and India. Whereas these official versions of history attempt to capture it for, in Adornian terms, identitarian authority, the disenchantments, disputatious and systematically sceptical investigations in the innovative work I have cited submit these fabricated identities to a negative dialectic which dissolves them into variously constructed components. What matters a great deal more than the stable essence or identity kept in currency by an official discourse is the contestatory force of a historical method whose material is made up of disparate, but intertwined and interdependent, and above all, overlapping streams of historical experience.

A major set of corollaries derives from this. For if the chief, most official, forceful, and coercive identity is the State with its borders, customs, ruling parties and authorities, and if that is questioned, then it must also be the case that other similarly constructed identities need to be similarly investigated and interrogated. For those of us involved in literature, our education has for the most part been organized under various rubrics – the creative writer, the self-sufficient and autonomous work, the national literature, the separate genres – that have acquired almost fetishistic presence. Now it would be insanity to argue that individual writers and works do not exist, that French, Japanese, and Arabic are really the same thing, or that Milton, Tagore and Carpentier are only trivially different variations on the same theme. Neither would I want to be understood as saying that an essay about *Great Expectations* and *Great Expectations*, the novel that Dickens wrote, are the same thing. But I do want to be understood as saying that a focus on identity need imply neither the ontologically given and eternally determined stability of that identity, nor its uniqueness, its utterly irreducible character, its privileged status as something total and complete in and of itself. I would much prefer to interpret a novel as the selection of one mode of writing among many others, and the activity of writing as one social mode among several, and the category of literature as something created, made to serve various worldly aims. Thus the focus that corresponds with the destabilizing and investigative attitudes I have mentioned in connection with active opposition to states and borders is to look at the way a work, for instance, begins *as* a work, begins *from* a political, social, cultural situation, begins *to do* certain things and not others.

Yet the modern history of literary study is strictly bound up with the development of cultural nationalism, whose aim was first to distinguish the national canon and then to maintain it in a place reserved for eminence, authority and aesthetic autonomy. Even where discussions concerning culture in general seemed to rise above national differences in deference to a universal sphere, it is very apparent that hierarchies (as between European and non-European cultures) and ethnic preferences were held to. This is as true of Matthew Arnold as it is for twentieth century cultural and philological critics whom I revere – Auerbach, Adorno, Spitzer, Blackmur. For them, their culture was in a sense the only culture. The threats against it were largely internal, like fascism and communism, so that what they upheld after a long period of siege, was European bourgeois humanism. Neither the ethos nor the rigorous training required to instal that *Bildung* and the extraordinary discipline it demanded has survived, although occasionally one hears the accents of admiration and retrospective discipleship without anything resembling work of the order of *Mimesis*. Instead of European bourgeois humanism, the basic premise of what literary scholars now do is provided by the residue of nationalism with its various derivative authorities, in alliance with professionalism, which divides material into fields, sub-divisions, specialties, accreditations and the like. In so far as it has survived, the doctrine of aesthetic autonomy has dwindled to the formalism associated with one or another professional method like structuralism, deconstruction, etc.

A look at some of the fields that have arisen since World War Two, and especially as a result of the newer non-European nationalist struggles with which I began these remarks, reveals a different topography and a different set of imperatives. Most students and teachers of non-European literatures today must take account of the politics of what they study right at the outset; one cannot postpone discussions of slavery, colonialism, racism, in any serious investigations of modern Indian, African, Latin American, Caribbean and Commonwealth literature. Nor strictly speaking is it intellectually responsible to discuss any of these literatures without specific reference to their embattled circumstances either in post-colonial societies or as subjects taught in metropolitan centres where, for example, the study of what are marginalized and/or subjugated literatures is confined to secondary spots on the curricular agenda. By the same token, discussion of literature today cannot hide inside positivism or empiricism and offhandedly require the weapons of theory. On the other hand I think it is a mistake to try to show that the 'other' literatures of Africa and Asia, with their more obviously worldly affiliations to power and politics, can be studied respectably, that is, as if they were in actuality as high, as autonomous, as aesthetically independent and satisfying as French, German, or English literatures. The notion of black skin in a white mask is no more serviceable and dignified in literary study than it is in politics. Emulation and mimicry never get one very far.

Contamination is perhaps the wrong word to use here, but some such notion – of literature as hybrid and encumbered, or entangled with a lot of what used to be regarded as extraneous elements, strikes me as *the* essential idea adequate for the revolutionary realities that face us today, in which the contests of the secular world so provocatively inform the texts we both read and write. Moreover I believe that we can no longer uncomplainingly afford conceptions of history that stress linear development or Hegelian transcendence, any more than we can accept geographic or territorial assumptions assigning centrality to the Natopolitan world, and ontogenetic peripherality to the non-Western regions of the world. If configurations like Commonwealth or world literature are to have any meaning at all it is therefore because by their existence and actuality in the late twentieth century they first testify to the contests and continuing struggles by virtue of which they have emerged not only as texts but as experiences, and second, because they interact ferociously not only with the whole nationalist basis for the composition and study of literature but also with the lofty independence and indifference with which it has become customary Eurocentrically to regard the metropolitan Western literatures.

What this means for Commonwealth no less than for English, French or American literatures classically differentiated is that once we accept the more actual configuration of literary experiences overlapping with one another and, interdependent despite national boundaries and coercively legislated national autonomies, history and geography are transfigured into new maps, new and far less stable entities, new types of connections. Exile, far from being the fate of those nearly forgotten unfortunates who have been dispossessed and expatriated, becomes something closer to a norm, an experience of crossing boundaries and charting new territories in defiance of the classic canonic enclosures, however much the loss and sadness of exile may also need acknowledgement and registering. Thus changed models and types jostle the older ones. The reader and writer of literature – which itself loses its perdurable forms and accepts the testimonials, revisions, notations of the post-colonial experience, including underground life and prison – no longer needs to tie him or herself to an image of the poet or scholar in isolation, secure, stable, national in identity, class, gender, or profession, but can think and experience with Genet in Palestine or Algeria, with Tayib Saleh as a black man in London,

with Jamaica Kinkaid in the white world, with Rushdie in India and
Britain, and so on.

I suppose what I am getting at is how we might expand the horizons
against which the questions of *how* and *what* to read and write are both
posed and answered. To paraphrase from a remark made by Auerbach in
one of his very last essays, our philological home is the world, and not the
nation or even the individual writer. For those of us who are professional
students of literature, for whom the literary life is principally teaching and
research, there are a number of quite astringent things to take account of
here, at the risk both of unpopularity and accusations of megalomania. For
in an age of the mass media and what has been called the manufacture of
consent it is little short of Panglossian to assume that the careful reading
of a relatively small number of works designated as humanistically, pro-
fessionally, or aesthetically significant is much more than a private activity
with some slender public consequences. Texts are protean things; they are
tied to circumstances and to politics both large and small, and these require attention and critique. No-one can take stock of everything of course,
just as no theory can possibly explain or account for the connections between texts and societies. But to read and write texts cannot ever be neutral activities: there are interests, powers, passions, pleasures entailed no
matter how aesthetic or entertaining the work. Media, political economy,
mass institutions: in fine, the tracings of secular power and the influence
of the State are now part of what we call literature. And just as it is true
that we cannot read literature by men without also reading literature by
women – so transfigured has been the shape of literature – it is also true
that we cannot deal with the literature of the peripheries without also
attending to the literature of the metropolitan centres.

Instead of the partial analysis offered by the various schools of national
or systematically theoretical approaches, I propose finally the contrapuntal
lines of a global analysis, in which texts and worldly institutions are seen
working together, in which Dickens and Thackeray as London authors are
read also as writers informed constitutively by the colonial enterprises of
which they were so aware, and in which the literature of one Commonwealth is involved in the literatures of others. Separatist or nativist enterprises strike me as exhausted, since the ecology of the new and expanded
meaning of literature that I have been discussing cannot at all be attached
only to one essence, or to the discrete idea of one thing. I do not think,
however, that global and contrapuntal analysis can itself be modelled (as
earlier notions of comparative literature were modelled) on the notion of
a symphony; rather we have more to do with atonal ensembles, and with
such spatial or geographical and rhetorical practices as inflections, limits,
constraints, intrusions, inclusions, prohibitions, all of them tending toward
elucidations of a complex and uneven topography. While it remains of
value in the work of a gifted critic, the intuitive synthesis of the type
volunteered by hermeneutic or philological interpretation (whose proto-

type is to be found in Dilthey) strikes me as the poignant restoration of a serener time than ours.

This brings us round in the end to the question of politics. No country is exempt from the debate about what is to be taught, written or even read. I've often felt envious of theorists for whom either a radical scepticism or deferential reverence before the status quo have been real alternatives. I don't feel them to be, perhaps because my own situation prevents any such luxury, any such detachment and satisfaction. Yet I do believe that some literature is actually good, and that some is of a bad quality, and I remain as conservative as anyone when it comes to, if not the redemptive quality inherent in reading a classic rather than staring at a TV screen, then the potential enhancement of one's sensibility and consciousness by it, and by the exercise of one's mind in dealing with it. I suppose the issue reduces itself to what the relatively humdrum and pedestrian daily work of what we do as readers and writers is really about, if on the one hand professionalism won't serve and on the other a belief in waiting for apocalyptic change won't either. I keep coming back – simplistically and idealistically – to the notion of opposing and alleviating coercive domination, transforming the present by trying rationally and analytically to lift some of its burdens, situating the works of various literatures with reference to each other and to their historical modes of being. What I am really saying is that readers and writers in the configurations and by virtue of the transfigurations taking place around us are now in fact secular intellectuals with the archival, expressive, elaborative and moral responsibilities of that role.

WILSON HARRIS

The Fabric of the Imagination

The fabric of the imagination! What is this fabric of the imagination? Such a
notion arguably implies that there has been a genesis of the imagination
somewhere within the interstices of unrecorded time, that the unique –
indeed inimitable – force of such a genesis imbues the human psyche with
flexible and far-flung roots in all creatures, all elements, all worlds and
constellations, all sciences, all spaces susceptible to visualisation.

Alas, we have been conditioned to freeze such an awe-inspiring and
wonderful notion of the genesis of the imagination into an obsession with
binding and homogeneous archetype. Cultural homogeneity tends to
extrapolate frail genesis, the frail, alien beginnings of consciousness, into
an unchanging sanction of identity. Thus pure cultures, so-called, tend to
fear or scorn what is mixed or apparently impure. Such fear or scorn was
directed at the early Christian gnostics because they challenged the
ground of an absolute imprint or invariant code of identity. And this in
the age of Constantine which stood so close to pagan perspectives.

Concepts of invariant identity function in the modern world as a block
imperative at the heart of cultural politics. The oppressor makes this his
or her banner. The oppressed follow suit. *Such is the tautology of power.*
There is comfort in this, no doubt, for those who command the destinies
of the human race (or those who aspire to occupy the centre, and claim
they are the establishment); no comfort whatever for those who descend
into themselves and seek to breach a one-track state of mind – seek to perceive that every window of changelessness that a culture constructs anew
brings back into focus the participation of a *fallible* humanity.

Alas, fallibility is a heresy in the mind of the ruler and the aspiring ruled
alike; fallibility is swiftly eclipsed in favour of hubris (or the sophisti-
cations that mask the paranoid anxieties of hubris). There follows a series
of manoeuvres by which humanity (all parties claim to work for humanity) reinforces a bias, reinforces its deprivations into a self-righteous cult,
a self-righteous polarisation, a self-righteous ghetto.

A culture, for instance, that has suffered grave disadvantages tends to
build on its humiliations as the everlasting model of experience, tends to
invest in a vocabulary that impoverishes being, tends to build on the way
it has been circumscribed by history.

The fascination with authoritarian character that held the Russian masses
spell-bound in the wake of the Russian Revolution, the ease with which

Stalin rose to power, the ease with which Third World regimes are susceptible to repetitive coups or the suppression of opposition, is rooted, I think, in levels of deprivation that are lifted into an institutional or sovereign imprint to sanction a block imperative.

It is ironic that deprived societies everywhere endorse the panoply of changing technologies; they stand confused, even as they do so, by changes in global environments, polluted seas and rivers, endangered species and forests, and so on; confused, even somewhat appalled perhaps, yet their entrenchment in binding archetype is so fixed that a *resistance* to re-visionary potential in texts of reality seems wholly natural within the very body of unnatural crisis that affects our civilisation. True, that crisis becomes a fashionable topic; the mechanics of intellectual protest is set in gear against a state of malaise that everyone is told by science exists. But the message, so to speak, comes home to prosperous societies, and societies that aspire to prosperity, as if it were unreal and distanced from a necessity for penetrative vision through surfaces of existence we have long taken for granted.

Such distance from a penetrative and complex vision settles in the universal unconscious and gnaws at the heart of cultures, to breed nihilism and mass media escapism in the arts of the world. In the degree to which one clings to a faith in what I have called 're-visionary potential within texts of reality', a current may be invoked in the fabric of the imagination that runs much deeper than the language of the so-called imperialist exploiter by which so-called subject peoples have been conditioned. It runs much deeper than this syndrome and trauma, for I am not at all engaged in a politics of protest against the language of the so-called imperialist master. History within my mixed antecedents, across conflicting generations, has brought the supreme blessing of a language I genuinely love. A living language is a medium for which one must be profoundly grateful.

English, in which I write my novels, is my native language *not* because of historical imposition or accident but because of numinous proportions that sustain originality within a living text. I do not believe any area of the world is historyless or a product of absolute historical accident. There are complex flaws in all cultures that led to the breakdown of homogeneous societies on every continent and to the dangers at the heart of the modern world, dangers as well as far-flung, regenerative, cross-cultural possibility...

There are hidden numinous proportions within the mechanisms of colonialism and post-colonialism. Such numinous proportions throw a different, inner light on the mould of accident to which some sociologists or historians may cling. They give to the imagination a memory that seems to belong to the future, as though the genesis of the imagination is ceaselessly unfinished and within it incalculable rhythms and incantations have their roots in antiphony and response from buried voices of lost antecedents (never entirely lost because they belong to the memory of the future).

When I refer, therefore, to 're-visionary potential' as an active and infinite ingredient within imageries and texts of reality – to which one responds intuitively at many levels – I am implying the ecstasy of complex counterpoint within a living medium, a changing language: complex counterpoint between partial origins, between partial imprints of unfinished genesis, partial absolutes.

I shall elaborate more fully on this a little later as it possesses, I believe, a crucial bearing on the cross-cultural imagination.

Complex counterpoint between cultures raises the old question of the mystery of 'oneness' and the mystery of 'otherness'.

Who is the other? Does he or she exist? Does absent deity, absent other, live within the complicated abysses that are opening up within the body of our civilisation? Fear of the conquistadorial other, the other human being, the other and stranger god, the alien native, the alien trader or merchant or lover or warrior, *et cetera*, has led to curious ambivalences, curious acceptances, in philosophies of the imagination.

Take the epigraph that Octavio Paz, the Mexican writer, places at the door of his book, *The Labyrinth of Solitude* (1967). It is a brief passage that Paz takes from the work of one Antônio Machado, with whose writings I am unfamiliar. I gathered by chance that Machado was a distinguished contemporary of the poet, Lorca. The passage runs as follows:

> The *other* does not exist: this is rational faith, the incurable belief of human reason. Identity = reality, as if, in the end everything must necessarily and absolutely be *one and the same*. But the *other* refuses to disappear; it subsists, it persists; it is the hard bone on which reason breaks its teeth. Abel Martin, with a poetic faith as human as rational faith, believed *in the other*, in 'the essential Heterogeneity of being', in what might be called the incurable *otherness* from which oneness must always suffer.

Antônio Machado's bleak assessment of 'the incurable otherness from which oneness must always suffer' is at the heart of some of the most disturbing fictions of the nineteenth century, that fell outside the mainstream nineteenth-century novel and were largely ignored.

James Hogg's *The Confessions of a Justified Sinner* appeared in the 1820s. It fell by the wayside, it was ignored by press and public, and was revived to become a curious Scottish classic in the twentieth century. In the vanguard of that twentieth-century revival was a famous French novelist. Cross-culturalism in action, it would seem.

The Confessions of a Justified Sinner wrestles with Calvinist nightmare, the incurable damned, the incurable saved, from which – in Antônio Machado's phrase – 'oneness must always suffer'. The role of the unconscious in that novel is unusual; the strange amnesiac immunity a murderer – or mass murderer – may have as he blots out the memory of the others he has killed. Think of the recent trial in Israel of an alleged mass murderer accused of atrocities in the holocaust. He claimed absolutely that he was innocent. Perhaps he *was* innocent, or perhaps he had blocked out the memory of his deeds. Indeed, the murdered other in Calvinist nightmare may have been damned from the foundations of the world and therefore does not exist in the memory of the 'justified' murderer. *The Confessions of a Justified Sinner* is a pointer into an abyss that breaks the uniformity of Calvinist faith. Dread arrives to seal that abyss afresh and to become a block manifestation of a diseased one-track state of mind.

More or less around the same time, in the 1830s, upon the heels of Hogg's masterpiece, *Arthur Gordon Pym* by Edgar Allan Poe appeared across the Atlantic in the USA.

The two novels, though different in texture and confessional fabric, could fruitfully be compared. I have a chapter on *Pym* in the only full-length critical study I have ever written, which is called *The Womb of Space: the cross-cultural imagination* (1983).

All I wish to say now about the novel *Pym* is that the 'incurable otherness from which oneness must always suffer' led to cannibal theatre on the high seas. The high seas were the nineteenth-century equivalent of twentieth-century space; the Arctic or Antarctic visited by Pym may be compared to a distant planet beyond or beneath the moon. Incidentally, both W.H. Auden and the Argentinean, Borges, admired the novel *Pym*.

In *The Confessions of a Justified Sinner* and in *Arthur Gordon Pym* an abyss existed but remained an abortive realm. The capacity of the abyss to secrete what I have called 're-visionary potential within texts and imageries of reality' was eclipsed by dread. Nevertheless, the two novels differed from the conventional expectations of homogeneous fiction that we associate with, say, the Dickensian and Tolstoyan novel. They implied that the great documentary stance of the classic Dickensian and Tolstoyan novel, which rested on faith in natural justice, had begun to secrete – in the hands of a James Hogg or an Edgar Allan Poe or a Herman Melville (to whose novel, *Bartleby*, I shall soon refer) – a new ominous light on the liberal pretensions of society, when characterisation encompassed alien masks and pigmentations and cultures. They implied a threat from the alien side as well: the threat of alien ascendancy within a so-called liberal context of values.

Melville's *Bartleby* appeared in the 1850s and is a subtle repudiation of the vocabulary of fate in his age. Fate here implies acquiescence in structures of communication by which a culture may be circumscribed. The character, Bartleby, refuses to toe the line and sinks by degrees into a silence that promises to disrupt the frame in which he is set. The Australian novelist, Randolph Stow, it is of interest to note, presents us with a character called Byrne (the burnt, disfigured poet in the novel *Tourmaline* (1963)) who shares something of the pregnant silence that Bartleby nurses. Byrne, too, is out of step; his 'satanic eyebrows' are as much an indictment of himself, his past betrayals of himself, as they are a mirrored spectre of complacency in others, complacent evil one absorbs in one's blood, complacent tyranny so tarted up it passes for the good cause, the charismatic, fiery and Luciferian ideology or banner that few are prepared to question deeply.

Stow's Byrne singes the heart within a shadow land of images that we need to read and re-read differently from structured and apparently pre-ordained technologies of communication. Byrne, like Bartleby, subscribes – it seems to me – to a script woven in uncanny densities yet diminutive poles such as *a grain of light or dust* in a famished chaotic landscape, *a blade of grass* that seems numinous and intact in the midst of aridity, through which – as I understand it – the unconscious may gestate and bring fertile motifs and clues into the mind of penetrative narrative art.

It is the life of 'diminutives' that may offer a peculiar key to the cross-cultural imagination. Each 'diminutive' exists as it were in a certain field, or upon a certain frontier or margin of being, to apprise us of the polar life of other fields, to warn us of the necessity to *read* the mutual attraction of apparently remote poles of existence, to warn us to create a new space or interrelationship in which to transform a threat that may overwhelm us if we adhere to block, institutional habit...

Antônio Machado's 'incurable otherness from which oneness must always suffer' is a block device. Let us make no mistake about this. The suffering that oneness is destined to endure – according to Machado – implies a uniform and continuing ordeal from which there is no creative escape, no therapeutic relief, whereas uncanny 'diminutives', diminutive poles, within the innovative imagination, are drawn together by a mutual attraction that I think unshackles the logic of perpetual nightmare, perpetual ordeal. Through such diminutives one reads apparently unbearable events as bearable art, bearable translation of impending events for which one is – in some degree – curiously prepared. It is as if one stands upon a new, however difficult, threshold to weigh both the density and the beauty of the cosmos within a *thread* of indestructible being, a thread, yes, nothing more, signifying a creation of frailty.

However frail, the substance of 'diminutives' is, I confess, utterly real to me because of intuitive discoveries I have made and tested in many ways over long years.

I do not wish to engage in an extended analysis of Melville's *Bartleby* except to emphasise the curious eruption of a 'blade of grass' in the hospice area where Bartleby spends his last days. Note the diminutive pole – as one may see it – in a 'blade of grass'. Let us imagine Bartleby in the depths of his silence bringing imaginary letters to non-existent families, to families who have perished or died, and stacking those imaginary letters against a frail blade of grass. Remember he once worked in a Dead Letters Office in Washington where undelivered letters are stored. Let us imagine him in his silence placing a batch of such letters that he recalls from his Dead Letters days against the diminutive pole or blade of grass that springs at his feet. In that way he begins to *disinvest* in a block identity that has plagued him. He sculpts non-existent families into existence. He surrenders himself to otherness. Abysmal otherness, it is true, but the focus of visualisation is so real, the non-existent is so real, he sees into the heart of an *unfinished* genesis of the imagination he must share with future generations, with men and women in all future ages, countries, islands, continents.

In my late twentieth-century novel, *Carnival* (1985), Bartleby metamorphoses into a woman called Alice Bartleby who lives in an alms house in Georgetown, British Guiana. She embodies a 'barren colonial age'. That is her abyss, her non-existence, so to speak. Thomas – one of her carnival nephews – seeks to sculpt her eyes, eyes that weep for mankind; his sculpture is real, however tormenting and ungraspable, because its roots lie in a field of uncanny diminutives that, in exercising mutual attraction one upon the other, break the tyranny of solid imprint to hint at therapeutic community, therapeutic genius of love within one and other, within parallel existences and non-existences. It is the translation of apparently absolute ordeal into infinite poles extending backwards in time, forwards into infinity, that offers a progress, so to speak, into genuine diversity-in-universality.

Such progress, I am implying, breaks the mould of habit, breaks a mould of reading that bypasses the enormity and the subtlety of *re-visionary potential* within imageries in texts of being, images that need to be consulted in new lights as they bear backwards and forwards upon their partial substance within a theatre of unfathomable wholeness.

Take this passage from *Carnival* that depicts Thomas's encounter with Alice Bartleby:

> 'Take the measure of any statue in a formal garden,' Masters said to me. 'It weeps with bird droppings ... the tear duct of a stone knight or a stone lady. But Thomas's comedy and tragedy was that much as he tried, Alice's eyes defeated him in the sculpture he sought to make of the animal/human kingdom. No material tear rose there, neither faeces nor fire. *The shadow of a rose perhaps, the decrepitude of a lily*, that was all. They wept for mankind. And *that* Thomas could not prove. She was the one creature, *shadow of a dancing rose*, he could not touch. And yet she was drawn to him ... she loved him, *she loved him*, imagine that! with the kind of love that is incapable of destroying its siblings. Some say she was a fraud that only a colonial, barren age could fabricate. I say she was the mystery of fame at the heart of families of non-existence. She was the mystery of genius within the most unpropitious economic circumstances, a mystery that ran deeper than proof or parody of the evolution of limbo into heaven.'

You would have spotted, I am sure, the diminutive poles in a theatre of half-conscious, half-unconscious mutualities; namely, 'tear duct', 'the shadow of a dancing rose' and 'the decrepitude of a lily', and recalled 'blade of grass' (the pole upon which Melville's Bartleby may have stacked his imaginary letters) and 'grain of dust or light' as the fire that apparently consumed, yet may have healed, the burnt Australian poet into becoming a seer of the living and the dead.

Such 'diminutives' bear upon what I would call *living texts*, and by that I mean uncanny re-visionary potentials within imageries that need to be consulted backwards and forwards within a canvas of the intuitive imagination. It is as if the *concentrate range* of capacities within such texts is curiously difficult because the texts are alive; the imageries appear difficult at first sight because they are inwardly and subtly revising themselves within the body of the fiction to which they relate. They are in that sense *alive*.

Within the last five hundred years we have been historically aware of the fall of a major civilisation relatively close to us in time: that of ancient Mexico and Peru. A brief word about this, as it bears on the theme we are exploring.

We may visualise an abyss opening up within the world of ancient Mexico and Peru in the sixteenth century when the conquest occurred. Indeed, I would argue that that abyss may have been in existence – within the pre-Columbian psyche – generations before the conquest happened and the pre-Columbian world was suddenly catapulted into a wholly different climate of social and physical servitude affecting masses of people.

We glean from the records that there were legends of dread circulating long before the conquest, in Mexico and farther south amongst the Arawaks, the Caribs, the Macusis, the Arekunas and others who occupied the middle ground Guianas and South Americas between Mexico and Peru. Such legends of impossible monsters helped to seal the abyss; they conformed to ritual habit, ritual circumscription of events, a ritual flatness in reading events. They turned away from the reality of the abyss as a true moment, a true goad to the psyche of innovative imagination, they shrank from new ways of reading reality, from the complex life of the abyss that counselled far-flung changes of heart and mind. The life of society in the main appeared smooth and normal up to the instant of sudden convulsion. Ritual ball games occupied the centre of the stage. Everything looked hugely normal as men and women tossed the ball from hand to hand. Yes, everything looked normal except for a hideous addiction to blood as the ritual nutriment of the sun.

Normality is a plague of habit few suspect. Surely one understands this in our times! Take the addiction to drugs, to crack, to heroin, cocaine, alcohol, excessive and brutal violence *et cetera* in our twentieth-century societies around the globe. Addiction and violence – even on such a horrendous scale – do not puncture a conviction of habitual normality as we go about our business. They have become modern legends with which we live. We are automatically subservient to a link between apparently immune identity (ethnic identity, cultural identity, *et cetera*) and unchanging reality. *Nothing changes under the sun*, so we have been told from times immemorial. In that respect the Aztecs were our blood brothers in their kinship to the identity of the sun. When the conquest toppled ancient Mexico in 1521 our blood brothers were so embedded in ritual conformity to fate that one wonders in what degree they really perceived the end of their age. I would like to think that a handful rid themselves of mass complacency and read reality differently through the plague of normality. I would like to think that the enigmatic and magical calendar, which Montezuma's poets and priests had completed not long before the end, possessed a different thread into space and time through and beyond convention and custom. If so – if that calendar and its mysterious codices were genuinely on the brink of inner confrontation, inner space confrontation with the abyss that had opened in a pre-Columbian age – then it came too late.

One may dare perhaps to draw a modern parallel in the late-twentieth century. Quantum physics and the new science of chaos correspond in some degree in our age to a possible breakthrough from ritual habit, ritual normality that seals our eyes and ears.

Only a few weeks ago, I learnt of the new science of chaos in which the subtle rhythm of a butterfly's wing may signal the coming eruption of a storm in the changing climates of the globe. I was fascinated to hear of this, for it validated my own long-held intuitive premises of diminutive poles, namely, 'the shadow of a dancing rose', 'the decrepitude of a lily' associated with Alice Bartleby, the 'blade of grass' associated with Melville's Bartleby, the 'grain of dust or light' associated with Australian Byrne.

To scan such frailties and diminutives in the text of fiction – my argument runs – is to unravel a thread in the dense loom or economy of being (density means economy), to unravel a thread that may sustain us to cope with an abysmal otherness whom and which we dread but which may also bring resources to alter or change the fabric of the imagination in the direction of a therapeutic, ceaselessly unfinished genesis.

I mention the fall of the civilisation of the ancient Americas to show how easy it is to succumb not only to cataclysm but to the deadly plague of so-called normality by which we resist innermost re-visionary potential in texts of nature and spirit and being. Perhaps the magical calendar of the Aztecs did imply a new possibility, but if so it came too late to register deeply in the consciousness of a doomed civilisation. Equally, how can one know whether the computers aligned to quantum physics and the new science of chaos portend – or run in parallel with – a subtle, complex breakthrough in the language of imagination? I would like to think they do.

I will give one more illustration of my involvement in 'diminutive poles'. If Alice Bartleby is an abysmal other in *Carnival*, then Ghost, who arises from the seas of space and time in *The Infinite Rehearsal* (1987), occupies an abyss at the heart of ancient and modern adventure.

Ghost's multi-faceted disguises include hunger as a driving force in the adventures of ancient and modern civilisations: hunger for territory, hunger for gold, hunger for power and so on. Hunger in these contexts would remain a block and incorrigible motivation were it not susceptible to disinvestments in charismatic imperative, through which the vessels fuelled by hunger may be set in uncanny reverse. Ghost is associated with rigging, pole and sail upon a wrecked ship 'battered and ribbed and gaping and glistening in the setting sun like a quicksilver goddess's hatpins in steep, elongated disarray'.

The slightly comic stress in these lines – 'quicksilver goddess's hatpins' – assists in a disinvestment in male hubristic adventure. Quicksilver mutuality between the wreck and regenerative seed or design releases a thread into a motherhood of adventure. Not that such female counterpoint does not carry its own paranoid dangers in the wake of male ascendancy. But motherhood implies re-visionary foetal perspectives into humanity, it implies a nursery of hope where one least expects to find it, it implies that age-old myth, however apparently lost, gestates in the unconscious and may evolve and return with new, renascent complications and edges.

Ghost's first utterance under the shadow of hunger is couched in three texts: one from Walter de la Mare's *The Listeners* (1912), the second from the ballad calypso, *Jumbi Jamboree,* and the third from T.S. Eliot's *The Waste Land* (1923). This is the passage:

Hunger was so real that I ascended the moon as if it were Glass in a shoe-string ladder and knocked on its door.

'Is there anybody there?' said the 'Traveller, Knocking on the moonlit door.

Belly to belly
Back to back
Ah don't give a damn
Ah done dead a'ready.

And I Tiresias have foresuffered all
I who sat by Thebes below the wall
And walked among the lowest of the dead.

I could not believe it. Ghost was speaking at last. No formal message. A repetition of familiar texts become however strangely cross-cultural, the strangest subversion, where one least suspected or expected to find it in hollow convention or solemn usage. An edge, nothing more above the malaise, the death-wish of an age.

Let us recall the significance of the 'diminutive' as apprising us of a field of attractions – a field of signals from diminutive pole to pole – in which the creative and re-creative chemistry of our interactions with nature and history is imbued with new apprehensions, new rhythmic edges (remember the butterfly-thread or wing in the science of chaos) that may prepare us for, or take us through, the polluted life of being and nature, or assist us to find new, flexible balances between the past and the future if we are to cope with the consequences of our own deeds in the past and the present, our own malaise or unwitting death-wish.

The 'strangest subversion' of which the passage speaks links us therefore to an 'edge above the malaise, the death-wish of an age', links us also to the 'shoe-string ladder to the moon' (another diminutive pole or signal in a field of attractions). 'Ladder to the moon' becomes a signal of a space-age civilisation in which the portents of new possibility or disaster need to be read against a backcloth that we have long tended to suppress. The imaginative psyche which is steeped in levels of the unconscious, subconscious and conscious – in raising the ladder to the moon – brings a new rhythm into cross-cultural genesis of the imagination. Within that rhythm, 'the moonlit door' may signal an entry into a corridor of hope or into a reversion to Middle Passage enslavement lifted into vessels of space. Thus the lament of the slaves, so to speak, from the bowels of the space-ship – 'Belly to belly, back to back, Ah don't give a damn, Ah done dead a'ready' – is all the more telling in revealing the measure of escapist frolic or dance or the measure of an eruption of chaos in which ancient civilisations, ancient Thebes, yield up the seer Tiresias as a player in the jumbi, calypso band.

The stress on 'hunger' in the passage is as much the hunger of the seer to alert us to new rhythms of possibility, a new way of reading reality, as it embodies in the tattered body of the seer an equation with the South American pork-knocker who knocks on a pork barrel in the gold and diamond fields to gain a few lingering scraps of meat in his shoe-string budget or larder of existence.

We are catapulted, because of all these associations and mutual signalling from pole to pole, into interrelationships that encompass the old yet new content of a crisis-ridden civilisation in all parts of the globe.

The narrator is catapulted back in memory and remembers playing as a child of three with a ragged doll with a hole in its chest. He remembers a man being shot in the street below his window. It was the occasion of an industrial strike in 1948 over 'starvation wages' – another aspect of 'hunger'. The man who was shot in the street was called Tiger. Tiger was a member of the Tiresias Tiger band of the sacred wood.

> I played with him (he was a ragged doll) on the drawing-room carpet until he vanished and I did not hear of him, or see him again, until I learnt of the Tiresias Tigers of the magic wood.
>
> Absent or present he was often around the corner in my sleep and through him I became a pork-knocker scientist who rattled the black hole of gravity in Tiger's chest with a teaspoon.
>
> A frightening eye of sugar or telescopic spoon with which to scrape the barrel of the cosmos, a frightening glimpse into the heart of Ghost...

A disturbing dream for it set into circulation all over again the origins of sensation – such as tasting, rattling silver in a teacup, slicing a bone or a piece of meat that cost a pretty penny.

I know for a fact that an industrial strike over starvation wages occurred on the sugar estates of Old New Forest in 1948 and several strikers were shot dead, one fell in the sugar bowl beneath our window embracing a woman and a child. A tight nightmare fit.

I was three when it happened. Three-year-old relic of memory on whose lips was a grain of sugar... I witnessed the clash with the police from our window above the square. It could have been happening in our drawing room. Alice and Miriam were staring. Staring eyes. Everything and everyone tumbled into a relic of memory as I now write as if I was there yet absent from myself. Absent living body. I saw the hollow ambulance with Doctor Faustus at the skeleton wheel. The commotion of the skeleton bands BOOM BOOM DOOM DOOM. Commotion, ceaseless sweetness bitterness elaboration, movement, voices.

Thus I was moved across the years to sift unreliable fact from true play or fantasy and to reconsider the origins of sensation: *an eye in the mouth of a sugar bowl and in the body of Tiresias, the seer.*

Take the seer's eye: in the wake of a shot a *blind* silence enveloped every rattling teaspoon, every gun, every drum, every bone in the crowd in the square beneath our window. Then came an explosion of appetite and anger. I dreamt I saw the dead man move and eat the grain on my lip as he whispered in the hole in his chest. 'Everything you have been tempted to consume recedes into me now, hollow me. See the sweets of violence in dead men's chests, in dead men's lungs, in dead men's hearts, hear the bitterness of explosive suns.

> Fifteen suns in a dead man's chest
> Yo-ho-ho and the taste of the lotus.

A different bottled ear or eye from the one I received when I reached out to seize the kingdoms of glass, the kingdoms of the globe, and was greeted by my mother's exclamation of joy. An ear and a mouth and an eye in a ragged man's chest... I was translated, I was confused, by the telescopic mind of Ghost in Tiger's body.

The drums now spoke to the dead seer, the dead tiger, on the ground...

Why should a beast's sudden death help us to map the ancient heavens anew within the radius of a star, a child's star? One child's star is another's bullet.

I dreamt I put the question to Ghost and thought I heard him murmur very faintly in the hollow of my ragged doll, 'Life needs death. Life needs death if it is to be. But remember it is *through* death that life measures itself, measures its achievements, its glories. Remember it is *through* death not *with* death – not in league with death as the ultimate violence, the ultimate deprivation. The distinction is a crucial one – it bears on the fabric of the resurrection within every extremity, every hollow...'

Needless to say, perhaps, the 'diminutives' in this passage, namely, 'ragged doll' with a numinous hole in its chest, gravity's 'rattling teaspoon', 'telescopic spoon with which to scrape the barrel of the cosmos', 'Doctor Faustus's skeleton wheel', 'an eye in a ragged man's chest', and so on, touch upon the alien, yet paradoxically intimate, humours and rhythms of a space-age civilisation that we need to *read*, I think, as affecting every grain of existence in the nursery of being and changing spectre of the universe.

Everything we tend to block away (or to sublimate into bravado or false modes of heroism – and sublimation incorporates into itself deadly patterns of repression to feed the block mentality), everything that we have sublimated and repressed, is pertinent to a space-age civilisation. A redistribution of signals and forces within inner spatiality, within inner space creativity, is pertinent to outer space, to the space-age civilisation that ours is becoming. The block imprints of history need to be re-opened and scanned within pressures that will otherwise erupt dangerously from the unconscious in nihilistic humanities and technologies. Eruptions from the unconscious may spell enlightenment within a psyche that seeks a profound attunement to space-age change, but they may also spell catastrophe to nihilistic being.

A post-modernism that is bereft of depth or of an appreciation of the life of the intuitive imagination is but a game for a dictatorship of technologies aligned to sophistry and nihilism. Cross-culturalism needs to breach nihilism. I repeat, CROSS-CULTURALISM NEEDS TO BREACH NIHILISM.

The mystery of chaos involves us in a precipice of strange and paradoxical order, a precipice of strange and uncanny hope – precipice, yes, but hope in an indestructible reality, a rare and chastening combination within the genesis of the imagination.

NAYANTARA SAHGAL

The Schizophrenic Imagination

I am a little dazzled, and more than a little intimidated, by all the scholarship I have heard propounded in the last few days. I have also wondered when 'post-colonial' is supposed to end. First we were colonials, and now we seem to be post-colonials. So is 'colonial' the new Anno Domini from which events are to be everlastingly measured? My own awareness as a writer reaches back to x-thousand B.C., at the very end of which measureless timeless time the British came, and stayed, and left. And now they're gone, and their residue is simply one more layer added to the layer upon layer of Indian consciousness. Just one more.

The title of my talk may be misleading in terms of studies made about the subject – of which I know nothing. So let me begin by explaining that I am thinking of schizophrenia as a state of mind and feeling that is firmly rooted in a particular subsoil, but above ground has a more fluid identity that doesn't fit comfortably into any single mould. A schizophrenic of this description is a migrant who may never have left his people or his soil. We are all somewhat divided selves, but I'm referring to the divisions that history and circumstance impose on the complex creatures we already are. Let me take the example of Jawaharlal Nehru, a product of colonial times who called himself a man of two worlds, but unlike the quotation describing one of these as dead, the other powerless to be born, both his worlds were alive and vigorous. He was not in any limbo. That was the trouble. His was a life lived in two-plus-one cultures, in many ways a story of assimilation, yet the times he lived in and the role he played in them placed his cultures in conflict and confrontation. The struggle for independence gave the conflict a historic setting, and his life and personality a very different direction from the one it would otherwise have taken.

Educated Indians had, of course, been in contact with western civilization since the British occupation, though most Indians, who lived by the sun, the rain and the seasons, were not touched by it. But many of the educated, too, were affected only in their outer lives. It had not become second nature except for those few whose class and opportunities made this possible. Of these, some related to the East-West encounter by discarding their Indianness to become brown carriers of the white culture they admired and adopted. But nationalism produced another breed of westernized Indian for whom his plural culture meant a bewildering reckoning with himself, a balancing act, where the priorities were never in doubt, but where 'Who am I?' remained an on-going search and question. Nehru was one such Indian, and it may be that many of his countrymen and women are still sorting out the meaning of this particular historical experience.

In contrast, Nirad Chaudhuri, a man of the same generation as Nehru, born when the words empire and colonial still had benign associations, seems not only an unanguished product of the same period, but one who became a philosophical observer and erudite chronicler of the colonial framework he was born and bred in. After independence, at an advanced age when few people emigrate from choice to set up house and put down roots somewhere else, he could leave India never to return, and could flourish heart-whole in what perhaps was, and is, the real country of his imagination, teaching the English how to stay English. For those who did not cross swords with the imperial order, it was simply the order of the day. For many it had a mystique, the elemental rightness, and right to be there, of a natural phenomenon.

A strong element of mystique attached to Nehru's outlook too, but it was the mystique of the fight for freedom, though that is not all it was. It was also traceable to his peculiar involvement with India, as fact, as dream, and as possibility. He wrote in *Discovery of India*: 'For we are very old, and trackless centuries whisper in our ears.' He was aware of that whisper. One incident toward the end of his life sums up the quality of his involvement. The family was at the breakfast table. A nephew said the country was in a mess, its problems would never be solved, and he, for one, was getting out to settle abroad. Nehru's daughter was listening sympathetically. Suddenly Nehru who had remained silent, spoke in a rage, 'Go where you like, but if I am born a thousand times, a thousand times I will be born an Indian.' It was a statement of almost mystical emotion and power. It had an echo of the cult of the motherland, for in the early years of this century these had been the last words of more than one Indian martyr after he mounted the gallows for his execution. This was Nehru's subsoil speaking though he was a man deeply identified with other nationalisms, as also with the science, learning and pleasures of the west, and was better known as an internationalist than perhaps any other figure of his time. He was also saying that to transform your society, you have to be in it. The ultimate battles, whether for freedom or after it, are fought on your own soil. He was implying 'My life is my message' as opposed to 'My text is my message'. But the impassioned ingredient in his make-up is common to those everywhere – from rebels against empire to iconoclasts in art and literature – who see that there are facts which must be denied, and that there is more than one way of looking at the world.

There is a story from the imperial era about an Englishman whose posting in the Sudan was over. He was to leave with his family for England and he was pleased when his little son begged to be taken to say goodbye to the statue of Gordon. The father was proud that his child remembered

all he had been taught about General Gordon's magnificent defence of
Khartoum, a heroic event in the annals of empire, and deeply moved
when tears ran down the child's face as they stood at the famous equestrian statue, until the boy asked, 'Daddy, who's that man sitting on
Gordon?' It is those who in all honesty and earnestness are looking at the
horse and not the rider, who can fit neatly into no tradition except one
that is in the making. If anyone wants to fit me into a tradition, it is this
tradition-in-the-making they will have to settle for.

My own divided experience starts with belonging to North India, a
region that has been spared no convulsion or folk experience, from epic
marvels and a matchless metaphysics to repeated invasion and slaughter.
My part of the Ganges plain is the cradle of Hinduism but it is home to
Islam as well, and Indo-English by virtue of the continuing impact and
fall-out of British rule. All three influences meet in the city of my birth
whose original name, Prayag, figures in the *Ramayana*, while its present
name, Allahabad, testifies to Muslim conquest and rule, and where every
road in my childhood was named after an Englishman, the public park
had a statue of stout old Queen Victoria, and down the road from our
house two nights a week came dance music from a club that did not
admit Indians.

Going to school was like arriving at the club that didn't admit Indians.
My school admitted Indians but ignored India. As I was quite sure that
India existed, I didn't place much faith in school. At home I was nourished on revolt. My elders were committed to rooting out foreign rule and
had made a personal beginning by giving up their scholarship and their
careers at the Bar to devote their lives and all their resources to the
struggle for freedom. They were so enthralled with organising for it and
being imprisoned for it that I thought going to jail was a career. They had
no regular incomes because they had given up their means of livelihood,
but they found it so exhilarating doing without the comforts, amenities
and certainties other people took for granted, that when I was introduced
to what is known as normal life after independence, it gave me quite a
shock with its very different priorities. I had never before met people who
earned livings, took holidays, joined clubs, went shopping, and knew what
tomorrow would bring, and they struck me as a quaint and exotic species.
Above all, the whole business of entertaining, of serving elaborate meals
to other well-fed people, and then going to *their* houses to be fed elaborate
meals by *them*, seemed to me an extremely curious way of spending time.
There are several aspects of normal life I still haven't got used to. I think
I started to write books as a retreat from it. I know I am ill-equipped to
be part of it. I will forever be an outsider looking in through its windows,
marvelling at the sequences and continuities of normal life. When I try to
read them, they look like hieroglyphics, a fascinating language for which
I lack the code.

In a childhood filled with the sights, sounds and folklore, and sometimes the furore, of the national movement, nothing estranged me from school more than the way history was taught. Its content and perspective were so different from what I learned at home, that I soon put school history in the same category as Kipling's 'Gunga Din' – a rousing, rollicking white man's fable that had everything to do with the conqueror's image of the bullied, beaten Indian, loyal to his last gasp, and nothing to do with India. In short I didn't believe a word of it. I was also surprised to learn that ancient times began with Greece, that the world had been created in six days, and that all of religion was down in one little book. Though the nuns did their best with me, privately I suspected God Almighty was my grandfather, and Jesus Christ must be my uncle, since he carried other people's sorrows on his back; that they, together with my father and mother, were special shining beings, and that the fight for freedom was the path to the Holy Grail. I knew I inhabited a huger, older universe of which school taught me only a meagre slice, yet paradoxically this little scrap filled the textbooks and ruled the world.

Home had its paradoxes, too, but they fell into place as part of a larger purpose. I can see my frail, spectacled, widowed grandmother sitting cross-legged on her bedroom floor reading in a low mutter from her enormous large-print *Ramayana*, and shrieking for a servant when a mouse darts across the floor, but she's the same woman who picketed foreign cloth shops not long before, and who once stayed firmly put at the head of a procession halted by the police. Let me quote what happened next from a written account. She was 'knocked down ... and hit repeatedly on the head with canes. Blood came out of an open wound in her head; she fainted and lay on the roadside.' Within these outer tensions there were inner tensions, for non-violence does not come naturally to the human race, and my father once got solitary confinement for knocking down a jail guard who insulted my grandmother when she visited him in jail. I used to wish the time would come when my parents would stay home like other parents. For one of them the time never came, for my father died of his last imprisonment. I'm not sure whether a childhood lived in this heightened state of national and world awareness was euphoric or wretched. It is probably best described by Pushkin's reaction when he read Gogol's *Dead Souls*. After laughing uproariously all the way through it, he exclaimed, 'Oh God, how sad our Russia is!' It has been said that a person who survives her childhood has enough information to last her for the rest of her days, and it must be true, or my novels would not have reflected the political idealism of an emergent nation, and its progressive destruction and decay. There is always an obstinate idealist hanging around in my fiction, usually with as much chance of success or survival as a snowball in Hades.

I did not set out to write 'political fiction'. I have no ideology except a vague sort that feels uncomfortable with title and privilege, with kings, queens and political dynasties. I have no message either unless it is the non-message that Europe is not the centre of the world. Politics for me was an environment in which every issue was a political issue, and personal and political fates were inextricably bound. If it has remained a continuing awareness, it is because I live in an unsettled order, one I am trying to change, one where I am witness to the public and domestic misuses of power. And politics was for so long dictated by other people's view of us that I have found it satisfying to give it Indian expression and interpretation. Yet though I use a political backdrop or events – since these happen to be the outer focal points that trigger my imagination, and also because I think we gain or lose significance in our relationship to events – I prefer to think of my fiction as having a sense of history, in a country where race, religion or caste can decide the course of a love affair, where it can take as much raw courage to choose a husband, or leave him, as to face a firing squad. The nuclear family with its attendant traumas is not for us. Our traumas like our families are built on a grander scale. From where I stand, looking at the horse and not the rider, it doesn't seem to me there *is* such a thing as a purely individual predicament. Too many other factors blur and burden it, including the weather. Fornication and adultery go on in India as anywhere else, but I'm not sure they can be given such free rein as in western fiction without becoming unrelated to a social condition where the individual is tied hand and foot, and often back-breakingly, to wider responsibility. For one thing he hasn't got the time. And she has even less. But as we approach western living conditions – as in my novel after next – there will be more time for adultery.

Then, societies that have lived long under foreign domination bring their own behaviour characteristics into play. Passivity can become an active choice, a strength, among people where invasion and re-conquest have been the pattern, because it is one's best chance of remaining whole. Sycophancy, too, is the hallmark of the survivor and all cultures have sycophants. But when I wonder why *we* produce them in such abundance – and this struck me strongly during the 1975-77 dictatorship known as the Emergency – then I have to ask, as I did in my novel *Rich Like Us*, whether Hinduism inclines a whole society to the status quo. Does it put out the fires of rebellion? Does it incline women to victimization, to individual and mass acts of horrifying self-sacrifice? Has the cult of virtue (female) and honour (male) been so ferocious and merciless in any other society that prides itself on its humane values? How do we explain this aspect of ourselves? I have been much preoccupied with the effects of Hinduism on character in my novels.

All Indians are not Hindus but all Indians must reckon with Hinduism since it is the dominant setting, the social and psychological atmosphere. Yet what it is we are reckoning with is hard to say when Hinduism has no beginning, no founder, no church, no commandments, no single bible, no single prophet or messiah. There can never be a law of blasphemy against Hinduism, or any other concrete religious measure to bring all Hindus into line. But memory and imagination are much the most powerful of human possessions, and give us almost unlimited scope for both enlightenment and bigotry. This, then, is the sky I and my characters live under, and in one sense I am nothing if I am not a Hindu. On the Indian subcontinent there is no escape from the aspect of cultural behaviour we call religious.

Some Hindus solve their problem of how to come to terms with Hinduism by dumping it and calling themselves atheists, agnostics, or secular. But this is no solution for a writer. If I change my name today to Henrietta von Blinkenstaff, who am I trying to fool? Can I quick-change my bones, my myths, my grandparents? Can I forget that my great-grandmother became a suttee? So I find it more useful to say, Believe it, you are a Hindu. Now figure out, if you can, what that means, and fiction is part of the process of figuring it out. Even if I were so inclined, it would be futile to wish away a force that has moulded hundreds of generations, that governs some countries and is a governing force in others, and whose absolutism has crossed national frontiers to sentence a writer to death for blasphemy. There is no safe distance from such a force any more than there is from modern weaponry. Literature can hardly ignore this unfinished question.

I used to try to integrate my overpowering heritage, feel relaxed and easy about it, but I've discovered I'm not supposed to feel integrated and relaxed. It is not only inevitable, it is also perfectly natural for the inheritor of one of the earth's oldest and most complex inheritances to feel fragmented. And I have learned to treat my own particular muddle as a priceless asset. It is for my Third Eye to reconcile these fragments through fiction, and through my sense of plural self to produce a fiction other than that which a less ancient, more homogeneous, more settled society produces. Time itself – an important event of the novel – is not the same in the Indian, especially the Hindu reckoning as in other societies, including other ancient societies that have suffered uprooting shocks and made clean breaks with the past. The city I grew up in had co-existing time zones. The past is so much with us, in the beliefs and routines people live by, in conversations whose allusions can go from legend to modern in minutes, that no time is ever entirely past. It is modern times that strain my own imagination, and I don't think anyone has succeeded in creating a modern Indian character, if by 'modern' we mean a basic alteration or transformation from what went before. I'm not sure such a creature exists, so real life cannot be much help in providing examples. Is 'modern' the frame of mind that descends from the European Enlightenment? Is it the position you occupy in the race for European technology? Is the contemporary western world still The World, and all other peoples to be judged by its yard-sticks of progress? I've made some play with the word 'modern' in my last novel, *Mistaken Identity*.

One of the effects of coming to terms with my own dividedness has been to ignore chronology and to free myself from Indian locale and characters in my fiction. This has been liberating for me, and I expect it must be so for schizophrenic fiction in general. Not only is it time for interpretation to flow many ways instead of only west to east, but the question of direction is itself no longer relevant when the migration of cultures is leaving cultures open-ended, and when migration can take place without ever leaving one's soil. Where does one culture begin and another end when they are housed in the same person? There are powerful winds blowing through English literature. English is being assaulted by cross-currents of racial experience, by a vast expansion of its frame of reference, by new uses of imagination and language. The day of pure literatures, like pure or ruling races, is over, and English, at least, is in a new flowering – one that expresses a vision, a vitality, an expansionism that Sir Francis Drake and other English gentlemen never dreamed they would be unleashing when they set sail on their swashbuckling adventures.

To end with let me give you an example of the schizophrenia I am talking about. My father, a Sanskrit scholar, a fairly arrogant Indian, and a dedicated freedom fighter who was to die of British imprisonment a few years later, wept when London was bombed in the blitz, and when Paris fell to Hitler's armies. His answer to the question 'Who am I?' would have been, 'I am a member of the human race – and all the rest is rhetoric.'

THE WRITER
IN A MULTICULTURAL SOCIETY

BRUCE KING

The Commonwealth Writer in Exile

I begin with three suggestions. The first is the obvious one that Commonwealth and other post-colonial literatures are the result of European expansion overseas and the meeting and conflict of two or more cultures. The second suggestion is that what we call the post-modern is an expression of the dislocations and decentring brought about by intensive social and cultural changes, especially those caused by rapid communications, ease of international transportation, information networks and multinational organisations. With such a constant flow of facts, ideas and people any notion of a tradition or centre will seem arbitrary. My third suggestion is that the expatriate Commonwealth writer, whether realist or metafictionalist, is likely to be most sensitive to and representative of the contemporary post-modern condition, as such a writer will be aware of the arbitrariness of local social forms and language and emotionally live simultaneously in a multiplicity of competing cultures. My paper will be concerned with this condition.

There are an increasing number of writers who exist some place between the new national literatures and the new immigrant communities and their literatures. They are related to those literatures yet outside of them, as they also participate in the literature of England or the United States. I have in mind such writers as Buchi Emecheta, Timothy Mo, V.S. and Shiva Naipaul, Salman Rushdie, Zulfikar Ghose, Randolph Stow, Meena Alexander and A.K. Ramanujan. Most are expatriates, Mo is British of mixed parentage, Alexander is an Indian raised in Africa now married to an American. I call these writers exiles because they are alienated from their place of origin, from the lands in which they live, and from the immigrant communities. Although they have adopted diverse strategies of survival, they are the successors of James Joyce's Stephen Dedalus in *The Portrait of the Artist*, with his silence, exile and cunning. But we live in a time when the new nations and multiculturalism have become important; consequently the writer in exile has become the intermediary, the interpreter, of the new nations to the former colonial powers. The self-exiled have become the new men and women of letters, both producing as creative writers and functioning as commentators, reporters and translators of the new nations to the metropolitan centres.

V.S. Naipaul first rediscovered and reinvented the role of the nineteenth-century observer of foreign lands, but with the significant difference that he speaks as someone associated with the West Indies and with the Indian diaspora in the Third World. Mo, Rushdie, Emecheta and others also write about their place of origin or other foreign cultures from the double perspective of a native and of the First World. While such a strategy may seem obvious for someone from the Third World, it is significant that Stow's last three novels also reflect the difficulty of assimilation. That these writers, whether from white or Third World nations, share a similar psychology, is shown by the ways Stow's *The Girl Green as Elderflower* is like Naipaul's *The Enigma of Arrival*. Both are semi-autobiographical novels in which the difficulties of taking root in England are transcended by writing about it. Both end by a celebration not of assimilation but of self-creation through writing. This, then, is another major theme of such writers, their own condition of alienation and exile and how through writing they have given order to life. Significantly, the two novels also end with celebration of family ties, not with actual integration into British society as a whole. The disrupted continuity of childhood into a wider mature adult life is, as in the poetry of Meena Alexander and A.K. Ramanujan, salvaged by creating an inner space of self in relation to family. While such writers are aware of themselves as part of a broader picture, ex-colonial in Stow's case, part of the Indian diaspora in the case of Naipaul, their emotional world is enclosed, that of the exile, and not integrated into that of society.

While Stow and Naipaul conclude by writing about the novel they are writing, their books are not so much about the artist as a young man, but rather about the mature uprooted artist trying to find a place in the world after a breakdown, a collapse caused in part by the difficulties of homelessness, of trying to survive in an alien world. Having lost their home they have found no other except through the self-creative process of writing.

Naipaul's often repeated remark that he might have committed suicide if he had not succeeded as a writer seems relevant; such writers are unlikely to be part of any society. Alienated early in life, they have remained unclubbable. Salvation comes through writing, but to be a serious writer is also to be different; the attraction of English literature is itself likely to be a form of alienation. The writer in a new nation overcomes the condition by protesting against what is seen as subservience or ignorance and in the process helps make a new culture which is both modern and focused on the native. The exile may, like Stow, Selvon, Naipaul or Ramanujan, at first participate in such cultural renewal, but because of personal circumstances or a basic sense of difference, reintegration can only be through success in the metropolitan centres as a writer rather than as part of the national culture.

Whereas Charles Brasch, Nissim Ezekiel, A.D. Hope, Mordecai Richler or Wole Soyinka return home and reintegrate as leaders of dissenting cultures which eventually become new establishments, the writers in exile need to find other strategies, especially as they are increasingly cut off from developing post-colonial societies. While each writer's strategy for coping with this situation will be unique, there are noticeable patterns.

Contemporary, unlike earlier, exiles are not nostalgic for any idealized traditional culture or childhood disrupted by colonialism or expatriation. The rapidity and ease of modern international travel prevents such idealization. A trip or two home is enough to convince a Naipaul, Rushdie or Emecheta that you cannot go home again; society has moved on and you have also changed. Moreover, the original attraction to what was felt to be a wider, more significant world continues even beyond the disillusionments of failed assimilation. The writers in exile, because of education or because of an initial anglophilia, are part of an elite highly acculturated to their new land and metropolitan English-language culture. They either went abroad seeking a cultural home or had the important years of their education abroad. Their assumptions include those of London and New York. While they may be compassionately involved in the Third World, they approach it with an irritability towards its provinciality, complacency, lack of modernity, and the rhetoric and mystique of nationalism, race or other means by which new nations assert their cultural difference.

This does not mean they are totally cut off from their origins. Rather the contrary. Lacking deep roots in their new society, they often adopt some strategy of redefining themselves in relation to the land of origin. Rushdie and Naipaul, for example, have become writers of the Third World. Emecheta has adapted the Nigerian novel of cultural assertion to a feminism learned in England. Essentially she writes a critique of the Nigerian novel from inside the genre, using its themes and conventions. Ghose has translated into metafictional, magic-realist novels about Brazil his own sense of how colonialism brought alienating modern thought to Pakistan and himself. Mo's novels treat of the incompatibility and untranslatability between European and Chinese society, culture and language. V.S. Naipaul is concerned with the failure of the Third World to remake itself when presented by the challenge of freedom and the need to modernize. There is also the constant concern with the fate of the Indian diaspora caught between black Third World nationalism and the need to adapt to survive. What I am suggesting is that with such writers nostalgia has been transformed into other concerns, other ways of expressing national, cultural or racial identification, rather than something which relates directly to some homeland.

This form of self-creation and of affinities is both through and within literature. Such writers have often claimed a national literary tradition as in Emecheta's relationship to Nigerian writing. V.S. Naipaul has tried to establish a tradition based on his father's writing, and at various times tried to differentiate it from both the protest writing of the black Third World and Indian philosophical spiritualism. Ramanujan has tried to express his own condition of being a modern man of the world who has his psychological roots in Indian culture by adaptation of Indian literary, philosophical and linguistic forms to modern English-language poetry. Rushdie imitates the written and oral literary forms of India and the Islamic world and acknowledges a forerunner in G.V. Desani's *All about H. Hatterr*. Mo indicates that the fulsome comprehensiveness of *An Insular Possession* has similarities to the conventions of the Chinese novel. If the writers do not go home again, they do seek some native literary tradition of which they are part, although looked at from the outside, such a sense of tradition may seem individualistic, arbitrary and assertive.

Because a product of the post-colonial world, with its rapid social and political changes, new cultural networks and rapid flow of information, the exile is conscious of the arbitrariness and provisionality of culture, social forms, language and the way reality is perceived. A product of the interfacing of more than one culture, unrooted in all, the exile is post-modern in being forced to find continuities where they have been badly disrupted and the fragments incongruously mixed together. Living between cultures, exiles are aware that they are representative of our times, when the margins have invaded and unsettled what was thought to be the centre. Naipaul has said he is part of what he is fleeing. The literature of exile is concerned with rapid social change. Learning to live in a world of seeming chaos and flux is a central theme in such writers as Mo, Naipaul, Rushdie, Ramanujan and Stow. Uprooted, unsettled, they are the voices of the instability of the modern world.

They are deconstructionists, not out of the logic that led others from structuralism to post-structuralism, but from the experience of divided, uprooted, unassimilated lives; but they are also reconstructionalists in that for those genuinely threatened by chaos the logic of survival requires some new order, even if only provisional. This is Naipaul's point in his later writings. After moving beyond writing as memory to research and observation, he now holds a view of narrative which, while based on the notion of the western novel as a story of individual will, sees story-making as a way of imposing a usable order on the disorderliness of the changing world. Such narrative is tentative yet an analysis of social change and a celebration of accomplishment. While Naipaul claims that only through narrative can we make sense of the world, there is the recognition that the stories we tell are provisional, not the whole truth, and must be continually re-written. If Naipaul appears a realist he knows that reality is constructed by each person and society to explain and celebrate itself.

Ghose is more pessimistic. His own sense of displacement, of living between cultures, has been channelled through the thought of later Wittgenstein and that philosopher's awareness of the arbitrary relationship between language and things. Ghose sees all narrative as a lie, a falsification; the only true narratives are those which make us aware of their falsity and the deceitfulness of fictions. Rushdie, from *Grimus* on, has been concerned with ways to give literary shape to the clashes and contradictions between various cultures and mentalities and to the exile's sense of living simultaneously on multiple levels of reality. His word play, love of sounds, imitations and parodies of literary forms, experiments with science fiction and general extravagance and playfulness are ways of creating a Joycean world of words in exile and cunning. But unlike Joyce there is no silence; his novels challenge existing forms of power. Each of his novels treats of arbitrary systems of values and power which are supported by such words as 'shame' or those of the prophet Mohammed. When Rushdie brought the methods of the South American magical realists over into English he showed that there need not be a contradiction between self-conscious metafiction and political commitment. While like the other writers in exile he is often autobiographical, his use of satire permits a political emphasis.

A writer's commitment, however, is to language. The commitment to English has made the writer an exile and it is in language where the exile finds a home to replace society. Living on the boundaries between cultures, each exiled writer has an unusual sensitivity towards language, along with awareness of the provisionality of words. Naipaul's stylized Trinidadian dialect in his early books is balanced by an unusual precision in the use of generalized terms. He regards imprecise speech as confused thought. His prose is flat and logical, yet continuity is provided by repetitions of words, sounds and syntactical patterns, as if only tight weaving could prevent chaos. The repetitions which hold the words together are the inverse of the threatening chaos outside the rhythmic movement and order of the prose. In Rushdie's writing the meeting of East and West and living simultaneously in a multidimensional experience is expressed through multilingual puns and allusions, the presence of many voices, accents, dialects, languages and kinds of speech. Ghose distrusts words as misleading, an alienation from experience. Stow's novels are filled with the notation of class speech, dialect, idioms, slang, native usages, and other signs of an outsider observing foreign societies. Ramanujan creates continuity by incorporating an Indian dimension into English words. Emecheta begins by mixing Nigerian with very British idioms, then later begins using idioms in a personal way as if she were recreating the language.

Such writers share an alien's awareness of the way language has local forms and meanings, and of its provisionality. English has come loose from its moorings and needs to be fitted to new experiences. The dynamic which powers the exile's writing is being highly acculturated yet not fully assimilated into a new society.

AMIN MALAK

From Margin to Main: Minority Discourse and 'Third World' Fiction Writers in Canada

Let me begin with an explanation of the term 'third world' in the title. This is a term that is viewed with some trepidation and suspicion by many of us 'third worldists'. It evokes associations of underdevelopment, poverty, famine, and more recently a debt whose payment has long been overdue to the fat multinational banks. However, the other alternative terms – 'ethnic', 'immigrant' or still worse that odious coinage 'visible minorities' – are even more problematic and condescending. So, for lack of a better appellation, 'third world' will have to do as a functional reference to a group of writers, mainly from the Caribbean or South Asia, who have emerged on the literary scene in Canada, ever since government policies have changed in the 1960s, allowing more immigrants from sources other than Europe. I am thinking of such writers as Austin Clarke (Barbados), Neil Bissoondath (Trinidad), Michael Ondaatje (Sri Lanka), Bharati Mukherjee and Rohinton Mistry (India).

Since all these writers are first generation immigrants, and, more significantly, since most of them had to operate without an established literary tradition reflecting their own nascent communities in Canada, they are in essence pioneer workers on the literary landscape: their major initial landmark appeared in Canada a mere quarter of a century ago. I am referring to Austin Clarke's first novel *The Survivors of the Crossing*[1] which depicts, sympathetically and humorously, the hardship of life on the sugar plantations of Barbados. Thus, this novel is perhaps the first of several acclaimed works to be published in Canada *by* a third world writer about the third world. Naturally such works exhibit in both motif and manner an excess baggage of psychological and social ethos that seems at times radically different from the 'norms' of the Caucasian culture. Significantly, they dramatize as well the trauma often associated with the immigration experience. As Bharati Mukherjee puts it in the introduction to her collection of short stories portentously entitled *Darkness*: 'In my fiction, and in my Canadian experience "immigrants" were lost souls, put upon and pathetic',[2] because 'I discovered that the country is hostile to its citizens who had been born in hot, moist continents, like Asia' (p. 2). More importantly,

Mukherjee articulates her own personal anguish for being singled out as a visibly and behaviorally different person:

> If I may put it in its harshest terms, it would be this: in Canada I was frequently taken for a prostitute or shoplifter, frequently assumed to be a domestic, praised by astonished auditors that I didn't have a 'sing-song' accent. The society itself, or important elements in that society, routinely made crippling assumptions about me, and about my 'kind'. (pp. 2-3)

While avoiding the clichés of self-pity and/or sentimentality often associated with the immigration experience, Canadian writers of third world origin had (and unfortunately still have) to dramatize the dislocation and marginalization of their characters in an adopted society that is congenitally, if politely, unwelcoming. Such an inhospitable atmosphere, together with the lack of full-fledged literary institutions (like cultural associations, journals, and publishing agencies) that could echo Canada's cultural polyphony, compelled most third world writers to wage solitary battles to circumvent the Eurocentric hegemony over the Canadian literary establishment which has remained dominant until recently. Naturally they had to start from the periphery. Naturally they had to face neglect, derogation and spurn. Moreover, third world writers in Canada have to combat additional internal challenges, to climb, as Henry Kreisel puts it, 'curious psychological ... [and] linguistic mountains' caused by 'ever-present doubts whether the material will interest the majority of people living in the country, whether indeed the material is inherently valuable'.[3] Of course, such a dilemma has been faced by other immigrant writers elsewhere: Conrad, Beckett, Naipaul, Nabokov. The danger for the emerging third world writer, however, is to try to conquer this quandary by making compromises: such as going universal; that means avoiding facing the problems of his/her particular community in Canada by not dealing with them at all, as if they were non-issues. Such a strategy, if it is intentionally so, *might* be pivoted on a perception propounding that for a literary product to be of 'interest' to the Canadian reader, s/he need directly experience the issues at hand; nevertheless, we know that a diligent sympathetic reader can (simultaneously and diversely) relate to the fury of Dostoevsky's peasants, to the anguish of Kafka's beleaguered souls, and to the playful meandering of Rushdie's rootless, restless figures. At any rate, the resort to universalization to avoid marginality is one such a charge pressed against Michael Ondaatje's writing because:

> Ondaatje's work gives few indications of his Sri Lankan background. Ondaatje, coming from a Third World country with a colonial past, does not write about his otherness. Nor does he write about the otherness of the Canadian society for him. Intriguingly enough, there is no trauma of uprooting evident in his poetry; nor is there a need for redefinition in a new context: the subjects that preoccupy so many immigrant writers. One scours his poetry in vain for any cultural baggage he might

have brought with him when he came to Canada. Also absent are memories of familiar places, people, and things.[4]

In his fascinating book *Running in the Family*,[5] Ondaatje's archaeological
pursuit of roots turns fully private. He looks for parentage, not people-
hood: we learn more about the snakes of Sri Lanka than about its masses,
ethos, and agonies; more about the foibles of an eccentric half-tragic, half-
heroic father than about Sri Lanka's colonial past or conflict-ridden present. But a legitimate question arises: does he have to? Shouldn't he be free
to render what he chooses to, especially when he does it so enchantingly
well? Besides, what a writer doesn't say is at times more illuminating than
what he does say. Yet the criticism of Ondaatje claims some validity and
can be equally carried over to his most recent book: the highly engaging
novel *In the Skin of a Lion*.[6] He portrays – with lucid, poetic concision – the
life of struggling, hard-working immigrants, not from the third world, but
surreptitiously close: from Macedonia. Again, such a context begs the
questions: why this deliberate avoidance? Does the writer find it futile to
be associated with his own 'immigrant' or 'ethnic' group, shunning it as
one would, to borrow a term from Joy Kogawa, a 'gaggle of ghettoized
geese'?[7] Does the pursuit of the main necessitate avoiding the margin? If
the latter is the motive (and we are admittedly imputing it), it is definitely
working, for surely he is the most celebrated 'third world' writer in
Canada. We may be misreading Ondaatje's motives, but his case certainly
raises tantalizing, if exciting, critical questions that ache for answers.

Unlike Ondaatje, the fiction writer Neil Bissoondath, equally gifted and
accomplished, writes mainly and intensively about a community with
which he is obviously willing to be identified: his work depicts movingly
the daily dilemmas facing the West Indian immigrants of Toronto as well
as the conflict and corruption that afflict life in his home country,
Trinidad. Significantly, however, Bissoondath's fiction reveals other pitfalls
that await any third worldist when writing amidst an audience that is not
quite familiar with the complexities of the socio-political issues in the
Caribbean. Two hazards exist: the writer may be tempted to dilute the discourse concerning remote and removed issues to a perniciously reductive
degree, or s/he may resort to flattering Western stereotypes about the
post-colonial problems of the third world. A highly readable text like
Bissoondath's recent novel *A Casual Brutality*[8] may flash alarm signals and
provoke some probing questions. Set in a West Indian, newly-
independent, island-state called Casaquemada, which bears similarities to
Trinidad, the novel is permeated with overt as well as subtle signifiers
denoting the social and political disintegration of the Caribbean country
after the demise of white, colonial rule. The concoction of the name
'Casaquemada' is quite suggestive: its Spanish roots, as the text itself
indicates, means a 'House burnt' (p. 37); this portrayal of a homeland
hopelessly self-destructing, together with a title that suggests gruesome,

gratuitous violence, augurs the bleakness of life in the post-colonial Caribbean. After two ominous epigraphs, the novel thus opens most morbidly: 'There are times when the word *hope* is but a synonym for *illusion*: it is the most virile of perils' (p. 1). The narrative shifts between Toronto and Casaquemada, with the chronology being skilfully manipulated to register the perceptions and recollections of its narrator-protagonist: Dr Raj Ramsingh. The young physician comes from a middle-class Hindu family, whose status has evolved from that of being indentured labourers – brought to the island in hordes from India during colonial days – to that of being the influential elite in business and government. Despite this happy twist in his family's fortunes, Bissoondath's hero does not see his country as the promised paradise, for there exists a subculture of racial tension between the Indians and the Blacks, who too were imported in hordes to the island but as slaves. As the tenor of the narrator's observations suggests, the cause of this racial crisis is rooted in the resentment the Blacks feel for not achieving a fair share of wealth and power. Such a social and political context, echoing the familiar discourse in V.S. Naipaul's works such as *Guerrillas*, endows Bissoondath's text with ideological undercurrents demanding deciphering from any diligent reader. (Indeed, one faces a similar challenge in several of the short stories in Bissoondath's first book *Digging Up the Mountains*, such as 'Digging Up the Mountains,' 'The Revolutionary', and 'Insecurity'.)[9] There are constant hints of corruption in high places in Casaquemada, of promises broken and dreams betrayed, and ultimately of a situation of total chaos and cruelty in the post-colonial island-state. Significantly, given the narrator's Indian identity, the novel's discourse artfully insinuates that Black activists and/or the Leftists are mostly to blame.

According to Bakhtin's original insight,[10] it may not be valid to reduce a novel's polyphonic discourse to a single voice; yet, one can observe that Bissoondath's work here has a privileged voice represented by the character of Grappler, the sympathetically-drawn figure, who, as his name suggests, handles efficiently his family's problems and who functions as a father-substitute for the hero. It is this Grappler who makes the novel's major political statements, denouncing what he terms 'radicalization' and 'imported ideologies' and 'people building their personalities on other people's ideas, other people's experiences' (p. 200). He further declares:

> Trust no one who claims to speak for the people.... He almost never knows what the people want, but what they should want. And he will make sure they get it, even if he has to batter them into accepting it.
> Who would've thought back then, in the excitement of the flag, the anthem, the hope and the promise, that we would devolve to this mishmash of race, religion and politics, this carnival of intolerance? (pp. 200-201)

Competent, discreet, and always supportive, Grappler turns cynical. In his disillusionment, he judges (rather harshly and simplistically) his country's intellectuals instead of the corrupt, manipulative politicians with whom he is mysteriously associated:

> This is where our intellectuals have failed us.... They've been so busy looking back-wards, so busy shouting the simple politics of blame, so busy throwing barbs at the British, the Americans, the first world, the second world and any other world that presented itself, that they forgot to help prepare us for our change. (p. 202)

He eventually sums up his slanted views on the whole post-colonial ex-perience of the country by declaring:

> We had absorbed the attitudes of the colonizer, and we mimicked the worst in him. We learnt none of his virtues, grasped at all of his vices. That is what people don't understand. And now it have [sic] only one question left, and I wonder if it's even worth asking: When will we grow up? We're a failed experiment in nationhood, ... one among many. (p. 203)

While one appreciates the skilful rendition of such an angry rhetoric, one nevertheless quite misses the counter-discourse; compared to Grappler's dominant eloquence and charismatic appeal, the argument for the other side of the racial and/or political divide is subtly depersonalized, often distanced, almost schemingly alienated from the reader. To compound matters, Bissoondath's articulation of the protagonist-narrator's ideological ambivalence lacks lucidity and conviction. Since *A Casual Brutality* is un-avoidably permeated by the rhetoric of post-colonial malaise, the eager fascinated reader cannot help but find the text ideologically bridled. More importantly, the impact of a text with such a skewed and suspect dis-course on a reader not familiar with the complex, multi-faceted dimen-sions of the post-colonial debate is to develop a limited perspective that enhances the already established cynical stereotypes of a chaotic, violence-ridden, poverty-stricken third world.

The seriously slanted tone, amounting at times to the effects of a *danse macabre*, that pervades Neil Bissoondath's otherwise engaging work, is counterbalanced by the resort to irony and humour prevalent in the writ-ings of Austin Clarke and Rohinton Mistry. It is instructive to note that both Clarke and Mistry appear committed to their respective communities: they write almost exclusively and with total sympathy about the South Asians or Caribbeans living at 'home' or in their diaspora: Toronto. Fur-thermore, the humour does not flatter the stereotypes about people from the third world but potently pokes fun at them. It does not simplify issues but rather shows how subtle and painful discrimination and hypocrisy can be. For instance, Austin Clarke's latest collection of short stories *Nine Men Who Laughed*[11] dramatizes the anxiety and agony West Indians undergo in Toronto. The laughter of the title is nothing but black humour (no pun intended), because it essentially involves tragic experiences of dislocation, failure, hurt, and even (in the story entitled 'Canadian Experience') suicide. According to Northrop Frye, in Canada 'the nostalgia for a world of peace and protection, with a spontaneous response to the nature around it, with a leisure and composure not to be found today, is particularly strong'.[12] Frye calls such a pursuit 'a pastoral myth, the vision of a social ideal'. Unfortunately, for Clarke's Toronto characters, victimized as they are by various forms of racism, this pastoral myth has metamorphosed into a metropolitan malaise. In such a context, then, and in order to overcome this malaise, humour or irony is not a luxury but a shrewd saving device; not a trivial pursuit but an effective defense mechanism. Besides, either humour or irony serves, in this instance, as a potent commentary on the sophisticated pretensions of the Metropolis to the ideals of human fraternity and fair play.

My favourite example of a clever use of irony is Rohinton Mistry's short story 'Squatter' from the impressive 1987 collection entitled *Tales from Firozsha Baag*.[13] Complexly structured to accommodate the narrative shift between Bombay and Toronto, 'Squatter' illustrates the clash between Oriental and Western values. Mistry uses the ingenious technique of story-within-story. Through the witty, sardonic storyteller, Nariman, he narrates the comic tribulations of the Indian immigrant Sarosh who is transformed into Sid on arrival in Toronto. Among Sarosh's innumerable maladjustments is his perennial difficulty with the toilet seat:

> At the point where our story commences, Sarosh has been living in Toronto for ten years. We find him depressed and miserable, perched on top of the toilet, crouching on his haunches, feet planted firmly for balance upon the white plastic oval of the toilet seat.
> Daily for a decade had Sarosh suffered this position. Morning after morning, had no choice but to climb up and simulate the squat of our Indian latrines. If he sat down, no amount of exertion could produce success. (p. 153)

As if anticipating his difficulties in his prospective land of promise, Sarosh's mother insightfully encapsulates the truth that every sensitive immigrant comes to embrace: 'It is better to live in want among your family and friends, who love you and care for you, than to be unhappy surrounded by vacuum cleaners and dishwashers and big shiny motor cars' (p. 155).

Sarosh's tragi-comic ordeals with the toilet seat and his symbolic inability to perform his normal bodily functions cannot be overcome until he resignedly returns to India. Retaining the story's ironic tone, Mistry closes off with a parody of Othello's last speech. He lets Sarosh derisively sum up his immigrant experiences: just as Othello remained alien to the confusing values of Venice, Sarosh remains unfit for the dizzying world of Toronto:

> I pray you, in your stories ... [w]hen you shall these unlucky deeds relate, speak of me as I am; nothing extenuate, nor set down aught in malice: tell them that in

> Toronto once there lived a Parsi boy as best as he could. Set you down this; and say, besides, for some it was good and for some it was bad, but for me life in the land of milk and honey was just a pain in the posterior. (p. 168)

The implication of such a sharp treatment of the immigrant's experience may seem pernicious, yet the story's psychological thrust creates an over-all humorous effect that counterbalances the cynicism, concluding with a humane scene of care and compassion involving the storyteller Nariman and his young audience (the children inhabiting the residential complex of Firozsha Baag of the title).

A skilfully crafted character in his own right, Nariman appears as the man of ritual and foresight. Like all storytellers, Nariman functions here as the tribal spokesman and the repository of the community's heritage. If, as Walter Benjamin tells us, storytelling is a dead profession in the literate culture of the West, it is still thankfully a flourishing art within the oral tradition of the third world; the work of that other talented writer from Bombay, Salman Rushdie, would attest to its artistic relevance. Mistry effectively demonstrates the sublime psychic affinity between the storyteller and his enchanted, loyal listeners: this creative interaction becomes an edifying process, blending instruction with delight. Amusingly, it is this Nariman who interjects the sardonic tale with a scathing comment on Canadian multicultural policy:

> The Multicultural Department is a Canadian invention. It is supposed to ensure that ethnic cultures are able to flourish, so that Canadian society will consist of a mosaic of cultures – that's their favourite word, mosaic – instead of one uniform mix, like the American melting pot. If you ask me, mosaic and melting pot are both nonsense, and ethnic is a polite way of saying bloody foreigner. (p. 160)

The strategy of this scatological drama involves, to borrow from the Russian Formalists, defamiliarizing the familiar and familiarizing the unfamiliar. More importantly, it makes the prejudiced reader surrender stereotypes, liberating him/her from any preconceptions. Alternatively or conjointly, it may intentionally recall those stereotypes (such as the referent 'bloody foreigner') then proceed surreptitiously to eliminate them by showing their absurdity and through winning the reader's sense of sympathy and bonhomie.

If we were to formulate common denominators for these third world writers in Canada, we could conclude that theirs is mostly a collective experience of 'otherness', engendering diverse responses and resulting in various modes of articulation. The language used to mediate that experience (English) is adopted out of necessity or compulsion rather than choice: one more relic of the colonial era. Consequently, this adoption creates a feeling of ambivalence for third world writers not only in Canada but elsewhere too: English is currently a dominant international language, yet it has predatory associations with a colonial past. On the other hand, third world users of the language levy, in their turn, a price on it: under their influence, English perpetually evolves or devolves (depending on the perspective). Third world writers in English constantly coin new idiomatic and syntactical patterns to the chagrin, perhaps, of scholastic pedants wishfully dreaming of codifying or freezing the flux of the language in an imperial mould.

The dominance of the English language in South Asia and the Caribbean explains, moreover, why most of the third world writers in Canada are from these two regions rather than other areas such as the Middle East, South America and Africa. However, as more immigrants from these other areas settle, we shall certainly witness fresh talents entering the fray. In fact, the signs are already quite promising.

What the efforts and energies of these third world writers amount to is, in essence, a merging of the minority discourse from the margin into mainstream; this development represents the fourth stage of the progress of any minority articulation of itself. Let me schematize:

Stage 1: Invisible and Inaudible:

This is the stage of total domination over the minority's destiny, in which its entire existence is denied. This situation copies colonial practices in their cruellest form.

Stage 2: Visible but Inaudible:

At this stage, the minority is accredited recognition, but denied the right to speak for itself. Usually somebody else does the representation, *'faute de mieux* for the poor' minority, as Edward Said would say.[14]

Stage 3: Visible, Audible, but Marginal:

At this stage, discrimination takes the subtle form of attributing the amorphous qualities of merit and excellence exclusively to the 'host' culture or the 'master' code, while relegating the minority's discourse to the margin. Such a derogation creates the 'crippling assumptions' that Bharati Mukherjee complained about.

Stage 4: Storming the Fort:

At this stage, the minority, through sheer tenacity, wrests recognition of excellence. The cardinal merits of works by third world writers in Canada can now be readily acknowledged. For instance, when Rohinton Mistry published his *Tales from Firozsha Baag*, it was speedily shortlisted for the Governor General's Award. This happy conclusion to a long and arduous voyage signals that the immigrant's ship is, at long last, in port. The immigrant has arrived!

Let me conclude where I began by returning to the term 'third world'. While these writers, all being immigrants, can claim two countries, two cultures, two worlds (Canada being one and the country of origin the other), they really belong to neither because the immigrant mind is dichotomous by nature, locked on the horns of a dilemma, neither affiliated with the old root culture, nor fully fitting with the new adopted one. Accordingly, writers negotiating and articulating such an experience have to inhabit an alternative world, a *third* world: a world of their imagination, their memory, their nostalgia. This third world can obviously be a lonely world, at times a painful, predatory world imposing compromise and surrender; but also a world where it is equally possible to test one's capacity to endure, to survive, and to triumph.

NOTES

1. Austin Clarke, *The Survivors of the Crossing* (Toronto: McClelland & Stewart, 1964).
2. Bharati Mukherjee, *Darkness* (Markham, Ontario: Penguin, 1985), p. 1. All further references are to this edition and are included in the text.
3. Henry Kreisel, 'Language and Identity: A Personal Essay', in Shirley Neuman, ed., *Another Country: Writings by and about Henry Kreisel* (Edmonton: NeWest Press, 1985), p. 128.
4. Arun Mukherjee, *Towards an Aesthetics of Opposition: Essays on Literature Criticism and Cultural Imperialism* (Ontario: Williams-Wallace, 1988), pp. 33-34.
5. Michael Ondaatje, *Running in the Family* (Toronto: McClelland & Stewart, 1982).
6. Michael Ondaatje, *In the Skin of a Lion* (Toronto: McClelland & Stewart, 1987).
7. Joy Kogawa, 'The Japanese-Canadian Dilemma', *Toronto Life* (December 1985), p. 59.
8. Neil Bissoondath, *A Casual Brutality* (Toronto: Macmillan, 1988). All references are to this edition and are included in the text.
9. Neil Bissoondath, *Digging Up the Mountains* (Toronto: Macmillan, 1985).
10. Mikhail Bakhtin, *Problems of Dostoevsky's Poetics* (Ann Arbor: Ardis, 1973).
11. Austin Clarke, *Nine Men Who Laughed* (Markham, Ontario: Penguin, 1986).
12. Northrop Frye, 'Conclusion', in Carl F. Clinck, ed., *Literary History of Canada: Canadian Literature in English* (Toronto: University of Toronto Press, 1965), p. 840.
13. Rohinton Mistry, *Tales from Firozsha Baag* (Markham, Ontario: Penguin, 1987). All references are to this edition and are included in the text.
14. Edward W. Said, *Orientalism* (New York: Pantheon, 1978; rpt. Vintage, 1979), p. 21.

EMMANUEL S. NELSON

Troubled Journeys: Indian Immigrant Experience in Kamala Markandaya's *Nowhere Man* and Bharati Mukherjee's *Darkness*

The twentieth-century has witnessed massive migratory movements of various peoples across national and continental boundaries. The reasons for migration vary; the destinations differ. Yet all immigrant experiences share certain fundamental characteristics. 'The history of immigration,' as Oscar Handlin points out, 'is the history of alienation and its consequences.'[1] The migratory experience invariably entails pain: 'For every freedom won, a tradition lost. For every second generation assimilated, a first generation in one way or another spurned. For the gains of goods and services, an identity lost, an uncertainty found.'[2] Therefore, the numerous creative texts that have evolved out of the diverse immigrant experiences around the world can indeed be legitimately placed in a single category and viewed as a unique genre of imaginative writing with its own assumptions, forms, and features. In other words, works as diverse as Maxine Hong Kingston's *The Woman Warrior* (which deals with Chinese-American experience), Albert Wendt's *Sons for the Return Home* (which explores the Samoan immigrant experience in New Zealand), and Azouz Begag's *Le Gone du Chaaba* (which examines the dilemmas of North African immigrants in France), despite their obvious differences, are also closely related texts. The Chinese, Samoan, and Arab protagonists of these novels – different though they are – share a common experience: the experience of growing up in an immigrant family in an alien, often hostile, country. Their lives, and the texts that contain them, therefore, have certain shared themes and patterns.

Some of the powerful voices in this international literature of migration belong to Indian writers of the diaspora. These voices emerge from a variety of places: from Fiji and Singapore, from Durban and Trinidad, from London and New York. These voices give shape and form to a wide spectrum of Indian immigrant experiences near and far from the Subcontinent. My commentary is limited to two writers from this diaspora – Kamala Markandaya and Bharati Mukherjee; my discussion, specifically, will focus on a representative text of each author – Markandaya's *Nowhere Man*[3] and Mukherjee's *Darkness*.[4]

Nowhere Man is a bitter novel about the Indian immigrant experience in Britain. *Darkness*, on the other hand, is a collection of angst-ridden stories about the lives of immigrants from the Subcontinent in North America. Neither artist is new to the craft of fiction: Markandaya had established herself as a major writer well before her publication of *Nowhere Man*, and Mukherjee had written two critically well-received novels prior to publishing *Darkness*. So both texts reveal their creators' refined control over the mechanics of fictional composition. *Nowhere Man* is poignantly eloquent in its depiction of the immigrant plight; many of the stories in *Darkness* are flawlessly executed. Both writers expertly handle the artistic challenges they face and inform the often predictable themes of immigrant fiction with refreshingly new insights. What I wish to challenge, however, is the practical value of these texts to the immigrant communities that Markandaya and Mukherjee write about.

The question of identity and a host of related issues are concerns central to the works of both Markandaya and Mukherjee. As individuals who have lived the immigrant experience – Markandaya in England since the fifties and Mukherjee in North America since the sixties – both writers have had to confront the issue of identity in highly personal terms. Expatriation, to both of them, has been considerably traumatic. The barely concealed anger in *Nowhere Man* no doubt is a reflection of the author's own rage at British racism. Mukherjee's frequent encounters with racism on the streets of Toronto actually prompted her to seek legislation that would criminalize racist name-calling.[5] Their personal exposure to blatant racism must have been especially debilitating to them, since both grew up in upper middle-class homes in India and, therefore, were protected from such humiliating and degrading experiences. Their felt vulnerability as Indians living in the imperial West no doubt accounts, to a considerable degree, for their preoccupation with aspects of the struggle for identity.

In *Nowhere Man* healthy acculturation proves elusive to all Indian immigrant characters. Vasantha does not even attempt to adapt to England. Her relocation from India to England was not entirely voluntary. Even after many years in England her definitions remain traditionally Indian and she grieves as she watches her semi-assimilated sons adopt 'un-Indian' attitudes. Srinivas, like Vasantha, does not make a conscious effort to integrate – at least not initially. When he does attempt to do so later in his life, England proves to be too hostile a place to allow such accommodation. Their son, Laxman, aggressively attempts assimilation but only to arrive at the bitter discovery that his 'place' in England is irrevocably defined by his Indianness. Even his marriage to an English woman – the ultimate assimilative gesture – does not provide the symmetry he seeks in life. And Markandaya effectively reinforces her characters' uncertain sense of identity by manipulating the language – through fragmented sentences, convoluted syntax, and abrupt closures – to reveal their confused and troubled lives.

One of the primary consequences of this failure to forge an authentic awareness of self is an incapacitating sense of alienation. Srinivas becomes a 'nowhere man', an uprooted and dislocated individual devoid of any sustaining sense of connection to his environment. His leprosy is a gruesome symbol of his status as a rejected outsider, a hideous emblem of his gnawing exile. The ravages of the disease on his ageing body are symptomatic of his doomed quest for personal and cultural wholeness. His illness defines his crippling isolation; it is a grim testimony to the unwholesome metamorphosis that his migration has spawned.

The loss of a relatively coherent earlier identity, a stock theme in immigrant fiction, is often initiated and subsequently complicated by a simultaneous loss of a supportive community. While Vasantha and Srinivas lose their sense of connectedness, the feeling of being an integral part of a community, upon their arrival in England, they are unable to forge a new community in their adopted county. Their friendships with their English neighbours are flimsy ties at best; those connections lack the nourishing and supportive quality that can sustain them and enable them to feel that they belong.

But Vasantha, and to some extent, Srinivas, manage to create for themselves a faint semblance of internal stability – fragile though it is – by clinging to certain traditional Indian values and attitudes. Laxman, on the contrary, is even less rooted than his parents – despite his seeming confidence. Caught between India and England, a country he has never seen and a country that does not want him, Laxman is truly a 'nowhere man'. As Alec Hargreaves argues in his commentary on the literature of second-generation North African immigrants in France, the plight of the children of immigrant parents can be especially traumatic because they are forced into dealing with a dual heritage. The 'different cultural strands often fit uncomfortably together' and reconciling them into a 'harmonious whole'[6] can indeed be problematic. A divided self becomes an inevitable part of their immigrant inheritance. Laxman, for example, rejects certain aspects of his parents' value system – the very aspects that had furnished them with a modicum of stability – but he is unable to forge a valid alternative value system that can nourish him.

British racism, of course, is at the centre of the mangled lives that Markandaya's characters lead. Her detailed exploration of the circumstances of Srinivas' emigration from India is part of her attempt to place migration from the Subcontinent to Britain in a specific historical context. She underscores the often disregarded (by the British) fact that Britain's contemporary problems with immigration are a direct consequence of Britain's imperialist past. British racism – both historical and contemporary – is a key factor in Markandaya's presentation of the troubled lives of her characters. The ending of the novel reveals her grimly pessimistic view of the future of race relations in Britain. Her apocalyptic vision of the fire that engulfs Srinivas' house is a chilling metaphor for the very real possibilities of large-scale racial violence in Britain.

This concern with racism and racially motivated violence is a significant aspect of Mukherjee's *Darkness* as well, though racism in its more virulent forms is present mostly in stories that have a Canadian setting. In her preface to the anthology and in her 1988 *New York Times Book Review* interview with Barth Healey, Mukherjee implies that Canada is many times more hostile than the United States to immigrants from the Subcontinent. In Canada she was 'frequently taken for a prostitute or shoplifter ... [or] a domestic' (*Darkness*, p. 2). Canada, she asserts, is a country that has 'officially incited its less-visible citizens to react' (p. 2) against the more visible minorities, that in Canada her Indianness for her was increasingly becoming a '"visible" disfigurement to be hidden' (p. 3). Her immigration to the United States in 1980, she adds, has been a liberating experience. Long before her arrival as an immigrant to the United States many of the major civil rights battles had already been fought and won by the country's minorities. To Americans she is 'just another immigrant' (p. 2); to Canadian rednecks, however, she was, 'after the imported idiom of London' (p. 41), a 'Paki'.

Regardless of the presence or the intensity of racism in the settings, her stories, like Markandaya's *Nowhere Man*, focus on the question of identity and related issues. 'The World According to Hsu' is an effective rendering of the protagonist's growing realization of her homelessness. While vacationing in a politically turbulent island-nation off the coast of Africa with her Canadian husband, she finds out that her husband has accepted an offer of an attractive job in Toronto – a city that she knows from her past experiences is a 'hell' (p. 41) for immigrants from the Subcontinent. Though her husband is sympathetic to her fears of living in Toronto, he hardly understands the depth of her dilemma. As she sits alone drinking wine in a restaurant full of exiles from everywhere, babbling in many languages, she realizes that 'she would never feel so at home again' (p. 56). Once the vacation under the tropical sky is over, she will have to face the snowy hell in Canada – a place she knows will never allow her to belong.

Even seemingly well-adjusted and materially successful immigrants in *Darkness* harbour an uncertain sense of identity. Dr Manny Patel in 'Nostalgia' is a well-to-do psychiatrist in a state hospital in suburban New York. America has been 'very good to him, no question' (p. 99), but there is a nagging sense of longing for the life he has left behind in India, a nostalgia that is symptomatic of certain larger discontents with his life in the United States. His marriage to Camille, an American, appears superficially successful, but he senses a vague disconnection from her. His hasty attempt to have an affair with an attractive Indian immigrant girl he notices in a shop is, in fact, a clumsy attempt to re-connect with his memories of home and his past, an attempt to regain a tangible sense of India which is fading away from him while leaving behind a feeling of loss, guilt, and despair.

Equally important in Mukherjee's works in general, in *Darkness* especially, is the marital stress that the migratory experience generates. Raised in conservative, often sexually repressive communities, Mukherjee's characters desire the sexual freedom of other Americans. The traditional concepts of marriage which immigrants bring with them are challenged by the values of a permissive foreign culture. The structures that keep marriages in tact in India are absent in the Western context, thus leaving the immigrants' marriages fragile and vulnerable. Having an affair is not merely a sexual temptation, but it offers a way of reasserting one's autonomy, one's control over one's life. The danger is alluring. But, as in the case of Dr Patel, the desire for intimacy outside the boundaries of marriage might also be symptomatic of larger discontents of immigrant life – the loneliness, the uncertainty, the emptiness. Vinita in 'Visitors', for example, has a devoted husband, a fabulous condominium, and an apparently satisfying life. Yet the romantic overtures of a lonely Indian student, Rajiv, creates in her a longing to leave her husband, 'the haven of his expensive condominium, and run off into the alien American night where only shame and disaster can await her' (p. 176).

Thus Mukherjee and Markandaya articulate, often with remarkable accuracy and flair, our experiences as Subcontinental immigrants in the West. They bring a uniquely Indian perspective to the standard themes of immigrant fiction: failed quests and thwarted dreams; nostalgia for a home that now exists only in memory; conditions of dislocation and isolation; marital stress and intergenerational conflicts caused by the demands of a new and hostile cultural environment; loss of a supportive community and often unsuccessful attempts to forge new support systems; crippling loss of a relatively coherent earlier identity; and painful searches for an orderly sense of self and a healing awareness of personal and cultural wholeness.

Both Markandaya and Mukherjee are artful storytellers. One cannot overlook the grace with which they appropriate the English language and the skill with which they re-create the themes of our immigrant experience. Yet, as readers, we are left with a feeling of dissatisfaction; there is something lacking, something that might offer us at least momentary transcendence. A closer look at their texts allows us a glimpse of the reasons for our vague sense of disappointment.

Markandaya's and Mukherjee's analysis of racism, for example, is disconcertingly superficial. Racism is sometimes presented merely as a manifestation of ill manners, a sign of poor upbringing; or, as in the case of Markandaya's portrayal of Fred's racism, it is merely a mechanism for underprivileged whites to cope with their own frustrating sense of inadequacy. But racism is a far more complex phenomenon. Neither writer fully explores the psychological, political, and cultural bases of racist behaviour. One longs to see the incisive perceptions of a James Baldwin or a Richard Wright or a Toni Morrison on the issue of white racism but one is merely offered relatively shallow perspectives on it. It is disappointing, because a fuller understanding of the peculiarities of British and Canadian racism can offer us the empowering logic necessary to counter it.

Equally disappointing is the authors' reduction of the Indian immigrant experience to a metaphor for the universal human conditions of alienation and dislocation. Their artistic visions are shaped primarily by the values embedded in the twentieth-century bourgeois literature of the West; indeed both writers share with their Western counterparts an obsessive preoccupation with the modern maladies of exile, loneliness, and disorientation. Mukherjee is explicit in asserting her metaphoric intent:

> Indianness is now a metaphor, a particular way of partially apprehending the world. Though the characters in these stories are, or were, 'Indian,' I see most of these as stories of broken identities and discarded languages, and the will to bond oneself to a new community, against the ever-present fear of failure and betrayal. (p. 3)

In her short story, 'Isolated Incidents', for example, the seemingly stable life of a white Canadian woman who works for the Immigration Department is ultimately revealed to be as disoriented and fragmented as the lives of immigrants whose anxious and insistent demands she has to cope with on her job. In Markandaya's *Nowhere Man*, too, the dislocations of immigrant life assume metaphoric significance. Mrs Pickering's loneliness and Dr Radclife's barely contained frustration are not unlike the dilemmas of the immigrant characters. This shift toward the symbolic, however, does violence to the uniqueness of our post-colonial and immigrant inheritances. Metaphorizing may be a convenient strategy, but the cost is an unfortunate retreat from exploring the complex dimensions of our lives.

The resolutely apolitical stance of both writers also perhaps contributes to our disappointment with their art. Neither informs her text with a clearly defined ideological perspective; the value of their artifacts to the immigrant communities they write about is, therefore, questionable. They re-create our pain splendidly but fail to frame it within a redemptive, transcendent vision. The purpose of their re-creation of our troubles may be cathartic, but catharsis for whom? Our pain is real enough; there is no need to imagine it as well. In the face of widespread hostility and raw violence against Subcontinental immigrants in Britain, Canada and, increasingly, in the United States, mere re-creation of our pain seems somewhat impertinent, if not politically irresponsible.

Why is it that the Indian characters in these works often find themselves in states of exquisite alienation rather than forging an empowering sense of community with fellow-immigrants? Are our communities so devoid of cohesion, as Markandaya and Mukherjee imply, that we cannot develop a healing sense of connectedness? Why do many of their Indian characters avoid introspection and seemingly exist in a suspended state of paralyzing dislocation? Do we not have a past that we can examine, understand, and affirm – as so many African-American characters do in the novels of Alice Walker, Gloria Naylor, and Toni Morrison – to find our anchors and achieve a sense of order and coherence? Do we lack a shared set of symbols and mythologies which we can reinvent, as Maxine Hong Kingston does brilliantly for her Chinese-American readers in *The Woman Warrior*? Do we lack the revolutionary commitment that allow Paul Di Donato's Italian-immigrant characters in *Christ in Concrete* to gain control over their environment? Do we not have the capacity to adapt to own new cultural realities and reshape them to our own sense of reality as Saul Bellow's Jewish-American immigrant protagonist, Augie March, accomplishes so effectively? What we need from our artists who give voice and form to our immigrant experience is an activist consciousness, not just helpless angst; sadly, neither Markandaya nor Mukherjee offers us such a perspective. I am not attempting to prescribe what Markandaya and Mukherjee should write about; I am merely assessing, as a practical reader, the value of their texts to us. They are writing about us, after all, and they have the right to do so – just as much as we have the right to evaluate and articulate the usefulness of their art in our personal lives.

NOTES

1. Thomas Wheeler, *The Immigrant Experience* (Baltimore: Penguin, 1971), p. 1.
2. Ibid., p. 1.
3. Kamala Markandaya, *Nowhere Man* (London: Allen Lane, 1973).
4. Bharati Mukherjee, *Darkness* (Ontario: Penguin, 1985). All references are to this edition and are included in the text.
5. Barth Healey, 'Mosaic vs. Melting Pot', *New York Times Book Review* 19 June 1988, p. 22.
6. Alex Hargreaves, '*Beur* Fiction: Voices from the Immigrant Community in France', *The French Review* 62 (March 1989), p. 661.

PAUL SHARRAD

'Temporary Suspensions':
Form and Multi-cultural Expression

> The job is to build bridges – not of stone or girders, for that would prove the
> permanence of the objective, but like the rope bridges in the Himalayas, you build
> temporary suspensions over green and gurgling space.[1]

This paper will explore the idea that writing which expresses multi-
cultural experience charts a shift towards images rather than objects,
parameters rather than what they contain, to processes of exchange where-
in the text itself functions as a porous surface instead of a solid-state
reification.

Discussion will be based on Michael Ondaatje's *Rat Jelly* and Keri
Hulme's *Te Kaihau/The Windeater*.[2]

Edward Said, in one of the essays in his book *The World the Text the
Critic*, talks about a modern post-colonial cultural formation that moves
from the 'filial' to the 'affiliative' – from automatic inheritance of parental
identities to an active, personal and eclectic accumulation of identifica-
tions.[3] The idea is expressed similarly by social psychologists engaged in
theorising the emerging multicultural personality – a fluid area of exchange rather than a self conceptualised as some core objectified ego to be
discovered, defined, developed and protected at all costs.[4] The shift is
described by Lacan as a move from the ego to the subject – a constant reformation of the signifying chain, of the interaction between self and Other
– and has become enshrined in current literary debate as Bakhtin's
heterogeneous 'dialogism'.[5]

I want to go on to examine two pluri-cultural writers to see to what
degree these theories are reflected in the vision and structure of their
work, but we should first signal the power of that outraged clinging to
family, clan, and ethnic and religious filiations which today is expressed
in sectarian violence across the globe, and also consider just what has
produced the idealising of a mutable self – the social need for tolerance in
mixed communities brought about either by first-world multinationals
shunting academics, advisors, businessfolk and troops from country to
country, or by refugees from communal conflict, religious persecution,
political oppression, war and famine moving to become 'factory-fodder'

abroad. This is the large-scale view; there are internal disruptions and inventions of pluralistic communities as well – the mixing of ethnic groups in national bodies such as the police force or large banks, the urban drift in developing countries, and the historical creation of hybrid communities as a result of colonialism.

It is easy for theorists to speak of pluralism, of the marginalised voices 'speaking back' alongside established discourses of power. In real life we are confronted by the drunken Anglo youth on an Australian beach shouting his rage against Asian immigrants whom he perceives as taking his job and housing; we are witnesses to the (white) police shooting of an innocent (black) Australian during a house-raid; and then there is Said's native Palestine.[6] Even in the realm of theoretical writing, the hysteric poetical intensity of Julia Kristeva's dramatic 'discussion' of abjection bears witness to the suffering that goes along with ethnic displacements and re-formations of identity.[7] We should be wary lest our generalisations obscure pain and prejudice, careful lest they simplify the complexities of social movement into brute figures of exploiter and victim. The pluralising of societies does not mean their bland homogenisation. Perhaps one generalisation that will stand scrutiny is that the writers who emerge out of this social process insist on differences, make plain their particular torments, and resist the erosion of individual choice while acknowledging the power of social forces and history. What is of interest to us is the variety of literary strategies they adopt to represent their experiences. I have chosen two writers from two hemispheres as case studies.

Michael Ondaatje comes from a 'burgher' family founded during the expansion of Western trade into the East – Ceylonese-Dutch becoming Anglicised under the Raj; 'white' to the 'natives', 'coloured' to the colonial administration. Ondaatje went to England for his schooling and ended up studying and settling in Canada. He has written several books of poems, two 'experimental' novels, and an autobiographical exploration of his family. I shall concentrate here on the anthology *Rat Jelly & Other Poems, 1963-78* and mention *The Collected Works of Billy the Kid*.[8] Keri Hulme's name is familiar for her Booker Prize-winning novel, *The Bone People*. Keri is part Scots, part Maori, and I shall look at her use of this dual heritage in the collection, *Te Kaihau/The Windeater*.[9]

Ondaatje has been berated for not assuming an Asian identity in solidarity with other Asian Americans/Third Worlders, and for looking at his country of origin (when he does at all) from an outside, Western perspective.[10] In fact, *Rat Jelly* includes quite a few poems that draw on family history and South Asian cultural references, culminating in poetic observations of Sri Lanka during the time he spent there preparing the memoir *Running in the Family*.[11] 'The Dainty Monsters' has an epigraph from Sanskrit, tropical jungle is encountered in Henri Rousseau's painting, a heron eats from a banana leaf, there are references to family history in 'Dates', 'Letters', 'Uswetakeiyawa' and 'The Wars'.[12]

Whatever the attitude towards his native land, Ondaatje cannot help but express his identity in his poems, and that has little to do with the fixity of self-definition implicit in images of the migrant Asian struggling to keep alive the native traditions of the homeland. Even in Sri Lanka, his family looked at local tradition with the detachment of a Europeanised class – 'Letters and Other Worlds' mentions his father as a 'semi-official, and semi-white at that', unwittingly helping to precipitate the independence movement by drunkenly sprawling in the roadway in front of a Perahara procession.[13] Michael himself left Sri Lanka at an early age, adopting the identity of a coolly displaced citizen of the modern world (not unlike Dom Moraes). To express this position he uses a detached, dispassionate voice, observing the minimalist details of here and now and avoiding grand moral or emotional gestures: 'But there is no history or philosophy or metaphor with us./ The problem is the toughness of the Adidas shoe' ('Walking to Bellrock').[14]

Identity is reduced to a human awareness of corporeal frailty and behavioral absurdity. Blood constantly surges out to remind us of mortality; dogs are forever on the sidelines casting our assumptions of dignity and superiority into doubt. This is a kind of radical marginalising of self which is at once universalist and dislocated. It is accompanied by the attempt to relocate within a Canadian landscape, within family, and gradually the sense of selfhood begins to fill out as more and more of the surroundings are 'possessed' (see the longer and more densely packed narrative poems towards the end of the collection: 'Pig Glass' and 'Walking to Bellrock'). But even here the detached observing self cannot find complete integration with local history or nature, being alongside rather than included within, save for that present moment of walking or thinking that is reproduced in the reflection of writing the poem. This in itself is an ambiguously balanced condition, but it is ultimately all there is to validate the poet's sense of being:

> My mind is pouring chaos
> in nets onto the page.
> ...
> And that is all this writing should be then.
> The beautiful formed things caught at the wrong moment
> so they are shapeless, awkward
> moving to the clear.
>> ('"The gate in his head"', p. 64)

> I admire the spider, his control classic,
> his eight legs finicky,
> making lines out of the juice of his abdomen.
> A kind of writer I suppose.
> He thinks a path and travels
> the emptiness that was there
> leaves his bridge behind

looking back saying Jeez
did I do that?

('Spider Blues', p. 62)

Indeed, we might say that the clearest sense of a self is found in the process of writing – that Ondaatje writes himself into being. The self that emerges is as thin as the line of verse – a surface tension, 'tracks left empty/ walking to the centre of the lake'; and as diffused as the wanderer's identity: 'Oh world, I shall be buried all over Ontario' – an image of dispersal found in other poems as well: 'the dog scatters her body in sleep' ('Birds for Janet – the Heron', 'Signature', 'Biography', pp. 3, 9, 12). This self comes to being only within 'a cell of civilised magic' that is the poem ('The Diverse Causes', p. 6) and even then – significantly in a poem titled 'Signature' – it slips from 'him' to 'you' to 'I' (pp. 8-9).

What we have here is certainly a different project than Wordsworth's, even though it might appear to be Romantic in using 'natural objects' as devices through which to discover meaning. This poet discovers intimations of mortality and separation from the natural world, looking on it not as something that will absorb him into the cosmic power 'that rolls through all things', but with the eyes of an alien registering and estranging most obvious surface sense-data (a canoe and a beaver dam get mixed up with a badminton net and a dragon – 'Dragon', p. 4 – 'nature breeds the unnatural', – 'Early Morning, Kingston to Gananoque', p. 5). There is little sense of the philosophic imposition of meaning via tranquil recollection, or of the rapture of identification through relived emotions: all is present process and spare disinterest perhaps striving towards a deliberately anti-sentimental stoic toughness: 'Looking on/ we wear sentimentality like a curse' ('"Lovely the Country of Peacocks"', p. 16), but curiously not far, perhaps, from a Buddhist sense of meditation on experience and the self as reducible to a fluid succession of atomised phenomena which properly have nothing to do with individual identity, action, and desire.

The idea of writing oneself into being suggests a post-modernist outlook, a textual play celebrating fragmentation and flux.[15] There is in Ondaatje's writing, though, a consistent voice and a recognisable structuring of images that rather indicates a modernist sensibility seeking, like Eliot, to shore up a stable structure out of the ruins of shattered history. (The poem becomes a Wallace Stevens-type jar that focuses its chaotic surroundings into a semblance of meaning.) Indeed, there is a fear of disintegration; while the poet admires 'those/ who sail to that perfect edge/ where there is no social fuel', he also dreads the silence that waits beyond the edges of the social:

There is my fear
of no words   of
falling without words

over and over   of
mouthing the silence

('White Dwarfs', p. 68)

The poetic collection declares its debt to Wallace Stevens (p. 61, 'King Kong meets Wallace Stevens') and looks at times like William Carlos Williams, though always with a more literary, conceptual bent. It is perhaps as Ondaatje settles into his Canadian world that he gains the stability from which to experiment with the post-modern, so that the 'Pig Glass' section, while it records homely things like 'Moving Fred's Outhouse' and friendships with other Canadian writers, takes a quotation from Italo Calvino's *Invisible Cities* as its epigraph.

This apparent shift is foreshadowed in the earlier 'left handed poems' of *The Collected Works of Billy the Kid* (1970). Here, the assemblage of free verse, photographs, historical interviews and press cuttings, extracts from dime novels, guide-book facts etc. seems to convey a self-conscious intertextuality, a post-modern semiotic play that mocks fixed identity and knowable history: shape-changing is the essence, surfaces are all ('there is nothing of depth, of significant accuracy, of wealth in the image, I know', p. 20) and texts are provisional. Ondaatje says he likes writing that has 'lots of spaces and inquiries but never fully rounded off and framed'.[16] Yet there is a clear drive in this book to some identification with the outlaw-hero as well as an implicit foregrounding of the sceptical author selecting, 'touching up' and combining his material into a personal significance.

In noting a change from *Billy the Kid* to the more radically post-modern project of *Coming through Slaughter*, Ina Ferris notes that 'The shift in the role of art and the artist is a difficult one to make for a Romantic writer like Ondaatje, for it means surrendering the dream of originality'.[17] We can, I think, speculate on an equivalence between the migrant's pleasure in being 'original' in a new setting and the pain in having to be original by virtue of combining the uniquely disparate elements of old and new into a personal conception of experience. The marginalised position of this originality corresponds to an outlaw transgression, a crossing of boundaries in life and art for which there is always a penalty to pay. Hence, perhaps the urge to hybrid post-modern experiment and its accompanying reluctance to shed a modernist hold on unifying narrative and referential access to the past.[18]

The photograph becomes an important idea in Ondaatje's work. An early mention of it is a telling one: he registers the night jungle of Sri Lanka as 'A landscape nightmare/ unphotographed country' ('Uswetakeiyawa', p. 90) in which smells cannot be defined, dogs are 'so mongrelled/ they seem to have woken/ to find themselves tricked/ into outrageous transformations', a cyclist becomes 'a white sarong/ pumping its legs ... like a moth in the headlights' and boats have 'their alphabets lost in the dark'. However, as the description of Sri Lanka suggests (and as some of the pictures of the old American 'badlands' also indicate in *Billy the Kid*) the photograph and the 'documentary' texts are constructed *fixings* of history (you don't get photos without a 'fixer', as the opening blank 'photo' indicates). The photo is the modern sign of identity, a technological validation of reality/presence, a form of autobiography. Billy the Kid's country is not, like Sri Lanka, a nightmare of unconnected fragments: it is not 'unphotographed country' – nor is the book. One thing a photo does is to frame things, to compose them. All we have on the opening page is a frame (the outlaw 'framed' by history, by a multiplicity of 'texts'?) and it frames a work that closes with another frame, identical save for the inclusion of a photo of a child (of the author as child?) in a cowboy suit. Thus the book becomes a framing, a fixing of self via textual metaphor exactly equivalent to Ondaatje's (auto)biography which is a collage of impressions largely assembled through family photographs – a modernist 'composing' of the fragments of a personal past: the title, *Running in the Family*, not only suggests motion, it also connotes continuity, even if that continuity is figured as the eccentric and the solitary.[19]

Another person who figures as something of a solitary eccentric (though this image is belied by her very sociable personality) is Keri Hulme. Unlike the peripatetic Ondaatje, she was born in Christchurch and grew up around Moeraki in the South Island of New Zealand, the location of her first collection of poems, *The Silences Between/Moeraki Conversations*.[20] After time in the North Island working in TV, she moved to an isolated town on the West Coast of the South Island where she fishes for whitebait when she's not writing.

A glance at the poetry shows, as the title suggests, an attempt to locate an identity in a place using a style that owes much to Modernist techniques. In *The Bone People*, the barely disguised project of self-construction (witness its Yeatsian tower) that is the displaced *alter ego* of Kerewin Holmes's story in the novel, indicates a Modernist sense of the subject and of art as the means to generate an artifice of integrated selfhood. Moreover, Hulme's personal history of growing up in the one country and almost the one place, by comparison with the more mobile Ondaatje, would not lead us to expect a more radical sense of personal or artistic fragmentation.

Nonetheless, if we turn to the most recent publication, (perhaps the most representative one, since it collects stories written across the author's entire career), there is evident a surprisingly post-modern consciousness and style. *Te Kaihau/The Windeater* carries a lyrical meditation as framing preface which envisages life itself and the human entity, physical and psychic, as fluid areas of interchange or spaces through which various forms of energy pulse:

> This isn't any kind of fantasy however: far from it. We are transit points and blubbery highways and temporarily fluid screens; indeed we are a finity of things to

every light wave and every light particle and sonic particle and sonic wave, but mainly somewhere to pass through in a hurry without so much as a by-yr-lve or a pardon.

...

Now I know all about the waves that barge through us because we're not really there – or here – and now I know that there are at least 21 meanings for *tara* grouped under everything from gossip to rays. Maybe it was because it all took place on hills similarly holy, identically named, or maybe it was because a sneeze and a sound sent the soiling dance of my synergy swirling through another plane and other people and even another time. Don't bother my head: set up the frame – one marvellous 21-jointed word, full of diversities – and because I am merely weaver, making senses for the sounds – I shall weave anew. (pp. 10-11)

This is a more positive embracing of disintegration than Ondaatje's reluctant vision of cosmic dissolution in 'White Dwarfs'. While Hulme's general concept owes much to mysticism and modern theories of science, some of the indeterminacy and clearly a lot of the mythologising in the stories is connected to the problem of cultural identity.

The overt declaration of Maoriness in Hulme's writing, quite apart from its genuine authority (Hulme does speak Maori, for example) and considerations of its political stand within New Zealand letters, has perhaps something to do with the fact that the author looks very rosy-cheeked Celt and lives a solitary life outside of the usual extended-family and communal life of Maoritanga. Consequently, what looks like an appeal to some unifying source of selfhood is in fact more problematic. The writer's ambiguous position is reflected in her having the detachment to look beyond the Maori world to its putative origins in South American culture (in the mysterious 'feathered serpent' figure of the title story). She talks about this double vision/displacement in an essay:

Intermarriage between Maori and Pakeha has been going on for practically as long as the two races have known each other. A sizeable number of New Zealanders have both Maori and European ancestry, and a large proportion of these 'mongrels' are familiar with both cultures. I am a mongrel myself. When the frightened seek to erect a fence between two peoples, we are on both sides of it. Such fence-making tries to separate yourself from ... yourself....

A dual heritage is both pain and advantage....

Because you are part of it [Maori life] you are never bitten deeply by the spiritual loneliness that seems to deaden the heart of so many Pakeha New Zealanders. But you are not wholly of that world, just as you are not wholly of the European world, and that can be a heart-rending experience.[21]

Biculturalism is reflected in the wide range of literary reference that Keri Hulme commands – a desperate attempt perhaps to encyclopaedically encompass both inheritances. It also perhaps leads to one of the definite continuities of this collection, and that is the Gothic sense of dislocation between the world of the body and the life of the spirit, which frequently takes the form of images of physical and mental deformity. Ondaatje, too, makes consistent allusions to individual mortality, but appears to attach to them little of the dramatic anguish typical of Hulme's stories. There is something in this, it seems to me, that goes beyond a merely literary interest in the grotesque and bespeaks profound vulnerability as well as a defensive rage against all the wounds that mortal flesh and mind can suffer. We can see something of this in the psychically fragile mute, Simon Gillayley in *The Bone People*, and in the story 'Hooks and Feelers'. Hall Riley in 'The Cicadas of Summer' has no legs and the shopkeeper of 'A Nightsong for the Shining Cuckoo' is paraplegic. Both stories also show emotionally crippled people, while physical and mental deformity come together disastrously in 'Kite flying party at Doctor's Point':

> There were two things about the child; her whole air of sly friendship, defiant friendship, friendship that is not real, that snares, that entraps – that was one.
> The other was the fact that she had a birthmark on her forehead, the port-wine kind, and she seemed unconscious of this deformity. She did not hide it or show herself ashamed.
> I have thought about these things a lot. They troubled me: they trouble me still.
> ...
> I have a theory about deformities. People are either fearful in the company of a monster, or they will worship it. Any other reaction is rare.
> ...
> The different, the abnormal, the alien, the malformed .
> Who – or what – selects a person for the torment of difference?[22]

The speaker here cannot contemplate the friendship that is a sign of complicity between deformed sufferers, and is too tied by convention to consider the guiltless flaunting of abnormality as anything other than a wicked temptation to worship the monstrous. Out of fear, she makes a schizoid inversion of her own alienated state and becomes a monster of retribution, trying to obliterate signs of her abnormality in the act of confirming it; scorning and yet invoking codes of normal existence – codes that both admit and refuse violence, and which finally pull her life apart.

As with so many of Hulme's stories, the fragile identity of a central character is here figured not merely in the voice and the action, but in the coastal setting: the marginal place of contending forces – man and nature, work and leisure, sea and land. The coastline is swept by wind, light, history and tides, and these forces may be positively energising. Moeraki and the Puketapu hill overlooking the bay are mentioned in the introductory section to *Te Kaihau* ('Tara diptych'), and gives a link to tradition (the landing-place of one of the original migratory canoes of the Maori) and a personal sense of belonging. The coast may also be a place of menace: the ghost-story 'A Tally of the Souls of Sheep' relies on the atmosphere of a deserted holiday settlement on the beach, the powerful 'Hooks and Feelers' is set on the sea-shore, and the title story of the collection presents us with the dissolution of beach bums on booze and dope as well as the encounter between a young woman and an ambiguously disturbing dae-monic lover.

In all the maritime stories there is a fusion of the animate presence of nature and the fragile maintenance of a personal identity. The obvious im-portance to the author of a spirit of reverence that in the cold terms of social reportage translates as 'conservation issues' is a culturally grounded phenomenon that goes much deeper. There is an apparent social critique underlying 'A Tally of the Souls of Sheep' where images of New Zealand as a slaughterhouse and its inhabitants as sheep are built on the social reality of the meat export trade and the white settler ethos which has been expressed in the adage: 'If it moves shoot it; if it doesn't chop it down.' The redneck exploitative attitude to life is figured as the yobbo *agents provocateurs* at the demonstration in 'Swansong'. (The story is based on the enormously important public opposition to the South African Springbok 'apartheid tour' that revealed to New Zealanders for the first time deep splits underlying what had been for ages accepted as a homogeneous har-monious society built on 'healthy' macho white Protestant rugby-playing values.) Hulme lives amongst the denizens of that other major New Zealand form of self-mutilation for material ends – the logging industry – and, significantly, her other profession of whitebaiting is a solitary activity relying on the balance of nature for its continuance. We can see this in the mythic folk-tale, 'King Bait'.

The reverential attitude towards a spiritualised landscape has its source not merely in environmental consciousness, but in Hulme's double cul-tural identity. She is part Celt and otherwise identifies strongly with her Maori heritage (Kati Tahu, Hapu Ngaterangiamoa, Ngaiteruahikihiki.) Both of these elements can be seen in *The Bone People*,[23] where the loosely but recognisably autobiographical Kerewin Holmes is descended from a Hebridean islander and cured of a tumour by a Maori spirit ancestor, and her lover is a Maori with the name of Gillayley. The land is mythicised according to the Maori blending of history and religion and there are places of power such as the one where the canoe bearing the original tribe to the South Island has come to rest. In *Te Kaihau*, the same kind of animistic view of the natural world is evident in 'One Whale,Singing', in 'King Bait' and the irruption of fantasy into a trendy party in 'Planetesi-mal'.

> The Maori relationship to the land is intense. Land is not an exploitable resource: it is Papatuanuku, earth mother. It used to be traditional for the placenta of a new-born child to be buried in the child's tribal area so the newborn would later know that he was truly part, truly nourished and truly born of that place. Land and rocks and trees, rivers and swamps and the sea, are regarded in a much more personal light than simply as a collection of inanimate objects.[24]

The Irish neer-do-well of 'A Drift in a Dream' maintains the Celtic presence in the story collection, and the sordid aspects of that tale are divorced from the world of nature, a separation which, from the Maori point of view, shows the soul-destroying aspects of city life – consider the gang members of 'Kaibutsu-san' and the dreary life of a shopkeeper in a rundown city suburb in 'A Nightsong for the Shining Cuckoo'. While there is always a distinction between Maori and Anglo-Celt, there equally seems to be the consistent suggestion that Irish emotionalism and spiritual attachment to landscape provide a point of contact between pakeha and Maori that is denied to a more orthodoxly WASP view of life. However, there can be no question that it is a Maori outlook which predominates, just as it is evident that this outlook is frequently represented in terms of loss and fragmentation. To quote Hulme again:

> In the cities you are cut off from the life of the land, the sea, your family marae, from your ancestral roots. You are generally first, or at most, second-generation city-dwellers, and this separation aches. You are a member of a highly visible minority, and you know only a few ways to deal with city pain. You can gather together with other Maoris, because that is familiar and comfortable. You can isolate yourself and drink away the pain. You can become a Brown Pakeha....
> Among many city youth, gangs have taken the place of family and tribe. Black Power, Mongrel Mob and Nga Tama Toa have chapters in most cities providing tight, violent but accepting groups for disaffected young people.[25]

Place and a place in nature, then (as for Ondaatje, but with a more far-reaching significance), is a marker for the attempt to generate a self that will combine identity with community, white with brown, stability with flexibility. The stories in *Te Kaihau/The Windeater* (like the poems and the novel) use the features of the natural world as a solid, authorising basis for an emphasis on lack of authority and process. There is also an appeal to the outlines of conventional literary structures (not unlike Ondaatje's frames in *Billy the Kid*, perhaps, but with a more intense feeling for their arbitrariness and fragility) for a scaffolding to support a fiction of fluctuating forms, indeterminate characters, and so on. What we have at first glance in *Te Kaihau* are familiar generic types: the ghost-story, the crafted short-story with a twist, the fisherman's tall-tale, the mystery story, the Maori recall-of-childhood-and-brush-with-spirits anecdotal yarn. The tendency is, on first reading, to think 'So what; it's been done before and done more tidily.' Each unit of the book, however, is shot through/penetrated by elements of other story-types, so that we are estranged and startled out of conventional responses.

The tall fishing tale, 'King Bait', takes on aspects of social criticism, folklore, and an unsettling apocalyptic quality which leads from a basis in realism to a mystical science-fiction treatment. A similar shift from social realism to fantasy occurs in 'One Whale, Singing' and 'Kaibutsu-san'. As Hulme says in the 'other wing' of the Tara diptych (notice the fragmentation of this 'bird'), there is the difficult struggle to say something 'that is clean, new untrammelled,/ free of smears and fresh from mother-tongue.' Part of the difficulty, and part of the potential here is the writer's multicultural consciousness, her hypersensitivity to a complex literary heritage. Perhaps the quest for original utterance is part of a Modernist project, but its results are far more problematic than even Pound could envisage.

Another penetration/fragmentation/transgression of literary expectations takes place at the level of characterisation. This is perhaps more familiar, since it harks back through Faulkner to Dostoevsky at least, and takes the form of a shift in the mental life of the speaker so that we are moved from an apparently stressed but normal outlook on the world to a view of things that is at least distorted if not psychotic. 'Kiteflying Party at Doctor's Point', the 'autobiography' of the horse knacker's daughter in 'Te Kaihau' and 'Stations on the Way to Avalon' are examples of this deconstructing of reality. The last story is useful in that it clearly shows the refusal even to be contained within the normal literary conventions of mental breakdown where (as in Janet Frame's early fiction or the middle period of Doris Lessing's work) dreams or schizoid imaginings are simply exaggerated and warped reflections of real life. The fancies of Hulme's demented (and sadly malnourished!) television director enter the realm of the fantastic with inventions of sandwhale hunting that sound like something out of the science-fantasy world of Frank Herbert's *Dune* series.

Television brings us to perhaps the major interpenetration of literary forms. As with the 'Avalon' story, it emerges from the author's real-life experience as a TV director for NZ Television One and a scriptwriter. This is the mixed-media filmscript-cum-poetic-scenario-with-notes 'A Tally of the Souls of Sheep'. Building on the 'Kiwi gothic' tales of pakeha writers like Ronald Hugh Morrieson and Maurice Gee, which reflect the white man's uneasiness in the face of an alien landscape, an isolated existence and a fiercely parochial Calvinist conformity, and taking in Maori myths of violent and arbitrary nature-spirits and gods such as Tu, the hunter/warrior, we have a dramatic and atmospheric spine-chiller that includes a critique of white presence, exploitative primary industry, and so on, but whose effects are counteracted by a self-aware, self-mocking flouting of literary conventions. It is these which turn the tale from a modernist experimental prose beyond the metafiction of John Barth or Peter Carey to something more fundamentally conceptual and post-modern – a construction that draws attention to its own constructedness, its game-like arbitrariness, its essential fictiveness not merely as an assemblage of literary codes, but as a string of words which (as the notes declare) are themselves possibly misleading and certainly ambiguous. There is rarely a sense that the game is merely cynical fun in the slick post-modern style of a writer like Tama Janowitz, say. Some lines do suggest a self-mocking jokiness, but any tough show of cleverness is also self-lacerating: vulnerability, ambiguity and angst mark most of the stories.

The same kind of deconstructive fragility obtains in relation to the collection as a whole. We normally think of an anthology of stories (more so stories than poems, perhaps) as having internal consistency; we look for a typical 'voice' or style or set of concerns that we can align with what we know of the society or the person behind the text. What we have here is a product that reveals the means of its production, shows the gaps in the scaffolding, and tells us that we are not to go beyond its limits – it is what it is: nothing more; it is a story cobbled together from stories and held together by myth – which is another kind of story based not on authors but on faceless tellers and built on trickster characters such as Maui, who cannot be pinned down to personalities or even to cultural rules.

Just as *The Bone People* declares its means of production in the credits, so *Te Kaihau* reveals its rag-bag challenge to a ready packaging. Keri Hulme has been particularly uncompromising in her relationship to her texts. Her refusal to tone down or edit the often extreme and quite long manuscript of *The Bone People* resulted in that work almost being converted into a doorstop. It took a collective of Maori women to publish it in a low-budget operation before it reached the public, and a Booker Prize before a 'mainstream' publisher would touch it. So the physical book is itself a statement of the cultural politics of gender and race, and of the individuality – even idiosyncratic perversity – of the author's aesthetic. In *Te Kaihau*, we find stories published and unpublished going back to Hulme's earliest work, probably in the sixties (she received her first award, as a Maori writer, in 1973) and ranging from the poignance of a 'standard' Maori story about cultural loss 'He Tauware Kawa, He Kawa Tauware' to a 'standard' white realist story of women's liberation, 'The Knife and the Stone', then to the more 'arty' material discussed already. In a way, as the cover of the collection suggests ('Author of *The Bone People*/Winner of the 1985 Booker Prize'), it seems like Hulme has cheekily decided to capitalise on her fame and pass off whatever happened to be at hand onto a hypocritically eager publishing industry. What is interesting and a redeeming feature of the book, though, is her creative use of this unusual assemblage. As Hulme points out at the end of 'Te Kaihau/The Windeater', the compound is more than just the sum of its parts, even when it looks clumsy and artificial, and often it can only be this when it declares its factitious nature – when it draws attention to the holes in the fabric rather than the 'pattern in the carpet'. Thus, the image of the windeater is not simply erected in the old symbolist/modernist way as a unifying organic metaphor for life and the novelist; rather we are confronted with the author's presentation of it as a word with various possible meanings, an arbitrary provenance and form:

There isn't such a word, eh. There's a lot of us around though.

I came across the term as a gift, if you like, a sort of found gift. For instance if you break up a perfectly respectable word, happily married in all its component parts: you know it means several things, like a loafer or a braggart. Or a woman who takes part in certain rites. Or it can mean the acquisition of property without any return being made, as well as a spell that is cast to punish somebody behaving in such an unmannerly fashion. That's when it's a whole unbroken word, but if you split it, a power leaks out and becomes a woman trying to make sense of her self and her living and her world. (p. 236)

Much of this play relies on the disjunctions of (gaps in) translation between Maori and English and the possibilities of gain and loss of expressive power resulting from that, as also from the working within or breaking of linguistic conventions in either system. While Hulme's writing evinces the pain and terror accompanying cultural pluralising in a more intense way than Ondaatje's work, there is a corresponding acceptance, and, overall, a kind of celebration of the modern, indeed, the post-modern condition. We have only to note how the 'package' surrounding the stories characteristically refuses unity and closure in both its content and its form ('[Foreword] *Tara diptych* [the first wing]; *tara* [the other wing]' and the contradictory '[Afterword] *Headnote to a Maui Tale*') to see that the collection makes an aesthetic virtue of such troublesome unevenness, openness, asymmetry and plurality. Paradoxically, it is the more travelled, 'migrant' writer, Ondaatje, who resists, or at least approaches more slowly such an artistic vision.[26] But both writers attest to the trials and rewards of the post-colonial shift from cultural 'filiation' to a stable source to a problematic personal synthesis of multicultural 'affiliations'.

NOTES

1. Raja Rao, *The Serpent and the Rope* (London: John Murray, 1960), p. 306.
2. Michael Ondaatje, *Rat Jelly* (London: Marion Boyars, 1980); Keri Hulme, *Te Kaihau/ The Windeater* (Wellington: Victoria University Press, 1986).
3. Edward Said, 'Secular Criticism', 'On Repetition', 'On Originality', in *The World, the Text, the Critic* (Cambridge, Mass.: Harvard, 1983).
4. See, for example, Louis Zurcher, *The Mutable Self* (Beverly Hills: Sage, 1977).
5. Malcolm Bowie, 'Jacques Lacan', in John Sturrock, ed., *Structuralism and Since* (Oxford & New York: OUP, 1979), p. 116. Mikhail Bakhtin, *The Dialogic Imagination*, ed. Michael Holquist (Austin: University of Texas, 1981).
6. Edward Said, 'Reflections on Exile', *Granta*, Autumn 1984, p. 159.
7. Julia Kristeva, 'Approaching Abjection', *Oxford Literary Review*, 5, 1982, p. 125.
8. References in this paper to *The Collected Works of Billy the Kid* are to the Penguin reprint, New York, 1984.
9. See the interview with Andrew Peek, *New Literatures Review*, 20, 1990, for a discussion of Hulme's family background.

10. Arun P. Mukherjee, 'The Poetry of Michael Ondaatje and Cyril Dabydeen: two Responses to Otherness', *Journal of Commonwealth Literature*, XX (1), 1985, p. 49.
11. Michael Ondaatje, *Running in the Family* (London & New York: Norton, 1982).
12. *Rat Jelly*, pp. 2, 16, 41, 44, 89, 92.
13. *Rat Jelly*, pp. 44-5.
14. *Rat Jelly*, p. 82. All subsequent page references for Ondaatje's poems relate to this book.
15. I am basing my categorisation here on the outlines usefully 'dramatised' by Ihab Hassan in *The Postmodern Turn* (Columbus: Ohio State University, 1987).
16. Interview quoted in Ina Ferris, 'Michael Ondaatje and the Turn to Narrative', in John Moss, ed., The Canadian Novel, Vol. IV, *Present Tense* (Toronto: NC Press, 1985), p. 80. Ondaatje is also interviewed by Elizabeth Alley, *Span*, 16-17, 1983, p. 79.
17. Ondaatje, *Coming through Slaughter* (Toronto: Anansi, 1976). Ferris, p. 78.
18. We might also liken the migrant to the jazz improviser who practices 'a continuous act of self-cancelling originality'. Ferris, p. 78.
19. While I concur with some of the differences Ferris finds in *Running in the Family*, I do not see it as altogether departing from the modernist mode. In fact, a more recent poem, 'Claude Glass', not only suggests a continuity with the earlier 'Pig Glass', but contains the Eliotian poetic project: 'And he knows something is happening there to him/ solitary while he spreads his arms/ and holds everything that is slipping away together' (*Secular Love* (Toronto: Coach House, 1984), p. 14).
20. Keri Hulme, 'Mauri: an Introduction to Bicultural Poetry in New Zealand', in G. Amirthanayagam & S.C. Harrex, eds., *Only Connect: Literary Perspectives East and West* (Adelaide: CRNLE, 1981), p. 290.
21. 'Mauri', *Only Connect*, p. 294.
22. *Te Kaihau*, pp. 151-2, 154.
23. Keri Hulme, *The Bone People* (New Zealand: Spiral Collective, 1984; London: Hodder & Stoughton, 1985).
24. 'Mauri', *Only Connect*, p. 302.
25. 'Mauri', *Only Connect*, pp. 293, 299.
26. I realise that Ondaatje ostensibly deconstructs history and pluralises narrative in his *In the Skin of a Lion* (London: Picador, 1987) but, relative to *Te Kaihau*, it still relies on a recognisable story-line and an alternative set of histories that do not necessarily undermine the modernist notion of a complex, multi-faceted, but essentially integrated life/art.

DAVID RICHARDS

'A History of Interruptions': Dislocated Mimesis in the Writings of Neil Bissoondath and Ben Okri

This essay is principally concerned with the fictional strategies adopted by two writers, one currently living in Canada, but with Indian and Caribbean origins, the other living in England but with West African roots. The works of Neil Bissoondath and Ben Okri bring to light, in different ways, what may be called the social text of the post-colonial subject. What I mean by that is the host of social practices which constitute the fabric of social experience: in that respect the social text is the antithesis of ethnography, which transforms social experience into disciplinary objects of knowledge. Ethnography makes maps of the world; the social text grasps at the fabric of experience.

Alone in his study, Raj, the narrator of Neil Bissoondath's *A Casual Brutality*[1], contemplates the maps of India, the Caribbean and Canada which cover the walls of the room. The maps crystallise many of the latent themes of the novel as forms of representation which the novel will increasingly challenge. The form of the map is a representation of codes of meaning which possess elocutionary force, special signs which will be found to be increasingly unfathomable. As emblems of space and time, the maps tell stories: narratives which correspond to Raj's past, present and future. But the maps are indices, not of situation of the self located in time and space but symbols of splitting and division and the consequences of history. Since the first act of *King Lear*, the map has been the image of domination: the world rendered as representation, for consumption or destruction. But Raj holds no such dominion; space is ungraspable and contradictory: too large, too small. 'I am, by birth, Casaquemadan; by necessity disguised as choice, Canadian. There was Canada, there was Casaquemada, the one unseizably massive, the other unseizably minute' (p. 34). Spatial representations evoke a crisis of identity in the relocated narrator, who cannot bring the maps to signify his situation. Bissoondath writes that 'a person moved, was driven by a spasm[2] beyond human control like a piece of meat moving through intestine'. The dilemma is in constituting a framework of representation for these spasms in space, time and narrative whereby the social text of the post-colonial may become apparent.

As it is with space, so it is with time, since the meaning of narrative representations inheres in their temporal structure, direction and rhythm. But the history of the dislocated will not take significant shape. Bissoondath's stories repeat the failed attempts of characters to fix the 'fluid holding pattern'[3] of time and to make coherent historical narratives or maps which do not dissolve into absurdity, negation and violence. Bissoondath's characters live with a past which has 'formed but does not inform' (p. 377).

'Time', Bissoondath writes, almost as an admission that the post-colonial cannot know history, only 'time', 'Time kaleidoscopes. The past is refracted back and forth, becomes the present, is highlighted by it, is illuminated by it, is replaced by it. In this rush of sparkle and eclipse, only the future is obscured, predictability shattered. Yesterday becomes today, today steps back from itself, and tomorrow might never be' (p. 18). When time is substituted for history, Bissoondath's characters are subject to the unpredictability of the endless present tense when even 'today steps back from itself'. The ubiquitous form of description is the present, which renders its subjects as objects in a process of denudation which it disguises as an all-encompassing naturalism. History is abolished, not only for the subjects of narrative, but for the reader also, as the world is bleached and emptied of significance. Language is not metaphor but nomenclature. The abolition of history succeeds by magnifying the ordinary and inconsequential to the level of being the sole standards of validity in the world, only eventually to disclose that they are *only* ordinary and inconsequential. Post-colonial naturalism freezes the social text into tragic predictability and repetition, since time and space are unitary and undeniable.[4]

Time and space are, of course, the co-ordinates most adhered to by realist narratives and myths of origin. The world is given its density by the sense that we begin in such a place and at such a time, lending a tangible authority to acts of naming. The fictional Caribbean island of *A Casual Brutality* is located by a myth of origins and naming in an era of Spanish colonialism. Lopez, a disputatious member of the crew of a Spanish galleon, is marooned on a small island, but not before a small house is built for him. The captain puts in at the island on the homeward journey to see if Lopez has mended his ways. His crew find only a blackened skeleton and the burned ruins of the house, 'Casa quemada'. Expelled from human society, Lopez initiates history as suicide. Casaquemada's social text is inscribed in the burning of its social body; the state of post-colonial historylessness condemns its inhabitants to perpetually relive the conflagration in the endless present. In the short story, 'There Are Lots of Ways to Die', a failed historian of Casaquemada recounts his reason for failure: it is 'because our history doesn't lead anywhere. It's just a big black hole. Nobody's interested in a book about a hole.'[5]

Yet this is not to suggest that the triangulation of space, time and myth in Bissoondath's writings does not produce narratives which make a sense of the past cohere into a realised historical vision. At the climax of the novel *A Casual Brutality*, Casaquemada jerks into an even more extensive spasm of random violence and police massacres. While Raj attends to his dying grandfather, the police raid his home and kill his Canadian wife and three-year-old son. Raj, in a state of anguished bewilderment, finds himself at the old colonial fort in the hills above Lopez City:

> And I felt that somehow those men who had sweated and strained here, making their little play at fortification only, just over a century and a half later, to cut their losses and run in a well-orchestrated theatre of brass-bands and flag-raising, were in no small measure responsible for the fact that my wife and my son were dead, that my home was a shambles, that Madera [a policeman], gun in hand, was down there somehow satisfying his bloodlust. Those men who had sweated and strained had had other, more valuable lessons to teach, but they had paid only lip-service to their voiced ideals, had offered in the end but the evils of their actions, had propagated but the baser instincts, which took root and flourished so effortlessly in this world they called, with a kind of black humour, *new*. (pp. 366-7)

If these two sentences are meant to account for the lacuna in the history of the dislocated, and that this is Raj's portion of truth – that Casaquemada is a failed experiment in nationhood – then it is, however true, ultimately painfully banal. Its elocutionary force derives from a naive, even simplistic realism, a strict linearity of historical mechanics connecting chains of events from cause to ultimate effects: from Lopez to murdered wife and child as if the apocalypse of Casaquemada was present in and sprang from its genesis. Raj literally and figuratively surveys time and space in a unitary field of vision which renders explicit their implicit meanings. Paradoxically, he is most powerful and commanding at his weakest and most defeated moment, since the textual nemesis proposes to solve the problem it has tautologically caused to exist. The reader finds the same imperial version of history which caused the problem of history to exist in the first place. The social text emerges as the solution to an apparent conundrum: the novel solves the riddle of history by seeing into and beyond human chaos to the immanent order of imperial history. While it is true that the substance of the vision – near theological in its insight – involves an historical and political apprehension of the social text, the form of that historical knowledge is a form of absentee colonialism. If this fundamentalism was all of Bissoondath's message then the adverse criticism I have implied of his work may have found its justification. But it is not, because Raj's myth of the fall of Casaquemada is only the threshold from which it is possible to begin to elaborate a counterpoint to Imperialism's dominant ideological categories.

To the dislocated, representation is a lie; Art, Bissoondath seems to feel, has the potential to be the most pernicious of lies, since it is willed self-delusion. For the dis-located, mimetic forms are not merely inauthentic representations, misrecognitions, but 'writings' in a different script, alien languages forgotten or unlearned. This self is not discovered in, nor recognised by, Art. To adapt an axiom of Foucault's: 'Representation is engaged in a war with the [social text] it is determined to render. It is the relation of power, not the relation of meaning, that is important.' It is only in the radical subversion of art, art subjected to violence, clinically violated or riotously delimbed, that the misrecognised image can be turned to gesture at the site of enunciation. Raj's epiphany of imperial history is interrogated as Bissoondath, to quote Homi Bhabha in a different context, conjures 'the evil eye that seeks to outstare linear history and turn its progressive dream into nightmarish chaos'.[6]

It is a commonplace of description, particularly descriptions of 'other' peoples, that the social text is evoked by synecdoche: the social whole is represented by its parts.[7] The body is preeminent in this respect – witness Menenius's tutoring of the people of Rome in the first scene of *Coriolanus* – it is a familiar trope of representation such that the social text is often interchangeable with the social body. I now want to evoke two such social bodies; the first concerns Vernon, the central character of Bissoondath's story 'Veins Visible', who has a dream which conjures the terrible but appropriate image of the *corps morcele*,[8] the self envisioned as a mutilated, truncated torso:

> Then as if it was the most natural thing in the world, he found himself lying on the sidewalk looking up at the sky, ink blue with curls of diaphonous white cloud. That something was not right he was fully aware, but only when he tried to get up did he realise that his torso had been severed diagonally from just under his ribcage to the small of his back. His hips and legs lay two feet away, beyond reach, like the discarded lower half of a mannequin. Curious, he examined his lower half. The cut had been clean. There was no blood. The wound appeared to have been coated in clear plastic and he could see the ends of veins pulsing red against the transparent skin. There was, he knew, no danger.[9]

The *corps morcele* recurs throughout Bissoondath's writings as people are framed in windows, caught in photographs, rendered in portraits, but in part, 'footnotes forming of themselves no whole'.[10] (This is, in a sense, to make these grim images more sombre, since there is a joke of kinds in the long quotation above; 'his hips and legs lay *two feet* away...') Likewise, the texts themselves are *morcele*, disjunctive, abridged, mutilated 'in imitation of the language of the unconscious'. Their repetitions, reversals, the journeyings between Casaquemada and Toronto, the framings of image and action show a wholeness perpetually cut and redistributed through the novel and stories. The narrative momentarily 'intensifies all that is within the frame', opening on to other frames of truncated information receding into opacity.[11] These framed, truncated images disrupt the strident linear narrative of imperial history with a different counter rhythm, causing it to stumble over obstacles laid in its path.

It was Hari. Then it was Peter. Then Hari again. Then it was no one again. Just a man. The man had no arms.
Despair.

The second is from Okri's story 'A Hidden History' where an unnamed narrator, an 'earthbound, black angel', records the destruction of an unnamed street in an unnamed city. The black immigrants are evicted, and the street becomes a rubbish dump for the white citizens. A tramp wanders into the angel's view:

> he was of the devil, cursed in the bible; his sperm was black, he was the descendent of an ape; remembering that he was one of those who tainted, took their jobs and their fathers' jobs, took their women; and that he had a member big enough to shame the human race, they held their breath as they watched him going up and down, circling inevitably towards the rubbish bin lining. he got to the lining and opened it and dipped his hand in. his eye twitched. he brought out a bloodied leg: its toes were big and blue-black with a strange rot of the feet. he brought out a hand that was gnarled and withered like a twig. he brought out the head of a black woman, roughly hacked, the eyes still open and bloated, the nose cut like a harelip that had repeated itself. he brought them out smelling, listening, thorough in his investigation. he was drawn by the temptation to list.[12]

The art historian Jean Louis Schefer argues that in paintings such as Rembrandt's 'The Anatomy Lesson', the body is opened as if for the purposes of discovering an interior body – spirit or soul – which can never be actually figured in such a picture. For Schefer, the conventions of representation of the body rest upon this lost evocation: the actual physical body is dismissed in favour of a body which cannot be figured.[13] Art endlessly circles around the problem of representing what cannot be represented. But Bissoodath and Okri compel us to gaze upon what we would wish to discard. Like the physical body, the post-colonial has been dismissed from representation or misrepresented in ethnographic maps and fantasies as primitive or exotic: Okri and Bissoondath turn to the mutilated social body of the post-colonial to force an 'objectifying confrontation with a world of misrepresentations', and these terrible images are heavily laden with political significance as social bodies, as social texts.

But these bodies should not be read as accomplishing the same goals. Ben Okri visits many of the same dark places of the post-colonial habitus as Bissoondath, but in his writing there is an underlying commitment to the explicability of human affairs: in metaphor, narrative structure or tragic-ritual shape. For example, the story 'Laughter Beneath the Bridge'[14] is, at one level, a reworking of the scapegoat myth; Monica, a young girl of the 'rebel tribe', dressed in the costume of an ancestral spirit, is the sacrificial victim required by the community to rid itself of the putrifying consequences of war in the shape of hundreds of rotting corpses which have blocked the river which runs through the town. She is the innocent 'sin eater' whose death must carry away the accumulated evil of the war so that social equilibrium can be reinstated. Yet having established this familiar trope, the story proceeds to interrogate it, displaying its insufficiencies. The centre from which this questioning radiates is the use the story makes of the *egungun* masquerade, which, in traditional society, was the chief means by which a community held itself up to scrutiny by evoking its past in the shape of masked 'spirits'. The *egungun* played a role in traditional society which was revered and regulatory; the *egungun* was the receiver of sacrifice, not the sacrifice; the story therefore enacts a travesty of the past, the destruction of the ancestral links with the world of the dead. This fracturing of ties with the rituals of the past is prefigured by the mask Monica wears, which had been broken across and glued back together, ominously predicting the larger fracture Monica's death would entail. The soldier unmasks the *egungun*, which is an act of sacrilege punishable by death; further destruction, not an end to war, will ensue when the community sacrifices its inner nature by making a scapegoat of its ancestral past. Thereafter, the community has lost its ability to grasp its meaning. The story appears to assume Soyinkan mythic proportions since present life, Okri seems to say, echoing Soyinka, contains within it 'manifestations of the ancestral, the living and the unborn', albeit as travesties of the codes by which the past makes its narratives.

Okri taps the radical roots of the metaphor of the social body to challenge the versions of reality which normalise the civil society of oppression. As Okri's narrator of 'Stars of the New Curfew' says: 'Time was to teach us that those who get on in society, those who rise high and affect events, do so by manipulating, by manufacturing reality.'[15] Okri's work shapes other realities, for only in alternatives can the writer be truly subversive of 'manufactured reality'. Njabulo Ndebele wrote: 'We have given too much of our real and imagined lives to the oppressor', there is an urgent need for the writer to 'look for that area of cultural autonomy ... that no oppressor can ever get at'.[16] Okri concurs with Ndebele in his search for a radical poetics of subversion, an anti-aesthetics precisely delineating the terrible image of the post-colonial social body.

By way of elaboration, let me cite another quotation from 'A Hidden History'. The street continues to decay:

> sulphurous smells rose from this festeration. Pink mushrooms sprouted. Strange vegetable life took root beneath the rubbish and spread wings in the nights and grew rings round the street. Then this vegetable life flowered into purple and green flora, beautiful to look at like the fata morgana with terrible blue eyes, but they gave off corrosive smells that drove the dogs to a restricted area of the street...[17]

Okri has evoked a decorum where the image structures perfectly suit the subject of English racism. The new index of history is the subversive imagery of dreams, or the nightmares of an isolated tramp who describes his hallucinations as 'lovely'. Okri's black angels, tramps and pickpockets, his social pariahs, live in a world of decay. Through such figures Okri establishes a contradictory triangulation, between the tradition, its evocation and its denial. The writing evokes a dominant representation with its attendant forms of aesthetics and naturalism, only to expose its capacity for misrepresentation, failure and delusion. Mythical discourses are scrutinised, parodied, dissolved or rendered objects of play. Okri's voice emerges from that oppositional encounter with a history of misrepresentation to present the 'hidden history' of social violence.

The voice which speaks in Bissoondath's writing is both intriguing and instructive, since it speaks by what it disavows. Its elocutionary force derives from a denial of a voice. The 'I' cannot be said except as a negation of its representation. The dislocated subject carries with him the Casaquemadan myth of self-imolation. How can narrative escape representation without fleeing towards negation? Or is it possible for fiction to emanate from a place which is always 'not'? A voice which makes, but is not 'in' its narrative? His narratives will not cohere into a unity which lends identity to its subjects. His language constantly reaches for the negative form. Not what is, but what is not; denial, negation, the mirror's reflection. In so doing, Bissoondath lays bare what Homi Bhabha (following Fanon) has described as the 'perverse palimpsest of colonial identity'[18] which uses words, as Raj says, not as tools of enquiry but in their most dangerous capacity, as agents of concealment. Bissoondath's writing perpetually attempts to uncover the true nature of the post-colonial, while at the same time, acknowledging that writing protects and hides, it effaces the colonised self. Bissoondath's writing is a problematised strategy of obliqueness both to the subject and form of the fiction. Fiction which attempts to lend a voice to those who are voiceless in accents which are someone else's must necessarily be circumspect. In 'Digging Up The Mountains', Bissoondath writes of this sense of necessity, in producing fictions which are always incomplete, unresolved: 'All in passing ... visions fraught with the insubstantial, footnotes forming of themselves no whole, offering but image and sensation as recompense for endless motion.'[19]

The place they occupy becomes an 'ellipsis',[20] a syntactical figure of omission, between two statements: an implied but unrealised presence. Recalling the failed historian, Bissoondath writes 'books about a hole'; a black hole from which a voice emanates. By evoking lives disrupted by the random events of 'kaleidoscopic time', the unpredictable and disruptive are the very means by which his writing reveals, not the subject himself, but the acts of concealment effacing that identity. This subject can only be evoked by the negative values of language; Bissoondath's characters exist in the interstices, the 'gaps' between narratives of origin, places of residence, representations of the self.

Bissoondath presents a much more complex formation of history than Raj's construction would permit. For Bissoondath, colonial intervention, migration, dislocation, neglect have wrought a perpetuating sense of fracture which continues to fragment both self and other. In Fanon's phrase, 'a constellation of delirium' enacts and re-enacts a tragic cycle from which no recuperation is possible and which renders the colonial subject silent, invisible and unformed, since the social text consists of the replicated divisions of colonial identity. Bissoondath's dispossessed live in an 'alienated image of man', where the 'otherness of the self' makes the Casaquemadan myth the only one which obtains. What is returned to us is fragmentation, misrecognition, delirium, isolation; the unelaborated sense of self is disclosed by omission as the dispossessed views himself as an object discoursing on its strangeness, or on the blankness of its social constructions. The world of the post-colonial subject is a subjunctive state, viewed obliquely, tilted at an angle. It is difficult, therefore, to know how to conclude; to summarise would be to restore the body to its wholeness, to suture the wound which Bissoondath insists on fingering to inflammation – to render the post-colonial subjunctive an imperial indicative, when the vision, refracted and concave, is contingent, *morcele*, hypothetical. Better to end in contingent compromise? Raj, in *A Casual Brutality*, begins by stating that 'Self, in the end, is the prime motivation', but, 'in the end', he glimpses his own constellation of delirium. 'So this,' he says, 'is how the world shatters, with a peep at the soul' (p. 367). Fictional acts of displacement become for Bissoondath the appropriate medium for the expression of a post-colonial social text. But what political or historical vision descends from Bissoondath's elliptical voices?

Bissoondath's voices are always alone, inspected, threatened, lost; the thin ellipsis of the self. Thus isolated from his social role, his class, his community, the individual cannot control the representations language throws up, nor embrace its history. But the very 'fact' of the unavailability of communal myths, languages and historical narratives in his writings is the process by which the post-colonial subject is 'known' or 'recognised'. Bissoondath's post-colonials cannot break the ellipsis out of its confining parentheses to uncover its 'hidden history' of alternative dreams or subversive myths. Yet, paradoxically, this evocation of a state of historyless-ness is accomplished by calling forth a great deal of history: Lopez's house must be constructed for it to be burned. The view of Bissoondath as Raj, as a naive or simple realist, perpetuates the dualistic interpretation of the marginalised post-colonial engaged in dialogue with the imperial centre. It fails to see the third figure, the hungry ghost at the feast, known by what it lacks.

NOTES

1. Neil Bissoondath, *A Casual Brutality* (London: Bloomsbury, 1988). All references are to this edition and are included in the text.
2. Neil Bissoondath, 'Man as Plaything Life as Mockery', *Digging Up The Mountains* (Harmondsworth: Penguin, 1987), p. 178.

3. 'Insecurity', *Digging Up The Mountains*, p. 14.
3. *A Casual Brutality* (London: Bloomsbury, 1988), p. 377.
4. I have found the work of several anthropologists helpful at this stage of my argument. See in particular Johannes Fabian, *Time and the Other: How Anthropology Makes
   its Object* (New York, 1983) and James Clifford and George Marcus, *Writing Culture:
   The Poetics and Politics of Ethnography* (London: University of California Press, 1986).
5. 'There Are Lots of Ways To Die', *Digging Up The Mountains*, p. 92.
6. Homi K. Bhabha, 'Interrogating Identity', *Identity*, ICA Documents 6, 1987, p. 8.
7. Cf. Clifford and Marcus, op. cit.
8. Cf. Jacques Lacan, 'Le Stade du miroir', in *Ecrits* (Paris, 1966) and Christine Brooke-
   Rose, *A Rhetoric of the Unreal* (Cambridge, 1981).
9. 'Veins Visible', *Digging Up The Mountains*, p. 221.
10. 'Continental Drift', *Digging Up The Mountains*, p. 146.
11. Cf. Christine Brooke-Rose, op. cit., pp. 161-6.
12. Ben Okri, 'A Hidden History', *Incidents at the Shrine* (London: Flamingo, 1986),
    pp. 88-89.
13. Jean Louis Schefer, 'Thanatography, Skiagraphy', translated with an afterword by
    Paul Smith, *Word and Image*, 1, 1985, pp. 191-6.
14. *Incidents at the Shrine*, pp. 1-22.
15. 'Stars of the New Curfew', *Stars of the New Curfew* (London: Secker & Warburg,
    1988), p. 117.
16. Njabulo Ndebele, *Fools and Other Stories* (London: Longman, 1985).
17. 'A Hidden History', *Incidents at the Shrine*, pp. 84-5.
18. Homi K. Bhabha, 'Difference, Discrimination and the Discourse of Colonialism', in
    F. Barker, ed., *The Politics of Theory* (Colchester: University of Essex, 1983), p. 121.
19. 'Continental Drift', *Digging Up The Mountains*, p. 146.
20. Cf. Homi K. Bhabha, 'Interrogating Identity', p. 9.

ISHRAT LINDBLAD

Salman Rushdie's *The Satanic Verses*: Monoism *contra* Pluralism

One of the first things that strikes the reader of Salman Rushdie's *The Satanic Verses* is the multiplicity of the narratives contained within it.[1] This apparent multiplicity can, however, be reduced to two main narrative strands. First, there is the story which occupies the present tense of the narrative, and constitutes the 'real world' framework in which the two central characters, Saladin Chamcha and Gibreel Farishta live. Second, there is the narrative which describes Gibreel Farishta's dream life and comprises a number of other narratives, among them the story of Mahound in Jahilia. Even though the sections in which Mahound and Jahilia figure occupy a relatively small proportion of the complete text, they have come to dominate discussion of the novel because of the importance of the issues they have raised. In comparison to questions of blasphemy, of censorship, of state terrorism and of the responsibility of the writer, it seems trivial and formalistic to raise 'literary' issues like the question of the unity of a work of art.

Nevertheless, the question is inevitably raised, especially in the secular world of Western literary scholarship, and it is evident that many critics are unwilling to grant the book artistic unity. Patrick Parrinder, for example, describes it as one of Rushdie's 'baggy monsters', and Robert Irwin wittily calls it 'several of the best novels [Rushdie] has ever written'.[2] There is however, a relationship between the two basic narrative structures which reveals a clear sense of artistic purpose. A study of the two shows that whereas the 'real world' narrative possesses the unity of a conventional romance centred on the hero's identity quest the 'dream world' narrative seems deliberately to resist it. In effect, the juxtaposition of the two narratives against each other brings the concept of identity into a dialectical relationship with the concept of plurality. Unity, identity and monotheism are shown to have a common denominator in that they are all a kind of monoism, whereas metamorphosis, amorphousness and multiplicity are associated with pluralism. By shifting between a unified narrative and a pluralistic one, Rushdie is using the form of his fiction to say something about the virtues of pluralism. The medium of this novel can truly be said to be its message: the unity of the conventional romance structure of the 'real-world' narrative is sharply contrasted with the plurality of the 'dream-world' narrative. The implication is that unity, identity or any closed monoism is to be rejected, while pluralism is to be endorsed.

Similarities between the highly unified structure of the romance and the 'real world' narrative are noticeable. According to Frye, the romance employs a stylized pattern for the delineation of an identity quest. It usually starts with some departure from a stable identity for the hero, often signalled by his becoming an orphan or setting off on a journey. This journey can also take the form of a descent into an underworld where he undergoes some kind of ordeal which enables him to return to a state of identity.[3] In addition, the action of a romance frequently makes use of gemination and metamorphosis to stress that the hero is embarked upon an identity quest, and places him in a world where good and evil are polarized. Frye suggests that this 'simplifying of moral facts' partly accounts for the popularity of the form since it 'relieves us from the strain of trying to be fair-minded' (p. 50). It is precisely this simplification of moral facts that the 'real world' narrative of *The Satanic Verses* contains and which the 'dream World' narrative subsequently undermines.

The novel's concern with an identity quest is clearly signalled by the implied narrator posing the question 'Who am I?' twice in the first chapter of the novel. This question is immediately linked with the concept of metamorphosis : 'to be born again ... first you have to die' (p. 3). That the two central characters, Gibreel Farishta and Saladin Chamcha, are starting a new life in a new world, is implied both by naming the airliner from which they fall 'Bostan' after one of the gardens of paradise, and by using a number of time words that are replete with associations of a new age. Not only is it just before dawn on New Year's day, but it is also suggested that the bang of the aircraft is like the original big bang which created the world: 'a miniature echo of the birth of time' (p. 4). Moreover, the tube of the aircraft is described through images of 'a seed-pod giving up its spores, an egg yielding its mystery' (p. 4). The concept of the aircraft as a progenitor is also reinforced through the metaphors that came to Saladin's mind when he flew to England for the very first time on another plane: 'an aircraft was not a flying womb but a metal phallus, and the passengers were spermatozoa waiting to be spilt' (p. 41). Thus the reader is prepared to regard the descent of the two main characters as the beginning of a new life.

Their quest for a new identity after their fall is complicated by the fact that Gibreel Farishta and Saladin Chamcha can be seen as two sides of a deeply divided self. Rushdie has admitted to his interest in writing about divided selves in an interview with Roger Burford Mason.[4] The description of the way in which the two men fall towards earth as if they were both within the same birth canal (p. 4), coupled with the spelling of their names as rolled into one, 'Gibreelsaladin Farishtachamcha', suggests that they have now become a new compound identity, a suggestion that is reinforced by the use of words like 'hybrid', 'metamorphic' and 'transmutation' in close proximity to the subsuming of their two separate identities in a compound name. That this new self is deeply divided is also signalled by the adjective 'angelicdevilish' to describe their united fall and by the opposition of their natural impulses – Saladin nose-dives while Gibreel refuses to fall, Gibreel celebrates his essential Indianness in his descending Bombay movie song while Saladin fights back with the verses of 'Rule Britannia' on his lips (pp. 5-6).

The early stages of Salahuddin Chamchawalla's metamorphosis from an Indian to a would-be Englishman are presented in a flashback which shows how his migration to England as a schoolboy affected him. Frye points out that a change of name is a simple device to signal a change of identity (p. 106), and in the case of Salahuddin, this takes place in two stages. First he changes his Muslim name to the anglicized version, Saladin. Then he literally cuts himself off from half his father's name by deleting 'walla', the last part of his surname, which also means 'person' in Urdu. His new name draws the scorn of his childhood friends during his brief return home: 'Salad, like a bloody lettuce' (p. 53) is Zeeny Vakil's epithet for his new name. His change of surname is even worse, for it is synonymous with the Urdu word for 'spoon', which is also a pejorative term for the Indians who curried favour with the representatives of the British Raj: 'You name yourself Mister Toady and you expect us not to laugh' (p. 54) is Zeeny's comment on his mutilated surname. Saladin is cutting himself off from half his identity but has not yet gained a satisfactory substitute for the old one.

Saladin's severance from his paternal roots is further emphasized by his father's decision to cut down the walnut tree that he had planted to commemorate the birth of his son. When his mother dies he becomes, at least symbolically, an orphan. His mother's death, caused by her choking on a fish-bone at a dinner party in her home, is contrasted with her son's ability to survive in England by determinedly chewing his way through his first mouthful of English kippers (p. 46).

When he finally chooses to identify himself with the country he has migrated to, he has rejected the appeal of his Indian mistress, Zeeny Vakil, to stay in Bombay. Not only does he have a return ticket to England in his pocket but also an English passport, and an English wife waiting for him at the other end. However dearly he may wish to identify himself with the English, however, it is made clear that he has not yet been recognized as belonging among them by the English themselves. Zeeny draws attention to this fact by pointing out that although employed as an actor he is not allowed to appear on British television. Instead, his voice is used to animate a variety of products for commercial purposes. This impersonation of products rather than people is an apt indication of his lack of a *bona fide* identity in the culture to which he wishes to belong (p. 61).

In contrast to Saladin, his alter ego, Gibreel is (to borrow Helen Tiffin's witty phrase), an 'alter native'.[5] In the 'real world' narrative he is not as conscious as Saladin of the need to create a new identity. He loves his native Bombay, and is consistently derisive about England. There are, however, similarities between the situation of these two characters. Like Saladin, Gibreel has changed his name: from Ismail Najmuddin to Gibreel Farishta. He, too, is orphaned, and an actor. Through his numerous impersonations of the countless deities in the subcontinent's canon for the Bombay movies, he is associated with metamorphosis. He also embarks on his journey on the Bostan after a crisis of faith followed by a new 'vision', represented in comic terms as his meeting with the 'ice maiden' Alleluia Cone, whom he determines to pursue to her native England. Unlike Saladin, however, Gibreel remains loyal to his Indianness. His descent into what is represented as the corruption of the Western world gives him many opportunities to gibe at the society with which Saladin wishes to be identified.

After their arrival in London, both undergo a metamorphosis related to the concept of the polarisation between good and evil that traditionally exists in romance. Gibreel acquires a halo, an outward sign of his having become an angel, whereas Saladin acquires the sulphurous breath, cloven foot and hirsute exterior of the stereotype of the devil. His demonic features are also those of the stereotype of the Indian as pictured by a prejudiced Englishman: he is dirty, hairy and black. By making Saladin undergo this metamorphosis the author makes him confront all that is most abhorrent to him about his original identity. In his new shape he is also brutally rejected by the English people with whom he would like to be identified. His claim to a British passport is disbelieved by the policemen who arrest and maltreat him, while his British wife insists on maintaining the fiction of his death in the air-crash. Indeed, she betrays him as thoroughly as it is possible for a wife to betray her husband.

While Saladin's metamorphosis brings him humiliation and suffering, Gibreel's brings him fame and glory. On the very shore where William the Conqueror landed, he conquers first Rosa Diamond (the former wife of a Spaniard – another citizen of the world's great imperial powers), and then Alleluia Cone, who is a stereotype of Northern beauty, clearly the type that Saladin would most admire.

The cost of Gibreel's apparent success in England seems to be the loss of his formerly stable identity: he enters a dream world as the archangel Gibreel and finds it increasingly difficult to distinguish between what is 'real' and what is dream. These dream sequences can be seen as the equivalent of Gibreel's break with his former identity, since, according to Frye, 'individual loss or confusion or break in the continuity of identity ... has analogies to falling asleep and entering a dream world' (p. 104). In this dream world Gibreel becomes the archangel Gibreel, and as such finds himself implicated in a number of different stories.

In spite of the apparent disjointedness of the second 'dream world' narrative, the reader is tempted to try and find an underlying pattern because of the way in which details in the different stories echo each other. Gibreel is not only the dreamer but also, in the guise of the archangel Gibreel, an active participant in all the different stories. Above all, there is a duplication of names which suggests relationship between the different characters even though they inhabit different stories. There is, for instance, Mahound's wife Ayesha, and a prostitute who assumes her name in the story set in the city of Jahilia; there is also a latter-day prophetess called Ayesha in the story about the Indian village of Titlipur. Similarly, there is a Hind in three of the stories, and a Mishal in two of them. Especially noteworthy are the echoes associated with a major character, Alleluia Cone, whose surname is the same as the name of the mountain Mahound climbs in Jahilia, and who, like Mahound, climbs a mountain. In addition, Everest, the mountain she climbs, appears again in Everest Villas, the apartment building in Bombay in which her lover, Gibreel Farishta, used to live. There is also specific evocation of the resemblance between her name, 'Allie', and that of the pagan goddess, Al-Lat, whom Mahound first accepts and then rejects (p. 459).

The repetition of the same name for several female characters suggests that like the pagan goddess, Al Lat, whom Hind staunchly champions, they stand for pluralism against the rigid monoism of several of the male characters. Indeed, in a number of the different dream episodes, a male character insists upon a rigid division between good and evil. In the key episode which has given the novel its name, Gibreel inspires Mahound with verses suggesting that he compromise his monotheistic vision and accept the most important goddesses, especially Al-Lat. At first Mahound accepts these verses as coming from a 'divine' source, but later rejects them as 'satanic'. The validity of Mahound's recognition of good and evil as coming from two distinct sources is, however, undermined by Gibreel's awareness that he was equally involved in both visions (p. 123).

That good and evil are essentially dualistic is also implied within the 'real world' narrative that Gibreel inhabits in his waking state. For example, when Saladin is outwardly most like the devil he gains the reader's sympathy for his plight. His movement downwards into a kind of hell is reversed, however, once he allows hatred to enter his heart. Thus the 'evil' of hatred paradoxically brings him a 'good'. Similarly, at what appears to be a culminating moment of recognition, the implied author juxtaposes Saladin and Gibreel as 'conjoined opposites' or 'two fundamentally different *types* of self' (p. 427). The difference between them that the implied author emphasizes is that Gibreel is '*continuous* – that is ... still a self which, for our present purposes, we may describe as 'true' (p. 427). Saladin, however, 'is a creature of *selected discontinuities*, a *willing* re-invention; his *preferred* revolt against history being what makes him in our chosen idiom, "false"' (p. 427).

Since the story of Saladin has been told in a more continuous form than that of Gibreel, the truth of such true/false opposition is undermined by the reader's experience of the text. It is further undermined by the implied author's having entered the book as its omniscient creator in the section that contains this opposition. The implied author warns the reader that a tragedy is about to be enacted in which Saladin plays the role of an Iago and Gibreel of an Othello. In other words, their roles are switched around and Saladin is 'false' and Gibreel 'true'. Thus both Gibreel and Saladin ultimately play 'angelicdevlish' or 'truefalse' roles. Here the simple polarisation of good and evil which characterizes the romance world is denied. Further, the implied author of this narrative states that the question he is interested in is 'the nature of evil, how it's born, why it grows, how it takes unilateral possession of a many-sided soul' (p. 424).

Once Saladin allows unilateral evil to take possession of his soul, he chooses to revenge himself in an manner that parodically echoes the incident of the satanic verses in the dream narrative. He decides to make diabolic use of his ability to change his voice to arouse Gibreel's pathological jealousy. By reciting slanderous verses about Allie to Gibreel over the telephone he convinces him of Allie's infidelity, so that Gibreel shoots first Allie, and then himself. Having thus rid himself of his pluralistic Other, Saladin is restored to a stable identity.

Saladin Chamcha's identity quest ends with his return to his father's house and a deliberate echo of Matthew Arnold's 'Dover Beach':

> He stood at the window of his childhood and looked out at the Arabian Sea. The moon was almost full; moonlight stretching from the rocks of Scandal Point out to the far horizon, created the illusion of a silver pathway, like a parting in the water's shining hair, like a road to miraculous lands. Childhood was over, and the view from the window no more than a sentimental echo. To the devil with it! Let the bulldozers come. If the old refused to die, the new could not be born. (pp. 546-47)

As soon as he decides to let the old die, Zeeny Vakil enters the room. Realising that she is giving him a second chance, Salahuddin (who has reverted to the original spelling of his name) turns away from the window and joins her.

The evocation of 'Dover Beach' – the window, the moonlight, the sea – plays a significant role here. It establishes a thematic connection with a poem in which the poet laments the loss of faith in his world and suggests that the only hope that remains for man is fidelity in love. There is yet another Arnoldian echo in Salahuddin's final acceptance of Gibreel's credo – the famous lines from 'Stanzas from the Grande Chatreuse': 'Wandering between two worlds, one dead,/ The other powerless to be born.'

What is the effect of this intertextuality? If Arnold is taken as a symbol of the English liberal humanist tradition, it is ironic that even as Salahuddin affirms his original identity, he reveals that his frame of reference is essentially English. At the same time, however, the words have become associated with Gibreel and his Indian philosophy of resurrection. This ambivalence serves a thematic purpose: Salahuddin has been able to reconcile his conflicting selves. He is no longer haunted by his alter ego Gibreel, he has laid his father to rest, he can accept the loss of his childhood home and is finally fit to 'inherit the magic lamp which he felt promised the end of his troubles and the gratification of his innermost desires' (pp. 36, 533). Like a romantic hero he has gone through an identity quest, been metamorphosed, and returned to his original identity, ready to claim his princess and live happily ever after.

How is the reader to interpret this apparently 'happy ending'? Is it an affirmation of the monotheism his father stood for and a rejection of the polytheistic worship of Gibreel's surrogate father? In trying to answer this question we need to look again at the opposition between the unilateral and the many-sided that was posited in the passage where Saladin embraced unilateral evil. It seems that the 'hero's' acquisition of identity is the product of his villainy! Not only has he driven Gibreel to suicide but he has also sacrificed Allie, a completely innocent woman. Instead of celebrating the hero's return to a stable identity, the reader laments the high price he has paid for integration.

This price is further underscored by the form of the novel. The 'real-world' narrative of Saladin and Gibreel does possess unity as a romance about the identity quest of its hero. But this is true of only a limited part of the novel as a whole. The dream world that the angel Gibreel inhabits is one where past and present, real and surreal mix, and where multiplicity is celebrated as an alternative to the limitations of unity. The amorphousness of Gibreel's dream world is ultimately more like the reality in which people have to live. The simplified story of Saladin's identity quest is only possible in the world of romance. Thus the apparent shapelessness of this novel has an artistic purpose – it questions by its very plurality all forms of monoism.

Rushdie's personal background as an ex-Muslim Indian writer who has migrated to Britain may help to explain why the author is so determined to valorize pluralism. Monotheism and polytheism have to exist side by side in present day India, and present day Britain has to accept ethnic plurality as the legacy of its imperialistic past. *The Satanic Verses* points to the need to accept plurality in a world where people are constantly on the move and all kinds of new hybrid cultures are coming into being. It is, however, too facile to equate the very real phenomenon of cultural antagonism with cultural plurism. Ironically, Rushdie's endorsement of plurality deconstructs itself when he fails to recognize that pluralism is not the *only* answer. His failure to perceive this irony, and to make room for monoism as well, has cost him more than most authors have to pay for their artistic vision.

NOTES

1. Salman Rushdie, *The Satanic Verses* (London: Viking, 1988). Page references will be to this edition and are given in the text.
2. Patrick Parrinder, 'Let's Get the Hell Out of Here', *London Review of Books*, 29 Sept. 1988, and Robert Irwin, 'Original Parables', *The Times Literary Supplement*, 30 Sept.-6 Oct. 1988. Kaukab Siddique's article 'A Look at the Literary Qualities of *Satanic Verses*: Did it Deserve Notice in Literary Circles?', *New Trend*, Aug. 1989, declares the book a failure on artistic grounds. In a panel session on the text of *The Satanic Verses* at the 1989 conference of the Association of Commonwealth Language and Literature Studies, University of Kent, Canterbury, where I discussed a preliminary version of this paper, several members of the audience raised the question as to whether or not the book had artistic unity. During the same session, the writer, Nayantara Sahgal, in spite of a highly appreciative account of the book, came to the conclusion that it lacked unity of form. Abdulrazak Gurnah was one of the few who suggested that it focused on the theme of migration.
3. My discussion of the structure of the romance is put together from various sections in Northorp Frye's *The Secular Scripture: A Study of the Structure of Romance* (Cambridge, Mass.: Harvard University Press, 1975). Page references will be to this edition and are given in the text.
4. Roger Burford Mason, *Poetry Nation Review*, XV, 4, 1989, p. 15. The publication of the text of Salman Rushdie's lecture 'Is Nothing Sacred?' (no publisher or date of publication), which was read in London by Harold Pinter on 6 Feb. 1990, and of his brochure *In Good Faith* (London: Granta, 1990) provides further confirmation of my argument. See particularly pp. 9 & 13 in 'Is Nothing Sacred?', and pp. 3-4 in *In Good Faith*. This article was already in press when they appeared so I have not been able to incorporate them in the text.
5. Helen Tiffin used this term in her paper '"Convertible Imageries": Cross Culture and Counter-Discourse' at the 1989 conference of the Association for Commonwealth Literature and Language Studies, University of Kent, Canterbury. See paper by Helen Tiffin in this volume.

ROGER LANGEN

Progresses of the Soul: Affliction in Three Novels of Colour – André Schwarz-Bart's *A Woman Named Solitude*, Jean Rhys's *Wide Sargasso Sea*, and Bessie Head's *A Question of Power*

> Pain is the colour of certain events.
> Simone Weil

What is offered here to the Commonwealth literary project is some 'pepper'. I mean philosophy, the discipline of distinctions, black or white (and shades between; this paper, in a sense, is the prolegomenon to a re-searching of the idea of colour). Principally I apply a concept. My sources are Continental, so that, mindful of the English setting, I must own my thought to be colonized from there. Decorum is otherwise preserved; theory is prevented from overpowering the sensible, empirical world and style kept plain. Certainly nothing appears here in the technocratic language of that conspicuous other colonist on English soil, the 'de-construction' worker. What signs of the Continental accent may be heard occur instead in the two abashed (and abashing) words, 'passion' and 'soul', necessary, if unscientific, to what follows, and preferable, I think, to the Anglophone alternatives, the American 'commitment' and the Eng-lish 'the person'.

The concept I employ, affliction, is borrowed from the metaphysical writer, Simone Weil. Weil was not only a penetrating and exacting philo-sopher but a visionary, one feels bound to say, with an extraordinary gift for empathic feeling. Her abstract work is distinguished almost *a priori*, therefore, by its close attention to human problems. Even her death at the regrettably early age of thirty-four (in 1943) is characteristic, vaguely reminding one of Joan of Arc, and inviting, perhaps for this reason, an 'English' reflection. My own specific suggestion is that the analysis of affliction has special relevance for Commonwealth Literature, which is noteworthy for a wide variety of afflictive sites. I adapt Weil's concept in this paper to three novels which show clearly, in my view, an afflictive temper: André Schwarz-Bart's *La mulatresse Solitude* (1972), translated as *A Woman Named Solitude* (1973); Jean Rhys's *Wide Sargasso Sea* (1966); and Bessie Head's *A Question of Power* (1974).[1] The critical reception of these novels reveals, in each case, problems of interpretation, attributable, as I argue, to the failure to recognize their afflictive structure.

Weil writes that 'the great enigma of human life is not suffering but affliction'.[2] Suffering is the relatively alleviable, universal commodity; affliction the intractable, special condition. In affliction, the soul is pervaded by great forces outside it, at once hostile and indifferent. This produces an absurd condition, entailing to an individual, blameless life a radically diminished existence. The soul in this condition is indelibly marked, Weil says, and it is this 'marking' of the soul which constitutes affliction. Some physical suffering is normal, even necessary (if only in the constant apprehension of it), but social degradation, degradation in the eyes of others, is the crucial element; otherwise, 'there is not really affliction' (p. 78). Where physical suffering abates, affliction leaves yet an 'irreducible core', the permanized effect of an entrenched scorn.

To this general condition, certain special absurdities pertain. One is that the afflicted, despite their severe distress, are beyond compassion; this because they are invisible. Whoever looks at them, Weil says, 'only notices that they have rather a strange way of behaving and ... [they] censure this behaviour' (p. 78), as Rochester does Antoinette's. Related to this is the incommunicability of an absurd reality – innocence seized (in the instances I consider) by an historical evil. Two personalities emerge in response – the familiar one which turns on itself, rationalizing its innocence into guilt or otherwise fleeing consciousness of its absurd position, 'realistically' acclimatizing itself to circumstances; and, more rarely, the soul which holds steady, instinctively rejecting guilt, as indeed all other avenues of false escape, or not feeling it; who is, therefore, 'most exposed to affliction' (p. 156) and upon whom, in consequence, the weight of affliction characteristically imposes silence. Such a one Weil calls a 'pure soul'. With reservations, the female protagonists in the three novels I briefly examine are each in this kind. Their particular affliction, it is worth mentioning now, consists in their mid-position, historically determined, between racially defined sources of identity. Solitude and Elizabeth are mulatto-born or 'coloured', while Antoinette is Creole at a time when indigenous white West Indian power has suddenly collapsed. I draw attention to the 'marking' character of the terms – mulatto, Creole, coloured.

A third absurd attribute which belongs to affliction touches upon a possible cure, but is expressed by Weil somewhat metaphysically: 'anonymous before all things, affliction deprives its victims of their personality and makes them into things' (p. 84). Between the afflicted pure soul, therefore, and the attainment of a coherent personality within some structure of meaning lies an infinite distance – logically so, inasmuch as objects are not subjects, obscurity not light, hatred not love. The afflicted, Weil concludes, against the indifference of the outside world, which touches them like a 'metallic coldness', and over their despair 'they will ... [ever] find warmth again' (p. 84), must keep their souls disposed toward the light, or God, whose infinite character alone can pierce the void. This is Weil's master concept, the patient waiting or attention directed to some indefinably spiritual source, which has the power to centre existence, to influence personality, to rescue a life. As Weil never defines the term 'God', I substitute there the less metaphysical but still suitably unclear term, Love, with a capital L.

A caution, however. Socially and politically, Weil was something of an activist and it would surely be a mistake to find in her idea of 'waiting' a passive spirit, or even a passive body. The silence of the pure soul in affliction can be assumed to be a very resisting one, with episodes of outward struggle. Having said this, I nonetheless feel that Weil has too little to say about active struggle within affliction, and I augment her analysis with Sartre's idea of a 'passionate revolt', expressed in his essay, *Black Orpheus*, an introduction to French West Indian and African poetry. He writes there: 'suffering carries within itself its own refusal ... [opening] itself toward revolt and toward liberty'.[3]

One of Sartre's points in that essay is that poetry is particularly adept at conveying suffering and that black poets like Aime Cesaire were radically refreshing French poetic language, giving it a new power of feeling. The translation of Schwarz-Bart's novel was met in the conservative American press with a contrasting opinion, that pain cannot be rendered in beautiful lyric language. It is perhaps not surprising that the book reviewer for the *National Review* would be deaf to a song of affliction. Jewish critics like Robert Alter were not. Schwarz-Bart, one of those solitary survivors of the holocaust, brings a special hearing to the *Solitudë* story, which he learned (one presumes) through his marriage to a Guadeloupan writer.

A more serious criticism is that a white European man cannot, should not, attempt to convey a 'black' female story, hidden deeply, moreover, in another time and place; and that the proof of this error is contained in how little realized and remote the character, Solitude, seems in the novel, how artificial and gratuitous her beauty. Undoubtedly, Solitude is an abstract figure. The historical details, if striking, are sketchy: born to a Senegalese woman about 1772 as the result of a shipboard rape; separated, perhaps rejected, from her mother early on and 'educated' to the plantation house; sold February 8, 1784 and again August 23, 1787; reputed to be a zombie for at least 15 years of this time and hanged finally on November 29, 1802 'immediately after the delivery of her child', as Oruna Lara reports in his *Histoire de la Guadeloupe* (1921),[4] for her part in the resistance to post-Revolutionary France's re-enslavement of black labour. Schwarz-Bart was evidently struck by the story of a woman who, a beautiful mulatto, could choose to live within black culture, and who could emerge from a long period of zombiedom to status as a rebel leader significant enough to earn her a historical mention. But outside of the plantation registers and other slight public records, the author is dependent on legend and upon his own considerable imagination, out of which the novel is really made.

My suggestion with the Schwarz-Bart novel is that an afflictive analysis justifies this imagination, not only for what the author estimates were true elements in the story, but also for his choice of literary technique. He does not, for example, attempt to bring us 'closer' to the story by inventing for the Solitude character a personality, by 'characterizing' her within a 'narrative'. Instead he 'sings' to her, setting down to her memory a succession of tactfully worked out, and occasionally beautiful, stills. The lack of substantive, historical detail proves convenient. He can, without distraction, present her life in a more or less stepwise, logical way. What he shows us by this method is the complete paradigm for affliction. Schwarz-Bart has clearly made that judgment about Solitude. He has estimated that in choosing negritude over the easier, customary mulatto path of white mimicry and association, she was one of Weil's pure souls; that her zombiedom was at least ambiguous, certainly psychological, perhaps even intuitively strategic, expressing both anonymity and patience (in which the seeds of rebellion 'waited'); that her birth was markedly absurd; and that her acquisition of a 'culture' was, in her special context, unusual, an evidence for affliction's miraculous event, the traversal of the infinite distance between non-personality and self-creation, which Schwarz-Bart imagines to have occurred through a significant encounter (actually there are two). An early sign of her precocity for this kind of treatment was her ability to retain for herself an interestingly intelligent name.

Whether or not a genuine transcendence took place Schwarz-Bart is careful to let legend decide. At the fountain on her way to the gibbet, she stands before the mixed crowd serenely, on the edge, it may be, of joy. A 'leafy twig' falls at her feet, tossed by 'an enormous black woman in a blue madras'; it was 'a fragrant, purple-flowering herb known as Christ Child, whole armfuls of which were traditionally given to young mothers' (p. 173). Solitude notices the 'kind thought':

> Turning away from the woman with the madras, Solitude contemplated the white audience and, so the story goes, said very distinctly in an excellent French French, which startled all about her: 'It seems one must never say: Fountain, I shall not drink your water ....'
> Then throwing back her head and opening wide the magnificent globes of her eyes – made by the Lord, says a legend, to reflect the stars – she burst out laughing. It was a strange laugh, deep in her throat, a gentle cooing, gay and barely tempered with sadness. All the stories, all the legends and fireside tales about Solitude end with that laugh, which some have likened to a song. (p. 174)

Whatever the accuracy of this last image – and it must certainly have been an extraordinary moment – Schwarz-Bart's abstract representation of the character's 'development' is both 'correct' and reasonable. He has made deductive assumptions about her life which are perfectly consistent (as it happens) with Weil's detailed, terrible observations on the afflicted state; and inasmuch as the observations are supplied by that suffering itself, it is possible we have in the Schwarz-Bart text holograms, so to speak, of the life of the real Solitude. This gives Schwarz-Bart's imaginative report, and imaginative reports in general, the value of a historical surmise, which is another way of saying that extreme sympathy has a methodical and tellable logic of its own, different from Locke, Berkeley and Hume's. The author's anchoring into Solitude's mind an obsessive attention to the memory of her mother is a striking instance of this, although only indirectly supported by an afflictive reading. Bayangumay is invented as herself a pure soul – Bayangumay, 'she whose eyelashes are transparent'. But where Solitude is a transparency in affliction, her mother was 'a flute which her ancestors played all day long' (p. 27). Nourished in the replete scene of a total identity, she has a culture, a name and roots. And when the 'fishers of men' come, isolating her and killing her world, she can in her brand new world hold up soul still and body erect. Solitude's attention to this memory is like the memory of a 'culture', again abstract, and preserves for the reader the reasonableness of her ability to wait in silence – for God or Love, the return of life.

With Rhys's novel we have not an allegorical recovery but a 'realistic' retelling, with direct access to the afflicted state of mind. Affliction is seen from the inside. Here, as with *A Question of Power*, the text itself is afflicted, with the difference that the afflictive character of *Wide Sargasso Sea* presents itself in a condition of memory, while in *A Question of Power* affliction is co-temporal with the text. In Rhys we are in the period following Emancipation, the metamorphosis, as Sartre calls it. Antoinette has the spectacular advantage of being physically white, but she is, like Solitude, spiritually black. Her affliction is acquired the moment she realizes, after the poisoning of her mother's horse, that there is no space for them in their native Jamaican world. Panicking, her mother, a Martinican, '"pretty like pretty self"' (p. 15), marries back into money; but the times have changed and the very English Mr Mason merely blunders past. Their strangely 'cultural' misalignment is a pre-figuring sign that Antoinette will have no location, no future, no escape from the peculiar limbo she finds herself in. Contemptuously misunderstood by her own race, at worst a 'white nigger', hated by the blacks – so long as she presents this weakness – as a 'white cockroach', she tells her husband, Rochester: 'So between you I often wonder who I am and where is my country and where do I belong and why was I ever born at all' (p. 85).

The afflictive point of interest in Antoinette's case is her awareness that she is beyond the reach of the compassion and perception of others. In logical terms, she is less afflicted than Solitude, because she has advantages – a personal consciousness, social position, cultural resources. But this elevation only changes the perspective, puts another face on the same reality; her power is a power of looking down. She perceives her dilemma with a full consciousness, emotionally, and is unable, or refuses, to turn away from it. She is another one of Weil's pure souls, concentrating on her absurd condition, binding herself to affliction. The knowledge of being lost, of being caught in a historical 'dead sea', constitutes in the sensible progress of the 'single' affliction I am tracing, a 'hopeless' phase. Antoinette's clairvoyant dreams express this in the ponderously repeated phrase, 'this must happen'. It is a knowledge whose fatefulness only enables her to struggle futilely in the descent into an abyss, in a pervasive atmosphere of an indispersible despair.

The sense in affliction of an ineluctable doom engenders what Weil calls an 'inert compliance'. It is a phenomenon which goes a long way toward explaining Antoinette's much-alleged 'passivity'. Compliance is not resignation, not the turning away or true despair which Weil warns is the greatest danger. In Antoinette, despite the absolute character of her foreknowledge, despair is also hope disguised, hope perpetually disappointed, a relentless contemplation of herself and her world. The hysterical or schizophrenic pattern of struggle alternating with compliance is familiar, the endemic, all-too-human, diminutive of absurd circumstances.[5] Antoinette's approach to the stranger, whom the 'order of things' has appointed to kill her, is the form also of a passionate resistance, and we are bound to sympathize.

The evidence for this pattern is clear exactly where critics find Antoinette's behaviour puzzling. Rochester, of course, is the stranger in her dreams. On their wedding eve, she baulks, explaining only that 'you don't know anything about me' (p. 66). Piqued at the prospect of being 'jilted by this Creole girl', he contracts, gently, to trust her 'if you'll trust me' (p. 66). She falls silent and willessly carries through. On the wedding day she tells the story from her childhood of waking to see, without feeling, two 'enormous rats ... on the sill staring at me'; then re-awaking later to extreme fear, having, she says, 'slept too long in the moonlight' (pp. 69-70).

In the other scene which has been taken for a culpable complicity in her own fate, Christophine is urging her to leave Rochester, or at least, to 'have spunks and do battle for yourself' (p. 96). Antoinette agrees to 'talk to him first' but on condition that she take away with her some of Christophine's obeah, a strong potion for 'getting back' the love of a man she knows is 'someone who hated me' (p. 23). What we ourselves, sensible to suffering but perhaps insensible to affliction, read here as perversity contains, in fact, an instinct for health. Antoinette has an intuitive grasp of where struggle should lead. She has, as Sartre expresses it, 'the passion of suffering in revolt', and a significant aspect of this passion, which Sartre identifies also in the 'erect patience' of the 'black soul', is a 'sexual sympathy with life'. Antoinette has precisely this. Her sensual relation to the garden at Coulibri and her sensitivity to colour and light in general make this clear. With Rochester she fixes obsessively on recovering the sexual abandonment of their honeymoon, justifying the acute observation – Sartre again – that 'between anguish and sexual desire' there is a direct relation, an 'indissoluble unity of suffering, of eros, and of joy'.[6]

The quality of desperation in Antoinette's passion fits in with her compliancy to make a package, or complex, of accession to her fate, the panicky hope of escape only sinking her down further. As Naipaul has observed, the Rhys passion is 'a further diminution of the capacity to survive'.[7] In choosing Rochester, in questing after love by embracing the 'chill hypocrisy of the English',[8] she commits a slow and agonizing suicide. At the same time, her choice to marry, and to marry Rochester, gives evidence of a daring calculation for eluding fate. Rochester is caught in history, too, the product of his time. He cannot respond to Antoinette in a human way because he carries with him the superior presumptions of his country, colour and class. Power – its attitudes and expectations, his own nervous familiarity with its icy thrill – forms the core of his personality; others – women, foreign worlds – must respond to him, not the other way round. Yet, as a human being and a man, Rochester is less English than Mason was; by way of creeping, insistent suspicions, he comes near the edge of another reality, another way of seeing. He is not callous or uncurious, as Mason was; he is even vulnerable and reflective. As a boy, Grace Poole remembers, he was ever 'gentle, generous, brave' (p. 145). But it was as a boy that he learned to hide his feelings, as all English were taught; a view, he says, 'that I have always accepted' (p. 85), the price for which is 'confused impressions [that] will never be written ... blanks in [the] mind that can never be filled up' (p. 64). The West Indies that he associates with Antoinette is 'too much' (p. 59); Antoinette's eyes, to him, are 'dark' and 'alien' (p. 56). The failure of his 'humanity' underscores Antoinette's isolation; secretly jealous, he must, in the end, 'pretend she is mad' (p. 132).

Antoinette is 'driven to madness'. She dreams her death in the image of her mother's parrot, Coco, falling to oblivion from the railing of flaming Coulibri, screeching and on fire. Mr Mason had clipped his wings. Before her fall Antoinette hears the parrot call, as he always did 'when he saw a stranger ... *Qui est la? Qui est la?*' (p. 155).

In Bessie Head's *A Question of Power*, affliction is, as I have stated, present to the text; the text itself is 'mad', not literary, not fictional. And this is its virtue. What it gives up in literariness, it gains in an intense intimacy of effect. The story it relates of a woman savagely struggling to fend off her demons is compellingly authentic. The 'backgrounds', for their part, the depiction of an ordinary town life, simply expressed, the coded references to Botswanan history, the mythological matter which figures in the character Elizabeth's spells of trauma, enacted nightly, make for absorbing, if strange, 'other reading'. The critic's task here is to bring the text through, to cure it of its ills.

The afflictive starting point is, primarily, Elizabeth's consternation with the problem of racism, especially as it affects her. She has expectations which Antoinette could not have known; hers is an affliction in an historically late stage The library becomes the centre for a restless, personal activity; her struggle is more engaged, more concentrated. But she is always reading the same book, staring down at the absurdity of her own life. The intellectualized consciousness of this absurdity, with some of its lived consequences, is what afflicts Elizabeth. Inevitably, she tries to escape the 'permanent nervous tension' (p. 19) of life in South Africa, to outdistance the legal label, 'Coloured'; she migrates to Botswana. But what she finds there is only another racism, only the opposite wall. The three-year period of breakdown which follows is, in reality, the slow eruption of a long-suppressed rage.

Her anger at the degradation which this double racism brings, with its denial to her of ordinary personality, is a mark of her own soul's more advanced progress in affliction, beyond Solitude's or Antoinette's. She is keenly aware of the injustice because in the contemporary world setting, organized stigmatization for colour is now the exception and not the rule. Paradoxically, this makes her experience, while a technically less afflicted one, more painful, more anxious, more immediate. It is like the sudden energy of struggle at the release point, after the exhaustion of a long captivity. She is impatient for relief, hostile to impediment. She has, moreover, a frustrated sense of her own power, a power she conceives as capable of representing the suffering and enlightenment of all mankind, of inducing in all men a faith in community where all belong. At the end, she is the prophet of 'the warm embrace of the brotherhood of man' (p. 206). Solitude's negritude is rejected, therefore, as a type of racism, while Antoinette's insistence on a personal love which would include her 'difference' as a white West Indian is, in Elizabeth, replaced by a desire for a general love which would exclude difference, including her own as the 'half-breed' (p. 104). This describes for this form of affliction an odd arc-ike 'progress', from Solitude as anonymous object to Elizabeth as an anonymous subject, from a zombie's pure imitation of serenity to its reality, after struggle, in a conscious, ordinary life.

The heat in Elizabeth's consciousness, her sense of the near possibility of an ordinary, inconspicuous existence, makes her quarrel with, or debate, her condition. This has the lofty dimension of a metaphysical struggle – of good with evil, of 'Sello' with 'Dan' – as well as the personal dimension of strenuous suffering. The one is a mask for the other. It is beyond the scope of this paper to decipher the jumble of signs in the large outer material, to peel off all the tape. Research will show that Head knew this material well; all the signs can be read. I conclude instead with a direct assessment of what lies under the mask, in Elizabeth's mind, in turmoil or at peace, at the centre of which is hidden (but 'expressed' in the text) a very private affliction. Does she, in the end, it might be asked, exorcize the demon?

The Osiris myth, in its benign agricultural form, contains coded suggestions for how we should interpret Elizabeth's 'inner hell'. Osiris's double death and recovery, like Elizabeth's two breakdowns and recoveries, is not a simple case of one-and-one-makes-two. Isis's recovery of Osiris the second time is incomplete; she never finds his sexual part, so that, despite his effective stewardship of the Egyptian crop cycle, he himself is without potency. This is a vital clue. The theme of sexual absence, or of its opposite, sexual excess, is a powerfully manifest element in Elizabeth's disturbance. Its connection with race is established in the novel by the figure of Medusa, turned by Athena, goddess of wisdom, agriculture, and civilized life, into an ugly Gorgon for a sexual misalliance, and slain finally in Egypt, where the drops of blood from her severed head infest Africa with its serpents.

Elizabeth's first breakdown is the result of Medusa's 'terrible thunderbolt' (p. 39), which passes into her body. With it Elizabeth's preoccupation with 'strange arguments' (p. 38) ceases and a shock of repugnant self-realizations charge through her, in 'wave after wave' (p. 39). She has no vagina, Medusa mocks; 'you're not linked up to the people' (p. 44); 'I can do more for the poor than you' (p. 38); and (worst of all) she, Elizabeth, 'never really liked Africans ... [but] only pretended to' (p. 51). The linkage of an abuse for sex with an abuse for colour is very clear in the novel. Early on, we learn that Elizabeth

> had lived for a time in a part of Africa where nearly all the Coloured men were homosexuals and openly paraded down the street in women's clothes. They tied turbans round their heads and talked in high, falsetto voices. It was so widespread, so common to so many men in this town that they felt no shame at all. They and people in general accepted it as a disease one had to live with. No one commented at these strange men in women's clothes ...
>
> An African man gave her the most reasonable explanation: 'How can a man be a man when he is called a boy? I can barely retain my own manhood'. (p. 45)

At night Elizabeth dreams how 'all these Coloured men lay down on their backs, their penes in the air, and began to die slowly'. And Medusa comments, 'You see, that's what you are like ... That's your people, not African people' (p. 45).

Her second breakdown is worse, with tremendous intensification of this theme. Dan, who rationalizes his own homosexual lapses, is merciless with Elizabeth: 'You are inferior as a Coloured. You haven't got what that girl has got'; she's a 'specialist in sex', with hair 'properly African' (p. 127).

Medusa, 'pitchblack in colour' (p. 37), loans Elizabeth the 'sensuous bomb' (p. 44) of her own orgasm; Dan and his girls include Elizabeth in theirs, either directly or as a shamed, impotent spectator. Either way she is their abominated host. Elizabeth resists but it is useless 'talking uphill against a terrible downward pull' (p. 135). Her silence, a 'makeshift replacement for love' (p. 136), we have seen before, the passive sign of a resistance, the mark in Elizabeth's case of a 'violent pride that could not endure humiliation' (p. 136).

We can now 'read out' the Buddhistic text in the novel. The evil which produces suffering is caused by natural desire, for power and for sex; give desire activity and it strengthens its hand. Enlightenment consists in the right mental poise, which the body endangers. The soul must renounce the body, just as Siddhartha renounces caste.

For Elizabeth, the renunciation of personal desire involves, initially, the projection of her psyche into the Medusan figure. Medusa first makes her appearance by stepping forward from out of the 'image of holiness' of Sello's 'wife', a woman who was 'almost the extreme of spirituality' (p. 37). In her corollary guise Medusa is at once Elizabeth's damaging self-critical voice and a growing grotesqueness of the passion of the body. Dan represents in this process a 'lived' context, the failure of sexual relationships with – and perhaps fear and distrust of – men. The working out of African politics in these relationships – Africa's history of 'brutal desire' – makes sex a politically volatile exchange, so that Elizabeth, as a Coloured, not rooted in African soil, finds she cannot situate her body in the social space. Sex has become the climaxing point of her affliction, the point where her amazement at the absurd founding of personality on race manifests itself. The sense of her own sexual debasement, together with her obsessive contempt for sexual 'perversions', finally quashes all instinct for a 'personal love' (p. 202). The body is divided from the spirit, African destiny from the 'brotherhood of man', and sex from love, in a 'buddhistic', negative transcendence. In place of personal love, Elizabeth substitutes international friendships among agricultural volunteers in Botswana, growing the resilient Cape Gooseberry in her yard and bottling it for jam.

Elizabeth's is a partial success. Her consciousness of the absurdity of her position privileges her in the end with a view of human suffering as universal. Her suffering 'is the suffering of others' (p. 70), the suffering of the 'black soul', which in turn, because it embodies suffering in our own time, is a suffering on behalf of all mankind. Ultimately, the 'black soul' is an all-soul – as Sartre describes it, a beautiful 'iridescence of being ... dedicated to its own destruction'.[9] The presence of 'colour', on the other hand, is a denial of being, an obstruction to 'the simple joy of being a human being with a personality' (p. 44). Considered together, the afflictive narratives of Solitude, Antoinette and Elizabeth represent a particular form of historical progress through colour, the passage between black and white. That Elizabeth acquires a liveable humanity suggests that this particular affliction has nearly mended, that black and white have approached an historical position of rapprochement, and that they have done this in part, perhaps in significant part, under the 'yellow' light, over 400 years, of their miscegenated children.

NOTES

1. André Schwarz-Bart, *A Woman Named Solitude* (San Francisco: Donald Ellis, 1985; English translation by Ralph Manheim, 1973, Atheneum Publishers); Jean Rhys, *Wide Sargasso Sea* (Penguin, 1968); Bessie Head, *A Question of Power* (London: Heinemann, 1974). All references are to these editions and are included in the text.
2. Simone Weil, *Waiting on God* (Fontana, 1959; English translation by Emma Craufurd, 1951, Routledge & Kegan Paul, from French edition, *Attente de Dieu*, 1950), p. 78. The two essays I rely on are 'The Love of God and Affliction' and 'Forms of the Implicit Love of God', pp. 76-166. All further references to these works are included in the text.
3. Jean-Paul Sartre, *Black Orpheus* (Paris: Présence Africaine, 1948; translated by S.W. Allen), p. 55.
4. Quoted in *Solitude*, epigraph page (unnumbered).
5. I am re-deploying Wilson Harris's use of the word 'diminutive' (as a small, contrary sign marking liveable ground within dead universes) given in an address to the ACLALS Conference, University of Kent, August 1989, where this paper was first presented. See Wilson Harris, *The Fabric of the Imagination* in this volume.
6. Sartre, p. 50 (all quotations).
7. V.S. Naipaul, 'Without A Dog's Chance', *New York Review of Books*, 18 May 1972, pp. 29-31.
8. Albert Alvarez, 'The Best Living English Novelist', *New York Review of Books*, 17 March 1974, pp. 6-7.
9. Sartre, p. 59.

CHANDANI LOKUGÉ

The Cross-Cultural Experience of a Pioneer Indian Woman Writer of English Fiction

Pundit Nehru, assessing from personal experience, the full result of the joint forces of East and West upon the Indian consciousness, says

> I have become a queer mixture of the East and West, out of place everywhere, at home nowhere. Perhaps my thoughts and approach to life are more akin to what is called Western than Eastern, but India clings to me, as she does to all her children, in innumerable ways; and behind me lie, somewhere in the subconscious, racial memories of a hundred, or whatever the number may be, generations of Brahman. I cannot get rid of either that past inheritance or my recent acquisitions. They are both part of me, and, though they help me in both the East and the West, they also create in me a feeling of spiritual loneliness not only in public activities but in life itself. I am a stranger and alien in the West. I cannot be of it. But in my own country also, sometimes, I have an exile's feeling.[1]

The experience of culture-conflict is, at varying depths and levels of consciousness, the theme of most English fiction by Indian women writers. One of the most recent of them, Bharati Mukherjee, makes the pendulum swing violently to the west in the attempt to locate her heroine's psychological centre in the free and easy life of New York in her new short story, 'A Wife's Story'. The wife describes her cross-cultural experience and her search for personal identity with the following words:

> In the back of the cab, without even trying, I feel light, almost free. Memories of Indian destitutes mix with the hordes of New York street people, and they float free, like astronauts, inside my head. I've made it. I'm making something of my life, I've left home, my husband, to a get a Ph.D. in special ed. I have a multiple-entry visa and a small scholarship for two years. After that, we'll see. My mother was beaten by her mother-in-law, my grandmother, when she'd registered for French lessons at the Alliance Française. My grandmother, the eldest daughter of a rich zamindar, was illiterate.[2]

She obviously prefers the new life and lives it to the hilt. But India clings to her, and she can only try to forget. She too floats like an astronaut between east and west. Today, there is an insecurity about the intensity of life of the modern Indian woman depicted in much of the most modern

Indian fiction in English, a formlessness about her identity that is frightening. The writings of Kamala Das, Namita Gokhale and Bharati Mukherjee bear ample witness to this phenomenon.

The genesis of this split personality of the Indian female psyche caught in the cross-currents of two cultures – the acquired western and the instinctual Indian – occurred in English fiction in India exactly a century ago, with Krupabai Satthianadhan.

Krupabai was born in 1862 and was the thirteenth child of the first Brahman converts to Christianity in the Bombay Presidency. Autobiographical and biographical records disclose that Krupabai belonged to that segment of Indian society most exposed to the 'new order of things – an order of things which at the present time [was] spreading its influence to a greater or less extent over the whole of her native land'. The new order was introduced to India, as most of us from nations conquered by the British at one time or another are aware, via Christianity, education, and political and socio-economic reforms. And awakened through these media to the western ideology of individualism and liberalism, Krupabai is seen, in the identity crisis, to challenge the doctrines of her own traditional culture and religion which defined female identity only in terms of a definite role at any given moment – of daughter, wife or mother.

Krupabai was informally introduced to education by her brother in early childhood. She then attended a Zenana mission school in Bombay. There, her close association with an American lady doctor and her outstanding academic success resulted in her qualifying for medical study in England. Debarred from foreign scholarship on the grounds of poor health she made do by attending the Madras Medical College. The first female student ever to enter the portals of an Indian medical college Krupabai distinguished herself academically by obtaining the highest results in her group. She married the Reverend Samuel Satthianadhan on his return from Cambridge and lived out her remaining brief life span with her husband. Biographical records disclose that while Krupabai's most significant role in life was that of devoted wife, she actively encouraged female emancipation when and where she could. She also had time for creative writing. Her articles were published in the *South Indian Observer*, in the *National Indian Journal* and in other papers and magazines. They have been called 'delightful accounts of life around her'. She died in 1894, aged 32 years.

Saguna,[3] which renders in imaginative terms the writer's autobiography and the biography of her mother, was first printed in the Christian College Magazine. It was published as a book posthumously in 1895. It is an excellent illustration of the unique identity that emerged from contra-acculturation.

In the autobiographical areas of *Saguna,* Krupabai admits to a childhood happily spent beneath the mantle of Christianity with a larger-than-life, Christ-like figure of a dead father and the live presence of a pious sister

constantly wielding their very christian influence over them all. Her
brother Bhaskar, following in his father's religious footsteps, was her
constant companion, guide and mentor, directing her spiritual growth
through life. She promised him faithfully to devote her life 'to God's glory,
wholly to God's glory'. They were alone at the time, she remembers,
'alone with God on the mountain top, and [they] fell on [their] knees and
prayed'.

Her own belief in Christianity and her adherence to this promise so
reverently given, shed an aura of Christian faith over her literary work. In
fact, one of her reasons for writing *Saguna* seems to have stemmed from
her promise. *Saguna*, among other things, is a celebration of Christianity.
It is also propagandist literature.

> ...for I thought I heard with the advent of light quite an outburst of song and merri-
> ment ... it is just like this, shadowy, dark, mystic, weird, with superstition and
> bigotry lurking in every corner, before the light of Christianity comes into a land....
> So it is when the sunbeams of Christianity dispel the darkness of superstition in a
> land. (*Saguna*, p. 7)

Krupabai's brother Bhaskar was her guru in all other matters pertaining
to the emergence of her personal identity. She was introduced by him, in
her early childhood, to English literature, to education and to the world
outside.

The small circle of people within which the Satthianadhans moved socially, representative of that Indian milieu liberated in a sense from conventional norms of orthodoxy by their exposure to western influence, was
another force that helped mould Krupabai's identity. She gives the following interesting anecdote which describes her initial encounter with the
English novel.

> One day she [a friend] told me as a great secret that her Ma had given her a novel,
> but that Pa did not know anything of it, and that she knew a great deal of the
> world now. (She always spoke of her parents as Ma and Pa).
> 'And what is a novel?' I said, afraid to show my ignorance and yet wanting to
> know what it was.
> 'A novel! a book, you know but you must not read one. Little girls should not
> read novels. It is different with me,' she said proudly. (*Saguna*, pp. 96-97)

She was not, however, to be restrained, and quietly developed her own
taste in English literature. Her favourite author in later life, and one who
had considerable influence on her literary work, was George Eliot.

Another influence in her life, rather more passive than those of the new
order, yet always present and no less significant, was her mother. An
Indian Brahman converted to Christianity like her husband, Radha was
subject to near-fanatic Christian devotion. However, Krupabai emphasizes
the fact that her mother was never really uprooted from ancestral beliefs

on account of the new religion. She explains in *Saguna*, 'My father died early, leaving us in the sole care of an orthodox mother, who though her faith in her new religion was strong, was still full of Hindu notions of things' (p. 1).

As a result Krupabai was, like Maggie Tulliver, sometimes reprimanded by her mother for her interest in what Indian gender-norms had decreed as being outside the woman's sphere. 'What is the use of learning for a girl? A girl's training school is near the school (the fire over which everything is cooked) ... and however learned a girl may be she must come to the school' (*Saguna*, p. 4).

However, unlike Maggie's thwarted ambitions, Krupabai's desire for the development of intellect through formal education was indulged not only because she was beloved of her family, but because the new order had taken firm root within her home.

India itself was the final active force. Capturing one moment of the elemental effect of her motherland on Krupabai's consciousness is her account of a ride in a simple bullock cart with her family to and from their mountain home. Her alienation from the quintessence of the indigenous is felt in her unconscious use of derogatory words like 'primitive' and 'clumsy' in the description of it. Yet this description (quoted below) also suggests a curious instinctual one-ness with the indigenous people, with the land and with its elements. It can only be described as a primal force.

> But what delight do these primitive cart journeys afford! What a wild breeziness and what freedom from restraint there is about them! We feel that all men are akin to us. The weary wayfarer, the peasant toiling in the fields, the chatty old dame that tells of her affairs loudly and walks briskly on, the sturdy farmer returning loaded with drooping sheaves of corn, their smiling faces a study in themselves, – all seem one with us. Safely we jog on in our two wheeled clumsy vehicle, ... straggling fields and solitary temples soon disappear, and we are face to face with nature in all her wild grandeur. The soul catches a responding note of wild, joyous freedom. Sometimes idly dreaming and watching, we seem to see in the sky-mingling distance fairy castles gently take shape and rise, revealing in the nearer view some ancient fortress of a ruined Mahratta power.... A little further and the forest disappears: we emerge in the sunlight, and look with a mysterious, superstitious dread on the dark avenue left behind. (*Saguna*, p. 85)

The personal identity of Krupabai that emerges from *Saguna* and from documented biographical records conforms to Nehru's definition of the Indian identity struggling to home in cross-cultural currents. In Nehru's words – 'her thoughts and approach to life are more akin to what is called Western than Eastern'. She is seen to embrace the study of medicine as a career and to reject would-be suitors defiantly asserting her independence from archetypal ideologies. Her voice is vehemently feminist.

> I would now throw aside the fetters that bound me and be independent. I had chafed under the restraints and the ties which formed the common lot of women,

and I longed for an opportunity to show that a woman is in no way inferior to a man. How hard it seemed to my mind that marriage should be the goal of woman's ambition, and that she should spend her days in the light trifles of a home life, live to dress, to look pretty, and never know the joy of independence and intellectual work. The thought had been galling. It made me avoid men, and I felt more than once that I could not look into their faces unless I was able to hold my own with them. So, like a slave whose freedom had just been purchased, I was happy, deliriously happy. (*Saguna*, p. 178)

Yet, India clings to her and she cannot rid herself of past inheritance.

I loved these two [English] ladies and stayed with them for months, and ... I lived very happily with them.... When I returned home.... I felt, however, a sweet happiness, a sense of security and safety in my mother's company. I had been all along vaguely longing for this. There was no fear of anybody misunderstanding me now, ... I had in a way enjoyed the refined surroundings, the pleasant occupations, the conversations and company of the life that I had just left behind. There is a subtle pleasure in having one's powers drawn out and in the consciousness of the thought that in some respects one is in no way inferior to others, but there seemed to be an artificiality in the life which I had shared.... Something seemed wanting, and what it was I failed to comprehend.... The conversation with simple folks, my mother's acquaintances, I enjoyed immensely, and I took a special delight in chatting with country peasants who came to our door to sell butter, milk, vegetables and other things.... The breath of their homes seemed to linger round them.... The thrashing of corn was in my ears, the voices of men and children mingled with the bleating of sheep and the lowing of cows... (*Saguna*, p. 157)

The many silent influences at work within her developed a critical awareness of both the eastern and the western life-styles in her which naturally alienated her from each of them, in turn. She indicts her own people who are mere superficial imitators of the west and boldly advocates middle-path moderation to both Indian women and men.

Her mother wore a saree. But she attended an English school, and her thoughts were influenced by those with whom she mixed. And who knows what a rising Christian community may not aspire to in the future? Nothing is so startling in these days as the unconscious imitation of English customs and manners of the people of India. The fault, if indeed it can be called a fault, is characteristic not only of native Christians, but of Hindus as well. It is not because the manners and customs are English that they are unconsciously imitated, but because they are looked upon as necessary concomitants of a higher stage of civilization. Probably the change is inevitable, and it is useless to try to prevent it, but I sincerely hope that my countrywomen, and for the matter of that, my countrymen also, in their eagerness to adopt the new will not give up the good that is in the old. (*Saguna*, p. 99)

She is equally repelled by the hypocrisies that characterized some of the Christian missionaries and their followers and does not hesitate to expose their petty prejudices and racial bias. To her truth was beauty, beauty –

truth, nothing else mattered. A disciple of truth and a nonconformist, she was, and inevitably, a maverick, 'at home nowhere'.

Kamala[4]

Kamala is Krupabai's only novel in English and it was published in 1894. Leaving aside the artist's compulsive desire to create, Krupabai's novel has surely been motivated by other aims. Primarily, strongly convinced that archetypal religious and cultural norms were the root causes prohibiting the Indian woman's emancipation, she attempts to eradicate them through social and religious reforms.

The writer's reformatory purpose calls for the representation of generalized types characterised by the social situation rather than of specific or individual characters. Kamala is consciously created in the mould of the archetype of Indian feminine consciousness.

Given that 'role expectations are highly specific and institutionalized' as in the Indian social structure, Krupabai's concentration on the archetype rather than on individuality in the illustration of her heroine's character is nothing other than realistic. Kamala typifies convention and lives only within the familial enclosure, in the personae of daughter, wife and mother, roles designated for the Indian woman by ages past. A nonentity in herself, she is conditioned from birth to live by the collective unconscious personified for her by the omnipotent twin components of her life – tradition and religion. Her unconscious absorbs the religion of her ancestors from dawn to dusk. The sacred tulsi grows on a pedestal in the enclosure in front of the home. Pilgrimages form an integral part of the life of women and children. The narrator often intervenes to explain the general situation and so ensure that Kamala is seen to be a representative figure. Puranic readings, timeless Indian myth and legend are ingrained early in the child heroine's psyche with the conscious purpose of inculcating denial of self, self-effacement and self-sacrifice.

With the collective unconscious thus constantly kept alive by this atmosphere of religion and tradition the female psyche early recognizes that the fulfilling of a great ideal, of duty before self, is and has always been her purpose in life. This ideal, entwined with an early acceptance of fate as all-powerful, forms the sum and substance of her simple moral code, and in times of suffering she faithfully embraces it.

The archetypal heroine is subjected to those life experiences and interpersonal relationships within the familial structure which best highlight the atrocities that the writer holds responsible for the retardation of her psychical growth. Kamala is barely out of childhood and ignorant of the world when her marriage ceremony takes place. She has no voice in the selection of her partner, the marriage is arranged by elders. There is no rebellion, she has been conditioned to believe that she was born for marriage and the procreation of sons.

Krupabai emphasizes the nihilistic role that the traditional Indian wife plays in marriage, the total annihilation of ego as she describes Kamala's marriage ceremony. 'Living or dead she was henceforth, the wife and the property of the man who-ever he might be. This was ordered by the shastras, and the law was never to be broken' (*Kamala*, p. 26). With reformistic zeal she digresses from the main story to offer explications like the following. With them she disrupts the traditional Indian institution of patriarchal matrimony and attempts to reconstruct it on European foundations.

> The relations between a husband and a wife in an orthodox Hindu home are, as a general rule, much constrained. The two have not the same liberty of speech and action that are accorded to them usually in European countries. The joint family system is the chief cause of this anomalous state of things. The Hindu wife, unless she lives with her husband in a house of her own, scarcely exchanges a word with him before other members of the family. They behave as if they were strangers to each other, the woman covering her head at her husband's approach, or leaving the room when he happens to come in, or standing aside, and when talked to, either not taking any notice of what is said, or, with head turned aside, answering in the most distant manner possible. The mother-in-law's jealousy prohibits the young people from having anything like liberty of speech or action in her presence. (*Kamala*, p. 64)

The quotidian routine of the child-wife's life, as described in *Kamala*, further establishes the empty identity of the wife/daughter-in-law in her husband's home. Sociological surveys carried out on this era prove that the writer is merely divulging contemporary realities as she describes Kamala's psychological immurement.[5]

She is physically and mentally browbeaten by the mother-in-law. Hardly more than a child, naive and innocent, she can neither comprehend the conflict with her mother-in-law nor deal with it with the maturity that it demands. Totally alienated from her in-laws who band together against her, and from her husband who is quite dominated by his family, she naturally takes refuge, as her sisters have for generations, behind the protective walls of her traditional and religious upbringing. She resigns herself to ancestral expectations of her and, according to the writer, languishes in a psychical stasis. Krupabai's comment on Kamala's timid moral submission (quoted below) discloses her conviction that it was concepts of ancestral religion and culture that, by suppressing the spirit, regressed the development of female individuality.

> Somehow Kamala became resigned to her lot, and it was her crude religious convictions that enabled her to do so.... But there was another kind of teaching that mingled with it all and that was ... whether she enjoyed pleasure or suffered pain, she ought not to grumble but accept it meekly, for it was her fate ... she wished to be exemplary like Savitri, Seeta and other noble women; but even they had to submit to fate and did not get their due in this world. (*Kamala*, pp. 57-58)

Unable to break free of cultural and religious conditioning, Kamala attempts suicide. In Krupabai's other literary creation, *Saguna*, she hails Christianity as the saviour of the orthodox Indian woman from psychical imprisonment. Radha, Krupabai's mother as portrayed in *Saguna*, triumphs where Kamala failed because she is given via the new religion a solid foundation on which to build individuality and attain liberation. With her conversion to Christianity she is directly exposed to the new order which advocates such a transformation. And she is transformed by it, to an extent, and it affords her happiness. 'There was now no feeling of constraint between Harichandra and Radha. The unnatural fetters of custom had fallen away, and they met and talked with the freedom of children' (*Saguna*, p. 70).

However, it was noticed that Radha remained rooted to ancestral beliefs. (See p. 4). The equity in marriage attained by Radha and her husband soon after Radha's conversion as described by Krupabai above, had its limitations. However, the limitations were imposed by Radha herself. That Christianity gave her licence to choose her own status in marriage and family is strongly endorsed. Writing her own autobiography Krupabai maintains that she was finally able to attain liberation of mind and soul to a greater extent than her mother. Born into a Christian family she is exposed to the new order from infancy. However, that she too is not completely liberated from the instinctual and primal forces of India has already been suggested above and will be discussed in greater detail later on.

Thus *Kamala* begins, in English fiction by Indian women writers, the female identity's metamorphosis from tradition to modernity. The three women together – Kamala, Radha and Saguna – form sequential links in the evolution of this identity. Kamala attempts personal identity and fails because she was bound fast to orthodox India. Radha, exposed to the new order in maidenhood, attains a vestige of it. Saguna, through her exposure to the new order from infancy absorbs it to a greater extent and is thereby liberated a step further.

While Krupabai utilizes art for the purpose of amelioration of woman's status, she also attempts through it to satisfy an intensely more private desire – the desire to orchestrate role identity, founded by ancestral cultural and religious norms, and personal identity emerging from identity consciousness induced by the exposure to the new order. This is articulated by Krupabai as she passionately attempts to create personal identity in her very archetypal heroine.

Kamala's new identity emerges when her *alter ego* occasionally desires to shake free the shackles of orthodoxy. Often in the novel, parallel to Kamala the type, the archetypal daughter and wife is her glimpsed *alter ego*, submitting to the first stirrings of consciousness that created the new woman of India, aware of her own soul, of her rights and liberties, in conflict with archetypal and alien ideologies. Kamala's *alter ego* in the final analysis can be identified with the writer's own inner-self representative of the new woman caught in the dichotomous, between world of inherited past and acquired present.

In the attempt to develop individuality in her heroine the writer exposes Kamala to certain unconventional experiences. For instance, while, being representative of the archetype, Kamala cannot be exposed to a system of formal education, she is yet given a glimpse into 'learning'.

> The greater part of the day however she spent with her father, who generally sat in the temple verandah which was densely shaded with trees. She would nestle by his side and listen to his learned talk; for he was a recluse and a scholar. Brought up in this way, unlike other girls of her own age, she was shy, retiring and innocent. (*Kamala*, p. 6)

This learning, and perhaps the affection with which she is surrounded in childhood, develops an unusual dimension in the child's consciousness. 'There was a certain grace and refinement about her which together with her unique beauty marked her out as distinct from other girls of her age. He [Ganesh] found her, moreover, eager to get information about everything, and wonderfully quick of comprehension' (*Kamala*, p. 79). Kamala is sometimes allowed to romp the countryside with untrammelled freedom by the doting old relative who cares for her in childhood. And her Wordsworthian intimacy with nature again distinguishes her from the masses. Her delight in it discloses the sensibility of a Lucy educated by nature.

> ...and Kamala, as she looked down into the valley arrayed in its fresh morning garb, was tempted to go down in spite of her grandmother's orders. She stepped over the cool dew washed stones, picking here and there a wild flower which she pressed against her cheek, and with each gust of wind she felt the happy buoyancy of life which made her forget that she was a bride. The song of the birds rang out sweet and clear. Tew Tew rose to the heavens, and filled the whole valley, and Kamala felt the melody dance in her veins, and in her wild delight she too danced round the trees with Tew, Tew, Whew, Whew, on her lips. It was very early ... she felt free to do what she liked. She ran and jumped over the stones like a mountain goat, and sang out in her joy whatever came to her lips. (*Kamala*, p. 24)

This exquisite communion with nature that Krupabai grants Kamala signifies literary influences quite alien to the traditional at work in Krupabai's own creative consciousness. Both literary critics Meenakshi Mukherjee and M.E. Derrit maintain that indigenous Indian literature generally contained highly stylized and idealized representations of nature which have no impact on character or reader. M. E. Derrit writes that 'Indigenous literatures overflow with stylized and (to us) monotonous, artificial references to nature. Sanskrit poetry is overloaded with nature, leaving a bewildering and uninspiring impression of rutting elephants, bees and creepers.'[6] Meenakshi Mukherjee admits that 'sonorous passages of nature description' are a 'convention of Sanskrit literature',[7] yet explains further that 'In traditional narrative fiction descriptions of landscape or nature tend to appear in a stylized manner, more to satisfy literary convention than as the actual observation of specific detail'.[8] On the other hand, the significance that the western novelist generally attributes to the female adolescent's relationship with nature is recognized by Simone de Beauvoir. She writes of the female adolescent:

> ...and the fact that she accomplishes nothing, that she is nothing, will make her impulses only the more passionate. Empty and unlimited, she seeks from deep within her nothingness to attain All. That is why she will devote a special love to Nature; still more than the adolescent boy, she worships it. Unconquered, inhuman, Nature subsumes most clearly the totality of what exists. The adolescent girl has not as yet acquired for her use any portion of the universal: hence it is her kingdom as a whole; when she takes possession of it, she also proudly takes possession of herself.[9]

Passages describing Kamala's intimacy with nature abound in Krupabai's novel. While stressing Kamala's innocent enjoyment of nature these passages express that nature is Kamala's reprieve from the repressions of her home. There is also a curious soul searching that results from this communion, leading to definitions of self-identity suggested by Simone de Beauvoir. The following passage in particular reflects a moment of transition, when Kamala the stereotype is momentarily subordinate to Kamala the individual whose stifled psyche trembles with self-awareness in a tremulous one-ness with nature. In these moments it seems that potential individuality cannot be suppressed for the sake of the archetypical; authentic selfhood is being searched for in alliance with nature, a unique and individual identity is labouring to be born.

> So Kamala reasoned while she bore meekly all the taunts and hard words of her sisters-in-law and wondered why she ever felt happy at all, as she did when she looked on the blue sky, the radiant sunset, or the swollen river – why she felt such longing to be lost in a great wild wilderness, where she might dream in silence and enjoy to her heart's content the glory and the magnificence of earth and sky. (*Kamala*, p. 58)

In *Saguna* Krupabai often reaches out for truth and self-possession in similar fashion. Obviously, she transfers her own intimate experience of nature to her fictional heroine Kamala. Thus a merging of identities – of the writer with fictional heroine – is suggested.

As a wife, Kamala conscientiously fits into the mould of the pativata. Yet, however rarely, the *alter ego* of Kamala the wife is exposed when she reveals qualities different from the stereotype. Kamala retaliates in the most unconventional fashion when forced to bear with the authoritative presence of her husband's mistress in her own home. By expostulating angrily against the injustice to which she is being subjected Kamala is articulating the rights of the individual in marriage, and her speech and action here revolt against the submissive role of the archetypical Indian wife of the traditional patriarchal marriage, and instead anticipate modern concepts of the marital relationship as practised in the modern west.

> She got up, suppressed the pain and facing him [Ganesh] said – 'You! You! to strike me for this. Take care that God does not strike you in return.' He felt awed. It was an unusual thing for a woman to behave in this fashion, but she faced him and stood her ground. And emboldened by her victory she cried to Sai – 'Leave my house forever. Leave at once. If you do not go I shall force you.' And with extraordinary strength she pushed her out ... and Kamala shut the door on Sai and returned and saw that her husband stood where he was. After that she felt lifeless. (*Kamala*, pp. 179/180)

Kamala's aggression and rebellion are short-lived. Her evolving self suddenly collides with society's imposed role identity of wife and her psyche shrinks back to traditional proportions. She leaves her husband but is decisive about where her future lies. 'Where shall I go? Not back to my child home at Anjinighur. No! Never! Never! a woman must die in her husband's house and never return to her own home' (*Kamala*, p. 82).

And so Kamala returns in resignation to the detested house of her in-laws where she submits to the usual atrophy of personality and premature senility that the orthodox deserted wife is sentenced to.

Kamala is given a significant pre-requisite for liberation when she becomes the heiress to an unexpected legacy. She is thereby given a voice of her own – liberated from one of the strongest fetters of the orthodox, economic dependence. The writer's conviction that economic independence was one sure path to women's liberation is directly suggested when Kamala's in-laws welcome her to the bosom of their family when they are made aware that she has suddenly come into a fortune and is no longer a penniless waif who must grovel in the dust for crumbs falling off their table.

But misfortune is ever at Kamala's heels. With the death of her infant daughter she suffers irreparable loss. Finally, with the death of her husband the widow's blight falls upon her and faithful to tradition, she retreats from life. Yet the end of the novel offers a glimmer of hope for the future Indian woman when Kamala is given the freedom to decide her own future whereas for generations it had been decided for the Indian woman by tradition. Ramachander, who has proved her devoted friend all her life and for whom she has nurtured a strange attachment, finally declares his love and offers her freedom. Kamala's rejection of Ramachander's proposal is very much in accordance with the norms of the archetype. However, the writer's own inability to cut through the shackles of tradition is strongly visible in her refusal to free her heroine from them. Kamala's refusal, quoted below, very obviously reflects the writer's reluctance to let go of the orthodox teachings as well as her attempt to justify her heroine's submission to them. By offering, like Toru Dutt in *Savitri*, a 'note of cultural explanation which contrasts the situation of women in the favourable past with the – by implication unfavourable – present'[10] Krupabai is seen to take a flying leap right back into the traditions from which she so compassionately attempts to extricate her heroine. India clings to her...

> 'Ask me not that' she [Kamala] said, with a shudder. 'It is too much for me to think of. Did we wives not die on the funeral pyre in days of old? Did we not court the water and the floods? What has come over us now? My heart beats in response to yours, but betray me not, thou tempting heart. I am ashamed of myself. Despise me and drive me away from thee. Look not on my face.... I am but a broken vessel, fit only to be thrown aside and to be spat on.' ... A cry rang from her heart and she uttered the word 'Ganesh' and ran to the house as if mad. It was the cry of a heart pierced to its inmost depth. Her religion, crude as it was, had its victory. She felt that her life would have been an unending remorse and misery; and thus she freed herself once and for ever from the great overpowering influence of the man before her. (*Kamala*, pp. 206-207)

These words given to Kamala recall the truth of Simone de Beauvoir's statement that 'woman exhausts her courage dissipating mirages and she stops in terror at the threshold of reality'! They also reflect the conflict within the writer, her inability to locate her own psychological centre in the cross current atmosphere of the mind. She is desirous of personal identity, is yet bound fast by preconceived concepts of religion and culture.

Krupabai's assessment of female identity in relation to male narcissism anticipates western feminist ideas expounded by Virginia Woolf and Simone de Beauvoir. Woolf maintains, 'Women have served all these centuries as looking glasses possessing the magic and drawing power of reflecting the figure of man at twice its natural size.'[11] The idea is reiterated by Beauvoir.

> Woman has often been compared to water because among other things she is the mirror in which the male, narcissus like, contemplates himself; he bends over her in good and bad faith. But in any case what he really asks of her is to be outside of him, all that which he cannot grasp inside of himself, because the inwardness of the existent is only nothingness, and because he must project himself into an object in order to reach himself.[12]

These universal feminist views today are shared by most Indian women writers of English literature. Contemporary poet/novelist Kamala Das uses the image of the looking glass in the above context to excellent effect in her poetry. In the nineteenth century, Krupabai, if less blatantly, expounded this same view, thereby establishing herself firmly in the tradition of western feminist literature. She more than illustrates this fact in her projection of the character of the protagonist's husband Ganesh.

Ganesh's nature was hard to comprehend ... he was indolent.... Everything was subservient to his pleasure ... she [Kamala] was his wife, his property, and he felt that
there was no need for him to exert himself to draw her near to himself. He did not
trouble in the least as to know what she was doing so long as his own hours were
spent in pleasure. He was intensely kind to her for it gave him pleasure to be kind
and to see the beaming look of gratitude on her face ... intelligent conversation gave
him pleasure and his mother's conversations satisfied his vanity, for he was the pet
son. (*Kamala*, p. 119)

Ganesh believed in a patriarchal structure of matrimony which expects the
following mode of behaviour from the wife:

...that woman who considers virtue as the foremost of all the objects of pursuits,
who observes the same vows which are observed by her husband, who adorned
with chastity looks upon her husband as a god, who waits upon and serves him as
if he were a god, who surrenders her own will completely to that of her husband's,
who is cheerful, who ... is completely devoted to her husband, so much so that she
never thinks even of any other man, is considered as truly righteous in conduct.[13]

Krupabai's censure of Ganesh, an Indian husband, even from the distance of the third person narrator, is daring. It emphasizes her anglo-
philian bias and her dislocation from indigenous concepts.

Paradoxically, the writer never advocates liberation for the Indian
woman at the cost of those ideals of virtue that Indian womanhood has
always been famed for. The disreputable Sai, the novel's antagonist, educated, independent and emancipated, is, in the novel, as much plot mach-
ination as a direct indictment of the liberated woman. Sai's moment of
self-awareness when she yearns for her virtue, a gem of rare value in
Indian tradition, and which is lost to her in the process of liberation
illustrates the above. 'Yes you took away something from me – my name
and my honour – I parted with them willingly, thinking of the glamour
that you cast over learning, independence, riches, and the power of
securing an influence over others. All these I possess. But what is all this
without my name?' (*Kamala*, p. 158). Krupabai thus celebrates the Indian
tradition of woman as the guardian of indigenous spiritual culture. 'Indian
women, with all their sentimentality and ignorance, have remained the
guardians of a spiritual culture which is of greater worth than the effi-
ciency and information of the educated.'[14]

To conclude, Krupabai attempts to belong, it could be said, to that paradoxical paradigm of the Indian woman as advocated by Bhaskar. His
words to her were: 'And you will help me? Won't you? You will speak
boldly to your countrywomen and yet be as your sister was, modest,
gentle, and kind, a real woman?' (*Saguna*, p. 12).

It is interesting to note that Bhaskar's ideal of the nineteenth century has
been cherished by other Indian patriots. Indira Gandhi, more than half a
century later, described her ideal of the modern Indian woman with the
following words: '[T]he modern Indian woman has a special responsibility

to be a catalyst of change synthesizing the best of the old and the best of the new.'[15]

Thus the novel *Kamala* in the final assessment is a confession of the writer's own conflict with herself as she attempts to establish her own identity in the in-between world of contra-acculturation. Her commitment to Anglophilia is expressed in her reformatory point of view, in her advocacy of liberation from traditional familiar and social norms. Meanwhile, her attachment to her own collective unconscious is clearly evident as she reaches out for the ideals of her ancient past through her fictional characters in *Kamala*.

NOTES

1. Jawaharlal Nehru, *An Autobiography with Musings on Recent Events in India* (1936; rpt. Bombay: Allied Publishers Private Ltd., 1962), p. 596.
2. Bharati Mukherjee, *The Middleman & Other Stories* (London: Virago Press, 1989). Ext. from uncorrected proof copy, pp. 28-29.
3. S. Satthianadhan, *Saguna: A Story of Native Christian Life* (Bombay: Srinivasa, Varadachari & Co., 1895).
4. S. Satthianadhan, *Kamala: A Story of Hindu Life* (Bombay: Srinivasa, Varadachari & Co., 1894).
5. This subject has been extensively researched and documented by historians, sociologists and social reformers. See, for example, Dr A.S. Altekar, *The Position of Women in Hindu Civilization* (1938; rpt. Delhi: Motilal Banarsidan, 1973); Kiran Devendra, *Status and Position of Women in India* (New Delhi: Vikas Publishing House, 1985); S.N. Mukherjee, 'Raja Ram Mohan Roy and the Debate on the Status of Women in Bengal' in Michael Allen & S.N. Mukherjee, eds., *Women in India and Nepal* (Canberra: A.N.U. Printing for the South Asian History Section of The Australian National University, 1982), pp., 155-179; Pandita Ramabai Sàrasvati, *The High Caste Hindu Woman* (Philadelphia, 1888); *Speeches and Writings of Sarojini Naidu* (Madras: Natesan & Co., 1918).
6. M.E. Derrit, *The Modern Indian Novel in English: A Comparative Approach* (Bruxelles: Institute of Sociology of the University of Bruxelles, 1966), p. 158.
7. Meenakshi Mukherjee, *Realism and Reality: The Novel and Society in India* (Delhi: Oxford University Press, 1985), p. 15.
8. Ibid., p. 22.
9. Simone de Beauvoir, *The Second Sex* (1945; edition translated and edited by H.M. Parshley; London: Picador Classics, 1988), p. 385. Beauvoir illustrates and supports the statement quoted with extracts from *Sido* by Colette and *The House in Dormer Forest* by Mary Webb.
10. S.C. Harrex 'The Strange Case of Matthew Arnold in a Sari: An Introduction to Kamala Das', in S.C. Harrex, ed., *CRNLE Writers Series, Number I, Kamala Das* (Adelaide: Centre for Research in the New Literatures in English, 1986), p. 161.
11. Virginia Woolf, *A Room of One's Own* (1929; rpt. London: Grafton Books, 1987), p. 35.
12. Simone de Beauvoir, quoted in *The Female Imagination: A Literary and Psychological Investigation of Women's Writing* (London: George Allen & Unwin Publishers Ltd., 1976), p. 21.

13. *Anushaasan Parva*, quoted in *Status of Women in Ancient India* by Professor Indra (Motilab Banarasidan, India, 1955), p. 29.
14. Ananda Coomaraswamy, *The Dance of Shiva* (New York: Noonday Press, 1957), p. 102.
15. Indira Gandhi, quoted in *Status and Position of Women in India* by Kiran Devendra, op. cit., p. 132.

KIRPAL SINGH

Inter-Ethnic Responses to Nationhood: Identity in Singapore Poetry

Many years ago, while still very young, the Singaporean poet Lee Tzu Pheng wrote a poem entitled 'My Country and My People'. Written probably as a poem to express her sense of personal anxiety, a personal search for a sense of self so vital to any human being, let alone a poet, 'My Country and My People' came to be regarded as a poem which expressed the anxiety of Singaporeans as a whole. The poem's opening lines have become more than familiar:

> My country and my people
> are neither here not there, nor
> in the comfort of my preferences;
> if I could even choose.
> At any rate, to fancy is to cheat,
> and, worse than being alien or
> subversive without cause,
> is being a patriot
> of the will.[1]

If these opening lines suggest and point to a tentative and cautious questioning of the nation's state, and, more significantly, of the position of the individual within it, Lee's conclusion is even more telling:

> My country and my people
> I never understood.
> I grew up in China's mighty shadow,
> with my gentle, brown-skinned neighbours;
> but I keep diaries in English.
> I sought to grow
> in humanity's rich soil,
> and started digging on the banks, then saw
> life carrying my friends downstream.
>
> Yet, careful tending of the human heart
> may make a hundred flowers bloom;
> and, perhaps, fence-sitting neighbour,
> I claim citizenship in your recognition

of our kind.
My people and my country,
are you, and you my home.[2]

Is the final statement convincing? If so, how does it balance the tentative-ness of the rest of the poem? Allusions to 'China's mighty shadow' and the blooming of a hundred flowers (we remember *that* from China of the mid-sixties) placed in close connection with 'my gentle brown-skinned neighbours' (an obvious allusion to the Malays in and around Singapore) cleverly raise issues which the official establishment would, when the poem was written, rather have avoided but which of late have begun to be openly discussed and debated. Related and interesting questions con-cerning identity, commitment and that vital sense of belonging which con-stitutes and assures the marvellous feeling of comfort we call home, are all pertinent to a deeper meaning embedded in Lee's poem.

Nationhood and nation-building may at least be discussed at two levels: one, as *political* constructs infusing an attitude of intellectual apprehension, and two, as *emotional* constructs, eliciting an attitude of passion and passionate conviction. Now, this word 'passion' has, recently, come into prominence in the vocabulary of ministerial pronouncement in Singapore. In the 1989 National Day Message, the Prime Minister, Mr Lee Kuan Yew, spoke of the *absence* of passion among young, liberal, English-educated Singaporeans. The immediate context was the loss, yearly, of at least about 4,000 Singaporeans to other countries, mainly Australia, Canada, New Zealand and the United States. The majority of these 4,000 were Singapor-ean Chinese who could, in the Prime Minister's words, contribute greatly to the growth and development of Singapore.

I recall that as far back as 1975, in a public speech given at the National Library of Singapore, I had charged the Singaporean writer in English with not possessing that crucial sense of conviction, of passion, which, for me at least, was necessary for the creation of a viable, *living*, literature. As to whether the English language itself can provide such a sense remains highly debatable and the issue has become quite complex. From a *second*, a *foreign* language, English in Singapore has now become, for most Singa-poreans, a *first* language – creating in this latest instance, yet another problem for the Government in terms of the question of values – the cherished Asian values seem to be visibly eroding in the face of extreme westernisation via the English language.

The poets writing in English have at least *one* advantage – they can cut across ethnic boundaries (subtle and complex in a small island state like Singapore) – hence there are Chinese, Malays, Indians, Eurasians, all of whom write in English. Their major poetic spokesman, Edwin Thumboo, has come closest to uttering the various issues related to the theme of nationhood. In several poems Thumboo has attempted to explore the meaning of Singapore – sometimes in a kind of prophetic, statesmanlike manner:

> But we have to work at a destiny.
> We stumble now and then. Our nerves are sensitive.
> We strive to find our history,
> Break racial stubborness,
> Educate the mass and Educated –
> Evacuate the disagreeable.
> *Bring the hill to valley, level the place and build,*
> *And generally cater for the people ...*
> Set all neatly down into Economy.
> There is little choice –
> We must make a people.[3]

In the same poem Thumboo makes the very disconcerting realisation that Singapore will almost always be regarded as a kind of 'boil' on the Mellanesian face. On other occasions Thumboo's voice is nostalgic, intensely aware of the histories that went into the making of modern Singapore:

> Peoples settled here,
> Brought to this island
> The bounty of these seas,
> Built towers topless as Illium's.
> ...
> Despite unequal ways,
> Together they mutate,
> Explore the edges of harmony,
> Search for a centre;
> Have changed their gods,
> Kept some memory of their race
> In prayer, laughter, the way
> Their women dress and greet.
> They hold the bright, the beautiful,
> Good ancestral dreams
> Within new visions,
> So shining, urgent,
> Full of what is now.[4]

Thumboo is here attempting to confront and chart the history of this very unique nation – that rare construction of modern politics and technology, a cosmopolitan metropolis, a modern multi-cultural city-state trying to carve a niche for itself in the very volatile region known as Southeast Asia.

Robert Yeo, younger than Thumboo, highlights the problem in another way –

Five years ago
        along Serangoon Road, Whampoa's bungalow
used to peel.
        Ten years ago
in the dining-room behind, probably,
where the towkay served Admiral Keppel
complete with chrysanthemum tea
from his Cantonese garden
        my uncle had a dance studio.
When I was away
the last tenants in the room next door
must have left.
        I wonder
were they his relatives?
                They must have known for sure
                when the engineers came
                to assemble the bridge
                and demolish the bungalow.

      We lacked a cause then,
      Five years ago
          we had no history
      and therefore no historical monument
          to preserve.[5]

This feeling of unease, a sense of dislocation is, perhaps jingoistically but significantly nevertheless, communicated in yet another poem in which Yeo sums up the ethos of modern Singapore:

But O the demands you make
on us Singaporeans!
Since you didn't choose us
But we chose you
(most of us, at any rate
and we still have that choice)
your demands shall be commands.
They shall be observed:
the school's daily litany
five mornings saluting
five stars and a crescent;
our young men shall bear arms
to deter unnamed enemies;
we shall accept as treasonable
strikes not in the national interest;
Southeast Asia's cleanest city
shall be Asia's cleanest city;
we shall enlarge the airport
for the Jumbos
and develop Sentosa
but only for the tourists;
our already low birth-rate

shall further decline;
the world's fourth-largest port
shall become the world's third largest port;
we shall keep our hair short,
we shall continue to view Art
as an adjunct to Culture
serving Politics.[6]

These are, essentially, intellectual statements, stemming chiefly from a rational and sometimes even rationalised capacity to explain, perhaps even clarify, the feeling of uneasiness experienced by many Singaporeans and which drives them to leave for greener pastures elsewhere. In recent discussions, even Members of Parliament have pointed out that the 'be number one' ethos is not going to endear Singaporeans to Singapore; that real emotions of national identity lie deeper and are not so easily, or so visibly, created.

The Prime Minister, Mr Lee Kuan Yew, in the same National Day Speech mentioned earlier, observed that those who have been leaving Singapore are well-educated, usually professional English-speaking Chinese Singaporeans – they are mobile, their skills and talents are useful in their new adopted countries and they are young. The implication is that those who do not leave, or find it difficult to leave, do not handle the English language with the same degree of competence. The emigration figures point out clearly that the Malays are the ones who *least* desire to leave Singapore – this is a significant fact in the light of the impression that Singapore is by and large, chiefly a *Chinese* city, and one where the Malays (on their own admission) feel marginalised.

With due respect to the Prime Minister's observations however, it may be suggested that there might well be other, more compelling factors for the state of affairs (i.e. the large numbers of talented young English-educated Chinese leaving Singapore) he laments. Some of these factors are, indeed, contained or at least alluded to in the Prime Minister's own ruminations on the nature of a passionate committment to the country. There are very few poems in English which *celebrate* Singapore as home in any fundamental, passionate way. By celebration I do not mean praise, but *relate*, in a manner that goes beyond cliché. Often celebration is ensconced in severe criticism, we criticise most drastically that which we hold most dear, that which we most love – hence my belief that in a very real sense the Singaporean poet who writes in the mother-tongue may hold the key to this question of inter-ethnic response to identity.

The poetry of Singaporeans writing in Mandarin, Tamil and Malay is available to most only through translation – and the translations are few. But even these few provide insights into the psyche and sensibility of their authors. The Indians who write in Tamil may be dealt with first. I have it on the good authority of K. Ellangovan, a contemporary Singaporean Tamil poet (and one who is quite closely associated with numerous artistic and literary activities in Singapore) that by and large the Tamil poets of Singapore have remained 'trapped in traditional forms and traditional thinking'. They either praise Singapore without the slightest hint of reservation or they praise God; or they write about villages in India or romancing under the moon. From the little that I have read I myself have detected a reticence, quite definite in its lack of articulate response, and a terrible reluctance to tackle the problems of nationhood in the way, say, suggested by Lee Tzu Pheng. This picture of the Tamil poets is quite contrary to the usual impression of the Singapore Indians being voiciferous in matters of politics.

The poets writing in Mandarin are bolder, and question much more incisively their role and position in society, especially a society that is changing so fast and therefore threatening a loss of ideology, of traditional ways of being. Hence this poem by Lee Sam Hong called 'The Young Ones', which laments and at the same time envisages a glimpse of hope:

> Two children are enough but their toys are never enough,
> After each holiday they leave pools of toys
> abandoned and out of favour.
>
> They might try the Hainanese Chicken Rice at Swee Kee's
> but it doesn't compare with Kentucky Fried Chicken
> where they can enjoy the in thing of finger-lickin'.
>
> Afterwards they will switch on Xiao Li to watch him play with the
> Flying Daggers,
> and also look for Brother Wu Ji who practises
> the art of the Dragon Sword.
> From nine at night in every housing board flat
> forest outlaws and swordsmen of the Chivalrous World
> appear on TV screens.
>
> Three years of primary education
> And their futures must be decided.
> They must be good in English
> and also speak a little Mandarin.
> Tests and exams are cold-blooded slaughters.
> They're not anxious – but their parents are.
>
> It is good that Sundays and holidays
> bring children's art exhibitions at the community centres,
> and concerts by little musicians at Yamaha as well.
> At New Year there is the Chingay Procession
> and during the mid-autumn festival they'll enjoy
> taking part in the lantern parades at the Chinese Garden.
>
> – holding the rays of happiness tightly
> in their little hands.[7]

Within the Singaporean context it is obvious that this poem speaks mainly – and possibly only – to the Chinese, re-confirming the widely-held belief that the poets who write in the mother-tongue write for a specific ethnic group.

In a very interesting and engaging sequence of poems entitled 'Wayang Kulit', Wong Yoon Wah, in one of those very valuable instances of cross-cultural interaction in poetic metaphor, speaks of how the puppet in the shadow play is sensitive to the needs of his country, and to his immediate environment from which his own sustenance is derived:

> Though only a shadow
> performing in darkness
> I am a child of the light
> deprived of whose love, I die.
>
> My country
> is a piece of white cloth.
> In this dark
> and dirty
> world
> I cannot find myself.[8]

'Shadow play' or 'Wayang Kulit' is a moving engagement with the process of nation-building as change dictated by powers beyond those who have to play a part, those who have to act. The stage metaphor significantly disguises the emotional depression so intensely conveyed in the poem:

> After the show
> our heads are removed
> one by one,
> our bodies heaped up
> and stored
> in a sealed box.
> Like convicts
> we wait patiently,
> for another sunrise.[9]

It is not at all re-assuring, this associational imagery of convicts in a shadow play. Chinese poetry always communicates through subtle images – more understatement than explicit posturing. When it does become explicit, as here in Chua Hiang Yang's 'The Highclass Cafe', it sounds very familiar, but the sensibility which informs the poem remains essentially Chinese:

> These cafes
> are meant for
> high class poets

> who say: In here we can buy a roomful of quietness
> in here we can buy a wisp of inspiration.
> Forget the fiery sun –
> in here we can buy a cool summer
> as cool as a season of ice-cream.
> ...
> The poets are, after all
> No Balzacs who like thick coffee –
> These only like pretty dresses and beautiful women
> and to raise their cups elegantly
> and speak foreign languages in refined accents.[10]

The poet-narrator concludes the poem by offering to lead the 'high class of cafe poets' out from a 'bewitching night' to the 'loud day outside'. This 'loud day outside' for the Singaporean Chinese poet seems unsettling primarily because it takes away the quiet and the certainty for which he yearns. Direct comment on Singapore as a nation, on Singapore as a multi-racial, multi-cultural Home in which all can mix and mingle without anxiety is infrequent – perhaps the loss of familiar values and cultural rituals is one way for the Chinese poets to register their sense of deprivation.

It is the *Malay* poet who crystallises the deep anguish and passionate conviction which, for me, speaks of a *fundamental* attachment to the land, to the soil, to the country as Home. And naturally so. Unlike the Indians and the Chinese who came as migrants to better their fortunes (repeat: fortunes) the Malay has been around the place for centuries. His notion of place is secure, for him there is no need to hark back to his past, his history is here. This provides the Malay poet with a perspective on Singapore which the others lack (including, I might add, those writing in English for whom history is intellectual knowledge, rather than experienced wisdom). It is interesting to note that Mr Lee Kuan Yew's discussion of 'passion' was in connection with Singapore's need to invite around 40,000 Hong Kong Chinese to makeup for the losses in the Singapore Chinese population. The number of Singapore Malays who leave the country are negligible – and this also explains why they view this latest Government move with a great degree of alarm. But let me offer you an example of the way in which one of Singapore's leading Malay writers has stated the case:

> My Singapore
> I do not understand
> here spilt the blood of my mother
> here my bones are decaying
> here grow my children
> like swamp that keeps enlarging
> and upon all these, sand and stones are enthroned
> and man for a thousand years shall be enslaved.
>
> The sea where I went fishing
> the hill where I searched for rambutans

have been forested by slabs of stones
Pak Lasim will no longer be a headman
his island has been unrooted from his memories
his kinsmen have been cast off
on the hot stones and sands

I've lost my sea
I've lost my hill
I've lost my soul.

...

And afterwards
the four songs echo again
at times one is unheard
I do not know whether only two will be left
finally, in time to come, we'll be left with one
here I am with my wife and children
for the time when the ship will leave.

My Singapore
I do indeed understand
here is my home
but I do not know when
I will regain what I have lost.[11]

I have only quoted, above, two parts of a longish poem, but even here the pain is registered with feelings that definitely spring from deep-rooted experience. S. Markasan, the poet, is fully literate in English and knows his history – yet there are very disturbing elements in his poem. (I might add here that in the original, in Malay, the rhythms are powerfully evocative and no one hearing it read in Malay can escape the impact, the resonance with which the statement is uttered). The question of languages, for instance (contained in the 'four songs' allusion in the poem), with the Government's policy of promoting chiefly English and Mandarin, the increasing Chinesisation of Singapore which is so acutely felt by the minorities, and, further, the crass materialism with which the Malay does not want to identify, all occasion Markasan's lament. Poem after poem written in Malay echoes Markasan's anger:

Walking along this path
makes me seek the certainty
of our insignificance
in this cosmopolitan city
where there are no melodies of *dondang sayang**
no more boisterous shouts
honouring *bahasa kebangsaan***.[12]

The Malays feel awkward and very uncomfortable in the face of so much that is blatantly promoting the Chineseness of the nation, and even the status of Malay as the national language (the 'bahasa Kebangsaan' of the passage above) remains now slightly uncertain. So when the Malay poets write, their poetry reveals a sense of loss, displacement and anger. And though, sometimes, there is the gentle resignation which a poet like Rasiah Halil expresses in her poem 'Like the Phoenix' it is unmistakably the resignation of one who feels unable to change the course of her destiny except by surrender to fate:

> how painful it is to forgive the past,
> and as difficult to forget, this sadness that
> has become so stagnant in the pool of experience,
> for they who should have cared,
> were indifferent and full of vengeance, a home
> is no longer a refuge, and love is a memory.
>
> varied are God's way in teaching us
> the meaning and value of maturity
> and like the phoenix, I rise above all miseries.[13]

In a very sensitive poem (perhaps the sensitivity grew naturally out of the theme and subject) Edwin Thumboo dealt with the problem of the Malay, recognising in him the multi-configurations which encapsulate the question of identity in Singapore. There is, in this poem (one almost never cited by any critic of Thumboo's work) a deep feeling of inadequacy, and an almost prophetic hint that if Singapore is to survive, the status and role of the Malay within the context of Singaporean identity must receive crucial notice. This poem, simply titled 'Ahamd', serves as a pertinent conclusion to this brief discussion of inter-ethnic response to Singapore identity.

> And there is an anger
> In that bronze patience
> Tied to the murmur of his fingers.
> Those speaking eyes,
> Squatting on me,
> Take up my educated helplessness
> Against his communal gestures.
> An apologetic fidget in the chair
> Adjusts his harshness.
>
> He is a son of the soil who roves
> The outskirts of our jungle;
> He is our brother who moves
> With the sun so easily.
> Still,
> His eyes have strange fires.
> Will there be time,

For us, for me
Groping for a neutral gentleness
To reach him without burning,
To lift into laughter?[14]

NOTES

1. Edwin Thumboo et al., eds., *The Poetry of Singapore* (Singapore: ASEAN Committee on Culture and Information, 1985), p. 518.
2. Ibid., p. 520.
3. Ibid., p. 468.
4. Ibid., pp. 475-6.
5. Ibid., p. 491.
6. Robert Yeo, *And Napalm Does Not Help* (Singapore: Heinemann, 1977), pp. 24-5.
7. *The Poetry of Singapore*, pp. 339-341.
8. Ibid., p. 363.
9. Ibid., p. 367.
10. Ibid., pp. 411-13.
11. Ibid., pp. 87-9.
12. Ibid., p. 115
13. Ibid., p. 129.
14. Edwin Thumboo, *Seven Poets* (Singapore: Singapore University Press, 1973), p. 44.

*) National language.
**) Traditional Malay love song.

KOH TAI ANN

On the Margin, in Whose Canon?
The Situation of Ee Tiang Hong
and Shirley Lim

Ee Tiang Hong, whose poems began appearing in the early fifties in little student magazines at the then University of Malaya in Singapore, has to date published four volumes: *I of the Many Faces* (1960), *Lines Written in Hawaii* (1973), *Myths for a Wilderness* (1976) and most recently, *Tranquerah* (1985). Shirley Lim, who belongs to the next generation of Malaysian poets writing in English, also had her work published while she was a student at the University of Malaya (by then located in Kuala Lumpur) in the mid-sixties, although her first volume of poems, *Crossing the Peninsula* (which won the Commonwealth Poetry Prize), appeared only in 1980. This was followed by *No Man's Grove* (1985) and *Modern Secrets* (1989). However, two thirds of this last volume consists of a selection culled from the two earlier volumes; only one-third, mainly those in the last two sections, 'Another Spring' and 'Song of an Old Malayan', are new poems.[1]

Read in bulk, both Ee's and Lim's poems have an unmistakable autobiographical flavour, their work in the main reflecting the impact of historical circumstances on themselves as poets and the directions their poetry has taken. Lim's characteristic habit of ordering her poems in significant sections (or re-ordering them, as in the case of *Modern Secrets*), invites the reader to see each section as stations along a personal journey or as the major pre-occupations of a poetic life. In either case, the impression is of poetry as fictional autobiography. (In fact, there is a poem about herself as poet actually called 'Biography'). Ee's poems are if anything more nakedly autobiographical, as is evident in the very titles of each volume and the exact historical detail to be found in many of his poems.

Although Ee emigrated to Australia in 1975, almost fifteen years ago, and Lim has been away in America for about twenty years, their poems refer repeatedly to their home country and dwell still on Malaysian themes. They are thus still regarded as Malaysian poets, not only because their poems record two Malaysian poetic lives, but mainly because the work of both conveys a deeply felt sense of home. Home is Malacca, an old town in Malaysia, vividly rendered and strongly recalled – all the more because it is the location of a landscape that is retrievable only as memory and as myth, belonging as it does to a lost past, and now proving to have been only a dream. 'Dream' is a recurrent metaphor, meaning also a dream future that failed to become reality. Ee's Malaya is 'the golden peninsula' ('Heeren Street') of a lost 'golden dream' ('Tranquerah Road', *Tranquerah*, pp. 51, 66). Lim, in her poem 'Crossing the Peninsula' (among her most achieved lyrical pieces), describes how

> Salt falls from our hair and traps
> In a dream the sailors motionlessly
> Rocking in the eye of the moon.
> We dream like grey gulls blown inland,
> Or as one-eyed ships, blown, espying
> The bright-shelled peninsula. (CP, p. 95)

The sailors, probably migrant forbears near the end of their journey, trapped in a dream, perhaps of their new country, are blown like gulls and ships, and thus as in a dream trance drift within sight of the land of promise, the 'bright-shelled peninsula'. But when generations later, the promise failed, Lim seems the better able of the two poets to relinquish the past, probably because she chose to leave. Her poem, 'Visiting Malacca' has the dry-eyed detachment of the expatriate, and is a record of what now must be the case:

> I dream of the old house.
> The dreams leak slowly like sap
> Welling like a wound: I am losing
> Ability to make myself at home.
> Awake, hunting for lost cousins,
> I have dreamed of ruined meaning,
> And am glad to find none. (CP, p. 93)

The loss of ancestral dreams, while painful, is counterbalanced by a sense of a clean break with the past: the poet finds no 'lost cousins' and, ambiguously, either no 'ruined meaning', the past still there intact, like the house, or no more meaning in the past. It is time to move on.

Ee, the older poet, whose family, as he tells us in his poem 'Patriotism' (*Myths*, p. 52), has been 'seven generations' in the Malayan peninsula, seems less able to relinquish the past because of a bitter sense of dispossession and deprivation, as he did not leave by choice. In tones restrained, yet full of pain, the poet says of Heeren Street in Malacca where his ancestral home was and where he had hitherto spent his life:

> But only it, there, here,
> not some remote village in China
> once upon a time
> was all the earth and sea and sky
> and rainbow, golden dream
> we owned,
>
> and were compelled to leave. ('Heeren Street', *Tranquerah*, p. 66)

In their different ways, the responses of the two Malaysian poets reflect changes in the history of our region and point to the future of the writing in English in formerly colonial countries where English has only a second-ary status. Race, culture, language – the potent components of identity both personal and national – have rendered both poets and the writing in English in the country of their birth quite marginal, almost a historical aberration, in danger of disappearing altogether with the current gener-ation of writers for lack of function, purpose and a local audience.

Ee's suddenly marginal situation and his condition of exile fuel the two later volumes of his poems, his angry protest appearing as the last sparks of a poetic urgency increasingly threatened by a sense of futility. The an-ger comes from the circumstance that the 'golden dream we owned' was not merely and only that of his immigrant forefathers who generations ago had put down roots in the peninsula; it was also that of Ee the poet and his generation in the late fifties and early sixties who had pinned much nationalistic hopes on first, the achievement of a pluralistic, multi-racial 'Malayan', and then later, 'Malaysian' identity. Ee's beginnings as a poet were grounded in colonial times, fuelled by the urge to form and express an identity liberated from a colonial history. He had meant his poetry, had written it as part of the task his generation of English-educated writers had set for itself, to 'domesticate' the English they had acquired in order to foster a 'Malayan consciousness'. They would write on Malayan themes, in a Malayan style and idiom, works that had reference to the Malayan landscape, local images, native circumstances. His first volume of poems has a pointedly titled 'Song of a Young Malayan' which attempts to repro-duce in local accents the condition of the English-educated, Westernised young Malayan who is unable to relate to western high culture, but who yet quite unselfconsciously embraces its vulgar forms. The volume con-cludes with a poem appropriately called 'Dead End', a warning of the con-sequence if the poet and writer should fail to develop his own language and continue to 'Waste all my time at singing well/ Some mimicry of foreign birds'. He poses to himself the central question facing poets of his generation: 'What power can drive Malaya's pulse/ Or tap a rhythm for its song?'

Thirty years later, that rhythm seems to be expressed less certainly in English and that power will not be embodied in Ee's dream of a 'Malayan' or 'Malaysian' literature in English. *In Myths for a Wilderness*, Ee seems not as yet to realise this. He ends this volume with a poem, 'Epilogue', the original title of which better indicates its theme, 'Apologia for the Dearth of Malaysian Writing' (meaning, the writing in English, of course). The poem is a protest against political repression of free speech and the poet sees this, not the new national language and literature policies, as the reason for the dearth of writing such as his. It is among his weakest poems, not least because, overcome by bitterness, the poet lacks a distancing and persuasive understanding of his situation, and hence the situation of the writing in English in post-independence Malaysia.

I of the Many Faces appeared a year before Malaya's (as it was then known) achievement of independence in 1957. Independence meant the constitutional enshrinement of Malay as the national language. But it was the racial riots of May 13, 1969, which produced a hardening of attitudes on language. After that, the status of Malay as the national language was rendered unquestionable, and moreover, it was declared that only the literature written in Malay would be recognised as the 'national literature'. Literatures in the other major languages such as Chinese, Tamil and English were relegated to the secondary status of being 'sectional' literatures, limited to their respective community of readers. To the literature in Malay would henceforth be given the central function of expressing a Malaysian consciousness, a Malaysian cultural identity in Malay accents and idioms. Deprived of an albeit self-appointed and self-perceived national function or role in Malaysian cultural life, sectional literatures such as that in English have become, in the words of a Professor of Malay Literature, 'sastera kehilangan'. This has been translated as a 'purposeless' or 'aimless literature', but as the root word 'hilang' in fact means 'lost', it strongly suggests a dead literature.[2]

It is not only as writers in English that Ee (and Lim) have been thus rendered marginal. After the 1969 riots, the Malays declared themselves the 'bumiputras' or 'sons of the soil', the only indigenous people, with consequent political, economic, and cultural advantages. Both Ee's and Lim's situation is rendered more painful because they also happen to be Baba or Straits-born Chinese whose term for themselves, 'peranakan', means 'native-born', in contrast to more recently arrived immigrant Chinese from whom they are culturally distinct. The Peranakan Chinese speak Baba Malay, a dialect of Malay, and share some cultural features with the Malays as a result of long domicile in the peninsula. Consequently, they were also marginal to the larger Chinese community, with whom they were now lumped as non-bumiputras. They were further distinguished from the other Chinese because the Peranakan community tended to be English-educated, unlike the majority of the Chinese who, being more recently arrived, tended to be more attached to the Chinese language. Their English education also meant a closer identification with the British colonial establishment, to the extent that they further distinguished themselves from the other Chinese by proclaiming themselves the 'King's Chinese'. As Ee records in his poem, 'Heeren Street',

> Here in the good old days
> the Babas paved
> a legend on the landscape,
> and sang their part –
> God save the King –
> in trembling voices. (*Tranquerah*, p. 51)

Abandoned as a class by the withdrawal of imperial rule, they found themselves further abandoned, given no equivalent place in the sun of the new order. Ee depicts the Babas and their 'memorabilia' as now but

> mute mementoes
> of service and loyalty
> to state and clansmen,
> ...
> in the hey day of Company and Empire
> justice, rule of law.

In a quite central way, the failure of the Peranakan and other Malaysian-born minority ethnic groups to obtain equality of status with the Malay majority deeply rankles; it is the motivating power now behind Ee's later poetry, replacing the earlier nationalistic impulse. The resultant sense of personal, social and political injustice which permeates *Myths for a Wilderness* becomes obsessive in *Tranquerah*. Published ten years after his emigration to Australia, the poems in this volume are those of a poet who, unlike Lim, cannot trample on the past and regard it as 'a dead land'. There is little sign, either in allusion or locale, of his response to fifteen years of living in Australia. Rather he is drawn back to the landscape from which he feels exiled. Significantly, the later volume takes its title from the Malacca road of his memories, while the title-sequence, 'Tranquerah Road' and 'Heeren Street' are part republication and part expansion of two of the three opening poems similarly titled in *Myths for a Wilderness*. These and most of the other poems exhume bitter memories to haunt the consciousness, complaining of dispossession and exile, telling the poet's very heart of loss, remembrance swelling at his breast and turning the past to pain when he contemplates his own lost village.

Tranquerah conveys a dawning awareness, too, of the poet's voice being now deprived of a native constituency by the post-1969 national policies. He is more acutely aware of making myths for and crying in a wilderness, this itself in turn being an enabling myth, allowing him to cast himself as an ignored prophet, a voice in the wilderness. This seems to be his way of continuing the earlier self-perceived role of writing a 'public' poetry of social concern, political comment and protest. We recall how the title poem of his first volume, 'I of the Many Faces', originally titled 'I of the Three Monkeys', chides both himself and those others who would see, hear and speak no evil – that is, would be silent, and hence compromised. This is the driving power which enables Ee to 'tap a rhythm for his song' and which explains why the more private lyrics of *Lines from Hawaii* lack the impact and force of the poems of public themes which count among his best work.

But one notes also the co-presence of a tension between this self-created myth of the poet passionately concerned to give voice in frank, fearless tones in Malayan/Malaysian accents on behalf of his people, and a deep, despairing sense of powerlessness. This often shades into a sense of guilt and paralysing powerlessness, so well expressed in his poem, 'Retreat'. The poet is there described as being trapped, 'tight cockles dumb within/ Dungeons of granite shells', while he informs himself, 'See how futile it is to shed/ One anger against the world' (*Myths*, p. 37). Like Blake's Romantic poet he has a touching faith in the power of poetry: 'Hear the voice of the Bard/ Who present, past, and future sees'. Yet at the same time, he seems to agree with Auden's tired, worldly-wise meditation, 'For poetry makes nothing happen: it survives.../ A way of happening, a mouth'. Ee dedicates *Tranquerah* to his mother who, like Eliot's sardonic, weary Tiresias, 'has seen it all'. Thus Ee himself, a refugee of sorts, declares in his poem 'On the Boat People', 'Nothing I can say/ Will change the situation'. Yet he must speak out still, as in 'A Poem':

> It will say
> what it must
> notwithstanding the threat
> to silence the throat. (*Tranquerah*, p. 24)

But who will the poem say it to? Ee's most successful poems show that the 'dead end' he feared would come from a failure to find a local rhythm, accent, and idiom or style, has been unfounded. Rather, it is national developments in Malaysia and Ee's response to the new directions which seem to be leading him to a personal dead end. The poem 'Epilogue' in *Tranquerah* expresses an uncertainty as to readership and even comprehension of his poems. This last is evident from the fact that *Myths for a Wilderness* has a one-and-a-half page Glossary, while *Tranquerah* nervously has eight pages of explanatory Notes. The 'Epilogue' of *Myths for a Wilderness* tries to explain the 'dearth of Malaysian Writing', but this later 'Epilogue' refers to a possible dearth of readers:

> All these may well
> come to nothing
> and all the hopes.
> World doesn't owe us poets
> a reading

'Or if it does attend', he fears that it 'should turn its meaning/ but where it will' (*Tranquerah*, p. 67).

Finally, one other factor that we often tend to forget – poetry is everywhere a marginal activity and a minority taste, even an elitist occupation, especially in Third World societies, including Malaysia. If valued at all, it is in these societies more often less for itself as such, than for its role and function in serving such purposes as nation-building on the one hand, or socio-political protest on the other. Thus to be a poet writing in English in such circumstances when, moreover, English has only a secondary status (if at all), is indeed to be marginal, isolated, and ultimately, seemingly futile – as Ee's frequent poetic expressions of powerlessness attest. But there is also a possible other view to this, suggesting why such poetry may survive and may find a small readership still. Another poet contemplating similar restricted and restricting circumstances has put it penetratingly:

> You need defeat's sour
> Fuel for poetry
> Its motive power
> Is powerlessness. (D J Enright, 'Cultural Freedom')[3]

In contrast to Ee, Lim protests less and has made a virtue of necessity. It empowers her in a different way when she willingly embraces marginality as her condition and frequently makes it the ground of her poetry. Her poetic development in this respect may be mapped in the distance travelled between 'Crossing the Peninsula' and 'No Man's Grove' which, significantly, are the title poems of her first and second volumes, respectively. 'Crossing the Peninsula' (as earlier discussed) lyrically celebrates the immigrant dream on 'espying' from a distance 'the bright-shelled peninsula', while 'No Man's Grove' shows the immigrants discovering the reality on landing. They arrive only to discover their alienation from the earlier arrivals – presumably Malay, already in possession of the cultivable land, 'knee-deep in padi', whose 'dream' the poet notes, they 'cannot enter'. Instead, the new arrivals, like the 'mammoth croakers', must content themselves with the tougher terrain of the coastal mangrove jungle located on the land's fringe, shut out by jungle from the sun, overshadowed, bending to circumstances in a tropical version of no man's land. As for the poet, she sees herself as inhabiting the fringe of even this fringe, for 'I choose to walk between water and land', to remain, in other words, on the margin.

In a discussion of Malaysian novelists writing in English, Lim indirectly points to her own situation when she observes that in the wake of Malay nationalism, these writers now 'find themselves doubly dispossessed. For, initially dispossessed by their use of the English language from their native cultures ... after the introduction of Malay as the national language [they] now find themselves dispossessed a second time in a country in which both their native and adopted cultures have only a minority status'.[4] Judging from the directions their novels have taken, she sees a turning away from 'nationality to identity' as expressed in 'ancestral religions' – that is, towards 'racial and individual identity'. Belonging to a later generation of writers in English and feeling less the burden of expressing a Malayan/Malaysian consciousness, creating a style and idiom in local accents, etc., which the older generation (among them, Ee) had assumed, she has found it easier, unlike Ee, to move away from the Malaysian landscape and its concerns. Her poems express therefore a poetic self that is variously expatriate Malaysian, Peranakan Chinese, woman (in her several roles as daughter, lover, wife, mother and feminist), poet, and lately, increasingly Chinese American. Noticeably, these are all marginal identities, too.

Alastair Niven, in his anthology of poems selected from volumes which have won the Commonwealth Poetry Prize, *Under Another Sky*,[5] shows a shrewd grasp of these characteristic directions in Lim's poetry in his three quite representative selections from her prize-winning volume, *Crossing the Peninsula*. 'Monsoon History' is a journey back in time, its climate, locale and cultural detail expressing her Malaysian Chinese Peranakan self and past. 'Modern Secrets' (which, significantly, re-appears as the title-poem in her latest collection) encapsulates her Chinese roots, English education and Asian American experience:

> Last night I dreamt in Chinese.
> Eating Yankee shredded wheat
> I said it in English
> To a friend...
>   The sallow child
> Ate rice from its rice bowl
> And hides still in the cupboard
> With the china and tea-leaves. (CP, p. 50)

The third poem that he selected, 'Women's Dreams', aptly represents a strong body of work, among her best, which are about female experience and which express aspects of her various female identities. Lim's modern frankness about female sexuality (as in 'Women's Dreams') and its power, and an often bitter exploration of the condition of being female, are likely to gain her an audience from a growing female constituency. Such poems rank among her most engaged and most achieved poems – poems like 'Mother's Song' (CP, p. 38), the poignant 'Inventing Mothers' (NMG, p. 33), 'Family Album' (NMG, p. 15), 'I Look for Women', and the chilling 'Pantoun for Chinese Women' (NMG, p. 63) about female infanticide, the more effective because of its technical virtuosity and formal tautness. It seems to me that she has sufficient poems expressing such experience to fill a separate volume.

But it is 'Bukit China' (NMG, p. 39) which to me best exemplifies the kind of poetry that she is adept at achieving, and which at its most successful combines unique locality and personal experience with an universal appeal, not least because of an unmistakeable poetic flair. 'Bukit China', in its blend of her Chinese roots, her Malaysian Peranakan experience and past, her female identity as daughter and her condition as exile, composes a complex self. The site itself, Bukit China (or Chinese Hill) in her home town, Malacca, and Malaysia's most famous Chinese cemetery (recently threatened by re-development) is poetically apt as symbol because Malacca is as close as the Peranakan Chinese community ever came to having an ancestral, and thus also, a cultural home. The poem turns out to be an act of ancestral worship, a meditation upon roots, family ties, filial piety, home, exile and future directions. The immediate occasion is her return to Malacca, too late to attend her father's funeral and it opens with an invocation, 'Bless me spirits, I am returning' as she burns joss in an act of filial piety at her father's tomb. In a telling pun, Bukit China is described as 'A dead land' – cemetery, lost home, dead past, but a site of hauntings in the memory and site also of mourning for more than dead parent. The burning of the joss sticks, besides being a ritualistic enactment of piety, also provides a metaphor to reinforce the sense of loss of more than only her father:

> country is important,
> Is important. This knowledge I know
> If it will rise with smoke, with the dead.

Where Ee chooses Heeren Street and Tranquerah Road as the site of child-hood memories and lost family home for obsessive re-visitations, Lim's choice of Bukit China cemetery is more economically suggestive and shows again the greater distancing power of her poetic stance – the mar-ginalised self.

An aspect of this self, which has distinguished her poetry, is herself as poet and a concomitant preoccupation with the problems of poetry, craft, and language. This is an interest evident from her first volume. Poems like 'Words Plague You', 'The Suicide Poet' and 'No Alarms' reveal the poet's acute sense of the poetic vocation, its responsibilities, its constant risk-taking and the subterfuges of the self in its attempts to grapple with and capture reality despite a despairing sense of the inviolable substantiality of things. As Samuel Johnson noted, 'words are the daughters of earth, and things the sons of heaven'. A saving self-ironical stance enables Lim to see with a sense of subverting realism in her poem 'Imagine' that

> All poetry
> necessarily
> begins with a lie (CP, p.4)

– 'necessarily' because 'words are significations / of things other than'. This is a tough-minded poet.

As poet, Lim also has a propensity to engage confidently on equal terms with other writers in the British and American canon, even referring in passing, to Yevtushenko. Scattered among her poems are engagements with and allusions to Marianne Moore, Robert Lowell, Whitman, Wallace Stevens ('I Defy You'), Thoreau, Conrad, Joyce. In this, the poet declares her identity with these other poets, shrugging off the identity usually asso-ciated with nationality. Thus in the appropriately named poem, 'Identity No Longer', she repudiates nationality, here represented by identity card and passport. Now as 'Citizeness of the world, she approaches the Republic/ of feeling'. Among the other inhabitants of this Republic, whom she refers to as her 'spirit-lovers', are Eliot, Pound, Joyce and her mentor, J.V. Cunningham (to whom she part-dedicates *No Man's Grove*). She joins, if one may put it thus, a common Western tradition, enabling her to draw upon a central bank of poetic forms and values from classical times to the present. She is however, too self-aware a poet to be unconscious of complication, as her poem 'To Li Poh' indicates. Referring to the Chinese poet as 'brother' and 'Countryman', she notes regretfully, 'Yet cannot speak your tongue with ease,/ No longer from China', and she has had to 'read you in a stranger's tongue' (CP, p.92).

Nonetheless, she is so securely at home in this tongue and its literature that among Commonwealth poets writing today, her poems are among the most versatile and ambitiously wide in their technical range and forms. She competently uses not only the by now almost standard, preferred free verse, but also casts her poems in forms as various as the sonnet, villanelle, epigram, epitaph, and even has a 'prose poem', the aptly titled 'Striving and Anarchy' (NMG, p. 25). She readily experiments with different kinds of strict stanzaic forms and dabbles with non-European forms such as the *haiku*, made familiar to the west by Pound, and the Malay *pantun*. An intense training in American and British literature with, perhaps, stints at creative writing classes, and an acquired habit of literary allusiveness, standard since the modernists, gives to her poetry an intertextuality that assumes an international audience similarly steeped in a shared Anglophone literary culture. A glance at only the titles of her poems alone will illustrate what I mean: 'The Book of Fevers', 'A Dream of Duty', 'In Memoriam', 'Portrait of...', 'Lines' (very gnomic, like Blakean Proverbs), and one couldn't miss references such as 'paring my fingernails' (Joyce, in 'The Critic'), or 'Master, he dead' (Conrad, in 'Inheritance') and 'Only what is is the flower' (Gertrude Stein, 'Lotus').[6]

It is of course English which has made all this possible. Although Lim's use of English marginalises her at home in Malaysia, it also enables her to become 'citizeness of the world', giving her as it does fellow poet, Ee, an international audience. Characteristically, Lim is aware, too, of her problematical possession of a language that she has seen in other ways as a cause of cultural dispossession. The ambiguity of her linguistic situation is well-conveyed in her poem, 'Lament':

> I have been faithful
> Only to you,
> My language. I choose you
> Before country,
> ...
> Before history and all
> It makes, belonging,
> Rest in the soil,

Although everyone knows
You are not mine.
They wink knowingly
At my stupidity –
I, stranger, foreigner,
Claiming rights to
What I have no right –
Sacrifice, tongue
Broken by fear. (NMG, pp. 61-2)

Where Lim chooses the language as such and is diffident about her claim
to it, Ee and his generation of writers in English had made it their project
to give English a local colour, a 'Malayan' accent and rhythm and thus
'domesticate' it to become their own tongue. Nonetheless, because of his
colonial experience and his generation's struggle for freedom from colonialism and their colonised selves, he is more uneasy, even edgy about his
writing in English. His satiric poem, 'O to be in England' represents the
poet as 'confounded' and his mind 'in a deep fog' when an Englishman
expresses surprise at his competence in the language and ironically asks
him

But why do you choose
To use English, why not Chinese?
Then you'd be famous. (Myths, p. 13)

The suggestion of course, is that as a non-native user he would never be
considered good enough when measured against the imperial standard of
the native user. Ee's poem reveals as well a deeper problem for the writer
than that of 'domesticating' and indigenising the language to such an extent that it becomes both recognisable and accepted as one's own tongue,
as part of one's identity. The problem is that when one writes in English
one then invites comparison with an achieved body of literature, with all
the writers in the canon, and becomes therefore subject to critical standards derived from the study of that canon's classics.

When Commonwealth Literature was constituted as a subject, a reiterated concern from the very first conference on Commonwealth Literature
(cropping up recurrently at the others), is that while the Commonwealth
writer's work was (and should be) written primarily for his people and
that while it may help define for himself and his local audience who and
what they are, such work if it wanted to be considered among 'the best'
should transcend its locality and possess (in A.N. Jeffares' words) 'supranational qualities', capable of appealing to others in the English-speaking
world beyond its national borders.[7] 'Naturally' enough, the 'international
standards' of critical judgement were implicitly derived from the classics
of the canon of English Literature or its off-shoots.

However, it is difficult for the Third World writer to avoid suspicion of ethnocentrism and critical imperialism at work here. Belonging to a generation sensitised to colonialism and whose first task had been to liberate their colonised selves, Ee understandably harbours such suspicions. A recently published (but as yet uncollected) poem of his titled 'Comment' does suggest this. The epigraph to the poem is a quote from Timothy Mo, who was reported in a regional magazine, *Asiaweek*, as saying that one has 'got no hope as a writer of Oriental themes living in the Far East; it's either England or America and I prefer England'. Ee then concludes of his own situation: 'Mine, especially, is a hopeless case – a *Baba* born and bred in Malacca, Malaysia, and now in exile in of all places, Australia, which is further east and right down under.'[8] With a touch of self-pitying irony, he declares that although he may be content 'if somewhere people read me', 'Unfortunately, they mightn't, unless, as you say England approves, or America says okay'. A writer such as Ee whose work expresses a strong sense of nationality and cultural identity and which is inescapably sociopolitical in purpose, its occasion being often a response to specific local circumstances, should be above caring whether or not he gains 'international recognition' as represented by 'England' and 'America'. Yet he must care, if he is to be included in even his own 'national' canon.

The fact is, writing in English enables a writer, if considered good enough by whoever decides such questions, to be published (in both senses of the word) abroad or to build up an audience beyond national borders wherever English is used. Paradoxically, however much local writers and critics chafe at this situation, if the writer is capable of a sustained achievement of 'supranational' critical acclaim, this helps ensure his installation in a 'national' canon of that international audience's or critics' making. This is the case with both Ee and Lim who have published most of their work in regional and international, and not only local magazines or journals. And it is in English-speaking Singapore and nearby Australia and wherever in the world there exists an interest in Commonwealth or the so-called new literatures in English that their works and those of fellow writers in English such as Lee Kok Liang, Lloyd Fernando and K.S. Maniam, established as the canon of Malaysian writing in English for purposes of study and discussion. This is the case whether the people at home in general read their work or the local literary establishment there recognises their work or not.

Partly because of a network of old ties or friendship and partly because of common history, and because Ee, for instance, left Malaysia for reasons basically similar to those which impelled Singapore's separation from Malaysia, Ee and Lim have currently an assured place in the canon of Malaysian and Singapore writing in English as constituted by Singaporean critics and curriculum planners. As Ee rightly notes in 'Heeren Street', 'The Malacca boys' must realise, if at all, their ambitions

especially in Singapore.
There if you're good,
sure to succeed, you know,
real justice, no racial nonsense,
that's the truth.

The local accent and idiom of the English intentionally suggest a solidarity with like-minded local readers. The fact, too, that English is the major and virtually first language in Singapore as a result of national policies and, as importantly, the fact that critical standards here since Ee's days at the University of Malaya have remained 'international', it is likely that their work will survive here at least. Both have spent stints at the National University of Singapore as writers-in-residence, and as 'fellows' at tertiary and other institutions in Singapore, and all their volumes of poems (except Lim's latest volume, *Modern Secrets*) were published and first reviewed here. In such ways, Singapore, and to some extent, Australian centres as well as other Commonwealth institutions, provide the institutional support and audience lacking in Ee's and Lim's home country. As the very constitution of Commonwealth literature as a subject shows, the reality (as always, but more so) today is that it is critics and university or school curricula that define the canon and provide canonical recognition. Thus, ironically, because of the growing international currency of English, the far larger body of the literature in Malay, the best work of which is in no way inferior in achievement to that in English, remains chiefly of national or regional interest, while the writing in English, declining in quantity, represents Malaysia 'internationally'.

Although writers in the Commonwealth are urged to achieve high standards of literary excellence if they wish to appeal internationally, yet nationality is still required for prior identification and recognition. This partly explains why despite being no longer Malaysian citizens, Ee and Lim are still seen and strategically regard themselves as 'Malaysian' writers. Ee especially continues to write poems that are Malaysian in setting and reference, while Lim, who has hitherto rarely written poems of socio-political statement of the kind characteristic of Ee, has poems such as 'Aborted' and 'Song of an Old Malayan' in her latest collection. The latter, especially with its echo of Ee's much earlier poem 'Song of a Young Malayan', is political protest, while the volume ends with a poem 'Fear and Friendship' which suggests a reconciliation between Malay and Chinese, a dissolution of fear and hostility in friendship and a vision of peace.

Thus, despite Lim's evident movement away for the most part in her work from nationality to race and individuality she, like Ee and writers everywhere including those in the Commonwealth, cannot escape the fact that writers in general are defined more by their nationality than by ethnicity and individuality for inclusion in canons (although one notes the existence of such canons as 'Black writing' and the creation of a canon of women's writing which might be the trends of the future). An established writer of wide international repute and readership such as V.S. Naipaul, for instance, began his career, as we know, by drawing upon his Indian immigrant and West Indian experience for his early work. International recognition of his work as part of the West Indian canon gave him the authority to attempt those later works which transcend locality and nationality and address transnational themes such as the postcolonial and modern condition of 'deracination, exile and alienation' which consolidated his international reputation. He could therefore afford to declare, against popular opinion, at the first ACLALS conference that 'In the end, it is the writer and the writing that matter. The attempt to perfect Indian English or achieve Canadian-ness is the private endeavour of an irrelevant nationalism'.[10] In Naipaul's case, consistent literary excellence, the result of a unique individual talent, and the later strategic assumption of the identity of a free-floating exile, render unnecessary a sense of home and belonging, homelessness becoming the very condition and ground of his writing. He can therefore also with conviction give the following advice through a character in *A Bend in the River*, a novel about post-colonial malaise:

> There could be no going back; there was nothing to go back to. We had become what the world outside had made us; we had to live in the world as it existed.... Use the airplane, trample on the past ... get rid of that idea of the past; make the dream-like scenes of loss ordinary.... And make a fresh start somewhere else.[11]

While Ee's recent poetry shows him trapped still by the past, Lim's shows many signs that this is the direction she is moving towards – making a fresh start somewhere else – probably as the poem, 'American Driving' and the poems in the section similarly titled indicate, as Asian American writer.[12]

NOTES

1. Ee Tiang Hong, *I of the Many Faces* (Malacca: Wah Seng Press, 1960); *Lines Written in Hawaii* (Honolulu: East-West Center, East West Culture Learning Institute; Mimeograph, 1973); *Myths for a Wilderness* (Singapore: Heinemann Educational Books, Asia, 1976); *Tranquerah* (Singapore: Department of English Language and Literature, National University of Singapore, Shell Literary Series, 1985). Shirley Lim, *Crossing the Peninsula and Other Poems* (Singapore: Heinemann Educational Books, Asia, 1980), thereafter referred to in the text as CP; *No Man's Grove* (Singapore: Department of English Language and Literature, National University of Singapore, Shell Literary Series, 1985); *Modern Secrets* (Sydney: Dangaroo Press, 1989).
2. Tham Seong Chee, 'The Politics of Literary Development in Malaysia', in *Literature and Society in Southeast Asia: Political and Sociological Perspectives*, ed. Tham Seong Chee (Singapore: Singapore University Press, 1981), p. 235.

3. *Unlawful Assembly* (London: Chatto and Windus with the Hogarth Press, The Phoenix Living Poets, 1968), p. 64.
4. 'Gods Who Fail: Ancestral Religions in the New Literatures in English from Malaysia and Singapore', *Commonwealth Novel in English*, 3,1 (Spring/Summer 1984), p. 49.
5. Manchester: Carcanet Press, 1987.
6. All poems mentioned are from *No Man's Grove*.
7. Introduction, *Commonwealth Literature: Unity and Diversity in a Common Culture*, ed. John Press (London: Heinemann, 1965), p. 14.
8. *Commentary*, 7,4 (May, 1989), p. 49.
9. 'Deracination, exile and alienation in varying forms are the conditions of existence for the modern writer the world over'. Andrew Gurr, *Writers in Exile: The Creative Use of Home in Modern Literature* (Sussex: The Harvester Press; New Jersey: Humanities Press, 1981), p. 2.
10. 'Images', in *Critical Perspectives on V.S. Naipaul* (Washington: Three Continents Press, 1977), p. 28.
11. *A Bend in the River*, (1979) (New York: Vintage Books, 1980), pp. 244-5.
12. She has sixteen entries as poet, writer and critic in *An Annotated Bibliography of Asian American Literature*, comp. King-Kok Cheung and Stan Yogi, (New York: Modern Language Association of America, 1988). But in an interview in Singapore she is reported to have said that she considers 'the weakest poems in *No Man's Grove* ... to be in the last section called American Driving, which speak of her isolation in a society constantly in movement. "Maybe they are weak because I have yet to integrate my experiences in America. I have yet to absorb them and make them part of me." She has yet to exhaust her reservoir of experiences in Malaysia, and that is why she is still reluctant to publish in America' (*Straits Times*, 22 Feb., 1986).

Since the delivery of this paper in August, 1989, Ee, to our great loss, died in April, 1990.

NEW SYNTHESIS

The ... writer should become a 'mulatto of style' by making 'creative use of his schizophrenia, an electric fusion of the old and the new'.

Derek Walcott, *Dream on Monkey Mountain*

T.J. CRIBB

Transformations in the Fiction of Ben Okri

I will begin with two quotations from Ben Okri's second novel, *The Landscapes Within*, published when he was twenty-one. The hero, Omovo, is a would-be painter, living in poor circumstances in Lagos; he has recently, for no particular reason, had his head shaved, and has just given a few small coins to the children of the compound, who rush away to spend them.

> As they went one of them shouted: 'Shine shine head.' Omovo could not tell which and he grinned forbearingly.
> He turned his gaze upwards, at the cloudless sky through the eaves of the zinc roofs. Staring into the strip of skyline he tried to conjure up images before his vision. He tried to imagine darkness. His focus shifted and went awry. Nothing happened. Then he tried to imagine tall dark trees. He could sense the remembered shapes of trees but could not see them as solidly as he wanted to. He found that as always he had to create the image within him, almost paint it with an interior deliberation. When he opened his eyes again he felt good and serene.[1]

When does he shut his eyes? When his focus shifts and goes awry? When he tries to imagine trees? When he finds that he can create the image only within? The blurring of the narrative may indicate the intensity of the forces it carries. Here, in the midst of a Lagos slum, a young Nigerian is standing with his eyes shut trying to see something, a spectacle simultaneously comical and impressive. The effort and energy exerted is considerable. His gaze goes 'upwards', 'at', 'through', 'into', 'up', 'before', 'awry', 'within'. Before turning inwards, it reorganizes space according to its own angle of vision: the slum drops away, the zinc roofs providing only a horizon-line, the abstract geometry for a space of infinite possibilities, like a television screen or a painting. Correlative with this first act of abolishing the actual space around and subjecting it to a physically mastering gaze is the turn to the landscape within. If there is effort involved in the first, there is even a certain weariness registered in the effort involved in the second: 'He found that as always he had to create the image within him...' What is being shown here is a young man inducing in himself by deliberate exercise a sense of Renaissance perspectival space and the psychology that goes with it; we witness the birth of what Raymond Williams has taught us to call a structure of feeling.[2]

The formation of this structure of feeling is by no means unimpeded. In the following paragraph Omovo reflects on 'the long silent periods it had taken him' before he could realise an image on canvas (again the effort), and this thought 'clouds' the inner sky of his mind so that life outside begins again to intrude.

> Babel. A baby was crying, a husband and wife were quarrelling, there was the shrill hissing sound of something frying, somebody's radiogram was blaring some native music, a woman was shouting and demanding to know whose baby had excreted at her doorstep, a wide-mouthed man with kolanut-stained teeth was calling his children, and there were the shuffling, scraping, slapping sounds of the dragging feet of passers-by. It was all sheer cacophony, assaulting and binging and vibrant. (p. 88)

Abruptly, the tenses all change. In the first passage we start in the past historic: 'He turned his gaze upwards', which then prolongs itself as 'staring', so that all the following past historics are suspended and sustained by and within this abstracting vision. In the second passage, everything happens simultaneously in a continuous, formless, overlapping process, without hierarchy or geometric organization. What can be controlled in the silent world of vision here assaults the ear uncontrollably. The opposition of these two sense-worlds helps to organize the whole book. Thus in the passage immediately following my second quotation, Omovo recovers his abstraction, only to be interrupted again, this time by Ifeyinwa, a married woman with whom he is in love. In conversation together they succeed for a time in creating a special space equivalent in value to that of Omovo's private vision. Then 'the little cocoon they had woven about themselves was shattered by the noises from the compound' (p. 89). She too aspires to a life beyond the cramped quarters of her marriage and that is the bond between them. Within the space created by the perspectival gaze the romance of Tristan and Isolde can come into being. In *Flowers and Shadows* it is the story of Romeo and Juliet.[3]

I might have chosen to enter on this commentary from a different angle, for example from the way the word 'soul' is deployed. The novel's epigraph from *A Portrait of the Artist as a Young Man* gives a strong cue for such an approach. Or I might have related it to the *Bildungsroman* and its economic base in the bankruptcy of an older generation, the self-assertion of a new. Either way, we have a novel intimately imagined within the Western tradition. There can be no going back on such an assimilation, which is as profound as religious conversion. But there can be a way forward, in Ben Okri's case into Modernism, and there can then be change of direction. It is this last which I hope mainly to show.

I chose the opposition of sound and silence because I want to link the themes and values I've mentioned to language considered as cultural system. In his supplement to Ogden and Richards's *The Meaning of Meaning*, Malinowski rejects the idea that grammar is either merely conventional or

that it enshrines any absolute logic: 'Language serves for definite purposes
... it functions as an instrument used for and adapted to a definite aim.
The adaptation has left its traces in linguistic structure.... Narrative speech
... is primarily a mode of social action.'[4]

Taking this view of language as a premise, what happens when a linguistic structure adapted for specific social and practical ends is superimposed on a quite different culture? This question can be answered quite
specifically in the case of the formation of pidgins and creoles. At the level
of phonology, the Consonant-Vowel-Consonant-Vowel structure that char-
acterises the sound system of most West African languages is carried over
into English and alters its diphthongs into distinct Consonant-Vowel
alternations: 'oil' for example becomes /aja/.[5] In linguistics this is called
calquing; the African phonological system is calqued onto the English lex-
ical system.[6] At a higher level, the syntactic representation of action and
agency in the indigenous language can profoundly modify the mode of
these concepts in pidgin:

> The functions of the sensory organs are seen as being independent, according to the
> principle of 'it thinks', and they have not entirely become part of a unitary 'I'. Thus
> Molibei says 'eye belong me he sleep', my eyes are asleep.... Thus it is the concrete
> organ, the manifest feeling as well as the manifest object of the external world to
> which reference is made without further reflection.[7]

If this is true of the basic narrative categories of grammar, it should also
be true of the larger narratives recounted in stories. I have already shown
the intimacy with which the two early novels assimilate Western structures of feeling. For the rest of this paper I shall try to show that in his
later work Ben Okri draws on West African resources to modify the structures of experience embedded in English, both at the level of narrative and
at the level of syntax. In doing so he creates a genuinely new and literally
intercultural form.

The narrative level is conspicuous enough. Several stories in his two
recent collections, *Incidents at the Shrine* and *Stars of the New Curfew*, draw
directly from the stock of tales that circulate in West African oral tradition,
best known to Western readers through Amos Tutuola.[8] These open out
onto a set of temporal and spatial coordinates quite different from those
prevailing in the Western narrative tradition. Contrast the feelings of serenity that Omovo enjoys as he attains to his ideal vision in the first passage I quoted with this from 'What the Tapster Saw': 'After the trembling
ceased a curious serenity spread through him. When he looked around he
saw that he had multiplied. He was not sure whether it was his mind or
his body which flowed in and out of him' (p. 186).

This kind of experience in the Western tradition would be accompanied
by feelings not of serenity but anxiety, for identity is defined in terms of
inner and outer, boundaries and separations. The same would be true for
Omovo. Only when integrated into some higher metaphysical whole,

whether in mysticism or Romanticism, can the self be surrendered with confidence and elation. The kinds of movement and tonalities of feeling in 'What the Tapster Saw' are quite different, and out of these different coordinates, different boundaries for identity, different narrative structures emerge.

For an example of such a narrative, consider the opening sequence from the beginning of the title story of *Incidents at the Shrine*. Anderson is sacked. 'He went home, dazed, confused by objects, convinced that he saw many fingers pointing at him.' He loses himself in the city and stumbles into a market: 'As Anderson went past he had a queer feeling that the goats were staring at him.' Shortly afterwards a fire breaks out and while he runs for his life 'it struck him with amazing clarity that the fire was intent upon him because he had no power to protect himself'. And in the midst of this confusion and realization he hears someone calling his names, not his city one but all the others as well, even those he has forgotten. At home he looks in the mirror and sees a complete stranger. He journeys to his home village and at the boundary is pursued by three rough forms with 'flaming red eyes' who again shout his names (pp. 53-56).

I do not think this kind of sequence could be generated from the Western narrative tradition. In the first place, the male heroes of Western stories are accustomed to look rather than be looked at. Only women and children are subjected to looking in this way, like Pip pursued by the eyes of the cattle in *Great Expectations*. There the feelings are internalised as guilt and never completely purged, here they are externalised as shame. On this basis the feelings can be located as substantial entities in the world, as it were independent of their subject.[9] It is only if this vector is open for traffic that the next move in the narrative can be made, in which the feelings transform into warnings and messages from the other creatures in the world to the man who shares it with them. Hence the significant look of the goats, the powerful revelation of the fire. By this stage we are experiencing a system of actions quite different from any that can be reached from Western premises of psychology and causality. Fire becomes a power, a meaning, an agency which tells us something about the world in which Anderson lives, not just about Anderson and his state of mind, although it does that too. There is an obvious continuity from this incident to the flaming eyes of the spirits who shout his names. Anderson's identity exists not only in himself but also outside, in his names, which are public property, they have indubitable, real existence, they are powers in themselves. So it follows that part of the reconstitution of Anderson's identity in the village consists of a dance during which the celebrants 'wove Anderson's names in songs', recomposing his various identities into a rhythm that will have power to sustain him in the world (p. 61).

The reverse of this is abuse:

'God hammer your head,' she shouted up at him.
'Who? Me?'
'Yes, you, your very wretched self,' she said, relaxing into an impregnable posture of derision. 'It is you I am talking to, you who spits water down at people. You are a goat. You are not a man. You are a shameless fool with nothing better to do but spit water at people. You will die spitting.' (pp. 23-24)

The man being abused is Agodi in 'Converging City'; he has just cleaned his teeth out of the window onto the passing woman. Praise and abuse are constructed on the paratactic principle of the list. There is no shaping by classification, as the speaker does not have to take on the responsibility of conferring a unity on the material; that exists outside the situation, as a stock or repertoire to draw from. Virtuosity is displayed, then, by surprising *dis*continuities and combinations, showing mastery of the repertoire.[10] By the same token, the independent existence of the names means they have reality and power; to use them is efficacious, verging on the performative. Hence, although the English used is perfectly standard, the way it is used is not; it is calqued on a quite different set of cultural and syntactic relations. In some situations Standard English itself is subtly altered.[11] Usually it remains superficially standard, but is made to respond to unfamiliar lines of force, like a mask occupied by a new spirit.

Because English is the international language of modernisation, the mask is also the modern world. I have argued that Ben Okri's stories achieve formal definition and authority by mobilising resources derived from a world where the arts of language and structures of feeling are organized acoustically rather than visually.[12] These supervene on a Western set of premises. But this does not produce a mere clash of cultures, relegating the stories to the level of sociological data, and still less is there any implication of nostalgic reaction. Quite the reverse, for what he mobilises are in fact genuine resources for understanding the world we live in, especially the modern city. From one point of view, what one might call the officially preferred one, the modern Western city corresponds superficially to its own map. One cannot perceive London and walk around it without having one's perception conditioned by knowledge of the map of the Underground - which is not even a map but a diagram. The Western city has been rationalised and made legible so that it can be treated as a utility for the extraction of information, money, entertainment, power. It is pictured as a function of its functions - transport systems, communication systems, commodity and service systems. But, to take another point of view, our perception of it changes drastically if we are mugged. Then the mapping is coloured in terms of safety, danger, the unknown, socially open or closed spaces, highly charged feelings and sensitivities to emotional temperatures. Many of Okri's stories occur when the systems are mugged, during traffic jams, power failures, collapses or hypertrophies of communication systems. In this respect, his recourse to African tradition for ways of articulating experience in these situations marries up with what he draws from European Modernism. It has not been my concern to show how the stories incorporate this last dimension, so suffice it to suggest that in Rilke, too, we can meet spirits in the street, that Joyce multiplies systems of signification beyond parody in comedy, and that Kafka opens up a space of anxiety in the heart of administered rationality. Since their day all the phenomena they address have increased and multiplied; we live in a world even more haunted, more loaded with meanings, more netted by systems, more administered, more chaotic, more dangerous, more absurd, more hungry for miracles and more daily miraculous than they knew. London and Lagos overlap in ways that Paris and Dublin only faintly foreshadow. We all know perforce what it is like to live in the gap, interstitially in the systems we credit ourselves with having created. Ben Okri's short stories are an A to Z for survivors.

NOTES

1. Ben Okri, *The Landscapes Within* (London, 1981), p. 87; hereafter cited in the text.
2. John White, *The Birth and Rebirth of Pictorial Space*, 2nd edn. (London, 1967); Raymond Williams, *The Long Revolution* (London, 1961; Harmondsworth, 1965), pp. 63-66.
3. Ben Okri, *Flowers and Shadows* (London, 1980).
4. Malinowski, 'Supplement I', in I.A. Richards and C.K. Ogden, *The Meaning of Meaning* (London, 1926 edn.), pp. 327, 313.
5. The example is taken from Loreto Todd, *Modern Englishes* (London, 1984), pp. 12-13.
6. The concept of calquing is explained in Thea Bynon, *Historical Linguistics* (Cambridge, 1977), pp. 232-37; I owe this reference to Dr Adamson of the Faculty of English, Cambridge.
7. Quoted from the early twentieth-century ethnologist R.C. Thurnwald in Loreto Todd and Peter Mühlhäusler, 'Idiomatic Expression in Cameroon Pidgin English and Tok Pisin', *Papers in Pidgin and Creole Linguistics*, No. 1 (Canberra, 1978).
8. Ben Okri, *Incidents at the Shrine* (London, 1986) and *Stars of the New Curfew* (London, 1988); hereafter cited in the text.
9. Cf. *Incidents at the Shrine*: 'He thought how every single person in the world had witnessed his shame' (p. 26); 'Agodi caught the lizard in a gaze and was surprised that it stared back at him' (p. 28); *Stars of the New Curfew*: 'He got the curious feeling that she was watching him from all the eyes of the animals, old men, and children' (p. 177). Cf. John Berger, *Ways of Seeing* (Harmondsworth, 1972).
10. Cf. Karin Barber's comments on disjunctivity in 'Interpreting *Oriki* as History and Literature' in *Discourse and Its Disguises: the Interpretation of African Oral Texts*, eds. Barber and P.F. de Moraes Farias (Birmingham, 1989), a collection of essays containing important revisions of received opinion about orality and literacy.
11. E.g., 'He hopped and goaded the man', *Incidents*, p. 26; 'He changed gear with such dramatic flourish', *Stars*, p. 106.
12. This whole area of difference was opened up by Eric Havelock in *Preface to Plato* (Cambridge, Mass., 1963) and in his last survey of the field, *The Muse Learns to Write* (New Haven, 1986), following the pioneering work on Homer by Milman Parry and Albert Lord.

OLIVER LOVESEY

Accommodation and Revolt: Ngugi wa Thiong'o's *Devil on the Cross*

Devil on the Cross departs from models of the classic realist novel, and from Ngugi's earlier narratives of home-coming and social accommodation, the epics of romantic disillusionment: *The River Between, Weep Not, Child* and *A Grain of Wheat*.[1] The novel marks a shift in focus from the individual's social integration to the economic and cultural alienation of the community, Kenya's new diaspora. Part of a process begun in *Petals of Blood*, Ngugi's discourse in *Devil on the Cross*,[2] his first novel using Gikuyu as a 'vehicle', constitutes a revolution in language, an ending of his 'self-colonization', a rejection of the distorting 'words of honey,' and a recognition that the power of naming has been displaced.[3] In *Devil on the Cross*, the 'firebrand of words' must inspire, but may also burn the holder of the handle. The novel also shows Ngugi's emergence as an engaged writer who sounds a call to action. As a result *Devil on the Cross* has a variety of metafictional elements, particularly obvious in the figure of the foreign-educated artist, Gatuĩria. Here I shall explore various aspects of Ngugi's attempt to create a new narrative form to match his revolutionary vision, examining in particular the novel's treatment of feminist issues and its implied audience. I am dealing with Ngugi's translation of the Gikuyu novel, and so am looking at this work at, at least, one vital remove from the original text.

Devil on the Cross is a radical departure in form, which demands to be read in the context of East Africa's post-colonial, post-uhuru struggle,[4] and against the 'horizon' of works like Soyinka's *The Man Died* and Ngugi's own *Detained*. The circumstances of the production of the 'toilet paper novel,' its very writing an act of protest, are well-known and form a vital element in its early reception. Moreover, the subtext of the novel's allegory of capitalist devils and angelic workers, 'who grow fat on murders',[5] is a text of political economy, clearly identifying the novel's intended program of struggle with the fight against neo-colonial and cultural imperialism, and looking to Nyerere's conception of a pre-colonial African socialism as a model for new Kenya. In the novel, in Nkrumah's terms, neo-colonialism is identified as the last stage of imperialism. The novel's self-reflexive demand for a 'national tradition' (p. 243) is a response to calls, such as Okot p'Bitek's,[6] for a redefinition of 'African literature', and for a genuine Kenyan 'cultural revolution'.

In its form *Devil on the Cross* ranges from a parody of the Biblical parable of the five talents to a revision of a Bunyanesque allegory. It contains an anatomy of prose forms: 'the seeds in the gourd are not all of one kind' (p. 215). As Gatuĩria says of his own composition: 'There is no difference between old and modern stories. Stories are stories. All stories are old. All stories are new. All stories belong to tomorrow. And stories are not about ogres or about animals or about men. All stories are about human beings' (pp. 61-62). The story gourd also resembles the transcription of a praise singing feast, only here the participants sing their own praises, and demand that they be awarded the prize for modern theft and robbery. The participants in the competition, grotesque, animalistic caricatures in appearance, represent positions ranging from national to international capitalism. One entrepreneur plans to steal, repackage and resell the blood and sweat of the masses. The ability of certain characters to distinguish such monstrous animal or witch-like qualities in others recalls similar abilities possessed by the elect in the prose of seventeenth-century Dissent, such as George Fox's *Journal*. These figures are contrasted with the six characters travelling to Ilmorog to attend the feast, such as the representative peasant, Wangari, the worker in blue overalls, Mũturi, and the *petit bourgeois* intellectual, Gatuĩria. These characters are not individualized but are representative types, located in a novel unconcerned with 'personal destiny but [with] the destiny of a community' (Lukács, p. 66).[7] Moreover, these figures are provided with revolutionary or counter-revolutionary histories to match their present economic and political positions. Such characterization, at least as theorized in the *Yenan Forum on Literature*, is justified by 'present conditions': 'life as reflected in works of literature and art can and ought to be on a higher plane, more intense, more concentrated, more typical, nearer the ideal, and therefore more universal than actual everyday life. Revolutionary literature and art should create a variety of characters out of real life and help the masses to propel history forward.'[8] Ngugi consciously worked out the formal difficulties of the novel, he explains, to 'overcome the isolation imposed by poverty and illiteracy' (Ngugi, *Decolonising*, p. 83).

Each character generates a tale and these are presented in sequence, the characters themselves forming embedded narratives. Episodic events such as the ride to Ilmorog and the devil's feast, interrupted by Warĩĩnga's thoughts, are linked through uncertainty about withheld information concerning Warĩĩnga's various rescuers, and about the identity of the Rich Old Man, presented in the first sentence of the main narrative. Like Bunyan's use of fantastic characters and battle scenes, Ngugi employs detective story techniques to intensify narrative interest. However, here, his purpose is not only to make the reader laugh, cry and wait, but to make the reader act. The novel's two main situations, the matatu and the speakers' cave, often only provide occasions for long polemical diatribes and sloganeering. Even Mūturi suspects his own inclination to 'preach' (p. 211). Like the imprisoned Bunyan, however, Ngugi is here a teacher, and an inspirational one. As in *Pilgrim's Progress*, epithets are attached to the characters' names, and the Puritan image of life as a battle is employed. The novel also shares Bunyan's strident tone, his work's moral seriousness and a certain degree of Puritan authoritarianism and anti-intellectualism. Ngugi has noted rural African familiarity with Bunyan's allegory, and he probably assumed his audience would identify his allusions to Bunyan as readily as those to the Bible. However, in *Devil on the Cross*, there is a certain ambiguity in the treatment of Christianity, also evident in *A Grain of Wheat*.[9] Here, however, Ngugi's awareness of his audience's 'horizon of expectation' regarding the Christian myth and Bunyan's interpretation of it is of sustained structural importance. Christianity is presented as an anthropomorphized moral system, in Feuerbachian terms, substituting the human being for God. In this light the student leader who rescues Warīīnga may say 'Maybe I'm a priest who has not yet been ordained.... But I belong to an order that has been called to serve by the poverty of the people of Kenya' (p. 27). Christianity is also, of course, a camouflage for imperialist intentions, a counterbalance to the sword in the hidden hand. Here, the eucharist has become a cannibal feast. At various points, the retelling of the parable of the five talents trails off, as if it has, opium-like, lulled its hearers to sleep.

However, as Ngugi has said, a further inspiration for the novel was the oral tales of 'maneating ogres' and the 'human shaped rocks' of Idakho in western Kenya (*Decolonising*, p. 81). The novel resembles an oral tale in its cyclical structure, movement from speaker to speaker, and use of recognizable place names and matatu stopping points in Nairobi, and even its extensive use of brand names. Gikuyu proverbs, seemingly used here as intensifiers and as appeals to authority and universality, are often repeated, causing them to accumulate a wealth of associative meaning in the process. Much of the novel has a performative, theatrical quality, speakers usually addressing groups of five or more, and occasionally breaking into choral song. This quality of the peasant opera may have in part resulted from Ngugi's use of popular theatre in his first writings in Gikuyu. Indeed, his next novel, as Ngugi has explained, was much influenced by film technique: 'the whole novel is a series of camera shots.'[10] Such media are 'the ideal means for breaking through the barriers of illiteracy' (*Decolonising*, p. 71). The novel is a written oral tale, and in Kenya it was read by assembled families, by workers during lunch breaks, by people in taxis and buses, and by 'professional readers' in bars: 'When the reader reached an interesting episode and he discovered that his glass was empty, he would put the book down. "Give him another bottle of beer!" some of the listeners would shout to the proprietor. So our reader would resume and go on until his glass was empty' (*Decolonising*, p. 83). In this way the novel was 'appropriated' into the 'oral tradition' (p. 83), through its reception by the group, which is an intrinsic, constitutive dimension of the work itself, as argued by Sartre and, more recently, Jauss.

The novel is also infused with the magic realism of Marques. Ngugi uses popular, folk forms and international models, and 'remoulds' the artistic forms of the past to make his work accessible to his targeted audience (Mao, pp. 27-39). In this way the novel is revolutionary, but perhaps its most radical element is its equation of feminism, of Warīīnga's movement from young promise to disillusionment, with the country's progress, and its linking of feminism with revolution itself.[11] Warīīnga's sexual exploitation is a metaphor for the nation's neo-colonial seduction. The nation is now pregnant, the product of the incestuous relationship of the capitalist and his motherland, and the product may be a demon baby. Like *Petals of Blood*, *Devil on the Cross* uses such images of nature and natural processes to show corruption in the traditional order. While, in many respects, it seems to be a story without a hero, or with a collective one, which is an explicit feature of *Matigari*, in *Devil on the Cross*, Warīīnga is prominent. In many ways she is a figure who subverts stereotypes of gender and culture. Surviving rape, suicide attempts and the possibility of incest, she is transformed, in a temporal setting which is both present-day Kenya and a generalized African 'metaphysical landscape'.[12] At the open-ended closure of the novel, she strides into the battlefield of the 'war without spectators' (p. 53). Warīīnga emerges through the course of the novel from disillusioned alienation, taking a role as heroic worker, equally adept at judo, engine repair and shooting. Between the novel's subtexts of Christianity and capitalism, and the art of Gatuīria, is Warīīnga, the 'people's judge', who rebels against the purchase of immortality in an economy of blood. In a novel in which capitalist exploitation is usually described through images of eating human flesh and drinking blood, sexual play, between sugar girls and their daddies, is associated with the predatory relationship of hunter and hunted. There is an implication that forgetting women's role in the national struggle, when they manufactured guns, is equivalent to ignoring modern theft and robbery: 'these days a woman's youth has become a rotting corpse, the warmth of her body a bonfire that consumes her life, her womanhood a grave in which her fertility is buried' (p. 136). Self-reflexively the narrator explains that the corruption of traditional styles of courtship was accomplished, partly at least, through the influence of foreign popular novels, songs and films, and of popular local forms mimicking their hedonism and apolitical stance.[13] Just as male exploitation of women is an image of political oppression, so the use of whitening creams and hair straighteners represents the corruption of the identity of the nation, conceptualized as a living organism in the process of constructing a heart.

Devil on the Cross, nevertheless, is not always radical in its treatment of Warĩĩnga. The 'engineering hero', the heroine of the workers (pp. 217-18), is also startlingly beautiful, even though the words used to describe this beauty, reminiscent of the Song of Solomon, link Gatuĩria with the voice of the tempter. As at other points in the novel, there is ambivalence in the treatment of Gatuĩria. He recognizes Warĩĩnga's beauty, and takes a certain national pride in her, and yet is criticized by implication for being concerned with mere personal beauty at a time of collective crisis, when such considerations are superfluous. Furthermore, while Warĩĩnga eventually avenges the workers, she is rescued twice by male guardian angels. There is, therefore, a certain accommodation to traditional, phallocentric narrative expectations; idealized elements in her characterization maintain a certain tension with the more radical components.

Devil on the Cross's first readers were prison guards. The novel assumes an implied audience of hearers, rather than readers.[14] The novel's implied reception is a collective and communal rather than private, secluded experience. Various narratees, 'the pleading cries of many voices' (p. 7), implore the narrator to tell their own story. They help this narrator/author to 'situate himself in relation to his story and the world it presents'. However, he and we assume a male narrator, 'felt this burden weigh heavily upon [him]' (p. 7). Later, he refers to a more generalized narratee, 'my friend', and to the 'lover of justice' (p. 215). His tale is partly a retelling of Warĩĩnga's story and a re-creation of historical events in actual settings for 'You who were there'. These narratees are represented by the characters of worker and peasant in the novel, which is also partly an account of things revealed in dream visions, 'of what I ... saw ... and heard ... when I was borne to the rooftop of the house...' (p. 8). The narrator is people's judge, visionary and beleaguered worker. Ultimate inspiration to tell the tale comes from his understanding that it is community property, and that he is merely the collective's voice: 'Who has told you that prophecy is yours alone, to keep to yourself?' (p. 8). This is where he departs from Gatuĩria, an artist who wishes to compose a 'national oratorio', praising the heroic deeds of the past. His work, moreover, like the narrator's, is not purely historical and revolutionary, but is an intertext of traditional and imaginary elements. However, Gatuĩria has been somehow tainted by his class background, his therefore divided allegiances, and his fifteen years overseas, the sign of which is his inability to speak Gikuyu without breaking into English. He has a colonised mentality. The implication is that, while he can observe and mimic the revolutionary struggle, he is motivated finally by self-interest, and at the end is helplessly caught in the knot of stasis, 'hearing in his mind music that lead him nowhere' (p. 254). This is particularly important in a novel in which hearing becomes a sustained metaphor for correct understanding. It is an ability which counters mental 'deafness', debilitating self-questioning, and the dread of hearing the echo of one's own voice betraying community secrets (p. 7). In this sense,

sense, Gatuĩria's anxiety is associated with the narrator's. Gatuĩria has missed the vital message of the novel which is that a choice must be made, a road taken, and that words must lead to action: 'It is our actions that show which side we are on' (p. 54). His love for Warĩĩnga, like his patriotism, stops at the boundary of hatred, which, as Warĩĩnga says, is entwined with true love. As an artist he is selfish and cannot translate musical themes into acts. Even when he can compose, it is implied that, because, in the predatory economy, he has sold his soul to the devil, he remains merely a 'shell of a human being' (p. 60), unable to 'believe in the existence of the subject of ... [his] composition' (p. 67), inasmuch as belief encompasses certain choices and actions. This is the artist's dilemma. Though Gatuĩria realizes that his own stuttering Gikuyu is a sign of 'the slavery of the mind' (p. 56), and laments the losing of 'our national heritage' (p. 59), he is flawed and will not be part of the struggle for the new society.

Devil on the Cross demands that the dream of the devil crucified and revived, the allegory of modern history, the naming of good and evil, love and hatred, must lead to direct, revolutionary political action. In this parable of naming, of separating fakes and forgeries, the artist cannot be, like Gatuĩria, an observer, attending the Devil's feast to accumulate musical themes. At this feast, he must learn the implication of Mao Tse Tung's words, 'A revolution is not a dinner party.' While he claims a spectator's objectivity, a proverb, one locus of authority in the novel, declares 'There is no difference between a thief and him who observes the act' (p. 158). Even the narrator must overcome the bewildering sense of betrayal he feels in telling 'the secrets of the homestead' to 'strangers' (p. 7). This equation of the telling of local tales with a sense of violation of taboos emphasizes the novel's regional nature. The quality of moral outrage which permeates the book impels the narrator out of his self-questioning reluctance. He retells history and prophecy, but his utterance is a warrant. It proceeds to accuse, pass judgement, sentence and execute. The sincerity of the narrator's moral tone, despite its pedagogical qualities, and the resultant restriction placed on the reader, is one of the novel's strongest elements. As a result, the western English reader, approaching the narrative from an obviously disregarded perspective, is positioned at a considerable distance and is necessarily rendered passive, and is therefore implicated in the novel's scheme of values. This is perhaps one cause of the uneasiness about the English translation notable in a number of Western reviews.[4] In a novel in which the only permissible consequence of reading is revolutionary action, passivity, and the passive reader's position as observer – even a knowledgeable and sympathetic observer like Gatuĩria – constructs this reader as a consumer of the novel, a contributor to the predatory economy. There is a certain ambivalence here, because, on the one hand, the narrator claims to merely present facts, allowing hearers to interpret, while, on the other hand, he severely restricts interpretative freedom, stressing instead action and the consequences of passivity.

Devil on the Cross's implied audience is a collective one, a class, represented by the group of characters in the novel itself. It is the real 'national oratorio', the story which has been and will be 'told over and over again' (p. 247). Through the act of telling it becomes not the product of 'the mouth that ate itself' (p. 7), but an inspiration for self-reliance, action and struggle. In this sense *Devil on the Cross* thematicizes its own production, the story of Gatuĩria's failure and Warĩĩnga's future paralleling the tale of the novel's creation. Just as the author struggled to use Gikuyu, so Gatuĩria has difficulties writing African music, for its notation has yet to be sufficiently differentiated from Western forms. The form of the novel, partly the result of a sense that the luxury of careful observation and detailed delineation of incident must be abandoned, carries the urgency of being written under real duress and marks the writer's decision to produce a literature of engagement.

The form of Ngugi's work, the very production of which was an act of defiance, is inseparable from its cultural and political program, and its telling subverts traditional notions of narrative form, and of gender and audience. In *Devil on the Cross,* there is a friction between accommodation with European and Afro-European narrative tradition, and revolt against it. This is apparent in the character of Gatuĩria and in the narrator's somewhat ambivalent stance. While all artistic production is communal and intertextual and in times of crisis must aid the struggle, the artist is independent and his work requires inspiration. At the novel's closure the narrator is frustrated and exhausted, and Gatuĩria is voiceless. In such a scenario the role of the artist is ambiguous. He doesn't compose new plots. He is more a chronicler and judge, and his work's effectiveness may only be evaluated according to its contribution to the struggle. Reading too is a performative act which must embody a necessary resultant action. While the sincerity of the novel's commitment is stirring, it is a different kind of literature, one of simplified problems and often caricatured characters, perhaps necessitated by the demands of the project of writing a true African literature, readily comprehensible to a mass audience. Necessarily, for the Western reader, it is an airy, though somewhat unsettling ride in a matatu, after the breakdown of the obsolescent, emblematic Mercedes Benz. Departing from the narrative conventions of Fielding's stage coach, Scott's flying carpet, and Eliot's tube, *Devil on the Cross* employs a really African narrative vehicle. Despite the romanticizing of the peasantry in the novel,[15] and the presentation of the pre-colonial past as a Golden Age, it is this focus upon a rural African implied audience that is almost as important as its language of creation and its use of oral conventions in signifying *Devil on the Cross* as a truly African novel.

NOTES

1. For discussion of novel form, see Georg Lukács, *The Theory of the Novel*, trans. Anna Bostock (Cambridge, Mass.: MIT, 1971), p. 117.
2. Ngugi wa Thiong'o, *Devil on the Cross*, trans. by the author (London: Heinemann, 1982). All further references are to this edition and are included in the text.
3. For comments on this, see Ngugi wa Thiong'o, *Decolonising the Mind* (London: James Currey, 1986), p. 63; David Cook and Michael Okenimkpe, *Ngugu wa Thiong'o. An Exploration of His Writings* (London: Heinemann, 1983), pp. 119-23; Ngugi wa Thiong'o, 'On Writing in Gikuyu', *Research in African Literatures* 16 (1985), p. 152.
4. Edward W. Said, *The World, the Text, and the Critic* (Cambridge, Mass.: Harvard University Press, 1983), p. 157.
5. David Diop, 'Certainty', *Hammer Blows* (London: Heinemann, 1975), p. 29.
6. Okot p'Bitek, *Africa's Cultural Revolution* (Nairobi: Macmillan, 1973).
7. Ngugi has said he intentionally created 'class types' in *Petals of Blood* (quoted in John Updike's 'Mised Reports from the Interior', *New Yorker*, July 2, 1979, p. 91). This technique is yet more explicitly used in the central figure of *Matigari*. The representative, symbolic quality in Ngugi's fiction, however, has been identified in works as early as *Weep Not, Child* (see Douglas Killam's 'Recent African Fiction', *The Bulletin of the Association for African Literature in English 1964-1966* (rpt. 1970, Nendeln: Kraus), p. 9.
8. Mao Tse Tung, *Talks at the Yeman Forum on Literature and Art* (Beijing: Commercial Publishing House, 1972), p. 45.
9. Goving Narain Sharma, 'Ngugi's Christian Vision: Theme and Pattern in *A Grain of Wheat*', *African Literature Today 10*, ed. Eldred Durosimi Jones (London: Heinemann, 1979), p. 169.
10. Hansel Nolumbe Eyoh, 'Ngugi wa Thiong'o Interviewed', *JCL* 21 (1986), p. 166.
11. Terry Eagleton, among others, has examined the similarities of the Marxist and feminist programs. He concludes: 'without the "feminization" of human history, the world is unlikely to survive', *Literary Theory* (Oxford: Basil Blackwell, 1983), p. 150.
12. Chinua Achebe, *Morning Yet on Creation Day* (London: Heinemann, 1977), p. 50.
13. Elizabeth Knight provides a useful exploration of the cynical consumption of pleasure in urban settings in much East African 'popular literature', *African Literature Today 10*, ed. Eldred Durosimi Jones (London: Heinemann, 1979), pp. 177-90.
14. This is a feature of reviews of Ngugi's work after *A Grain of Wheat*. For example, Updike notes the use of Swahili and Gikuyu words in *Petals of Blood*, 'as if to warn non-African readers away' (p. 91). Reading *Devil on the Cross*, David Sweetman suggests, 'the white reader is in for a rough ride' ('Adding to the Howl of Anguish', *TLS* June 18, 1982, p. 676). Similar sentiments are noted by Andrew Gurr ('*JCL* and the Implied Reader', *JCL* 21, 1986, pp. 4-8), and Reed Way Dansenbrock (Review of *Devil on the Cross*, *World Literature Today*, Winter, 1984, p. 153). The latter, in an otherwise sympathetic and insightful review, holds that 'Anyone who does not share these views [Ngugi's 'extremely crude Marxism'] is going to find parts of this extremely didactic novel hard to take' (p. 153). Most recently, Michelle Quinn notes that 'something essential is lost to the English reader' in reading *Matigari*, 'both in translation and in our unfamiliarity with Ngugi's intended audience' ('A Parable of Anger', *Manchester Guardian*, June 18, 1989, p. 29). This points to the movement in Ngugi's fiction, traced by Adele King in the work of Laye and Beti, from an address to an implied foreign reader to an implied African reader ('Audience and Exile: Camara Laye and Mongo Beti', *Audience and Artist: African Literature as a Shared Experience*, eds. Richard K. Priebe and Thomas A. Hale (Washington: Three

Continents, 1979), pp. 141-48). In another useful essay in the same volume, Thomas Hale and Gerard Pigeon examine the effect of 'Africanisms' in African literature upon the foreign and the African reader unfamiliar with the source language ('Artist and Audience', pp. 77-83).

15. Chinweizu, Review of *Decolonising the Mind*, *TLS*, 8 May 1987, p. 499.

OYEKAN OWOMOYELA

Yoruba Folk Opera: A Cross-Cultural Flowering

Introduction

In the following pages I will revisit the theatrical phenomenon in Nigeria that has attracted so much scholarly attention, and attempt a clarification of some persistent confusions surrounding it. I will also respond to certain questions that scholars have raised about some of my earlier statements on the subject, in the hope of contributing to a better understanding of the true nature of the historical event and the dynamics that have determined its fortune.

My title hints at some of the points at issue: some scholars are not agreed on the propriety of the designation, 'opera', some object to 'folk', and many would contest some of the implications embedded in the quali-fication, 'cross-cultural'. For example, to what extent is the 'opera'[1] a new form, and to what extent a continuation, albeit somewhat altered, of tradi-tional performance? To what extent was it influenced in its form by tradi-tional 'theatre'? Was it (and is it) the brain child of individual artistes or of the people as a whole, with the artist serving only as its expressive medium? And how do we assess the extent and value of foreign input into it?

Opera and Traditional 'Theatre'

For the most part scholars who write on Yoruba opera, if they consider its relationship to traditional ceremonies featuring dramatic elements, stress its separateness and independence. For example, Ola Rotimi writes that while traditional Nigerian drama developed from ritual, Yoruba folk opera, like Nigerian drama in English, 'developed individually, and not in direct response to an already existing native form or to one another'.[2] In the same vein Akinwunmi Isola observes that in pre-colonial days drama among the Yoruba was limited to ritual drama and *alárìnjó*, itiner-ant performing masqueraders, and 'dramatic aspects' in religious and secular festivals. He sees the 'modern travelling theatre' as a new breed that arose from 'Christian inspired operas and service of songs until Ogunde changed the orientation and moved it to a play form'.[3]

In her study of Hubert Ogunde's career Ebun Clark seems ambivalent on this point. She objects, for instance, to my contention that Ogunde's professional theatre company was the first such in Nigeria. 'To say this,' she argues, 'is to ignore the long establishment of another valid theatre – the Alarinjo Theatre of masked strolling players...' She continues, however, to cite differences between the two while still conveying the idea of innovation within a continuing tradition: *alárìnjó* uses masks while Ogunde does not, and 'Ogunde ... withdrew the theatre from the traditional patronage of the court and religious organizations to rely solely on the patronage of the public'. He also took indoors 'what was traditionally an open-air theatre'.[4]

Other scholars in effect posit not only a continuity between traditional performances and the opera but attribute their development to the same cultural impulses. Thus Kacke Götrick complains in her book, *Apidán Theatre and Modern Drama*, that although I entitled an earlier study 'Folklore and the Rise of Theatre Among the Yoruba', I paid no attention to *apidán* theatre. 'By Yoruba theatre,' she writes, '"the creators" of which he appoints Hubert Ogunde, Kola Ogunmola and Duro Ladipo, Owomoyela means the Yoruba opera only, thus excluding all types of traditional theatre...' While I admitted the influence of traditional festivals on Yoruba theatrical art, she continues, my 'thesis seems to be that Yoruba theatre did not really exist before Ogunde'.[5]

Finally, in an article on the 'opening glee' Adedeji says that 'the Yoruba Masque Theatre (Alarinjo or Eegun Alare) and the Yoruba Operatic Theatre (the Travelling Theatre Parties)' are 'the two theatrical developments in Yorubaland which are indigenous and are products of Yoruba cultural history. Both are professional theatres with travelling troupes or companies which developed from religious rites'.[6]

The Debate on Genre and Terminology

The disagreement over what is African theatre and what is not is unlikely to be resolved in the near future, and I will not repeat arguments which I have made earlier.[7] The objections I have cited above to some of my positions do, however, deserve a response. The disagreements, as I see them, result from a certain inconsistency in our approach to the subject, and in our theory about how to deal with imported concepts and borrowed terms. To confine ourselves to terminology for the moment, one can assert without fear of contradiction that, as Oyin Ogunba pointed out,[8] 'theatre' and 'drama' do not occur in any African language; that they are borrowed from other cultures and traditions. The very necessity to borrow a word from another culture and language to describe a phenomenon indicates its newness, since if it was not new it would presumably already have a name. Unfortunately modern African realities, one feature of which is the effective rejection of African languages for foreign ones, have robbed that argument of some of its cogency. Whether the phenomenon is new or not, however, the borrowing of a foreign word for it we can construe either as an indication of exact correspondence between it and the thing that bears the name in the lending culture, or as suggesting a similarity of both *in certain respects*.

That far I believe there will be general agreement. Problems begin to arise when we venture beyond that point. 'Biodun Jeyifo, for example, believes that the effort expended on distinguishing between African traditional performances some scholars describe as 'theatre' or 'drama' on the one hand and what I will describe as conventional Western drama on the other is wasted; it appeals to 'a reified, narrow and Eurocentric concept of theatre', and leads to 'ignoring the most basic fact of the experience of theatre in all cultures and at all times; it is historically and formalistically variable...'. He continues: 'The concept of "European", "African" or "Asian" theatre is of course intelligible at a certain level of abstraction and generalisation; but for comprehending theatre as a cultural mode charged with the changing, variable experience of living generations, these concepts are of little worth.' He adds, 'when such concepts are not deductively derived from the available diverse and concrete traditions and forms but are inductively and arbitrarily applied to any theatrical phenomenon whatsoever, they become a methodological dead-end'.[9]

I willingly concede his point that the appeal is to a Eurocentric view of theatre, but with the qualification that it is Eurocentric only in the same sense that the use of the terms 'theatre' and 'drama' is Eurocentric. I do not concede, though, that it is reified. I submit that, contrary to his observation, the procedure of those of us who appeal to that Eurocentric concept of theatre has not been arbitrary or inductive, but strictly *deductive*, with the properties of Eurocentric theatre as a starting point. My defence of the Eurocentric measure will come in time, but first, a justification of the assertion of deductiveness.

'Theatre' and 'drama' are by no means abstract concepts in the cultures from which we have borrowed them, but refer to a concrete performative genre, one, besides, that has centuries of tradition and scholarship behind it. If our borrowing is held to imply no more than a suggestion of *approximation* or *metaphorical affinity* I doubt that we would be involved in this tiresome debate. But that is not the case; we are meant to take the designation as having the same order of applicability to Yoruba traditional performances as to, say, Edward Bond's plays. Normally, if one sought to borrow a term from a foreign culture for a local phenomenon the deductive path to ascertaining the suitability of the candidate term (in this case 'theatre' or 'drama') among the many available in the lending culture would be as follows: the properties of theatre or drama are a, b, c (the major premise); the properties of the phenomenon on whose behalf we seek to borrow a name are x, y, z (the minor premise); if a, b, c correspond to x, y, z, we conclude that the new phenomenon has justified the designation. If not, we conclude that it has not, in which case proceeding to apply the name in any case would be arbitrary, or an indication that we are satisfied with a metaphorical affinity only.

The procedure Jeyifo recommends is attractive to a number of scholars. Witness two quotations from Götrick which succinctly make the same case. She introduces her study with the statement:

> The Western theatre terminology, too, has of course grown out of the Western experience and thus cannot cover the requirements for description and analyses of other theatrical traditions. An all-embracing terminology can be created only when we have better knowledge of the entire theatrical field to which it is meant to be applied. Primarily there is a need for a careful documentation of as many theatrical traditions as possible, together with their own respective aesthetics. A widening of the present Western theatre concept is a likely result.[10]

Much later, after applying a standard dramaturgical criterion to *apidán*, the fiction of the presence of a world known to be hypothetical, she finds that it does not always apply. She concludes, therefore, that this fictional requirement 'is not true of all traditional African drama. Instead, a new definition of drama is needed, which includes enactments that are at the same time presentational and representational, that are efficacious, and that are conceived of as a duality by appropriate spectators, comprising reality and fiction simultaneously'.[11]

Both Jeyifo and Götrick assume an *a priori* knowledge of what drama and theatre are, knowledge which, apparently, has no reference to 'drama' and 'theatre' as they are commonly conceived in their original context, for that is what they wish us to move away from. But we need to be guided *somehow* to the appropriate 'concrete traditions and forms' and away from inappropriate ones. What criteria shall guide us if not the customary ones associated with our borrowed terms? If one may use a scientific analogy, their suggested procedure would be as though a scientist were given a clear liquid substance and asked to determine what it is. Because the liquid is clear, he decides that it must be water and proceeds to test accordingly. In the course of testing, however, he finds that the liquid turns litmus paper red. Rather than give up his presupposition that what he has is water, he insists that the properties of water must be revised to accommodate his new finding. What he has under analysis simply has to be water! We cannot simply assume, *a priori*, an 'experience of theatre in all cultures and at all times', although we may assume an experience of *performance*, for the same reasons that we cannot assume an experience of sonata, although we may assume that of music.

By now it is quite clear that I am using these terms, 'theatre' and 'drama', in their specialized and academic sense rather than in their vulgar sense, because I believe that in our discipline we are obliged to do so. I am insisting on a precise definition of the terms, and on appropriate stated qualifications when we depart from accepted usage, for nebulous, open-ended definitions are of little use. Carolyn Porter, citing Samuel Weber as authority, warns us that 'exclusion is the necessary act by which an object of study is constituted; discursive analysis cannot proceed without such exclusionary acts'.[12]

Eurocentrism; the Necessary and the Contingent

I earlier conceded Jeyifo's point that the criteria I am applying in my definition are 'Eurocentric'. My reason is because 'theatre' and 'drama', the concepts and the terms, are undeniably European. This is not to say that one doesn't find performances in traditional Africa and elsewhere in the world which have certain elements in common with theatre and drama. However, my point is that the institution that most scholars of theatre and drama think about when either of those terms is mentioned originated once, at a particular time and a particular place, and has evolved to our day as a European cultural phenomenon, gathering influences from various cultures and spawning offshoots along the way. The charge of Euro-centrism against those of us who insist on 'Eurocentric' definitions is considerably weakened in any case when we note that those who make it, do so in the interest of an unrestricted right to the European terms 'theatre' and 'drama'. Besides, how credible is a rejection of Eurocentrism when we operate in European languages and in a generally European cultural orbit?

The scholars who favour the licence to unconditionally use 'theatre' and 'drama' for traditional performance, to broaden the definition of European terms to accommodate African rituals, contend correctly that African drama does not have to replicate European drama in every detail. Few reasonable people would be inclined to dispute that contention. But, para-doxically, they also object to statements like Finnegan's that the phenom-ena such scholars so designate are different from theatre and drama as they are customarily conceived in the West, a qualification that would seem to correspond to their assertions.[13] Their point is of course important, if only they would press it consistently: we must acknowledge cultural specificity and difference. If we do, then we must allow that simply be-cause the West developed drama and theatre, *as they are known in the West*, we cannot insist that other cultures must show evidence of having also developed them or be judged inferior or incomplete. The sentiment often expressed that European ideas and definitions are not universals[14] is abso-lutely correct, and so is the fact that the structures and institutions of Europe (or the West) are not paradigmatic.

We might borrow from philosophy the concepts of the necessary and the contingent and assert that theatre and drama do not fall in the first cat-egory but in the second. They are not imperatives like food, and not a necessary part of a culture's development nor a requisite for a people's meaningful existence. On this score J.C. de Graft's otherwise excellent essay, 'Roots in African Drama', falls into error in my view. He suggests five conditions a culture must have to produce drama: a propensity for role-paying, narrative habit based on local history and lore, social solidarity, a recording system, and freedom — religious, political and economic.[15] Theatre and drama did not develop in Africa, in his view, because the last two were lacking at some point. But we have no reason to suppose that if all of the conditions were present we would have drama and theatre as they do in Europe. Moreover, the implication that Thespis' Athens is the only place in history where they have ever converged is simply unacceptable.

The Legacy of Culture Contact

I suspect that a great deal of the effort that has gone into establishing what Clark describes as 'a valid theatre' in Africa before the arrival of Europeans is a manifestation of a well-meaning intention to assert African sufficiency. But it is futile to suggest that our contact with Europe resulted in nothing new in either European or African cultures. For all the statements that have been made about the brevity of the colonial period in the context of the totality of the African experience, and the truth that the vast majority of the continent's population was little affected by it, there were some new developments, even if one stops short of conceding the sea-change Irele postulates.[16] The fact is that those who were intimately associated with the colonial processes, or in some way absorbed in its institutions, developed a subculture, bastard European, let us call it, along with supporting institutions that hark back to European originals, but, to be sure, with varying degrees of African input. Karin Barber's study of the popular arts in Africa[17] illustrates how the partially assimilated urbanites concocted arts for themselves, creatively adapting European forms with the use of traditional elements. The opera we are here considering is one such example; it is distinct in its origin and development from any traditional 'theatre' or 'drama'.

Origins

While there are disagreements on the existence of professional theatre in Nigeria before Ogunde's emergence, there is no question that he inaugurated the professional Yoruba opera. That does not mean that there was no theatrical activity in the country before him. Michael Echeruo's pioneering studies on elite entertainment in 19th century Lagos[18] have established the European derivation and flavour of the theatrical fare, as well as its progressive devolution to churches and their schools; Lynn Leonard[19] expanded the investigation to the 1920s, pointing out the process of its progressive indigenization. My later study[20] concentrated on arguing the contribution of folklore to the development of the opera.

By way of underscoring the decisive role of non-indigenous institutions in the emergence of the form I will briefly direct our attention to the pertinent activities in the decade or so before Ogunde took his historic step.

The Gold Coast Connection

Kwabena Bame's history of Concert Parties in Ghana[21] credits Teacher Yalley, an elementary school headmaster in Sekondi, with originating the form in 1918.[22] Yalley began his performances in connection with the annual observance of Empire Day and drew heavily on Western influences.[23] Bame singles out three features of these performances as significant: 'the elite character of his audience, which the use of English in the performances and the very high ticket prices helped to maintain; other significant non-African influences; and the importance of music in the evening's entertainment' (p. 8). But the new art went on to shed its elitist nature and adopted local languages, themes and form, 'while retaining buried though recognizable aspects of non-African influence' (pp. 8-9).[24]

Better known than Yalley was Bob Johnson, who had been impressed by Yalley's performances and church-organized moralities and 'cantatas', by silent cinema and Charlie Chaplin, and by Liberian seamen who visited a Club near his home in Sekondi. There 'Liberian seamen sang "sea-shanties and highlifes to the accompaniment of guitar and musical saw", and Black Americans performed "comedy sketches and [sang] foxtrots and ragtimes"' (p. 10). Other influences came from the black American vaudevillian couple Glass and Grant, who lived in Accra between 1924 and 1926 and performed minstrel shows. In 1930 Johnson founded a professional concert party, on the demise of which he joined the Axim Trio founded soon after his group, when it embarked on the first of two successful tours of Nigeria.[25] The new group became the prototype for a number of others.

The Lagos Scene

In Lagos meanwhile, although there was no professional troupe the elite entertained themselves in very much the same manner as those of the cities of Accra and Sekondi. What follows is a detailed account of one representative example of elite entertainment in the Lagos of the 1930s.

On Thursday, August 13, 1931, the *Daily News* of Lagos carried a story under the heading, 'The Lagos Concert Party', and the subheading, 'A Grand Thrilling Performance'. It began:

In the theatrical history of Lagos of the last ten years there has not been an occasion when a small party of six young men has given so excellent a concert as the one by the members of the Lagos Concert Party headed by FATHER OF THE TROUPE, Barrister Ayo Williams and presided over by the local Joynson Hicks, the popular Hon. Dr. C.C. Adeniyi Jones on the Night of the first of this month.

The other member of the Concert Party were: J.O. Smith, E. Olumide, A.S. Euba, E.A. Meadows, and C. Sowande. The account continued:

The Concert Party appeared at about 9.26 p.m. singing the following opening chorus written and composed by our local Jock Hylton, Mr. C. Sowande:

We are the Lagos Concert Party: We are the happy Family—There's old Jack there is old Joe, There's old Chappie and There's old Bill—there you see the Pianist—Four-eyed stead of two there you see the Humorist the Father of the Troupe we all surely welcome you to-night dears and we shall try our best to do welcome again and welcome welcome from the Lagos Concert Party.

The chorus was followed by a pianoforte solo (Rachmaninoff's Prelude in C Minor) by Mr. C. Sowande, and Chopin's Prelude in A as encore. He came on later to sing 'the Samoa' and when encored 'Pack up your troubles'. The reporter, one Mr. Adetayo, observed that 'Mr. Olumide's performance would have been perfect if his songs were rendered with moderation and his cake-walk dancing carefully regulated'. After some more songs the party presented 'a dialogue' entitled 'The Making of a Will' by Euba and Meadows, about a destitute dying man trying to draw up a will. A 'quartet' by members of the Party made up for the 'dialogue', which Mr. Adetayo considered a failure. There were three songs, including: 'Don't wait too long', 'Rosery waiting at the end of the road'.

The report was continued in the paper's August 14 issue, with the information that 'The Humorist – Father of the Troupe' when he gave his performance 'disguised his face with white, black and red paint: his mouth was painted round in white'. The ensemble did 'plantation anthems' with appropriate props – sticks of sugarcane, cutlasses, lanterns, mandolin, guitar, and so forth, and they concluded the evening by singing 'Good Night Ladies. Good Night Gents'. The reviewer hoped they would give a repeat performance after the completion of the Glover Hall renovation.

I have devoted so much time and space to the Sekondi and Lagos developments in order to highlight some significant details: the adoption of the 'concert party' designation, the elitism of the participants, the European flavour of the performances, the introductory 'opening glee', the sandwiching of a 'dialogue' (as the drama was called) in the Lagos instance between musical numbers, the use of minstrel make-up and props, black face and mandolin for example, and the conclusion of the evening with a valedictory 'closing glee'. Since the Axim Trio was not formed until 1935, the similarity of the performance described above (which antedates the group's first tour of Nigeria) to the elite fare in Gold Coast's cities, must be attributed to the operation of the same influences on the elite of both British colonies who had a great deal in common.

Ogunde dates his debut with *Garden of Eden* to June 12, 1944 at the Glover Memorial Hall in Lagos.[26] For that reason it is interesting to note as examples a couple of performances in Lagos in the months immediately before that. The *Daily Service* of Monday February 21, 1944 announced the performance of a 'Yoruba Native Air Opera entitled "Joseph and His Brethren" by the Yaba Methodist Church Choir, assisted by specially selected ladies'. The stage, it said, would be directed by A.B. David, the composer of the play.

Another news item, this one in the paper's issue of Saturday April 8, 1944, speaks of another influence. It stated: 'The Lagos Opera Club Will Present A Local Hollywood on Easter Monday.' After announcing the venue as the tennis section of the Yaba stadium it continued: 'The aim of this Club is to experiment on instituting theatres and operas in this community and the coming show is intended to be an opportunity of visualising what a local Hollywood might be.' Among the performers would be the Lagos City Orchestra, Rhythm Brothers, and the Moonlight Club Orchestra. The first example indicates that the pattern of church sponsorship of theatrical entertainment was unabated, and that Ogunde's *Garden Of Eden* was part of a routine. The second reveals the conscious effort of those involved in theatrical entertainment to duplicate what was glamorous and effective in Western theatre practice as epitomized by Hollywood.

Influences

In the course of describing how he embarked on his professional theatre career, Ogunde recalled that he was asked by the prophet of his church, the Church of the Lord, to compose 'a sort of service of songs'. Already in the field, he said, were Mr. Onimole, Mr. Layeni and A.B. David; 'they were composing songs; it was a sort of cantata ...., service of songs they called it in those days'. But thinking that a program of mere singing before a large audience in Glover Hall would be dull he asked the prophet if he could insert some movement, even though movement and dialogue were then thought to be inappropriate in such performances. The prophet agreed, and the success of the show changed Ogunde's career and his life.

With regard to the subjects of his first shows – *Garden of Eden, Africa and God, Israel in Egypt, Nebuchadnezzer's Reign,* and *King Solomon* – he said: 'You will notice that all the first plays were biblical, because ... the thing started from the church. St. Jude's Church, Lafiaji; U.N.A., Eleja; and because it was started by the church, the church didn't want anything that would not be of biblical interest to the people. But I broke away...'

Suggestions that the opera emerged from traditional institutions like *egúngún* or had any connection with it ignore the reality indicated in Ogunde's reminiscence. The attitude he mentioned – keeping extra-biblical materials out of church-related activities – was not confined to his particular church but was shared by other churches and their schools. At the same forum with Ogunde was Ladipo, who revealed that when on being asked by his church at Osogbo to compose a Christmas cantata he introduced *bàtá* drums into the music, he was stripped of his office as lay reader, because 'it was an offence to bring the pagan drums into the Christian church'. His father, a reverend gentleman who had hoped that his son would also join the ministry, was so disappointed in him and in his subsequent career that it took the intervention of Bishop Philips to bring about a reconciliation between father and son barely three days before the senior Ladipo died.

In my mission-school days in Osogbo in the 1940s the headmaster of the school, and sometimes the pastor of the church, pulled some unfortunate young boys out of morning assembly to whip them publicly because they had been seen earlier participating in *egúngún* processions. It did not matter that their families had a ritual obligation to 'carry' a particular *egúngún*; the church and school sought to override such traditional obligations. Those familiar with the *aládùúrà* churches, of which Ogunde's Church of the Lord is one, will be aware that, far more than the larger main-stream churches, they are inveterately hostile to traditional institutions. H.W. Turner has written that the founders of the sects announced their calling by 'destroying idols and charms in large quantities', among other similar acts of piety.[27] These they did while still members of established denominations, but after receiving the call to 'commence preaching judgement and repentance, the destruction of idols, and healing through prayer' (pp. 16-17). He adds: 'It must not be thought that the attitude of the missions was entirely negative, for they were impressed with the burning of the idols and all the apparatus of native charms and medicines' (p. 27).

Adrian Hastings' history concurs with Turner's. He notes that

> one of the roots of the prophetism which swept across so many parts of Africa in those years [the 1920s] was no other than the mission church's catechist, run a little wild. It was the catechist with his limited training and simple message but great authority who really carried the mission church into the bush in the first decades of the twentieth century...[28]

The Yoruba Cherubim and Seraphim movement, a faction closely allied to the Church of the Lord, harks back, according to Hastings, to the activities of William Wade Harris, 'a Liberian of Methodist and Episcopalian background who erupted upon the Ivory Coast and the Gold Coast in 1913 an 1914.... [W]hat Harris did in 1914, with his powerful message of the Bible, the One God, baptism, healing in faith, the utter rejection of fetishes, countless other prophets were to do in the coming years.' Apart from stressing the rabid antipathy of the *aládùúrà* sects to African tradition, Hastings' words testify to the fact that the colonies of West Africa (in this case both French and British) were more often than not subject to very much the same social and cultural influences.

In some cases the imputed connection between the opera and *egúngún* is not outright derivation, but of the two enjoying an intimate relationship, for example that *egúngún* inspired the opera. Thus according to Adedeji,

> In spite of the forces which had committed [the *alárìnjó*] to antiquity, its members are being raked up and its undying influence is now visible in the organizational and operational practice of the practitioners of the contemporary travelling theatre led by Hubert Ogunde.
> Hubert Ogunde, who became the first Nigerian artist of the contemporary theatre to turn professional and assume the leadership of a flourishing theatre troupe, recalled that his experience and source of inspiration belonged to the Alarinjo theatre. 'I was playing drums with the masqueraders in my home town when I was young, and these Egungun people gave me the urge inside me to start a company of actors.'[29]

Adedeji attributes the quote to 'personal communication', but when Ogunde spoke about his career at the aforementioned seminar he said:

> Now, if you like to know how I started, I will tell you I started the very time I was born. Because born into the house of fetish priests, the babalawos [*Ifá* diviners], I was born into the sound of drums. Drumming ... you know the babalawos in the olden days ... is a sort of idol worshipping; it is drumming and drumming all day and night. So I think this even had an effect. And, curiously enough, my father was a priest in the church. He was a reverend in the Baptist church, but he was not staying at home at the time I was born. And so, before I saw him, this fetishness had something ... impact in me, because what I knew then was drumming, dancing, babalawos, the olorisas [traditional priests], and I was even taking part in the drumming.

At the time he either did not recall the *alárìnjó* part of the experience, or he did not consider it significant.

Adedeji's researches into *egúngún* and opera have certainly yielded a number of influential publications. One of the issues on which his statements may be confusing is the 'opening glee' that usually opens the 'operas' and their derivation. In an article he writes concerning *ìjúbà egúngún*: 'The *Ijuba* was the formal or ceremonial opening very much like an "opening glee". It contained the "pledge" and the "salute"' (p. 45). He adds later: 'The significance of the *Ijuba* (salute), the entrance song of the traditional theatre, was in evidence in Ogunde's "Opening Glee" and at the early part of his career, having introduced some modifications which are a reflection of his Christian outlook and contemporary viewpoint' (pp. 49-50). This sounds very much like suggesting that Ogunde learned about *ìjúbà* from *egúngún* practice and adopted it from there. But in another context he traces the 'opening glee' to the Lagos Glee Singers, 'veteran performers of European Operettas' in the year 1910.[30]

Ìjúbà as a concept and as a practice is so entrenched in Yoruba etiquette that it would be inappropriate to attribute it to any one product of the culture rather than to the culture itself. The Yoruba believe firmly that before anyone embarks on any venture he or she must acknowledge (and beg leave of) the powers that have authority over the pertinent domains of the universe and existence, and also acknowledge fellow human beings. Having done so the person secures the blessing and protection of the powers, and wards off the malignant obstructionism of malevolent people. Proceeding without such acknowledgement is *àdáse*, trusting solely in one's own powers, and a well known proverb says, *Àdáse ní ńhunni; ìbà kì í hunni* (Trusting solely in one's own powers is what leads to disaster; paying homage does not lead to disaster). Another, equally well known, assures us, *Bí ekòló bá júbà ilè ilè á lanu* (If the earthworm pays homage to the earth the earth will open for it). We can occasionally see evidence of the cultural entrenchment of *ìjúbà* even in popular musical entertainment.[31]

Incidentally, I have been described as 'categorical and dogmatic' about the structure of opera performances generally and about the 'opening glee' in particular.[32] I do not believe the description is correct. I gave an outline of what I said *generally* obtained, and added: 'Within the broad limits defined, some variations are possible, and do occur, but these are insignificant and are not such as would have any bearing on my subject.'[33]

Ulli Beier and Yoruba 'Opera'

Ulli Beier's extensive and intimate involvement in Nigerian arts in the 1950s and 1960s is common knowledge, and few will doubt that his impact was considerable. It was, in fact, so profound that it has generated strong resentment in some Nigerian scholars to whom he was nothing but a meddler. When he gave a talk in Drapers Hall at the Institute of African Studies, University of Ibadan, on February 12, 1983 as part of the observance of the anniversary of Ladipo's death, he was subjected to blistering attacks by some of the Nigerians present. Among other things, he was accused of speaking for Nigerians and pre-empting their voices in the years he spent working in the country.

Demas Nwoko, who believes his meddling was dangerous, characterizes his relationship with Ladipo as follows:

Ulli Beier is not an artist, but he developed very clear ideas of what should constitute African art and theatre and went on to produce them. To realize this theatre, he created by suggestion a theatre troupe basically after the style of the existing Ogunmola and Ogunde vernacular troupes. He suggested a historical theme from the legends, a subject that gave ample opportunity for the exhibition of 'traditional African culture'. Through further suggestions during production, original indigenous music and appropriate dances (along with poetry) were used. Added to this, for decor, were back-cloths of typical modern art school colours which were the result of the art workshop he had organized. The result was an exhibition of slices of African customs and traditional art forms, loosely linked by improvised dramatic movements and speech. *Oba Koso*, as the play was called, was a very exotic presentation and it was sent round Europe as a demonstration of our fine culture.[34]

In his tribute to the late dramatist Yemi Ogunbiyi disagrees with Nwoko, at least on the extent of Beier's influence. Nwoko is not fair to Ladipo, Ogunbiyi argues, citing the latter's long experience in theatre before he met Beier: 'Duro Ladipo himself was for ever eager to acknowledge the assistance of Ulli Beier in helping him to achieve his artistic objectives', but he also knew that 'assistance in matters of creativity is a very limited factor, because in the end, the real artist is his own man, on his own, alone'.[35]

On both scores Ogunbiyi is correct. During his presentation at the 1970 seminar, for example, Ladipo said: 'But for the interest some Europeans took in what I was doing, I could never have been heard of at all.' He was obviously referring to Beier. One cannot doubt, either, that Ladipo had dramatic and musical inclinations before meeting Beier, because *they* account for Beier's interest in him in the first place. Furthermore, there must have been some reason for his church to commission him to write a festive cantata. But having granted those points, one must also argue that they are not incompatible with Nwoko's observations.

Beier's wish to be not only a commentator on African art but also a creator of it is a matter of record, especially in his assumption of the pseudonym Obotunde Ijimere under which he wrote and published a number of plays. Through Ladipo he was able to place his stamp on Yoruba and Nigerian art in a more legitimate way. He does not claim to have introduced Ladipo to theatre, for he says, 'I knew Duro a long time before I knew of his interest in theatre.'[36] Beier conducted Extra-Mural classes at Osogbo for the University of Ibadan, and got to know Ladipo when he went to the latter's Popular Bar in the evenings for a beer. 'Then there was the trouble about the cantata he wrote for the church,' Beier recalls. 'The church wanted to throw him out. He was very upset, and he came to me. I discussed his interests with him and told him not to worry; he could develop them outside the church.' He thereafter took Ladipo under his wing, arranging performances for him at Osogbo and Ibadan.

The first play he wrote, Beier says, was 'very bad: slapstick and music like church music. He tried to imitate Ogunde, who was then very popular'. Beier asked him why he wrote like that, telling him it was nothing like the sort of thing he said he was interested in, and nothing like his cantata music. Then Beier gave him Johnson's *The History of the Yorubas* to read. From the book came the materials for *Oba Moro* (read *Oba Amórò*) and *Oba Kò So*, the greatest of Ladipo's achievements. Beier also provided the material for *Eda* (Hugo von Hoffmansthal's *Everyman*), and *Oba Waja* (a true story which he said he first offered to Soyinka, but which the latter did not use until much later in his *Death and the King's Horseman*).

Beier gives Ladipo a good deal of artistic credit:

> He had a very good imagination and was very inventive.... When he was composing *Oba Kò So* I would look at a passage and ask, 'What is the message?' or, 'What is the mood?' After that I would ask, 'What kind of music would best convey it to the audience?' Immediately he would turn to his wife and say, 'We will try a, b, and c.' Just like that.'

Rejecting criticisms such as Nwoko's that he was a puppeteer manipulating Ladipo from behind a screen he said:

> I helped him because he wanted to write for a particular kind of theatre, and I knew more about it than he did, so I gave him advice. I encouraged him to write; there is nothing wrong in that. The relationship between us was a perfect one between an artist and his friend.... I also suggested stories to him, but he had his own ideas also.

Beier says that after *Moremi* (1966) he wanted to separate himself from Ladipo's group because of all the talk that Ladipo was not a *bona fide* artist. Ladipo was very upset because he thought Beier was deserting him. That was the reason, said Beier, why he left Nigeria for New Guinea. We are free to interpret this information as we choose, but it does seem to vindicate Nwoko's assessment of the degree of Ladipo's dependence on his mentor.

There is another reason to believe that Nwoko is right on the mark, and that is the state of the Ladipo company since Beier's departure. Revealing of this is the performance of *Èkù Idà* by the Duro Ladipo Theatre at the Cultural Centre in Ibadan on March 15, 1983. It was to be one of the events marking the fifth anniversary of Ladipo's death, but it was hardly a fitting memorial to him. The show started an hour late, and when it did begin, it was slow, the dialogue was hardly audible, the characters engaged in interminable horseplay with frequent musical interruptions, and at times the horseplay was so drawn out that members of the audience shouted, 'O tó! E sèmíì!' (Enough! Go on to something else!). The plot of the opera is based on Shakespeare's *Hamlet*; after two and a half hours the performers got to the appearance of Hamlet's ghost! It is true, of course, that Ladipo was no longer there to discipline the group, but it is also true that it did not have any great success even during Ladipo's lifetime after Beier left.

The Designation 'Folk Opera'

In passing I will at this point comment on some controversy about the designation 'folk opera'. Rotimi says that it is 'a term coined by Ulli Beier'[37] (Karin Barber also notes that 'folk' is 'Beier's term for popular'.[38]) Although Rotimi does not question its applicability we may see the attribution in the context of the discussion of Beier's role in Nigerian arts, and in that of the complaint that 'opera' as a term 'mystified rather than explained the aesthetic and structural features of the form', while 'folk' suggests a dichotomy between the low art of the people and 'the high art of talented and sophisticated individuals'.[39] The word 'opera' was in use to describe performances well before Beier arrived in the country. Note, for example, the description of A.B. David's 1944 program as a 'Yoruba Native Air Opera'. In using the word Beier undoubtedly meant to acknowledge the relationship between Ogunde's art and the earlier operas. I do not agree with the charge of mystification because, unlike those who insist on 'theatre' and 'drama' for traditional rituals and festivals, those of us who use 'opera' for the type of performances under discussion will willingly concede that we use it for want of a better word, and that its use is by no means an insinuation that the thing so described is the same as opera as it is known in the west.

As for 'folk', Jeyifo appears to concur with Adedeji's opinion that its use for the opera 'unequivocally repudiates its artistic worth, the creative dynamism of its artist and the unfettered and adventurous experimentation of its singular practitioners'. Using the qualifier 'folk', according to him, is 'relegating the form to a folk genre'.[40] Jeyifo believes (if I understand him correctly) that the critics who adopt the dichotomy have increasingly promoted the 'Yoruba Travelling Theatre (the designation he prefers), 'initially dubbed a "folk" art', as 'the exclusive creation of the leading actor-managers ... this change being supposedly an indication of a "progressive" evolution from the "folk" to the "sophisticated"' (p. 3).

Such statements as the foregoing assume, I believe, a contempt for folk forms that I certainly do not share. Rather than intending to disparage the opera or repudiate its artistic worth, the use of 'folk' represents a desire to indicate, as Jeyifo first surmised (p. 2), its closer proximity to the vast majority of the people than to the elite theatre in its personnel, language and theme. The alternate designation 'popular' seeks very much the same end, to situate the form between the traditional and the elite, without however making value judgments regarding its worth compared to either. Karin Barber's definition of 'popular' art as 'the new unofficial arts of colonialism and post-colonialism, produced by the profound and accelerating social change that has characterized these periods' (p. 13) is quite apt. I would not object to substituting 'popular' for 'folk', especially because at least it avoids the confusion inherent in the fact that 'folk' is also used to describe traditional forms. But one must observe that even 'popular' is susceptible to the accusation that it suggests inferiority to the sophisticated or elite.

With regard to the figure of the troupe leader as an 'individual artiste', or as a mere depersonalized expression of the will of the masses, the weight of the evidence (and of opinion) is that such people as Ogunde, Ogunmola and Ladipo operated as individual artistes – as entrepreneurs. Their operations, in Barber's words, 'revolve around personal rather than purely financial relationships' (p. 30), and were conducted in an 'individualistic entrepreneurial climate' (p. 65). Michael Etherton also stresses that the popular theatre is based on personality,[41] and adds categorically, 'Ogunde's theatre company is Hubert Ogunde' (p. 48). Adedeji's point in the passage quoted above is that the opera was always the creation of 'unfettered ... singular practitioners'. We may also recall here Ogunbiyi's comment (quoted earlier) that 'in the end, the artist is his own man, on his own, alone'.

Themes

Some further observations about the subjects of the operas may help to clear some misunderstandings about the motivating impulses of the dramatists, especially Ogunde and Ladipo. I am responding here in particular to a comment[42] that Ogunde did not come up with a performance critical of the recent regimes in the country, whereas in the past he rose to the occasion whenever there was some crisis, as he did with *Strike and Hunger* (1945), *Human Parasites* (1946), *Bread and Bullet* (1950), and *Yoruba Ronu* (1964). Jeyifo cites Irele's view that Ogunde had not responded to the events simply because they had not sufficiently challenged 'his sense of event'. That rationalization does not, however, match Clark's portrayal of the artiste as 'a pure nationalist' whose theatre fought bravely for independence,[43] and who vacated politics in the 1950s only because of threatening rivalry from Bobby Benson. That he produced *Yoruba Ronu* in 1964 would seem to indicate that he had by then rid himself of the threat, and it is difficult to credit any view that events in Nigeria since 1964 had not been much more horrendous than anything that happened in the early 1960s.[44]

I suggest that we look at Ogunde's career and the choices he made in it for the clues for his motivation. The first thing to recall is that although he began within the church, and for the first few operas chose biblical themes, he soon broke away, as he put it, from both church context and biblical themes. He did not do so because he had undergone some conversion, but because he read the market well and adjusted to it. Clark correctly places *Human Parasites* in the context of the long-running controversy about *aso ebí*, and we may do the same with *Highway Eagle*, which came also in response to a crime wave so intense that the *Daily Service* of

January 20 and 21, 1944 carried the item, 'Cut This Out And Keep It For Reference: Thefts and Burglaries.' It listed thirty steps citizens could take to help the police force in preventing and detecting various crimes. With regard to *Herbert Macaulay* (1946), Ogunde said, 'when our old father Herbert Macaulay died, I thought it was a good opportunity to recall, to relive his life...' (1970), and, of course, it was also guaranteed to be extremely popular with the masses.

Ogunde has always been quick to make the adjustments necessary for commercial success. In 1970 he told the story of the trip to the Gold Coast which had a profound impact on his style. He made the trip in 1947 with *King Solomon*, toured the cities for three months, and returned to Nigeria with five pounds sterling. He had yet to pay his rent and his performers. The people of the Gold Coast not only did not understand the Yoruba of his opera, but they also did not think much of the sedate style of his music. Before he left for home, he said, someone advised him that if he came back he should 'come with some trumpets, saxophone, play highlife, play jazz....' He took the lesson to heart and did as he was advised. 'That was what started my using saxophones, trumpets ..., musical instruments, in my shows.' He went back nine months later, and after a twenty-day tour, he said, 'I came back with a thousand eight-hundred pounds.'

During an interview I had with Ladipo in his Ibadan residence in 1969 he said: 'Ogunde called me one day, and told me that I cannot be successful with the kind of plays I perform. He said that people do not like dirty clothes. My costumes are all ancient costumes. He said I have nothing shining. He advised me to create something light, something that will attract people.' And during his presentation at the 1970 seminar, with Ogunde sitting at the same table, he repeated essentially the same story:

> Hubert told me one day, as a father advising his son, that this line you are taking is very interesting, but I doubt very much how you can live comfortably, because these plays may not fetch money. But I advise you that any time you are putting on some plays, try as much as possible to introduce some social satire to bring in money. And that is his advice I followed that brought *Eda*, and *Eda* has been very successful.

In his own presentation Ogunde cited the differences in the tastes of various audiences – the Yoruba, the Eastern Nigerian, the Northern Nigerian, the Ghanaian, the Togolese – and differentiated among what sorts of performance he would offer to each. His move from stage to screen in the years before his death may also be seen as one calculated to capitalize on the greater profit potential of the new medium. These comments are not to say that he has no political interests but to caution against over-emphasizing the wrong element in his career as an artist.

To return to our main question, we may justifiably assert that the opera did not evolve from *egúngún*, and that it is an error to lump its practitioners together with the performers of traditional rituals. It owes its origin to the social dynamics engendered by the contact of Africa and Europe in a particular part of West Africa.

Conclusion

Although de Graft sees the 'cultural admixture' that resulted from Africa's contact with Europe as not totally devoid of saving graces, he does believe that 'as far as the growth of dramatic art is concerned ... we may say that the effect of the last few centuries of Europe's impact on African expression has been largely disruptive'.[45] He holds that view because he blames Europe for depriving Africa of one of his five conditions necessary for a society to develop drama, which he apparently believes to be a necessary component of any culture. I believe that it is more correct to see the development of the opera as a creative achievement of a new social class, the partly assimilated elements of the urban centres, people responding to new circumstances and adapting the inventions and affectations of the elite class.

As for the involvement of foreigners, I do not think it is necessarily bad, for it is entirely possible for a person not born into a culture to understand it through study, and to be capable of contributing to it at its frontier with other cultures. Input from a foreigner, in other words, could be mutually rewarding. Besides, it is not so outrageously illogical to say that African writers have been (and are) busily contributing to European cultures.

Finally, it is not out of place to observe that despite the charges made by some scholars that other scholars disparage the opera or popular arts in general, the fact remains that they share the same fate with traditional arts in the academic world – they are studied and written about as curiosities, but they are not created or performed by academic types, nor is the teaching of their creation and performance a part of the educational curricula. Robert G. Armstrong complained to me in 1970 that while there was no shortage of Nigerian scholars writing *on* the opera, there was no academic interest in actually creating and performing operas. Wande Abimbola once wrote regarding oral literature: 'Scholars interested in oral literature should not limit themselves to collecting, transcribing, translating and analyzing. They should cultivate an active interest in the chanting of the material. Oral literature, an interesting and fertile aspect of our culture, cannot be preserved on tapes and tape-recorders, nor can it be preserved through analysis and translation.'[46] Anyone who has heard him chant *Ifá* verses will know that he practises what he preaches. If those of us interested in the opera could follow his prescription we would be demonstrating in the most practical way our respect for the form. Rather that trading accusations about which scholars champion the opera and which regard it as inferior to elite art, we might see ourselves, all of us, as accomplices in the inferiorization of folk and popular forms, as long as we treat them only as objects of study and not as activities we would ourselves become involved in.

NOTES

1. Henceforth I will use this word to refer to the Yoruba phenomenon without enclosing it in quotation marks, and without any suggestion that it belongs in the same genre as Wagner's or Puccini's operas.
2. Ola Rotimi, 'Traditional Nigerian Drama', in Bruce King, ed., *Introduction to Nigerian Literature* (New York: Africana Publishing Corporation, 1972), p. 36.
3. Akinwunmi Isola, 'Modern Yoruba Drama', in Yemi Ogunbiyi, ed., *Drama and Theatre in Nigeria: A Critical Source Book* (Lagos: Nigeria Magazine, 1981), p. 399.
4. Ebun Clark, *Hubert Ogunde: The Making of Nigerian Theatre* (Oxford: Oxford University Press, 1980), p. 4.
5. Kacke Götrick, *Apidan Theatre and Modern Drama* (Stockholm, Sweden: Almqvist & Wiksell International, 1984), p. 32.
6. Joel 'Yinka Adedeji, 'Trends in the Content and Form of the Opening Glee in Yoruba Drama', in Bernth Lindfors, ed., *Forms of Folklore in Africa: Narrative, Poetic, Gnomic, Dramatic* (Austin: University of Texas Press, 1977), p. 188.
7. Oyekan Owomoyela, 'Give Me Drama Or...: The Argument on the Existence of Drama in Traditional Africa', *The African Studies Review*, 28/4, 1985, pp. 28-45.
8. Oyin Ogunba, 'Traditional African Festival Drama', in Oyin Ogunba and A. Irele, eds., *Theatre in Africa* (Ibadan: University of Ibadan Press, 1978), p. 9.
9. 'Biodun Jeyifo, *The Yoruba Popular Travelling Theatre of Nigeria* (Lagos: Nigeria Magazine, 1984), p. 6.
10. Kacke Götrick, op. cit., p. 10.
11. Ibid., pp. 130-131.
12. Carolyn Porter, 'Are We Being Historical Yet?', *The South Atlantic Quarterly*, 87/4, 1988, p. 771.
13. Ruth Finnegan, *Oral Literature in Africa* (Oxford: The Clarendon Press, 1970).
14. For example, Oyin Ogunba, op. cit., p. 25.
15. J.C. de Graft, 'Roots in African Drama', in Eldred Durosimi Jones, ed., *African Literature Today, No. 8: Drama in Africa* (London: Heinemann, 1976), p. 11.
16. F. Abiola Irele, *In Praise of Alienation*. Inaugural Lecture delivered on 22 November 1982 at the University of Ibadan, p. 12.
17. Karin Barber, 'Popular Arts in Africa', *African Studies Review*, 30/3, 1987, pp. 1-78.
18. Michael J.C. Echeruo, 'Concert and Theatre in Nineteenth Century Lagos', *Nigeria Magazine*, 74, 1962, pp. 68-74 (reprinted in Yemi Ogunbiyi, ed., *Drama and Theatre in Nigeria: A Critical Source Book* (Lagos: Nigeria Magazine, 1981), pp. 357-369); and *Victorian Lagos: Aspects of Nineteenth Century Lagos Life* (London: Macmillan Education Limited, 1977).
19. Lynn Leonard, 'The Growth of Entertainment of Non-African Origin in Lagos 1866-1920', M.A. Thesis, University of Ibadan, 1967.
20. Oyekan Owomoyela, 'Folklore and the Rise of Theatre Among the Yoruba', Ph.D. Dissertation, The University of California, Los Angeles, 1970.
21. Kwabena N. Bame, *Come to Laugh: African Traditional Theatre in Ghana* (New York: Lilian Barber Press, Inc., 1985).

22. E. J. Collins' account of the development of the form ('Comic Opera in Ghana', *African Arts*, IX/2, 1976, pp. 50-57) corresponds with Bame's.
23. 'The shows were performed in English and tickets were expensive, with the result that most of the audience were from the educated Ghanaian elite. According to people who saw these shows, Yalley's sketches were assisted by a tap dancer and a harmonium player who together provided a program of then-current popular Western dance music, such as Black American ragtime and ballroom dances like the foxtrot, quickstep and waltz' (Kwabena N. Bame, op. cit., p. 8; further references are included in the text).
24. In an earlier article ('Comic Play in Ghana', *African Arts/Arts d'Afrique*, 1/4, 1968, Bame saw the origin in 'the use of dramatization and mime in story-telling' (p. 30).
25. Kwabena N. Bame, *Come to Laugh: African Traditional Theatre in Ghana*, p. 12; E.J. Collins, 'Comic Opera in Ghana', op. cit., p. 52.
26. Ogunde's testimony that I will quote from in the following pages was part of his presentation during the seminar held in Trenchard Hall at the University of Ibadan early in 1970 to commemorate twenty-five years of the operatic movement in Nigeria. Joel Adedeji, then the head of the department of Theatre Arts, organized the seminar in conjunction with the Institute of African Studies. The chairman was Wole Soyinka. The account by Duro Ladipo that I will later refer to comes from his own presentation on the same occasion. I taped the seminar for the Institute.
27. H.W. Turner, *History of an African Independent Church, I: The Church of the Lord (Aladura)* and *II: The Life and Faith of the Church of the Lord (Aladura)* (Oxford: The Clarendon Press, 1967); p. 7. Further references are included in the text.
28. Adrian Hastings, *A History of African Christianity, 1950-1975* (Cambridge: Cambridge University Press, 1979), p. 81.
29. Joel 'Yinka Adedeji, 'The Literature of the Yoruba Opera', *Spectrum: Monograph Series in the Arts and Sciences* III, 1973, p. 49. Further references are included in the text.
30. Joel 'Yinka Adedeji, 'Trends in the Content and Form of the Opening Glee in Yoruba Drama', p. 193.
31. The following are the lyrics to an opening song by Ebenezer Obey, the popular *jùjú* artiste, and a thoroughly devoted Christian:

> Olójó òní o, ìbà!
> A júbà ká tó seré.
> Ágbààgbà ìlú o, ìbà!
> A júbà ká tó seré.
> Omodé ìlú o, ìbà!
> A júbà ká tó seré.
> Bómodé bá ti júbà fÓlúwa
> Ònà á là, ire á wolé.
> Bágbààgbà bá ti júbà fÓlúwa
> Ònà á là, ire á wolé.
> Mo júbà, mo júbà, kíbà mi se o;
> Mo júbà o, ìbà!
> Ìbà fómodé ìlú,
> Mo júbà o, ìbà!
> Ìbà fágbààgbà ìlú.
> Mo júbà o, ìbà!
> Ìbà Olórun, ìbà èèyàn!
> Mo júbà o, ìbà!

(Oh, Owner of this day, homage!
We pay homage before performing.
Oh, elders of the town, homage!
We pay homage before performing.
Oh, youths of the town, homage!
We pay homage before performing.
If a youth pays homage to the Lord
The path will clear and good will enter.
If an elder pays homage to the Lord
The path will clear and good will enter.
I pay homage, I pay homage, may my homage be heeded;
Oh, I pay homage, homage!
Homage to the youth of the town,
Oh, I pay homage, homage!
Homage to the elders of the town.
Oh, I pay homage, homage!
Homage to God, homage to people!
Oh, I pay homage, homage!)

32. 'Biodun Jeyifo, op. cit., p. 11.
33. Oyekan Owomoyela, 'Folklore and the Rise of Theatre Among the Yoruba', op. cit., p. 30.
34. Demas Nwoko, 'Search for a New African Theatre', in Yemi Ogunbiyi, ed., *Drama and Theatre in Nigeria: A Critical Source Book* (Lagos: Nigeria Magazine, 1981), pp. 469-470.
35. Yemi Ogunbiyi, 'The Popular Theatre: A Tribute to Duro Ladipo', in *Drama and Theatre in Nigeria: A Critical Source Book*, p. 339.
36. In this context I am quoting from an interview I had with Ulli Beier on his visit to the University of Ibadan in 1983 in connection with the anniversary of Ladipo's death. The interview has been published in my contribution to Tayo Olafioye's *Critic as Terrorist*, with the title, 'Ulli Beier and Yoruba Theater: A Conversation'.
37. Ola Rotimi, op. cit., p. 36. He refers to Ulli Beier's 1954 article with the title, 'Yoruba Folk Operas'. But D.W. Macrow also published in the same year an article on the same subject with the title, 'Folk Opera'.
38. Karin Barber, op. cit., p. 10. Further references are included in the text.
39. 'Biodun Jeyifo, op. cit., p. 2. Further references are included in the text.
40. Joel 'Yinka Adedeji, 'The Literature of the Yoruba Opera', p. 55.
41. Michael Etherton, *The Development of African Drama* (New York: Africana Publishing Company, 1982), p. 30. Further references are included in the text.
42. 'Biodun Jeyifo, op. cit., pp. 107-108.
43. Ebun Clark, *Hubert Ogunde: The Making of Nigerian Theatre* (Oxford: Oxford University Press, 1980), p. 91.
44. This discussion was written before Ogunde's death in 1990.
45. J.C. de Graft, op. cit., p. 14.
46. Wande Abimbola, 'Notes on the Collection, Transcription, Translation and Analysis of Yoruba Oral Literature', in Adebisi Afolayan, ed., *Yoruba Language and Literature* (Ibadan: University Press Limited and University of Ife Press, 1982), p. 80.

CHRISTOPHER BALME

The Caribbean Theatre of Ritual: Derek Walcott's *Dream on Monkey Mountain*, Michael Gilkes's *Couvade: A Dream-Play of Guyana*, and Dennis Scott's *An Echo in the Bone*

The 1950s and 1960s were decades of considerable programmatic as well as practical theatrical activity in the Caribbean. As the various islands prepared for and moved into independence, so too did the calls for an indigenous Caribbean theatre, free from the taint of colonial influences, gain in number and volume. Although the political idea of federation very quickly proved to be unworkable, the notion of a Caribbean national drama and theatre as a culturally unifying force remained a vital idea at least until the early 1970s. The various plays and programmes aimed at demonstrating and promoting an indigenous West Indian theatre all sought to quarry the rich mine of the expressive 'folk' culture: the musical, dance, story-telling and processional traditions, which contained a pronounced performative component. First the patois and dialects, the Caribbean 'first' languages, were found to be stage-worthy, and then by the late 1950s the performance forms themselves began to be co-opted for the new theatre.

In review, it is possible to discern two main lines of development in the process of indigenizing West Indian theatre. The first and most widespread movement can be termed the Theatre of Exuberance. Here the colour and celebrative nature of Carnival and the various indigenous masquerade traditions were supposed to provide the basis for a theatre and drama incorporating and exploiting the 'Gesamtkunstwerk' of Carnival. The most eloquent theorist and practitioner of the Theatre of Exuberance was, and perhaps still is, Errol Hill. In 1974 Hill outlined the central points of his programme in the article, 'The Emergence of a National Drama in the West Indies',[1] which he concludes with a seven point credo for a national theatre, an idea which Hill had been propagating since the 1950s. He is very eclectic in his choice of folk forms adaptable for the stage. Referring to his own efforts as a promoter of a folk-based theatre in the 1950s, Hill writes:

He urged theatre artists to seek inspiration from the indigenous theatre of the folk, not as curiosities but as the fibre from which a national drama is fashioned: the carnival and calypso, John Canoe and dead-wake ceremonies, Shango and Poco-mania, Tea Meetings, La Rose and Vieux Croix festivals, the Hosein and other Indian customs, native music and rhythms, dialect as a serious medium of expression.[2]

While Hill himself tended to favour the exuberance of Carnival and calypso, the theatrical possibilities of wake ceremonies and the hieratic worlds of Caribbean syncretic cults began to exert a fascination on other dramatists and directors. Hill had already exploited some of the theatrical potential of the Shango cult in his musical comedy *Man Better Man*. Here however the ritualistic acts are depicted in a comic light and ridiculed as quackery and bush medicine. By the late 1960s and early 1970s plays were being created which took the ritualism of such cults very seriously indeed and ushered in a whole new development in Caribbean theatre.

In 1970 Marina Maxwell, co-founder of the Yard theatre in Jamaica, propagated a combination of the two trends. Like Hill, she considered Carnival to be the seedbed of West Indian theatre. In her programme (which, as the name suggests, sought to set up theatre in the backyards of Kingston ghettos, open to the people and using performance forms famil-iar to the people), the impulses of decentralized political popular theatre practised by European and American ensembles conjoined with the in-digenization process in Caribbean writing and art. In her manifesto 'Towards a Revolution in the Arts' (1970), Maxwell divided the Caribbean artistic community into 'unconscious' (folk, Rasta) and 'schizoid' (Western influenced) artists:

Throbbing at the heart of our identity is the drum, our African identity [...] the rhythmic possession of and by the drum [...] They [the unconscious artists] are pos-sessed by the gods of the drum. We, the schizoid artists, torn between our educa-tion and our instinct, stand outside the *hounfour* as the ceremony continues despite us.[3]

Maxwell's choice of the *hounfour,* the arena of Vodoun ceremony, as a metaphor for Caribbean folk art is symptomatic of the increasing interest in ritual forms. Representative and artistic highpoints of this movement are Derek Walcott's *Dream on Monkey Mountain* (1967), Michael Gilkes' *Couvade* (1972) and Dennis Scott's *An Echo in the Bone* (1974).

Before continuing, it is necessary to clarify what is meant by ritual for the purposes of this investigation. In performance theory, particularly in the writings of Richard Schechner and Victor Turner, the term has been expanded to encompass any number of socially or religiously significant stereotyped actions that are conditioned in some way by a ceremony of prescribed order. Schechner concurs with Eric Berne's definition: 'A ritual is a stereotyped series of simple complementary transactions programmed by external social forces.'[4] This definition becomes so all-encompassing that it is of very little intellectual use: sponge-like, it soaks up phenomena rather than providing them with clear conceptual contours. Scholars working in the area of non-European performance forms have had to, out of necessity, find a more clearly defined distinction between terms such as theatre, performance and ritual. Anthony Graham-White postulates for example that in African cultures 'the distinction between ritual and drama is not formulated', but that the 'ultimate distinction lies in the attitudes of the performers and spectators'; a ritual contains 'expectations of consequences beyond itself'.[5] The expectation of efficacy on the part of the spectator-participant is thus the crucial defining factor. This limits the understanding of rituals here to those performed in some kind of religio-spiritual context. In specific terms, the Caribbean rituals that Walcott, Gilkes or Scott have incorporated into their plays stem for the most part from the rites and ceremonies of Afro-Christian syncretic cults such as Shango, Pocomania and Revivalism.

Both the Theatre of Exuberance and the Theatre of Ritual are examples of syncretic theatre. This is a widespread movement of theatrical reform and programmatic renewal observable in most postcolonial societies since the 1950s. Syncretic theatre in its broadest sense can be defined as the attempt to marry the traditional performance forms of a (usually colonized) society with the Western theatrico-aesthetic tradition. Caribbean cultures abound of course in examples of syncretism; it is moreover especially observable in the revivalist cults and folk religions such as Vodoun, Shango, Kumina and Pocomania. Here, however, the interpenetration of European, African and Indian influences is the product of an osmotic process of absorption; the syncretic theatre of Walcott and the others is a conscious aesthetic, and to some extent also a political programme.

Although the focus here is on anglophone dramatists, it should be pointed out that in Haiti dramatists had begun experimenting with the theatrical possibilities of Vodoun. The psychiatrist Dr Louis Mars, son of Jean Price-Mars, the first theorist of négritude, outlined in 1966 how an autochthonous Haitian drama and theatre could or should be based in Vodoun ceremony and its practice of spirit possession:

> (1) The Vodoun ceremony is inspired by motives of exceptional gravity: it is concerned with death, illness, economic and social crises, all those things which plunge the human soul into confusion.
>
> (2) The various gods are incarnated in their devotees on the basis of a fixed typology transmitted by tradition.
>
> (3) The divine figures constitute ceremonial procedures whose role is central to the course of the religious celebration, but here the Vodoun devotee is not satisfied with just playing a role like a character in ancient Greek drama, he identifies totally with the god, he is (the) god.[6]

The singing, dancing, acts of possession and the fundamentally religious nature of the ceremony moved the Haitian critic Robert Bauduy to hail Vodoun as a form of 'total theatre' marrying these elements into a 'harmonious synthesis which opens the way to renewal of our drama.'[7] The catchwords 'Greek drama', 'total theatre', 'synthesis' and the idea of replacing psychologistic, word-based European drama by a new type of theatre rooted in ritual ceremony – and thus existentially 'vital' in some way to the spectators/participators – are the leitmotifs of the Caribbean Theatre of Ritual. Vodoun represents an important model because it was the first Caribbean cult whose practices were 'marketed' as a tourist attraction: its ceremonial procedures were recognised to have a performative facet which could be appreciated on a purely spectative and not participatory level.

Equally important as the religious practices and their performative expression for the Caribbean Theatre of Ritual were developments in the avant-garde theatre of Europe and America aimed at creating theatrical events (plays is too narrow a term here) based on some kind of ritual experience. This movement has been analyzed by Christopher Innes in his book *Holy Theatre: Ritual and the Avant Garde* (1981). The title is drawn from the writings of Antonin Artaud, the movement's posthumous high priest. Innes' summary of the 'dominant interest' of Holy Theatre could apply equally well to the central formal and thematic features of the Caribbean Theatre of Ritual:

> Beneath variations in style and theme there appears a dominant interest in the irrational and the primitive, which has two basic and complementary facets: the exploration of dream states or the instinctive and subconscious levels of the psyche, and the quasi-religious focus on myth and magic, the experimentation with ritual and the ritualistic patterning of performance.[8]

The other names associated with the catchword 'Holy Theatre' are Peter Brook and Jerzy Grotowski, both of whom are themselves influenced by and openly acknowledge the writings of Artaud. And all three names play a prominent part in Walcott's most important essay on the theatre, 'What the Twilight Says: an Overture' (1970).

The problem of enacting ritual on stage is a complex one and, as Brook cogently demonstrates in the chapter 'Holy Theatre' in *The Empty Space*, a highly questionable theatrical practice. Whether it be a mass, a Nine Night ceremony or Vodoun worship, the presence of religiously disinterested but aesthetically engaged spectators must invariably render the ritual, if not meaningless, then at least spiritually disembowelled. This is by no means a contemporary insight, but rather a predicament which has accompanied all theatre artists and theorists who have attempted to rejuvenate the stage on the basis of its supposed ritual origins. In the European tradition, the full-scale assault on the theatre of words in favour of a theatre of music, choric chants, dance and dream predates Artaud by at least 60 years. Its theoretical program can already be found in Nietzsche's essay, *The Birth of Tragedy from the Spirit of Music* (1872), to give his elliptical apology for Wagner's music drama its full title. Whatever misunderstandings his pamphlet may have caused, the vision of ancient Greek theatre as a dionysiac celebration based on music and dance and attended by a congregation of concelebrants, plus the notion of a dramaturgy based on the logic of dreams, exerted an influence on the European theatre which is still at work today. By framing ritual or ritualized acts within a dream, it is possible to marry a European aesthetic convention with any kind of ritual. The stage tradition of dream dramaturgy dates from Strindberg's proto-expressionistic *A Dream Play*. Its highly influential preface in which Strindberg propagated a dramaturgy based on the associative logic of dreams can be detected in Walcott's 'A Note on Production' to *Dream on Monkey Mountain*.[9]

Turning now to the play itself, one can observe how Walcott has incorporated ritual elements such as spirit possession, revivalist faith-healing, masking and Shango dancing in the fabric of Makak's dream. The dream itself is occasioned by a fit of possession, a psychological state frequently associated with Caribbean cult practices. In the prologue Makak falls into a 'frenzy' of possession and at the same time reflects on this state: 'I fall in a frenzy every full-moon night. I does be possessed'.[10] is his comment as he relates his encounter with the White Goddess. A few minutes later, he actually begins to act out this possession: 'And in that frenzy I began to dance/ With the splendour of a lion/ faster and faster/ Then my body sink' (p. 229). This action is accompanied by drumming and a high level of affective arousal which has a strong similarity to Shango or similar cults which involve spirit possession. What we see is both immediate – the act of possession is acted out – and diegetic – Makak is telling us and those in the prison his story. This is an important filtering and distancing device for the ritual elements. The ensuing action is transported/transformed into the oneiric realm of spirit possession and is the product of a ritual act.

Walcott has explained that this dramaturgical device is necessary in order to mediate the raw power of ritual: 'In *Dream*, the frenzy comes out of a man's relationship to his dream. If this had been realized more heraldically, its power would have been akin to the power of Shango. Yet this might have been impossible, for if the play becomes that powerful, it becomes the ceremony it is imitating.'[11] This is the point which is crucial for the whole question of depicting ritual on stage. Walcott is an artist and not a houngan (a Vodoun priest); he is keenly aware of the need to keep the ritualistic material within the bounds of the aesthetic. This is an important point which separates him from the European promulgators of a ritualistic theatre such as Artaud or The Living Theatre. Of these Walcott writes in 'What the Twilight Says' that their experiments are nothing more than 'the enactment of remorse for the genocides of civilization': 'These self-soiling, penitential cults, the Theatre of the Absurd, the Theatre of

Cruelty, the Poor Theatre, the Holy Theatre, the pseudo-barbarous revivals of primitive tragedy are not threats to civilization but acts of absolution, groping for the outline of pure tragedy, rituals of washing in the first darkness' (p. 6).

The other crucial problem involved in the depiction of ritual on stage concerns the mythology and cosmology on which it is based. Here Walcott's comments on Soyinka's theatre illuminate the problem of the Caribbean theatre artist working in the Afro-European syncretic culture. The Trinidad Theatre Workshop staged a production of Soyinka's *The Road* in 1966. Very much propelled by the ground-swell of the Africanist movement which was gathering strength throughout the Caribbean at the time, Walcott and his actors were confronted with the predicament of coping with the complex cosmology of the Yoruba belief system. Despite the manifold influences of West African culture in the Caribbean, the group was ultimately struggling with an alien mythology. Walcott comments on the highly problematic undertaking of resurrecting 'dead gods' as he calls them: 'Ogun was an exotic for us, not a force. We could pretend to enter his power but he would never possess us, for our invocations were not prayers but devices' (p. 8). In the final analysis, the Theatre Workshop was struggling with the same problem as the Artaudian epigones in the experimental theatres Off-Off-Broadway and in London.

Besides drumming, dancing, and spirit possession, the use of masks is another striking feature which transcends the purely theatrical and attempts to lock into something closer to masking in primal cultures where the wearing of masks involves the transformation of the performers; where they are actually animated by the spirits they are representing.[12] Walcott's comments suggest that the mask on stage can be something more than just a theatrical convention: 'A mask is not, as it is in metropolitan theatre, a device: it is a totem. [...] Modern playwrights who use masks (Brecht and Genet for example) are not avant-garde, but are returning to the primal formalities of Chinese, Japanese and African theatre.'[13] The mask as a totem means that it is not just an aesthetic but is a religious cult object of considerable spiritual power for the wearer/possessor. In *Dream on Monkey Mountain* the white mask with black sisal hair is both a potent image and metaphor within the play, and also a totem for Makak. It is among his few possessions that the Corporal itemizes after his arrest. It is at once a totem of his White Goddess, who is also a *diablesse*, in St Lucian folk mythology, a diabolic, seductive creature,[14] and the catalyst which spurs him into his spiritual odyssey and quest: 'MAKAK: I never see this [the mask] before. [*Pause*] Saddle my horse!' (p. 240). Walcott's description of the mask, especially its black sisal hair, evokes associations with African masks. At the same time it evidently has the power to metamorphose black into white. On its second appearance in Scene 1, after Makak has related his vision to his friend Moustique, the latter discovers the mask, dons and dismisses it as 'cheap stupidness black children putting on [*He puts it on, wriggles and dances*]'. Moustique's fooling has a galvanising effect on Makak. For Moustique, however, it has the association of subterfuge and deceit, which is closer to the connotation masking has on the Western stage. He asks Makak in desperation: 'You think this damn stupidness going to take us there?' (p. 255). Moustique also associates the mask with the schizophrenic attitude of the colonized black towards his own skin colour that Frantz Fanon analyses in his seminal study, *Black Skin, White Masks* (1952). In the market scene, after he has been 'unmasked' for impersonating Makak, Moustique holds out the mask and lambasts the villagers for this naivety: 'All I have is this (*Shows the mask*), black faces, white masks! I tried like you!' (p. 271). The allusion to Fanon's analysis of black alienation, self-hatred and racially conditioned role-playing suggests that Moustique embodies the labile, imitative type of black personality of which Fanon speaks, and that the mask is a metaphor for this condition.

In the Epilogue, after the action has returned from the dream world to reality, the mask reverts to its status as an everyday object, devoid of totemic power. The Corporal protests: 'Everyone round here have one. Why you must keep it, cut it, talk to it?' (p. 323). Makak, however, leaves the jail without the mask, and in so doing, liberates himself from both his nightmares and, it is suggested, from his feeling of racial inferiority. He no longer feels the need to transform himself into a white man.

Other depictions of ritual acts include the faith-healing scenes in Part One, numerous dances and Makak's beheading of the White Goddess. Whereas the latter act, a ceremonial execution, and the nightmarish dance scenes are part of Makak's fantasy world, the faith-healing scenes are very much rituals drawn from contemporary Caribbean reality, although located dramatically in his dream. The opening stage direction of Part One, Scene 2, underscores the theatricality inherent in certain practices of revivalist cults: 'White-robed women, members of a sisterhood, bearing torches, swirl onto the stage [...] They kneel and pray, clap and sing, trying to exorcise [the patient's] sickness' (p. 243). The whole process of attempted healing and Makak's successful cure is accompanied by drumming, dancing and singing. Makak's healing stunt, performed by holding red-hot coals, is similar to the acts of possession involved in Vodoun ceremonies, where possessed devotees may pick up dangerous objects such as red-hot coals without suffering harm.[15] This is not the only device which locates the scene, and the following one in the market-place, in the realm of Vodoun or Obeah. Visually, this is underlined by the presence of Basil, the carpenter, who is dressed like 'Baron Samedi', a well-known figure from Haitian mythology. Basil warns Moustique that he is standing at the crossroads, the renowned cult place in Vodoun practice, where the 'legba' or spirits are supposed to gather. The market-place where Moustique is killed is called significantly Quatre Chcmin crossroads.

The faith-healing scenes may also have some link to traditional Jamaican Jonkonnu, a syncretic performance form dating back to the 17th century and incorporating West African elements – mainly derived from Egungun masquerades, English and Scottish Morris dances, and Carnival processions. Sylvia Wynter has noted in her study of Jonkonnu that apart from the central dance component, these performances formerly included short dance-pantomimes known as 'doctor-plays', 'in which the mock doctor with his assistant was called upon to revive the dead protagonist'. These are death and rebirth plays, known in many pre-Christian cult practices, and as Wynter comments, 'plays about death and resurrection were a feature of many other cults taken to the Caribbean'.[16]

If we take the idea of Makak's 'humiliation' as the core from which the action emanates – Makak and Moustique represent between them the whole gamut of racially conditioned psychic disorders Fanon describes – then the positive movement of the play revolves around the power of dream, possession and hallucination to effect transformations, to be therapeutically efficacious. The emancipatory moment of the play is not just Makak's dream of beheading the White Goddess, although this clearly has some form of therapeutic effect, but the process of the dream odyssey itself. It is suggested that the therapeutic and aesthetic experience of his dreams and hallucinations are in some way ennobling: in this 'zone of occult instability', to use Fanon's term,[17] even the humble woodcutter can undergo an uplifting and ennobling experience, as the final speech unmistakably suggests.

In Michael Gilkes's 'dream-play from Guyana' *Couvade*, first performed in 1972, the two areas, dream and ritual, are also closely entwined and dictate both the structure and the thematic core of the play. In his perceptive introduction to the published play script, Errol Hill has summarized the action as follows:

> The literal tale is about Lionel, a tormented black Caribbean artist-teacher who seeks to resolve the question of his identity through his paintings. In his background lurk African, Amerindian, East Indian and Portuguese ancestors. His young wife, of East Indian and African stock, is pregnant with their first child. The more Lionel strives to unify the competing traditions of his Caribbean past, working feverishly day and night on his canvases, the deeper he sinks into a world of dreams and hallucinations [...] Eventually his mind cracks under the strain, even as the new baby is born to carry on the struggle.[18]

The realistic setting is for the most past Georgetown, Guyana in the present. This milieu accounts, however, for only about 50% of the action. The rest of the play consists of various rites and ritualistic acts, most of which take place within the framework of Lionel's dreams. The rituals and dreams are inextricably linked with (a) the process of artistic creation: the central character is a painter, struggling to find expression for the hieratic worlds of Amerindian, West African and Hindu myth he has immersed himself in; (b) the attempt to objectify a 'dream' of a new Caribbean society composed of a harmonious mixture of this disparate cultural heritage.

Like *Dream on Monkey Mountain* the ritual material is performed within the fictional frame of dream, and like Walcott's play, the central character's psychological and spiritual odyssey involves substantial changes; the rituals Lionel experiences are efficacious in the sense that they are injurious to his mental health. Like Makak and Lestrade, Lionel regresses in order to be reborn. Gilkes has structured his play into four parts, the cryptic titles of which name the play's central thematic concerns. Part One is entitled 'The Sleepers' and connotes primarily the title of the play itself, 'couvade', which as Gilkes explains in a prefatory note, 'is an extremely widespread ritual among so-called "primitive races" like the Carib Indians where the father of the new-born child confines himself to his hammock, and must observe certain rules and taboos aimed at ensuring the child's health and happiness in the future' (p. v). The couvade here is the sleeping, dreaming Lionel. The play opens with a prophetic incantation intoned by an Amerindian shaman. This incantation, given in the original Black Carib language, functions as a leitmotif throughout the play. The shaman addresses a figure asleep in a hammock: 'Sleep, Couvade/ Dream your dream/ When you awake/ Forest will die [...]/ Our people die' (p. 2) This scene, set in a rainforest, glides into Lionel's house, where he is asleep in a hammock. The previous scene has been dreamt and like the ritualistic scenes to follow is an emanation of Lionel's ego, to use the terminology of Expressionist dream dramaturgy.

Part Two is called 'Game of the Stone' and constitutes the play's political thread. It begins with a scene (presumably) from the past involving three gold prospectors ('porkknockers' as they are called in Guyana), one of whom, possibly Lionel's missing grandfather, has hidden a 'carat-stone' from his two partners. This character, called Buckman John-O, is present only as a sleeping figure in a hammock. He is abused by his two partners as a 'trickster bitch' and because of his racial heritage: he is apparently part Amerindian. This buried stone, like many a similar precious object in folk-tales and legends which appeal to man's avarice, seems to emanate a divisive, destructive influence, and sows dissension among the partners. This motif is echoed in further scenes in Part Two. The first (Scene 5) involves a debate, mainly on political and racial questions, between Lionel and his Black activist friend, Arthur, and Lionel's apolitical brother-in-law Eddie; the latter two characters are played by the same actors who played the gold prospectors. The motif receives a ritual treatment in Scene 4 when an Ashanti priest conducts an elaborate ceremony accompanied by talking drums, in which he invokes the god Tano and makes offerings of wine and, more significantly, 'dust of gold' (p. 15).

The title 'Game of the Stone' receives its exegesis in Scene 6. This is a political address by a speaker of the PNP in the inland town of Manoa.[19] He is recognisable as the Shaman from the opening scene and in the course of the speech 'metamorphoses' back into this character. He is thus also a 'trickster', who tells an Anansi story. The politician, a populist, speaking to the economically deprived country people, urges his listeners to political action:

> 'Here in Manoa you have flung a stone into the water [...] Soon these ripples will touch the cities on the coast and people in comfortable houses will feel the shock and be disturbed. [...] But when the gold lies at the bottom of the creek, how else is it to be reached? [...] Yes comrades, the game of the stone is a dangerous game. For he who casts the stone must harbour no stone in his own heart.' (p. 29)

The game of the stone thus seems to mean the competition for an equitable distribution of economic and political power which will bring with it substantial political ripples.

Part Three, the 'Masque of the Ancestors', comprises the thematic core and transports the 'message' of the play primarily in a series of impressive 'coups de théâtre'. It invokes the vision of a syncretic merging of cultures as the key to harmony and a new society in the Caribbean. The idea is concretized in a complex theatrical vocabulary of visual and acoustic signs which underscore perhaps even more than the spoken text Lionel's vision of the new, syncretic culture. For example, the Ashanti priest re-enters, this time accompanied by the music of Chinese cymbals not the African talking drums. Contemporary Caribbean syncretic culture manifests itself in a Jordanite revivalist meeting. The syncretic nature of this cult, which dates back to the beginning of this century, is made particularly tangible in the figure of the preacher, who is the barely disguised Ashanti priest. His costume and ceremonial regalia also underline the convergence of Judaio-Christian, African and Eastern elements: 'He wears heavy bead necklaces and an elaborate, turban-like headdress. He carries a ceremonial staff, like a shepherd's crook which gleams smooth as mahogany' (p. 42). The preacher articulates in standard revivalist manner the message of re-birth and spiritual renewal which Lionel is grappling with on an aesthetic and politico-cultural level. The scene ends with a hymn 'you must be born again' and switches back to Lionel's studio where he is at work on a new painting, 'A Composite Man'. The stage direction reads: 'the figure of a Composite Man, something like an Aztec/Toltec totem, made up of African/Amerindian/Hindu elements' (p. 46). The scene glides into another dream sequence in which Lionel literally dreams a *Masque of the Ancestors*. In this dance a composite mandala figure representing Amerindian, African and Southern Indian gods assumes the form of the god Shiva. The dance culminates in Lionel's sacrificial death and rebirth: he is engulfed in an oversized version of his painting 'The Robe' – 'the whole thing is mostly a blend of African and Amerindian motifs. But there are other elements, too. Indian, Chinese...' (p. 19), Lionel explains to Arthur – from which he emerges, foetus-like, streaked with blood. Transposed into the real world, Lionel has suffered a kind of mental collapse; his wife, Pat, finds him lying on the floor, 'his face streaked with paint' (p. 51).[20]

The final part, 'Child of the Vessel', refers unmistakably to images of birth: directly to the imminent birth of Lionel's and Pat's child – Lionel sees his child as the embodiment of his syncretic vision – and indirectly to the birth, the outbreak of political unrest up-country as a result of the murder of the PNP politician Buckman. The play ends as Lionel, now hospitalized after his breakdown, 'squats on the bed, having assumed [...] the DREAMER'S "foetal" position' (p. 64). This image fades into the rainforest setting of the opening scene. Now, all the figures of his ritualistic dream world – the Shaman, the Ashanti priest, Carib dancers – are grouped around a cot. The priest and the Shaman close the play by invoking their respective deities and the sleeping couvade.

Thematically, Gilkes is grappling with some of the most complex and pressing questions facing (not just) the Caribbean writer. Indeed, the braid of mythic, political, artistic, racial and interpersonal strands Gilkes weaves may even obscure the play's ultimate capacity for communication on a once-seen theatrical level. More crucial for this discussion is, however, the use he makes of the rituals and the theatrical form they are expressed in. To stage the rites and ceremonies of Amerindian shamans and Ashanti priests runs the risk of resurrecting Walcott's 'dead gods'. While the theatrical power of these incantations and rituals is undoubted, their ability to invoke more than an aesthetic response must be questioned. This assumes of course that Gilkes the dramatist, like his character Lionel, is wanting to probe into the submerged layers of the middle-class Guyanese (and perhaps wider Caribbean) consciousness in order to stir up some form of resonance to this heritage. With the exception perhaps of the Jordanite revivalist meeting and even allowing for the Amerindian population who live mainly in the inaccessible parts of the country, the rituals shown have very little immediate religio-spiritual foundation in contemporary Guyanese society.

In 1974, with the production of *An Echo in the Bone* by the Jamaican poet, playwright and theatre director Dennis Scott, we see a ritual which is an essential part of the spiritual fabric of its society forming the framework of a play. The work is based on a Nine Night ceremony, a widespread death ritual practised throughout Jamaica. A wake is held nine nights after the deceased person's death to ensure that the spirit is expedited away and will leave the family in peace. The ceremony consists of singing, dancing, games and story-telling and, depending on the denomination or sect performing it, can vary considerably.[21] The social milieu of *An Echo in the Bone*, poor farm labourers, and the ritualistic elements of the ceremony – drumming, spirit possession, rum drinking and ganja smoking – suggest that the participants are followers of a revivalist cult such as Pocomania or even Kumina, syncretic cults with a high retention of African culture.

First performed in Jamaica in 1974,[22] the play has been widely performed in the Caribbean and other countries. The action takes place in an old

barn, nine nights after the disappearance of Crew, a peasant labourer, and
the murder of the landowner Mr Charles. Crew is suspected of the murder
and his wife Rachel believes him drowned. She decides to hold a wake,
a Nine Night, and gathers around her sons, Jacko and Son Son, her
daughter-in-law, Brigit, a mute drummer and various other friends. The
play is structured around this ceremony but is interspersed by a number
of historical flashbacks going back to the slave trade and ending with the
murder.

Apart from newspaper reviews, the only substantial critical and interpretative comment on the play is provided by Errol Hill in his introduction to the anthology *Plays for Today* where it is published. Hill emphasizes
the ritual framework which enables the play to range widely in time and
space. Through 'the transforming power of ritual ceremony' the 'mundane
stage picture becomes a slave ship moored off the African coast, the
auctioneer's office, a grocer's shop, a wooded hillside, a Great House, a
field, and a room in Rachel's cottage'. The characters themselves also
undergo changes and take on a number of roles. 'Here the act of possession, which is the central objective of the ritual, induces a change of
persona in the possessed individual without any obvious change in facial
make-up or dress' (p. 11).

Of the three plays considered here, *An Echo in the Bone* is the one which
explores to the greatest extent the theatrical possibilities of ritual. In so
doing Dennis Scott establishes, or better perhaps, re-establishes the link
between the aesthetic stage of Western theatre and the transforming
power of ritual-based performance. Scott's play comes closest to actual re-
enactment on stage: the drumming, rum-drinking, libations and recital of
the dead-wake litany (cf. p. 84). The act of possession becomes a kind of
paradigm, a ritual equivalent, for the modern convention of role-playing
on the stage where one actor can assume a multiplicity of roles. The play
employs the aesthetic framework of film – the action is structured around
a series of flashbacks – yet its belief-system is fundamentally Afro-
Caribbean.

The acceptance of causal links between a family in the present and the
slave ships of 1792 is one that tends to strain the credibility or even deeply
disinterest the Western spectator. However, for cults such as Pocomania
and especially Kumina, where strong links with the ancestors and ancestor
worship are key notions, such causality is an integral part of the belief-
system and ceremonial practice.[23] It is a characteristic of many non- or
semi-literate cultures that the oral tradition functions to a far greater
degree than in scribal cultures to keep the memory of past generations
very much alive and immediate through frequent invocation of their lives
and deeds.[24] The memory of degradation, both racial and personal, is
clearly something that cannot be forgotten or erased through political
independence and a change in political structures. As the old cannabis
grower P puts it:

'Three hundred years crying into the white man's ground, to make the cane green, and nothing to show. [...] Nothing to show! That's what he always said. And then they plough you back into the canes, and nobody remember how strong you was. [...]'

RACHEL: 'I remember. I remember. Thirty years long like three hundred.' [*Hums and the others follow*] (pp. 86f.)

On the one hand the 'echo in the bone' is personal and familial memory kept alive by the oral tradition and ritual ceremonies, on the other, it is deeply ingrained racial memory, transmitted by and located in the collective unconscious of the race or culture. Scott seems to be operating with a concept which is close to C.G. Jung's definition of the collective unconscious as primal images and archetypal symbols which connect all races and form the common psycho-mythical bedrock of all mankind. It is important to remember, as Jung himself stresses, that it is not the images themselves which are transmitted but the ability to imagine them.[25] Just as Freud explored and deciphered the symbolic language of dreams as a *via regia* to the unconscious of the individual, so too can the act of spirit possession be seen as a means of unlocking the racial memory of a cultural group.

The formal theatrical devices Scott uses are drawn from a wide range of non-illusionistic theatrical techniques. The characters assume other roles during the flashbacks, both black and white, although Scott specifies that all characters are black. This was facilitated in at least one production by the use of masks when playing white characters. Not only does this technique effect a nice reversal of traditional racial stereotyping and the Black and White Minstrel image of the negro on stage, but as Victor Questel remarked in a review: 'the use of the mask enables the actor to explore the echo in the well of his unconscious.'[26] In the final, climatic scene in which Son Son, in the role of his father, acts out the murder of Mr Charles, the landowner, the clear shifts between the immediate stage time of the Nine Night ceremony and the past begin to blur. In the previous scenes drumming moved the action effortlessly by means of a kind of acoustic cross-fade from the present to the past. As the action approaches the immediate past, the murder of Mr Charles, and coupled with the affective arousal engendered by the events leading up to the act, Scott employs a form of scenic foreshortening to emphasize the growing excitement. The murder is acted out in the present by Son Son, who is possessed by his father's spirit. He trudges on the spot while the other actors/characters (the distinction is difficult to make at this point) form a chorus; they block his way and utter fragments of speech which appear to bombard Son Son's/Crew's consciousness:

CHORUS: What's one more nigger more or less
Lazy bitch
[*laughs*] Lost your tongue? You dumb?

[...]
Overboard, and tell the Captain (p. 130)

The scene climaxes with Son Son/Crew holding his machete high over the prostrate body of Stone/Mr Charles. The drumming stops, the chorus utters a 'long building scream' (p. 131) which ends in a blackout.

Drumming and choric screams are not, however, anything quintessentially Caribbean – London theatre audiences had seen exactly the same devices in action a year earlier (1973) in Peter Shaffer's *Equus*, where Alan Strang's equestrian rites were accompanied by drumming, choric incantations, flashbacks and cathartic climaxes. As Christopher Innes indicates, *Equus* was a *summa summarum* of avant-garde techniques of ritual theatre which finally found their way onto the mainstream stage.[27] Despite similarities in theatrical vocabulary, the fundamental difference between a play like *Equus*, in which Western man's need for ritual experience is thematicized and indeed acted out, and *An Echo in the Bone* lies in the ritual framework of the latter. A Nine Night ceremony is a widely practised ritual and an integral part of the belief system of large sections of Jamaican society. The identificatory potential in a play like *An Echo in the Bone*, at least when performed in its Caribbean context, is far greater. The convergence of the religio-spiritual horizon of the spectator with the ritual practice shown is a necessary ingredient for a more intense theatrical experience which goes beyond a voyeuristic delectation of the rites performed. Although Scott's play comes very close to '[becoming] the ceremony it is imitating', to refer back to Walcott's admonition, it manages to fracture the actual ceremonial procedure by the many flashbacks and include an historical and critical dimension which clearly situate the play finally in an aesthetic context.

All three dramatists display an impressive grasp of the theatrical power of the rituals they adapt. It is clear that director-dramatists are at work who have complete command of the anti-naturalistic theatrical vocabulary. Their plays move swiftly in time and space, their characters shift between states of consciousness ranging from dream to hallucination to spirit possession. This dramaturgy presupposes or at least looks to an audience which is also familiar with this array of devices and conventions. These plays demonstrate that a dramatist in the late sixties and early seventies can assume if not an audience *au fait* with avant-garde theatre, then at least an audience which is cine- and tele-literate, adept at deciphering flashbacks, time-jumps and fade-outs. It is fascinating irony of theatrical development that a theatre which attempts to tap into something as primal and ancient as ritual should be doing it with the dramaturgy of theatrical modernism and the techniques of the visual mass media.

NOTES

1. Errol Hill, 'The Emergence of a National Drama in the West Indies', *Caribbean Quarterly* 18:4 (1974), pp. 9-40. Cf. also Hill's book *The Trinidad Carnival: A Mandate for a National Theatre* (Austin: University of Texas, 1972).
2. 'The Emergence of a National Drama', p. 34.
3. Marina Maxwell, 'Towards a Revolution in the Arts', *Savacou* 2 (1970), pp. 19, 21.
4. Eric Berne, *The Games People Play* (New York: Grove Press, 1964), pp. 33ff. Cited in Richard Schechner, *Performance Theory* (London: Routledge, 1988), p. 33.
5. Anthony Graham-White, *The Drama of Black Africa* (New York: Samuel French, 1974), pp. 16ff.
6. Louis Mars, *Témoignages* (Madrid, 1966), p. 41; cited in Robert Cornevin, *Le théâtre haitien des origines à nos jours* (Montreal: Leméac 1973), p. 193. (My translation.)
7. Robert Bauduy, 'Aux sources du théâtre populaire haitien', *Conjonction* 24:3 (1969), p. 28; cited in Cornevin, p. 193. (See note 6.)
8. Christopher Innes, *Holy Theatre: Ritual and the Avant Garde* (Cambridge: Cambridge University Press, 1981).
9. This debt has already been noted by commentators; cf. Hill, 'The Emergence of a National Drama', p. 33; and Robert Hamner, *Derek Walcott* (Boston, 1981), p. 85.
10. Derek Walcott, *Dream on Monkey Mountain and other plays* (New York: Farrar, Straus & Giroux, 1970), p. 226. All further references are to this edition and are included in the text.
11. 'Reflections before and after Carnival: Interview with Derek Walcott', *The Chant of Saints: A Gathering of Afro-American Literature, Art, and Scholarship*, ed. Michael S. Harper and Robert B. Stepto (Urbana: The University of Illinois Press, 1979), p. 299.
12. Cf. Richard Schechner in his account of the Hevehe festival in Papua New Guinea; Schechner, op. cit. p. 46.
13. Walcott, 'Reflections', p. 297.
14. 'A *diablesse* appears to be a beautiful white woman, one who is capable of enticing a young man to follow her into the woods where he dies or goes mad.' Daniel Crowley, 'Supernatural Beings in St Lucia', *The Caribbean* 8 (1955), pp. 264f.; cited in George E. Simpson, *Religious Cults of the Caribbean: Trinidad, Jamaica and Haiti*, 3rd ed. (Rio Piedras: Univ. of Puerto Rico, 1980), pp. 316ff.
15. For a description of a Vodoun ceremony where such acts were performed, see Wade Davis, *The Serpent and the Rainbow* (London: Collins, 1986), p. 50.
16. Sylvia Wynter, 'Jonkonnu in Jamaica: Towards the Interpretation of Folk Dance as a Cultural Process', *Jamaica Journal* (June 1970), pp. 34-48; here pp. 38ff.
17. Frantz Fanon, *The Wretched of this Earth* (New York: Grove Press, 1962), p. 227.
18. Michael Gilkes, *Couvade: A Dream-play of Guyana* (London: Longman Caribbean, 1974), pp. viiif. All references to the play are to this edition and are included in the text.
19. The People's National Party is a fiction, as is the town of Manoa. The name refers to the fabled country of gold, El Dorado, located according to legend somewhere in South America.
20. Wilson Harris has singled out Gilkes's play, and especially this scene, for special mention in a recent essay: 'What is the The Robe? One may say I think that it is a body of absences that the painter comes to don or wear without quite understanding the consequences of his involvement with ancestry (non-being) and futurity (unborn-or-not-yet-present-being). The painter's penetration of The Robe implies the birth pangs of a world he carries within his art in parallel with his wife's pregnancy.' Wilson Harris, 'Oedipus and the Middle Passage', *Landfall* 43:2 (June 1989), pp. 198-208, here pp. 207ff.

21. See G.E. Simpson, *Religious Cults of the Caribbean*, pp. 201ff. for a detailed account of the ceremony. The scholar of Jamaican culture Martha Warren Beckwith recorded in 1929: 'The Jamaican Negroes believe that for nine nights after death the ghost rises out of the grave and returns to its familiar haunts...During this period every relative and friend gathers at the house of the dead to entertain the ghost, welcome his return, and speed him back to the grave.' *Black Roadways* (Chapel Hill: University of North Carolina, 1929), pp. 77-8; cited in: *Dictionary of Jamaican English*, ed. F.G. Cassidy and R.B. Le Page, 2nd ed. (Cambridge: Cambridge University Press, 1980), p. 321.

22. The play is published in Errol Hill, ed., *Plays for Today* (London: Longman Caribbean, 1985). References are to this edition and are included in the text.

23. For a detailed account of Kumina and ancestor worship, see Maureen Warner Lewis, *The Nkuyu: Spirit Messengers of the Kumina* (Mona: Savacou Publications, 1977).

24. The anthropologist Melville J. Herskovits cites an example of ritualized 'acting out' of the slave past in a dance performed by a group of negroes [sic] in Paramaribo in then Dutch Guiana: 'Spectators who had been sitting joined the ring of dancers, and circled about close behind each other until one of them shouted: "You'll have to get up early tomorrow. There's a lot of work!" The character was that of the "overseer"; the action had thrown back to the time of slavery.' 'Dramatic Expression Among Primitive Peoples', *The Yale Review* 33 (1943-44), pp. 683-698, here pp. 693f.

25. Cf. C.G. Jung, *Über die Psychologie des UnbewuBten* (Frankfurt a.M.: Fischer, 1975), pp. 65ff.

26. Victor Questel, 'Unlocking the Gates of History', *TAPIA*, Sunday 19 December, 1976; p. 12.

27. Innes, op. cit., pp. 239ff.

CAROLYN COOPER

Words Unbroken by the Beat: The Performance Poetry of Jean Binta Breeze and Mikey Smith

In a tersely sardonic *meta-dub*[1] poem, 'Dubbed Out', Jean Binta Breeze distinguishes her work from the rub-a-dub-a-dub monotony of facile performance poetry in which meaning is rubbed out in the dub:

> i
> search for words
>
> moving
> in their music
>
> not
>
> broken
>   by
>
> the
>
> beat[2]

The s/pacing of the lines jerking to a halt enacts the beating down of sense and lyricism; the double-entendre, 'moving', extends the conventional conceit of poetry as music – emotive sound – to include the fluidity of the word released from the mechanical rigidity of the beat, and from the fix of the page. Poetry becomes verbal dance, transmitted word-of-muscle. This reading of 'Dubbed Out' not only evokes the embodied word in performance, but also requires a distinction between the poet as maker and as performer. For not only are the words in motion, unbroken by the beat, but the poet/performer, uncontained by the boundaries of the book, speaks face to face with an immediate audience. In an act of performative transference the speaker gets across the closure of the printed page.

The performance itself thus becomes a privileged reading of the text.[3] For example, the audio/visual/kinetic integrity of Breeze's repeatedly spectacular performance of her 'Riddym Ravings' classic cannot be fully anticipated from reading the relatively static (though richly allusive) words on the page. Somewhat like a musical score, the poem pressed to the page encodes performance. Breeze, fully possessing the rhythms of the body/text, achieves the music. She engenders the mad woman's despair with such absolute artistic control that the comfortable distance between madness and sanity, between actuality and the act is uneasily contracted. The audience becomes a collective *voyauditeur*, enjoying the aesthetic pleasure of exquisitely recreated suffering. The dissonant pain of the mad woman's debased condition is dignified, but not diminished, by her fleeting moments of total lucidity. The radio DJ in her head keeps her 'sane', comforting her in abject distress. In the passage below, the thin narrative thread of sanity stretches on the disturbing image of the living dead and snaps:

> Wem mi fus come a town
> mi use to tell everybady 'mawnin'
> but as de likkle rosiness gawn outta mi face
> nobady nah ansa mi
> silence tun rags roun mi bady
> in de mids a all de dead people dem
> a bawl bout de caast of livin
> an a ongle one ting tap mi fram go stark raving mad
> a wen mi siddung eena Parade
> a tear up newspaper fi talk to (p. 59)

The capacity to make metonymy and metaphor – rosiness and the rags of silence – is the privilege of the poet and the lunatic: 'The Lunatic, the Lover, and the Poet,/ Are of imagination all compact.'[4] In performance, Breeze's articulate dramatization of 'the mad woman's poem', as 'Riddym Ravings' is ambiguously subtitled, confirms and obscures that cunning distinction.

Similarly, Mikey Smith's signature statement, his indelible voiceprint, 'Me Cyaan Believe it', is a howl of incredulous anguish that dares to speak the unspeakable. That heart-rending 'Lawwwwwwwwwd',[5] the penultimate line of the poem, is the protracted pain of generations of sufferers whose affirmative voice the poet becomes in a single gesture of communal defiance. The poet/performer seems to assume the *persona* of woman for whom belly pain – 'me ban me belly/ an me baw!' (p. 13) – is the specific anguish of child-bearing in a society that defies the poor to survive. Woman-pain is both an act of survival and evidence of defeat:

> Doris a modder of four
> get a wuk as a domestic
> Boss man move een
> an bap si kaisico she pregnant again
> bap si kaisico she pregnant again
> an me cyaan believe it
> me seh me cyaan believe it. (p. 14)

The refrain, 'bap si kaisico she pregnant again', in its adaptation of the nonsense words and rhythms of children's verbal play – 'bap si kaisico pinda[6] shell' – is a brilliant image of the generation of cycles of impoverishment. The woman's fertility is itself entrapping; her body bears its weight of nuts, and is then discarded, an empty shell. 'Boss man' sexual politics defines the rules of the adult game: no p/lay, no pay. The search for work thus exacerbates the repetitive pain of sexual exploitation that is often the poor woman's unwanted lot.

The power of the poem derives, in part, from the righteous anger of utterance. But the poet's performance, however privileged, is not authoritative. Indeed, the very 'text' of performance poetry, and its meanings, are dependent on complex variables beyond the absolute control of the poet as maker. Mervyn Morris, both poet and critic, defines the performance text/context thus: 'If the poem in print does, however minimally, alter with the specific context of its reception, the "performance poem" is even more difficult to fix, dependent for its meanings on the variable interaction between text, performer, audience and occasion.'[7] This fluidity of the text in performance is not inherently problematic except, perhaps, for the scribal critic wishing to keep the subject fixed in place and in proper perspective. In the two-way flow of the immediate moment of performance a discriminating audience, in contract with the poet/performer, functions as communal critic, endorsing (or not) the craft of the wordsmith and the authority of particular performances. The audience's familiarity with the words of the poem does not reduce the distinctive pleasure of each succeeding performance. For as the work becomes appropriated by the community – is known – an enjoyable tension between the new and the familiar is sustained, as in numerous other communal speech contexts: Anansi story-telling and political speech-making, for example.[8]

This inter-dependent relationship of performer, word, audience and occasion that invigorates the work of Jean Breeze and Mikey Smith is often compromised in the efforts of less accomplished practitioners who quickly become dubbed out. In the words of Gordon Rohlehr, '[d]ub poetry is at its worst a kind of tedious jabber to a monotonous rhythm'.[9] The search for the exact word and rhythm is abandoned as the dubber settles for the automatic reflex of cliché. The song-and-dance of 'performance' struggles to animate nonsense that cannot stand alone on the page or on the stage. In addition, an indiscriminate audience, relinquishing its responsibility to the artist and the medium, can simply opt out of the critical contract, applauding a noisy belch of vacuity as great oral art. Or the occasion for performance may not readily arise. Performance is often occasioned by commemorative events, for example African Liberation Day, International Women's Day; or festivals – Reggae Sunsplash in Jamaica, the International Bookfair of Radical Black and Third World Books in London; or 'poetry readings' where performance itself is the celebrated occasion. The professional performance poet wishing to make a living must often seek out occasions for performance in which the essential interplay of word and audience may be subverted. Without patronage, whether State or private endowment, the performer, reduced to hand-to-mouth circumstances, often drivels.

In a punningly titled essay, 'Dub Poetry: Selling Out', Stewart Brown frankly assesses the contradictions of the commercially successful dub poet, cut off from a knowing community and in quest of a mass audience:

> As dub poetry becomes a commercial product, as its performers like Benjamin Zepphaniah (sic) or Mutabaruka or Ras Levi Tafari become media Stars and strive to entertain a mass, multicultural audience, there seems to me to be a real danger that the protest, the anger, the fire, becomes an act, while the image, the dub/rant/chant/dance becomes the real substance of the performance.[10]

Muabaruka, himself, derides the notion of the incongruously entertaining 'revolutionary poet':

> revolutionary poets
> 'ave become entertainers
> babblin out angry words
> ...
> yes
> revolutionary poets
> 'ave all gone to the
> creative art centre
> to watch
> the sufferin
> of the people being dram at ized by the
> oppressors
>   in their
>   revolutionary
>   poems[11]

The easy transformation of rage into entertainment disfigures the masquerading actor. For the 'act' is both performance, in literal theatre terms, and fraud, in the metaphorical, derogatory sense of that word. Mimicking performance, the commercial dub poet can put the audience on, assuming an anger that has not been earned. Particularly in a 'multicultural' context like Britain, where negative stereotypes about Black culture seem to prevail, the act may become an un/conscious fraud perpetrated both by performers who exploit the low expectations and ignorance of their uncritical audience, and by the perversely 'liberal', patronising art establishment. For example, the sad case of Benjamin Zephaniah and the Professorship of Poetry at Oxford University.

The *Guardian* of Saturday, 20 May 1989 carried a witty front page article by Maev Kennedy headlined 'Dark horse in poetry contest bridles at sporting metaphor': the dark horse is and is not Zephaniah. It is, first of all, Duncan McCann, a renomination, who, according to the report 'was very indignant when he was described as "the bar room poet" five years ago, on being nominated by some friends from the King's Arms in Oxford'. McCann's objections to the sporting metaphor are sent up by Kennedy: 'The Professor of Poetry at Oxford University is still backing his own runner in the succession stakes despite the entry of a dark horse who bitterly disapproves of sporting metaphors cantering over sacred literary turf.' The newspaper article begs for deconstruction. The likely performance of the jockeying horses is forecast. The bar room poet is handicapped by his petulance; Seamus Heaney, the favourite, has the backing of the right credentials – '[i]t has been murmured that he is in line for a Nobel Prize for Literature'. According to Kennedy's pre-race analysis, Heaney's

> ... strongest competition comes from the Somerset-based poet, author and translator, Charles Sisson, and the Rastafarian dub-poet, Benjamin Zephaniah, whose work includes a New Year Rap for the *Guardian* with the prophetic lines:

> And when it comes to Nuclear Arms
> Where does Neil Kinnock stand?
> And where's that Marxist Theory dat dey told us dey
> had planned?

Pure greeting-card doggerel, despite its clairvoyance. Intriguingly, in Kennedy's sporting review of the ratings, Zephaniah is the only entrant whose work is allowed to speak for itself. The black horse is unbridled and nothing further need be said about its chances. In the *Weekend Guardian* of the same date, the page 5 'Sound Bites' column reports a more viscerally outspoken appraisal of Zephaniah's work: 'Benjamin Zephaniah's chief claim to fame is finding the functions of the bowel a suitable topic for verse. Francis Bennion, barrister (letter to the *Daily Telegraph*).'

It is in this context of honest contempt, or worse, conspiratorial silence that Breeze, in a *Marxism Today* interview, makes a plea for accountability on the part of both the actor/poet and the critic/audience:

> 'I'd rather we had only two or three artists in our community that represent what is finest and truest about ourselves than a host of poseurs who have been allowed to take on the title of artist simply because they are black.... I'm tired of people preaching to the converted and saying it's art.'[12]

For the poseur the image and the act are the degenerate substitute for genuine poetic ability. But for poet/performers like Breeze and Smith, both of whom are trained actors and talented poets, the act does indeed become quite literally 'the real substance of the performance'. It is the fulfilment of the promise of the words on the page.

Mervyn Morris, in his introduction to Mikey Smith's collection of performance poems which, as editor, he shaped for the medium of print, cites an oral account given by Honor Ford-Smith, one of Mikey's tutors at the

Jamaica School of Drama, which stresses the poet's studious preparation for performance:

> he would work hours and hours, sometimes the whole day, with his tape recorder which would have the booking tracks for the music, trying out different variations of rhythm. He was very very conscious of the variety that he could get in his voice. And you hear it in the voice, and you hear his consciousness of pace, when you listen to his recording, and when you hear him perform you would hear that he had worked hours on the pacing of his poetry, you know. So it wasn't just something that he improvised when he got on stage.[13]

What is illuminating in this account is the suggestion that the process of making the poem is organically connected to the rhythms of its performance. In the programme notes to the 1988 Creation for Liberation national poetry tour of England done by Ntozake Shange and Jean Breeze, Mervyn Morris gives a similar sense of Breeze's theatrical control of the non-verbal elements of performance:

> Jean 'Binta' Breeze is, I think, the best of the performers. I think when Mikey Smith was alive he could have competed with her as a performer, but some of the things that I've seen her do in performance are really quite astonishing. I remember, for example, an occasion in London when the Mikey Smith book was being launched. Although I'd heard the poem, it was the first time I saw her perform the 'Mad Woman's Lament', 'Riddym Ravings'. A couple of gestures she made at that time were really astonishing; like a gesture, a sudden gesture for sort of putting the plug back in. It was really alarming you could feel everybody freeze at that moment. Obviously that kind of detail, I think, is very carefully calculated.[14]

This calculation and crafting are not to be expected when performance poetry is reduced to mere protest, anger and fire. The mode is declamatory and the emotional range of the poetry is accordingly contracted.[15] 'Riddym Ravings' is a brilliant performance poem; a 'dub' parody could read like this:

oman a bawl
lice a crawl
een her head
waan fi dead
man wid gun
a come fi fun
belly big
like pig
a wallow
land fallow
pure gutter water
fi bathe di daughter
etc., etc.

The primary characteristics of this non-poem are its exteriorization of consciousness; its facile word association dependent on rhyme; its short, lobotomized lines.

Mutabaruka's humorous, generic poem, 'Dis Poem', anticipates the parodic response of the jaded critic/audience fed up of *poetics* passing itself off as poetry. It both illustrates and subverts the anxiety that the glib performance poem can generate. The wit of the poem depends on Mutabaruka's deliberate exploitation of the audience's uncomfortable suspicion of being put on. The hearer's dismay at the seeming nonsense of the many of the poem's lines thus becomes incorporated into the play of the text: 'dis poem is watchin you tryin to make sense from dis poem.'[16] Not only is there this mockery of the audience's expectation of immediately intelligible lines – instant aural gratification – but the poet as non-entertainer insists that the audience actively participate in making the meaning of the poem. The poem therefore does not come to a fulfilling end; the listener is left hanging: 'dis poem is to be continued in your mind in your mind in your mind your mind.'[17] An ironic reverberation. This dub poem is thus self-satirical, consciously making fun of its own conventions. The genre has come of age: *meta-dub*.

Indeed, a broad thematic and tonal range characterizes the work of the sophisticated performance poets. It is not all protest, anger and fire, an exclusively apocalyptic idiom. In Mikey Smith's 'Give Me Little Dub Music' the aggressive anger elicited by debilitating economic deprivation struggles for release in the sweet melancholy of the dub:

> Give me little dub music
> right ya so
> tonight
>
> A have dis haunted feelin
> so meck we bat een
> an ketch a reasonin
>
> No bodder talk bout anyting too tough
> Skip de usual stuff
> dat yuh out a luck
> a look fi wuk
> an meck we seat up
>
> We no mourners
> We naw go watch weself
> go down de road
> like witherin flowers
>
> An jus
> give me little dub music
> right ya so
> tonight. (p. 32)

On the Island Records performance of this poem the elusive 'haunted feelin' of the plaintive voice is supported by the grounded instrumental accompaniment. Then there is the muted celebration of Breeze's 'Simpie Tings' which on the 1989 LKJ Records release, 'Tracks: Jean Binta Breeze', quietly affirms, *a capella*, the solid peasant values of rural Jamaica, in particular the endurance of women: '(for Miss Adlyn and Aunt Vida).' The counterpoint of English and Jamaican voices authenticates the poet's tribute. She is herself the product of both worlds:

> de simple tings of life, mi dear
> de simple tings of life
>
> she rocked the rhythms in her chair
> brushed a hand across her hair
> miles of travel in her stare
>
> de simple tings of life
>
> ah hoe me corn
> an de backache gone
> plant me peas
> arthritis ease
>
> de simple tings of life
> leaning back
> she wiped an eye
> read the rain signs
> in the sky
> evening's ashes
> in a fireside
>
> de simple tings of life. (p. 33)

This is not a sentimental pastoral. The seer divines the rain signs and the ashes of evening with equal calm; decline is simply accepted as part of the natural cycle of things.

In its sustained use of the imagery of radio transmission Breeze's 'Eena Mi Corner' is reminiscent of the harrowing 'Riddym Ravings'. But whereas the tone of the latter is dread melancholy, the former is drily humorous. The poem is a witty treatment of the theme of easy channel-changing men, whom the woman must learn to tune out in order to get rid of static:

> flip a switch
> tun mi receiva
> to transmitta
> checkin anadda one
> wanderin troo
> de sonic boom of a bassline
> but wen mi see seh

```
dis one a forward pon de same riddym station
breed een
breed out
mi memba
how it easy
cho
mi haffi
mi haffi
mi haffi jus
check out  (p. 27)
```

'Holly', a bitterly ironic warning to beware the power of sexuality and the corresponding shortness of the male attention span, is developed in naturalistic imagery that suggests the organic nature of the perennial problem:

```
so hole strang gal
fi wen man look pon yuh
like im is sun
talk
like breeze
run im han oba yuh
wid cool coconut cream
waiting to flow troo yuh
like im is ribba
nex ting yuh know
flood yuh wid crop
draw back
an lef yuh liddung
fallow
a tiad
hardened soil
weh ongle macka grow  (p. 67)
```

In Jamaican folk etymology, the biblical injunction to dig up one's fallow ground often becomes the digging up of folly ground. The sexual imagery of the poem, for example the crop/crap/clap overtones, grounds multiple levels of meaning.

'Lovin Wasn Easy', transposed into a blues/jazz idiom in the LKJ 'Tracks' recording, is an equivocal celebration of mutual affection that survives, for a while, the harshness of material poverty threatening to erode it:

```
wasn easy at all

cep wen
warm
eena de tear up tent
a we blanket
jine wide we glue
```

```
we use to watch mawnin star
rise
troo de hole
eena de bamboo shack  (p. 69)
```

In 'Ordinary Mawning' despair prevails. In its very ordinariness, the
sameness of the struggle to eke out an existence is overwhelming:

```
was jus anadda
same way mawning
anadda clean up de mess
after dem lef mawning
a perfectly ordinary
mawning of a perfectly
ordinary day
trying to see a way

out

so it did hard fi understand
why de ordinary sight of
mi own frock
heng up pon line
wid some clothespin
should a stop mi from do nutten
but jus
bawl  (p. 49)
```

In Smith's 'Sunday a Come' the pathos of the speaker's impotence is
imaged in the dark disjunction of skin and world:

```
Sometime a siddung
wid me heart full up an me face wet up
for is a shame when yuh mumma breast wither up
an yuh waan cry and yuh cyaan bawl
for darkness between yuh world and yuh skin  (p. 25)
```

In the prophetic 'Sunday' this pain is transmuted, quite unsentimentally,
into a visionary acceptance of both the necessity of earthly sacrifice and
the possibility of martyrdom:

```
I sit
Sunday

not meditating on
people clapping
shouting
meek
shall inherit earth
```

but meditating
freedom

I
shall not die
a natural death
but fighting (p. 37)

Then there is the grim humour of 'I an I Alone' that records the verbal
battles between the buyers and sellers in the market place, as both sides
struggle to keep flesh on the bone. Hustling becomes a way of life. The
folk thrift encoded in the proverb 'every mickle meck a muckle' – it all
adds up – is devalued into a raw competitiveness for scarce goods that
commodifies human relations:

De people-dem a teck everyting meck a muckle
Dem a try fi hustle down de price
fi meck two ends meet,
de odder one a try fi push up de price
fi meck de picni backbone get sinting fi eat.
But two teet meet an dem a bark
dem cyaan stan de pressure,
dem tired fi compete wid hog an dawg,
but dem mus aspire fi someting better
although dem dungle-heap ketch a fire. (p. 28)

The insults fly in a dissonant mix of market noises: the warnings of the
preacher and the sales-pitch cries of other unperturbed sellers:

'Shoppin bag! Shoppin bag! Five cent fi one!'
'Green pepper! Thyme! Skellion an pimento!'
'Remember de Sabbath day, to keep it holy!
Six days shalt thou labour,
but on the seventh day shalt thou rest.'
'Hi, mam, how much fi dah piece a yam deh?'
'No, no dat; dat! Yes; dat!'
'Three dollars a poun, nice gentleman.'
'Clear out! Oonoo country people too damn tief!'
'Like yuh mumma!'
'Fi-me mumma? Wha yuh know bout me mumma?
Look ya, a might push dis inna yuh!'
'Yuh lie! A woulda collar yuh!'
'Bruck it up! But, dread, cool down!'
'Alright, cool down. Rastafari!' (p. 27)

Even a less accomplished poem like 'I Sight Up Tacky' which is rather
prosaic in its loose rhythms, facile rhymes and glib, up-beat exhortations:

> If yuh waan two ends fi meet
> only yuh can do it,
> by awakenin yuh soul to yuh reality
> an determine not to devalue yuh dignity.
> Stan up like Tacky!
> Regardless of de term
> Yuh haffi stan firm
> fi we chart we destiny. (p. 48)

is redeemed from absolute banality by the sudden switch to an altogether different register: 'Yuh feel de heat?/ Who will suck anodder kisko-pop?' (p. 48). The intrusive practicality of the seller's question takes the heat of the poem's rhetoric down several degrees. This kind of incongruity is funny, intentionally or not.

It is the range of poems such as these that makes one sympathetic to Mervyn Morris' privileging of the term 'performance poetry', a more inclusive designation than 'dub':

> ... if we say that 'dub poetry' incorporates, or is performed to the accompaniment of reggae rhythms, we are forced to acknowledge that 'dub poetry' constitutes only a fraction of the output of the writers/performers we call 'dub poets'. 'Performance poetry' encompasses more of the work they do, and the term may have the further advantage ... of encouraging the recognition that there are performance poems among the works of many poets we more often associate with print.[18]

An excellent example of the latter is the poet Lorna Goodison, whose performances resonate with the oracular authority of 'chant' and in whose work metaphors of 'calling', 'mission' and 'channel' recur. Goodison often assumes the public *persona* of 'sojourner poet carolling for peace/ calling lost souls to the Way of Heartease'.[19] In performance, seemingly translucent lines such as these – that can indeed look like doggerel on the page – acquire opacity and weight in the phrasing. A pensive pause on 'poet' and between 'souls' and 'to', for instance, slowing down the brisk pace of the dactylic feet, subtly alters the rhythm and meaning of the seemingly glib lines. An understated, counter-rhythmic reading allows the subversive possibility of self-mocking irony. The poet's mask does not always fit smugly in performance.

But the 'further advantage' of the broader term 'performance poetry' includes its own limitations. What is lost is the allusive power of the emotive label 'dub', with its onomatopoeic drum resonances and its recognition, in the naming, of the roots of this artistic movement in the reggae culture of urban revolt: working a rhythm that is the dub-side of both middle-class respectability and the somewhat constricting conventions of the iambic pentameter, to use Kamau Brathwaite's metaphorical turn of phrase in *The History of the Voice*: 'What English has given us as a model for poetry, and to a lesser extent prose (but poetry is the basic tool here), is the pentameter.... There have, of course, been attempts to break it.'[20] He continues: 'It is nation language in the Caribbean that, in fact, largely ignores the pentameter.'[21] Oku Onuora's definition of dub poetry similarly focuses on its distance from the conventions of English metrics: 'It's dubbing out the little penta-metre and the little highfalutin business and dubbing in the rootsical, yard, basic rhythm that I-an-I know. Using the language, using the body. It also mean to dub out the isms and schisms and to dub consciousness into the people-dem head. That's dub poetry.'[22] When 'dub' poetry is dubbed 'performance' poetry it goes genteely up-market, somewhat like the Third World Band.

Nevertheless, the all-encompassing term does have the decided advantage of confirming the breadth and complexity of the performance/print, oral/scribal literary continuum along which both 'performance' and 'non-performance' poets operate. For before performance comes composition, the conceiving, writing and rewriting of the script. With bad 'performance' poets it is all an organic process of decomposition. Though Breeze, herself, images the creative urge as a natural bodily function – composition versus constipation[23] – the evidence of her words on the page and in performance is not flatulence. By her own admission she engages in a search for the moving word. Similarly, Mikey Smith acknowledges both the flash of inspiration and the slow, evolutionary process of making the poem:

> A man seh, 'Boy, me can't believe it, that the thing gone up, yu know.' Me seh, 'Rahtid, a it that, you know! We can't believe it. And when you can't believe it and you look and you see the things that you can't believe!' And then me go home now and me seh, 'Yeh. Poem now. I waan get a poem. "Cyaan believe it". That's the poem I want.' And then it slowly evolve. It might work out. You might jot it down – line, piece a line – and you go weh and you leave it, and then you come back an you build on it. Or it might come 'roops', right out. The whole intensity just come right out and you just really – release it. Or sometimes a rhythm come to me first. You know, is a rhythm, and me seh, 'Dah rhythm-ya feel nice, you know, feel nice.' And then me try remember the rhythm ... and then I build up under that and catch me breaks and the bridges. Just like how a musician a work out.[24]

It is evident from an account such as this that the disjuncture of sense and sound, of word and beat that often characterizes simple-minded performance poetry is likely to be less a function of the orality of the medium and more a measure of the skill (or lack of it) of the composer. For like literacy, oracy requires the mastery of hierarchies of knowledge: the concrete and the abstract, the literal and the metaphorical. Indeed, oracy is not merely the absence of literacy; it is a way of seeing, a knowledge system. Practitioners like Breeze and Smith who are both literate and orate employ the conceptual conventions of both discourses. Thus in the process of creating and in the later analysis of the product it may be difficult, if not impossible, to discriminate between orate and literate constructs. Mikey Smith's statement above illustrates the difficulty. It used to be possible to employ purely linguistic criteria: English was the language of literacy; Jamaican the voice of orality. But the gradual spread of literacy in Jamaican, largely through the efforts of our creative writers, raises the politicized issue of the degree to which the authority implicit in English as the official language of literacy, may now be assumed by/for Jamaican. Experiments in Caribbean Creoles as literate languages of *analysis* suggest their extended range of possibilities.[25] Determining a functional, generally agreed upon Creole orthography is essential for the full development of Creole literacy.

In his 'Introduction' to *Voiceprint: an Anthology of Oral and Related Poetry*, Gordon Rohlehr provides a brisk summary of the historical problem, especially as it relates to Caribbean poetry:

> Nowhere has the 'dialect' versus 'standard' polemic been more bitter than in the question of whether serious poetry can grow out of a dialect base. Since it was widely believed that dialect was a restricted code, incapable of expressing abstract ideas, sublimity or complexities of thought and feeling, the functions permitted dialect were those of drama and energetic folksy humour.[26]

Acknowledgement of the *oraliteracy* of Jamaican might come to mean not only a recognition of the capacity for abstraction and subtlety of feeling and expression on the part of speakers/writers in Jamaican, but it may also require a de-privileging of abstraction; or at the very least, a revaluation of the making of metaphor as a kind of literal-minded process of abstracting: The metaphorical is to oracy what abstraction is to literacy – a way of generalizing. I am not proposing a simplistic opposition of the form:

literacy:abstraction : orality:metaphor

as though literacy is not itself rooted in metaphor. Rather, I wish to suggest that Caribbean literary criticism (and linguistics) needs to more fully investigate *how* Creole orality uses metaphor to generalize. Devonish's work, cited above, represents an important development. Like Louise Bennett, he recognizes, for example, the weight of the metaphorical proverb in translating the abstractions of English into a readily accessible form for Creole speakers.

But poetry, whether performance or not, is not a language of generalities. It is a celebration, in the making, of particulars. It is a return to the roots of language in oracy. Unlike the transmitter of traditional Jamaican oral texts – for example, Anansi stories, riddles, duppy stories, Big Boy jokes, proverb – who inherited a body of knowledge that was memorized and re-presented with or without modification by the performer, the contemporary performance poet makes his/her own text. Elements of traditional lore are inevitably incorporated into these texts. Mikey Smith's use of tags from ring games and folk sayings is particularly effective. In the following verses he fuses a children's ring game ('Room fa rent, apply widin, when I run out you run in'); a proverb ('Waan good/ nose haffi run'); allusions

to two English nursery rhymes – with ironic wit. In a metaphorical slide
the horn-blower seems to become an unwelcome, self-aggrandizing suitor
– perhaps politician, or lover bearing the seeds of more children:

> Room dem a rent
> me apply widin
> but as me go een
> cockroach rat an scorpion
> also come een
>
> Waan good
> nose haffi run
> but me naw go siddung pon high wall
> like Humpty Dumpty
> me a face me reality
>
> One little bwoy come blow im horn
> an me look pon im wid scorn
> an me realize how me five bwoy-picni
> was a victim of de trick
> dem call partisan politricks
>
> an me ban me belly an me bawl (p. 13)

Similarly, in Breeze's 'Warner', ironic Biblical imagery – Herod's sword –
merges with the apocalyptic sing-song rhetoric of the Afro-Christian,
Kumina Warner Woman, Mother to the flock, who breeds fear in the presumably promiscuous baby-mother:

> an de baby madda
> clamp dung pon er stomach muscle
> lack er foot tight
> fah Herod sword nah come een tonight
> an river nah rush no more
>
> Madda tek pickney by de han
> and de cymbal start sing
> she sayin I
> I come to bring a warnin
> fah de Lawd Gad say to tell you
> dat de day of your sins is upon you
> dat de day of tribulation is nigh (p. 22)

It is this inter-weaving of disparate elements from oral and scribal literary sources that characterizes the neo-oral performance poetry of both
Breeze and Smith. Poems such as these will inevitably become part of the
communal repertoire just as Louise Bennett's poems have been appropriated and performed by other actors. This process of communal appropriation raises the paradoxical issue of originality: that which already existed

or that which is newly made. Old-fashioned Western, scribal definitions of the poet as maker – a lonely individual talent – collapse into broader oral notions of the poet as transmitter of 'pre-packaged' cultural forms and values which are realizable only in specific contexts of production and reception. Karin Barber, of the Birmingham School of African Studies, argues in a brilliantly eclectic essay on 'Yoruba *Oriki* and Deconstructive Criticism' that 'Deconstructive criticism, despite its rhetoric of writing, of inscription and textuality, appears to have moved silently and, as it were, surreptitiously into a position from which oral literature takes on a paradigmatic quality; oral texts are what the deconstructive critics say all literature is – only more so'.[27] In traditional oracy performance is, quite literally, the making of the text, which has no 'existence' or authoricity independent of its voicing. Performance itself is thus a privileged skill. Indeed, would-be performance poets with limited abilities in composing might well be advised to forfeit the attractions of short-term originality and concentrate their efforts instead on performing well the classic works of our accomplished poets. To subversively paraphrase Derek Walcott's homage to Gregorias, such lesser talents ought to abandon apprenticeship to the errors of the communal soul, and thus repossess aboriginal force.[28]

As composed text, the performance poetry of Jean Binta Breeze and Mikey Smith illustrates the sensitive deployment of a range of rhetorical styles of both Jamaican and English provenance. The pure orality of Jamaican folk poetics (both rural and urban, folk song and reggae) engages in constructive dialogue with the scribal conventions of English metrics – in which both poets have been schooled, Breeze somewhat more so than Smith. As performance text, the *meta-dub* script of these skilled actors allows them to fully demonstrate their command of a broad repertoire of theatre idioms. In performance, the word – unbroken by the beat – speaks volumes.

NOTES

1. I use *meta-dub* to suggest the transformation of the somewhat more limiting term 'dub' into 'performance' poetry. See the discussion of the pros and cons of the terms, below.
2. Jean Binta Breeze, *Riddym Ravings and Other Poems*, ed. Mervyn Morris (London: Race Today Publications, 1988), p. 29. Subsequent references cited in text. For my somewhat limited analysis of individual poems as performance (I am aware that my critical vocabulary is largely print oriented), I depend on my memory of events in which I have participated, and on recordings.
3. I am indebted to Stewart Brown, in conversation, for this formulation/wording of the process.
4. Theseus in *Midsummer Night's Dream*, Act I, Sc. 1, 6-7.

5. Michael Smith, *It A Come*, ed. Mervyn Morris (London: Race Today Publications, 1986), p. 14. Subsequent references cited in text. The Island Records LP album ILPS 9717, *Me Cyaan Believe It*, and again, my composite reconstruction of performances, is the 'performance text'.

6. 'peanut' – '<Kongo (Angola) *mpinda*, ground-nut, peanut', *Dictionary of Jamaican English*. '[ad. Pg. *pinda*, ad. Congo *mpinda*, Mpongwe *mbenda*; carried out by negroes to America.] W. Indian and Southern U.S. for the ground-nut or pea-nut', *O.E.D.*

7. Mervyn Morris, 'Gender in Some Performance Poems', unpublished conference paper, Seminar on 'Gender in Caribbean Culture', Women and Development Studies Project, U.W.I., Mona, June 1987, p. 2.

8. See, as well, Erna Brodber's subtle fictional account of the paradoxical pleasures of familiar story-telling ritual, which is introduced thus: 'At New Year's eve our clan gathers never tired of tears and never weary of the warmth of sadness.' *Jane and Louisa Will Soon Come Home* (London: New Beacon Books, 1980), pp. 13-14.

9. Gordon Rohlehr, 'Introduction' to Stewart Brown, Mervyn Morris and Gordon Rohlehr, eds., *Voiceprint* (London: Longman, 1989), p. 18.

10. Stewart Brown, 'Dub Poetry: Selling Out', *Poetry Wales*, Vol. 22, No. 2, 1987, pp. 53-4.

11. Paula Burnett, ed., *The Penguin Book of Caribbean Verse in English* (Harmondsworth: Penguin, 1986), pp. 80-1.

12. Jean Breeze, Interview with Andrea Stewart, *Marxism Today*, Nov. 1988, p. 45.

13. *It A Come*, p. 10.

14. Leila Hassan, ed., *Women of the Word* (London: Creation for Liberation, 1988), p. 13.

15. See, for example, Victor Chang's review of Christian Habekost's presumably indiscriminate selection/editing of *Dub Poetry: 19 Poets from England and Jamaica* (Michael Schwinn: Neustadt, 1986): 'Thus, while dub poetry covers a range of topics, its tonal range as represented here is essentially limited: protesting, threatening, accusatory. And we need to recognize this.' Chang proceeds to generalize: 'I am not saying that this poetry does not have its value or that it should be like traditional poetry. I merely want to suggest that we cannot often expect any subtlety of approach, anything that is inward-looking, musing, quiet, reflective, tender, delicate, registering a complexity of position or feeling.... And for those who value and want more than the broad effects, the clout on the head, the deafening roar, the enraged shout this poetry is just not enough.' *Jamaica Journal*, Vol. 21, No. 3, Aug-Oct 1988, p. 50.

16. Mutabaruka, 'Dis Poem', poster, Kingston, Jamaica, Lithographed by Stephenson's, n.d.

17. Ibid.

18. 'Gender in Some Performance Poems', p. 1. See also Morris' review of Paula Burnett, ed., *The Penguin Book of Caribbean Verse in English*, in *Journal of West Indian Literature*, Vol. 1, No. 2, June 1987, pp. 73-75, in which he questions the editor's segregation of the poets (and texts) into 'oral' and 'literary' camps.

19. Lorna Goodison, *Heartease* (London: New Beacon Books, 1988), p. 41. In an unsympathetic review of *Heartease*, 'Exiles and Heartlands: New Caribbean Poetry', *Third World Quarterly*, Vol. 11, No. 4, Oct 1989, p. 273, Stewart Brown somewhat sceptically allows that 'performance' might redeem what looks like clearly bad poetry on the page: 'Lorna Goodison is renowned for her public readings, and one can see how the admirable sentiments that underpin many of these poems would be well

received in such circumstances. Some of them, however, read as rather limp and self-indulgent on the page.' This critical dissatisfaction with limpness may very well be an exclusively male, performance-related anxiety; admittedly, the female recipient of a limp performance (poem) may also feel, self-indulgently, that it is not enough.

20. Kamau Brathwaite, *History of the Voice* (London: New Beacon Books, 1984), p. 9.

21. Ibid., p. 13.

22. Statement made at a seminar on 'Dub Poetry', Jamaica School of Drama, 17 January 1986. Transcript of excerpts done by Mervyn Morris.

23. *Marxism Today*, p. 44.

24. Mikey Smith, Interview with Mervyn Morris, 27 May 1981, in *Jamaica Journal*, Vol. 18, No. 2, May-July 1985, p. 41. Quoted by Morris in the 'Editor's Notes' to *It A Come*, pp. 9-10.

25. See, for example, Hubert Devonish, *Language and Liberation* (London: Karia Press, 1986), particularly Chapter 7, pp. 122-34, which eloquently answers the question, 'How does one go about expanding the linguistic resources of Creolese in order for it to adequately perform its new functions?', p. 129. See also my own experiment with Jamaican as a language of literary analysis in 'Writing Oral History: Sistren Theatre Collective's *Lionheart Gal*', in *Kunapipi*, Vol. XI, No. 1, 1989, pp. 49-57.

26. *Voiceprint*, p. 1.

27. Karin Barber, 'Yoruba *Oriki* and Deconstructive Criticism', *Research in African Literatures*, Vol. 15, No. 4, Winter 1984, p. 498.

28. Derek Walcott, *Another Life* (London: Jonathan Cape, 1972; 1973), p. 59: 'Gregorias abandoned apprenticeship/ to the errors of his own soul/ .../ he possessed/ aboriginal force.'

VELMA POLLARD

Dread Talk – The Speech of Rastafari in Modern Jamaican Poetry

Brathwaite, writing about Caribbean poetry of the 1960s,[1] says of that time that it released the 'revelation of the word'. The poet he singles out as exemplifying that revelation is Bongo Jerry, the best known of the Rasta-farian poets of the sixties. And that is just. For when mention is made of the 'word', certainly in the language of Jamaica, it is to the Rastafari that one immediately looks since that group re-organized the vocabulary of Jamaica Talk to force the word to reflect a particular philosophy, a particu-lar point of view. The requirement was for a certain consistency of mean-ing, and a certain relationship between sound and meaning within what has been described variously as 'I-tally' (Ras Boanerges),[2] 'I-ance' (Nettleford),[3] 'Dread Talk' (Peart[4] and Pollard),[5] and 'Iyaric' (Birhan).[6] Jerry in the oft quoted poem 'Mabrak' identified the need for the use of the code of Rasta to carry the message of Rastafari, decrying the prevailing situation in which 'man must use men language to carry this message'. 'Man' here signifies the Rasta man, the poor black man, scorned by the establishment, while 'men' is not the English plural of 'man', but the non-Rasta individual representing the establishment and identifiable in this context by his language – English.

This paper looks at the language of Rastafari in the poetry of Jamaica, particularly at its use by poets whose regular vehicle is Standard Jamaican English (SJE) or some variety of Jamaican Creole (JC). Dennis Scott and Lorna Goodison are the poets of particular focus.

In 'Mabrak', published first in a volume (*Savacou* 3/4) which was to be-come highly controversial in Caribbean literary circles, Jerry articulates a language policy which is personal but which may be thought of as repre-senting the feeling of a cohort of conscious young people of Jamaica during the sixties. The situation in which English, the official language of the country, is given primacy, is seen as one which needs to be righted. The poet sees himself as having a mandate to change it:

> ...now I and I come to recreate:
>
> sight sounds and meaning to measure the feeling
> of BLACK HEARTS – alone – ...
>
> The coming of light to the black world.[7]

The colonial impact is identified as having its well-spring in language. Black people may try to get rid of their colonial orientation by wearing dashikis and no longer straightening their hair but 'mostofthestraighten-ingisinthetongue'.

Bongo Jerry accuses English of deluding black people with double talk, with turning things around. The example he gives is instructive: 'SAR' instead of 'RAS'. 'Sar' is the Jamaican pronunciation of 'Sir' while 'Ras' is an Ethiopian royal title adopted by many Rastas; hence Ras Boanerges, for example. The irony of Jerry's position becomes clear if one examines the way the speech code of Rastafari transforms words within the common pool it shares with Standard Jamaican English and Jamaican Creole, the dominant languages of the society, giving them new meanings and new significance. It is the code of Rastafari, the newcomer on the linguistic scene, which turns old meanings around.

The official language of Jamaica is Standard Jamaican English (SJE). It is the language of the formal motions in the society and of education. Jamaican Creole, the speech of the man in the street and the language of informal interaction in the society, is a creole of English lexicon; the code of Rastafari is an adjustment of the lexicon of either of the languages, to satisfy certain requirements of speakers sympathetic to the philosophy of Rasta. All language within the Jamaican speech community may be de-scribed as 'English related'. The significance of this fact is that writers are able to include usage and meaning from within the conventions of Rasta, while writing either in English or in Jamaican Creole.

The intention behind this manipulation of word is usually to establish a kind of identification with the man at the bottom of the social ladder, the suffering Jamaican. The traditional Rasta man comes from this sector of the society. He is a 'sufferer', though not all sufferers are Rastafari. Scott's poem 'No Sufferer' from his collection *Uncle Time* is a good example of the use of words from the vocabulary of Dread Talk (DT) within a poem written in SJE to rationalize the inclusion of one who might be thought of as an 'establishment' sympathiser within the ranks of the sufferers.

Admitting that his social and economic position do not permit him to accept the label 'sufferer' justly, the speaker in the poem makes a case for himself as a sufferer in a metaphorical (psychological) sense: 'I have my version.' The term 'version' has as its primary meaning in DT the flip side of a record usually played with instrumentals only, largely drum-like sounds. There is a pun on that word so that both the SJE and the DT meaning apply. The body of the speaker is a city in which a tortured self roams. He asks that this, his version of suffering, be recognized:

> : in the dread time of my living
> while whatever may be human chains me
> away from the surfeit of light, Mabrak
> and the safe land of my longing,
> acknowledge I.[8]

Pollard divides the lexicon (Wordology) of the code of Rasta into three categories, in terms of its relation to English, as follows:

Category I   In which known items bear new meanings.
               e.g. *chalice* = pipe for smoking ganja.

Category II   In which words bear the weight of their phonological
               implications.
               e.g. *downpress* = oppress.

Category III   /ai/ 'I' words
               i. Pronominal function, e.g. I, I-man = I; me.
               ii. Initial syllable replacement
                   e.g. I-lalu = calaloo.[9]

'Dread' is one of the more significant words in the Rasta vocabulary. It belongs to category I in the sense that its primary meanings are not the same as those accorded it in English. As an adjective, it conveys the ultimate of either suffering or joy; good or bad. The connotations in Scott's lines quoted above are negative. The 'dread' time is one in which the human being goes through extensive and intensive tribulation. Morris, commenting on the use of the term in this poem, describes it as suggesting 'cool anger, a sort of menacing stillness'.[10] More significant perhaps than its meaning, however, is the fact that it is used in preference to other likely adjectives ('troubled' or 'difficult', for example). It signals the acceptance of the Rasta man as one unit of the manscape with which the poem is concerned. It is this man with whom the poet wishes to identify.

The use of the pronoun 'I' at the end of the verse where English would expect 'me', is similarly significant. For it is the Rastas who have dispensed with 'me' even in the object position. 'I' is used as both subject and object in Dread Talk. 'I' may also be the second person pronoun translating to English as 'you' singular or plural. This sub-category marks one of the few instances of the code of Rasta altering more than the lexicon of Jamaica Talk. This is interference at the level of grammar. Morris allows the following multiple significances for the last line of the quotation above: '"I acknowledge", "acknowledge me", "acknowledge my Rastafarian brothers"'.[11] The preferred translation might be 'acknowledge me as one of you'. The term 'Mabrak', Morris says, is a Rastafarian concept meaning 'black lightning'. Note that this term is the title word of Bongo Jerry's poem to which reference was made earlier.

In the poem 'Solutions' from the same collection (*Uncle Time*) 'I' is made to serve both SJE and DT briefly in a line where it hangs suspended like a bridge between the two:

> ...I stretch, I am
>   reaching
>   out, *I*
>   wrench its wings into stillness.[12]

The grammar of English is not disturbed but in the speaking of the lines, the 'I' in the third line by its position at the end, by its separation from its verb, suggests an emphasis which is able to take it beyond English to Dread Talk where it would become a term of address.

Compare Scott's use of the same pronoun in two examples where there is no ambivalence – one from SJE within that same collection:

> Now
> heart-sailed
> from home *I* name them[13]

the other from JC from the later collection:

> *I* wearing de ring dem tonight –
> one gainst hate and de red pepper
> tongue of malice, a snake-eye
> bone-ring to touch
> if *I* buck up de tempter[14]

In these the English first-person pronoun and the Creole alternative to the more frequently used equivalent, 'mi', retain their position near to their respective verbs.

The use of the Rasta 'I' is perfected in the title poem of Scott's second collection, 'Dreadwalk'. The strategy continues to be to end the line with that sound and to separate it from its accompanying verb. In four of the seven stanzas this usage appears. Examine the opening stanza:

> blackman came walking I
> heard him sing his
> voice was like sand
> when the wind dries it

The 'I' at the end of the first line, shared between DT and SJE, allows 'blackman' to be a Rasta man (in case there was any doubt): 'blackman came walking I' and allows as well for the presence of his interlocutor who is not: 'I heard him sing'. This feature is what Rohlehr describes as the 'fluid interplay of personae'.[15] The poem traces a deeply philosophical discourse between two speakers each representing a different population of the society, a different philosophical position. The future of the nation is the issue. Whoever wins will teach the children. There is near violence after the request from blackman 'give I the children'. Somehow a knife gets drawn, but peace prevails as the interlocutor gently chides blackman for his inefficiency in handling the weapon. On the linguistic level 'I' again does double duty as term of address (after 'wrong') and as first-person pronoun (before 'said'):

> but you holding it wrong I
> said love the fist opened
> the knife fell away...

Note that the interlocutor uses the Rasta term for peace and goodwill 'love' to dissipate his new friend's anger. The balance maintained between the characters, the deftness displayed in handling the codes and above it all the philosophical significance of the discourse[16] make this one of Scott's finest pieces.

The kind of manipulation of the words illustrated above allows the poet to write in language which is accessible to the English-speaking outsider and to the Jamaican insider. Obviously the insider here has access to far deeper levels of meaning than the untrained outsider.

It is worth noting that the category of word associated with the sound /ai/ 'I' (category III), is the most popular category. In fact any individual who wants to seem to be using the code of Dread easily adapts that sound to the several functions it embraces: personal pronoun (first, second and third person), possessive pronoun and adjective, term of address and finally, though not illustrated here, initial sound of any number of nouns. Note also that the sound is the same as that which represents the organ of sight and that 'seeing' is the most highly valued sense in Rastafari theology. Alleyne, commenting on the Rastafarian division of the world into positive and negative forces, says with regard to seeing: 'The most positive force is perception physically realized through the eye by means of the sense of sight and leading to the metaphysical realization of the self, the ego, the "I".'[17] And the Rasta man himself, comparing his ability to perceive with that of the non-Rasta man ('Babylon' in the code of Rasta), says, 'Eyes have they and see not, only Fari could see'.[18] Note the pun on 'fari' which becomes both part of Rastafari and 'Far eye' suggesting 'far-seeing eye'.

In 'More Poem' from the same collection the idiom, if not the concepts, becomes more complex as Scott exploits different categories of word together:

> Only I-tongue have the right
> to reason, to that sense of dread.
> Man must keep silence now, except
> man without bread.
>
> No. See the flesh? It is a cave, it is
> stone. Seals every I away from light.
> Alone. Man must chant as Man can
> gainst night. (p. 35)

The pronominal 'I' of the earlier examples returns but this time it translates into English 'my'. The significance of its use here is that the tongue
becomes the Rasta man's tongue. Only he has the right to hold discourse
about important matters, which is the force of the word 'reason'. It does
not indicate discussion towards a logical conclusion as it might in English.
Note also the pun on 'I' in line two of the final stanza. From the context
it is clear that 'eye' is one of the intended meanings. A Rasta man might
write 'I' but draw an eye next to it or above it.[19] 'Chant' is also used in a
special way. Its meaning does not necessarily include the intoning of
words after the fashion of psalms in a church service. It is allowed to
mean simply 'speak'. The use of 'man' and 'dread' have already been
commented upon in other contexts. The message of the lines is one of
almost aggressive assertion of the right of the Rasta man (the man without
bread) to speak his piece.

Like Scott, Goodison uses the code of Dread to include the Rasta man in
the environment she describes and to add his particular focus or interpretation to any discourse. So words appear to mean one thing (English
meaning) but in fact have at least one other meaning (Dread Talk meaning). Goodison does not restrict herself to any one category of DT word
but exploits all the categories. This includes new words which might be
strange in form as well as meaning to the non-Jamaican reader, and which
emerge as a category IV (new items) in the ongoing analysis of DT.[20]

Goodison's descriptions have been compared to painting.[21] The Jamaican
environment in all its diversity is graphically represented. But murals
rather than simple pictures are what Goodison offers. Backdrop and foreground activity vie for the reader's attention on any one canvas. Language
is one of the means of indicating the identity of the representatives of the
different social groups interacting in the display. It is in the delicate overlap of the codes of the Jamaican speech community that Goodison excels.
The poem 'Ocho Rios II' from the collection *Tamarind Season*,[22] analyzed
in detail elsewhere,[23] is a good example of this. The situation is a tourist
city – Ocho Rios. Comments representing at least three social groups from
the society are included. The poet begins the observation with the voice
of the Rasta man soliloquizing: 'Today I again I forward to the sea.' The
significance of the ever-present sound /ai/ 'I' has already been commented upon. The first-person pronoun used initially might be SJE or DT
but the ambiguity is resolved by the repetition of the 'I' suggesting the DT
alternative 'I an I'. The item 'forward', which in SJE is an adverb of place
or a verb meaning 'to send', is in DT a very positive verb meaning to
'walk', 'advance', 'step', or simply 'go'. And so a line, intelligible to the
speaker of English, is unmistakeably a DT utterance. The Rasta man is indicating that he is visiting once more a site frequented by tourists. Later
in the poem, apologizing for the poor weather, the Rasta man tells the
tourist: 'man need rain for food to grow', and while man may include

'mankind' in its meaning, the primary reference in this context is to Rasta man.

In another picture, an urban one from her second collection *I am becoming my mother*, Goodison describes an open market 'Bend-Down Plaza' (one literally bends down to purchase). At the end of the description the Rasta man, who in Jamaica reserves the right to have the last and uninvited word on any subject, speaks to a prospective purchaser. His voice is recognizable by the word he selects for reference to the power he worships – Jah (abbreviated form of 'Jehovah'):

> Bend down nice lady
> bend down
> but try not to bend too deep
> for Jah inna this plaza
> distributing diseases
> and it look like God a sleep[24]

Note here the juxtaposition of the Rastafarian deity Jah and the Christian God who, at the time of the comment, is 'sleeping'. Jah threatens to give diseases to people who bend low enough to be available for carnal sin. And the God of mercy is not available to intervene.

Earlier in this poem the voice of the Rasta man is recognizable in the kind of effortless punning which has become part of his stock-in-trade. The guard, asleep with the alert guard dog beside him, is described as 'a sleeping *form*' and the voice, critical of the guard's irresponsible behaviour, suggests: '"Dem shoulda give the dog the *uniform*"'. This poem is written for the most part in a version of JC and illustrates very well the fact that DT interacts with SJE or with JC or with both, doing what Bongo Jerry accuses English of doing: 'word rearranging/ ringing rings of roses, pocket full of poses'.[25]

Sometimes, in order to include the Rasta man in the human environment of a poem, some lines are made to give the same meaning twice, once in SJE and once in DT. But the repetition is not obtrusive because the words are different. Category I words are useful for this exercise. In the poem 'Ceremony for the Banishment of the King of Swords' in her third collection, *Heartease*, for example, Goodison uses a word from this category. Note the lines: 'go through this again so you can/ *penetrate* it'.[26] In terms of SJE there is unnecessary repetition here because to 'penetrate' is to 'go through'. But in DT to 'penetrate' is 'to understand, to get the full meaning of'. So speakers of both codes are represented and the sentence really means: 'go through that again so you can understand it'.

A strategy close to this one, but different in its detail, is used in 'A Rosary of Your Names' from the same collection. God is worshipped here in a litany of fine words:

Your names are infinity
light and possibility
and right
and blessed
and *upfull* (p. 58)

'Upfull' is a DT term (Category IV) whose meaning includes both 'right'
and 'blessed'. The repetition is not obvious to the reader who is unaware
of the code of Dread. To the initiated, however, the intention of the addition of that word to the list is the inclusion of Rastafari in this act of
worship.

Equally hidden from the uninitiated is a reference to the Rasta man in
one of the title poems of that collection: 'Heartease I'. Note the closing
lines:

Believe, believe
and believe this
the eye know how far
Heartease is

Here 'the eye', the organ of sight, is also the Rasta individual, 'the I'. He
is here doubly represented as the 'eye' which can truly perceive and the
Rasta man who is in fact the possessor of such an eye. This is the reverse
of the usage recorded in Scott above where the representation on the page
is 'I'.

In Goodison's first collection there is a poem which is reminiscent of
Scott's 'Dreadwalk'. There are some differences, however. Scott in his
poem depends chiefly on the manipulation of one item, the significant 'I',
to give the dimension of Rastafarian involvement. The linguistic environment of his poem is predominantly SJE. Goodison makes use of the 'word'
in a JC environment. This is in fact the more natural environment of DT,
a code which arose out of a need of the lower-class Jamaican, whose language is JC, to find an identifiable voice. (Of course Scott is treating
dialogue between a Rasta man and a speaker of English.)

'The Road of Dread' might seem to be written in JC, but if you try to
read it aloud the pauses dictated by the phrasing encourage the tone and
pace regarded as typical of the Rastaman's speech. In addition the content
and the biblical references considered typical, mark this poem as a soliloquy by a Rastaman walking along the road. In Jamaica such a man is a
very familiar sight and sound. The Rastafarian is known to go miles on
foot conversing with himself and occasionally shouting with much verve
'Jah Rastafari!' Of the road the Rasta man in the poem says:

That dey road no pave
like any other black-face road
it no have no definite colour...

Pan dis same road ya sista
sometime yu drink yu salt sweat fi water
far yu sure sey at least dat no pisen,
an bread? yu picture it an chew it accordingly
an some time yu surprise fi know how dat full
man belly[27]

(That road is not paved like any other black-faced road. It has no definite colour.
On this same road sister, sometimes you drink your salt sweat for water for you are
sure that at least that is not poison. And bread? you picture it and chew it accordingly and sometimes you are surprised to know how that fills your stomach.)

At the end of the road there is hope in a final stanza which bears quotation in its entirety not only because it is valuable as a place where the central philosophy of Rastafari is neatly articulated but because from the
linguistic point of view, it illustrates (in line five) Goodison's ability to
move from a JC association to an SJE association.

The joy of the road of the dread, the recompense for all the tribulation,
from the point of view of the traveller, is the meeting with a kindred
spirit:

and better still when yu meet another traveller
who have flour and yu have water and man and man
make bread together.
And dem time dey the road run straight and sure
like a young horse that cant tire
and yu catch a glimpse of the end
through the water in yu eye
I wont tell yu what I spy
but is fi dat alone I tread this road   (p. 23)

(and better still when you meet another traveller who has flour and you have water
and two people make bread together. At that time the road runs straight and sure
like a young horse that can't be made tired and you catch a glimpse of the end
through the tears in your eyes. I won't tell you what I spy but it is for that alone
that I tread this road.)

Note the almost English of the line 'like a young horse that cant tire'.
English might require a passive verb here, but JC requires the predicate
adjective 'tired'. 'Tire' is a fine compromise.

The cultural movement that is Rastafari is perhaps the boldest statement
of rejection of the values associated with European supremacy to have
been made anywhere in the New World. Nettleford describes it as one of
Plantation America's 'most authentic expressions of organic revolt in
appropriate if anguished response to some of the deepest social forces that
have shaped and still determine the discrepancies of our Caribbean
society'.[28] It would be more than surprising if the effect of the movement

had not been felt in the literature of the region. The language is the organ of the movement.

It is not the intention of this paper to suggest that the influence of Rastafari has been on language only, nor that the influence has been on the work of Jamaican creative artists only. Rohlehr's discussion[29] is ample evidence of the influence of Rastafari on the thought and language of at least one non-Jamaican, Kendel Hippolyte, a brilliant young poet from St. Lucia.[30]

The accomplishment of Scott and of Goodison must be seen as a refinement on earlier attempts to write the Rasta man into the poetry of the region. Perhaps the language of Rasta had not developed enough in the sixties for non-Rastafarians to be able to manipulate it in the way these two do. Perhaps the level of understanding they have attained was not reached by the earlier writers. The fact is that if the Rasta presence may be described as 'intrusive' in Scott and Goodison, it is 'extrusive' in the writing of some of the earlier poets. The work of Brathwaite and of McNeil provide some examples of early experimentation with the language and philosophy of Rasta.

Brathwaite, in 'Wings of a Dove', uses the 'I' forms and the Dread terminology to discuss the condition of 'Brother Man the Rasta man':

> And I
> Rastafar-I
> in Babylon's boom
> town, crazed by the moon
> and the peace of this chalice, I
> prophet and singer, scourge
> of the gutter, guardian
> Trench Town, the Dungle and Young's
> Town, rise and walk through the now silent
> streets of affliction...[31]

Scott's 'Dreadwalk' may in fact owe something to Brathwaite's description. Note the place of 'I' at the end of the line, a feature discussed at length, in Scott's work, above. Yet there is something more convincing about Scott's lines which is not merely the result of a different craft. The single term 'Dreadwalk', for example, by the time Scott published, could conjure up everything that Brathwaite's lines above describe. Equally, Goodison's description of the road of the Dread with its weight of literal and metaphorical meanings is capable of conjuring up a more complete picture than the 'streets of affliction' from the passage above.

McNeil's 'Saint Ras'

> ...had
> not learned to fall in with the straight
> queued capitalistic for work.
> He was uneasy in traffic.[32]

All this is contained in Scott's line 'blackman came walking I' or Goodison's 'dat de road no pave'.

The dramatic movement over the decade or so which allows for the space separating these artists as far as this influence is concerned runs parallel to the movement within art, music and dance as the culture of Rastafari has moved like yeast through the Jamaican society infusing all these expressions with its power.

NOTES

1. Edward Brathwaite, ed., *New Poets from Jamaica* (Mona: Savacou Publications, 1979).
2. Ras Boanerges, 'Now we shall be a Nation', *Youth Black Faith*, Vol. I, No. 1, 1984.
3. Rex Nettleford, *Caribbean Cultural Identity – the Case of Jamaica* (Kingston: Institute of Jamaica, 1978).
4. Joshua Peart, 'Dread Talk', Caribbean Study Undergraduate Requirement, Faculty of Arts, University of the West Indies, Mona, Jamaica, 1977.
5. Velma Pollard, 'Dread Talk – the Speech of the Rastafarian in Jamaica', *Caribbean Quarterly*, Vol. 26, No. 4.
6. Farika Birhan, 'linguistic language lattitudes – the queen's "english" and the emperor's iyaric', in *itations of Jamaica and i RASTAFARI* (New York: Ragner and Bernhard, 1982).
7. Bongo Jerry, 'Mabrak', *Savacou* 3/4, p. 15.
8. Dennis Scott, *Uncle Time* (University of Pittsburgh Press, 1973), p. 53.
9. Velma Pollard, 'Dread Talk – the Speech of the Rastafarian in Jamaica', pp. 35-36.
10. Mervyn Morris, 'Introduction' to *Uncle Time* (Scott, 1973), p. xx.
11. Ibid., p. xx.
12. Dennis Scott, op. cit., p. 52.
13. Ibid., 'Homecoming', p. 6.
14. Dennis Scott, 'Guard-ring' in *Dreadwalk* (London: New Beacon Books, 1982), p. 44.
15. Gordon Rohlehr, 'The Problem of the Problem of Form', *Caribbean Quarterly*, Vol. 31, No. 1, p. 39.
16. For extensive commentary on this aspect of the poem, see Gordon Rohler, op. cit., and Ian Smith, 'Poetics of Self – Dennis Scott's Dangerous Style', *Caribbean Quarterly*, Vol. 30, No. 1, 1984.
17. Mervyn Alleyne, *Roots of Jamaican Culture* (London: Pluto Press, 1988), p. 148.
18. In Velma Pollard, 'The Social History of Dread Talk', *Caribbean Quarterly*, Vol. 28, No. 4, 1982, p. 21.
19. See, for example, in Senya, *Senya Poems* (Frederksted: Ay Ay, 1988), pp. 98-99.
20. Velma Pollard, 'The Social History of Dread Talk'.
21. P. Mordecai, 'Wooing with Words – Some Comments on the Poetry of Lorna Goodison', *Jamaica Journal*, No. 45, 1981.
22. Lorna Goodison, *Tamarind Season* (Kingston: Institute of Jamaica, 1980).
23. Velma Pollard, 'Overlapping Systems – Language in the Poetry of Lorna Goodison', *CARIB*, No. 5, pp. 33-47.
24. Lorna Goodison, *I am becoming my mother* (London: New Beacon, 1986), p. 11.
25. Bongo Jerry, op. cit., p. 14.
26. Lorna Goodison, *Heartease* (London: New Beacon, 1988), p. 53.
27. Lorna Goodison, *Tamarind Season*, p. 22.

28. Rex Nettleford, op. cit., p. 188.
29. Gordon Rohlehr, op. cit.
30. For detailed comment on the influence of Dread Talk on the languages of St. Lucia, see Velma Pollard, 'The Speech of the Rastafarians of Jamaica in the Eastern Caribbean – the Case of St. Lucia', *International Journal of the Sociology of Language*, No. 85, 1990.
31. Edward Brathwaite, *Rights of Passage* (London: OUP, 1967), p. 41.
32. Anthony McNeil, *Reel from 'The Life Movie'* (Kingston: Savacou Publications, 1972), p. 39.

POLITICS AND LITERATURE

The writer is witness to the public and domestic misuses of power.
  Nayantara Sahgal, 'The Schizophrenic Imagination'

ELLEKE BOEHMER

Motherlands, Mothers and Nationalist Sons: Representations of Nationalism and Women in African Literature

The point which this paper will try to keep in its sights is that the nationalist ideology or ideologies which inform African literature (especially
that of the immediately pre- and post-independence periods) have worked
to limit representations of and by women. The idea is that nationalism
generally, both in its past and its present manifestations, bears a clear
mark for gender, and that this gender marking, rather than being referred
to a monolithic or trans-historical concept of patriarchy, can be explained
as a specific historical development of gendered power. Therefore,
whether nationalism speaks the languages of emptiness, dream and desire,
or whether of fulfilment and the achievement of meaning, the codification
of that meaning – of self and also of the objects of desire – is gendered.
But this is the idea to which I am moving. My beginning is rather in story
– two stories in fact: one about a hero, the other about a 'girl'.

The hero is Matigari, eponymous messiah-fighter of Ngugi wa Thiong'o's
most recent novel.[1] The story opens with Matigari, as old Land and Freedom guerilla, returning to his homeland, and goes on to relate the various
trials and adventures which befall him as he attempts to reclaim his
family, that is, the true Kenyan nation, by sowing a message of patriotism
and peace in a land of fear and betrayal. Matigari's full name, which
means, 'the patriots who survived the bullets' (p. 20), points to his status
as the people's collective hero. He has fought for the people, and has now
come again to guide and save them; he is the nation in ideal form – a
'little man' and yet a prophet. His mission is that the people will grow to
be more like him – will become *matigari*. Yet, if this is so, if Matigari is
representative, then his gender is also significant. This is especially so if
we set him in relation to Wariinga, the powerful central figure of Ngugi's
previous novel, *Devil on the Cross*. As beautiful and bionic all-rounder,
Wariinga, flinging out of the pages of that novel bearing a gun, was, like
Matigari, the symbol of a struggle for justice and a new order. In a polemical text, her womanhood presaged one of the freedoms which that new

order would bring. With Matigari, then, Ngugi has returned to the trope
of the nationalist actor as masculine, as conventionally a fighter-figure and
a leader of men.

Matigari is aided in his liberation campaign by a prostitute, Guthera,
whom he has saved from sin and exploitation in the manner of a Christ,
bidding her to 'Get up ... Come, stand up, mother' (p. 32). Guthera resembles Wariinga in that she doubles up as strong woman and as desirable object: her clothes are said to fit her 'as though she was created in
them' (p. 28).[2] Yet, at the same time, her role relative to Matigari's is
primarily one of support: she accompanies him courageously into his final
moments but it is he who leads. Within this sort of gender stereotyping,
it is quite appropriate that, when Guthera and Matigari disappear in a
raging river, a boy-follower, Muriuki, is left to carry on the struggle. In the
familial triad she forms with Matigari and Muriuki, Guthera, acting as at
once prostitute and surrogate mother, can be seen as representative of all
Kenyan womanhood (or of that body of human beings carefully addressed
as 'the women' when inclusive references are made to the Kenyan nation).
If this logic of family and generation is taken further, it also becomes clear
that the boy child, Muriuki, prefigures the new Kenyan nation. The true
successor of Matigari is to be neither a mother nor a Wariinga-type re-
formed prostitute – in simple terms, the inheritor is not to be a woman.
For if Matigari is a man and a fighter, and if he returns to his people so
that his people in turn will become *matigari*, then the conclusion which
seems inevitable is that Matigari can bequeath his AK 47 to no one other
than a son.

The 'girl' of my second tale is called Gladys; she is the (at first nameless)
young woman whom the narrator of Chinua Achebe's story 'Girls at War'
encounters at three representative moments during the years of the Biafran
War.[3] Though Achebe has seemingly been long intrigued by the power
granted to women in myth and ritual (Ani, Idemili), what is at issue in the
present story is not so much mythical presence as the 'girl' Gladys's signifying condition – she is in effect a sign of the times. 'Girls at War' was
written out of the exhaustion and disillusionment which was the aftermath
of Biafra. Three distinct phases in the worsening conflict are charted out,
each phase corresponding to a meeting between the narrator, Reginald
Nwankwo, an official in the Ministry of Justice, and Gladys, the 'girl'. As
Reginald is the narrator of the story, it is he who will index each phase in
the action relative to Gladys's various incarnations as a 'girl at war'. The
term, 'girl' or 'girls', with its compound implications of vulnerability, im-
maturity, helplessness and sexual provocativeness, is used throughout.

The first time the two meet, Gladys is off to join the militia and Reginald
gives her a ride. This was, we are told, in 'the first heady days of war,
when thousands of young men *and sometimes women too* were coming forward burning with readiness to bear arms in defence of the exciting new
nation' (my emphasis, p. 98). Reginald tells her that 'girls [are] not

required in the militia' and instructs her to go home (p. 100). The second time they meet, he is again in his car, she on the side of the road, but because she is supervising a road block, it is she who can now give instructions. Reginald's irritation registers the extent to which this contravenes his expectations as a privileged government official and as a man. Yet his feelings are somewhat mitigated by the pleasure he takes in her appearance: he notes that despite her military look, she is 'a beautiful girl in a breasty blue jersey' (p. 99). He is even more impressed when she reveals her identity. 'Yes, you were the girl', Reginald says as he recognises her (p. 100). As he drives off Reginald's preconceptions have been sufficiently shaken for him to acknowledge that 'the girls' must now be taken seriously; they are no longer to be compared to children imitating their fathers' drilling exercises (p. 100). Significantly, though, despite the potential subversions implicit in their new military jobs, it is still primarily the time-honoured role of self-dedication, 'their devotion' to an external cause, that has redeemed them. The cause itself remains not only of the first importance, it is also firmly in the hands of those at the top. As he drives away, Reginald repeats to himself the words his new friend used to describe her activity: 'we are doing the work you asked us to do' (p. 100).

Reginald and 'the girl' meet for the third time eighteen months later. The war is going badly; the once free and hopeful nation of Biafra is now crippled by heavy casualties and mass starvation. Reginald has gone out for food supplies for his family – as he puts it, in 'search of relief' (p. 101). On the way home relief comes in the form of his old friend, 'the girl', once again hitch-hiking by the side of the road, and again in a different garb – the military look has not lasted long. Reginald soon observes: 'You were always beautiful of course, but now you are a beauty queen' (p. 103). Her appearance secures her a measure of individuality; she is no longer a generic figure, an example of devoted national service. It is time for Reginald to learn her name. He is not entirely comfortable though with the way that Gladys has turned out. He notes her high-tinted wig and expensive shoes and concludes that these are smuggled goods and that the girl has been corrupted. An attack-trader, one who deals in foreign currency and looted goods, Reginald decides, is at the bottom of it all. Once again the girl is not entirely in charge; she is susceptible to being manipulated. 'Too many girls were simply too easy these days', Reginald comments to himself, 'War sickness, some called it' (p. 106). The girl's physical state, as well as her assumed status as a pawn in a some underground enterprise, becomes an emblem of the general state of the nation. Reginald himself acknowledges this: 'Gladys ... was just a mirror reflecting a society that had gone completely rotten and maggoty at the centre' (114).[4]

The girl's corruption intrigues Reginald. After she has '[yielded]' to him, he offers to drive her to her home, hoping in this way to find out more about her. En route, having picked up another hitch-hiker, a disabled young soldier, they are caught in an air-raid. Gladys runs back to help the soldier and the two of them are caught in the bombardment, immolated in one another's arms. This final image, reinforced by the presence of the soldier, confirms Gladys's emblematic role. We witness in this moment of conflagration the destruction of young Biafra, of brave loyal soldiers and dutiful girls, united in a hopeless and yet ennobling national struggle. Moreover, through her final (?) heroic act, Gladys either wins back or reasserts the integrity which she seemed to have lost. She does this though by remaining unambiguously 'female'. Her actual physical death catches and fixes her once again in the time-worn attitude of giving herself (like Guthera, she is granted a support role). She is made available for carrying both the positive and the negative meanings of war, of national conflict as glorious, and of double-dealing and civil strife as diseased and corrupting. The representation of the male soldier, who is anyway introduced only at the point of glorious immolation, is more simple. If 'girls', crudely speaking, represent the state of the nation whatever that state may be, male figures exemplify honest-to-goodness integrity and national character.[5] This would seem to be so not only because men command the action – driving the cars and carrying the guns – but also because they determine its meanings. This is so whether we look at the arena of national politics – at national pageantry, presidential cavalcades, garlanded grandstands – or within the somewhat more secluded spaces of national literatures.

Gender in nationalism as elsewhere has to do with symbols and signifying practices. Everyday speech, then, would presumably be similarly marked. Consider, for example, the metaphors buried in the terms 'motherland' – and/or '-continent', '-country,' '-tongue' – and 'fatherland.' What immediately attracts notice here are, perhaps unsurprisingly, the differing symbolic valencies of these terms, suggesting, like the two tales, that images of mothers and of men occupy different spaces and levels in national iconographies. Syntactically, the epithet 'father' cannot be used interchangeably with that of 'mother'; so too the meanings which collect around the mother metaphor when applied to lands, languages and other national entities, are incommensurate with and preclude the idea of the father. The image of the mother invites connotations of origins – birth, hearth, home, roots, the umbilical root – and rests upon the frequent, and some might say 'natural', identification of the mother with the beloved earth, the national territory, and the first-spoken language, the national tongue. In contrast the term fatherland has conventionally lent itself to contexts perhaps more strenuously nationalistic, where the appeal is to *Bruderschaft*, filial duty, the bonds of fraternity and paternity.

Taken together with the roles assigned the male and female characters in the two stories, these metaphors limn a paradigm for the symbolisation of gender in nationalism. As the outgrowth of a time that 'en-lightened man', nationalism makes its appeal, or professes to make its appeal, to all citizens equally. The controlling idea is of a homogeneous society; all have

equal access to power. In practice, however, and certainly in its iconographies of power, nationalism may be characterised as a male drama.
National actors are cast in conventionally masculine roles: as soldier,
leader or representative of state, official orator (or artist) or faithful
citizen-hero – in most cases either as a fatherly or as a fraternal figure.
Woman as actor or equal participant is strangely absent from this drama.
She is rarely assigned a role alongside that of the male actors, neither does
she set the scene or swell a progress. External to the 'serious' affairs of the
nation, she is most often found in the form of inviolable ideal or untouchable icon – that is if she is not excluded from the action entirely as an
unknown subversive quantity and a threat. Her role is that of emblem,
two-dimensional and either tainted or sacrosanct. Even if she is granted
the part of single glorified heroine, she is seen as superhuman ('no normal
woman could be this way') – once again removed from real life, once
again inviolable.

The symbolic economy of nationalism, then, would seem to be strictly
delineated by gender – or even more precisely, by tropes which fit into
gendered categories. Male roles in nationalism may be characterised as
metonymic: as author and subject of nationalism, the male is a part of the
nation, or contiguous with it; his place is alongside that of his brother
citizens. If he appears as a personification of the nation, he is both an
individual and individualised – a John Bull, an Uncle Sam. In contrast, the
figure of woman in nationalism is usually seen as generalised and generic
(not to say generative also). Her form swells into a trope closer to metaphor. In some special cases, when for example she takes the androgynous
form of woman fighter or soldier (the latter-day Wariinga, the early
Gladys), a woman character may be ranked together with her nationalist
brothers. Yet, despite the male dressing, her status as single woman remains, as I have suggested, idealised and totemic. In general, then, the
woman – and usually the mother – figure stands for the national territory
and for national values: symbolically she is ranged above the men; in reality she is kept below them. As, for example, in the imagery of African
nationalism, as also that of pan-Africanism,[6] the idealised woman figure
can take on massive, gravid, even continent-wide proportions – she is
Great Mother, both Africa and mother, embracing each and every nation
in her generous arms. Yet, as elsewhere, it is also the case that, right
across the continent, subsisting as they may despite the bright myths of
motherhood, women make up the greater part of Africa's illiterate, oppressed and poor.

It may be that some of this seems rather obvious and uninspiring. The
female form has long been deployed as a repository of value in patriarchal
societies. In the shape of Madeleine, Britannia, Liberty, she has taken upon
herself the personification of national virtues even as women within nations have been marginalised and subordinated. In answer to the proposal
that nationalism, say, has patriarchal features, it might simply be argued

that this is only another incarnation of the worn though resilient figure of
the father. So, if women are placed as the stuff of nations, the womb and
ground of origin, we know who is doing the placing. The assumption here
is that the symbolic baggage nationalism has inherited from older social
formations need not necessarily impinge on the ideology itself. My response to this is quite simply that no matter how familiar the symbols, nor
yet how iconoclastic or recuperative the ideology, its symbols and its
vocabularies of self-representation do matter – fundamentally so. Metaphors of self, place and history reveal not simply how national entities
identify themselves, but also how and why that identification can work as
misrecognition. If these tropes of identity are examined more closely, it
becomes possible to suggest ways in which this misrecognition might take
place. Who is located where in the processes of identification? What sort
of groups get to compose national meanings and which groups are composed by those meanings? Who masters the languages of selfhood? It is
precisely because of the persuasive representation of nations as collect-
ivities of equals, that such questions are too infrequently asked and that
the codification of (in this case) gendered power within nationalism is insufficiently scrutinised.

If women are portrayed as the objects and men the subjects of national
aspiration, this would seem to have two main implications for nationalism:
one, that the structures of nations or nation-states are soldered onto the
struts of gender hierarchies; and two, that imagining nations[7] may be a
process profoundly informed by those structures, that it may be extremely
difficult to conceive of nationalism outside of gender. Rising out of this,
my claim then is that gender as iconic language of nationalism is both
reflective of and reproduces concentrations of power within nationalist
movements and in nation-states. To make this claim, I draw on the insights of Joan W. Scott who, speaking of the informing effects of gendered
meanings, has convincingly argued that 'gender [is] implicated in the conception and construction of power' and so of politics.[8] Or, as Maurice
Godelier has also put it, though in more general terms: 'It is not sexuality
which haunts society, but society which haunts the body's sexuality. Sex-
related differences between bodies are continually summoned as testimony
to social relations and phenomena that have nothing to do with sexuality.
Not only as testimony to, but also testimony for – in other words, as
legitimation.'[9] If metaphors organise and contain meanings, then the gendered metaphors which are used to legitimate nationalisms may be said
at once to embody the organisation of power in the nation and to delimit
the national participation of women. Gender, I would argue, thus operates
at a primary level of structuration in nationalism – its symbology is both
constituted by and is constitutive of patriarchy in nationalism.

From this it is clear that the dominance of mother images in nationalisms
cannot simply be read as natural, nothing more than the expression on a
national level of a respect for mothers built into social attitudes. Yet

having said this, I want also to add that such respect cannot be discounted in any analysis. The ways in which the category 'mother' is named and conceived will vary from culture to culture. Where families are traditionally extended, as in Africa, and where mothers and matrons accrue status as they grow older, the noun or name, mother, may refer to a wider generic category than is the case in societies which feature predominantly nuclear families. Moreover, as Unterhalter and Gaitskell have observed: 'in vernacular African languages ... the word for adult woman and the word for mother are the same.'[10] Taking these considerations together, it is clear that in cultures which assign power to women in accordance with their age and position in the community as well as with reproductive capacity, 'mother' may be an honorific title for a woman, designating high status. The gender construction is thus different from the biological role. As Ifi Amadiume informs us in her study of Igbo communities, gender concepts and identities need not be aligned with sex differentiation based on biology.[11] Practically speaking, women – or mothers – have also become the veritable guardians and keepers of the African earth. Due to the socio-economic pressures of urban migration and (in the South especially) migrant labour, men leave women on the land where they work to produce Africa's food: 'mothers' hold the earth in safekeeping. To bring in another sort of point entirely, it must also be recognised that the ubiquity of the trope of the mother, and more generally, the predominance of generic women figures in literatures shaped by new (and not only African) nationalisms may be partly the result of a particularly polemical, pictorial phase in the emergence and growth of those new nationalisms – of a need to connect with home and origins and to establish authenticity.

Perhaps the significance and impact of the mother totem in nationalism becomes more distinct if it is set alongside its related trope, that of 'her' nationalist son.[12] The 'family romance' in which the male artist, leader or citizen-hero addresses himself to his national mother (land, home, concept of nation) in tones variously deferential or reverential, is enacted again and again in the literature and history of national movements. The hierarchical relationship depicted in this romance, as also the aspect of its actors – their identities, assigned characters, even their relative sizes and allocated speaking times – say much about the particular configurations of power which operate in national formations. The 'family drama' may therefore be read as supplying the corroborative script and choreography for the larger symbolic dramas staged in nationalist histories. Literature is a singularly appropriate medium for such 'acts'. This is not only for the obvious reasons: that literature permits self-articulation; or that it serves to display and to validate national customs and 'traditions' – or to enshrine talismans of fatherly power. On a more metaphoric level, it is also, I believe, because in literature, nationalist traditions of 'sonship' are crossed with and reinforced by the vocabularies of patrimony and filiation which inform literary mythology.[13] I will try to illustrate these ideas in some greater detail, drawing on more examples from African literature.

Ranging across a fairly wide terrain in the African literature of the fifties, sixties and seventies, the nationalist hero, often exiled or alienated from home (mother and heart(h)land), may be cast as resilient and courageous (the soldier, the leader); idealistic or visionary (the poet); or resourceful, even omnicompetent (where women are absent from the arena of action, men must learn to 'do' for themselves). Michael Udomo in Peter Abrahams's *A Wreath for Udomo*[14] is a representative case. *A Wreath* is a tale of exile and return to Africa embodied in Udomo's efforts to claim self-government for his nation and identity for his people (significantly, the novel appeared a year before Ghanaian independence and was later seen as presaging developments in that country). Udomo as chief liberator stands in the strong dominant position in the text; its positive terms (reason, assertiveness, resourcefulness, conviction) are reinforced and confirmed in his character and action. Udomo is also vigorously male; he is the leader of '[o]ur young men [who] must ceaselessly prepare themselves for the fight' (p. 15).

Contrasted with Udomo and highlighting his status as true national leader, are two centres of rival power, each in some way a negation or aberration of those characteristics and qualities which Udomo incarnates. On the one side are those of the exiled elite (all of course male) who are at first suitably rational and freedom-loving, but who eventually fall from grace, turning to 'tribalism' and subverting Udomo's plans. On the other are 'the women', all of them in some way either inconsequential or deviant. The single positive female symbol is that of Africa. Only as ideal, purged of her materiality, it appears, can the feminine be strong, single and pure. As her one upright and constant devotee, Udomo then wins the right to be consort of Mother Africa and her most eloquent worshipper. On returning to Africa after exile, Udomo salutes the shoreline in tones of annunciation and adoration. Note that in identifying with sun imagery, Udomo claims agency and 'sonship' for himself:[15] 'Mother Africa! Oh, Mother Africa, make me strong for the work that I must do. Don't forget me in the many you nurse. I would make you great. I would have the world respect you and your children. I would have the sun of freedom shine over you once more' (pp. 122-123).

The sentiment of Udomo's cries, the yearning to cleave and champion and unite, recalls something of the longing and striving of (the somewhat earlier) Negritude poetry, recently correctly described as a 'vindication of the black *man*'s humanity in the face of the white man's racism' [my emphasis].[16] The speaker in Negritude poetry is again – invariably – male; the object of his desire female. Assuming the attitude of a supplicant and worshipper, the Negritude poet addresses himself to Africa, location of past memory, continent of his people, and conceived of in womanly form. Once again, Africa is never so much Africa as when the land is incarnated as woman, as manifestation of the people's (alleged and acclaimed) corporeality, mystery and sensuality. In Senghor's much-quoted poem, 'Femme Nue, Femme Noire,'[17] the woman is apostrophised as Beloved and as desirable body. Her physical form is glorified and reified; it is a body triumphantly corporeal, entirely body, and thus, in terms of the values endorsed by the poetry, a true embodiment of Africa. Yet her form is also maternal; she is the nurturing presence of the past: 'J'ai grandi a ton ombre; la douceur de tes mains bandait mes yeux' ('In your shadow I have grown up; the gentleness of your hands was laid over my eyes'). This same comforting gesture the poet begs from the woman he invokes in 'Nuit de Sine' (pp. 12-13 and 5). Both desired and nurturing, the Beloved comforts the poet. And she comforts all the more because she is one with the home earth. In 'Femme Nue' she is 'Terre promis', 'savane qui fremis' ('savannah shuddering'), beneath the homecoming force of the East Wind. Thus love for home and Africa is expressed simultaneously as sexual desire and as filial adoration – a yearning to cleave with a/the body of the land that is at once maternal lap and lapping flesh of the desired woman. The conjuncture is possible because the land of the poet's desire is both the place of his childhood dreams, associated with his mother, and the cherished object of his present need and future hope.

Camara Laye is not strictly a Negritude writer, yet his terms of apostrophe in recalling Africa and the African woman are similarly lyrical, even rhapsodic. *L'Enfant Noir* (1953) (*The Dark Child* (1955)),[18] which is roughly contemporaneous with *A Wreath*, is the autobiography of Laye's childhood. Though the African son figure is not yet mature and must still come into his own, the novel charts the first stages in that process of growth. The hankering for the African heart(h)land is therefore all the more mother-bonded. The narrative insists on the pre-eminent position of Laye's mother: she is there as a constant within the progression of the memoir and the life; a still point – though far from voiceless – to which the wandering and increasingly more alienated Laye returns for sustenance. Whereas a European presence resides in the city down at the coast and dominates the cold north, the hinterland, the warm heart or bosom of Africa, is suitably presided over by the spirit of the mother. In accordance with her centrality to the writer's life, the novel begins with a dedication which is also, as with Udomo, an invocation from an exiled son: it is a call to 'my mother', who is also a Mother, a generic 'Black Woman, Woman of Africa', a muse of belonging and nostalgia: 'Black woman, woman of Africa, O my mother, let me thank you; thank you for all that you have done for me, your son, who, though so far away, is still so close to you!' (p. i) In contrast to the mystic mother force which presides over the land, male characters in the autobiography have specific work and a more localised power – the father is a goldsmith, the son an engineer-to-be. But, far from this signifying some sort of deficiency, the male char-

acters are therefore presented as the more normatively human. They are
the practical actors and authors of African life.

In his appropriately-named survey of sub-Saharan African culture, *The
Breast of the Earth*,[19] Kofi Awoonor, the Ghanaian writer, deploys comparable terms of identification: the mother is idealised but man is the social
actor. Awoonor builds his initial comments on an implicit symbolic sub-
structure which represents the mother as the presiding genius of the home
and the community. Some way into the work he makes this link-up clear.
The mother in African society, he notes, is 'sustainer', 'inspirer', 'path-
finder' and 'the nerve centre of the homestead'. She doubles up as multi-
mammia and mage. So it follows, Awoonor asserts, that 'The mother in
the African world represents not only the most steadfast person in the
homestead, but also the symbol of the eternal giver, the earth itself'
(pp. 99-100). At the same time, however, on occasions when spiritual arte-
facts are being sculpted, her gaze is said to be 'profane' (p. 60). And again,
at important rituals where the spirits of the community are worshipped,
her presence is a defilement: she is forbidden entrance. It then becomes
significant that in his own poetic work of reconstituting African traditions,
Awoonor has taken over a form – the Ewe dirge – which is 'normally performed by women' (p. 84). Is it possible to deduce from this that the male
artist alone is to speak for his land as nationalist; and that he is the one
who officiates at national ceremonies also?

To demonstrate the temporal and geographical spread of support for the
Mother Africa ideal, more recent work by nationalist sons from the south
of the continent can also be quoted. In the long poem, 'No baby must
weep', Wally Mongane Serote, like Awoonor, expands the meanings of the
mother metaphor.[20] The township mama whose attention he as prodigal
son insists on in the first part of the poem, gradually swells into the more
generalised and generic shape of Mother Africa. By the end of the poem
he is calling on Africa, as maternal presence, to take him home (pp. 72-92).
As with the other writers, the mother image evokes sentiments of love and
longing for Africa as place of authenticity and origin and thus focuses
nationalist aspiration. Yet in a pattern that is by now becoming familiar,
though the honoured iconic personage is feminine, the poet is concerned,
both in this and in other poems, to tag his own identity as male. He is
'manchild' (pp. 34-35), 'ofay-watcher' (pp. 38-41), concerned for his fellow
brothers (pp. 17, 31) and the rape of his mothers (p. 17), and wielding
what would seem to be a phallic pen (p. 45). In Ingoapele Madingoane's
anthology *Africa My Beginning*,[21] the dichotomies are even more clear: the
poems offer an unambiguously seminal statement of the gender categories
which operate in nationalism. Again, the mother is custodian of tradition
and identity, of Africanness (pp. 14-15). She is interpellated as comforter
and granted status in proportion to the support she offers (pp. 4-5, 6-7).
However, we discover that this is all to guarantee the 'manhood' of
Africa's blackmen (pp. 4-5). They are in charge of meanings; the identity

they seek is indistinguishable from an assertive maleness. To quote from yet another dedication: 'I did not know,// but had to know,// that we in Africa are blackmen, born of women who loved oppressed men.// This book is dedicated to the women who love us in bondage.' As Valerie Smith has remarked of the Black Nationalist Movement in the United States, the discourse of liberation and cultural assertion 'enshrines the possibilities of black male power'.[22]

As symbolic figure, then, the substantial bulk of Mother Africa embraces with some liberality and largesse nationalist imaginations. In nationalist iconography male filial figures experience the gravitational pull to the national ground; women constitute part of its gravid mass. As I have tried to demonstrate, this symbolic drama of nationalist action repeatedly enacts and so repeatedly reproduces itself across the pages of literature. At the least, then, it is possible to say that binary gender terms compose and organise nationalist symbology. I have not yet shown, however, or not explicitly, what I have set out as a reciprocal formation or tendency in nationalism: that is, its specifically gendered state as ideology. This assertion is stronger than that which would refer only to the legitimating force of gender tropes. The claim is rather that nationalism articulates and consolidates itself through gender because it is deeply imbricated in, not to say structured by, gendered forms.

Earlier in this argument I made reference to the determining powers of symbols in literature and history. Having now spoken at some length of literature, it is time to speak (in what will have to be a more summary and tentative way) of history. What this will involve is a refusal or at least a qualification on the grounds of androcentrism of the broad liberatory claims made by nationalist formations, including those which have arisen in the South or so-called Third World. As the mother-son literary drama has suggested and as I will now try to argue further, this androcentrism has co-existed comfortably with and in fact subtends the dominant orientation to mother images. My intention is not however to dismiss or to disparage those for whom nationalism works, or has hope of working – those who may believe that nationalism offers ways of recovering self and reclaiming cultural integrity after colonial occupation. For such nationalists it may be that the various discriminations imposed by national structures in the post-independence era can be interpreted in the main as a hangover from the time of colonialism, an expression therefore of the failure of the moment of so-called liberation. In the case of Africa, say, it might be contended that at independence the framework of the colonial system, taken over virtually intact by the new national elites, was only superficially africanised. Those who take this view would then believe that a solution to the trauma of a derivative politics is to be found in fostering a national and also a populist consciousness. A truly rooted nationalism will provide innovative and indigenous means of conceiving of the nation. Yet such proposals, no matter how optimistic or even expedient, do not adequately address the problem of agency as this pertains to gender (and also in some cases to class distinctions). It is important to ask once again, in a putatively national culture, in creating a national consciousness, given that certain hierarchies of power remain in place, who is it who gets to set the meanings? Whose national consciousness are we speaking of?

Acknowledgement must be given once again to what could be called the originary ground of nationalism, its own historical roots. This however is by no means the same as saying that there is necessarily anything essential, fixed or inbuilt in nationalism in its various incarnations. Nationalism travels well precisely because it is constructed and thus protean in form and in definition. National identities, as I have already suggested, are not innate but incorporative, working within and remaking the political and cultural materials which lie to hand. At the same time though, no matter how many processes of replication, splitting and reformation nations may have undergone in the course of their various histories, nationalism as a modern movement has itself been constructed in time, and bears the mark of that history or histories. Models for national movements and for thinking about nations which reached Europe's occupied territories, were informed and catalysed in the Europe of the Enlightenment.[23] Such models inevitably owed something of their form and coherence to the pre-existing social structures of that time. However much the new age of nationalism was regarded as a break with the past, nationalism whether as ideology or movement was not *sui generis*; it relied on what was available, and what was available in this case were the formations of the old dynastic state and the patriarchal family.

Though such rudimentary analyses simplify rather brutally what was a complex and lengthy historical process, it is possible to trace a determining link-up between the formation of modern states and the rise of nationalism. Since feudal times, as other older forms of authority such as the church, the monarchy and the aristocracy disintegrated, state structures found in the nation a new means of representation and legitimation. This was tied in with the rise of the bourgeoisie: if nationalism endowed the new middle classes with an ideology allowing wider and more democratic access to power, state structures provided the means of establishing and maintaining political and economic control. Both the older state formations and the new economic system, however, operated according to principles of gender-domination; in the state, as in the new workplaces, as also in the new middle-class home, lines of control emanated from the feared and/or revered figures of fathers. What happened then was that nationalism, in its first incarnations, was projected upon the gender hierarchies based in the state. In a world where other orders were changing and falling away, such hierarchies were then reinforced by parallels which were seen to exist between public and domestic patriarchies. The new nation-state secured a controlling metaphor for its existence in the unitary and hierarchal structure of the patriarchal family. De Tocqueville made note of this fact in his comments on American society:

> Nor have the Americans ever supposed that democratic principle should undermine the husband's authority and make it doubtful who is in charge of the family. In their view, every association, to be effective, must have a head, and the natural head of the conjugal association is the husband. ... They think that in the little society composed of man and wife, as in the great society of politics, the aim of democracy is to regulate and legitimate necessary power.[24]

An interesting analogy to this appears in the African Charter of Human Rights which, while also using the generic pronoun 'he' throughout, observes that 'the family shall be the natural unit and basis of society' (Article 18).[25] From the trope of the family and of male rule, the move towards embracing concepts of mother-bondedness and state-mothers was an easy one. Through reproducing the male sphere of the family at a national level, the state guaranteed not only its stability but its survival or reproduction over time.

Perhaps one could go even further than plotting only structural homologies. There is, though it might be tricky, a case to be made for nationalism as itself bearing a patriarchal cast, which would imply that nationalism did not become gendered simply through transmission and association. This argument rests on the supposition that the masculine, whether expressed in thought, ideas, or social norms, favours rationality, homogeneity, and unitary order. Nationalism similarly works itself out through unitary forms, promoting standardisation, fixed meanings, one interpretation of the past, one homogeneous national identity and one national destiny for all. The national then is monologic, as is the patriarchal – 'a world', as Bakhtin would say 'of fathers and of founders of families'.[26]

But whether intrinsically or institutionally gendered, the nationalism which was exported to the colonies of Europe bore, so to speak, an in-built mechanism or historical memory which primed it to co-ordinate with state and patriarchal hierarchies. Quite predictably, then, with independence, the new national masters moved smoothly and easily into the halls and offices of power vacated by the colonizer. These state formations, as instruments of colonial rule, had themselves been exported from Europe, and remained in form and expression elitist, patrimonial, and alienated from civil society. Legitimation of such state power, if it was sought, could again be made through an appeal to pre- and co-existing structures of authoritarian and/or patriarchal rule at family and at community levels. The family metaphor was again readily and usefully incorporated, being as it was at once local and familiar and yet recognisable in one or other form to all concerned. As emblem of patriarchal authority, it also made available a convenient variety of roles: 'Father of the nation' (Kenyatta and

Kaunda for example), the 'Great Mother', and all their 'sons', the collective of loyal national functionaries and citizens.

It is again important to stress that the replication of national forms on the colonial periphery – and in this case in particular the patriarchal transposition – was even at the state level not a straightforward cloning process. If nationalism is a reconstruction from existing materials rather than a pure invention, the multiple variables of cultural difference, including inventive and syncretic forms of opposition to the colonial master, would modify and re-form nationalism in the process of its being transferred. Yet where, as in Africa, colonialism was a continent-wide experience, it would everywhere have been the case that the most successful forms of colonial power worked through exploiting existing power relations of hierarchy and subordination. Just as the (stereotypical) mother of the Victorian middle class may have had her formal or moral power in the family circumscribed in practice by male authority, so at the state level in independent African nations, a national ideology privileging mother symbols did not in reality empower mothers; the authority of fathers had been entrenched. Far from being only an outward manifestation of colonial rule, patriarchy, the intersection of indigenous and imported forms, thus became its medium. Women in the various nations came to be subjected to a syncretic fusion of male rules, encoded as principles of law and often enforced as tradition. Taking into account that power is consolidated through gender and that successful power is self-confirming, the usefulness of this system guaranteed its ubiquity and its survival beyond independence both in national and in pan-national ideologies.

I suggested earlier that, as a figure transcending national boundaries, the mother symbol has also provided a powerful talisman for pan-Africanism. An important reservation which should be made is that pan-Africanist ideology is not necessarily equivalent to African nationalism – not only the boundaries it recognises but its aims and motives are not coterminous with strict nationalism. Yet the ideology can still be construed as strongly nationalist in certain of its postulates. Perhaps, as does Tom Nairn in his descriptions of British nationalism, pan-Africanism may be characterised as the 'a-national nationalism of a multi-national entity'.[27] Within such 'non-ethnic nationalisms', as Nairn has also argued, 'a personalised and totemic symbolism' (p. 11), in the case of Britain the monarchy, in Africa the image of Mama Afrika, goes a considerable way towards creating and arousing supra- or transnational loyalties. It is ironic then, given its potency, that the identification of the entire continent as mythical mother betrays certain affinities with iconic material from Europe. Africa in popular colonial mythology was personified as dark alluring woman – Rider Haggard's She, Kurtz's African woman. The woman as unknown and dangerous other is, as Freud once pointed out, the dark continent.

It has been my thesis that national independence in Africa represented a take-over rather than a radical transformation of power, and, following from this, that the strong patriarchal presence already built into nationalist ideologies and state structures continued by and large to dominate unchallenged. The new nationalisms married the symbolic legacies of two patriarchal systems and so men, as elsewhere, remained manifestly in charge: they defined the shape and meaning of post-colonial nationhood on behalf of 'their' people. Ways of representing the land or the national territory which formed a part of the colonial rhetoric of nationalism were thus transferred and assimilated to local conventions of respect for the mother and the land. At the same time, the nation as a body of people was imagined as a patriarchal family in which the leaders had the authority of fathers and, in relation to the maternal national entity, adopted the position of sons.

Processes of compensatory representation also had their effect. Given that Manichean allegories of colonialist representation portrayed the colonized as the other, as deviant, passive and disorderly – as 'female' – it followed that national leaders on achieving power might well try to arrogate dominance, autonomy, 'maleness', to themselves.[28] In literature, too, the ethos of literary authority transmitted to the (in most cases male) colonized in university colleges and via literary canons was explicitly masculine – writing was represented as instituting and forwarding a male tradition, establishing or challenging rights of paternity, mastering an art. Were he a writer, then, a nationalist's maleness could not but be confirmed and enhanced: his two roles were mutually reinforcing. Yet this reciprocity also announced precisely through its structure of equivalence the non-presence of women. Clearly, if both writing and nationalism involved the articulation of being and of consciousness, then women were barred from both kinds of activity. If, according to the normative definitions, nationalists were not female, then how much less would females be not simply writers, but writers of a true nationalist persuasion? Whether in nationalist literary iconography or in nationalist literary practice, if she refused the mother title, woman had neither voice nor name.

The obvious conclusion to all this is that the unshackling of the African continent from colonial rule through nationalism has precluded a corresponding full emancipation of women. In the iconographies of nation-states, there are few positive roles on offer for women that are not stereotypes and/or connected in some way to woman's biological capacity for mothering. Gladys, in Achebe's story for example, becomes suspect the moment she abandons national 'service'. In reality the situation is worse: the queenly status of mother icons only serves to point up by contrast the actual lowly status of women within the new nation-states. Instances of the nation-state mobilising against women appear right the way across the continent. Maria Mbilinyi mentions measures taken in Tanzania during the '70s and '80s to control the migration of women from the rural areas.[29] The Zimbabwean state has throughout the '80s undertaken campaigns against prostitution, baby-dumping, squatting and uncleanness – ways of

obtaining control not simply over unplanned urban settlement, but specifically, of disciplining women as urban dwellers. The Campaign against
Indiscipline of the Federal Military Government in Nigeria in 1984-85 targeted women-petty-traders, single women in cities – as the prime
offenders.[30]

It is by now high time to address a question that has been urging to
speak itself throughout most of this paper: how are women, specifically
in this case women writers, to work with the patriarchal in nationalism,
especially as African literature has been so deeply imbued with nationalist
themes? In nations that are less mother- than father(ed)-lands, where and
how are women to find a voice? How are they to interrupt the duologue
of colonial master and national father? The seriousness of these sorts of
questions demands that the subject be treated at much greater length than
will be possible here; it certainly does not deserve to be placed in the
position of appendix. Yet it is also important to acknowledge the possibility of confronting the gender inconsistencies and spaces in nationalism.
These inconsistencies are not, it seems to me, sufficiently redressed simply
by participating in or even revamping the patriarchal myth of the continental mother. In a type of coda to the foregoing discussion, I will thus
look for a moment at potential ways of re-placing the unplaced space in
the national drama with the concrete figures of 'daughters' – of women.

As nationalism, in its past and current interpretations, is monologic,
single-voiced, the first answer to these questions seems to lie in simply
giving voice: women speaking for themselves, telling their own histories,
countering the monologic with multi-vocality. For women writers this
would mean addressing the quietness of their gender in text: recounting
national and what might be called ante-national experience from their
position on the sidelines of public life and on the margin of accepted national traditions. Such vocalisations and rewordings, unsettling if only by
virtue of their emergence, might in turn bring about shifts and changes in
the canon of nationalist texts, the exploration of new generic forms, possibly new versions of 'tradition'.

However, to propose ways in which women writers could be rereading
nationalism is to run the risk of conflating the predictive with the prescriptive. I should therefore confine my comments to existing work by
women writers, specifically in the field of the novel. The novel in Africa
has been dominated by historical and hence nationalist themes; it thus
offers itself as a pre-eminent site for active confrontation and contestation.
Buchi Emecheta, for example, though assuming on most occasions a self-
consciously metropolitan stance, has drawn from the memories of her
Nigerian past, and of her mothers' tales, emblems of women's experience
which may be counterposed to iconic images in male nationalist texts. Her
metaphors for the condition of woman in pre-colonial, colonial and
present-day societies are those of the slave girl – the woman bought and
sold; of the deeply ironic 'joys of motherhood' and of the double yoke, the

interlocking forms of oppression to which women are subject.[31] Flora Nwapa, another Nigerian novelist, situated her first two novels outside the conventional narrative of nationalist history, that is history as an account of the deeds and exploits of men. These novels, *Idu* and *Efuru*, resemble *Things Fall Apart* in so far as the subject matter has to do with rural Ibo life before the time of overt domination of the white man.[32] However, as the focus of both novels is on the women's community rather than the group of male leaders, the medium of narration and also the narrative concerns bear few resemblances to Achebe. The chorus of anonymous women's voices relating and commenting on the lives of the central characters and on village affairs in general becomes a pervasive if not dominant presence in the text. What happens in the novels is often no more than such voicings and verbalisations. The implication seems to be that what happens beyond the women's conversation is of no real concern. This technique of sharing responsibility for narration with a chorus of voices is one also employed by Bessie Head in her historical account or collected colloquy, *Serowe: Village of the Rain Wind*.[33] More explicitly than Nwapa, Head here engages with history, the experience of a community under political and climactic change, yet she consistently avoids the single perspective, the conventional or official line. In order to speak in others' tongues, or to allow those tongues to speak, Head has sought to gather together the actual testimonies of village members. Multi-vocality has become for her a method and a form. In this way, by foregrounding and commemorating voice and babble, women writers may, at least stylistically, begin to irrupt their presence into the national 'community'.

NOTES

1. Ngugi wa Thiong'o, *Matigari* (London: Heinemann, 1989).
2. Cf. Ngugi, *Devil on the Cross* (London: Heinemann, 1982), pp. 216-221.
3. Chinua Achebe, *Girls at War* (London: HEB, 1972), pp. 98-118. All further references are to this edition and are included in the text.
4. Gladys's moral 'easiness', however, gives Reginald a license that the resilient, impersonal and chaste figure of the militiawoman would not allow. He takes Gladys home and she 'yields' (p. 108) to him in a bunker after an air-raid, clinging to him in fear. Transformed from a stern national figure into an individual woman, Gladys is reduced to a more appropriate element and attitude – she is helpless, unresisting, weak, as well as, from Reginald's point of view (with which we collude), disturbingly though conveniently corrupt.
5. It is not necessarily paradoxical that Reginald could, like the woman, be seen as corrupt. Reginald is not a symbolic figure. Being highly placed in the government, his own improprieties are of course significant. Yet, as official and narrator, he also represents an ordinary, normative male humanity and national citizenry. Masculine roles in national life are, as I will suggest, largely metonymic.

6. As a trope that would appear to overarch and so subsume the impositions of national boundaries, the attractiveness of the Mother Africa symbol to pan-Africanists is understandable. This comparison is not, however, to be read as a simplistic equation of pan-Africanism with nationalism. More will be said of this later.

7. The concept of imagining nations is taken from Benedict Anderson, *Imagined Communities: Reflections on the Origin and Spread of Nationalism* (London: Verso, 1983).

8. Joan W. Scott, 'Gender: A Useful Category of Historical Analysis', *American Historical Review* 91 (1986), p. 1069.

9. Maurice Godelier, 'The Origins of Male Domination,' *NLR* 127 (May-June 1981), p. 17. I am indebted to the Scott essay for this quotation.

10. Deborah Gaitskell and Elaine Unterhalter, 'Mothers of the Nation: a Comparative Analysis of Nation, Race and Motherhood in Afrikaner Nationalism and the African National Congress', *Woman-Nation-State*, eds. Nira Yuval Davis and Floya Anthias (London: Macmillan, 1989), p. 72. I am aware of the problems of over-generalisation in this particular comment.

11. Ifi Amadiume, *Male Daughters, Female Husbands: Gender and Sex in an African Society* (London: Zed, 1987).

12. Who may also have a role as 'father' of the nation – in which case he could still honour the nation or land as his 'mother'.

13. In other words, in a variety of literary traditions, including that of African nationalism, writing has been characterised as a masculine activity, and the tradition as a struggle between 'author'-itative fathers and their sons. The theory of the anxiety of this influence as also the term 'sonship' is obviously adapted from Harold Bloom. See Gilbert and Gubar, pp. 5 ff, in particular, for a critical discussion of the 'legal fiction' which is literary patrimony. Sandra M. Gilbert and Susan Gubar, *The Madwoman in the Attic* (Yale UP, 1984).

14. Peter Abrahams, *A Wreath for Udomo* (London: Faber, 1979).

15. This bears comparison with Edward Kamau Brathwaite's *Mother Poem* and *Sun Poem*, in which the mother is identified with the land, while the poet, the son of the 'i:land', draws on sun-god myths to present himself as the inheritor of that land, who will restore it to itself and grant it i:dentity. *Mother Poem* (Oxford: OUP, 1977); *Sun Poem* (Oxford: OUP, 1982).

16. Clive Wake, 'Invitation to Dissent', review of Julio Finn, *Voices of Negritude, Third World Quarterly* 11.1 (Jan 1989), p. 178.

17. Leopold S. Senghor, *Poèmes* (Editions du Seuil, 1973), pp. 14-15, and *Selected Poems*, trans. John Reed and Clive Wake (OUP, 1964), pp. 16-17.

18. Camara Laye, *The African Child*, trans. James Kirkup (London: Fontana, 1980).

19. Kofi Awoonor, *The Breast of the Earth* (Nok, 1975).

20. Wally Mongane Serote, *Selected Poems*, ed. Mbulelo Mzamane (Donker, 1982).

21. Ingoapele Madingoane, *Africa My Beginning* (Ravan, 1988).

22. Valerie Smith, 'Gender and Afro-Americanist Criticism', *Speaking of Gender*, ed. Elaine Showalter (London: Routledge, 1989), p. 60.

23. A cautionary note should be added here. Though this analysis tends to represent nationalism in Africa as imported, indigenous concepts of, say, community cohesion may have existed which could with hindsight be characterised as proto-nationalist. Islamic nationalists, for example, argue that the concept of the Islamic community – *umma* – can be read as the precursor of modern nationalism.

24. Alexis de Tocqueville, *Democracy in America*, ed. J.P. Mayer, trans. George Lawrence (Doubleday, 1969), p. 601.

25. 'The African Charter on Human and Peoples' Rights', Appendix 1, *Human Rights and Development in Africa*, p. 320.

26. Mikhail M. Bakhtin, 'Epic and Novel', *The Dialogic Imagination*, ed. Michael Holquist, trans. Caryl Emerson and Michael Holquist (Austin: University of Texas Press, 1986), p. 13.
27. Tom Nairn, *The Enchanted Glass: Britain and its Monarchy* (London: Radius, 1988).
28. See Abdul R. JanMohammed's elaboration of Fanon's term 'Manichean' in 'The Economy of Manichean Allegory: The Function of Racial Difference in Colonialist Literature', *'Race,' Writing and Difference*, ed. Henry Louis Gates Jr. (Chicago: University of Chicago, 1986), pp. 78-106.
29. Maria Mbilinyi, 'Runaway Wives in Colonial Tanganika: Forced Labour and Forced Marriage in Rungwe District 1919-1961', *The International Journal for the Sociology of Law* 16.1 (Jan 1988), pp. 1-29.
30. See Carolynne Dennis, 'Women and the State in Nigeria: the Case of the Federal Military Government 1984-85', *Women, State and Ideology: Studies from Africa and Asia*, ed. Haleh Afshar (London: Macmillan, 1987), pp. 13-27.
31. Buchi Emecheta, *The Joys of Motherhood* (London: HEB, 1985); *The Slave Girl* (London: Fontana, 1981); *The Double Yoke* (London: Fontana, 1984). In this context the heroine of *Destination Biafra* (Fontana, 1982), Debbie Ogedemgbe, should also be mentioned, though I see her in the first instance as conforming to the 'masculine' stereotype of the bionic woman fighter mentioned earlier, rather than as a convincing liberatory symbol.
32. Flora Nwapa, *Efuru* (London: HEB, 1987); *Idu* (London: HEB, 1987).
33. Bessie Head, *Serowe: Village of the Rain Wind* (London: HEB, 1986).

PAULINE DODGSON

Culture and Literary Production in Zimbabwe

In this article I want to give a brief overview of Zimbabwean literature in English, but before I do that, I would like to consider the wider issues of culture and cultural policy.

In September 1981, at a seminar on 'Education in Zimbabwe – Past, Present and Future', Ngugi wa Thiong'o gave a talk entitled 'Education for a National Culture' in which he stated:

> The world outlook of a people is embodied in their moral, aesthetic and ethical values which are in turn embodied in their culture. Their culture is itself a product and a reflection of the history built on the two relations with nature and with other men. Thus education is part of culture and culture is part of education. They run into each other, and one way of looking at education is as a process of integrating a people into the dominant culture of that community.[1]

Yet after its first decade of independence, Zimbabwe still does not have a clearly defined cultural policy, despite the publication of two national development plans and the transfer of the Culture Division from the Ministry of Education to a new ministry in 1984.

The Ministry of Education had been given responsibility for culture at independence but the ministry was already overburdened. It had been charged with the task of changing the colonial education system and bringing education to the masses and it had to do this with very little pre-planning and with only limited resources. However, there were other reasons why the Ministry of Education ignored culture. The government had embarked on a policy of reconciliation and unity, and cultural transformation would inevitably have involved cultural and political conflict. Education was meeting enough resistance in its attempts to make the white schools change from a race and class oriented system; similar conflicts in the field of culture would have meant more clashes with the unity policy. This was not the only practicality to be considered. The Ministry of Education had a reactionary civil service which would have done all in its power to resist the social transformation which a new cultural orientation would have entailed.

Therefore, it might have seemed a good move when the Culture Division was transferred to the new Ministry of Youth, Sport and Culture which had been created out of the old Ministry of Youth, Sport and Recreation. This ministry would have more time and resources to develop culture. However, to return to Ngugi's point about the interrelatedness of education and culture, there are ideological problems which arise when you separate them. As a guest writer stated in *Moto* (an independent magazine whose pages provided a rare forum for the cultural debate):

> The absence of the cultural component in education may be used to strengthen the narrow concept of education; where it is seen only as a producer of skilled man-power for the economy. This concept ignores completely the fundamental principle that the quality and harmony of a people is achieved by safeguarding the cultural component of education, in both formal and informal spheres.[2]

I think it is arguable that if the Ministry of Education had been forced to work on the cultural component and take it seriously, then there would have been a better chance of producing a new education system which would have benefited the majority of children and of not retaining the rigid structures of the past, many of which remained after independence.

What is more, a progressive education system would have revitalized culture. With that component missing, the Ministry of Youth, Sport and Culture has tried to contain and control culture without encouraging or shaping it. It has endorsed cultural practices and traditions which are not progressive, retained institutions such as the National Arts Council which favour established elitist groups when it comes to funding and, with the introduction of culture houses in the rural areas, the ministry has tried to take art and culture to the people instead of learning from and helping to stimulate the people's art and culture.

One cannot entirely blame the ministry for this. This lack of cultural direction had taken root before independence. Of course, there would have been no point in expecting cultural innovation to come from the largely reactionary white minority whose outmoded culture evolved around the myth of white and Western supremacy. What is surprising is that a culture of resistance similar to that of South Africa did not develop, except in popular music, and that culture was not used consciously by the political leadership of the liberation and nationalist movements as a dynamising force. There was some poetry which drew its inspiration from the liberation struggle; claims have been made for Solomon Mutswairo's Shona novel *Feso*, which was banned by the Rhodesians.[3] However, what was missing was the integration of politics, literature and culture which can be found in Mozambique and Angola, where literature, specifically poetry, was used as a cultural weapon. It was not just that Zimbabwe did not have a developed written literature of resistance; it also did not have the kind of public debate on cultural theory which takes place among writers and intellectuals inside South Africa and in exile.

An obvious reason for this difference is that South Africa has become a more urbanised society with a number of universities and a cultural infra-

structure in which it is possible to set up theoretical journals and oppositional video groups, whereas Zimbabwe is a predominantly rural society
with a culture which is based on oral tradition.

There was a cultural opposition at grassroots level in the rural areas of
Zimbabwe but the leadership was not directly in touch with it and did not
incorporate it in a cultural programme, either before or after independence. David Lan has shown how the traditional culture of the *mhondoro*
mediums was used by the ZANLA guerrillas to legitimize their resistance
to colonial rule in the Zambezi Valley.[4] Research and extension workers
in rural Zimbabwe report that people have many creative stories to tell of
events which took place during the struggle which have not been collated,
transcribed or published. Nor has an attempt been made to document the
way drama was used for conscientization in the villages and in the camps
in Mozambique.

In his theory of the formation and development of intellectuals, Gramsci
has argued that intellectuals who come from peasant societies tend to lose
their class identity and become *traditional* intellectuals, whereas within the
urban proletariat movement *organic* intellectuals emerge who work within
a specific class formation.[5] In South Africa there are moments when the
traditional and organic intellectuals can work together. In Zimbabwe those
intellectuals who were born in peasant communities appear to have lost
their class solidarity and to have worked outside their communities. These
include many of the political leaders, the writers and the academics. The
Willowgate Scandal shows how distant many of those with political power
are from the masses in the rural areas and, increasingly, also from the
urban proletariat.

Perhaps because of this lack of a cultural and intellectual debate, the
literature of pre-independence Zimbabwe was not a unifying element in
the anti-colonial movements. This is especially true of the fiction, which
can be placed roughly in three categories. Firstly, there were novels in
Shona and Ndebele, published by the Rhodesia Literature Bureau, which
were on non-political 'safe' subjects, usually domestic and moralistic.
Secondly, there were the quasi-historical or 'documentary' novels. This
category includes Mutswairo's novels and those of Stanlake Samkange
which rely on history and myth, sometimes paraphrasing historical documents. Although these works do create an awareness of the past, there is
a problem in the way they use myth to evoke historical consciousness,
since this can lead to mystification. The last category and the one most
widely discussed is writing in English which uses colonialism and the
liberation struggle only as a backdrop to the main narrative. It is precisely
this reluctance to put the struggle at the forefront which has led to charges
of pessimism and disillusionment being levelled against the writers of this
fiction.

Four novels which are said to fall into this last category are Charles
Mungoshi's *Waiting for the Rain*, Wilson Katiyo's *A Son of the Soil*,

Dambudzo Marechera's *The House of Hunger* and Stanley Nyamfukudza's *The Non-Believer's Journey*. The last novel was published in London in 1980, the year of independence.

Of the four, *A Son of the Soil* is the least pessimistic, since it shows a young man growing up under colonial oppression in the village and the town who makes the decision to become a freedom fighter. In the opening section of this tripartite novel, the *sekuru* tells the village children the story of how whites came to Chief Makosa's village, stole the oxen and enslaved the young men. One of those captured, Shonga, is given to a missionary as an assistant and is converted to Christianity, but he later helps to defend his village from the whites and dies with his hands gripped round a dead white man's throat. It is one of Shonga's descendants who is the central character in the book, the man who takes up arms. Thus, through the device of traditional story telling, the novel relates the independence struggle of the 1960s and 1970s to the resistance to colonialism in the previous century. It effectively delineates the divide and rule tactics of the Rhodesians but does not look at the contradictions within the struggle.

Mungoshi, who remained in the country during the years of UDI in the thankless task of working as an editor at the Rhodesia Literature Bureau, has written a novel which shows the disintegration of traditional society under colonial rule and which suggests that there may be no way out of the impasse. Education results in alienation and eventual exile. It is the grandfather in *Waiting for the Rain* who comments on the irony of the African trying to fight the white man after he has abandoned his own culture and adopted alien customs. His grandson John wants political change but the Old Man thinks it is too late for change: 'What kind of fighting is it when you are clutching and praying to your enemy's gods? I don't know what he was talking about but he is certainly playing someone else's drum. Each time I see my wife Japi take in a handful of sugar, I know how complete and final the white man's conquest has been.'[6]

For Marechera, the most maverick of the Zimbabwean writers, the one who refused to conform before and after independence, there are no heroes. Anyone who has ever been in the 'house of hunger' has what he calls 'gut-rot', a physical and mental degeneration. *The House of Hunger* illustrates Fanon's theory of auto-destruction: Marechera's blacks fight with each other and they fight themselves.

Nyamfukudza has a similar story to tell although he is a more socially and politically aware writer than Marechera. The central character Sam in *The Non-Believer's Journey* dies an outsider. He is asked to supply medicines to the guerrillas, but he refuses and when one of the fighters calls him a coward, he senselessly attacks him and is shot dead. Sam cannot conform either to the dictates of Rhodesian society or to the 'rousing, emotional politics' of the liberation army in the bush. Nyamfukudza has said that he wrote the novel to show the leadership that there were problems with the way they were conducting the struggle.[7] The message came rather late to be of use in the pre-independence struggle, but the course events have taken in the new society suggests that *The Non-Believer's Journey* offered a warning for future times.

I should say that I do not share the generally held opinion that there was a malaise in Zimbabwean fiction before independence. All these writers offer useful insights into the nature of oppression and Marechera raises questions of power and sexuality and power and gender, albeit in an oblique way. There is no doubt that the pre-independence writers of fiction in English wrote from an individual stance. It is interesting that the title of one of Marechera's stories is 'Black Skin What Mask' in parody of Fanon's *Black Skin, White Masks*. It was Fanon's early work on the psychology of oppressed people which interested Marechera, not the anti-colonial discourse of *The Wretched of the Earth*.

Given this background, it is perhaps not entirely surprising that there was no immediate renaissance of Zimbabwean literature after independence. Those who were writing before were silent or, at least, very quiet. Nyamfukudza published a collection of short stories, *Aftermaths*, some of which had been written before independence, and which tended to reinforce the anti-heroic label which had already been given to his work. Marechera, claiming that he was as uncomfortable in independent Zimbabwe as he had been in racist Britain, went further into his own private world. His second novel, *Black Sunlight*, fell foul of the Censorship Board and was banned in 1981. Even when the ban was lifted, the book was generally regarded as obscene and almost unreadable.

Marechera remained in Zimbabwe until his premature death in 1987. His was always a useful dissident voice. His third work, *Mindblast*, a collection of plays, poems and stories, is at times only just coherent but it points to the corruption and hypocrisy of a neo-colonial society. Marechera, in public and in his writing, dared to ask the questions that others were afraid to ask. Ostensibly the least political of all Zimbawean writers, yet Marechera was the one who was detained, even if only for a few days, in 1984. After the death of the allegedly elitist and obscure author of *The House of Hunger*, the dissident voice most often heard in Zimbabwe was that of the populist and didactic Edgar Tekere, the resurrected politician who formed an anti-corruption party. The irony of that would not have been wasted on Marechera.

The euphoria that independence had brought was short lived. There was a flourish of activity. The Harare Book Fair, with its writers' workshops, was established in 1983; later, a writers' union was formed. Yet artistic expression remained muted for a number of years.

The first colloquium on Zimbabwean literature in English was held at the university in April 1987 and, in a keynote speech, Charles Mungoshi, who had become the university's Writer-in-Residence, speculated as to why those who were productive before independence had such a meagre post-independence output. Mungoshi suggested that the mood in

Zimbabwe was still apprehensive. He pointed to a tentativeness in the Zimbabwean social sphere and said that it was as if writers, like everyone else, were waiting to see what was going to happen, what direction the country was going to take.[8] Clearly, with that kind of attitude writers were not going to be in the vanguard.

But why was there such reticence? At the 1985 Harare Book Fair, the then Minister of Information had declared that 'African writers should be allowed to express their views without fear of victimisation from intolerant governments'.[9] The Zimbabwe Writers Union (ZIWU) had welcomed this statement, stating in the words of its Chairperson Chenjerai Hove, that victimisation of writers 'kills creativity and deprives society of change'.[10]

Yet the previous year Marechera had heckled Nyamfukudza and prevented him from reading at an event sponsored by ZIWU. He had asked Nyamfukudza why the Writers Union had not protested when he was detained. Nyamfukudza, a member, not an official of the union, could not give an answer; none of the officials present cared to do so. Two and a half years later, Nyamfukudza was himself to criticise the Writers Union for not being strong enough when the government acted against the drama group Amakhosi's play *Workshop Negative*,[11] to which I shall refer later.

However, I do not want to give the impression that there has been no interesting writing in Zimbabwe since independence because that simply would not be true. What is significant is that much of the more stimulating and challenging writing is by women. A number of women writers have become prominent: Barbara Makhalisa, writing in English and Ndebele, Bertha Msora, Tsitsi Dangarembga, who has written a play *She No Longer Weeps* and a novel *Nervous Conditions*, and the poets Kristina Rungano and a former combatant, Freedom Nyamubaya.

Issues which are of concern to women have come to the fore since independence. Women played a significant role in the liberation struggle and then found that they were expected to return to a traditional domestic role within a family structure and patriarchal society. In this sense women have suffered continued oppression. Freedom Nyamubaya, whose work integrates the personal and the political, has shown in her poem 'A Mysterious Marriage' how independence does not necessarily bring liberation:

Independence came
But Freedom was not there.
An old woman saw Freedom's shadow passing,
Walking through the crowd, Freedom to the gate.
All the same, they celebrated for Independence.

Independence is now a senior bachelor
Some people still talk about him

Many others take no notice
A lot still say it was a fake marriage.
You can't be a husband without a wife.
Fruitless and barren Independence staggers to old age,
Since her shadow, Freedom, hasn't come.[12]

There were minor gains for women after independence. A women's ministry was set up although it has not been able to do very much for women; the Legal Age of Majority Act passed in late 1982 was an attempt to give women independence from their male relatives. But there were also setbacks which showed how a double standard operated. Men could be sexually promiscuous; women were condemned at the mere hint of any impropriety. In 1983, the Ministry of Justice, Legal and Parliamentary Affairs ordered a round-up of women and 'undesirables' who were on the streets of Harare and Gweru after a certain time on one particular night. There was also an outcry against 'baby dumpers'. Abortion is illegal in Zimbabwe and, in a spate of cases, women who were perhaps suffering from post-natal depression and who were certainly alone and afraid had been found guilty of abandoning or even killing their unwanted babies. The local press carried out a campaign against the women and there were threats of harsh punishment; only a few commentators discussed why 'baby dumping' took place and what could be done to prevent it and to help the mothers.

Not only were women vilified as uncaring, immoral and incapable of leading independent fulfilled lives in the local press but they also had to suffer stereotyping in literature. Rudo Gaidzanwa has illustrated this in detail in her book *Images of Women in Zimbabwean Literature* where she studies the way women are portrayed in Zimbabwean literature in English, Ndebele and Shona.[13]

It is the women writers who have taken a questioning approach to the portrayal of women in literature and tried to find an alternative practice. Dangarembga's *Nervous Conditions* uses the stereotypes in order to subvert them and offer insights into the complexity of motherhood, female physiology and psychology and women's social subordination. The novel tells the story of two young women, the cousins Tambu and Nyasha, and of their mothers, one a village woman and the other a graduate 'been to' trying to cope with the frustration of returning to a domestic role.

The narrator Tambu understands her cousin's descent into anorexic immobility but realises that it is not a solution because the individual withdrawal into the self will not ease the pain of colonialism or of women's oppression. It is interesting, though, to note the self-consciously analytical style of the writing. The writer organizes and dissects her female characters' thoughts and actions rather as Nadine Gordimer does. Women under a double yoke in a repressive situation where they cannot immediately act to free themselves are perhaps forced to analyse as a necessary prelude to action.

I would like to bring in one male writer at this point. Chenjerai Hove is one of the few writers of the pre-independence generation who has continued to write and develop. His poetry collection *Red Hills of Home* uses a complex metaphoric language to accentuate his concern with the erosion of the environment and the disintegration of human relationships. His first novel in English, *Bones*, is a powerful work, deeply rooted in Zimbabwean life but also influenced by Hove's reading of Latin American writers. The central woman character, Marita, who is almost a mythical figure, provides the link between the past and the present. The interior monologue, contrary to what one might expect, opens out possibilities for social understanding, reconstruction and transformation. It seems that Hove has taken up Lewis Nkosi's plea for more experimentation in Southern African writing.[14]

Drama is also concerned with social transformation, and there is much to be said on the subject of drama in Zimbabwe. It is not possible in a brief survey to do justice to the movement away from the white minority enclave theatre to the non-competitive drama of the community theatre groups but I shall attempt to outline some of the developments which took place between 1982 and 1987.

The innovative drama which had been used for conscientization in the camps in Mozambique and in rural Zimbabwe did not have much influence immediately after independence. Despite some attempts to introduce drama which was politically, socially and culturally more appropriate than the usual Harare Reps fare, there were no major changes. Innovation came with the introduction of community drama and the promotion of drama as an extra-curricular activity in schools.

A community based theatre programme was launched at Zvamanyanga, near Shamva, in early 1983. It was reported that the government was committed to 'setting up community cultural centres and a progressive theatre movement all over the country'.[15] Since then, community drama groups have been formed in both rural and urban areas and have produced plays which are relevant to the lives of the group members and their audiences. The Zimbabwe Association of Community Theatre (ZACT) was formed in February 1986 and took a strong stand against the competitive theatre festivals organized by the National Theatre Organization on the grounds that these competitions encouraged elitism and discouraged collaborative working practices. Drama has also developed in schools where teachers and students have written their own plays in the languages of Zimbabwe. Although drama is not on most school syllabuses, the Ministry of Education held a workshop at Ranche House College in 1987 to launch the National Drama Teachers Association and to help teachers implement drama across the curriculum strategies.

I do not want to give the impression that drama is a workshop or talk oriented activity in Zimbabwe, so let me turn to the drama performed in the Faculty of Arts at the university. Robert McLaren, Senior Lecturer in

Drama, prefers the term 'democratic theatre' to community theatre and generally dislikes what is termed 'theatre for development'. He sees democratic theatre as being concerned with problem solving, dialogue and discussion. The drama groups at the university have been prolific and I can cite only a few examples of their work: their first production *Mavambo* (an adaptation of *A Son of the Soil*), a revue focusing on the role of women in society, *The Adamant Eve*, a play based on actual cases in a community court, *Seri Kwesasa/Okusemsamo* and adaptations of *The Good Person of Szechwan* and *Macbeth*.

McLaren has implied that the most important and significant work undertaken in university drama is the agit-prop and Southern African political solidarity work which could be seen in the productions, *Katshaa!* (1986) and *Samora Continua* (1987), both performed by Zambuko/Izibuko, a group largely composed of students. These two plays are partly derived from the *pungwe* or night gathering the guerrillas held in the bush during the liberation struggle.[16] However, in terms of conscientization, the plays appear to function in a fairly limited way. Zimbabweans are already aware of South African oppression and the reiteration of this oppression does not suggest how Zimbabweans can play a more active role in the region's liberation.

The university production of *Macbeth* raises similar issues. It is preceded by a statement that the teaching and performing of Shakespeare in Africa has been a weapon of cultural imperialism and that, therefore, *Macbeth* and other plays by Shakespeare must be reinterpreted through performance. There were some interesting changes – the use of modern English and Shona, male witches, and the final denouement in which it is suggested that rather than bringing a period of stability to a troubled country, the overthrow of Macbeth will lead to further struggles for power – and yet, the adaptation fails to rewrite the play in a way that is culturally or politically relevant.

But then there are dangers in referring too specifically to political and social conditions in Zimbabwe. In conclusion, I would like to discuss a play which has caused considerable controversy in Zimbabwe, *Workshop Negative*, written by Cont Mhlanga and performed by Amakhosi. Amakhosi started out as a karate club in Bulawayo before switching to drama and their theatre is a popular theatre which includes fight scenes. Their first play, *Nansi le Ndoda*, which looked generally at corruption in terms of nepotism, ethnicity, seduction and bribery, was welcomed by the cultural pundits. It was *Workshop Negative* which caused problems.

This time the corruption shown in the play was more specific and it made some people in the Culture Division very uncomfortable. The play revolves around three men – a black former combatant, a white former Rhodesian soldier (both now the workers) and their boss Mkhize, a political commissar who owns the workshop. Mkhize plays off the two former antagonists against each other while he gets rich; he preaches socialism while the 'money mountain' grows. Not surprisingly, the workshop was seen as a microcosmic representation of Zimbabwe.

The Ministry of Youth, Sport and Culture did not stop the play from being performed in Zimbabwe – it was too late for that – but it did with-hold permission for the company to take the play to Botswana and other neighbouring countries. The play was said to present a negative view of Zimbabwe and to be anti-socialist. In fact, it shows what happens when the public face of socialism is smeared by the private practice of capital-ism.

A performance of the play was staged at the university, followed by dis-cussion. After listening to a panel of experts, Mhlanga specifically raised the issue of class. He said he was not interested in what the academics and officials said about his play, that he would listen only to what a workers' committee said and that if a member of his own class, the work-ing class, rejected the play, then he would 'get on the cross and hang there'.[17] Far from having to do that, Mhlanga, who said he was utilizing what he heard in the beer halls, has had the satisfaction of seeing what he only hinted at quite blatantly exposed as one minister after another has been indicted by the Sandura inquiry into corruption. *Workshop Negative* may even have played a role in this in that discussion about the play allowed what had been rumoured for some time to be talked about more openly. With Amakhosi and some of the community theatre groups, we see the emergence of organic intellectuals in Zimbabwe.

However, it seems unlikely that there will be a union with the traditional intellectuals despite demonstrations at the university which resulted in its temporary closure in 1989. One of *Workshop Negative*'s most vociferous critics was fellow playwright Stephen Chifunyise, who, in his then capac-ity as Director of Arts and Crafts, denounced the play as anti-government and an affront to Zimbabwe. As I listened to Chifunyise, a man who had previously been sympathetic to new writers and performers, I could not help remembering the time when I had interviewed him on the origins of Zimbabwean drama for an educational radio programme. On that occasion Chifunyise had talked of how drama was used in traditional society to criticize the chief. If you criticized him openly, Chifunyise explained to the school children, you would have your head chopped off. Drama allowed you to be critical and stay alive.[18] It seems it was a different story when drama was used as criticism in the 1980s.

However, the cultural critics are still alive. Mhlanga was elected as Chairperson of the Writers Union in 1989; the extent to which the union's executive will support writers who deviate from the official line remains to be seen. Clearly, there are major political, economic and educational difficulties in Zimbabwe and the Southern African region but a dynamic culture is beginning to emerge in Zimbabwe which has the potential to oppose all forms of oppression.

NOTES

1. Ngugi wa Thiong'o, *Education for a National Culture* (Harare: Zimbabwe Publishing House, 1981), p. 2.
2. 'Reshuffle Brings New Hope for Culture Division', *Moto*, 21 (March 1984), p. 12.
3. Mutswairo himself referred to the influence he believed *Feso* had had on the liberation struggle in a talk recorded at Audio Visual Services, Harare, in 1986. See also Emmanuel Ngara, 'The Role of the African Writer in National Liberation and Social Reconstruction' in Kirsten Holst Petersen, ed., *Criticism and Ideology: Second African Writers' Conference Stockholm 1986* (Uppsala: Scandinavian Institute of African Studies, 1988), pp. 131-4.
4. David Lan, *Guns and Rain: Guerrillas and Spirit Mediums in Zimbabwe* (Harare: Zimbabwe Publishing House, 1985).
5. Antonio Gramsci, 'The Intellectuals', in Quinton Hoare and Geoffrey Nowell Smith, eds., *Selections from the Prison Notebooks of Antonio Gramsci* (London: Lawrence and Wishart, 1971), pp. 5-25.
6. Charles Mungoshi, *Waiting for the Rain* (Harare: Zimbabwe Publishing House, 1981), p. 115.
7. Stanley Nyamfukudza, in a panel discussion on 'The Novel and the Short Story' recorded at Audio Visual Services, Harare, in 1986.
8. Charles Mungoshi, 'Towards a Definition of Zimbabwean Literature', First Colloquium on Zimbabwean Literature in English, University of Zimbabwe, 24 April 1987.
9. 'Give Writers Free Rein – Minister', *The Herald*, 30 July 1985, p. 1.
10. Report in *The Herald*, 5 August 1985, p. 4.
11. Stanley Nyamfukudza, in a talk in a series organized by the Zimbabwe-German Society, Alliance Française and the British Council, Harare, 4 March 1987.
12. Freedom Nyamubaya, 'A Mysterious Marriage', in *On the Road Again: Poems During and After the National Liberation of Zimbabwe* (Harare: Zimbabwe Publishing House, 1986), p. 13.
13. Rudo Gaidzanwa, *Images of Women in Zimbabwean Literature* (Harare: The College Press, 1985).
14. A point often emphasized by Lewis Nkosi in discussion in Harare and elsewhere.
15. 'State to Boost Folk Theatre', *The Herald*, 2 February 1983, p. 3.
16. Robert McLaren in 'Where From – Where To: The New Theatre of Zimbabwe', *Kaleidoscope*, BBC Radio 4, broadcast 21 October 1988.
17. Cont Mhlanga after a performance of *Workshop Negative* at the University of Zimbabwe, 20 March 1987.
18. Stephen Chifunyise in an interview on 'Drama in Zimbabwe' recorded at Audio Visual Services, Harare, in 1986.

CAROL SICHERMAN

Ngugi wa Thiong'o as Mythologizer and Mythologized

As Ngugi wa Thiong'o's preoccupation with myth and history continues unabated in his latest novel, *Matigari*,[1] Ngugi himself remains the subject of the Kenyan government's fantasies of subversion: the mythologizer mythologized. In this paper I have two purposes: first, to suggest ways in which *Matigari* contributes to the theme of mythologizing; and second, to discuss the government's mythologizing campaign depicting Ngugi as a political ogre. Both the government and Ngugi have identical aims; each wishes to portray the other as ogres. In *Matigari* Ngugi alludes to 'the ogres currently running the country' in terms of the *marimu* of Gikuyu folktales (56);[1] and collaborating journalists call Ngugi a 'Communist stooge' – surely an ogre in modern political terms. In a replay of colonial days, 'honest efforts for making the truth known' are 'construed as seditious and revolutionary' ('Memorandum from the Kikuyu Land Board Association', in Mockerie 77).

In *Matigari*, the Provincial Commissioner attempts to counter truth by labeling it fiction. He therefore bans an incendiary song that 'claims that when Matigari ma Njiruungi stamps his feet, the bullets tinkle'. Matigari, he declares, does not exist: 'Let us with one accord, like loyal parrots, agree that Matigari ma Njiruungi was just a bad dream' (119).[2] By extension, the Mau Mau struggle is 'just a bad dream'. All history, Joyce said in *Ulysses*, is a bad dream, 'a nightmare from which we are trying to awake'; Ngugi implies that Matigari, who persistently seeks truth and justice, can help Kenya awaken from the nightmare of its history.

The address 'To the Reader/Listener' declares that the novel could take place 'in the country of your choice ... in the time of your choice'. Although this is true – Kenya's is hardly the only government attempting to silence truth – any reader familiar with contemporary Kenya will immediately recognize local references. The banning of the song about Matigari and the mention of 'loyal parrots' are bound to remind the historically aware reader/listener of actual events and persons in twentieth-century Kenyan history. Such a reader would recall the banning in January 1930 of the famous *Muthirigu* protest song expressing the 'people's rejection of forced labour, their disgust with cultural imperialism, their uncompromising opposition to political oppression, and their strong condemnation of Kenyan collaborators with colonialist enemy occupation'

(*Detained* 65).[3] And such a reader would find many parallels between colonial and present-day Kenya.

As for 'loyal parrots', who in the novel include professors of the science of Parrotology, they are President Daniel arap Moi's sycophants, who heeded his call (on 13 Sept. 1984) for government officials 'and every other person to sing like parrots' following his tune (qtd. Umoja, *Struggle* 21). Three weeks before Moi's notorious demand, the Annual Conference of the Historical Association of Kenya[4] demonstrated parrotological proficiency, parodied by a Provincial Commissioner in *Matigari*:

> Wasn't it only the other day that all the university professors and specialists in Parrotology had a history conference? What do they teach us? That, according to their research, those who joined hands with colonialists in protecting the law – *loyalists* – are really the ones who made the colonialists give us independence on a platter. (103)

Thus the Mau Mau struggle vanishes from the history books, replaced by the Kenyatta gospel that 'we all fought for freedom' (*Devil* 177; cf. *Matigari* 88), which, in turn, paves the way for Moi's 'nyayo'[5] philosophy of 'peace, love, and unity', a 'philosophy' mocked by the well-known torture chambers in the basement of Nyayo House in Nairobi. The call of Matigari, himself a Mau Mau veteran, to resist parrotology must be seen as the call of the people, for he is at once a character in the novel and a composite hero of resistance (his name is actually a Gikuyu plural meaning 'those who survived the bullet').

The Provincial Commissioner hopes to rewrite history by banning the song and indeed all verbal art concerning Matigari – that is, all art concerned with truth and justice: 'No song, no story or play or riddle or proverbs, mentioning Matigari ma Njiruungi will be tolerated.... We are not interested in fiction' but in 'new history' as written by professors of parrotology (118). Ngugi's novel is a kind of fiction, but it is also a kind of truth, and it is the capacity of fiction to tell the truth that has alarmed the Kenyan government into fighting what the Minister of Truth and Justice calls 'the kind of *distortion* you find in some of those *fiction* writers' (*Matigari* 103; italics indicate English words, not emphasis). Just as the fictional Matigari was banned, so was the actual book. As Ngugi recounts in his note to the English edition, when government intelligence agents heard 'that peasants in Central Kenya were roaming the whole country making demands about truth and justice', they gave orders for his arrest. Finding that he was 'only a fictional character', they raided every Kenyan bookshop and seized all copies. By that time, 3,346 copies had been sold (Chakava 241) – not bad for five months of sales of a novel in a language spoken by only twenty percent of the population, many of whom are not sufficiently literate to read it. These sales figures of a novel by Kenya's only literary figure of international stature compare with a total of 405 copies sold in three years (1985-87) of a Gikuyu-language Mau Mau detention camp diary by Gakaara wa Wanjau, the only promoter of writing in Gikuyu prior to Ngugi – a book that won the Noma Prize in 1984 (Chakava 240). Why should this book – not only Gakaara's 'crowning work' (Ngugi, *Decolonising* 24) but 'the single most significant historical document of the entire resistance literature from Kenya' ('Kenyan and Black South African') – have sold an average of 135 copies a year while Ngugi's novel sold twenty-five times as many in five months?

There can be only speculation to answer such a question,[6] but Gakaara does have indisputable links with Ngugi: they are the only significant writers in Gikuyu; and Gakaara was forced to contribute to the political mythologizing of Ngugi – that is, to the creation of the Ngugi-ogre who is the *bête noire* of the Kenyan political establishment. Gakaara was in detention not only in colonial but in postcolonial days. Released in May of 1986 after three weeks, he gave a widely publicized press conference in which he claimed (or was forced to claim) that Ngugi was leader of the December 12 Movement and its successor, Mwakenya. Gakaara asserted that Ngugi had attempted to recruit him in the early 1980s when both were members of a study group at the University of Nairobi – a study group that, Gakaara said, was a front for the 'diabolical' dissident movement, the objective of which was to 'bring about a socialist change and install a Marxist regime' (statement qtd. 'Freed Author Exposes' 24). In fact, according to a member of the group, they were exploring a revision of heretofore standard, missionary-designed Gikuyu orthography under the leadership of a professor of linguistics at the University; they had no political agenda.[7] In the present political climate, even orthography can be dangerous; Ngugi used this collaborative linguistic research in writing *Caitaani Mutharaba-ini* (*Devil on the Cross*) and *Matigari*. The Provincial Commissioner in the novel is one with the real-life government officials who arrested Gakaara, forced him to confess falsities as a condition of his release, and then, a month later, arranged a car 'accident' in which he was nearly killed.[8]

In researching Ngugi's career and the background to his works, one quickly encounters mythologizing of historical figures: not only Ngugi himself in the 1980s but also such figures as Waiyaki in the early 1890s, and Dedan Kimathi and Jomo Kenyatta in the 1950s. The forces that encourage mythologizing are various, including needs – both human and political – for heroes and for villains. Ngugi himself has been frank about his creation of heroes. It is imperative, he has said, not to 'forgive and forget', as the accommodationist Jomo Kenyatta preached, but to 'choose your side' (*Petals* 200), for – we repeatedly hear in *Matigari* – people are either 'patriots' or 'sell-outs'. And in choosing your side, you also choose your heroes. He told an interviewer who criticized his elevation of resisters like Dedan Kimathi and his denigration of colonial chiefs: 'When writing history for our children, which things do we want them to admire? Should they emulate traitors or heroes? We must draw a line between those who held out consistently and those who collaborated' (Omari 1). Increasingly Ngugi himself has been one 'who held out consistently' – who refused while in prison to permit himself to be chained and therefore gave up family visits and dental care, who refused to write in the colonial language, who refused to curb his tongue and who therefore is condemned to an exile with no clear end.

One more point has to be made about the creation of heroes and villains out of actual historical figures. Sometimes they develop through oral traditions; sometimes they are artificially created – for example, by novelists or politicians; and sometimes they emerge through a combination of the natural and the artificial methods. 'The truth of the past', Eldred Jones has written, 'is history, while the penumbra cast by an extraordinary event or personality ... constitutes the weighty metaphor that is myth' (1). Myths that endure may cross the line and affect history. In an example of oral tradition causing action in real life, Waiyaki, the late-ninteenth-century Gikuyu leader whose death while in custody made him a martyr, was said to have issued a deathbed command that his death be revenged through killing a European in the manner of Waiyaki's own legendary death – burial alive and face down. Such a death took place when Arundell Gray Leakey, an apparently harmless elderly cousin of L.S.B. Leakey, was murdered in 1955 (Itote, *Action* 26-27; Hofmyer 74-75; *Times* [London] 26 Oct. 1954: 6; and 23 Nov. 1954: 7). The spirit of Waiyaki was likewise said to have been infused into Jomo Kenyatta, who was also – in a typical intermixture of African and Christian – like both Jesus and Moses as well.

In Kenya, makers of history have often been cannily aware of the possibility of deliberately entwining myth and history, producing something close to legend, that 'combination of fact and fiction' (Okpewho 12). When Kenyatta was about to go off to prison, there was some discussion whether his last supper should be modeled on the Last Supper of Jesus.[9] Similarly, the Mau Mau leaders fostered belief in Kimathi's magical omnipresence by signing his name to threats made by others when Kimathi was actually in another location.[10] Ngugi may be seen, then, as a mythologized figure in the line of Waiyaki, Kenyatta, and Kimathi. In the remainder of this paper, I will focus on Ngugi himself as hero or villain, with emphasis on the Kenyan government's attempted suppression of the London 1984 production of *The Trial of Dedan Kimathi*, Ngugi and Micere Mugo's 1976 play. My object is to restore history, to expose the deliberate myth-making of the Kenyan authorities, who have, in the Gikuyu idiom, added salt to the story (*Matigari* 69). Salt has its place – but not in history.

The thirteen performances of *The Trial of Dedan Kimathi* scheduled in October 1984 at the Africa Centre in London were part of the Centre's annual or semiannual 'Focus' program, which that year featured Kenya.[11]

There was also a November 2 performance at the Commonwealth Institute in London as part of the African Writers Conference (co-sponsored by the Africa Centre) that had opened the previous day, with Ngugi as keynote speaker. The group then took to the road, with sold-out performances in Oxford, Manchester, and Leeds, returning to London for three performances in outlying areas that concluded with one in Brixton on 17 November. The performances were preceded by a series of open rehearsals. By 1984 *The Trial* had become transformed (in the eyes of the Kenya government) from the official Kenyan entry at a pan-African cultural festival – FESTAC 1977 in Lagos[12] – into a symbol of dissidence. One obvious reason for this transformation was the two intervening plays by Ngugi – *Ngaahika Ndeenda* (written with Ngugi wa Mirii), which was a main cause of his year-long detention in 1978; and *Maitu Njugira*, the suppression of which in 1982 was followed by the razing of the theatre and the fleeing into exile of three of the principal people involved (see Björkman, 'Mother', *passim*).

The group presenting the London production of *Trial*, Wazalendo Players 84,[13] operated as a collective, much in the manner of Ngugi's theatre group at Kamiriithu, with certain people taking main responsibility for particular tasks but with much sharing and doubling up. 'All of us', says a note below the cast list in the program, 'have contributed to the play in various ways, in composing songs, choreographing movements', and so on. There was very little change to the basic text, however, although a main element in the government-created myth was the alleged 'communist slant' given the text (Warsama, 'Campaign Provokes' 3). The London cast did not compose significant sections, as happened in the development of the script for *Ngaahika Ndeenda* at Kamiriithu, where the play 'became the central experience of the community' and individual participants did not so much 'perform' as *be* themselves (Kidd 53; Björkman, 'Ngugi' 128).[14]

Although the cast in London, coming from widely varying backgrounds, could hardly have become a community in the Kamiriithu sense, they did encourage contributions from the audience during rehearsals, a method that was also used at Kamiriithu for *Ngaahika Ndeenda* (and later for *Maitu Njugira*). Audience participation extended past rehearsals into performances: at Kamiriithu the audience joined in the dances and 'many people came three, five times to watch a play they had participated in creating, that they had read, that they had seen develop' (Ngugi wa Mirii, interview, Harare, 6 April 1987).[15] Of course, the London audiences could not have such a close connection, but publicity prepared by Wazalendo Players 84 stressed another kind of relevance to Thatcherite Britain: by bringing theatre to 'the culturally excluded and the economically exploited' through free public rehearsals, the production gave encouragement to the 'defiance, appeal, hope and determination of working men and women', and it challenged stereotypes by presenting courageous and intelligent blacks, strong and resilient women ('Wazalendo Players 84 Present ...' 1).

According to both Ngugi and Ahmed Sheikh, who played the lead, the production – but not the text – was considerably altered by the processes of group consultation during rehearsals as well as by interaction with the audience during the public rehearsals. As Ngugi has said, 'If you take a stage movement or a street scene, it will develop differently. It's not as if it's a different text; it's a different production' (interview, London, 4 Aug. 1987). The main directorial issue was how best to give dramatic weight to various parts of the text by (for example) introducing songs (Micere Mugo, interview, Canterbury, 29 Aug. 1989). The one change in the text recalled by Sheikh was in the character of the Woman. Members of the cast felt that in the text 'she only got her importance through Kimathi': 'We felt that Kimathi's speech in the forest, when he says look at how many dangers that woman has faced [*Trial* 72-73], was a bit patronizing: why not let the woman speak for herself?' (interview, London, 10 Aug. 1987).[16] Other alterations, which Sheikh described as 'minor', resulted from the 'fifteen or sixteen different nationalities' of the cast members, who added 'new songs, sung in different languages, that added to the richness of the play' (interview).

The Kenyan government, which had not objected during discussions between the Africa Centre and the Kenya High Commission back in July, reacted to the production in several ways. The first sign of trouble came on 31 August in a curt letter from G. N. Nyaanga, the Acting High Commissioner, declining 'involvement ... in a programme that includes subjects that do not make any sense to the Kenya government' – presumably a reference to the play. Then, as the play was about to open, Foreign Minister Elijah Mwangale, in London for consultations, tried to persuade the British Foreign Secretary, Sir Geoffrey Howe, to suppress the production. This effort having failed, the Kenya government sent security personnel to every Africa Centre performance, or so rumor had it (Perry) and immediately undertook a more successful disinformation campaign that is well illustrated in Arnold Raphael's front-page article in a Nairobi daily on 18 October, announced by a banner headline: 'NGUGI'S PLAY UPSETS LONDON.' It was Nairobi, however, that was upset. Describing the script as 'updated' and 'revised', the article fully reflects the government line:

> The script of the play has been considerably changed to incorporate contemporary and imperialist material well-larded with references to the neo-colonialist exploitation of African peasants and workers.
>
> It has, indeed, been turned into a kind of communist musical set in Africa, with much clenching of raised fists and brandishing of automatic rifles.
>
> A lavish, coloured programme has a cover of the British and American flag ... intertwined to form a hangman's noose.
>
> The *Soviet Weekly* took a fullpage advertisement in the programme.

Raphael goes on to allude to the alleged 'Communist bloc backers' of both the production and of Kenyan exiles. The Kenya government claimed as well, Raphael reported, that the exiles' activities 'are also damaging to race relations in Britain' and were 'undermining British foreign policy', with a 'ripple effect in Kenya of the group's propaganda'. It was the potential 'ripple effect', presumably, that alarmed the Kenya government.

There was some factual material in Raphael's journalistic farrago: the talks between Mwangale and Howe, the boycott by the Kenya High Commission of the Kenya Focus project at Africa Centre, and the characterization of a Kenya factsheet in the program as 'an outright attack on the post-independence government'. Otherwise the article is a tissue of lies and distortions.

The *Standard*, for which Raphael was the London correspondent, featured a front-page follow-up article on 19 October, illustrated by photographs of the two authors of the play and entitled 'Ngugi Communists [sic] Stooge'. The article reported Mwangale's airport speech on his return from his failed mission in London: 'A bunch of Marxist communists who are hostile to Kenya' were funding the play with 'huge sums of money', Mwangale said, assuring 'Ngugi wa Thiongo'o, Michere Mugo and a Mr. Kihoro, that their activities in London were well known'.[17] Mwangale's dismissal of Kenyan exiles in London (a few 'non-starters' who 'are no more important than a fellow shouting at Hyde Park for the sake of it') was belied by his attempt to quiet them. His claim that the text was substantially changed was made in response to an incredulous question from a reporter, 'Is this the same play which was the official Kenyan entry in FESTAC in 1977?' When the reporter followed up with a request for information about the alleged new version, Mwangale answered, 'No, no, it's a matter of security' (Ngugi, interview, London, 4 Aug. 1987).[18] Later on, Mwangale's line was echoed by the editor of the Nairobi monthly *The Express*: Ngugi was 'the spiritual head of the *Pambana* group', 'misty-eyed revolutionaries' whom 'the Soviet Union is now openly backing' with 'vast sums of money' and a steady supply of briefings from 'the Soviet KGB Disinformation Department' (Warsama, 'Ngugi Plans' 5-6). In 'stable and healthy' Kenya, the writer said reassuringly, it would take years to establish 'a Kenya Communist Party' (Warsama, 'Ngugi Plans' 6).

The much-reiterated charge that the play was financed by 'huge sums of money from some communist embassies' (Raphael, 'Ngugi Communists Stooge') is dismissed as false by Nigel Watt, who became director of the Africa Centre just as planning for the Kenya Focus began. According to Watt, the production received £2,000 from the Greater London Arts Association and £5,820 from the Greater London Council but 'absolutely no' money from Communist sources.[19] Africa Centre was willing to take a financial risk in supporting the production because the play 'reveals a significant moment in the history of both Kenya and Britain and ... would stimulate considerable interest in London and contribute to a fuller understanding and interest in Kenya' (letter, 16 July 1984, from Nigel Watt to B.K. Kiplagat, Kenya High Commissioner). The 'fullpage advertisement' for the *Soviet Weekly* alleged by Raphael in fact occupied a half page;[20] there were many other advertisements, mainly for British anti-racist organizations and publications. The program included as well a two-thirds-page statement from the Committee for the Release of Political Prisoners in Kenya.[21]

Nairobi newspaper readers were treated to additional confusions, first being told (by Raphael in a front-page article on 25 Oct.): 'NGUGI PLAY BANNED'[22] – this being the November 2 performance at the Commonwealth Institute – and then, the following day, learning (from Raphael in a quieter headline on page 3), that there had been a 'Rethink on Ngugi "Trial"' and that the performance would take place after all. The second of these articles, characterizing the Africa Centre and the play as 'violently anti-Kenya', explained that the Kenya High Commission 'did not want to gag its author' – an astonishing statement in view of Mwangale's failed mission. The supposedly democratic government included in its attack a call for the expulsion from England of all Kenyan dissidents ('"Exiled" Dissidents' 3). In response to this publicity, the Writers Association of Kenya removed Ngugi as its chairman; Micere Mugo, his co-author, as its assistant secretary; and Kimani Gecau (director of *Ngaahika Ndeenda*) and Al-Amin Mazrui as executive members (Warsama, 'Campaign' 9); the move was symbolic, since Mazrui had been in detention since 1982, and the other three were already in exile. In apparently orchestrated moves, Ngugi was widely condemned in Kenya by high government officials parroting Moi's characterization of the dissident exiles as 'disgruntled idlers'; protests included a Kamiriithu rally addressed by the Limuru M.P. (during which 'the people of Kamirithu' allegedly 'publicly disowned Ngugi') (Warsama, 'Campaign' 9). A cover story of the influential *Weekly Review* (Oct. 26), entitled '"Exiled" Dissidents Come Under Fire', suggested that Ngugi was 'the mastermind behind the anti-Kenya propaganda campaign' (3) and supplied additional disinformation, implicitly endorsing the view that after publishing *A Grain of Wheat* Ngugi became 'an intellectual demagogue producing propagandist literature' (4).

A more virulent attack appeared in a special report in the November issue of *The Express* announcing: 'Ngugi Plans to Form Communist Party.' In a long article replete with disinformation, the *Express* editor, Mohamed Warsama, asserts that 'Ngugi would readily accept to work with' Oginga Odinga, the once-influential opposition leader ('Ngugi Plans' 7), something that a person who introduced Ngugi to Odinga in 1982 roundly denies, reporting Odinga's annoyance at Ngugi's refusal of an active political role.[23]

Apparently acting as Mwangale's mouthpiece, Warsama enlarges to mythic proportions the Foreign Minister's canard; Ngugi – 'rightfully described' by Mwangale as 'a communist stooge' – and 'his companion-in-exile, Micere Mugo'[24] rewrote the play: 'The script ... bore no resemblance to the original Kimathi play.... It had been changed to a communist propaganda piece featuring contemporary anti-imperialised [sic] material with lots of references to the neo-colonialist exploitation of African peasants and workers' ('Campaign' 8-9). Echoing Mwangale, Warsama then quoted him: 'It is not the old Ngugi', just as it was supposedly not the old *Trial* ('Campaign' 9) – an argument obviously intended to explain how the play, which had been a set text in the Kenya Advanced Certificate of Education only two years earlier, could have been earlier presented under official auspices. Two other articles in the same issue of *The Express* reinforced the message. The historian William R. Ochieng' protracted his long-standing vendetta with Ngugi in even stronger terms while denying 'personal animosity': Ngugi, a tribalist, was 'a hopelessly devious and dishonest man', and Ochieng' was 'allergic to liars' ('Ngugi wa Thiong'o and I' 10-11). George Godia, author of the other article (and of an exposition of Moi's 'philosophy', *Understanding Nyayo*), provided a far more measured analysis of 'How Ngugi Used the Pen for Political Involvement', which more subtly supported Warsama's and Ochieng's remarks.

The attempted repression of *The Trial* in London probably stemmed from two causes: its historiography and its public implication of defects in independent Kenya. The broader cause may have been the interpretation of Mau Mau. Ngugi takes the nationalist interpretation of the radical historian Maina wa Kinyatti, who maintains that Mau Mau, despite being predominantly Gikuyu, was the peak of *African* – not narrowly Gikuyu – nationalism.[25] Maina argues, further, that it was African nationalists who wrested freedom from the British. The main opposing interpretation sees the movement as a Gikuyu civil war; denies it any importance in speeding the achievement of independence; and, in the words of the accommodationist Politician in *The Trial*, maintains that Kenyan Africans passively 'receive[d] uhuru' – an interpretation that Ngugi and Mugo's Kimathi rejects scornfully as the view of 'beggars', not patriots (46).

That this is no mere literary or academic debate appears in the comment of a minister in the Kenyatta government, who sounds much like the *Trial* Politician: 'I believe we obtained our independence in a very nice way at the instigation of the British Government but not through fighting in the forest' (Stanley Oloitipitip, qtd. Srinivasan, 'Theatre' 27). This is the dominant official attitude today, so dominant that a wealth of documentary material on Mau Mau lies untapped in the National Archives as historians play it safe and silent. Were the struggle to be more fully analyzed, many of those in power today would be revealed as collaborators with the British government, which would certainly not appear as the 'instigator' of independence. 'If MAU MAU was accorded its rightful place at the apex of Kenya's nationalist upsurge', write two defenders of the Maina/Ngugi position, 'many in state power [would be seen] as impostors, renegades, collaborators, home guards and as the DO-NOTHING chicken hearts' (Omondi and Karanja 19). The historians' debate on the interpretation of Mau Mau mentioned above occurred in August 1984, when the London production was about to begin rehearsals. The debate, protracted for weeks in the press, inevitably made a Mau Mau play exhibiting the dissident interpretation too hot to tolerate.

A second and more immediately apparent cause of the repression of *The Trial* was resentment that Kenya's dirty laundry was being washed abroad. Telling 'the secrets of the homestead' to 'strangers' is so shameful that the truth-teller is bound to be hated: 'Is it not said that the antelope conceives more hatred for him who betrays its presence with a shout?' (*Devil* 7-8). In *The Trial*, the government-antelope felt, Ngugi and Mugo betrayed the presence of neocolonialism 'with a shout'. The Kenyan press and politicians repeatedly compared Ngugi and his fellow exiles to 'people who abuse their mothers', and such people 'according to African custom ... "always stand condemned"' (Warsama, 'Campaign' 9).[26]

But a more important reason for the attack was a probably justified fear that success abroad would encourage the burgeoning dissident movement at home. A model for the attempted London repression was the previous twofold repression at Kamiriithu. The first of these Gikuyu plays, *Ngaahika Ndeenda* (*I Will Marry When I Want*), was, as Ngugi wa Mirii, the co-author, recalled in an interview,

> an eye-opener to the writers, the people, the artists, everybody who was involved. When they were banning it, the District Commissioner told the newspapers that that play was creating [social] classes. We were ... just reflecting the socio-economic classes in Kenya. But ... we created a threat. There is a proverb that if you awaken the sleeping dog, you sleep yourself.... Once all these people are conscious, then they will want their own share of the wealth. So their fears were correct. (Harare, 6 April 1987)

The same was true of the second play, *Maitu Njugira*, as Ingrid Björkman's recent book amply demonstrates. Whether the government's fears about *The Trial* in London were correct cannot be clearly ascertained; certainly both the dissident movement and its repression grew after 1984. Two years later newspaper headlines took up the familiar line: Kenyan dissidents were 'A Bunch of Cowards'; 'Ngugi a Vagabond, Says Mwangale';[27] 'Ngugi Behind "Mwakenya"' (Aboge). Ngugi as the scheming head of all Kenyan opposition is an ogre invented by Moi, Mwangale, and their loyal collaborators. One way of dealing with ogres is to pretend that they do not exist, and this tactic, too, has appeared; Ochieng', Ngugi's most persistent antagonist, recently summarized 'the first generation of African literature lecturers at the University of Nairobi' as 'people like Okot p'Bitek, Taban Lo Liyong, David Rubadiri – the lot' ('String' 31). Omitting the one Kenyan in 'the lot' from this list was no accident.

We come, then, full circle. A version of Ngugi, the creator of fiction, has been created by the Kenyan government. He cannot go to Kenya; his latest novel cannot be bought in Kenya. Furthermore, his work after *A Grain of Wheat* – that is, after his early writings – cannot be discussed in Kenya as literature. Because it challenges the status quo, all Ngugi's work from *The*

Trial onward has to be lumped together as mere 'marxist propaganda' by 'the *Enfant Terrible* of the Literary World' – not art at all, just intellectual demagoguery by a 'tribal nationalist' ('Best-Known Writer'). 'Ngugi stopped being an artist' after *A Grain of Wheat*, says Ochieng', who calls him both 'a Marxist-Leninist' and 'a Kikuyu nationalist'; everything after *Grain* is just 'political propaganda' that 'bores me to death' ('Ngugi' 11).[28] There can be no comprehensive discussion of the leading writer of East Africa in the Department of Literature that owes its name and curricular design to that very person. Speaking for Ngugi, Matigari asks the teacher, who represents Kenyan intellectuals, to 'take your chalk or your pen' and explain 'where in this country ... a person girded with a belt of peace [can] find truth and justice' (92). The teacher responds anxiously: 'Sssssshhh, stop talking so loudly.... Didn't you hear that teachers and lecturers are being detained without trial? Look at me. I have a wife and two children. What will they eat if I am sent to prison?' Anyone who has attempted to do literary research in Kenya has met that teacher.[29] 'Kenyan Writers: What Went Wrong?' asked a feature article in the *Weekly Review*, complaining of the 'serious drought in the production of creative writers' (Manzo 3). The answer is one that cannot be spoken in Kenya: creative writing dries up or goes into exile in the face of political repression because, as the proverb reiterated in *Matigari* declares, 'too much fear breeds misery in the land' (31, 76, 87, etc.).[30]

NOTES

1. This theme had been sounded earlier in *Devil on the Cross*, in which the 'modern-day ogres' (175) are seen as 'latter day Marimus' (*Decolonising* 81).
2. Cf. the modern ogre in *Devil* (177) who declares 'all that business of fighting for freedom ... just a bad dream, a meaningless nightmare'.
3. Ngugi included *Muthirigu* in *Maitu Njugira* (Björkman 31), his music drama in Gikuyu written the year before *Matigari*, which similarly reflected colonial and neo-colonial conditions was dense with specific allusions to Kenyan history.
4. At this conference Ngugi's interpretation of Mau Mau as a nationalist movement was a 'sore point'; see 'Academic Confrontation' and my 'Ngugi wa Thiong'o and the Writing of Kenyan History', *Research in African Literatures* 20.3 (1989).
5. Literally, 'footsteps'. Initially Moi used the term to suggest that he was loyally following in Kenyatta's footsteps, but it quickly became a sinister command that Kenyans follow in his own footsteps.
6. The answer may have little to do with politics. Gakaara had developed a small, faithful group of readers, and this group may not have expanded when the diary was published. Still, the fact that the book sold 271 copies in 1985 but only 91 in 1986 and 43 in 1987 has to be seen in a political context: repression escalated sharply in 1986, the year in which Gakaara was arrested and detained.
7. An article in the *Guardian* (London) saw Gakaara's 'confession' as a 'dreary and un-convincing' attempt to feed the Kenyan authorities' 'paranoia about East Africa's most distinguished writer' ('Conspiracy "Confession"'). According to my source,

who must remain anonymous, the group was founded in 1979 when a diverse group including writers, church leaders, journalists, printers, and scholars asked Dr. Karega Mutahi of the University of Nairobi Department of Linguistics to help develop a more scientific Gikuyu orthography; the basic problem was indicating vowel length, according to this source and also according to Ngugi in *Decolonising* (24). Ngugi initiated the group shortly after he came out of detention, having discovered that Gikuyu speakers could not read his play *Ngaahika Ndeenda* – he thought because of the orthography; the group met for three years, disbanding in 1982, the year Ngugi went into exile (see Gakaara viii for members of the group). Not everyone accepts Ngugi's assertion that orthography was what troubled his readers; Henry Chakava, Managing Director of Heinemann Kenya and Ngugi's Kenyan publisher, says that readers' difficulty came simply from inexperience (interview, Nairobi, 28 April 1987).

8. A character in *Devil* who is insufficiently conformist is killed in a 'car accident' (214). Such events are common in real-life Kenya. Bishop Alexander Muge of the Church of Kenya, a long-time critic of the government, was killed on 14 Aug. 1990 in a car 'accident' widely believed to be a government-ordered assassination; three days earlier, Peter Okondo, the Minister of Labor, had threatened Muge with death if he visited his constituency, Busia. A former UN official in Nairobi estimates that at least 10% of Kenyan car 'accidents' are planned.

9. The Kenyatta/Jesus analogy appears in *A Grain of Wheat*: 'He was arrested, sent to Lodwar, and on the third day he came home from Maralal' (219). The Waiyaki/Jesus analogy, anticipating the Kenyatta myth, appears in a Mau Mau pamphlet by Mbugua Njama translated by Ngugi that also describes Kenyatta as Waiyaki resurrected (see Mbugua, *Mahoya ma Waiyaki* ['The Prayers of Waiyaki']).

10. The British also engaged in strategic disinformation during the Mau Mau struggle, spreading rumors about detention camp atrocities and staging fake shootings (Blundell 198-99). The Moi government suppresses information regarding its massacres of its own citizens; in *Matigari* (122) Ngugi alludes to the 'bloody Sunday' massacre on 10 Feb. 1985, when – said the official report – one student was 'trampled to death by other students', while eyewitnesses claimed anywhere from three to more than twelve dead at the hands of police (see *Kenya News* no. 8 [Mar. 1987]: 5); *Kenya News* no. 9 [Jan. 1989]: 4). A massacre in northern Kenya in 1984, officially said to have cost 59 lives, is now said by an anonymous government official to have killed 2,169 (*Africa Confidential* 30.1 [6 Jan. 1989]: 6).

11. According to Anne Walmsley – a member of the Africa Centre Programme Committee and a former publisher with Longman Kenya – the Kenya Focus was conceived as a deliberate corrective to the generally held image of Kenya, which featured its prehistory and its touristic attractions. It was prompted by advance notice of a major exhibition of Richard Leakey's archaeological work in Kenya, to be held at the Commonwealth Institute. (Walmsley, letter, 18 Sept. 1989.)

The intention of the Focus was to discuss problems as well as achievements of contemporary Kenya; talks at the Africa Centre included panel discussions on 'Education in Kenya' (3 Oct.) and 'Population and Land Use in Kenya Today' (9 Oct.), a lecture by the poet Abdilatif Abdalla on 'The Tradition of Resistance in Swahili Poetry' (10 Oct.), and four film programs (4, 11, and 25 Oct.; 1 Nov.), with Ngugi lecturing at the second on 'The Rise of African Nationalism: Struggles for Independence in the Early 50's'. Besides the thirteen performances of *The Trial* originally scheduled, two more performances were given because of public demand, for which tickets were sold out in two hours.

12. Despite 'a clash between the authorities and the authors', the FESTAC performance took place (Ngakane); the previous run in Nairobi (Oct. 1976) had been restricted

to five performances. Ngugi was then Chairman of the Literature Department at the University of Nairobi.

13. 'Wazalendo' is Kiswahili for 'progressive'. The Kenyan singers and dancers who came together in 1983 as Wazalendo Players were supported by African Dawn, a group of six artists from Kenya, Zimbabwe, Senegal, and Ghana that, according to the Africa Centre *Trial* program, 'has toured extensively in the UK and has supported many political campaigns'. The objective of the group, a program note by Maasai Karioki explains, is to 'resuscitate' the 'useful art' of poetry 'as a means to articulate their crusade of liberation and also as a stimulus to the appreciation of the traditional African values'. Karioki quotes 'Our Song', a poem by Wanjiku Kiarie on *The Conversation*, a record produced by African Dawn, in which the poet 'castigates the rallying mottos of "Harambee-pull together" and "Nyayo-follow footsteps" as rhythmless rhythms that have helped to "plunder granaries" of the masses' – motifs, of course, of Ngugi's work from *Trial* onward (Ngugi contributed a comment to the jacket of this record). See Owusu, Ch. 8 ('The Wazalendo Experience').

14. Srinivasan concludes that the performers of *Maitu* were not *'actors* in the accepted sense of the term', because the play was such an intense 'living, felt reality', not the 'make-believe world of theatre at all' ('Historical Self-Assertion' 11, 13).

15. Besides the Kamiriithu model, the production also had behind it the experience of the Free Travelling Theatre sponsored by the Literature Department of the University of Nairobi, a group founded in 1974 (when Ngugi headed the Department) and supported by funding from embassies, cultural centers, and publishers and other businesses. In September and October of 1976 the group performed *The Trial*, as well as plays by Brecht, Soyinka, and Sophocles, in twenty-nine locations from the Coast to Kisumu (Mwagiru).

16. Other witnesses of the development of the production confirm this view. Reviewers, apparently unaware of any textual changes, commented on the successful prominence of women's roles; see Brooke 37 and Perry. Owusu – a member of the cast – asserts that the cast altered the script 'in significant ways', introducing not only songs but dances and 'whole scenes and sequences' (153); he does not, however, explain what these were, and the four persons intimately involved in the production whom I have interviewed all stressed the trivial nature of the textual changes, except those in the Woman's role.

17. Although seemingly not well known to the government at the time, Wanyiri Kihoro – a lawyer who was the play's production manager – paid for his activities in London and for earlier political activity in Kenya when he was detained some six months after his return to Kenya early in 1986. He was released three years later and, threatened with re-arrest or assassination, fled over the border to Tanzania in 1991; promptly expelled from Tanzania, he joined his exiled wife and children in London. He was described as 'another communist' in one of the 1984 attacks (Warsama, 'Ngugi Plans' 6). In continuing disinformation, the *Weekly Review* article on Kihoro's 1989 release described him as the 'administrator' of Africa Centre, where he in fact worked as a program officer on a time-shared basis with his wife, Wanjiru. The article invents history retroactively: while at Africa Centre, 'Kihoro was accused of turning the centre into a propaganda forum and a venue of theatrical and other activities by self-exiled radicals, Ngugi and [Micere] Mugo being foremost among them' ('No More Detainees', 9 June 1989: 7). The same issue of the *Weekly Review* calls Ngugi 'a symbol of anti-Kenya government propaganda' ('Life After Detention' 7).

18. The supposedly enlarged text was reported as well in the British press: Nicholas De Jongh complained in the *Guardian* that the play was now 'submerged in new

material supplied by the cast ... which swell[s it] to nearly four hours', thus lending uninformed support to Mwangale's allegations; in fact, the opening-night perform-ance in Nairobi in 1976 also lasted four hours (Hirst 27). The *Guardian* added insult to injury by printing a deprecatory article derived from a two-part review in the *Standard* by Harry Hilton, a self-described 'ex-Kenya copper' who recalled being 'chased off the slopes of Mount Kenya by a band of 40 irate Freedom Fighters'.

19. Interview, London, 22 Aug. 1989; see also Owusu 153 and Hall. This amount, even when increased by a few minor grants, was far below what was needed; Africa Centre made up the difference, and the cast in effect subsidized the production by accepting low salaries (£20 a week) and performing multiple tasks (Ahmed Sheikh, interview, London, 10 Aug. 1987). Kitchener incorrectly says that there was no public funding.

20. The charge of a fullpage advertisement was repeated by Mohamed Warsama the next month, in an article interpreting the advertisement as 'the first open gesture of support' from the Soviet government 'for the dissident movement led by Ngugi', which Warsama links with the 1982 attempted coup in Kenya ('Campaign' 8).

21. The Kenya government claims the Committee is an organ of dissident Kenyans; however, the chairman was (and is) John La Rose, a publisher and London book-store proprietor originally from Trinidad, and the rest of its membership was divided approximately equally between Kenyans and Britons who had worked in Kenya and who assisted in mediating between the Kenyans and British politicans and the media.

22. This article calls those involved in the play 'extremists' and the production 'a political stunt'.

23. Private information. My informant erroneously claimed that Ngugi and Odinga had not met before.

24. During a summer visit to London, Mugo helped with auditions and rehearsals, up to the point of open rehearsals, and composed the lead song. Returning to London in time for the 2 Nov. performance at the Commonwealth Institute, she was struck by the many changes in production introduced during open rehearsals (interview, Canterbury, 29 Aug. 1989).

25. Maina 17 completed a six-and-a-half-year prison sentence for possessing a 'sedi-tious' document on Oct. 1988 and fled over the Tanzanian to exile in the United States, where he is preparing his prison memoirs. The sentencing appears to have been at least in part an attempt to repress his kind of history and, more specifically, his view of Mau Mau.

26. Martin Shikuku, a fellow detainee of Ngugi who resumed his political career after his release, chided him for 'abusing his mother country' while in 'cowardly' exile (qtd. Kimondo 1).

27. Mwangale's appeal was made in a speech to Kenyan students in New York in which he claimed that Ngugi (then in the United States on a speaking tour) 'had been given a cool reception' – surprising news to anyone who had been in one of his rapt and enthusiastic audiences. Mwangale repeated in New York the charge of abusing the mother country, labeling exiled Kenyan dissidents 'a bunch of cowardly criminals and opportunists'. A 1985 anthology prepared by the Kenya Institute of Education for secondary schools, *Chameleon's Second Delivery*, was withdrawn as a set text when a government official read the minutes of the committee that devised it; the minutes recorded one member's premonition that 'somebody' wouldn't like the book because it included two satirical stories by Ngugi, 'A Mercedes Funeral' and 'Wedding at the Cross' (private information). By 1986 a single sentence alluding to Ngugi – referring to *The River Between*, his most inoffensive work, and accom-panied by photographs of Ngugi and Micere Mugo – sufficed to cause the offend-

ing journalist, David Kimotho, to be picked up for questioning. Photographs of Ngugi and Mugo, along with Soyinka, decorate a 1991 article on the suffering of 'great writers' in exile, but the article itself, which details the suffering of Dostoevsky, Tolstoy, Gogol, and Hemingway, omits any comment on Mugo and confines its comments on the other two pictured writers to the following: 'In Africa, Wole Soyinka and Ngugi wa Thiong'o have spent some time in detention' (Wanjohi). It is true that Ngugi serves as chairman of Umoja, an umbrella organization of Kenyan dissident groups, and he has come out as a leader of Mwakenya, although it is not clear whether he does much more than lend his name; this is the closest he has come to heeding Matigari's call for 'armed words' (131). In the spring terms of 1989, 1990, and 1991, he has served as visiting professor at Yale University, a location even less convenient than London for fomenting political subversion in Kenya.

28. The claim that Ngugi's post-*Grain* (or, in more liberal versions, post-detention) writing is not real 'art' sometimes extends to the unquestionable lie that he has written little in recent years; see, for example, Manzo, who asserts that Ngugi is now engaged in 'popularising his political beliefs ... while engaging in little creative writing'. Between *Grain* and his detention he published a novel and wrote a play while working as a full-time academic; since his release from detention he has published a play and two novels. This is not a creative drying up. And one should note that since *Grain* he has also published five books of nonfiction, two translations of his own works, and occasional journalism.

29. One member of the Department of Literature, for example, had to face questions from the press about the London production of *The Trial*. What did he think of it? He explained that he could think nothing, since he had not seen it. The next day the newspaper trumpeted his views; he had attacked Ngugi. He explained to me that he could not repudiate the views attributed to him: 'I have a wife and children.' Another member of the University of Nairobi Department of Literature, a one-time friend of Ngugi whose dissertation included ample discussion of his works, now turns the class over to a graduate assistant when Ngugi's works come up. A panel discussion on 'What Ails Kenyan Literature?' at Paa ya Paa Gallery on 23 June 1991 treated Ngugi, when bothering to mention him, as if he were from an irrelevant older generation; the panelists pussyfooted around the obvious cause of the ailment, government repression.

30. See the annual bibliographical roundups by R. N. Ndegwa in *The Journal of Commonwealth Literature*, in which she echoes Taban lo Liyong's famous lament for East African literary barrenness. Despite recent releases of political detainees, the prospects are not bright. On 11 Nov. 1988 the *Weekly Review* ran a cover story, 'Message to Dissidents', with a cover photograph of a loyalty demonstration in Kiambu feature a man holding up a homemade poster attacking, among others, Ngugi. In January of 1991, an attempted revival of *Ngaahika Ndeenda* at the Kenyatta International Conference Center was banned 'at the eleventh hour', apparently because of Ngugi's reputation as 'the Salman Rushdie of Kenya' and the 'uncomfortable truths about society' contained in the play (Mutahi).

WORKS CITED

Aboge, Paul. 'Ngugi Behind 'Mwakenya', Claims Kariuki Chotara.' *Kenya Times* 8 Apr. 1986: 3.

'Academia Confrontation: Wa Thiong'o a Sore Point at History Conference.' *Weekly Review* 31 Aug. 1984: 5-6.

'Best-Known Writer Now 'Enfant Terrible' of the Literary World.' *Weekly Review* 20 Sept. 1985 (Life and Leisure section): 6-7.

Björkman, Ingrid. 'Mother, Sing for Me': People's Theatre in Kenya. London and Atlantic Highlands, New Jersey: Zed P, 1989.

Björkman, Ingrid. 'Ngugi wa Thiong'o.' *Kunapipi* 4.2 (1982): 126-34. [Interview.]

Blundell, Sir Michael. *So Rough a Wind: The Kenya Memoirs of Sir Michael Blundell.* Foreword by the Earl of Kilmuir. London: Weidenfeld and Nicolson, 1964.

Brooke, Stephen. 'The Trial of Dedan Kimathi.' *Artrage* no. 8 (Spring 1984): 36-37.

'Bunch of Cowards, A.' *Weekly Review* 10 Oct. 1986: 9-10.

Chakava, Henry. 'A Decade of Publishing in Kenya: 1977-1987: One Man's Involvement.' *African Book Publishing Record* 14.4 (1988): 235-41.

'Conspiracy "Confession".' *Guardian* 30 May 1986: 18.

De Jongh, Nicholas. 'The Trial of Dedan Kimathi.' *Guardian* 25 Oct. 1984: 12.

'"Exiled" Dissidents Come Under Fire.' *Weekly Review* 26 Oct. 1984: 3-5, 7.

'Freed Author Exposes Mwakenya: Ngugi's "Methods" Listed.' *Standard* 21 May 1986: 1, 24.

Gakaara wa Wanjau. *Mau Mau Author in Detention.* Trans. Paul Ngigi Njoroge. Nairobi: Heinemann Kenya, 1988.

Godia, George. 'How Ngugi Used the Pen for Political Involvement.' *The Express* Nov. (1984): 11-13.

Hall, Richard. 'Kenya Protest at Play.' *Observer* 21 Oct. 1984: 14.

Hilton, Harry. '"Trial of Dedan Kimathi" in London.' *Standard* 29 Nov. 1984: 6.

Hilton, Harry. 'Ngugi's View of Dedan Kimathi.' *Standard* 1 Dec. 1984: 4.

Hilton, Harry. 'Play Back.' *Guardian* 2 Nov. 1984: 17.

Hofmyer, Agnes Leakey. *Beyond Violence.* Nairobi: Jomo Kenyatta Foundation, 1990.

Itote, Waruhiu (General China). *'Mau Mau' General.* Nairobi: East African Publishing House, 1967.

Jones, Eldred. 'Editorial.' *African Literature Today* 11 (1980): 1-3.

Kenya Institute of Education. *Chameleon's Second Delivery: A Short Stories Anthology.* Nairobi: Kenya Literature Bureau, 1985.

Kimondo, James. 'Shikuku Blasts Ngugi.' *Standard* 20 Oct. 1984: 1.

Kimotho, David. 'Why Nationalists Consider African Literature to be Unique.' *Kenya Times* 26 Mar. 1986: 10.

Kitchener, Julie. 'Keeping Kimathi Alive.' *New African* 1 Oct. 1984: 49.

Liyong, Taban lo. 'Can We Correct Literary Barrenness in East Africa?' *East African Journal* 2.8 (Dec. 1965): 5-13.

Maina wa Kinyatti. 'Mau Mau: The Peak of African Political Organization in Colonial Kenya.' *Kenya Historical Review* 5.2 (1977): 287-311.

Manzo, Henry. 'Kenyan Writers: What Went Wrong?' *Daily Nation* (Life and Leisure section) Sept. 1985: 3-5.

Mbugua Njama, *Mahoya ma Waiyaki.* Nairobi: Mbugua Book Writers, 1952. Trans. as 'The Prayers of Waiyaki' by James Ngugi, Nov. 1968. In Brian G. McIntosh, 'The Scottish Mission in Kenya, 1891-1923.' Diss. U of Edinburgh, 1969. 474-79.

Mockerie, Parmenas Githendu. *An African Speaks for his People.* Intro. Julian Huxley. London: Hogarth P, 1934.

Mutahi, Wahome. 'This Censorship Smacks of Sanitising Rot in Society.' *Daily Nation* 4 Feb. 1991.

Mwagiru, Ciugu. 'The Traveling Theatre for the People, by the People.' *Umma* no. 3 (1976): 29.

Mwanzi, Henry. 'Men of Literature and Kenya's History.' *Weekly Review* 5 Oct. 1984: 39.

Ngakane, Lionel. 'Africa Through Kenyan Eyes.' *Africa: International Business, Economics and Political Monthly* no. 160 (Dec. 1984): 49.

'Ngugi a Vagabond, Says Mwangale.' *Daily Nation* 4 Oct. 1986: 1, 4.

'Ngugi Communists [sic] Stooge – Mwangale.' *Standard* 19 Oct. 1984: 1.

Ngugi wa Thiong'o. *Decolonising the Mind: The Politics of Language in African Literature.* London: James Currey; Nairobi: Heinemann Kenya; Portsmouth, NH: Heinemann; Harare: Zimbabwe Publishing House, 1986.

Ngugi wa Thiong'o. *Detained: A Writer's Prison Diary.* London: Heinemann, 1981.

Ngugi wa Thiong'o. *Devil on the Cross.* Trans. by the author from the Gikuyu. London: Heinemann, 1982.

Ngugi wa Thiong'o. *A Grain of Wheat.* London: Heinemann, 1967.

Ngugi wa Thiong'o. *Matigari.* Trans. into English by Wangui wa Goro. Oxford: Heinemann, 1989.

Ngugi wa Thiong'o. *Petals of Blood.* London: Heineman, 1977.

Ngugi wa Thiong'o and Micere Githae Mugo. *The Trial of Dedan Kimathi.* Nairobi: Heinemann Kenya; London: Heinemann, 1976.

Ngugi wa Thiong'o and Ngugi wa Mirii. *Ngaahika Ndeenda: Ithaako ria Ngerekano.* Nairobi: Heinemann Educational Books, 1980. [Trans. by the authors as *I Will Marry When I Want.* London: Heinemann, 1982.]

Ochieng', William R. 'Ngugi wa Thiong'o and I.' *The Express* Nov. (1984): 10-11.

Ochieng', William R. 'A String of Words That Rhyme.' *Weekly Review* 10 Feb. 1989: 31-32.

Okpewho, Isidore. 'Rethinking Myth.' *African Literature Today* 11 (1980): 5-23.

Omari, Emman. '"I Am Not Above the Contradictions Which Bedevil Our Society".' *Standard* 28 Aug. 1981: 11, 15. [Interview with Ngugi.]

Omondi, Timothy, and Jackson R. Karanja. 'Scholarship and Politics in Kenya: Reply to Backward Scholars.' *Forward* 7.2/3 (1985): 19-20.

Owusu, Kwesi. *The Struggle for Black Arts in Britain: What Can We Consider Better Than Freedom.* London: Comedia Publishing Group, 1986.

Perry, Alison. 'Whose Country Is It Anyway?' *West Africa* no. 3 506 (29 Oct. 1984): 2193.

Raphael, Arnold. 'Ngugi Play Banned.' *Standard* 25 Oct. 1984: 1.

Raphael, Arnold. 'Ngugi's Play Upsets London.' *Standard* 18 Oct. 1984: 1.

Raphael, Arnold. 'Rethink on Ngugi "Trial".' *Standard* 26 Oct. 1984: 3.

Srinivasan, Padma. 'Historical Self-Assertion or Traditional Drama? – The Case of Kenya.' Occasional Paper. Centre of East African Studies, University of Bombay, Bombay, 1987.

Srinivasan, Padma. 'Theatre as Political Dissent: The Kenyan Experience.' *Freedom First* no. 391 (Oct. 1986): 27-28.

Umoja. *Struggle for Democracy in Kenya: Special Report on the 1988 General Elections in Kenya.* Preface Ngugi wa Thiong'o. London: Umoja, 1988.

Wanjohi, Kimaru. 'Lives and Times of Great Writers.' *Sunday Nation* 9 June 1991: XIII.

Warsama, Mohamed. 'Campaign Provokes Anger at Home.' *The Express* Nov. (1984): 8-9.

Warsama, Mohamed. 'Ngugi Plans to Form Communist Party.' *The Express* Nov. 1984: 5-8.

Watt, Nigel. 'Africa Centre.' *Weekly Review* 9 Nov. 1984: 2.

'Wazalendo Players 84 Present "The Trial of Dedan Kimathi".' Publicity material prepared by Wazalendo Players 84. Africa Centre (London) files. 2 pp. typescript.

KATHRIN M. WAGNER

'Both as a Citizen and as a Woman'? Women and Politics in Some Gordimer Novels

> I believe the truth about any subject only comes when all the sides of the story are put together, and all their different meanings make one new one. Each writer writes the missing parts to the other writer's story. And the whole story is what I'm after.
> Alice Walker[1]

Nadine Gordimer's problematic status as a woman writer, and as a writer *about* women and their experience in apartheid-ridden South Africa, has attracted increasing critical attention over the past few years, and has recently given rise to a number of short critical studies specifically focused upon the question of whether she may be termed to be 'feminist' in her approach and in her concerns.[2] Critical focus upon this issue has arisen at least partially out of an interest in the fact that a large number of her works offer us female protagonists,[3] whose voices are manipulated with increasing sophistication by an authorial consciousness which is itself, of course, female.

However, Gordimer's own repeated denial of a specifically feminist thrust in her work has problematised such an enquiry considerably. In her many statements on what it is to be a writer, she has quite unambiguously dissociated herself from a 'feminist' perspective: she has said that she is simply 'a writer who happens to be a woman', and has amplified this by emphasising that she is *'not a feminist* except in so far as I carry, still, the tattered banner of full human rights for all human beings' (my emphasis).[4] In 1975 her view of the essentially androgynous nature of the writer became the subject of a few paragraphs in her 'Introduction' to *Selected Stories*, in which she stated:

> As for the specific solitude of the woman-as-intellectual, I must say truthfully that my femininity has never constituted any special kind of solitude, for me. Indeed, in that small town, walled up among the mine dumps, born exiled from the European world of ideas, ignorant that such a world [sic] existed among Africans, my only genuine and innocent connection with the social life of the town ... was through my femaleness. As an adolescent, at least I felt and followed sexual

attraction in common with others; that was a form of communion I could share. Rapunzel's hair is the right metaphor for this femininity: by means of it, I was able to let myself out and live in the body, with others, as well as – alone – in the mind. To be young and in the sun; my experience of this was similar to Camus...

In any case, I question the existence of the specific solitude of the woman-as-intellectual when that woman is a writer, because when it comes to their essential faculty as writers, *all writers are androgynous beings.* (My emphasis.)[5]

Gordimer's perspective here may of course be understood as arising out of an adolescence and early adulthood spent in a relatively isolated colonial outpost in contexts untouched by any feminist ideology; the first major post-war resurgence of feminist consciousness, which only reached South Africa in 1964/5 with the publication of Betty Friedan's *The Feminine Mystique*, came too late to alter the thrust of her already clearly established aesthetic and political commitments, and it should not surprise us that her representation of her youthfully uncritical embrace of conventional ways of being female in the thirties and forties is here only marginally ironical and quite in harmony with her consistent unwillingness to be seen as embarking upon a 'feminist' polemic in her fiction. That her rejection of a 'feminist' label has remained consistent over several decades was made clear once again as recently as November 1988, when, at a COSAW conference in Johannesburg, she returned to the idea of the writer as essentially androgynous:

One gets the feeling often, talking to feminist writers, that the women feel that it's their destiny to write simply from the body of a woman, from the mind of a woman.

But I think this is denying what a writer is and what a writer can do. Because a writer can be many things in the imagination, in the creation of a character...

What I am saying is that there is a certain gift or ability in writers, a certain gift which comes from observation, cultivated, that comes from hypersensitivity to other people's faces, to hear beyond and behind their words, what they are really saying...[6]

And, in Gordimer's view, this is a 'gift' in no way determined by gender. Thus the androgynous writer consciously chooses his or her perspective, unconstrained by the vagaries of authorial gender or personal autobiography, and subject only to the requirement that [she] cultivates [her] sensitivity to the gap between the said and the unsaid.

Gordimer in fact appears to see the feminist thrust as a middle-class self-indulgence on the part of women who both resent, and aspire to participate in, traditionally male domains of power in a capitalist, patriarchally-ordered world. As such it is seen to be largely irrelevant both to the apocalyptic battle against racism within the single-issue society she seems to understand South Africa to be, and to the life-experience of the vast majority of (Black) women, whose struggle forms part of the overall struggle against apartheid. It has indeed been claimed that her position is at times even anti-feminist, as her work reflects her sense of the need to privilege the urgent political and public issues of her time over the merely personal and private that she appears to understand feminist concerns to be: for her, as she emphasised again in 1983, 'the feminist issue withers in comparison with the voteless, powerless state of South African Blacks, irrespective of their sex'.[7]

In the light of such statements, attempts to read her within the context of some current (Anglo-American) definitions of what it is to be a feminist – that is, as one who 'is primarily concerned with the oppression of women in an androcentric society', and whose chosen perspective thus represents 'political act in which the politics of gender-oppression are confronted',[8] – have met with significant difficulties; and the search for a feminist thrust in her work by such critics as Lazar (1988, note 2) and Cooper (1989, note 2) has to date only uncovered a plethora of sexist stereotypes in her fiction which keep company uneasily with those other, sharp and dismissive analyses of the inadequacies of characters whose personal and political deficiencies she so ruthlessly dissects. Being a woman writer quite clearly has not to date allied Gordimer (even unconsciously) with feminism *as a movement* in the sense in which Rosalind Coward defines it: 'feminism', she insists, 'must always be the alignment of women in *a political movement* with particular political aims and objectives. It is a grouping identified by its *political* interests, not its common experiences' (my emphasis).[9] But Gordimer appears to be willing to understand politics only in terms of the dynamics of the struggle against racial, rather than sexual, oppression. Thus it is not surprising to find that feminist critics, who cannot exonerate her on the grounds of ignorance and who find it difficult to read her sometimes bluntly reductionist statements as merely ingenuous, have come increasingly to criticise her work as simply 'insensitive' to precisely those issues we might expect to find her, as a woman in the post-feminist era, directly concerned with; we need a study, suggests one such critic, which will 'account for her willingness to recognise racial oppression, the oppression of others; but not to perceive that, in terms of gender politics, it is *she herself* who is the other' (my emphasis).[10]

Is the particular accusation which is implicit in such a plea, that Gordimer (as a major female voice) has failed to become sensitised to feminist issues, despite their centrality in the current intellectual life of women writers, in fact justified? Recent attempts to suggest that there has been some development in her response to contemporary feminist thrusts were briefly encouraged by a comment made by Gordimer in an interview with Stephen Gray in 1981, in which she claimed that she had become 'more radical ... both as a citizen and as a woman':[11] a comment which seemed to suggest an awareness that her stance had been in need of some critical reassessment, and had indeed been revised and developed. Yet critics have, nevertheless, looked in vain for evidence of such a growing, feminist, orientation in her work. I would suggest, in fact, that the particular context within which Gordimer made this statement has not been fully taken into account, a context already firmly established by a large number of earlier pronouncements which clearly delineated her sense of the nature of the relationship between the individual and society. Thus, her comment must be read as implying not so much a new commitment to the development of feminist perspectives in her work, as a restatement of her well-documented belief that both men's and women's lives are embedded in the political developments of their times. Women, she suggests, should not be shown as in retreat from the public world, operating primarily within the personal and subjective complexities of a privately constituted world: both men and women must be shown to be shaped, as much in their innermost consciousnesses as in the external forms their lives take on, by the political nature of the times they live in and through. What this amounts to is a conscious rejection of the division between the public and the private as an inappropriate luxury in the world Gordimer inhabits; already in 1965 we find her stressing that her characters – and people in general – 'are what they are because their lives are regulated and their mores formed by their political situation ... politics *is* character in South Africa' (my emphasis).[12]

And yet Gordimer's comment that she had become 'more radical ... both as a citizen and as a woman' is illuminating at another level, if only by default. It raises, for instance, the question of how Gordimer has conceptualised the role of the citizen (on the one hand) and of the woman (on the other). To be a fully-fledged *citizen*, for example, suggests to her not only that one is embedded within a shaping society, but also that one bears a moral responsibility to assist in the further shaping of that society. In Gordimer's work, such a sense of a moral responsibility to her society is reflected in both her belief that the writer possesses unique qualities, and that these qualities ought to be put to work in a particular way in the service of society. In 1975 she brings these two strains together in a particularly illuminating passage, in which she claims (without any qualification) that the writer possesses

> powers of observation heightened beyond the normal [which] imply extraordinary disinvolvement, or rather the double process, excessive preoccupation and identification with the lives of others, and at the same time a monstrous detachment.... The tension between standing apart and being fully involved; that is what makes a writer.... The validity of this dialectic is the synthesis of *revelation*; our achievement of, or even attempt at this is *the moral, the human justification for what we do*. (My emphasis)[13]

In the Wordsworthian conflation of the moral and the human, in the use made of the concept of revelation, and in the emphasis on the writer's faculties as being in some way superior to those of the 'ordinary' man, – claims repeated in the 1982 essay, 'Living in the Interregnum'[14] – we find

Gordimer's sense that the writer-as-citizen has a mission to fulfil already hinted at. That she is fundamentally a moralist, and that her work is obviously shaped by quite clearly defined ideological commitments, which bring it at times perilously close to collapse into the merely polemical and didactic, has recently been increasingly clearly recognised.[15] Yet she herself appears quite unaware of the extent of this element of didacticism in her work, arguing (again in 1975) in a well-known passage that

> in a certain sense a writer is 'selected' by his subject, his subject being *the consciousness* of his own era. How he deals with this is, to me, the fundament of commitment, although 'commitment' is usually understood as the reverse process: a writer's selection of a subject in conformity with the rationalisation of his own ideological and/or political beliefs.[16]

Ten years later, in an interview with Susan Sontag, she again denies the presence of a consciously didactic thrust in her work:

> [t]he political aspect is something that came into my work implicitly, because the life around me was imbued with it, even the most private aspects of life were penetrated by the effects of politics ... [yet] I saw [politics] as something completely separate from what I was doing as a writer ...
> ... being answerable to some political or social problem, in which I may be involved as a citizen: the day that becomes more important than being a writer, I think I'm discounted in the world.[17]

What is of interest to us here is the obvious contradiction embedded in the two prongs of these observations: to have 'become more radical both as a citizen and as a woman' (1981), because of a growing perception of the extent to which 'even the most private aspects of life [are] penetrated by the effects of politics' (1985), leaves little room for the line Gordimer nevertheless attempts to draw above between her commitments as a citizen on the one hand and as a writer on the other.

What is also becoming increasingly clear to contemporary critics of Gordimer's work is that both her representation (as a citizen) of the South African reality and the *political* position she takes up in the fiction are governed by somewhat narrow perspectives. Thus when Gordimer claims above a 'commitment' to the faithful representation of 'the consciousness of [her] own era', it is a commitment which expressed itself in the incorporation of what is being increasingly seen as a simply reductive version of the doctrinaire positions of the South African radical left. As I have argued elsewhere,[18] her fiction frequently reproduces in an essentially uncritical way the mainstream positions of this segment of the political spectrum, as they have developed over time; (Clingman has pointed this out too, for somewhat different critical purposes, in his interesting 1986 analysis of the relationship between the fiction and the historical processes reflected in it).[19] The encoding of such ideological clichés at certain levels in her work has begun to attract some negative critical attention, such as that reflected in a recent comment by Brenda Cooper, who points out that 'The repressive laws, the bannings, the bombings, the torture, underground activity and guerilla warfare, encompass Gordimer's South African history entirely, rather than consisting of one aspect of it ... by privileging race she underplays the realities of social class and compromises on issues of gender'.[20]

Not only does Gordimer follow a well-trodden path in her overt political philosophy: I would also argue that her position is shot through with the kind of contradictions that one might expect, given her particular position in the South Africa she inhabits. For example, despite her fierce and contemptuous dismissal of the pretentions to liberalism on the part of her white protagonists, the values in terms of which those characters are measured and found wanting may be seen to be at root themselves shaped and formed by an essentially liberal philosophy. Recent definitions of liberalism have glossed the term as meaning – originally – 'To be free from narrow prejudice or bigotry', and from 'unreasonable prejudice in favour of traditional opinions or established institutions', and as then coming to embrace the additional ideas of being 'open to the reception of new ideas or proposals for reform', and of being determined to live in accordance with the dictates of conscience:[21] it is clear that Gordimer's own convictions are rooted in a liberalism understood within these parameters, and that her much-discussed 'critique of liberalism' grows out of her sense of the extent to which liberal values have been debased and corrupted by white South African smugness, hypocrisy, and greed: in essence she mourns liberalism's failure to triumph rather than rejecting its fundamental precepts, which continue to inform most of her responses. It is clear that, although she emphasised in an interview in 1984 that she now sees herself as a radical and not as a liberal,[22] her fictional analyses remain politically naive, and the extent of her commitment to the radical Marxism to which she pays some lip-service remains still to be examined and assessed in more detail than has been done to date. It is in fact not difficult to argue that her radicalism is rooted not so much in a commitment to Marxist ideology as in basic Christian values: for example, the 1979 novel, *Burger's Daughter*, interestingly stresses Lionel Burger's explanation that he was drawn to the Communist Party of the day because it was the only non-racial political party available to idealists and humanists like himself: in essence, he understands and practices socialism almost exclusively within the parameters of mainstream Christianity's command that one be one's brother's keeper.[23] That Gordimer's representation here is not merely a response to the demands of plot and characterisation but also reflects the moral content of the world Gordimer herself inhabited as a young intellectual is suggested by an interesting comment made by Gordimer's contemporary, Doris Lessing, in a 1985 interview; the link between liberalism, Christianity, and 'Communist' affiliations among young radicals in the

decades of the fifties and sixties is perceptively laid bare in her unequivocal statement that

> Marxism didn't create these ideas of harmony and happiness and equality. It [sic]
> comes from religion. Utopias long predate Marxism ... So Marxism is in fact struc-
> tured like Christianity, with Heaven and Hell – Hell being capitalism, and Paradise,
> and suffering redeeming you. It's exactly the same structure. And the idea of para-
> dise in the classless society. It predates even Christianity. It's the old Golden Age
> theme.[24]

Gordimer's depiction of the ideals informing political activism in South
Africa in the era with which she deals not only fails to contradict but
rather fleshes out this perspective more fully. In fact, I would argue that,
although Gordimer allies herself with what the South African regime has
termed radical positions within a particular political spectrum, her sympathies are rooted in essentially Christian and (in the widest sense) *conservative* (rather than innovative or original) convictions, especially in the
sphere of what it is to be a 'citizen'.

It should not surprise us, then, to find her representation in the novels
of what might be allowed to women, both in a private context and in the
public sphere of active involvement in political change, to be equally fixed
in what have increasingly come to be thought of as outmoded and sexist
paradigms – perhaps predictably so, since both she and Lessing served
their political apprenticeships during a period in which women's roles in
left-wing circles were allegedly defined by a characteristically unpoliticised
and cheerful sexism. Thus, for example, the dimensions that women's lives
are allowed to take on in Gordimer's fictions – indeed, at times their very
identity – depend repeatedly upon the nature of their relationships with
the *male* characters. And so Rosa, in *Burger's Daughter*, finds herself in
prison at the novel's end not because of what she has *done* but because of
who she *is* – that is, her father's daughter; while Antonia, in *The Conservationist*,[25] who has 'done' nothing but suffers the indignities of interrogation, about her connections with radical groupings with which she is in
sympathy only, flees the country on an exit permit made possible only by
her access to expensive lawyers as a spin-off from her relationship with
the male arch-capitalist, Mehring. It is also clear that the actions of
Gordimer's women are determined more by stereotypically 'feminine'
emotional and sexual responses to the situations they find themselves
caught up in (within the parameters of traditional sexist clichés), rather
than by the so-called 'male' quality of rational analysis or even ideological
commitment. Her female characters, for example, repeatedly romanticise
and sexually idealise the figure of the male black guerilla (see Elizabeth
van der Sandt's response to Luke Fokase in *The Late Bourgeois World*
(1966);[26] a response which comes to maturity in Hillela's fascination with
her 'obsidian god' in *A Sport of Nature* (1987).[27] We might also note the
extent to which Gordimer's women remain, in a sense, camp-followers

throughout the fiction, rather than being themselves doers and shakers: they react and are acted upon, rather than initiating action themselves.

And yet, despite Gordimer's insistence upon representing women's lives as essentially subordinated to the more active and aggressive activities of men, the fact remains that the fiction betrays a powerful interest specifically in the precise and subtle nuances of *women's* experience in an apartheid-ridden world. Among the novels, six out of a current total of nine mediate events chiefly or entirely through a central *female* consciousness; thus a significant majority of the novels concentrate upon a muted analysis of the options and roles available particularly to *women*, both in the various resistance groupings depicted, and more generally in relationship to a world devastated by the cumulative actions of men. Although it is the men who act, the focus is frequently upon the impact of these actions upon their women: men are in fact repeatedly pushed off centre-stage by the novels' insistence upon examining the confusions about roles and identity which beset the psyches of the *female* narrative voices – as in, for example, *The Late Bourgeois World*, which privileges Elizabeth's meditations about the origins and impact of Max's actions, and the choices these present her with, rather than focusing upon Max's perspectives upon those actions.

If, however, we accept Gordimer's denial of a 'feminist' impulse behind her work, how are we to explain such a tendency in her work? We cannot simply argue that Gordimer's own gender-identity 'naturally' predisposes her towards women's perspectives in her work: she has herself recently emphasised again that she wishes to make 'a case for the powers of writers to write not only within the confines of their own sex. I think that women write very well about men.'[28] Nor is it a solution to accept her own, recent, somewhat flippant suggestion that there are autobiographical origins for her focus upon strong and independent women: 'I came from a very female-dominated background.... My mother was the stronger character in more or less everything we did and learnt. That might account for [my concentration upon women's perspectives].'[29] The reductive inadequacy of such an explanation is obvious, although some critics continue to suggest that such autobiographical material supports their claim that Gordimer is in fact, despite her denials, a 'closet' feminist.

I wish to suggest, on the contrary, that, beyond the accidents of autobiography and authorial gender, we might attempt to locate the origins of Gordimer's interest in developing female narrative voices in her fiction *not* in an as yet unacknowledged commitment to the *political* goals of an activist feminist stance, but as arising out of the specific, emotionally and subjectively experienced quality of her adult life both as a woman and a citizen in South Africa. It has been a life which, despite its appearance of privilege, has been arguably defined – though perhaps only at a subliminal level – by the twin experiences of powerlessness and marginalisation (at both a personal and a political level) in an authoritarian and patriarchally ordered world. For Gordimer has from birth been a member of at least four groups which have been effectively pushed aside in South African history in this century: she is a *woman* within a male-dominated world, a *liberal* and an *English*-speaker within a nationalist and Afrikaner hegemony, and she has – more recently – experienced the painful consequences of being *white* within the context of the rise of Black Consciousness politics amongst those with whom she has identified herself. If we ask, then, what it is that welds together the three prongs of Gordimer's work: her withering denunciations of the moral hypocrisies of the specific class she belongs to (at a particular point in its history), her valorisation of the political aspirations to power of a black majority marginalised by a white hegemonic minority, and her consistent interest in the specific nature of the options open to women involved in the struggle – women who are presented as trapped within a particular kind of society and a particular set of expectations – we might argue that the ultimate link between these three thrusts should be sought precisely in Gordimer's fascination with that experience of powerlessness and marginalisation which all three of these groups share. It is, then, the tensions arising from the relationship between her own quadrupled powerlessness and those other forms of marginalisation identified above which appear subliminally to direct and shape Gordimer's focus upon her female protagonists, rather than the more facile equation between sexism and racism suggested by some critics as an explanation for her interest in what it might be to be both a citizen *and* a woman in the South Africa she inhabits. Thus Gordimer's frustrated sympathies with the predicaments of both her own class and sex 'naturally' ally her with those other marginalised and dispossessed peoples, black South Africans in general, whose quest for a voice and for power she perceives as even more fully frustrated than that of white women in the historical era of which she writes.

Given the conservative nature of Gordimer's response to the pressure of feminist politics on her work, it is not surprising to find that the connections between the personal and the political outlined above express themselves rather more in the form of an ironically powerful emotional logic, operating at a subtextual level in the fiction, than as an overt shaping principle in the textual foreground. In this reading of Gordimer's work we have 'history from the inside' in a dimension rather different than the one suggested by Clingman: we are offered the interior histories of developing fictional female consciousnesses as they seek to find appropriate ways to respond to *both* political *and* gender contexts, and as they struggle to find space for their voices within the fictions' overt and often didactic commitment to the struggle against apartheid. Yet such a space is both difficult to find and to maintain, given the pressure of the political agenda Gordimer sets herself, and I would in fact argue that her decision to privilege her political commitments over her tentative history of women's consciousness, as outlined above, generates tensions which repeatedly undermine the power and credibility of her fictional project in unexpected ways. An understanding of these tensions will go some way, in particular, towards illuminating the novels' not infrequent collapse into relatively contradictory and unsatisfactory endings, despite their often successful juggling of the conflicting claims of the public and the private dimensions of Gordimer's interests in the bodies of the works.

Such tensions, for example, demonstrably undermine the conclusion to *July's People*,[30] Gordimer's examination of the possible fate of liberal whites in a South Africa in which the Armageddon of violent revolution has finally arrived. I would suggest that the credibility and power of this novel is seriously undermined by Gordimer's uncertainty about the precise nature of her project here. On the one hand, the Smales couple are clearly intended to be representative of the 'decent', fair-minded, liberal response of Johannesburg's northern suburbs to the impossible contradictions inherent in being affluent, liberal, and white in the post-Sharpeville era; the weaknesses and internal contradictions of this position are exposed by Gordimer with a characteristically detached, cold, and merciless eye. Here she focuses on human relationships within the South African family structure: husband, wife, children, and servants, and suggests that the artificial separation of human beings from one another brought about by the apartheid regime, and the patterns of guilt and often involuntary collusion that this has forced upon even the liberal white grouping the Smaleses represent, has created a society in which the fullness of emotional response between human beings has been stunted, and the deeper dimensions of a spiritual life appear to be entirely absent. The shallowness and sterility of the emotional relationships this family is caught up in are suggested by Maureen's and Bam's inability to relate to one another except in terms of the playing out of the roles their society has provided them with: thus Bam is the provider and later the hunter, Maureen is consigned to the domestic sphere, and, later, to the hut. At this level they operate as stereotypes of what late bourgeois/capitalist man under the cumulative impact of the apartheid regime has been reduced to, and the authorial narrative voice takes care to distance itself from an identification with the moral sordidness of their dilemma: there is, for example, the tonal patterning of the opening stress on what July's 'kind has always done for *their* kind' (my emphasis; p. 1). It is also at this level that names are assigned: for example, the children, Royce, Gina, and Victor, are (perhaps too obviously) named to signify their paramountcy over their mostly nameless black countryman; while the satiric intentions in the naming of July and the link established thus between Gordimer's text and *Robinson Crusoe*'s naming of Friday are only too clear.

At this level, then, the morally didactic thrust of the novel is unambiguously presented. It is clearly implied that the Smaleses' attitudes are to be understood as *typical* of the morally culpable stance of liberal white South Africans as such; the affluence of their life-style has an emblematic significance, and their futile and rather absurd attempts to behave 'decently' and within the parameters of a liberal 'correctness' towards July are sharply and mercilessly satirised. No sympathy softens the element of self-flagellation implicit in the quite un-ironic description of the Smaleses as 'sickening' 'at the appalling thought that they might find they had lived out their whole lives as they were, born white pariah dogs in a black continent. They joined political parties and "contact" groups in willingness to slough privilege it was supposed to be their white dog nature to guard with Mirages and tanks' (p. 8). It is predictably their attachment to precisely these non-exportable privileges which prevents them from following the promptings of their drive for self-preservation by emigrating in time, and encourages in them that characteristically ostrich-like stance which finally makes them first fugitives from and then prisoners of history. The total destruction of all they have clung to is presented by the authorial voice with so fertile a wealth of improbable detail about how the revolution erupts and progresses (pp. 6-12), and in a tone of such implicit satisfaction, that their losses cannot be read as anything other than morally and poetically just within the wider scheme of things.

They then, still true to the *typos* of the morally didactic *Entwicklungsroman*, embark on that odyssey into the 'heart of darkness' which becomes, of course, for Maureen at least, also the classic journey of self-discovery. The fable softens and extends as Gordimer begins to move beyond the purely polemical dimensions sketched out above to develop the character of her female protagonist more fully (Bam and the children remain one-dimensional characters, whose flatness fades into insignificance as Maureen's perspective comes to dominate the narrative). It is at this point that Maureen's origins in the class and milieu from which Gordimer herself has emerged begin to significantly colour the narrative, allowing the narrative voice to develop the specific details of Maureen's 'appalling' experience 'in the bush' with an element of empathy and a complexity of insight which contrasts sharply with the novel's detached and coldly ironic treatment of the Smaleses' predicament at the level of fable. The story of Maureen's response to her incarceration in the bush becomes a subtly-developed narrative of both destruction and transformation, as her old certainties are progressively broken down and she is forced out of the dead shell of the past into an uncertain present, as a moth – doomed nevertheless to self-destruct against the light – might emerge from the dead chrysalis within its cocoon. Initially it is the family and the roles it has imposed upon its members and required them to play out which becomes the focus of interrogation and the primary casualty in the novel: as Maureen begins to move towards painful and incomplete glimpses of the true nature of her situation, one defined by the inescapable realities of her race and sex, Bam metamorphoses from a husband into merely a chillingly distant 'blond man' (p. 138) – a 'man who had nothing now' (p. 145) – and her children are reduced first to a 'litter' (p. 47), and then cease to be invested with any clear emotional significance for her whatsoever, their voices (in the final sequence of the novel) blending unintelligibly with Bam's by the river in the meaningless chatter of strangers which represents danger only because they speak in the English that might betray them all as fugitives to a listening enemy (p. 159). Maureen's tentative moves to connect with July as a friend and/or as a man, and her attempts to establish some relationship with the black women of the village (on the basis of her superficial notions of universal sisterhood) are frustrated not only by language and race barriers but also by July's obdurate refusal to allow her to escape from her class-role as the white madam: and although he strips her of her illusions about her adequacy in that role, he will not allow her sentence to be transmuted.

Such painful disillusionments are, however, shown to be also accompanied by muted and embryonic forms of transformation. Maureen's initial alienation from her body, which has stood as symbol of a more general and pervasive alienation from reality as such, and which has informed her 'disgusted' scrubbing at vagina and anus as she realises for the first time in her life that her body might smell (p. 9),[31] begins to break down: she even discovers the possibility of a fierce possessive joy in it when she performs her solitary dance in the rain (p. 48), a dance which represents the beginnings of a movement towards a self-awareness and a self-possession which will ultimately express itself in her flight from the village at novel's end.

But it is precisely at the point of flight that the novel breaks down into a problematic inconclusiveness which causes both its political polemic and its tentative feminism to collapse into a confusion which undermines the whole project. How are we to interpret Maureen's flight away from the village? Is it to be read as a 'suicide run' into the arms of an enemy, a suicide which is ironically intended to 'liberate' her from the unbearable actual and emotional isolation which is the consequence of her alienation from family and society in the village? Or is it an affirmative action, a gesture which represents an attempt to take control of both herself and her destiny, 'trusting herself with all the suppressed trust of a lifetime, alert, like a solitary animal at the season when animals neither seek a mate nor take care of young, existing only for their lone survival, the enemy of all that would make claims of responsibility ...[?]' (p. 160). Is her flight intended to break the cycle of fear and impotency by a confrontation with the feared? Or are we to read this as a pathetic attempt by a deranged consciousness to recover a lost, familiar past as Maureen is drawn on by 'the smell of boiled potatoes (from a vine indistinguishable to her from others) [which] promises a kitchen, a house just the other side of the next tree' (p. 160)? (In this latter reading, the novel may be understood to encode that long and familiar tradition in which women are driven into insanity both by their inability to play out the gender-roles assigned to them, and by Africa's refusal to mould itself into forms familiar to them.[32])

Or is Maureen perhaps fleeing back not only into domesticity but also from third-world deprivation into first-world comfort, in so far as the helicopter (regardless of whether it contains friend or foe) may be understood as a symbol of modern technology and of the resources of an urban civilisation Maureen is desperate to recover? That the helicopter must at one level represent not only the unknown future but also some kind of redemption is strongly suggested by the baptismal imagery which accompanies Maureen's improbable fording of the river, in waist-deep water through which she wades with her shoes held above her head, in defiance of the dangers posed by unseen rocks in the waters underfoot: she does after all, in the heavy-handed imagery of the passage emerge 'born again' (p. 159): but as what?

Gordimer offers us no assistance in our attempt to make sense of the contradictory elements in this passage. That Maureen has achieved some sort of personal liberation as a woman and as an individual is strongly suggested, but her political redemption remains in question, and any attempt to read the novel's ending as one articulating a feminist solidarity with Maureen's struggle to achieve a fuller sense of self also finds itself in conflict with the overwhelming emphasis in the tonal patterning of the text as a whole on the Smales's inadequacies, on almost every level, as fully human beings. I would argue that, although this emphasis is made necessary by Gordimer's determination to offer her readers a political fable, her morally didactic thrust here cannot simultaneously accommodate a true sympathy for or sense of solidarity with Maureen's struggle: the Smaleses are to be condemned as both the typical products of, and the guilty collaborators with, a regime which (within the framework of an essentially clichéd conception of historical process) must be seen to be finally brought to a richly deserved and catastrophic end by the triumphantly victorious forces of a successful revolutionary thrust.

The naivete of both the political analysis and the political vision embedded in this novel has been rather fully commented upon (by implication) in Heribert Adam's incisive analysis[33] of the weaknesses in Gordimer's argument in her influential 1982 article for *The New York Review of Books*, 'Living in the Interregnum', a piece which expresses in discursive form those perceptions of white South Africans' position in relationship to historical cycles of change which were encoded in the fictional representations of *July's People* a year or so earlier. Little work has however so far been done on the significance of Gordimer's decision to tell the story through Maureen's eyes and to concentrate specifically on *her* experience. That her movement towards rebirth *must* be represented as still-born in terms of the politically didactic purposes the novel has been designed to serve (which will of course determine that white South Africans such as the Smales cannot be granted any form of redemption in a vision of the future almost as completely dominated by an implicit Black Consciousness perspective as *The Conservationist* (1974) was, seven years earlier), reduces and skews the novel's imaginative thrust in ways which prevent it from achieving that degree of fullness, depth, and humanity of analysis which would save it from being little more than an interesting political tract.

Such tensions are not confined to *July's People* alone: similar difficulties beset Gordimer's endings in many of her other novels as well. In *Burger's Daughter*, both Rosa's decision to return to South Africa, and the idealised images offered us of her final sense of well-being in her prison cell at the novel's end, are only explicable in terms of the political project the novel is made to serve; they cannot be read as necessary consequences of the complex and subtle analysis of Rosa's dilemma as Burger's daughter which has been the subject of the body of the novel. And in *The Late Bourgeois World* it is interesting to note that, although Elizabeth's decision to agree to the request Luke Fokase makes of her is determined not so much by her tentative attraction to the idea of helping the struggle onwards as by the extent to which she is powerfully sexually attracted to him, it is an attraction both she and Gordimer attempt to discount – to the novel's detriment – in the heavy-handed musings upon the American space-walk and its significance which form an uneasy conclusion to the novel. Here too Gordimer's characteristic insistence upon making sexual preference an indicator of the individual's potential for moral and political salvation or redemption within the context of the apartheid state undermines, and threatens to negate the subtlety and intelligence of the analysis in the novel as a whole, and reduces aspects of the work to the level of stereotype and caricature.

Not only does Gordimer fail to do herself justice in allowing her novels to collapse repeatedly into such conclusions, but the weakness of such endings betrays a conflict in her work between her twin roles as both a citizen and a woman which remains largely unresolved. The two streams of interest frequently work against each other in unproductive ways, and their dissonances contribute to a significantly damaging diffusion of focus which is most apparent in the novels' problematic resolutions.[34] That this is so must encourage us to treat her denials of both a feminist impulse and a politically didactic thrust as shaping and directing her work with caution: we might regard them at best as ingenuous, and at worst as suggesting a genuine confusion in her grasp of the nature of her fictional project: a confusion which predictably expresses itself not only in contradictory public statements but also in tensions within the works. As I have suggested above, these tensions undermine the fundamental impact of her fiction in an important way, and go some way towards explaining the dissatisfaction with her work which is currently developing some critical impetus in South African academic circles.

NOTES

1. Alice Walker, *In Search of Our Mother's Gardens: Womanist Prose* (London: The Women's Press, 1984), p. 49.
2. See for example Brenda Cooper, 'New Criteria for an "Abnormal Mutation"? An Evaluation of Gordimer's *A Sport of Nature*', unpublished paper, University of Cape Town, August 1988; also Karen Lazer, 'The Personal and the Political in some of Nadine Gordimer's Short Stories', unpublished M.A. thesis, University of the Witwatersrand, 1988. This contains an interesting interview with Gordimer which touches upon some of the issues developed in this paper; also Dorothy Driver, 'Nadine Gordimer: The Politicisation of Women', *English in Africa*, Vol. 10, No. 2, Oct. 1983, pp. 29-54; and Dorothy Driver, '"Woman" as Sign in the South African Colonial Enterprise', *Journal of Literary Studies*, Vol. 4, No. 1, March 1988, pp. 3-20: this also develops observations which might usefully illuminate aspects of Gordimer's work, although it does not deal directly with Gordimer's period; also Cecily Lockett, 'Feminism(s) and Writing in the South African Context', unpublished paper read at the AUETSA conference held at the University of Pretoria, July 1989.
3. In six out of a total of nine novels the central consciousness through which events and concerns are mediated is female.
4. Quoted in Driver, op. cit., note 2, p. 33 and p. 45 (both statements made by Gordimer in 1981).
5. Nadine Gordimer, 'Introduction' (1975) to *Selected Stories* (Penguin, 1983), p. 11.
6. Nadine Gordimer, *Women Speak*, 1989, p. 55: a publication in which papers presented at a conference held by COSAW in November 1988, in Johannesburg, have been made available to the general public.
7. Nadine Gordimer, 'Review of *Olive Schreiner: A Biography*' in *Olive Schreiner and After: Essays in Southern African Literature*, eds. Malvern van Wyk Smith and Don MacLennan (Cape Town: David Philip, 1983), p. 17.
8. Lockett, op. cit., note 2, p. 1.
9. Rosalind Coward, 'Are Women's Novels Feminist Novels?' in *The New Feminist Criticism: Essays on Women, Literature, and Theory* (Virgo, 1986); quoted in Lazar, p. 238.
10. Lockett, op. cit., note 2, p. 27.
11. Nadine Gordimer in an interview with Stephen Gray, in *Contemporary Literature*, Vol. 22, No. 3, Summer 1981, p. 291.
12. Nadine Gordimer, 'A Writer in South Africa', in *London Magazine*, May 1965, p. 23.
13. Nadine Gordimer, 'Introduction', p. 12.
14. Nadine Gordimer, 'Living in the Interregnum' (1982), rep. in *The Essential Gesture*, ed. S. Clingman (David Philip/Taurus, 1988), pp. 232-3.
15. See Don MacLennan, 'The Vacuum Pump: The Fiction of Nadine Gordimer', in *Upstream*, Vol. 7, No. 1, Summer 1989, pp. 30-3; and Brenda Cooper, op. cit., note 2.
16. Nadine Gordimer, 'Introduction', p. 15.
17. 'Nadine Gordimer and Susan Sontag: In Conversation', in *The Listener*, 23 May 1985, pp. 16-17.
18. K. Wagner, '"History from the Inside?": Text and Subtext in Some Gordimer Novels', in *Crisis and Conflict: Essays on Southern African Literature*, ed. G. Davis (Essen: Verlag die Blaue Eule, 1989).
19. Stephen Clingman, *The Novels of Nadine Gordimer* (Ravan, 1986).
20. B. Cooper, op. cit. note 2, p. 10, p. 4. Another critic comments that 'she has on the whole translated existing political philosophies into fictional form and ... toed a straight-forward political line': Driver, op. cit. note 2, p. 32. Maclennan has also recently suggested that Gordimer's 'main theme is her attachment to a certain ideo-

logical notion of History ... a complex rhetoric has persuaded me to take fiction for fact: with one eye to watch the claustrophobic dance of inadequate characters in their frail humanity, and with the other to watch an inexorable historical process that seems to be disconnected from their lives, and which yet dictates how we shall see their emptiness and futility' (Maclennan, op. cit., p. 32).

21. Elie Kedourie, 'The Limitations of Liberalism', *The American Scholar*, Spring 1989, p. 265.

22. 'I'm a white South African radical. Please don't call me a liberal', said Nadine Gordimer in 1974 in an interview printed in *The Times* of London. Her dissociation of herself from 'liberal' positions from the early seventies onwards is explained by the changing definitions the term has been given in the South African context; in 1987 she gave a brief account of what the term now means to her in an interview with Anthony Sampson, reprinted in *The Sunday Star* (5 April), in which she said: 'Liberalism used to mean, to whites and blacks, that blacks should be allowed into the existing white structure, legal and governmental ... The definition of liberal, now, is one who believes in incremental reform.' Gordimer's political commitments obviously distance her from so narrow and historically-specific a definition of liberalism. See too the entry on 'Liberal' in Raymond Williams, *Keywords* (Glasgow: Fontana Books, 1976).

23. Nadine Gordimer, *Burger's Daughter* (London: Jonathan Cape, 1979), p. 172.

24. See Eve Bertelsen in interview with Lessing in 'Doris Lessing', *The Journal of Commonwealth Literature*, Vol. 21, No. 1, 1986, pp. 156-7.

25. Nadine Gordimer, *The Conservationist* (1974; Penguin, 1978).

26. Nadine Gordimer, *The Late Bourgeois World* (1966; Penguin, 1982).

27. The sentimentality of this image is by implication sharply satirised in Christopher Hope's choice of title for his new novel, *My Chocolate Redeemer* (1989).

28. Nadine Gordimer, in *Women Speak*, op. cit.

29. Quoted in Lazar, op. cit. note 2.

30. Nadine Gordimer, *July's People*, (Johannesburg: Ravan/Taurus, 1981).

31. Cooper (op. cit. note 2) has suggested that Gordimer's apparent hatred of white women such as Maureen arises out of a deep-seated self-hatred: implicitly acknowledged here is the impossible position women occupy in South Africa, as both victims of sexism and of apartheid. White women in particular are in an ambiguous position; they benefit as women from a system which oppresses black women as domestic servants, and thus in effect find themselves allied with the male oppressor class, despite themselves; see Driver, 1988, on this issue as well.

32. See for example Doris Lessing's *The Grass is Singing*, J.M. Coetzee's *In the Heart of the Country*, Olive Schreiner's *The Story of an African Farm*, Jean Rhys's *Wide Sargasso Sea*, etc.

33. Heribert Adam, 'Reflections on Gordimer's Interregnum', in *Occasional Papers: Series No. 1: Center for Research on Africa* (University of the Western Cape), Dec. 1983.

34. An extreme reaction to these tensions has been articulated recently by a critic who claims that 'as historian, Gordimer has presented us with faceless, hollowed-out characters, who seem to have consented ... to be mere products of their age and nothing more' (MacLennan, op. cit., p. 31).

SHIRLEY GEOK-LIN LIM

Social Protest and the Success Motif in Singapore Novels in English

Twentieth-century world literature, according to Jameson, has to be conceived in its third-world manifestation as a cultural struggle between first-world imperialism and newly decolonized national states.[1] His thesis, however, does not explain the centrifugal forces of 'local' events, which include rapidly multiplying rivalries among linguistic, tribal and ethnic identities, tensions between competitive economic systems made intolerable by increasing populations and climactic disasters, the break between the scientific and secular spirit associated with first-world countries and the continued emphasis on religious superstructures, all of which and more compose the dynamic context in which third-world writers are producing.[2] In countries such as Sri Lanka or Uganda, ethnic or tribal groups are seemingly more intransigently resistant to national convergences; violent political fragmentation mirrors global fissures and paradoxically appears to deny the technological advancements and capitalist penetrations which have made national boundaries collapse into an international corporate and media market.

Singapore, which has enjoyed almost unprecedented stability since its emergence as a city state in 1967, also presents an excellent case of a different kind of model from the one Jameson totalized for the entire third world. It is possible to read into the Singapore literary scene not the death-and-life struggle between first-world imperialism and third-world nationalism that Jameson envisions but a culture-specific national debate between class struggle and class striving which may also incidentally reflect the dialogics of the (personal) value of the individual against the (economic) value of an ever-more-technological global market-place.[3]

In Singapore, English was a foreign language brought in by colonizing British and used for colonial administration. The internationalism of English itself, with its firm base on western rationalism, secularism, scientific thought, individualism, and scepticism becomes a tradition. From the margins of this tradition writers from new national societies can and do write to assert their counter-identities and to subvert their national centres. In Singapore, the place of the English-language novel is complicated by a situation where its producers come from the English-educated elite. Their criticism of their society is (double)crossed by their complicity of success in that very society. Their versions of national identity therefore present a subtle and nuanced reflection of interests based on the dominant ideology of state and class.[4] This essay will consider three Singapore English-language novels, Goh Poh Seng's *If We Dream Too Long*, Lim Thean Soo's *Ricky Star*, and Phillip Jeyaratnam's *Raffles Place Ragtime* as critiques of aspects of Singapore society and values which can be subsumed under the success motif.[5] The essay will examine the ways in which their criticism, expressed as a form of class struggle, is itself undermined and contradicted by their thematic concern with class striving, in which, consciously or unconsciously, bourgeois characters and values pervade and/or triumph over working class protagonists.

These novels are self-conscious productions and show a pre-occupation with social identity other than as British colonial subject. They deal specifically and urgently with the relationship between the individual and the economic, material world. Goh Poh Seng's *If We Dream Too Long* (1972), Lim Thean Soo's *Ricky Star* (1978), and Philip Jeyaratnam's *Raffles Place Ragtime* (1988) have as their protagonists ambitious yet thwarted characters who are finally defeated by their own weaknesses and by the cruel competition of an urban society. All three novels are *romans-à-clef*. They each portray the mis-education of a male protagonist as he attempts to survive and succeed in a material(ist) context, in order to educate their readers to a moral apprehension of the just society. In all three novels, the invested libido we associate with the twentieth century western genre of realistic fiction becomes detached from representations of male/female relations and attaches itself instead to desire for social success. Psychosexual motivations are less in evidence; in fact, we can read the 'failed' desires of the protagonists for the women characters (Lucy, Connie) in all three novels as symptomatic and expressive of transformations of psychosexual desire to psycho-economic desire. The success motif can thus be read as a fetishization dynamic so largely accepted as a social good as to function as an ideological frame for individual explanation and action. The dialectic between character and this social/material ideology of success allows these novels a sharpness of social criticism which can be said to involve them in a debate on national identity.

In the earliest novel, *If We Dream Too Long*, the working-class protagonist, Kwang Meng, hates his meaningless lowly clerical job, yearns to escape through upward mobility or immigration, finds sex and alcohol as compensations, and is trapped finally in his dead-end position by his father's illness and family responsibilities.[6] The young Kwang Meng's frustrations permit Goh to write a classical critique of the post-colonialist society. The novel begins with Kwang Meng taking a sick day off from work and observing the activities of the colonialist English, a class so removed from him that he can only approach it in ironic imagination: 'the same English masters were seen going in for their Whiskey Stengahs and their Brandy Drys. He caught a glimpse of the white uniformed Chinese "boys". It's funny how the English can unselfconsciously call these old Hainanese men, "boys"' (p. 4).

Kwang Meng lives at home with his parents and two younger brothers. Privacy is a middle-class luxury he cannot afford, and he finds it only in his stolen swims. In early post-colonial Singapore, limited economic opportunities signified class-identified destinies:

> Those with well-to-do parents did not worry: they could afford the university, or failing that, go abroad. The rest of the class....knew what was to come.... Most saw themselves become like their fathers, fated to their fathers' lives. In the space of a few weeks they assumed adulthood, they assumed an undespairing and undramatic resignation. (p. 9)

Kwang Meng, however, is seen as more sensitive, indeed, perhaps more morbid than his cohorts. Still, his future is already imaged in the figure of Balthazar, the role he played in his school production of *The Merchant of Venice*. Balthazar is a character with only one line, 'Madam, I go with all convenient speed', and the line is for an exit. Goh portrays Kwang Meng as that insignificant player in society whose only role is to exit expediently. The novel ends with this figure of Balthazar. His affair with the bargirl Lucy over, his hopes of moving to Sarawak for a more adventurous life ended, and even the beginning of a romance with middle-class Anne nipped because of his father's illness, drunk and distraught, Kwang Meng takes on the role of Balthazar one more time in response to an elderly English lady's request for directions to Raffles Hotel. This single irrational act completes the implicit authorial frame of social commentary. Kwang Meng's tentative attempts to move out of his working-class existence having failed, the novel ends as he abruptly exits. In short, the character is vivid so long as he maintains the sensitivity and dissatisfactions which drive him to escape his class origins. Once escape is closed off, he becomes only a bit player. In this way, *If We Dream Too Long* is very much a middle-class fiction, critical of narrow proletarian interests (portrayed in Kwang Meng's parents' obsession with security and money), valorizing middle-class mores and aspirations (in the pleasures in books and classical music of the paragon couple, Boon Teik and Mei-I) and presenting in Kwang Meng's entrapment in poverty the truly middle-class nightmare.

Lim Thean Soo's *Ricky Star* has a more malevolent protagonist. Coming from a mercantile family (his father was a fast-dealing middle-man), Ricky struggles to educate himself in order to succeed as a business executive. Following his rise and fall, the novel foregrounds a modern, urban society in which the emphasis on money and social success results in family and individual deterioration. Socially ambitious, Ricky measures everything and every individual in material terms. He approaches paintings as consumer items exhibiting material status. Similarly, he courts and marries a middle-class woman as part of his campaign to move out of his lower-class position. In Ricky's capitalist-oriented discourse, the woman is reduced to a commodity: 'He never felt endearingly towards his wife, as some husbands did, and always measured his wife in material terms.... He had unjustly concluded that she was, all in all, a marginal liability' (p. 3). The success thematic displaces sexual desire and is itself a fetishization of desire. When it becomes clear that Ricky's wife cannot help him attain success, she becomes both marginal, unimportant to the plot of social striving, and a liability, an actual debit in its accounting.

Ricky's obsession with success and his manipulative dishonesty are partially explained by his psycho/cultural anomie. He finds his father's (ancestral) values distasteful at the same time as he is insecure with western customs. The protagonist has not successfully integrated the bicultural forces of Chinese social origin and Western social influence; instead, his attempts to leave behind the former for the latter indicate a profound inferiority and over-privileging of the things western which mark his colonized mentality. Lim provides a number of sharply detailed instances of the protagonist's colonized identity. Contemptuous of his father's racial thriftiness, figured in the old man's one shabby pair of pyjamas, Ricky indulges in expensive although uncomfortable western-style bathrobes (p. 4).

Chinese cultural identity is not presented as superior to western cultural modes. Indeed, the destructive model for the protagonist's adult life is located in the patriarchal oppressiveness of his childhood. 'There had never been a fixed time for meals at home.... It was rare that father, mother, and children had any meal together, even on Chinese New Year's Eve' (p. 39). The father has a mistress and an illegitimate son, the mother withdraws into a catatonic state and finally kills herself. Ricky abandons his loveless paternal home to pursue his own career.

Ricky Star portrays a society in material transition. Unlike the economic dead-ends which Goh's novel indicts, *Ricky Star* reflects a dynamic society in which fortunes can be readily made. The authorial frame is stringently didactic. The dishonest are always punished (Ricky's father dies a penniless penitent, Ricky is last seen 'a social pariah'); the good rewarded with success. Teck Soon, 'an honest, sober man with hidden talent for business', marries the boss's daughter, and the author tells us, 'One day, he would be immensely rich and he could look back without bitterness to the early years' (p. 185). The fiction, therefore, is predictably structured with less of psychological and moral complexity and more of straightforward social instruction. If the fiction has allegorical resonances, it is not that Ricky is the Singapore Everyman. Minor characters such as Teck Soon or Ricky's business antagonist Jimmy or his brother-in-law, Graham, are held as the model Singaporean businessman. In fact, Ricky is the dark side of this figure, the morally deficient, inadequately cultured, business failure whose life can teach by dis-exemplar.

Similarly, Philip Jeyaretnam's *Raffles Place* is the most recent expression of this peculiarly Singaporean moral vision, the fear of corruption and of emotional bankruptcy brought on by the social pressure to succeed. In

Raffles Place, this society is no longer static, as in *If We Dream Too Long*, nor is it merely dynamic. Instead, it is a supercharged society, running on high technology in the workplace; luxury western consumer items such as Mercedes Benzes and French wines and cuisine; and a multi-national-corporation network. But the class/moral outlines remain the same. Under the enormous material changes in Singapore, reflected in the three novels' changed material descriptions, the thematic focus on the success motif as a problematic affecting individual happiness and social/moral coherence remains basically unchanged. In Jeyaretnam's novel, the protagonist, Vincent, comes from a working class family; his parents are food hawkers, and he shares a bedroom with a younger brother in a public housing apartment. Vincent is on the fast track; working for the Singapore Monetary Exchange, he courts Connie, daughter of a socially prominent family. Like Ricky, Vincent's drive to economic and social mobility distorts his moral vision. Every one and every event is perceived only in terms of material outcome for him.

Vincent's point-of-view is shared by others. His best friend, Yeow Khoon, a kind of choral commentator on the action, is equally economic about human relations. About Connie, he tells Vincent: 'You have rung up the jackpot, Vincent.... Don't waste time. Dig in' (p. 4). Here the sexual woman is again transformed into an economic fetish: Connie is a 'jackpot', a resource for wealth. Unsurprisingly, Connie and Vincent have a hard time making out together. The author draws a more damning portrait of Singapore society than the earlier works. Vincent's ambitions, after all, coincide with and reflect national aspirations:

> He alone truly appreciated the magnitude of Mr. Lim's rise from carpenter's son to stewardship of a banking empire.... It was Vincent's vigour and his ability that would propel Singapore forward in the twenty-first century, building on Mr Lim's achievements a generation earlier. Only a week ago Mr. Lim had indicated that he would propose Vincent for membership of the Pyramid Club. Life was falling into place! (p. 24)

Raffles Place demonstrates a greater self-consciousness about national identity and the place of the individual in the sociopolitical process; this self-consciousness is expressed in satirical and ironic mode, so that the moral dimension to which the fiction is pinned is not always simply addressed, as it is in *Ricky Star*. Instead, for the greater part of the novel, the interrogation of social/national identity is subtly carried out through the portrayal of the protagonist's contradictions.

Vincent works long hours, is sober and ambitious. His personal ambitions are often conflated with national ideological aspirations, as in the passage above, so that selfish careerism is equated at points with national-istic idealism. (We are reminded throughout the novel that patriotism is the scoundrel's best defence!) The fiction, therefore, satirizes the national drive for success at the same time as it satirizes the individual who embodies it. Vincent is, after all, an insecure, manipulative character who has an affair with a secretary at the same time as he is courting Connie, who denies his true feelings in order to climb the slippery ladder of mobility, and who is finally betrayed by his own working-class lack of savoir-faire and loses both his job and his rich girl.

The novel's didactic dimension is rather more sophisticated and perhaps even more stringently bourgeois in socio-political reflections than either Goh's or Lim's novels. In all three novels, the working class protagonist is seen as failing in his attempt to leave behind his class origin. But only *Raffles Place* specifically assigns the anti-hero to a class resolution; Vincent loses his rich girl/future, but he discovers happiness in the arms of his true working-class girl. He is only punished for desiring a social position which is not for him.

Connie, on the other hand, rejects Vincent because he is a loser: 'Go back to your HDB flat,' she taunts him. 'Mother always said you were not good enough for me' (p. 77). Depressed, she spends the next day shopping and drives home 'exhausted but happy...she would survive' (p. 102). Strangely, however, the novel concludes with this shallow materialist as its moral centre. Released from her proletarian lover, disillusioned by the discovery of her father's marital infidelity, Connie is given the privilege of moral recognition. 'She felt suffocated in here with this crowd of people in a rush, a rush for degrees, jobs, careers, spouses, houses. The words tangled in her mind and the faces in the room sped toward her from all sides.... She needed once and for all to escape' (p. 123). The same claustrophobic existentialist nausea which afflicted the working class Kwang Meng afflicts the upper-class heroine here. The escape is both moral ('too readily accepting the lash of the whip that sought to drive her on, blindly like a horse in blinkers') and physical, to escape the nation's geographical confines for a larger, more adventurous location: 'perhaps teach English in Papua New Guinea.... Travel round India' (p. 124). The whip, while never identified with person or cause, is undoubtedly that same drive for success which defeats Kwang Meng, Ricky, and Vincent. Ironically, the character who *has* the resources to succeed in Singapore turns her back on success in search of a more meaningful life:

> 'But what sort of life will I have had? ... And what about the rest of Singapore? Is everyone to sit around comparing husbands like motor cars?'... Her refusal to stay in the race would be resented, seen as a presumptuous condemnation of the other runners.... Going abroad would not be enough. Unless she found there some real meaning to her life, meaning that she could practise here in Singapore. (p. 125)

Raffles Place concludes on this diminutive allusion to 'Paradise Lost': 'The world was all before her, but Connie was in no hurry' (p. 125). Significantly, the fiction has slipped from the opening male anti-hero to the closing female heroine, from an examination of working-class pressure to climb up the social-economic ladder to an expression of bourgeois dissatisfaction and idealistic rejection of the success motif. The novel's unacknowledged slippage demonstrates the split between working-class and bourgeois consciousness in the same fiction. While working-class striving for material success is satirized, the bourgeois revolt against such crass materialism is taken seriously. The fiction, however, even as it expresses this revolt in Connie's closing mood, does not successfully depict it. Her sudden moral growth is unearned; in the early depiction of her shallow concerns and her equally crass rejection of her crass lover, nothing prepares the reader for that kind of epiphany which falls upon her in the conclusion like a spiritual mantle upon a Pauline convert. Connie is after all a creature of the author who uses her to express his own bourgeois position once the protagonist, Vincent, has collapsed into his working-class origin.

All three novels criticize a society in which the dominant values of money, position and career success are seen as corrupting a working class protagonist whose intelligence, energy and dreams become all too directed towards attaining these elements of social good. In the process of striving for these middle-class possessions, the heroes fail both in class aspirations and in their humanity. They lose hope and reason, as in Goh's novel, hope and decency, as in Lim's novel, or are allowed to retain their humanity only when failure in the class mobility project is conceded, as in *Raffles Place*. The problematic of this success motif is the insurmountable division between working class and bourgeois which all three novels construct. The motif itself lies beyond criticism. In Goh's novel, the books and classical music of the happy middle-class married couple are offered as the working class antagonist's glimpse of a utopia not for him. Lim offers as a foil to the failed hero the minor character of Singapore success, the hardworking, clean-living Teik Soon, whose deferment of present pleasure ensures him, as the author assures us, a place of wealth in the future. And finally, in the most recent incarnation of the success/class striving problematic in Singapore fiction, Jeyaratnam's Connie, the progeny and product of the economically successful class, is endowed with that other success of attained humanity, that sensitivity and perception of character which permits her a liberal, although not yet a materialist, critique of Singapore social values.

NOTES

1. Fredric Jameson, 'Third World Literature in the Era of Multinational Capitalism', *Social Text* 15, Fall 1986, pp. 65-88. Jameson has noted among American intellectuals an 'imprisonment in the present of postmodernism' (p. 66) which results in their

reading of third-world literature as 'outmoded stages of our first-world cultural development' (p. 65). He suggests in place of 'this particular mirage of the "centred subject" and the unified personal identity, we would do better to confront honestly the fact of fragmentation on a global scale; it is a confrontation with which we can at least make a cultural beginning' (p. 67).

2. Fanon's theory of postcolonial literature is such a systemic thesis: that it will move from an aping of the colonialists' literature to a stage of provincialism to a national and finally international identity. Fanon's progressive theory was based on the social reformer's utopianist vision of liberated societies.

3. Jameson, op. cit., 'Third-world texts, even those which are seemingly private and invested with a properly libidinal dynamic – necessarily project a political dimension in the form of national allegory: *the story of the private individual destiny is always an allegory of the embattled situation of the Public third-world culture and society*' (p. 69; italics the author's). For a discussion of the allegorical issue, see Stephen Slemon, 'Post-Colonial Allegory and the Transformation of History', *Journal of Commonwealth Literature*, Vol. 23, No. 1 (1988), pp. 157-168.

4. See Peter Chen, 'Elites and National Development in Singapore', *Southeast Asian Journal of Social Science* 3:1, 1975, 17-25; and Tham Seong Chee, *Literature and Society in Southeast Asia, Political and Sociological Perspectives* (Singapore: Singapore University Press, 1981).

5. Goh Poh Seng, *If We Dream Too Long* (Singapore: Island Press, 1972); Lim Thean Soo, *Ricky Star* (Singapore: Pan Pacific Books, 1978); Philip Jeyeratnam, *Raffles Place Ragtime* (Singapore: Times Books International, 1988). Page references to these novels will be given in the essay.

6. Koh Tai Ann calls *If We Dream Too Long* by Goh Poh Seng 'the first serious novel (in English) set in Singapore by a Singaporean' in Colin E. Nicholson & Ranjit Chaterjee, *Tropic Crucible: Self and Theory in Language and Literature* (Singapore: Singapore University Press, 1984), p. 163. Elsewhere, however, she contends that 'the existing prose work in English is generally lacking in literary merit' and that it 'is better studied as sociological documentary than work, which although of sociological significance, is chiefly of literary significance' (in Tham Seong Chee, op. cit., note 4, p. 177).

POWERFUL CANONS

The 'armed version' of modernism *is* colonialism itself.
Ashis Nandy, *The Intimate Enemy*

I'm part of the established Australian social structure, he
would say, *and I can't help it.*

> *mate*
> *horse*
> *dog*
> *missus*
> *wog*
> *poof*
> *boong*
> *that's*
> *the*
> *pecking*
> *order.*

See, he would say, *a poem, a kind of poem of structure. And
as many girls as you can get on the side.*
Do they count? someone might ask.
You're kidding, he would say.

Thea Astley, *It's Raining in Mango*

VINEY KIRPAL

Has the Indian Novel Been Understood?

Unless the Indian novel is read as a distinct form of fiction, it will continue to appear blemished, deformed, deficient and incomplete in comparison with the Western (English/European) novel whose tributary it is perceived to be. Until then, its strengths will appear weaknesses. The reasons for critical hegemony have already been spelt out by me in 'What is the Modern Third World Novel?'[1] In that piece, I generalized on some of the outstanding characteristics of the novel from the Third World. Here, I wish to make an in-depth study of a certain specific aspect of the Indian novel, namely its structure. During this investigation, I hope to achieve two things. First, to show the effects of reading the Indian novel as a derivative form and the unreliability of such Eurocentric readings. Secondly, to demonstrate that a fair understanding and evaluation of the Indian novel becomes possible only when the oral narrative elements embedded in its deep structure are methodically foregrounded.

T.D. Brunton, in his article 'India in Fiction: The Heritage of Indianness',[2] questions the very need of the Indian novel to be Indian 'in some peculiar and essential fashion' (p. 200) since in his conception the novel can be adapted to any culture which shares 'some of the rational, scientific, inquisitive tendencies of the West, and also the modern, almost world-wide curiosity about society' (p. 203).[3]

Brunton then proceeds to demolish the reputations of recognized classics of the Indian novel in English. For example, Raja Rao's *The Serpent and the Rope* comes in for adverse criticism for its 'unhurried pace which a less partial critic might well regard as the book's prolixity' (p. 202) and its total lack of 'dramatic motivation or purpose' (p. 203). His evaluation of the novel concludes thus: 'This critique is not meant to be polemical, but perhaps it registers the dismay of one who had been led to expect a finished and original achievement' (p. 204).

Kanthapura is similarly damned for lacking in 'analysis and probing human motives', while Rao's prefatorial statement, publicizing the episodic structure of the *Puranas* and the epics as the model for his novel, is dismissed by Brunton as 'a startlingly trivial narrative model for a novelist to follow' (pp. 204-5). Mulk Raj Anand's *Untouchable* – translated into more than twenty world languages – is then pronounced to be a 'minor classic' (p. 205). The evaluation of *Untouchable* is comparatively favourable because of 'its coherence while eschewing a formal plot and the density of "felt life"' (p. 206). Interestingly, its episodicity, almost as evident to me as that of *Kanthapura*, goes unnoticed because of the confinement of the action in the novel to a single day.

Again, R.K. Narayan's *The Maneater of Malgudi* is criticized as a novel 'about nothing' (p. 207) while his other novel, *The Bachelor of Arts* is commended as 'a work of great charm', with a definite theme 'made fully dramatic with the adventures of Chandran', that is, possessing sufficient logic in its construction. However, it is Narayan's *The Guide*, a Sahitya Akademi award winner, which comes in for all the flak. It is described as 'radically flawed' (p. 208) and lacking in 'real continuity' by which is presumably meant, lacking in motivation, unity of action and a cause-effect relationship. To sum up Brunton's estimation: it is the formlessness, episodicity and absence of coherence in *The Serpent and the Rope, Kanthapura, The Maneater of Malgudi* and *The Guide* that render these novels inferior. By contrast, *The Bachelor of Arts* and *Untouchable* pass the 'acid test' as, according to Brunton, they fulfil the usual norms of good Western/English fiction: unified action, motivation and logical development.

The novels of Narayan also provide grist to the mill of T.C. Ghai in his article, 'Pattern and Significance in R.K. Narayan's Novels'.[4] In an evaluation, typical of most criticism on Narayan, the novelist is censured for being 'too undeliberate' (p. 33), that is, lacking in awareness of modern novelistic techniques.

Narayan's *Swami and Friends* is described as 'hardly a novel' and regarded as 'a series of amusing or pathetic episodes linked together only by the presence of the hero but lacking in intrinsic unity' (p. 34). Ghai finds 'little improvement' in Narayan's next novel, *The Bachelor of Arts*. He asks: 'But what is the novel about? Is it about love? Does it purport to justify arranged marriages? Does it portray a conflict between a rebellious young man and a conservative social [sic] in which horoscopes override human emotions? ... Incidents in Chandran's life are too loosely threaded together to have a cumulative effect' (p. 35). Oddly, the very novel that Brunton, employing the yardsticks of unity and motivation, has found 'charming' and 'fully dramatic', is found wanting in Ghai's evaluation, employing the same criteria.

Conceding that there are individual differences among critics and that all artistic or critical endeavour is relative and subjective, can two critics applying much the same norms – coherence and causality – perceive the same novels in diametrically opposite ways? Surely, there ought to be some objective means of evaluating literature if we are to believe that criticism is also a systematic study and not merely an uncontrolled overflow of powerful critical feelings?

We borrowed the novel from the West but adapted and modified it so that it would authentically mirror the Indian mind and society. But we failed to evolve suitable critical strategies to interpret this new form. As a consequence, critical norms borrowed from Western/English fiction critical theory were taken up to explicate the Indian novel written not only in English but also in the regional languages. Consider the following critiques of two regional language novels:

(i)   It is difficult to call [*Phaniamma*] a novel because it lacks a coherent plot. A few events in the life of the central character are mentioned without much elaboration. The novel simply and directly presents the development of Phaniamma.[5]

(ii)   The novel [*Aranyak*] has little plot. It is rather a string of episodes, and presents a succession of portraits, some of which are touchingly human.[6]

It is obvious that on applying Eurocentric norms, both these famous novels appear to be deficient and deformed works. As against these unfavourable estimates, there is the response of the readers – Indian and non-Indian – who love Indian fiction, study it, teach it, value it. Their verdict ought to caution Eurocentric critics about the possible wrongness of their judgment.

To rectify the situation, a group of distinguished scholars – Edwin Gerow, C.D. Narasimhaiah, Krishna Rayan, S.K. Desai, G.N. Devy, M.K. Naik – have undertaken a search for critical strategies in the ancient Indian past.[7] They advocate Sanskrit Poetics as the alternative to Eurocentricism. But there are limitations to this approach, too. First, the theory precedes the product instead of the other way around. Secondly, Sanskrit criticism was designed to interpret Sanskrit poetry and poetic prose and not modern prose. Thirdly, these scholars have offered theoretical explications of Sanskrit Poetics but provided hardly any examples of applied Sanskrit criticism. The only exceptions are Gerow's two articles, one on a novel each by Bhabani Bhattacharya, Bibhuti Bhushan Banerjee and Bankim Chandra,[8] and the other on the early novels of R.K. Narayan.[9] Despite the usefulness of his work, there are obvious limitations to the application of Sanskrit criticism to modern Indian novels, and Gerow admits them.[10]

My own position is that the Indian novel is an inheritor of two literary traditions and not one, as both Eurocentric criticism and neo-Sanskrit criticism make it out to be. It employs constructive devices from the Western/English novel (with which most contemporary writers are well acquainted), but more so from the indigenous oral narratives (on which almost every Indian has been reared).[11] The oral traditions that it draws upon are both the Sanskrit classical tradition and the popular, folk tradition (a fact that gets overlooked in neo-Sanskrit criticism). Since the Indian novel draws upon multiple traditions, it is easy to see why both Eurocentric and Sanskrit critical norms succeed only partially and also why they prove to be unreliable norms for reading the Indian novel. To

understand the Indian novel, it is necessary to systematically foreground
the techniques and elements that it has borrowed from the Sanskrit narratives and the Indian folk forms. Then, using the relevant aesthetic and
critical theories, one could explicate this well-synthesized new form.

The Indian novel has evolved in response to the challenge of depicting
a colonial society with a valuable ancient heritage of its own, a society
changing under the impact of Western thought and technology but also
trying to preserve its native value system. The Indian world view, which
is cyclical and non-linear, has persisted through the centuries despite
recent changes in attitude towards time measured by the clock. Brought
up on the cyclical, episodic, digressive, exile-return pattern stories of *The
Ramayana*, *The Mahabharatha*, the *Puranas*, the *Kathasaritasagar*, the *Pancha-
tantra*, the *Jatakas* and the folktales – the Indian person's world view gets
so structured that he/she responds almost spontaneously to the digressive
mode of narration and thinking. This is reflected not only in the construction of the Indian novel, but also in the structure of Indian autobiographies, histories and films, as against the linear, ratiocinative, analytical,
cause-effect structure of Western writings.[12]

Consider Jawaharlal Nehru's *An Autobiography*. The book is clearly cyclical: it ends where it begins, that is, in Kashmir.[13] The structure of *The
Discovery of India* is similarly episodic and digressive.[14] Nehru says at one
point, 'But I have digressed and wandered away' (p. 47). And again later,
'To go back. The Afghans had settled down in India' (p. 154). His famous
speech, 'Tryst with Destiny' begins in the storyteller's manner: 'Long years
ago we made a tryst with destiny...',[15] an opening that compares favourably with the recitation of the legandary battle between the demon and
the goddess in *Kanthapura*: 'Kenchamma is our goddess. Great and beaute-
ous is she. She killed a demon ages, ages ago, a demon that...'.[16]

The same episodic manner characterizes many a newspaper article and
even ordinary discourse. Right from the illiterate peasant to the highly
educated person, Indians are a very anecdotal people. Indian TV serials
are usually slow, episodic and ponderous (for example, *Buniyaad*, *Humlog*,
Ganadevta). The same is true of Indian films. Commentators at film festivals have remarked upon the difference between Indian films which, by
and large, have a strong narrative mode and are episodic, and Western
films, which usually emphasize novelty and complexity of technique.

Derek Bose, in an insightful essay entitled 'Emerging Idiom in New
South Asian Cinema', contrasts Western films and cinema from Asian
countries. He says: 'While Western models present the spectacular, frenetic
and linear aspects of cinema, their Asian counterparts have evolved the
pure, suggestive, slow and even the static form, germane to their social-
cultural ethos.'[17] One recalls the films of Satyajit Ray and G. Aravindan.
Bose connects 'Epic Cinema' – as he calls Asian cinema – to the manner
in which an Asian film maker perceives reality. He says, 'Whereas western
thought is conditioned by the linear view of life, the Asian sees it as a

cycle – birth – life – death – rebirth.'[18] He cites the example of the famous Chinese film, Yao Sougang's *The Outcast*, the story of a young girl ostracized for adopting a child. The film, he observes, 'moves rhythmically back and forth, snatching glimpses of the child growing up, the resistance he faces, the problems of the "mother" and son, all the while establishing a harmony in visual metaphors and similes ... until the whole composition appears a grand collage on celluloid'.[19] How close that gets to the description of Indian oral narrative and how near to a description of the Indian novel!

E.M. Forster in *Aspects of the Novel* has distinguished between *Story* and *Plot*. He describes the former as lacking in a cause-effect connection, the latter as possessing it. In his estimation, the former is inferior to the latter.[20]

Interestingly, the Indian novel displays more affinity with the *Story* than with *Plot*, though it must be conceded that the Indian novelist is *writing* a novel and is not as free as is the creator of oral narrative. The 'story' is not inherited (as it is in the case of the traditional narrator) and the aesthetic situation is characterized by an autonomy of space and time. Yet, through the loose placement of episodes and chapters, and the clustering together of 'irrelevant' details (though it is difficult to say how much of this is deliberate on the part of the Indian novelist), the novelist does create the impression of having demolished causal as well as temporal-spacial relationships. While a traditional artist is 'traditional first and artist later',[21] the Indian novelist is both 'traditional', and an artist/ craftsman, that is, a person who is knowledgeable about the latest techniques of fiction. The Indian novel cannot, therefore, be evaluated only by the norms of Western fiction, though it employs some of its techniques. Rather, it has also to be judged by the norms endemic to this independent form of fiction, with its constructive principles drawn more from oral art than from Western fiction.

The first prominent constituent element of the Indian novel is its episodicity or the absence of motivation and cause-effect relationship between scenes. Episodicity is the central constructive principle of oral narratives. It is, in my view, also the structural principle of the Indian novel.

Consider Bhisham Sahni's Hindi novel, *Tamas*, which I regard as a typical example.[22] Capturing the pre-partition communal tensions that led to the Partition, homelessness and the massacre of a quarter million people, the novel has no sense of progression, no particular hero, no outstanding crisis in the usual manner of Western fiction. There are numerous characters and episodes in the novel and the situations and characters are juxtaposed like variegated pieces in a collage. In *Tamas*, there is no climax; only a series of tiny dramatic moments. The book is quiet like an unexploded bomb. The enormous tragedy of the people is unobtrusively placed against the backdrop of base politics, colonization and colonized native minds. The novel, merely 236 pages long, exhibits epic dimensions, while its whirlpool-like structure suggests affinities with the technique of oral art, though irony (a technique of Western fiction) is also an important device in the novel. The structure of *Tamas* (presented diagrammatically below) defies causal connection between chapters and clearly manifests itself as an episodic construct. Judged by Eurocentric criticism, the structure might be described as 'involved', 'defective', 'trivial', 'lacking in real continuity', and so on. Evaluated by the aesthetic norms of oral narrative, it is a structure that makes for a rich and reverberating novel which gains its power from the cumulative accretion of detail.

Chapter 1

Nathu paid by Murad Ali to kill a pig.

Chapter 2

A meeting of the Congressmen Bakshiji, Mehta, Shankarlal, etc.

Chapter 3

Nathu returning home
+
Congressmen confronted by a group of Muslims.

Chapter 4

Richard, the D.C., and his wife, Liza.

Chapter 5

Congressmen clean up drains
+
A dead pig found on the steps of the mosque.

Chapter 6

A religious congregation of Hindus
+
The terrorists Ranvir and Bodhraj
+
Ranvir assults a confectioner.

Chapter 7

Richard meets the deputation of Congressmen
+
Tension in the city
+
Liza's response to India.

Chapter 8

Communal tension continues
+
The Muslim section
Digression: a story
+
Digression: another story
+
Nathu and wife
+
Richard and wife.

Chapter 9

Lala Lakshmi Narain (Ranvir's father) and his family.

Chapter 10

The communal divide
+
The brutalization of Shahanawaz, a good man.

Chapter 11

Comrade Dev Dutt
+
The death of the 'general'.

Chapter 12

The terrorists
+
The murder of a poor Muslim hawker.

Chapter 13

Nathu suspects Ali
+
Nathu and wife.

Chapter 14

Harnam Singh and wife Banto.

Chapter 15

A Sikh congregation
+
The drowning of the voice of the moderates.

Chapter 16

The flight of Harnam and Banto from communal crowds
+
Sheltered by Ramzan's wife.

Chapter 17

Ramzan and others forcibly convert a Sikh to Islam. Irony: he is Harnam's son.

Chapter 18

Sikhs in a guru-dwara, preparing for a 'war' against 'Turks'
+
Sikh women commit suicide in a well to save their honour.

Chapter 19

The main city
+
Richard orders disinfection of the well.

Chapter 20

The Relief committee and the refugees
+
The tragedy of the uprooted.

Chapter 21

A peace meeting
+
Told that Nathu had died long ago in communal riots
+
Richard and Liza
+
Richard's transfer.

Mulk Raj Anand's *Untouchable* is similarly episodic.[23] It is also amorphously structured and is constructed in the whirlpool style of the episode-within-episode of oral narrative. Like *Tamas*, the novel grows centrifugally from the microcosm to the macrocosm; from the oppression of the low castes to the oppression of an entire nation. The fight for freedom at the individual, social level is for liberation from native oppressors, while the fight at the political level is for emancipation from the British. Episodicity, therefore, is an important attribute of the Indian novel.

The second constituent element of the Indian novel is that it is *digressive*. Digressions occur frequently in the Indian novel and are quite unique. Although it is possible to cite a few examples, particularly from early European/English/American novels that employ digression as a technique, the Indian novel is almost as a rule digressive. At least four types of digressions are seen in the Indian novel.

First, digressions are often made in order to introduce a parable or an incident from ancient lore that provides a living paradigm to the characters in modern times. U.R. Anantha Murthy's *Samskara* has several such digressions, the most dominant among them being the stories of Jaya and Vijaya, and of the gambler brahmin from the *Rig Veda*.[24] In the novel, these digressions become both technique (as in modern Western fiction) and substance (as in ancient Indian literature). These stories underscore the anxiety of Praneshacharya, the protagonist, to find a release from the frustrating cycle of birth and death. The inclusion of the stories in the novel is, however, quite unmethodical and at random. There is no clue as to why a story is being told. It is for the reader to infer that.

A second kind of digression is also present in the Indian novel. It is the deviation to re-create a *sthala-purana* or the legendary history of a place. *Sthala-purana* means ancient lore about a place, lore that is handed down for the most part by tradition.[25] The Indian novel has many a *sthala-purana*, its purpose being to provide linkages between the living ancient past (that is, the pantheon of gods, goddesses and saints) and the contemporaneous present. In the 'Foreword' to *Kanthapura*, Raja Rao has written: 'There is no village in India, however mean, that has not a rich *sthala-purana*, or legendary history of its own. Some god or godlike hero has passed by the village – Rama ... Sita ... or the Mahatama himself.... In this way the past mingles with the present.'[26] Rememoration of a *sthala-purana* is an effective method of evoking the deeply religious character of a people who see god in everything and invent legends easily.[27] Place-legends are not included in order to paint the landscape or to add colour to the picture of India, but to depict the mythic, religious imagination of the Indian people. In that sense, place-legends do not contribute directly to 'development' in the Indian novel, but they also do not distract the reader because they converge on his sensibility to provide him with a rich glimpse into the world-view of a people whose anchorage in the past and present is co-simultaneous and whose view of time is cyclical. In *The Serpent and the Rope*, *Samskara* and *Midnight's Children*, we get *sthala-puranas*, where the novelists try to evoke a sense of place not in geographical, physical terms but through mythological, legendary-historical lore. Consider these excerpts from *The Serpent and the Rope* and *Samskara*:

(i)   Tulsidas had written the *Ramayana* just there, next to the Rewa Palace and Kabir had been hit on the head by Saint Ramanand.... Farther down the Buddha himself had walked and had washed his alms-bowl....[28]

(ii)   The name of the agrahara was Durvasapura. There was a place-legend about it.... They believed Sage Durvasa still performed penance on it. In the Second Aeon of the cycle of time, for a short while, the Pandava brothers had lived ten miles from here, in a place called Kaimara....[29]

In *Midnight's Children*, Salman Rushdie gives us a *sthala-purana* to evoke the legendary, mythological origins of a primeval Bombay now submerged in the welter of the metropolitan city:

The fishermen were here first ... at the dawn of time when Bombay was a dumbbell-shaped island tapering ... [I]n this primeval world before clocktowers, the fishermen – who were called Kolis – sailed in Arab dhows, spreading red sails against the setting sun....

There were also coconuts and rice. And above it all, the benign presiding influence of the goddess Mumbadevi, whose name – Mumbadevi, Mumbabai, Mumbai – may well have become the city's....[30]

Thirdly, digressions in the Indian novel are employed to depict ceremonies, festivals and rituals that have sociological significance. These are described at a slow, leisurely pace and they represent those signs of Indian culture which define the essential framework for expressing and experiencing reality in the Indian context. For example, in K.S. Karenth's Kannada novel, *The Whispering Earth*, a whole page has been devoted to the description of the marriage celebrations of Laccha and Nagaveni. The scene has no motivation or 'relevance' in the Western/English fictional sense because it leads to no later crisis – major or minor – as, say, does the wedding scene in Forster's *Howard's End*. Judged by the standards of Western literate art, the scene could even be eliminated:

> The women of the bride's party welcomed the women of the bridegroom's party. The pipers piped and the band struck up, fireworks and crackers filled the air with noise and sparks....
>
> The whole party then entered the pavilion which was beautifully decorated with mango leaves and other green shoots. From the roof and the pillars hung bunches of plantain and betelnut. Carpets were spread on the floor and there were cushions for the guests to lean against.... Nagamma's dance party were there too....
>
> ...The sacrificial fire blazed brightly. Rose water was sprinkled on the guests, fans were waved, and there was cool sherbet for the thirsty....
>
> The women had just begun to sing wedding songs.[31]

It is sections such as these in the Indian novel which have been criticized for being incoherent, episodic, loose and disconnected from the main 'plot'. They have also been wrongly placed in the nineteenth century realistic tradition. Yet, it is these scenes, appearing almost as independent units, that cumulatively expand, amplify and re-construct the Indian *Weltanschauung* in the novel.

Marriage in India is an important, almost compulsory stage in a person's life because it is only after its performance that a person can fulfil his *dharma* as a householder. Much significance is therefore attached to the event. The entire community participates and blesses the couple. The guests and the bridegroom's party are treated with great respect. In the passage quoted above, for example, it won't do, in the interests of structural tightness, to abbreviate the opening sentence to: 'The bridegroom's party were welcomed'. It has to be written as in the original: 'The women of the bride's party welcomed the women of the bridegroom's party' because that alone conveys the cultural and sociological significance of the ritual even if the description slows down the pace of the narration. Scenes such as these can never be understood or appreciated from a Eurocentric position because they appear to be 'extraneous', 'meandering', 'involved'.

Interestingly, it is scenes of this kind, marked by great festivity and gaiety, which capture the sensuous side of Indian life and subvert the impression that Indians are a life-denying, life-negating people. As several scenes from the Indian novel show, Indians need no excuse to eat, sing, dance or to be sociable. Elaborate descriptions of rituals and customs, of meals cooked and served, abound in the Indian novel and bear testimony to that quality of sensuousness and joyousness which, paradoxically, goes hand in hand with the Indian's quest for self-realization, also an important theme in the Indian novel. Nehru, in *The Discovery of India*, quotes Arrian, the Greek historian of Alexander's campaign (in India) as having remarked that 'No nation is fonder of singing and dancing than the Indian'.[32] Songs and dances form significant digressions in the Indian novel. This is the fourth type of digression.

Classical singing has always occupied an important position in Indian society. But it is the popular folk song (or the film song often based on a folk song), sung by a group or for a group, that really characterizes the Indian sensibility. There are folk songs sung only by women or only by men, and there are folk songs sung by mixed groups. Be it a birth, a marriage, a festival, a victory in cricket or the elections, there is much evidence of group singing. On more solemn occasions, the *bhajan* is sung.[33]

In the Indian novel, folk songs appear with fair regularity, whereas in the Western/English novel they rarely do. For example, consider this tender love song from *Samskara*. It is sung by the newly-married Putta, whose wife has gone visiting her parents, leaving him lovelorn and lost:

> He beats his wife
>   but cries in his heart
> so falls at her feet
>   and at her feet he pleads
> Who's sweeter, tell me
>   Me or your Mother's place?[34]

In Amrita Pritam's Punjabi novel, *The Skeleton*, Pooro's mother, about to give away her daughter in marriage, is overwhelmed by the impending agony of separation. Tearfully, she sings a 'daughter's lament':

> I have got out my spinning-wheel,
> I have my wads of cotton,
> I'll spin sheets with square patterns
> To sons are given homes and palaces;
> Daughters are exiled to foreign lands.[35]

In *The Serpent and the Rope*, Ramaswamy sings an enchanting Kannada cradle song to Vera, the infant daughter of his friends, Catherine and Georges:

> The Swan is swinging the cradle, baby
> Saying 'I am That', 'That I am', quietly.
> She sings it beautifully, baby
> Abandoning actions and hours.[36]

In this novel, there are also a number of *bhajans* to Shiva, sung by the Advaitin protagonist.

In concluding this paper, I would like to say that digressiveness and episodicity are the two outstanding attributes (and not the defects) of the Indian novel. This inference is as true of the English language Indian novel as of the regional language novel. In reading the Indian novel, therefore, these characteristics should be assiduously identified and acknowledged so that the rich and autonomous form is not needlessly reduced or marginalized. This paper has, in a small way, tried to show how this can be done.

NOTES

1. Viney Kirpal, 'What is the Modern Third World Novel?', *Journal of Commonwealth Literature*, XXIII:1 (Aug. 1988), pp. 144-56.
2. T.D. Brunton, 'India in Fiction: The Heritage of Indianness' in M.K. Naik, S.K. Desai and G.S. Amur, eds., *Critical Essays on Indian Writing in English* (Dharwar: Karnatak Univ., 1968), pp. 199-209.
3. 'In an "instant" world of communication, there is no reason for cultural lag or for a difference between sophisticated writers in large centres and naive writers in smaller ones. A world like ours produces a single international style of which all existing literatures are regional developments....' Northrop Frye, in the 1980s, makes the same point, as Brunton, in 'Across the River and Out of the Trees'. Quoted in Arun Mukherjee, *Towards an Aesthetic of Opposition: Essays on Literature Criticism and Cultural Imperialism* (Ontario: Williams Wallace Publishers, 1988), p. 12.
4. T.C. Ghai, 'Pattern and Significance in R.K. Narayan's Novels', *Indian Literature* (July-Sept. 1975), pp. 33-58.
5. K.D. Kurtkoti, 'Two Novels by Mrs M.K. Indira', *The Literary Criterion*, 20:4 (1985), pp. 55-61.
6. Umashankar Joshi, 'The Novelist's Quest for India', *Indian Literature*, No. 1 (1965), pp. 58-81.
7. One collection which is quite representative of this school of thought is S.K. Desai and G.N. Devy, eds., *Critical Thought: An Anthology of 20th Century Indian English Essays* (New Delhi: Sterling Publishers Private Ltd., 1987).
8. Edwin Gerow, 'The Persistence of Classical Esthetic Categories in Contemporary Indian Literature: Three Bengali Novels' in Edward C. Dimock Jr. et al., *The Literatures of India: An Introduction* (Chicago: The University of Chicago Press, 1974), pp. 227-238.
9. Edwin Gerow, 'The Quintessential Narayan' in Meenakshi Mukherjee, ed., *Considerations* (Delhi: Allied Publishers Pvt. Ltd., 1977), pp. 66-83.
10. Edwin Gerow, 'The Persistence of Classical Esthetic Categories in Contemporary Indian Literature: Three Bengali Novels', p. 232.

11. 'How do our village folk develop their "Indianness" which I may describe as the essence of their culture? ... [D]uring my childhood days, I had listened to my father read out verses from the great Indian epics. This, incidentally, is a regular practice in the Kerala households: verses from the Hindu classical texts are read aloud in the evenings, after supper.... I don't think there is any other place on earth where literature forms the basis, the very life-style of a people...' T.S. Pillai, 'On Indianness in Literature', translated by K. Narayana Chandran, *Indian Literature*, No. 111 (Jan-Feb 1986), pp. 66-70.

12. Arnold Toynbee has questioned the deterministic cause-effect, scientific-methodical Western histories. In a bid to break away from this model, in vogue since the times of Plato, he resorts to the language of mythology to construct history. *A Study of History*, a new edition revised and abridged by the author and Jane Caplan (London: Oxford University Press, in association with Thames and Hudson, 1972), p. 97.

13. K. Chellappan, 'The Discovery of India and the Self in Three Autobiographies', in H.H. Anniah Gowda, ed., *The Colonial and the Neocolonial Encounters in Commonwealth Literature* (Mysore: University of Mysore, n.d.), pp. 95-106.

14. Jawaharlal Nehru, *India Rediscovered*. Abridged from *The Discovery of India* by C.D. Narasimhaiah (London: Oxford University Press, 1954), p. 47.

15. Available in Sudhaker Pandey, Shridhar Gokhale and Vidya Netrakanti, eds., *Rose Petals: Selections from Jawaharlal Nehru* (Bombay: Oxford University Press, 1989), pp. 15-16.

16. Raja Rao, *Kanthapura*, with an introduction by C.D. Narasimhaiah (1938, rpt. Madras: Oxford University Press, 1974), p. 2.

17. Derek Bose, 'Emerging Idiom in Asian Cinema', *Maharashtra Herald*, 18 April 1987, col. 2, p. 5.

18. Ibid., col. 2.

19. Ibid., col. 5.

20. E.M. Forster, *Aspects of the Novel* (London: Edward Arnold & Co., 1927), pp. 43, 116-17.

21. Rekha Jhanji, 'Creativity in Traditional Art', *British Journal of Aesthetics*, 28:2 (1988), pp. 162-72.

22. Bhisham Sahni, *Tamas*, translated from the Hindi by Jai Ratan (1974; rev. edn. N. Delhi: Penguin Books (India) Ltd., 1988).

23. Mulk Raj Anand, *Untouchable*, Preface by E.M. Forster (1935; rpt. Delhi: Orient Paperbacks in arrangement with The Bodley Head Ltd, London, 1970).

24. U.R. Anantha Murthy, *Samskara: A Rite for a Dead Man*, 1967; translated by A.K. Ramanujan (Delhi: Oxford University Press, 1976).

25. F.E. Pargiter, 'Puranas', in *Encyclopaedia of Religion and Ethics*, edited by James Hastings with the assistance of John A. Selbie and Louis H. Gray (Edinburgh: T & T Clark, 1918), pp. 447-55.

26. Raja Rao, 'Foreword' to *Kanthapura* (1938), p. v.

27. U.R. Anantha Murthy repeats a story told to him at a conference by a painter. The painter was travelling and he wished to photograph a stone god kept outside a peasant's home. He photographed it with the peasant's permission and then asked him casually if he had polluted it by moving it outside. 'It doens't matter,' the peasant replied, 'I will have to bring another stone and anoint *kumkum* on it.' Any piece of stone on which he put *kumkum* became God for the peasant. What mattered was his faith, not the stone. This is the manner in which the essentially mythical and metaphorical imagination of the peasant worked. 'The Search for an Identity: A Kannada Writer's Viewpoint' in Guy Amirthanayagam, ed., *Asian and Western*

Writers in Dialogue: New Cultural Identities (London: The Macmillan Press Ltd., 1982), pp. 66-78.

28. Raja Rao, *The Serpent and the Rope* (1960; rpt. Delhi: Hind Pocket Books by arrangement with the author and John Murray (Publishers) Ltd., London, 1968), p. 11.
29. Anantha Murthy, *Samskara* (1976), p. 16.
30. Salman Rushdie, *Midnight's Children* (1981; rpt. London: Pan Books Ltd., 1983), p. 92.
31. K.S. Karanth, *The Whispering Earth*, translated from the Kannada by A.N. Murthy Rao (Delhi: Vikas Publishing House, 1974), p. 70.
32. Nehru, *India Rediscovered* (1954), p. 57.
33. A.K. Ramanujan, 'The Relevance of Folklore', working draft for private circulation (now available in *Another Harmony*), p. 11.
34. Anantha Murthy, *Samskara* (1976), p. 119.
35. Amrita Pritam, *The Skeleton and That Man*, translator's name and first date of publication not stated (Delhi: Sterling Publishers Private Ltd, 1974), p. 5.
36. Rao, *The Serpent and the Rope* (1968), p. 405.

KETU H. KATRAK and BEHEROZE F. SHROFF

On Film: Indian and British Perspectives on Partition

'The Longest Journey' – a cover story in a recent issue of *The Indian Express*[1] – effectively portrays the traumatic history of Partition through interviews and personal testimonies from Hindus and Muslims who had witnessed and survived the horrors of that period, forty-two years ago. Ironically, at the same time that the two nations were 'created' on 15 August 1947, ten million people were uprooted. 'There were then, at least ten million histories of individual courage and endurance,' reports Shailaja Bajpai, 'ten million histories of friendship that transcended barriers of religion and prejudice, of betrayal and violence. There was, above all, the virtually indescribable anguish of leaving a homeland forever.'

Refaqat Ali Khan, one of the survivors of that time, remarks, 'There is only one word for what was happening those days: horror.' He continues:

> I was only ten years old at that time. But I was very conscious of what was happening.... We heard of murders everywhere.... We had no weapons only kitchen knives but these were being prepared because there was the likelihood of an attack in our area.... For us divided families [part of his family now lives in Pakistan], our feelings are always divided. During the 1965 war [between India and Pakistan], when there was the expectation that the Indian Air Force would bomb Lahore, I was not worried about Pakistan. I was not rooting for an Indian victory. I was praying for the life of my brother there.

A similar sentiment is echoed by M.A. Rahman – he and his brother 'are now on opposite sides of the fence'. The story of how Partition not only divided two countries but tore apart people's lives is poignantly recorded by Vimla Sindhi:

> My father, for instance, refused to believe that there would be any violence. There were forms, those days, issued to all of us, asking us which country we wished to live in. My father not only refused to fill out the form, he urged others not to also.... One of my brothers was working in Delhi and we came [from what is now Pakistan] to visit him. All the time I had this terrible feeling that I had left something behind that I would never see again. And this is what happened.... On September 17, my father had gone to the railway station to see off the first batch of Hindus who were leaving for India. He was stabbed there.... So whether they were rich or poor, landlords or villagers, they simply abandoned everything and got onto the

trains, trucks, whatever means of transport they could find and left for India.... My mother was left stranded in Khanewal.... We had come to Delhi for a holiday, now there was no going back.

The cost not only of human lives, but of psychological and emotional devastations for the survivors is documented in the same story. Vimla Sindhi notes how her mother went into

a state of shock after his [her husband's] death and that never really left her. The same is true of my youngest brother who was only 14 at the time. He never recovered from the loss. He didn't study much after that, he didn't do anything.... In my family there was one other tragedy. My cousin's 4-year old son was cut into two pieces when the train that was bringing the family to India was attacked. As many people as possible hid under the berths and though the child was hidden, the mob saw him and just cut him into two. We never mention his name.

One way of grappling with this history is to contrast the ways in which this historical event is represented artistically. Here, I focus on different points of view in visual representations of Partition in films made by Indians and by the British. Given the nearly 200-year-old contact between Britain and India, it is understandable that Western representations of India are often produced in Britain. Today, there are some independent film-makers of Indian and Pakistani descent who live in Britain. However, in terms of a general and wide distribution, their work is less easily accessible than say switching on a PBS channel in the U.S. and seeing any number of re-plays of the British Raj disseminated through the BBC.

How history is made and re-made in its very representation in film is fascinating when we analyse the impacts of this theme when seen in India itself, and in Britain and the 'West'. Historical fact and fiction are controversial matters debated in text and counter-text (recently, with the re-issue of Maulana Azad's version of Partition in his book, *India Wins Freedom*, a battle in print has broken out – Rajmohan Gandhi's *India Wins Errors* challenges many of Azad's 'facts'). In film specifically, the entire technical machinery – framing of shots, close-ups, visual symbols – itself manipulates audience response. Cumulatively when we see several shots of the 'civilized' British discoursing over glasses of sherry about the difficult political situation which culminated in Partition, and we simultaneously see several shots of 'mindless' Indians engaged in massacre, a powerful statement is made visually, without words. The particular appeal and impact of film, while certainly potent for largely illiterate populations such as that in India, works more insidiously for literate populations which, to use Bertolt Brecht's words in another context, 'hang up their brains along with their coats in the cloak-room' as soon as they enter the theatre, or, I would add, switch on the television.

In general, Partition as a theme is not popular in Indian cinema or visual arts. It is a heavy, non-celebratory, violent theme, one that is likely to stir up religious sentiments and conflicts in India to this day. As Gayatri Sinha points out in her article, 'The Canvas of Partition', painters generally stayed away from this theme.[2] As painter B.C. Gujral remarks, 'Partition is a disgusting memory ... you don't like to show the horrors.' Another artist, Satish Gujral, acknowledges that Partition was his major inspiration; however, his work didn't sell easily because people are reluctant to relive this nightmarish history.

In British-made films about Partition – *Mountbatten: The Last Viceroy*, or in parts of *Gandhi* – the emphasis is on the large canvas. By contrast, in Indian-made films about Partition – *Garm Hava* and, more recently, *Tamas* – the emphasis is on individual tragedies among the communities. History is represented in ways that make clear for instance that communal violence and hatred are politically instigated, and are often transcended by personal friendships among individuals of the two communities. The history of Partition brutalities, 'communal violence' as it is called, is rooted in the British divide-and-rule policy, and religion is often used to mystify political and economic agendas.

Such a history is absent from British-made films, which display epic proportions, pomp and splendour, and the role of prominent leaders. The impact of this horrific history on the lives of ordinary Hindus and Muslims is absent. The ordinary people are rendered invisible as the masses, as part of the backdrop in crowd scenes. It is worth adding that these crowd scenes are relatively cheap to film in a country like India; it is much more expensive in Britain or the U.S. to pay each individual in a crowd scene.

In *Gandhi*, the history of Partition is encapsulated through a couple of familiar symbols, and through the use of long shots – crowded trains, people fleeing, all seen only from a distance. Through the use of a helicopter shot, we see ant-like people moving in two directions – the issue was much more complex than the simple, directional emphasis given through this shot. We do not get to see, for instance, that many of these trains were mobile morgues carrying dead bodies. Attenborough ignores the actual horrors of the history underlying Partition, though he does deal satisfactorily with Gandhi's role in it without romanticizing the 'Mahatma's' message of Hindu-Muslim unity.

The contrasting representations of Partition in British and Indian films reveal the underlying issues of power and domination of the very making and dissemination of knowledge itself. In British India, personal power invested in an individual like Mountbatten-the-Viceroy can translate a personal story into official facts. Edward Said has discussed in *Orientalism* how 'personal document gets translated into the enabling codes of orientalist science'.[3] Mountbatten's personal experiences assume the authority of officialdom and, within the same text, one finds a subtle metamorphosis from a personal to an official statement. Colonial history offers many examples of this kind of transference. And in film particularly, one responds on a somewhat visceral level, as opposed to the way one responds to the written word. In film official versions, frozen visually, assume an incontrovertible power; often they are deceptively brief, though more lasting on subconscious levels of images and symbols. When we take a step away from that visceral response, and look again analytically, and use historical experience, such as the personal testimonies presented at the outset, we can contest those unanalytical responses and discover a very different view of history.

Another reason that delays the analytic response in films such as *Mountbatten* and *Gandhi* is that we never get any discussion of the reasons behind certain visually powerful scenes of human massacre. The bloodshed is presented only as scenes of people mindlessly indulging in killings supposedly rooted in 'religious fanaticism'. That is the official discourse we get from the British who are empowered with speech and reason; the Indians who are actually on the sites of history are voiceless numbers simply exacting justice for their religious beliefs.

The movement from 'a personal to a professional Orientalism' leads to a construction, a representation of the Orient which is insidiously broad. Such 'official stories' are useful only if we recognize their limits, namely, that they are rooted in personal experience, and personal vision.[4] However, when we deal with the personal experience of someone like the Viceroy, the story is already overdetermined, and it is difficult to separate the personal from the official line. Lady Mountbatten says to her husband, 'The birth of India would never be possible without you.' And Nehru is complicit in this type of history-making when he remarks to Mountbatten, 'Together, you and I have done a great thing [Independence].'

The blending, then, of the personal with the official story is to be problematized in British-made films about Partition. On the other hand, in Indian representations of this history, the opposite limitation is perceived: the canvas shrinks and, although a much-needed emphasis is placed on individual stories, what is often missing is the backdrop of British power and responsibility. In particular, British complicity in setting up communal divide and rule as a strategy had disastrous results for 'native' populations. So, in a film like *Garm Hava*, otherwise excellent for its evocation of individual pain and suffering rooted in the larger political scenario of Partition, we don't find any broader analysis of British responsibility for Partition. The recent TV serial *Tamas* by Govind Nihalani (based on the novel by Bhisham Sahni) does attempt to incorporate that history.[5]

The controversy surrounding *Tamas* had to be deliberated in the Bombay High Court: would a film like *Tamas* stir up emotions which have been buried and repressed? Interestingly, 'in 1974 when the novel was first published' remarks Nihalani in his Introduction, 'no such questions were raised'. The Bombay High Court's judgement that *Tamas* rather than inciting communal strife and violence was directed against 'the sickness of communalism' was endorsed by the Supreme Court of India, which stated:

It is out of the tragic experience of the past that we can fashion our present in a rational and reasonable manner and view our future with wisdom and care. Awareness in proper light is a first step towards that realisation.... *Tamas* takes us to a historical past – unpleasant at times, but revealing and instructive.

Among the few Indian films which deal with Partition, M.S. Sathyu's 1973 film *Garm Hava* is one of the most moving and effective portrayals of how political history affected the personal, day-to-day lives and struggles of a Muslim family in India. The film opens with stills recapturing a Nationalist history – Congress leaders, Gandhi's assassination captured in a long freeze frame. As the credits unfold we see the familiar image of Partition – trains, and a frightened and weary people fleeing disasters. This broad canvas immediately narrows as the narrative opens and we see the protagonist, the head of the Muslim family, played superbly by Balraj Sahni. He is bidding farewell to someone at the train and then gets into a tonga. This image returns as a motif throughout the film whenever he bids farewell to one more member of his family leaving India for Pakistan. Sahni's steps get visibly heavier, more despairing as he perseveres to remain in the land that is his home, and not flee to a newly created 'home' for all Muslims. The tongawalla remarks on this sentiment: 'Allah has created Pakistan for us.'

The film poignantly traces the many struggles that Sahani's family suddenly faces because of Partition and newly ingrained prejudices. Business partners and money-lenders suddenly become uncooperative. The family is forced, as the eldest son puts it, to 'live as beggars in this country, not as businessmen'. They also face discrimination in housing – in a heart-rending scene when they are forced out of their home, the old mother hides, crouched under a low wall, refusing to leave. She has to be literally carried out, howling and protesting. Why should she have to give up her ancestral home for larger political battles which she did not create and over which she has no control?

As in the above scene, the subtle blending of the personal and the political is most effectively accomplished throughout the film, particularly and most tragically in the case of the young daughter. The audience feels an intensely personal involvement and sympathy towards the daughter who must first be separated from the cousin to whom she is betrothed since he leaves with his family for Pakistan. The skilled interweaving of the personal – her affection, love – and the political – the cousin is arrested as an illegal 'foreigner' when he comes to visit her – is beautifully accomplished. When the cousin is deported we recognize how suddenly, through political realities over which an ordinary family has no control, he is considered a traitor because he has moved to Pakistan.

The daughter is devastated but gradually recovers and almost wills herself to become responsive to another suitor. Within a tradition-bound family, she has no choice except to marry – that is her destiny, no matter that new nations are being created, and battles waged over issues larger than the sad and narrow parameters of what is available to her. When this suitor also leaves with his family for Pakistan with promises to send for her, we are filled with misgivings. After a long wait, his mother returns and in a heart-rending revelation scene remarks callously that the sarees, etc. which she has come to purchase are for a bride selected for her son in Pakistan.

The daughter's desperation leads her to commit suicide. She becomes the unfortunate victim of larger political forces which impose new restrictions on what might have been a straight-forward event – marriage – in her life. The disastrous end also reflects that this might have been her only option in a society which grants not only status, but a sense of self to women only as wives and mothers. Although she has loving parents, this is not enough. Besides, after two disastrous rejections, she is shamed – questions of honour and shame are so intense in tradition-bound families that they can lead to suicide. Related to the question of shame, the film had depicted a scene which subtly suggested love-making between the young couple after they had pledged to spend their lives together. The daughter then has broken the strict codes of morality, of 'izzat', and would dishonour both herself and her parents if, no longer a virgin, she were to be given to another man. The oppressive, even fatal controls of female sexuality imprison her. Nor is she able to verbalize or find support for such conflicts which are totally silenced in her death.

The film's resolution seems to be interestingly gendered – male members of the family emerge out of the political disillusionments by the end. Not so the females. As a woman, the daughter would not be allowed by the family to join a political group. Her brother can situate his frustrations and anger within a larger political framework, attend meetings late into the night and attend demonstrations. He survives; the daughter's grief is turned inward so that it consumes and destroys her.

The father too, although fairly conservative throughout, conciliatory rather than radical about the various discriminations he faces as a Muslim, recognizes by the end of the film that religious and political issues are inextricably bound. He becomes aware of the fact that religious issues are always also political, particularly within the circumstances of an event such as Partition – a political event with tragically fatal communalism. He steps out of the tonga, tells his family to return home, not leave for Pakistan, and he joins the street demonstration along with his son. His politicization emerges convincingly as a result of his personal struggles.

In conclusion, I would like to remark that there are different kinds of contradictions involved for Indians on the one hand, and for Britishers on the other in both producing and viewing this history on film. Given a colonial history, there is a dialectic relationship between the viewer and the viewed, between the insider and the outsider. And within this dialectic there are ironies, perhaps sharper today than twenty years ago given the growing number of immigrant populations from the ex-colonies who now live in Britain and in other parts of the 'western' world. How do the British look back on who they were at the height of the Raj? And as the sun has most certainly set on the British Empire, does one perceive a more urgent need to re-create a glorious past? Perhaps as a way of forgetting the awful realities of the present? Perhaps as a way of recapturing 'what we once were'? Given these kind of questions, British versions of their history in India are more about themselves than they are about India, Indians, or Indian history. British versions of their history in India attempt to resolve various shades of guilt and complicity in certain non-celebratory, historical episodes such as Partition.

During the Raj, the question of insider/outsider might have been clearer than such a question today. During the Raj, the insider/outsider dichotomy could be viewed along the dialectic of shifting power and powerlessness. An insider could be determined by virtue of a consolidation of power, whereas an outsider could be the one without it. Today, the insider/outsider dialectic involves a complex mediation along the trajectory of race, class, ethnic group, language, geography. For writers, critics and film-makers, colonial and post-colonial histories require us to challenge the very notions of insider and outsider, identity and belonging.

NOTES

1. *The Indian Express* (Bombay), Sunday Magazine, 13 August 1989, pp. 1-3.
2. Ibid., p. 4.
3. Edward Said, *Orientalism* (New York: Vintage Books, 1979), p. 157.
4. The insidious blurring of lines between the personal and official story is not only an 'orientalist' problem common in the realm of politics. In literature too one finds examples of personal vision taken as universalist, nationally representative, and so on. Such attitudes are often buttressed by conditions of the market-place, and by say, race, relations industries in the 'West'.
5. Bhisham Sahni, *Tamas*, trans. from Hindi by Jai Ratan; Introduction by Govind Nihalani (Penguin, India, 1988, first pub. 1974).

GANESWAR MISHRA

Problems of Transmissibility of Culture: a Comparative Study of an Oriya Novel and Its English Translation

Translating Oriya fiction into English involves the problems of translating a text in the language of one culture into that of another. It is true that some translators are better than others and some texts are more translatable than others. But the problems, as discussed in this paper, pertain to the nature of language and culture and, hence, the competence of the translator is no answer to such problems. It can be said, however, that the more authentic an Indian-language text is – the more rooted in Indian culture, ethos and linguistic tradition – the more difficult is the task of rendering it into English, the language still alien to the masses. This paper compares an Oriya novel, K.C. Panigrahi's *Matira Manisha* (1931) with its English rendering, Lila Ray's *A House Undivided* (1973) to suggest how the translator fails to carry over the subtle cultural and linguistic nuances to the translated text and, as a result, how the translated text is a 'shift' of the original.

K.C. Panigrahi's *Matira Manisha*, generally acclaimed as a classic in modern Oriya literature, is a portrait of traditional Indian village life in pre-independence India and is in some ways similar to Raja Rao's portrait of village life in *Kanthapura*. The novel deals with Indian peasants who are innocent of modern education and the English language and for whom anything hardly matters except the moneylender and the temple. Written and published in the thirties, the novel unmistakably shows the author's inclination towards Gandhism and Socialism. Panigrahi does not refer to Gandhi or the Indian National Congress in his novel, but writing at a time when Gandhi and Gandhism dominated the Indian political and even literary scene, Panigrahi makes his protagonist, Baraju, practice Gandhism in his domestic life in much the same way as Moorthy does in *Kanthapura*. The translation of *Matira Manisha* into English as *A House Undivided* is done by Lila Ray, whose qualifications as a translator are quite impressive. She is a native speaker of English; she has translated several Bengali novels into English; and she is married to the Bengali novelist Annanda

Shankar Ray, who has also written fiction and poetry in Oriya, and is an intimate literary associate of Panigrahi. Lila Ray presumably has translated *Matira Manisha* from its Bengali version, but Bengali and Oriya as languages are so close that the Bengali translation is not likely to be substantially different from the original; and Lila Ray, as the wife of an Oriya poet and literary associate of Panigrahi, can be said to have certain additional advantages when translating a work of Panigrahi.

The nature of the languages more than any other factor seems to create problems in the translation of the Oriya novel into English, so much so that the English text is unrecognisably different from the Oriya; and the artist who has drawn the cover design for the English translation perhaps had no way of knowing that the novelist has portrayed a set of characters hardly resembling the ones he has drawn on the cover.

Indian languages differ from English in several general ways: in syntax, in semantics, in matters of cultural associations and so forth. It is possible to suggest how the syntactic structure of an Oriya passage differs from the same in English. But it is not easy to explain how and where Panigrahi changes conventional syntax patterns to add a sense of novelty to his style, how exactly, by the use of a single word or phrase, he reminds the reader of Oriya folklore, or where he is closer to poetry in his style and so on. Many of the linguistic experiments, achievements or failures in an Indian-language work are not likely to be carried over to the English translation; and the greater the merit of an Indian-language work for its linguistic achievement, the less its possibility of success in English translation. Panigrahi's work, written in colloquial idiomatic Oriya, is almost impossible to translate into English. Here is the first passage from the opening chapter of the novel, first in word-for-word translation, and then in literal translation:

> Our this very intimate very old sun like crore crore sun universe in everyday rise everyday set. One one sun around crore crore planet satellite *chaka chaka bhaunri* play – day, night, season, month, year create. Them out of one very small planet our this very ancient mother-earth, that in Bharatabarsha still smaller one country. That in Orissa. That in again [of] Cuttack district Birupa on the back Padhanpara – very small very tiny [of] human settlement one. Of Sham Pradhan very tiny cottage that village in. His place in universe what – atom or a fragment of an atom – who will calculate.
>
> That land which generation first coming set foot, of that no footstep left. That land who first coming seeds sowed, fruits ate, that story might this Birupa river tell, this sun-moon might tell. But today that land in paddy hay is smiling; that land today in human noise has come to life. That on road many children games playing have gone – Sham Pradhan his father grandfather seven generations. Birupa on the bank village *oseities* joyous *huluhuli* has rung; village of dead people's flames have burnt; in the ritual for the ghost to bathe coming many widows' bitter weeping of Birupa this dry sand in tears wet has many many years for, who knows.[1]

Literal translation:

Like this very intimate, very ancient sun of ours, crores and crores of suns rise and set every day in the universe. Crores and crores of planets and satellites play the game of *chaka chaka bhaunri* around their suns and create days, nights, seasons, months and years. This ancient mother-earth of ours is one of those planets and Bharatabarsha, still smaller, is a country in that. And inside that, Orissa. Inside that, again, Pradhanpara, in the district of Cuttack, on the bank of Birupa, a very small very tiny human settlement. The tiny cottage of Sham Pradhan is in that village. What is his place in the universe? Is it an atom or fragment of an atom? Who can tell?

There is no mark of the footsteps of the generation that first stepped into that land. River Birupa and the sun and the moon might tell who first sowed seeds in that land and ate the fruits. But today that land is smiling in paddy and hay; that land has come to life in the noise of human beings. Countless children have played on that road – Sham Pradhan, his father, grandfather and seven generations. Who knows for how long, on the bank of Birupa, the joyous *huluhuli* of village *oseities* has resounded; the pyres of the countless dead of the village have burnt high; and the dry sand of the river has been drenched by the bitter tears of widows coming to bathe in the ceremony of the ghost?

Had Panigrahi written in English, he might have rendered his thoughts in English approximately as I have done in the above passage. He might have observed, while rendering his narrative presumably thought out in Oriya, that the syntactic structure of English sentences being different from that of the Oriya, the emphasis on words and ideas in his narrative was being distorted in the process of the rendering, that the words and images which were meant to convey the subtle cultural nuances of the life of the characters or the locale of the story had often no equivalent in English, and so forth.

How the syntax of language determines the emphasis on words and images is of course difficult to explain. The syntactic structure of Indian-language sentences is often different from that of English sentences and that perhaps suggests a variation of thought-process, sense of proportion, etc. between Indian-language and English speakers. The Oriya sentence in the word-for-word translation begins with 'Our this very intimate, very ancient sun...' etc. and the English sentence in the translation with 'Like this very intimate, very ancient sun of ours...' etc. It could be that in the Oriya sentence the word 'our' is more emphasized than 'of ours' in the English sentence. One can perhaps change the English sentence so as to start it with 'our' or to suggest a greater emphasis on 'our', but one cannot continually change the English syntax to fit the Oriya sense of syntax without making the English unreadable. The second Oriya sentence in the word-for-word translation begins with emphasis on each individual sun ('One one sun...' etc.) that is the centre of crores of planets and satellites whereas in the English rendering the emphasis shifts onto the planets ('Crores and crores of planets...' etc.). To make the English rendering of Oriya sentences readable and intelligible, it is impossible not to violate the

Oriya syntactic pattern, and the emphasis on words and images, however skilfully the rendering is done.

In Lila Ray's translation of *Matira Manisha*, the first two sentences of the opening chapter go like this:

> Suns in hundreds of millions, suns like the Sun we know so well, the familiar Sun of our earth, rise regularly and set as regularly in the larger world of the cosmos. Planets ring them around, circling in an unending game of blind man's buff, a mighty game in the course of which nights and days, months, years and seasons come into existence.[2]

In Ray's translation of the first sentence, the reference to the word 'sun' is made four times while in the Oriya sentence, 'sun' is referred to only twice. The Oriya sentence starts with 'Our this ... sun' etc., but in Ray's translation the sentence starts with 'Suns in hundreds of millions...' etc., and 'our this sun' becomes 'the familiar sun of our earth'. In the Oriya sentence there is no mention of the word 'earth'. The second English sentence starts with 'Planets ring them around...' etc., and the word 'sun' which occurs once in the Oriya sentence, is not mentioned in the English at all. The individuality and importance of each one of the suns ('One one sun...') as the centre of crores of planets and satellites ('Crore crore planet satellite...' etc.) as suggested in the Oriya sentence is hardly carried over to the English in a phrase like 'Planets ring them round'.

The shift of emphasis on words and images seems almost inevitable in the rendering of an Indian-language text into English, and this could lead to several other changes, that is, the change of syntax might lead to addition and deletion of words, variance in the length of the sentence and so forth. All these changes could create a style entirely different from that of the original.

At least two other changes, besides the change in the emphasis on words and images as the result of the change in word order, are likely to happen in any rendering of an Indian-language work into English: firstly, the change of tense; secondly, the change of voice. What is known as sequence of tense in English grammar is not so significant in the context of Indian languages. An Indian-language passage might apparently contain verb forms of the past, present and the future tense and yet be quite consistent.[3] It is the context more often than the form of the verb that indicates the tense. One can for instance use the past or the present form of a verb to indicate the past tense. In the English rendering both may look alike, but in Indian languages, the use of the two forms of verb, though indicating the same tense, might suggest a subtle difference unlikely to be carried over to the English rendering. One may compare an Oriya passage with its English translation to see the difference in the tense of verb-forms. An Oriya passage from the first chapter, translated faithfully and retaining the original verb-forms, would go roughly as follows:

The old woman's attention *is* a little more on the younger of the two daughters-in-law. There *is* no other reason for that, except that she *is* the younger. People *take* a little more pity on those who *are* small and weak. That *is* why the old woman *would* always *see* whether the younger daughter-in-law *had* her bath and *had* the meal, *had* done her hair and *put on* the *haldi*. The elder daughter-in-law *cannot tolerate* all this. Her feet *do* not *touch* the floor as she *is* the mother of four children. She *claims* to be the favourite of the mother-in-law, father-in-law and the husband. (pp. 8-9; emphasis added)

In Ray's English translation, among other differences, the difference in the tense of the verb-forms may be noted:

Old Mother Pradhan *kept* an eye on chhakari's wife, Netromani. Netromani *was* new to the family and she *was* the youngest. Those who *are* weaker and younger usually *get* more attention than others. Mother Pradhan always *asked* her if she *had rubbed* herself *down* with tumeric paste, *taken* her both, *had* her meal or *dressed* her hair. Baraju's wife *did* not *like* this partiality. She *was* the mother of four children and *considered* herself entitled to the most attention for that reason. She *was* very proud of her motherhood, so proud that she *was* virtually puffed up with conceit. (p. 12; emphasis added)

In the Oriya passage, all the verb forms except in one sentence ('That is why the old woman would always see...' etc.) are in the present tense, whereas in the English, all the verb forms with the single exception ('Those who are smaller and weaker usually get more attention...' etc.) are in the past tense. That is, in the two passages, except in one sentence, the verb forms change in all the sentences. It is possible to point out such difference in the tense of verb forms throughout the two texts. But does this matter? Apparently it makes only minor difference and many readers and critics would not think it important. This difference is perhaps less important than the difference in the syntax. One can even argue that the verb forms in the Oriya and the English passages are really in the same tense (the past tense), and the verb forms in the Oriya passage, though in the present, are indicative of the past. Without exaggerating the way the change in the tense matters in making the English text different from the Oriya, it might be said that the tense, being indicative of time, might have something to do with the concept of time of the narrator, or the context of time of the narrative. Narrating a story in the present tense, however distant and old the story may be by implication, is suggestive of a sense of contemporaneity which a story narrated in the past tense might not carry. The predominance of the verbs in the past tense in the English rendering of *Matira Manisha* could suggest greater consistency and coherence in the time sequence but less sense of contemporaneity than the Oriya text does with its predominance of the verbs in the present tense. Because of the change in the tense, the tone and mood of the narrative does not remain the same. The Indian concept of time, with its emphasis on the eternal rather than the concrete and the transitory, could be related to the verb forms Indians use to indicate their sense of time. In *puranas* and folk tales the narrative is often in the present tense to indicate a sense of relevance and nearness.

Voice is another significant factor that differentiates English from Indian languages. In English, speakers perhaps take more liberty in changing the voice, and quite often it may not matter whether the sentence is in the active or passive voice. In Indian languages, however, the active voice is much more common than the passive and the change of voice may be quite significant.[4] Here are some sentences from *Matira Manisha* literally translated with the original voice retained. Lily Ray's translation follows each of them:

(A) Between the two daughters-in-law, the old woman's attention is a little more on the younger. (Lit. tr., p. 8)

Old Mother Pradhan kept an eye on Chhakari's wife... (Ray, p. 12)

(B) Call Sham Pradham if there is a quarrel inside or outside the village; if someone is sick or has any trouble, call Sham Pradhan; if a list of purchases for someone's household is to be made, call Sham Pradhan. (Lit. tr., p. 4)

When a dispute arose between two of the villagers Shyam Pradhan was called in to settle it. Pradhan was consulted when shopping lists had to be drawn up for weddings and purchases made and it was to him anyone in trouble turned for help. (Ray, p. 8)

(C) Old Sham Pradhan thinks, the naughty boy will be all right when the yoke falls on the shoulder. (Lit. tr., p. 14)

Shyam Pradhan had hoped the boy would lose his restlessness and steady down when he became accustomed to the yoke. (Ray, p. 17)

In (A), in the Oriya sentence, it is 'attention' (the Oriya word for 'attention' is *najar* which literally means 'eye-sight') which is the subject, whereas in the English rendering 'Old Mother Pradhan' is the subject. The author could have made 'Old Mother Pradhan' instead of 'the old woman's attention' the subject of the Oriya sentence without making much difference to the meaning. But by making 'the old woman's attention' the subject of the sentence, he adds a suffix to the Oriya synonym of 'attention' (*ta*) and this makes the sentence a little different from the one with 'Old Mother Pradhan' as the subject. The Oriya sentence suggests both the seriousness with which the old woman keeps an eye on the younger daughter-in-law and the sense of irony which is implied in the situation that the younger daughter-in-law is not as weak as the old woman thinks her to be.

In (B), the Oriya clause 'Call Sham Pradhan' and the English rendering 'Shyam Pradhan was called in' or 'was consulted' show not only a difference in the voice, but also in the 'person'. In the Oriya clause, the subject is 'you' whereas in the English it is 'they' (by them). The English clause suggests the popularity and importance of Sham Pradhan as much as the Oriya clause. But, by using the Oriya expression 'Call Sham Pradhan', the author refers to Sham Pradhan exactly the way a villager might do in his conversation, and the Oriya reader might feel as if he was hearing a villager praising a co-villager, Sham Pradhan.

In (C), the meaning of the two idiomatic expressions 'when the yoke falls on the shoulder' and 'when he became accustomed to the yoke' might not really differ much, although there is perhaps a little more emphasis on 'the yoke' in the Oriya sentence than in the English.

The changes in the syntax, the tense and the voice matter if one is to adequately render an Indian-language work into English. But they seem far less significant when it comes to transmitting cultural nuances of the Indian people as expressed in their languages to an alien language like English.

Comparing the literal translation with Ray's translation of the first passage of *Matira Manisha* (given earlier), we can notice considerable differences between the two. In the Oriya passage, the planets and satellites are described as playing the game of *chaka chaka bhaunri*. *Chaka chaka bhaunri* literally means circling round and round. It is also the name of a game which children play in the village street. In the game, a number of children circle round and round one child, singing a popular song which opens with the words, *chaka chaka bhaunri*. The novelist by bringing in the image of the game suggests a sense of playfulness and ordinariness though at the same time referring also to the profound significance of the planets circling round the sun. The circling of the earth and planets around the sun is an image which is repeated in the novel a number of times. For instance, in the third chapter, the novelist describes the death of Old Mrs Pradhan thus: 'The old woman died. The earth did not change, not even a thread. This old earth of ours went on circling round the familiar sun, as usual, with its usual speed' (pp. 21-22). And this is how, in chapter ten, the novelist refers to the fact that human nature has not undergone any change even though modern man is living in cities instead of jungles: 'Jungles were transformed to cities. Human nature remained what it was. Jealousy, envy and vanity continued to thrive. The earth is circling round the sun creating days, nights, months and years. The human race is flowing like a current. Kings, emperors, wars, acts of jealousy, pride and vanity have vanished from this earth' (literally translated from Oriya, p. 122).

Ray deleted the image of *chaka chaka bhaunri* from the first passage presumably for fear of making the image unintelligible to the reader. Since there is no equivalent in the English language of the phrase *chaka chaka bhaunri*, the translator had one choice – to retain the original expression and add a couple of words to explain the phrase. Instead, Ray introduced the phrase 'an unending game of blind man's buff' which is not in the original and is rather against the spirit of the image of *chaka chaka bhaunri*.

The passages in the original Oriya and in Ray's translation differ in several other ways. In the Oriya, the universe is referred to as *bishwabrahmanda*. *Brahmanda* meaning the 'universe', is a term of religious significance implying something like the manifestation of Brahma. In the Oriya *Bhāgabata*, the most popular and widely read religious work in Oriya villages, from which the novelist has quoted several times, one famous couplet describes God as one in whose hair-roots exist innumerable *brahmandas*. Ray's phrase 'the larger world of the cosmos' does not quite correspond to *brahmanda* with its Hindu association. Again, Oriya terms like *pruthibimata* (mother earth) are considerably distorted by Ray's use of words like *basundhara*. *Basundhara* is a Sanskrit word which is not there in the original and which, being a much used and hackneyed expression, the novelist has taken care to avoid.

Besides deleting expressions or changing expressions suggesting social and cultural nuances, Ray goes on interpreting facts which are just mentioned in the original, and such interpretation makes the translated text significantly different from the original. Here are some of the sentences translated literally followed by those translated by Ray:

(A) ... and the dry sand of the river has been drenched by the bitter tears of widows who came to take bath in the ceremony of the ghost. (lit. tr., p. 2)

The dry sand is flooded with the wild weeping of widowed women who came to take the cleansing ritual bath as required by custom on the conclusion of their husbands' last rites. (Ray, p. 6)

(B) From ancient times all the *dharma* of Padhanpara has been accumulated at the shrine of mother Mangala made up of black stone, under that Mandara plant. (lit. tr., p. 3)

Since time immemorial the faith of the people of Pradhan Para has centred around the black stone image of goddess Mangala which was set up a long time ago in a shrine at the base of a spreading tree. (Ray, p. 6)

In (A), the novelist uses the term *preta-kriya* (ghost-ceremony) which means the ceremony performed for the dead, and the bathing of the women in the river is a part of that ceremony. Ray translates the term in a long phrase, 'the cleansing ritual bath as required by custom on the conclusion of their husbands' last rites'. In (B), she adds a phrase 'image of goddess' which is not there in the original, and translates the Mandara plant as a spreading tree. The Mandara plant with its bright red flowers is associated with the Goddess Mangala with the red vermillion pasted upon her, and the omission of the tree distorts the original idea. The Mandara plant is not a spreading tree and the translator moves away from the original still further. Explanatory words like 'custom', 'ritual' and 'image', which are a part of the anthropologist's or the literary critic's jargon, are simply not to be found anywhere in the original.

As suggested earlier, it is not always possible to explain how several subtle linguistic devices of a work in an Indian language cannot be carried over to the English translation. Panigrahi's achievement in *Matira Manisha*, more than anything else, is in the way he uses the Oriya language; and it is not easy to convince a reader acquainted with the English translation alone that *Matira Manisha* is a fine work of art. The linguistic innovations which seem significant in the context of an Indian-language literature may even seem trivial to an English reader.[5]

Two examples might suggest Panigrahi's supple use of language which cannot be reproduced exactly in English translation. In the first passage referred to earlier, the novelist brings in the image of crores and crores of planets and satellites playing the game of *chaka chaka bhaunri* around their suns. In the Oriya passage, the contrast between 'one one sun' and 'crore crore planet satellite' (literal translations of the Oriya phrases) creates a poetic effect in the sense that the Oriya equivalents of 'one' and 'crore' (*Gotie* and *Kotie*) alliterate. Panigrahi presumably prefers the numerical adjective 'crore' to 'million' or 'thousand' to create a poetic effect. Ray replaces 'crore' by 'million', as the English reader might find it an easier number to comprehend.

Panigrahi, referring to the various dynasties that have ruled over the country leaving Padhanpara unaffected, introduces the image of the grass and the giant tree. The Oriya sentence can be literally translated thus: 'As Padhanpara, in all times, is the humble grass. Big trees tumble down in storms, but the news does not reach the grass' (p. 2). The contrast between the grass and the big tree is a hackneyed image in Indian literature. Panigrahi renders it fresh by contrasting the two terms at a linguistic level. He uses the colloquial word for grass (*ghasa*) and the Sanskrit word for big tree (*druma*). He could have referred to 'grass' and 'big tree' in several other ways – by using colloquial words for both, Sanskrit words for both or by using a Sanskrit word for 'grass' and a colloquial word for 'big tree'. He prefers a particular combination for a particular effect. Any of the combinations perhaps could be translated in the same way in English.

The difference, thus, between Panigrahi's novel in Oriya and its English translation suggests that Indian-language novels in English translation often fail to convey the original flavour.

NOTES

1. *Matira Manisha* (Berhampur, 1959), pp. 1-2. Subsequent page references are to this edition and are included in the text.
2. Lila Ray, *A House Undivided* (New Delhi: Hind Pocket Books, 1973), p. 5. Subsequent page references are to this edition and are included in the text.

3. My observation here is based on my knowledge of Oriya, Bengali and Hindi; but I presume that this is true of all Indo-Aryan languages, if not of Dravidan languages like Tamil, Telugu, Malayalam and Kannada. No systematic study seems to have been done so far comparing the tense of Indian languages with that of English, but some scholars have casually noticed the difference between Indian languages and English in regard to their tense. Nirad C. Chaudhury, interestingly, observes that in Sanskrit *puranas* the past and the future are very often not distinguishable (see *The Continent of Circe* (London: Chatto and Windus, 1965), pp. 57-58).

4. My observation here is again based on my knowledge of Oriya, Hindi and Bengali. S.R. Mukashi-Punekar, who writes both in Kannada and English, complains that by translating English sentences into Kannada, without changing the voice of the original, some translators working for the All India Radio, Indian-language dailies, etc. sometimes distort the meaning of the original. A sentence like 'National emergency was declared', translated in Kannada in passive voice, might change the meaning of 'emergency' to something like 'no danger at all'. (See S.R. Mukashi-Punekar, *The Indo-Anglian Creed* (Calcutta: Writers Workshop, 1972), p. 48.)

5. Adil Jussawalla in his 'Introduction' to *New Writing in India* (Penguin, 1974) rightly points out that linguistic innovations are among the major preoccupations of contemporary Indian writers. He observes, 'A large measure of a contemporary Indian writer's relevance to his own people depends on what he does to language – the degree to which he may break out of a classical mould, the extent to which he may make his written language approach the spoken' (p. 19). M. Mansinha suggests that the success of *Matira Manisha* can be understood in the context of the tradition of Fakiramohana Senapati (the first major Oriya novelist; a contemporary of Bankim Chandra Chatterjee). Mansinha writes, 'The novel [*Matira Manisha*] has carried forward the tradition of Fakiramohana in being written in a fluent colloquial style, and in not giving an incorrect pen-picture of Orissa's rural society' (*History of Oriya Literature* (New Delhi: Sahitya Academy, 1962), p. 250).

D.C.R.A. GOONETILLEKE

Sri Lankan Poetry in English: Getting Beyond the Colonial Heritage

In its continuing and growing vitality during the last three decades, Sri Lankan literature in English seems to be disproving the prophecies of gloom and even of doom made periodically with regard to it. In 1964, in *The Ceylon Observer*, Ashley Halpe said: 'Now, after more than a hundred years of Ceylonese writing in English, we can at last see the approach of the end. For those who have kept a finger on the pulse, the realisation must surely be accompanied by relief. Nothing of major significance has been achieved, nor is such an achievement likely in the short future that remains.'[1] In 1971, in his review-article 'New Ceylon English', T. Kandiah argued: 'there is no distinctively *Ceylonese* style for creative writing in English. If a distinctively Ceylonese style of writing had ever had a moment when it could have come into being, the creative writers had missed it.'[2] In 1981, in her 'Introduction' to *An Anthology of Modern Writing from Sri Lanka*, Ranjini Obeyesekere asserted: 'For the most part, the prognosis for creative writing in English in Sri Lanka is gloomy. As has been the case with the English theatre in Sri Lanka, creative writing in English is unlikely to have the chance for survival that its counterpart in India has.'[3] However, in the field of poetry in particular, Sri Lanka's English writers have reached a degree of achievement which compares favourably in quality with good poetry in English or in any language anywhere.

As in many countries, the colonial period in Sri Lanka was, despite fitful flashes, generally an era of mean achievement as far as original writing in English was concerned; it did produce the novel *The Village in the Jungle* (1913), still the finest imaginative work about the island, but that was by an Englishman, Leonard Woolf, just as the best creative work in the 19th century, *Forest Life in Ceylon* (1854), was by another Englishman, William Knighton. The presence of the colonial masters had a suffocating effect on the creative energies of the local inhabitants and it was only after Independence (1948) that a body of literature in English by Sri Lankans began to emerge. Actually, this had to wait till after 1956.

Sri Lanka was granted independence by Britain mainly as a consequence of the freedom struggle in India. Because this independence was won more easily – in fact, too easily – the Sri Lankans did not forge as strong a national consciousness as the Indians. In fact, neither country has been fully successful in this regard, if we are to judge by the separatist tendencies in both countries at the present time, but Sri Lanka has been much the less successful of the two, especially given the comparative smallness of scale of its problems, though these are no less acute than India's. Frantz Fanon, in *The Wretched of the Earth*, argues that violence is necessary in the process of decolonization to unify and truly liberate the native people. This is a stand I do not endorse, for I am mindful of the fact that violence can in itself be an evil responsible for great costs in both human and other terms. Even after Independence, the ruling and social elites in Sri Lanka consisted of 'brown sahibs'. But it did not take long for nationalist currents to surface, however extremist they might have been, and 1956 is, in several ways, a watershed in Sri Lankan history. Symbolically speaking, a national dress replaced the top hat and coat-tails, and English was displaced from its pre-eminent position as the official language and the medium of instruction in schools and universities. English had to be relegated to the status of a second language, sooner or later, despite the regrets of the English-educated classes, but it was not properly treated as such; it was neglected for two decades and even reviled. Paradoxically, it was in this context that literature in English by Sri Lankans came into prominence. Faced with the loss of, or at least a significant diminution of, their privileges, the English-educated became more aware of themselves and the social, cultural and literary response context in which they lived. Their response to the changes of 1956 was negative rather than positive, yet it led to fruitful results in the field of creative writing.

Of course, before 1956, poetry in English did exist in Sri Lanka. In fact, Ashley Halpe, in his article 'George Keyt: A Felicitation', claims that Keyt, who is well-known as a painter of extraordinary talent but who published three volumes of poetry around 1935-37 (*Poems*, *The Darkness Disrobed* and *Image in Absence*), is 'Sri Lanka's first modern poet', 'Sri Lanka's first authentically modern poetic voice',[4] but it seems to me that there is nothing of what one usually associates with modernity in spirit or form in Keyt's poetry even at its best and as art, modern or not, his poetry does not engage my interest:

> In a lonely place, among leafless branches,
> There are images seated in a circle,
> There are placid faces and unseeing eyes.
> In everlasting silence
> There are words spoken with voices from somewhere else,
> Very soft, very distant.
> The words are spoken, uttered in vibration,
> Around that lonely place,
> And the desolation listens.[5]

This is the abstract, pseudo-metaphysical kind of poetry one would expect Professor Godbole[6] to write if he were so inclined.

Around the mid-1930s and early 1940s, poetry was being written by the contributors to the Blue Page of the *Ceylon Daily News*[7] and the Kandy Lake poets, poetry which was not satisfactory or satisfying as art but did reveal tendencies of interest, both literary and social. Characteristic of this kind of poetry are these lines of Sunetha Wickremasinghe, a Kandy Lake poet:

> See the nights are dewy, sister; see the winds are friends to me
> Lone the moonlight breaths a whisper o'er the dreaming Mahaveli.....
> You may call it madness, sister, but to stay me, O 'tis vain,
> For the winds of freedom beckon, hark they call again, again –
> Yours the call of glorious wisdom, Learning's pathway high and steep
> But for me the starlit forests and the wonders of the deep.

These poets were obviously heavily influenced by the Romantics and Tennyson, to whom their literary education was restricted at school then, and also inspired partly by Indian poets such as Rabindranath Tagore and Sarojini Naidu and, even more so, by Rev. W.S. Senior's effort to be a bard of Lanka. It is a curious coincidence that, like the great Romantics who died young (Byron when he was 36 years old, Shelley when he was 30 and Keats at 26), most of them (Sunetha Wickremasinghe, Helen and Hector D'Alwis, Earle Mendis) suffered a similar fate. Nature and the human heart, treated in a manner reminiscent of the Georgians, were their main preoccupations and 'dreaming' was a keynote of the Kandy Lake poets. The human tendencies in the poetry reflect their well-to-do, alienated (that is, alienated from the mass of the people, their traditions and their problems) though well-meaning existence.

When our writers began to feel nationalist currents keenly after 1956, whatever their reaction to them, their central problem was that which faced all writers in ex-colonies at the same stage of literary development – that of reconciling their own sensibility, indigenous traditions and realities, on the one hand, and Western literary and other traditions and influences, on the other. The problem can be extremely difficult and lead to cultural dislocation: in his poem 'Stanley Meets Mutesa', David Rubadiri clearly wishes to suggest that the meeting of the two men represents a penetration of his own culture by the West, but the poem verges closely on the stereotyped Western account of the coming of the white man. But Gabriel Okara, in his poem 'Piano and Drums', is able to present the conflict of cultures more effectively from an African point of view.

In Sri Lanka, the predicament of the writer at this stage is partly illustrated by Ashley Halpe's poem 'The Boyhood of Chittha'. It is an account of, and a reaction to, his upbringing under the influence of two cultures. He first imbibes his native culture in the form of stories of old, which blend history and legend:

> Gemunu, tearing out brilliant ear-rings
> for the starved monk, reeked copious blood
> on golden shoulder-blades; his famous elephant
> was huge as a double-decker, wise as father;
> and Yasodhara blushed in every breeze,
> so fine her noble skin.[8]

His kind of progress is towards Western culture which moulds his early poetry:

> And so to Robin Hood, Drake-filled Devon,
> Prince Arthur, and Lancelot of the Lake,
> (Abridged and Simplified). At seven
> he versified – after a fashion –
>
> Horatius, Columbus, the evening star.[9]

Significantly, whatever he learnt of his own culture was from a servant who, moreover, 'not surprisingly, was sacked', and his bitterness towards both the circumstances into which he was born and his own divided personality is evident.

Given this kind of conditioning, it came naturally to a poet in the 1960s, Gamini Seneviratne, to write of his personal predicament in this vein in 'Two Songs of Myself':

> Am a lone wolf
> in the winter forest gnawing the ice.
> If I should see a man
> stamping into warmth on covered thighs
> I'd pull him down
> and tear at him.[10]

It is not illegitimate for a poet to use culturally alien (in this instance, extended) imagery. The poet has the right to exploit every area of experience and every resource of language, alien or not, and this kind of Western experience and language may even be regarded as having become international through common knowledge and currency. In a way, the crucial question is whether the poet communicates his meaning and, in this case, Seneviratne certainly does so on his own rather adolescent level. But all this is less than complete justification and *how well* he conveys his meaning is an important question: that Seneviratne should write in this manner is evidence of his deracination and his style is thereby less immediate.

It is a commonplace in literary criticism to adopt the position, as Ashley Halpe and D.M. de Silva do, in their 'Introduction' to *Selections of English Poetry for G.C.E. (A/L) 1973-74*, that 'the most characteristic problem of the Commonwealth poet is that of being caught between old and new, between inherited and acquired'.[11] What is more, this is stated as if this problem is everywhere and always true of Commonwealth poetry.

Actually, it is only partly true, and the problem ceased to be central or important a decade or two after independence from a colonial rule. With 'the clash of cultures' phase now over and behind them, the poets in the Commonwealth write as do their counterparts in Britain or America – out of their personal situations.

Another commonplace of literary criticism concerns what is regarded as a major problem for the Commonwealth writer, the choice or adoption of language, English. In the words of David Carroll (referring to African writers), in his book *Chinua Achebe*, 'We are faced with the paradox of a people describing and identifying themselves by means of a foreign language which embodies the values and categories from which they are seeking to free themselves'.[12] In Sri Lanka, the English language was taken for granted by many writers and posed no problem to many even during the early stages of our literary development, whereas, in others, it excited strong feelings and even contributed to dislocating personality. In 1965, in his 'Note' to his collection of poems *Lustre*, Lakdasa Wikkramasinha wrote:

> I have come to realise that I am using the language of the most despicable and loathsome people on earth; I have no wish to extend its life and range, enrich its tonality.
>
> To write in English is a form of cultural treason. I have had for the future to think of a way of circumventing this treason; I propose to do this by making my writing entirely immoralist and destructive.[13]

On the other hand, Yasmine Gooneratne takes to the English language without trauma and even approaches it as a lover in her poem 'This Language, This Woman':

> So do not call her slut, and alien,
> names born of envy and your own misuse
> that whisper how desire in secret runs.
> She has known greatness, borne illustrious sons,
> her mind's well-stored, her lovely nature's rich,
> filled with these splendid warm surprises which,
> now the distorting old connection's done,
> fit her to be your mistress, and my Muse.[14]

The diverse responses of the creative writers to English and their tendency to make the language of literature an issue especially during the early stages (that is, immediately after Independence) of Commonwealth Literature are valid, but not the arbitrary and the simplistic demands of critics. It is the generally accepted view of twentieth-century poets and critics that the language of poetry is more effective when it reflects the idiom of everyday speech. In his essay 'The Social Function of Poetry', T.S. Eliot argued:

> ... poetry has primarily to do with the expression of feeling and emotion; ... Emotion
> and feeling are best expressed in the common language of the people – that is, in
> the language common to all classes: the structure, the rhythm, the sound, the idiom
> of a language, express the personality of the people which speaks it ... a poet must
> take as his material his own language as it is actually spoken around him.[15]

In his essay 'Discoveries', W.B. Yeats thought: 'In literature, partly from
the lack of that spoken word which knits us to normal man, we have lost
in personality, in our delight in the whole man – blood, imagination, intellect, running together,'[16] and he sets out to make good this supposed loss
in his own later poetry, whilst in *Revaluation*, F.R. Leavis, perhaps the
most influential critic of this century and the counterpart of Johnson,
Coleridge and Matthew Arnold in their day, consistently lauds the poets
who employ the 'utterance, movement and intonation ... of the talking
voice'[17] (Donne, Hopkins, T.S. Eliot, for instance).

But it seems to me that this point of view is vulnerable. It ignores key
questions, though it is true that modern poets made a contribution to literature by re-introducing conversational tones after these had been virtually
banished for a long time in Romantic rhetoric and musicality (during the
Victorian period). Modern linguistics has sharpened our awareness of the
varieties of speech and dialects, of regional, class, group and individual
variations in speech of the same language within single countries. From
which kind of speech should the language of poetry draw sustenance?
Can there be universally applicable touchstones? How much does it
account for the achievements of modern poetry itself? Despite Yeats' declared view and though F.R. Leavis in *New Bearings in English Poetry*
praised Yeats' later poetry for employing 'the idiom and movement of
modern speech',[18] the language of Yeats' great poems such as 'Sailing to
Byzantium and 'Among School Children', though incorporating elements
of polite educated speech, is basically and in an overall way, stylized.
Really, what matters is whether poetry works as poetry, whatever the kind
of language that is employed.

Sri Lankan critics have adapted the position of the West in regard to the
language of poetry. In 'New Ceylon English', T. Kandiah argued that the
language of the Sri Lankan writer should reflect 'in an ideal form the
actual rhythms and idiom of living Ceylon English speech'[19] and even
further that the language of the Sri Lankan writer in English gains vitality
if 'derived from Sinhala', from the vernacular. The argument is also put
in a crude and dogmatic form by Quadri Ismail in his article 'Wanted: An
Offensive Poetry': 'no Lankan poet, seeking to evolve through his work a
Lankan identity, can hope to do so without an equal commitment to the
Lankan language.'[20] My criticism of Western writers and critics applies to
their Sri Lankan counterparts. Moreover, to be so conscious of language
and pay it special attention is to separate language from content and experience whereas, in the case of a truly creative writer, his experience will

find the language that comes naturally to it; this will determine its components, whether Sri Lankan or British or whatever mix. Lakdasa Wikkramasinha is often eulogized for employing Sri Lankan English in his poetry, yet his use of language is not a simple matter of doing so but is original, incorporating expressions derived from a variety of sources. Moreover, as Wole Soyinka said in a recent interview with Biodun Jeyifo, 'Soyinka at 50', 'we are now beyond the "Prospero-Caliban" syndrome of the complexities which attend the adoption of a language of colonial imposition', 'the "Prospero-Caliban" syndrome is dead'.[21] In our own region, Kamala Das in her poem, 'An Introduction', expresses the right spirit in regard to these matters:

> Why not leave
> Me alone, critics, friends, visiting cousins,
> Every one of you? Why not let me speak in
> Any language I like? The language I speak
> Becomes mine, its distortions, its queernesses
> All mine, mine alone.[22]

Probably, poetry will gain if writers and critics look upon language as their counterparts do in other fields. Kurt Vonnegut Jr, the American novelist, and Robert Penn Warren, in his fictional masterpiece, *All the King's Men*, took liberties with language; but no-one has taken them to task on a purely linguistic level for doing so. Writers everywhere, working in all genres, including poetry, should enjoy the same kind of freedom.

Yasmine Gooneratne is, probably, best known, especially outside Sri Lanka, for her work as a critic, but it seems to me that equally valuable is her poetry, found in her first two collections, *Word Bird Motif* and *The Lizard's Cry and Other Poems*. She possesses a mastery of the English language and literary forms in her poetry, whilst perhaps her greatest gift is her ability to think in images, especially when she transcends the Westernized upper class to which she belongs. In 'Peace-Game' she does so when she satirically and allegorically contemplates class conflict.

> We Evens were a well-fed lot
> and tough, so that the little patched
> and scrawny Odds would never dare
> to say the teams were not well matched.
> That was the beauty of the game,
> we chose the ground and made the rules,
> they couldn't really do a thing
> about it, stunted little fools.[23]

Satire is her strength, yet she is capable of combining it with deep feeling as in 'Words to a Daughter' and writing moving love poetry too as in 'Rocks on Marine Drive' and 'White Cranes'.

She was a Lecturer in English at the University of Peradeniya and then emigrated to Australia. Her first collection of poems appeared in 1971, her second in 1972, while *6000 Ft Death Dive* contains poems written in Australia, Honolulu and Sri Lanka between 1972 and 1981, nine years for a slim volume of 29 short poems, a performance disappointing for a poet so prolific earlier and explicable in terms of her emigration as portrayed in the poems themselves. She is still capable of writing warmly on the theme of love, but Australia has diminished her satiric fire and wrought changes. Lakshmi de Silva, in an unpublished radio review of the book, noticed a new tendency in her technique: 'It is as though the clarity and predictable precision of her earlier style has ceased to satisfy her and she is now exploring the resources of resonance, the depths and echoes that rim the edge of a poet's line.' More significant, however, is her new preoccupation with exile, the main subject of the volume, especially the difficulty of the writing of poetry in Australia. Like Coleridge in the 'Ode to Dejection', Yasmine Gooneratne in her new vein is communicating about an inability to communicate. Her position at the time as an alienated emigrant is, I think, responsible for the poetry in this volume not quite achieving the quality of her earlier works.

In point of actual poetic achievement, Yasmine Gooneratne and Patrick Fernando are Sri Lanka's most talented poets. Fernando's first book of poems was published in 1955 and the momentous changes of 1956 were not important in his case. In an interview with Yasmine Gooneratne published in the *Journal of South Asian Literature*, he said: 'A Ceylonese writing to be read by anybody anywhere cannot move in a field that is exclusively Ceylonese, or "oriental"' (p. 104). Perhaps he arrived at this point of view deductively: his poems possess a framework provided by Christianity (Roman Catholicism) and Western Classics; his poems have been published abroad (his 1955 collection was published in London and occasionally his poems have appeared in foreign anthologies too). However, it seems to me that, contrary to his pronouncement, he writes for a Sri Lankan educated public. Indeed, it is presumptuous to think that one is writing for an international reading public, not for those in one's own country.

Fernando's poems fall into several categories. His personal poems such as 'The Way of the Adjutant Stork' and genre pictures of Negombo fisherfolk such as 'The Fisherman Mourned by His Wife' and 'Sun and Rain on the West Coast' are among his weaker efforts. 'The Fisherman Mourned by His Wife' is generally praised by Sri Lankan critics and readers, but it appears to me that the effectiveness of the poem is undermined by its sentimentality, and such incidents as the wife recalling her deflowering seem inappropriate to her character and situation. The satirical poems such as 'The Late Sir Henry', 'Chorus on a Marriage' and 'Obsequies of the Late Anton Pompirelli, Bishop' are first-rate. It may appear as if the satire inhibits feeling, but the case is more complex: Fernando, concerned with feeling, satirises that lack of it. In fact, feeling is present in poems in all the categories. The Classical poems, written early in his career, are also fine. They capture the spirit of the originals, and those who know the Classical background will understand and appreciate them best. But these poems do possess a contemporary interest and Fernando is really writing of such permanent themes as the enduring power and tragic destiny of love in 'The Lament of Paris'. Later in his career, Fernando grew increasingly fond of writing symbolic poems, usually investing Nature with symbolic meanings such as the theme of procreation in 'Survivors' or the destruction of things beautiful and splendid by violent and incongruous forces in 'Life and Death of a Hawk'.[24]

At every stage in Fernando's career, irony is crucial to his work; it is a feature of his technique as well as what shapes his vision of life. It enables him to see contradictions as inherent in, and central to, life, and to reconcile himself to these. 'Folly and Wisdom' begins: 'Though her mind was rather small and its thoughts were quite absurd' and ends: 'The sparrows hop and wink and chirp 'But how could we have erred,/ We who in spite of all you say are not yet embittered?'[25] As M.I. Kuruvilla suggests in his seminal essay 'Modern Sri Lankan English Poetry', Fernando's language, like John Crowe Ransome's, is polished, minted, yet familiar, conversational, and his forms well crafted and orthodox.[26]

Yasmine Gooneratne, in her article 'Unhelpful Isolation: The Literary Correspondence of Patrick Fernando', observed of Fernando: 'He was firm in dissociating his own poetic practice from the technical experiments made by some poets in the 1960s and 1970s (including Lakdasa Wikkramasinha and myself) with a view to introducing a local sense into their English verse.'[27] Their view of the language of poetry is oversimple. In fact, in tone and quality, Yasmine Gooneratne generally resembles Patrick Fernando and both are different from Lakdasa Wikkramasinha. The latter is a radical, his radicalism being brought about partly by his traumatic reaction to his English affiliations. He spells out his credo in 'The Poet'; the images in the poem do not flow one into the other but they all cohere under the general banner of the poet as a rebel with a social and political consciousness.[28] Notwithstanding Wikkramasinha's posturing, the poem has an impact and helps us to understand him and others of his ilk. But Wikkramasinha had an aristocratic ancestry and, while his compassion would flow towards the underprivileged in society such as, for example, the servant girl exploited sexually and otherwise in 'The Death of Ashanthi'[29] and though he expresses scorn and anger towards his own kith and kin in the same poem, an ingrained aristocratic streak remains, suggested, for instance, by the fulsome praise accorded the feudal lady in 'From the Life of the Folk-poet Ysinno'.[30]

Wikkramasinha's, then, is not an integrated personality and it is from the tensions within him that his poetry and its vitality spring. He was conscious of his own worth as a poet: this lies behind the cheap humour he levels at the Professor in 'Work of a Professor', a deterioration of the satirical stance in his better poems:

> What does the Professor do?
> He plants brinjals
> all day because he's too
> intelligent
> to do anything else.
> But he loves his country;
> He loves poetry ...[31]

Wikkramasinha is the most original of our poets. His genius (evident in his ability to create a new stanza-form for each new experience) resides in his ability to unite Western and Sinhalese traditions in his poetry and in his ability to express himself freely as a Sri Lankan, exemplified for instance in the violent denunciation of imperialist exploitation in the guise of art in 'Don't Talk to Me About Matisse'.[32] These are abilities that belong to any major writer and Wikkramasinha has made the impact of a major writer in the small world of letters (in English) in Sri Lanka. Unfortunately Wikkramasinha died young (at the age of 37) and left behind only a handful of good (short) poems, without suggesting in what directions his undoubted talent might have developed.

To date Yasmine Gooneratne, Patrick Fernando and Lakdasa Wikkramasinha are our three important poets. The insurgency of 1971 and the present ethnic crisis have proved traumatic experiences and given rise to poetry. But our recent poets have not been able so far to reach the levels of their important predecessors, perhaps partly because they do not draw upon the Western traditions available to them as their predecessors did. But the very fact that the output of our recent poets is abundant, including good poems such as Jean Arasanayagam's 'A Question of Identity' and 'A Country at War' (published in the local journal *Navasilu* Volumes 7 & 8, 19-20, 21-4), augurs well for the future.

NOTES

1. Ashley Halpe, 'Contemporary Writers of English Poetry in our Country', *The Ceylon Observer* 14 September 1964, p. 2.
2. T. Kandiah, 'New Ceylon English', *New Ceylon Writing* (1971), pp. 91-2.
3. Ranjini Obeyesekere, 'Introduction to Part I', in Ranjini Obeyesekere & Chitra Fernando, eds, *An Anthology of Modern Writing from Sri Lanka* (Arizona: University of Arizona Press, 1981), p. 17.
4. Ashley Halpe, 'George Keyt: A Felicitation', *Navasilu* 1 (1976), p. 32.
5. George Keyt, *Poems* (Kandy: Gamini Press, 1936), p. 18.
6. The character in E.M. Forster's *A Passage to India*.

7. 'The Blue Page was actually a four-page pull-out on light-blue newsprint which came out each Friday as a magazine of features. Three-quarters of it were taken up with longish pieces on art and architecture, photographs by Lionel Wendt and essays by the famous Lankan writers of that time such as Andreas Nell, Major Raven-Hart, Dr R.L. Spittel, D.B. Dhanapala and E.M.W. (Sooty) Joseph. The back page was given over to young writers of English.' Tarzie Vittachi, 'Short Takes from the Past', *The New Lankan Review*, 4, 23.

8. Ashley Halpe, *Silent Arbiters* (Dehiwela: Tisara Prakasakayo, 1976), p. 2.

9. Ibid., pp. 2-3.

10. Gamini Seneviratne, *Twenty-Five Poems* (Colombo: Privately published, 1974), p. 1.

11. Ashley Halpe and D.M. De Silva, 'Introduction', *Selections of English Poetry for G.C.E. (A/L) 1973-74* (Colombo: Educational Publications Department, 1972), p. v.

12. David Carroll, *Chinua Achebe* (London: Macmillan, 1980), p. 23.

13. Lakdasa Wikkramasinha, *Lustre: Poems* (Kandy: Ariya, 1965), p. 51.

14. Yasmine Gooneratne, *Word Bird Motif: Poems* (Kandy: T.B.S. Godamunne & Sons, 1971), p. 48.

15. T.S. Eliot, 'The Social Function of Poetry', *On Poetry and Poets* (London: Faber, 1971), pp. 19, 22.

16. W.B. Yeats, 'Discoveries', *Essays and Introductions* (London: Macmillan, 1961), p. 266.

17. F.R. Leavis, *Revaluation* (London: Chatto & Windus, 1953), p. 11.

18. F.R. Leavis, *New Bearings in English Poetry* (London: Chatto & Windus, 1942), p. 42.

19. T. Kandiah, op. cit., p. 92.

20. Quadri Ismail, 'Wanted: An Offensive Poetry', *Lanka Guardian* 7, 6 (1984), p. 24.

21. Biodun Jeyifo, 'Soyinka at 50', *West Africa* 27 August 1984, pp. 1730, 1731.

22. Kamala Das in Yasmine Gooneratne, ed., *Poems from India, Sri Lanka, Malaysia & Singapore* (Hong Kong: Heinemann Asia, 1979), p. 10.

23. Yasmine Gooneratne, *Word Bird Motif*, p. 61.

24. See Patrick Fernando, *Selected Poems* (Delhi: Oxford University Press, 1984).

25. Patrick Fernando, *The Return of Ulysses* (London: Hand and Flower Press, 1955), pp. 26-7.

26. M.I. Kuruvilla, 'Modern Sri Lankan English Poetry', *Studies in World Literature* (Delhi: Sterling, 1984), p. 239.

27. Yasmine Gooneratne, 'Unhelpful Isolation: The Literary Correspondence of Patrick Fernando', *ACLALS Bulletin* Seventh Series 2 (1985), p. 103.

28. Lakdasa Wikkramasinha, *Lustre*, p. 46.

29. Lakdasa Wikkramasinha, *O Regal Blood* (Colombo: Praja Prakasakayo, 1975), p. 12.

30. Lakdasa Wikkramasinha, *Nossa Senhora Dos Chingalas: Poems 1965-1970* (Colombo: Praja Prakasakayo, 1973), p. 16.

31. Lakdasa Wikkramasinha, *The Grasshopper Gleaming* (Colombo: Felix Press, 1976), p. 20.

32. Lakdasa Wikkramasinha, *O Regal Blood*, p. 5.

RAJEEV S. PATKE

Canons and Canon-making in Indian Poetry in English

THE RELATION OF CANON TO HISTORICAL PERIOD

Canons are best seen as necessary evils. In a literary world beset by the clamour of a populous mediocrity, the principle of selection cuts with an elitist edge. Only thus can room be cleared – ostensibly, to preserve against fashion and time the authors and texts that the age would have us read and cherish; but also, and often covertly, to establish specific kinds of writing by displacing others in the polemic process that we call literary history. I propose to examine the dynamics of canon formation in such a perspective, and with particular reference to contemporary Indian poetry in English.

A convenient point of entry into the topic in its most general aspect is provided by Frank Kermode's 1987 Northcliffe lecture on 'Canon and Period':

> Judgements of value ... cannot possibly avoid assumptions about the workings of history.
>   It seems necessary, therefore, to say something general and elementary about the ways in which history is manipulated in the interests of literary valuation. There seem to be two main ways in which we try to make history manageable for literary purposes: by making canons that are in some sense transhistorical; and by inventing historical periods. (Kermode, pp. 108-9)[1]

The application of these general principles to the cultural situation in India, both to the contemporary literary scene as well as the literary accumulations of the past, may be clarified as follows: The usual way of making sense of such a body of writing is to treat it not as a mere sequence in time but as a historical process. The notion of process recognizes change as the effect of a cause which may be located in the literary sensibility of a culture. When a change in literary sensibility is shared by a number of authors, we see it nominalized as literary period. Canons are the textual embodiments of the values shared by a literary period. This notion of canon treats them as thoroughly historical, contingent on the values of specific periods. It should be distinguished from Kermode's notion of 'canons that are in some sense transhistorical', to which I shall return later.

THE INDIAN LITERARY SCENE

If we look closely at the history of Indian poetry in English we see that the management of literary periods has been accompanied by, and is indeed an outcome of, the struggle for power between alternative canons. As Kermode reminds us: 'canons are complicit with power; and canons are useful in that they enable us to handle otherwise unmanageable historical deposits' (Kermode, p. 115). In India, cultural independence has not necessarily followed upon the political independence of 1947. But at least in the field of Indian poetry in English, the 1950s are generally seen to mark the rise of a new kind of writing. This new writing was consolidated slowly by a few individuals in the 1960s; the next decade saw it well established; and it has for some time now been readily available, encapsulated and canonized, in the form of the anthology. The critical assumptions implicit in this new writing have generated a very sharply focused view of history. This has been achieved for the most part, and curiously enough, by the poets themselves, but in the role of anthologists.

Its double-edged principle of inclusion and exclusion makes the anthology an ideal instrument for canon formation. Every literary culture exhibits in some degree the desire of each generation to identify the significant authors and to put together a set of poetic 'touchstones' for its time. The anthology has been useful in serving both these ends. But the practice of poetry is an individual pursuit. Poets inevitably read other poets from the perspective of their own practice. This makes them, of necessity, subjective in preference and bias. When a poet compiles an anthology, a poetics may be inferred from what is chosen and what is kept out. When a whole generation of poets shares the same beliefs, and reflects them in a number of influential anthologies, we see the principle of inclusion operating in the service of a specific set of values as these are reflected in a canon. Concurrently, the principle of exclusion promotes a polemical differentiation of literary history into periods. Both phenomena may be seen writ large on the current Indian literary scene.

If we glance briefly at other cultures: in England, while Palgrave retained his popularity well beyond the Victorian period, the polemics of Georgian and Imagist poetry were primarily conducted through anthologies (whose principles and canons now wear a distinctly dated, historical look). Subsequent compilations by poets have only achieved notoriety: Yeats and Larkin come obviously to mind. It is in Eliot and Richards, and in Leavis and his *Scrutiny* that a truly significant new canon gets established. In America, there is a slight historical counterpart in the *Spoon River Anthology*; but with the exception of the expatriate Pound, the major poets have scarcely lent their names to anthologies at all, leaving the creation and academic absorption of a canon to the New Critic.

The Indian scene is interesting in that it is not academics nor critics but the poets themselves who have industriously set themselves to editing anthologies. This phenomenon has analogues in Australian poetry after the Second World War, and also in more recent poetry from Ireland. In the case of India, there are many compilations made by the interested outsider (e.g., Alden, Sergeant, McCord, Cevet), or by the academic (e.g. Gokak, Bandyopadhyay, Dwivedi), but the effective ones have been those compiled by the better poets themselves. These reveal a remarkable degree of concurrence in the choice of poets and even poems.[2] The consensus is accentuated by an emphatic and severe principle of exclusion. This has carved out a highly selective canon which has been widely and gratefully accepted by critics and academics. The institutional consolidation is evidently well on its way in a scholarly and historical work like Bruce King's *Modern Indian Poetry in English* (1987).

ANTHOLOGIES AS INSTRUMENTS OF CANON FORMATION

Why has the anthology proved the most expedient force for defining canons in India? And why or how have the poets proved so effective in this work of proscription and prescription? The efficacy of the anthology as an instrument for the dissemination of standards and values is related to the peculiar position occupied by English in India. While ubiquitous and virtually indispensable, it still functions as a poor second cousin of a language. It is learned only through books and bad teachers. Its general use is characterized by a stilted vocabulary, an impoverished idiom, and a poor control over expressive nuance, deprived of sustenance from any kind of spontaneous local rhythm except of the inadvertent kind.

1. Undeterred by the obvious hazards of putting such meagre command to literary use, the sheer quantity of versifiers and free versifiers threatens to swamp the reader of poetry. In this predicament the anthology offers a convenient short-cut.

2. The limits of poetic stamina necessarily dictate an almost universal preference for the short poem, and this is ideally suited to the narrow confines of the anthology (since very few venture, like Kolhatkar, into the long poem).

3. The Indian academic is a culturally derivative and diffident creature outside the already fenced in pastures of English and now American poetry, generally unable or unwilling to venture into the disorienting jungle of Indian verse; the anthology offers obvious comforts.

4. Where few read poetry but other poets, friends (perhaps enemies), and captive students, inclusion in an anthology can be more crucial for status among fellow-practitioners than publishing individual volumes,

which signify nothing beyond the willingness to pay for bringing out a book (generally with P.Lal). This status naturally brings with it the promise of eventual recognition abroad, which can then translate itself to academic ingestion at home.

5. The anthology is the only viable solution to the economics of marketing poetry in a relatively poor society inundated by the other mass-media and patronized reluctantly by the educational establishment.

6. The generally modest nature of the talent available hardly needs much more space than what an anthology provides.

These are some of the probable explanations for the dominance of the anthology in India. If the academic and the critic have fought shy of basic issues, the poets have been very eager, indeed anxious, to compose a canon and make explicit notions of value and period which would otherwise remain obliquities and implications of their own poetic practice.

The roll-call of significant anthologists is virtually a roll-call of the more prominent poets today: Saleem Peeradina (1972), Gauri Deshpande (1974), Adil Jussawalla (1974), R. Parthasarthy (1976), Keki N. Daruwalla (1980). There have been many other anthologies, which I deliberately omit from mention here, because they do not appear to have worked purposively or effectively enough in any specific direction. Their editorial principles or lack of principles are generally evident as a taste for the individually interesting poem, line, or image, rather than the significant poet. They dilute the strength of the deserving with the catholic inclusion of much dubious verse and worse. They either promote canons which do not achieve general recognition (e.g., Mallik & Bandopadhyay, 1981); or they form no sort of canon at all, abjuring the very function of the anthology.

In such a context, the current formation of a polemic canon should be seen as a necessary manoeuvre, undertaken in the spirit of a task better done by the poets rather than having it botched by academics, journalists, hacks or bureaucratic busybodies. There is litle doubt that the trend is a healthy one, and we should hope that it will continue even when the shy or arrogant academic has overcome his reluctance to engage with contemporary writing. It is of course possible, and even very tempting, to deal directly with alternative canons in terms of specific individuals and anthologies. For the moment, however, I find it useful to continue in a more generalized vein, both in order to disengage issues from personalities, and also in order to conceptualize these issues in a more comprehensive way.

IMITATION AND ADAPTION: AN EXPLANATORY MODEL

My first manoeuvre is to stipulate two sets of traits as characteristic of the Indian sensibility: imitativeness and adaptability. I submit these two characteristics as typical of the Indian, even if not prerogatively or uniquely so. Some such general set of binary terms is unavoidable in making sense of the sociology of any post-colonial culture. G. N. Devy, for instance, finds an identical dialectics between 'imitation-assimilation' in his survey of the problems of historiography in African and West Indian writing (Devy, pp. 82-3). It is clear that imitation can be the necessary first step toward adaptation and assimilation. But pure imitation is a form of identification with one's model, whereas true adaptation and assimilation recognize the need for differentiation from the model. In this sense adaption should be seen as moving away from pure imitation, and antithetical to it.

My second step is to take the most abstract approach possible to what may be described as the basic aspects or relations of any literary situation. Treating these relations as axiomatic, I shall map the struggle of canons in Indian poetry in terms of an explanatory model:[3]

reality	audience
X	B
.	.

poem
.

.	.
A	Y
poet	poetic medium

The model offers a representational map of the four principal aspects of a poem's existence: on one axis (A-B), its relation to the poet and to his audience; and on another axis (X-Y), the poem's relation on the one hand to the world of general human experience, the presumed common ground shared between the uniquely personal experiences of the writer and the reader; and on the other hand, to the microcosm of language and literature, to all the rules and conventions which enable language to communicate and express.

Now if we turn to the tension between imitation and adaptation that I have noted as the common or recurrent factor of the post-colonial literary experience, it becomes easier to perceive that the imitative and the adaptive tendencies imply differing poetics. These, in turn, affect and determine in different ways the set of relationships that I have mapped:

1. between the poet and his poems; in general, his sense of his literary identity and role;
2. the relation between the poet and his implied or actual audience;
3. the human issues and experiences which are the 'subject-matter' of the poetry, that which it refers to or is in some sense about;
4. the notions of linguistic usage and literary convention implied in the poetry: the dimensions of sound, tone, rhythm, metre, rhyme and prosody, as well as diction, syntax, idiom, grammar, style, and the literary semantics of genre.

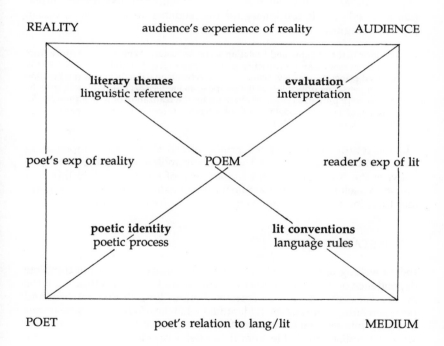

REALITY   audience's experience of reality   AUDIENCE

literary themes   **evaluation**
linguistic reference   interpretation

poet's exp of reality   POEM   reader's exp of lit

poetic identity   **lit conventions**
poetic process   language rules

POET   poet's relation to lang/lit   MEDIUM

IMITATION AS FREEDOM

Cultures like those of India, which have been subjugated and ruled over for extended periods, exhibit a long process of involuntary assimilation.

The values of such a culture reveal a combination of ones superimposed or borrowed with those developed indigenously. When these values are seen reflected or embodied in a literary canon, it serves as an ideal or a model, to implement or imitate. If we look momentarily and deliberately outside Commonwealth literature, we shall see these general truths exemplified in the tenets of the so-called Neoclassical tradition. English and European literature of the late 17th and the 18th centuries set up a self-conscious and complex set of relationships of dependency on Roman models in its practice of the whole gamut from imitation to adaptation, from pastiche to parody.

In an essay significantly titled 'Imitation as Freedom', W. K. Wimsatt asks of these imitations: 'When does this mesothesis of likeness and difference succeed in being a free, original, interesting, genuine and poetic expression?' and his own answer and explication of the oxymoron – imitation as freedom – is cautionary for the tendency to imitation in Indian poetry in English:

> The idea that burlesque and imitation were Augustan avenues of departure from the solemn models and constricting genre norms of the tradition ... [is a] commonly received principle, which we can invoke to advantage – if only we keep reiterating the compensating principle that the escape from models *was* fun, only so long as the models were present as fields of reference for the realization of new meanings. An imitation of a classic model is always a reference *to* and only thus a departure *from* the model. (Wimsatt, p. 464)

I shall return to the 'received principle' and Wimsatt's 'compensating principle' in due course, but I note in extrapolation that the difference between the Augustan and the Indian form of imitation lies in this, that imitation itself threatens to become for the Indian poet a constricting norm and tradition rather than an avenue of departure or freedom.

THE IMITATIVE CANON

Indian writing in English began in the 19th century in a spirit of complete dependence on the English poetic tradition, and more specifically on the norms and conventions then current: those of English Romanticism and post-Romantic Victorianism. It identified wholeheartedly with those norms and conventions, practising a craft which aimed at being seamlessly one with and indistinguishable from its model. Consider, for instance, verse like Sarojini Naidu's: 'She skims like a bird on the foam of a stream,/ She floats like a laugh on the lips of a dream' (in Parthasarthy, p. 3).

One must do more than just agree with R. Parthasarthy, that 'prosodically, her verse is excellent; as poetry, it disappoints', for indeed many a poetaster has done worse, and her lines could serve as a textbook example of efficient if facile anapaests; but that is not the point at all, for such craft resembles too sedulously a model which an ironic twist of history has ruled as of very little worth: in this case, Swinburne.

The poet's literary sensibility is adept in reproducing mannerisms of diction and metre and general 'poetic' effect, and in that sense, the copying is very intelligent and clever. But it is no way to cope with one's actual context of being, nor with the responsibility and burden of having to be distinctively oneself. Unconsciously, it vulgarizes itself before an English audience while patronizing and insulting the Indian. In identifying totally with the model, two crucial things are permitted to go disastrously wrong. Swinburne in his time and place may write which way he will. He may even be guilty of occasional self-parody. In the completely different world of experience that is India, for a woman to write as if she were a kind of Swinburne accidentally transposed to a charming garden from which she is to cull exotica for the English Southern Counties, is to abandon poetry for pastiche, and to be (not the nightingale of India, but) an ostrich in her own sand-plot.

That Swinburne is currently out of fashion is only partly relevant; though it does probably give the lie to Kermode's notion that canons are 'in some sense transhistorical', for perhaps they are never really outside history, but only as history dissembles provisional notions of transhistoricity. The kind of effect created by Sarojini Naidu would remain pastiche even if Swinburne were currently in high critical esteem, as he clearly was in her time. But fashions in India are notoriously slow in their emulation of the West, and poetry is still regarded widely among the literate as virtually synonymous with Victorian post-Romanticism. Modernism has had little impact except on the authors of the last two generations. A taste for poetry nurtured on the more imitable aspects of Romanticism finds perfectly acceptable condiments of both Swinburne and Sarojini Naidu.

The real issue lies in the difference between conscious and unconscious parody. An author like Shakespeare could be said to have transcended the vagaries of critical fashion, but Max Beerbohm's '"Savonarola" Brown' still remains a pastiche of Shakespeare. The vital difference between the amusement afforded by these two kinds of pastiche is that in dramatizing his imitator Brown, Beerbohm practises the conscious irony of parody, whereas Sarojini Naidu falls victim to the bathos of unconscious travesty. That the reputation of Shakespeare is higher than that of Swinburne, and with a much greater consensus through history, is actually beside the point. The issue is not one of the intrinsic worth of one's models at all (since worth is relative to history anyway), but depends on the manner of relating to one's models: with intelligent differentiation rather than rapt identification. The very style Sarojini Naidu adopts is aimed at expressing an affinity through total stylistic and rhetorical identification. This nullifies the scope for adaptation. She not only backed the wrong horse but, within the same metaphor as it were, she forgot that she was to run herself.

The moral exemplified in the lines from her would apply to a large portion of the verse written in India until quite recently. The models change ever so slightly, but always within a decadent post-Romantic canon. Such verse aims at little more than mimicry. Within the modest confines of its chosen humility, there is limited scope for skill: the prosody can be more or less fluent, the diction more or less vapid or turgid, the syntax more or less copious or stilted, the rhetoric more or less fulsome or flatulent; but the overall derivativeness hardly ever changes. This is the verse of the imitative canon of Indian writing: all the Dutts and the Naidus, and also the Tagores and Aurobindos when they write in English. It is a stunted tradition, stultified by its own affectation of fluency.

On the map of relations that I have proposed, it will be evident that the problem is located primarily at one end of the axis X-Y. It is to do with too slavish an adherence to the norms and register of a style which originated and belongs most naturally to a completely different literary context: that of the model culture, not a parental but a foster-parental or even mock-parental culture. The more completely faithful the act of imitation, the more successful may be the feat of stylistic ventriloquism, but the more exacting the price paid at all ends of the literary axiom: constrainment of audience; neglect or perversion of the demands of personal experience and environment; loss of poetic selfhood and identity.

In the routine verse of the imitative tradition, prosody and rhetoric, tone and nuance, all find a place; but only as a gigantic and unfunny joke, as an act of brutally insentient misappropriation. It would be difficult, thought not impossible, to define some redeeming criteria with which to salvage any part of this heavy deposit of history. In its own time, such verse had the novelty and charm of a distinctive and favoured manner of writing applied to a new and for the Westerner an exotic, and for the Indian, a native set of themes, images and topics. The manner underwent little change in adapting itself to new matter. Often the very notion of what should be the subject-matter of such poetry was conditioned by a priori notions of what might interest a patronizing audience.

The literary historian will continue to find extenuation in the argument that the 19th century Indian poet wrote chiefly for the English reader, and his later counterparts continue to write with an eye to the West, only adding a small like-minded elite from within India to their implied audience. However the argument will not rescue this form of imitative dependence from the charge of a snobbery which is venial only because it is so pathetic. In those rare cases where the imitation clears some free ground for genuine linguistic and stylistic adaptation, the verse manages to rise above its own self-imposed limits.

SINCERITY AND AUTHENTICITY: A WESTERN ALLEGORY

I have been looking so far at how the imitative strain in Indian poetry has suffered for its manner of following its models. But there is yet another dimension to consider: the fate of Indian post-Romanticism is subsumed in the fate of its very models. The forces of canon-making have been revising their view and valuation of what Kermode described as the deposits of history. The Western world has seen – through the 19th into the 20th century – a change of culture which is a change of literary sensibility and attitude. This syzygy is best explicated in terms of Lionel Trilling's Charles Eliot Norton lectures of 1970, where he traces the history of 'the moral mutation' between *Sincerity and Authenticity* (Trilling, p. 1). His terms define a master-plot for the familial supersession of Romanticism by Modernism.

The history traced by Trilling will serve as a virtual allegory for the struggle between alternative canons in Indian poetry in English. Let me briefly recapitulate some of its essential features. Sincerity 'refers primarily to a congruence between avowal and actual feeling ... sincerity is the avoidance of being false to any man through being true to one's own self' and 'the value ... attached to the enterprise of sincerity became a salient, perhaps a definitive, characteristic of Western culture for some four hundred years' (Trilling, pp. 2, 5, 6).

I would argue that it is precisely this concept of sincerity that we see unconsciously at work in the verses of Sarojini Naidu, Toru Dutt, Tagore and Aurobindo: it is the very principle of the tradition of imitation in India. In terms of my diagram, we can locate this as a shift in focus from point Y (the medium) to the relation A-X (between poet and his subject-matter, as this dictates a new sense of poetic identity). The imitative kind of poetry has suffered because there has been a 'sharp diminution of the authority' once exercised by the underlying concept. 'The devaluation of sincerity is bound up in an essential way with the mystique of the classic literature of our century' (Trilling, p. 6).

In the case of the Moderns:

> the criterion of sincerity, the calculation of the degree of congruence between feeling and avowal, is not pertinent to the judgement of their work ....they figure in our minds exactly as persons, as personalities, of a large exemplary kind, asking, each one of them, what his own self is and whether or not he is being true to it, drawing us to the emulation of their self-scrutiny. (Trilling, pp. 7-8)

THE CANON OF AUTHENTICITY

Turning now to persons and personalities, I remark that in India, and especially for the last two or three decades at least, one individual at least has been made exactly such a figure of an exemplary kind: Nissim Ezekiel. In asking his own self whether or not he is being true to it, he has succeeded, willy-nilly, in drawing younger poets to emulation. His slightly younger contemporary, A.K. Ramanujan, from abroad, and the slightly younger Kamala Das from at home, have pursued with an almost obsessive rigour (and varying degrees of success) a similar inquiry into what makes up their true being, and how they may be true to it. The modernist quest for the insecure certainties within selfhood, as exemplified in the Western tradition, has thus found eventual adepts in India.

One of our poet-anthologists, and an influential force in contemporary Indian poetry in English, Keki Daruwalla, concedes that the language of even his canonical writers 'remains a hybrid orchid raised on the mulch of classical dictionaries', and then procedes to quote from Ramanujan, and from Ezekiel's 'Philosophy':

> The landscape in its geologic prime
> Dissolves to show its quintessential slime.
> A million stars are blotted out. I think
> Of each historic passion as a blink
> That happened to the sad eye of time.

> (Daruwalla, p. xxxi)

If we look for the spirit of imitation here we shall see it, at the most obvious level, in the metre and the rhymes. In his own way Ezekiel is just as good a metrist as Sarojini Naidu. The syntactic role of that 'I think' is rather different from what she might have managed or appreciated, but otherwise, there is at work the same craft that she respected. How then is such poetry different from that of the earlier canon? At what level does the imitation move and develop toward adaptation, toward what Wimsatt in his context called 'imitation as freedom'?

It is in part a matter of subtlety and sophistication, of discrimination and nuance in balancing dependence with independence. Not all the verse by Sarojini Naidu or others of her persuasion is as bad as the example I have used, and it is both possible and necessary to perform a careful act of salvaging with the remnants of the imitative tradition, precisely because it is now so hopelessly out of currency.[4] Ezekiel's kind of verse too has its models, and is, in that sense, still loosely within a derivative framework. But, it might be argued, a less restricted sense of poetic identity, and a more flexible and discriminating notion of what constitutes adaptation is at work. It could be taken to represent a greater assimilation of its own models of metre and tone. In other words, it attempts to replace the principle of identity and identification with the principle of differentiation. In terms of style and tone it may be called post-lapsarian.

But at a more fundamental level the answer must remain a relativist or a purely historical one: the current model is Modernist rather than

Romantic. That which the poets think worth striving for – the underlying principle of rhetoric – is no longer sincerity, but authenticity. Trilling explains that :

> for the present I can rely on its suggesting a more strenuous moral experience than "sincerity" does, a more exigent concept of the self and of what being true to it consists in, a wider reference to the universe and man's place in it, and a less acceptant and genial view of the social circumstances of life. At the behest of the criterion of authenticity, much that was once thought to make up the very fabric of culture has come to seem of little account, mere fantasy or ritual, or downright falsification. (Trilling, p. 11)

It is at an identical behest that the entire fantasy or ritual of Indian post-Romanticism is in danger of being put away. In the complicities of power, one of the grimmer ways in which we handle the 'otherwise unmanageable deposits of history' (Kermode, p. 109) is to abandon them as mere detritus.

If we glance at our diagram we shall recognize that the issue is now focussed on the relation between X-A on the one hand, and A-Y on the other; the issue is the poet's conception of his own role and identity as these depend upon and arise from the needs and demands of his specific world of experience. It finds expression along the axis A-B, creating and conditioning its own specific kind of audience. Once again we see in India that it is the individual with finger alert on the pulse of authenticity who most completely fits Trilling's description of the modern canonical writer and 'his increasing concern with the actual, with the substance of life in all its ordinariness and lack of elevation':

> To emphasize the intractable material necessity of common life and what this implies of life's wonderlessness is to make all the more wonderful such moments of transcendence as may now and then occur. This, it will be recognized, is the basis of Joyce's conception of the 'epiphany', literally a 'showing forth'. The assumption of the epiphany is that human existence is in largest part compounded of the dullness and triviality of its routine, devitalized or paralysed by habit and the weight of necessity, and that what is occasionally shown forth, although it is not divinity as the traditional Christian meaning of the word would propose, is nevertheless appropriate to the idea of divinity: it is what we call spirit. Often what is disclosed is spirit in its very negation, as it has been diminished and immobilized by daily life. (Trilling, p. 89)

The transcendence that Trilling talks of is particularly difficult to earn in India, where the factors of daily living which diminish and immobilize are perhaps even more insidious than elsewhere. But when poets do struggle long and hard with these intractable factors, we get a poetry which is rooted in and grows out of these realities in a way that does not generally happen with Sarojini Naidu or Toru Dutt. The very notion of what are the realities of life in India is now conditioned by such verse. Its poetics is entirely at odds with the rhetorical assumptions of a Tagore or an Aurobindo. The new notion of 'real' or 'relevant' would question the older vision, negate it as blinkered and blurred. The reverse might very well be possible in a virtual sense, but it has little real consequence, because time and history function like a one-way path of no return. Once criteria of authenticity have become established, sincerity can no longer continue to function oblivious of the change which has overtaken it. There are many highly literate and literary individuals in India who still subscribe to what one might term the fallacy of anachronistic canons, denying that the notion of realism now established renders the old 'realities' obsolete. They might do well to reflect on the history of American poetry, where the Longfellows, once overtaken by the Whitmans, have had to call it a day for ever since. Once the hothouse roof is gone, it is no use cherishing the orchids, for the weeds must take over. It is in this context that lines like the following are significant, as the foundation of an alternative, modernist canon in Indian poetry:

1. Unsuitable for song as well as sense
    the island flowers into slums
    and skyscrapers, reflecting
    precisely the growth of my mind.
    I am here to find my way in it.
    ...
    How delight the soul with absolute
    sense of salvation, how
    hold to a single willed direction?
    I was born here and belong.

2. I have made my commitments now.
    This is one: to stay where I am,
    As others choose to give themselves
    In some remote and backward place.
    My backward place is where I am.

                                           (Nissim Ezekiel, in Peeradina, p. 7)

THE AESTHETICS OF AUTHENTICITY

It need not be supposed that this modernist commitment to the sheer ugliness or the mere ordinariness of the quotidian is necessarily remote from Romanticism. When pursued too hotly, as – for instance – by the many Bombay imitators of Ezekiel, it can become a tiresome shibboleth, no less an unconscious mockery of its own model than Sarojini Naidu in her worst moments was of her. But when truly epiphanic, the poetic insight, in its 'sudden disclosure transfigures the dull and ordinary, suffusing it with significance' (Trilling, p. 89). Trilling is careful in showing us how the archetypal modern epiphany, the heart of modern poetics, is not far removed from at least one of the two kinds of epiphany in Wordsworth, the sort which

> has as its locus and agent some unlikely person – a leech-gatherer, a bereft and deserted woman, an old man on the road – who, without intention, by something said or done, or not done, suddenly manifests the quality of his own particular being and thus implies the wonder of being in general....Lowness of social station, lowness even in a biological sense, is a necessary condition of the persons who provide Wordsworth's epiphanies.... We wonder, indeed, whether people as marginal to developed life as these can be thought to partake of full humanity; yet this is of course why Wordsworth has chosen them, for what epiphanies disclose is that these persons forcibly exist as human beings. (Trilling, p. 91)

Now consider how this offers a new perspective on all the ancestral figures invoked and exorcized with such an unrelenting passion in Ramanujan's poetry. It also places in a new light the engagingly misshapen figures of Ezekiel's very popular poems in Indian English: say his well-wisher of Miss Pushpa, or the completely total teetotaller. We are familiar with the effect, in these poems, of a different kind of imitation: socio-linguistic mimicry. The *dramatis personae* offer themselves in self-caricature: their uncouth vocabulary and mangled syntax, their outrageously funny but obviously sincere sentiments are set down for us to recognize as truly authentic: not as mere parody or the kind of satire that has even its Indian butt sniggering in fascinated self-recognition, but subsuming them, as a form of epiphany, as the inglorious but forcible truth about how meaning and significance inhere, for contemporary India, somewhere in the tragi-comic mismatch between human language and human being. The revolution in canon aesthetizes the mundane, the comic, the ugly, and the ridiculous. It makes it authentic.

Daruwalla's canonical sample from Ramanujan confirms the transfiguration from his personalized perspective:

> I smell upon this twisted
> blackbone tree the silk and white
> petal of my mother's youth.
> From her earrings three diamonds
> splash a handful of needles.

> (Daruwalla, p. xxxi)

So do the agonistic poems of Kamala Das, of whom R. Parthasarthy says: 'The despair is infectious' (Parthasarthy, p. 22), although he is not clear about how we might react to the infection. Authenticity is a blade that cuts two ways: 'Authenticity ... is a word of ominous import.... That the word has become a part of the moral slang of our day points to the peculiar nature of our fallen condition, our anxiety over the credibility of existence.' Moreover:

authenticity is implicitly a polemical concept, fulfilling its nature by dealing
aggressively with received and habitual opinion, aesthetic opinion in the first
instance, social and political opinion in the next. One topic of its polemic, which has
reference to both aesthetic and social opinion, is the error of the view that beauty
is the highest quality to which art may aspire. (Trilling, pp. 93, 94)

India is the ideal location for a tropology of despair. But 'beauty' in some
more or less traditional way was precisely what Sarojini Naidu or Toru
Dutt were after. Nathalie Sarraute's rejection of Flaubert's Emma has an
analogue in the Indian situation: 'the inauthenticity of Emma Bovary consists in her using as the stuff of her dreams the "cheap images drawn from
the most debased, discredited forms of romanticism"' (Trilling, p. 104). It
is precisely these facile, derivative notions that the alternative canon of
Indian poetry in English rejects. It replaces them with its own inverted
romanticism of the dull, the ugly and the negative. The polemics of
authenticity exhibit a remarkable congruence in their pursuit of what
might repel the conventional aesthete. This can be sampled at will from
the three anthologies generally recognized in India as instrumental in con-
solidating the canon (in chronological order): 1972 Saleem Peeradina; 1976
R. Parthasarthy; and 1980 Keki N. Daruwalla. The choice of subject-matter
and the manner of treating it form a virtual archetype through the three
anthologies. Consider, in passing, just the titles of some of the most
frequently anthologized poems from this canon: 'The Epilectic', 'The
Dance of the Eunuchs', 'The Freaks', 'Madness is a Country', 'Migraine',
'The Gnomes' (King, pp. 286-88, Chart 3). The choice of subject-matter and
corresponding range of tone, style and rhetoric bespeak a common poetics
and a shared notion of poetic role and function. In what it prescribes, the
new role and function is just as narrow, and in what it proscribes it is just
as sweeping, as the neo-Romantics; the only difference is that the directions are contrary. Prescription and proscription have reversed themselves.

Two other poets, or erstwhile poets, P. Lal and Pritish Nandy, have been
ubiquitous, tireless and very visible as anthologists. But, as Bruce King –
and Eunice de Souza before him (Peeradina, pp. 125-29) – remarks, 'Lal's
indiscriminate publication of writers came into conflict with the need to
establish standards', that is, the standards of good writing upheld by the
new canon, and pretty much the same objection is taken against Pritish
Nandy (King, pp. 73, 63). They fall in between the two traditions by trying
to accomodate poets randomly drawn from both; whereas the other three
anthologies tacitly recognize the mutually exclusive nature of the two
affiliations.

The canon formed by these three poet-anthologists comprises: Ezekiel,
Ramanujan, Kamala Das, Daruwalla, Arvind Mehrotra, Gieve Patel, R.
Parthasarthy, and Arun Kolhatkar.[5] To this two of the three editors add
Mahapatra. These nine poets constitute the substantive body of modern
Indian poets in English, a corpus to be identified more meaningfully with

poets and their shared poetics than simply with poems. To this select group one or the other anthology adds either Adil Jussawalla or Shiv Kumar, and to this future anthologies will no doubt, in time, add other names born after the 1921-1947 span covered by the present lot, or some older poets like Kersy Katrak or G.S. Sharat Chandra, whom Daruwalla admits to his canon.

What unites them is in part the principle of negation: the rejection of sincerity is accompanied by a complete alienation from most other kinds of past value-systems. The spirit of negation severs contact with and affinity for the traditions of thought, religion and culture indigenous to Asia and India. Consider the ambivalence and 'infectious despair' of one of the most well-known of the new canonical poems:

TASTE FOR TOMORROW

At Puri, the crows.
The one wide street
lolls out like a giant tongue.

Five faceless lepers move aside
as a priest passes by.

And at the street's end
the crowds thronging the temple door:
a huge holy flower
swaying in the wind of great reasons.

(Jayanta Mahapatra, in Daruwalla, p. 120)

Many of the Indian poets do translate, but nevertheless, the wealth of literatures in the other Indian languages has not been found a fruitful influence to writing in English. Even in the case of the bilingual Kolhatkar, as B. Nemade has remarked (1985), it is not clear what his English poems do that is not done better in the Marathi. In a positive light, what unites the new canon is the affiliation to a poetics of authenticity, and a general amenability to influences from Western Modernism and its sequels. Ezekiel's poetry practises principles not far removed from the Movement poets in England; and readers familiar with the Confessional examples of Lowell and Plath in America can greet the poems of Ramanujan and Kamala Das with ready recognition. Impressionism, Expressionism and Surrealism are more obviously at work in Kolhatkar and Mehrotra than Tukaram or Kabir. What this indicates is that the models sustaining contemporary writing in India are drawn from the West rather than from the past nearer home.

So long as the criteria and norms of the authenticist tradition continue to dominate, this canon will rule. But if the complicities of power displace or replace authenticity with some old or new principle, the more mechanical and glib parts of this canon too will become a deposit of history. This is as inevitable and no less paradoxical than that the canon of English poetry co-opts without coercion the poems of a neoclassical poetics alongside the Wordsworth who explicitly rejected it.

THE QUESTION OF 'TRANSHISTORICAL' CANONS

The most interesting question raised by this spectacle of the supersession of canons in India (and anywhere else) is the question of what Kermode describes in general terms as 'transhistorical' canons. Is there really any such thing as the true transcendence of history? Samuel Johnson clearly thought so when he announced with suitable aplomb that Shakespeare, in the eighteenth century, was finally ready 'to assume the dignity of an ancient and claim the privilege of established fame and prescriptive veneration' (Johnson, p. 58).

One may conclude then that an author is acknowledged as admissible into a privileged, transhistorical canon if two and more periods, each distinct from the other, find common value in the author. Such authors are the proof that there can be any common ground at all between the values and ideals of differing periods of literary culture. That this is possible is the only reason why any part of the past retains relevance for posterity. Transhistorical canons are thus the highest common factor between historical canons. But they should not be confused with the more ubiquitous sort of historical canon. All the general anthologies of poetry implicitly claim an identical transhistorical status for their canons. A good part of college and university teaching in the humanities treats the curriculum of primary texts as just such a 'transhistorical' canon, even when the methods of study recommended are historical, and the processes by which authors are let in or kept out are part of the polemics and politics of historical canons. After all, only a few are predestined for the neo-Calivinist election to transhistory. The longer a text retains a place in such a canon, the less the taint of history, and the more concealed the polemics which enabled it to enter the historical canon in the first place.

The present focus is on India in a temporal or diachronic perspective. If, for a moment, we move synchronously in geography, the cutting edge of the canonical scythe retains all its transhistorical sweep: thus, for instance, D.J. Enright's *Oxford Book of Contemporary Poetry* (1980) admits only Ramanujan into his canon, while B. Nemade has long been asking why the nightingales of India do not get the place of even crows in such anthologies. But then, Sarojini Naidu would not gain admittance to an authenticist canon even in India. So perhaps the reason has to do with *when* a canon is being formed, rather than *where* or *by whom*.

We have seen that the poets' politics of contemporary India reflects in its polemics a much larger rejection of the canon of sincerity. When a dependent literary culture breaks its historical process into two mutually hostile periods, there cannot be the common thread required for the choice items of a transhistorical posy or rosary. The same is perhaps also true of synchronous canons. What we are left with, for the time being, is simply disjunct threads. To tie them together to the spine of a single anthology is a matter of mere convenience. The tension can be sustained in meaningful debate only as oxymoron: two canons clearly distinguished as alternatives in a historical composite, whose claims to transhistory must yet wait on the ratification of succeeding periods. This might seem no better than the lame statistical crutch of consensus and longevity of reputation. But then, neither Samuel Johnson nor Frank Kermode base their notions of trans-history on anything other or better.

THE ROLE OF AN ANTHOLOGY FOR INDIAN POETRY IN ENGLISH

That is not to deny the use of such anthologies and their dissembling of transhistorical canons. On the contrary, one can even welcome it. But the only proper way to do this is to admit an historical awareness of period and canon directly into the organization of the anthology. Since the authenticist canon follows upon and displaces the imitative one, such an anthology would have to define chronology into two periods. This division would reflect the corollary to Kermode's axiom, that canons themselves constitute historical period. Such an anthology would have to raise and attempt to settle the question of what within the imitative tradition can be salvaged: of what if anything is adaptive within the imitative framework, to correspond to the freedom achieved in its rival and successor, the authenticist framework.

The efforts of Lal and Nandy did not represent this kind of anthology because they were far too catholic and indiscriminate and because they recognized no such period distinctions. Gokak's Sahitya Akademi collection does follow chronology (as does Dwivedi) but only in the sense of naive sequence, with no real attempt at defining a sense of historical period, and with little awareness of the implications of plural canons. These anthologists are much more comfortable with Tagore and Aurobindo than say Ramanujan or Kamala Das. There is little awareness of the irony inherent in quoting with gratification A. Norman Jeffares' praise of Aurobindo as 'the greatest Commonwealth poet of the 19th century' (Gokak, p. xxxvii), and yet going on to include poets completely at odds with the practice of Aurobindo. Likewise, Dwivedi is innocuously naive in reporting that 'During the fifties ... a definitive movement [arose] which was not restricted by a specific infrastructure of values or ideological considerations' (Dwivedi, p. 32). Gokak is only slightly better, conceding that 'A particular verbal mode of expressing romantic sensibility may have ended with Sarojini Naidu and her generation', but then misses the whole point of this historical perception by claiming that: 'it does not mean that romantic sensibility itself came to an end with her' (Gokak, pp. xxxvi-xxxvii).

He wants to keep his cake and yet has it spat on too. Opposing and mutually hostile poetics are made to lie side by side, uneasy bed-fellows unwillingly sharing the sheets of the same book. The coercion ought to fill the anthologist with much more unease and anxiety. Any such meaningful compilation would have to be much more explicit and cogent than Gokak's work about the criteria of transhistoricity. Alternatively, it ought to have adopted a pragmatically historicist approach, arguing for each of the two canons as valid for its time and age, although placed by historical process and sequence in a spirit of opposition and mutual exclusiveness, presenting them together as part of a historical dialectics rather than mere sequence and accident. Of all such miscellanies one can only say in exasperated malapropism:

> Reason, in itself confounded,
> Saw division grow together,
> To themselves yet either neither,
> Simple were so well compounded.

('The Phoenix and Turtle')

However, the attempt by Lal to provide some kind of a context for his poems is worth taking several steps further. It is a pity that his notion of help is limited to tiny photographs and wordy credos. Eunice de Souza is no doubt justified in her dismissal of all this as *frou frou* (in Peeradina, p. 126). But an editorial apparatus of information and sources, comments, insights, interviews and other related primary as well as secondary material, when selected and presented with a due respect to the text, could provide an enhancing – and not at all insurbodinatory – context. It would also place the two alternative canons in their true antithetical relation, providing for the present time the materials for a debate which today only gets resolved out of hand in the false favour of this or that canon, in its hasty effort to preempt a remote posterity. John Press, in his *Map of Modern Verse*, and Geoffrey Summerfield, in his Penguin collection of contemporary poets, *Worlds*, are instances of what I have in mind in terms of the kind of enhancing ambience a good anthology can create around its poems. Where the poets have done their work as anthologists – while Ezekiel or Ramanujan or Mahapatra can be persuaded to give us *their* anthologies – it is perhaps time now to call for a canonical stand-off, or perhaps, double-bluff. Anthologies too, like canons, are necessary evils.

NOTES

1. All page references to authors quoted by me are incorporated within the text in a parenthesis which gives name and page numbers; for full bibliographical details see the list of WORKS CITED given below.
2. cf King pp. 285-88: Chart 3.
3. I am indebted to M.H. Abrams, p. 7; whose model I modify.
4. Cf Eunice de Souza in Peeradina, pp. 128-9.
5. Cf King, p. 283, Chart 2.

WORKS CITED

Abrams, M.H., *The Mirror and the Lamp: Romantic Theory and the Critical Tradition* (New York: Oxford University Press, 1953).
Alden, Daisy, ed., *Poems from India* (New York: Thomas Crowell, 1969).
Bandyopadhyay, P., ed., *The Voice of the Indian Poet* (Calcutta: United Writers, 1975).
Beerbohm, Max, '"Savonarola" Brown' (1917), in *Seven Men and Two Others* (London: Oxford University Press, 1966), pp. 195-240.
Cevet, David, ed., *The Shell and the Rain: Poems from New India* (London: Allen & Unwin, 1973).
Daruwalla, Keki N., ed., *Two Decades of Indian Poetry 1960-1980* (Delhi: Vikas, 1980).
Devy, G.N., 'The Wind and the Roots: The Problem of Historiography of Commonwealth Literature', in Dieter Riemenschneider, ed., *The History & Historiography of Commonwealth Literature* (Tubingen: Verlag, 1983), pp. 78-90.
Dwivedi, A.N., ed., *Indian Poetry in English: A Literary History & Anthology* (Delhi: Arnold-Heinemann, 1980).
Gokak, V.K., ed., *The Golden Treasury of Indo-Anglian Poetry* (Delhi: Sahitya Akademi, 1983).
Johnson, Samuel, 'Preface' [1765], in W.K. Wimsatt, ed., *Dr Johnson on Shakespeare* (Harmondsworth: Penguin, 1969; sel. 1st pub. 1960).
Kermode, Frank, 'Canon and Period', in *History & Value: Clarendon & Northcliffe Lectures, 1987* (Oxford: Clarendon Press, 1988), pp. 108-127.
King, Bruce, *Modern Indian Poetry in English* (Delhi: Oxford University Press, 1987).
Lal, P., ed., *Modern Indian Poetry in English: An Anthology & a Credo* (Calcutta: Writers Workshop, 1969).
Mallik, K. & M. Bandopadhyay, eds., *19 Poets: An Anthology of Contemporary Indo-English Poetry* (Delhi: Prachi Prakashan, 1981).
McCord, Howard, ed., *Young Poets of India, Measure 3* (Bowling Green: Tribal Press, 1972).
Nandy, Pritish, ed., *Indian Poetry in English Today* (Delhi: Sterling, 1973).
Nemade, B.V., 'Arun Kolhatkar and Bilingual Poetry', in G.S. Amur, V.R.N. Pradhan, B.V. Nemade & N.K. Nihalani, eds., *Indian Readings in Commonwealth Literature* (Delhi: Sterling, 1985), pp. 71-86.
Parthasarthy, R., ed., *Ten Twentieth Century Indian Poets* (Delhi: Oxford University Press, 1976).
Peeradina, Saleem, ed., *Contemporary Indian Poetry in English: An Assessment and Selection* (Madras: Macmillan, 1972).
Press, John, *A Map of Modern Verse* (London: Oxford University Press, 1979).
Sergeant, Howard, ed., *Pergamon Poets 9: Poetry from India* (Oxford: Pergamon Press, 1970).

Summerfield, G., ed., *Worlds: Seven Modern Poets* (Harmondsworth: Penguin, 1974).
Trilling, Lionel, *Sincerity and Authenticity* (London: Oxford University Press, 1972).
Wimsatt, W.K., 'Imitation as Freedom: 1717-1798', in *Literary Criticism: Idea and Act. The English Institute, 1939-1972, Selected Essays* (Berkeley: University of California Press, 1974), pp. 463-82; first read at the Institute in 1968, and published in *Institute Papers: Forms of Lyric*, 1970.

ANNE WALMSLEY

From 'Nature' to 'Roots': School Anthologies and a Caribbean Canon

A canon of Caribbean literature? In 1964, at the first ACLALS Conference, a paper on any aspect of the literature and language of this newly independent, fragmented corner of the Commonwealth must have been a rarity. Even in 1974, a new collection of its short stories, poems, essays and plays was subtitled, 'The emerging English Literature of the West Indies'.[1] It seemed to me at first outrageous that already we should be asked to consider the formation of the 'canon' of a literature which is still so comparatively young, so vital and varied and self-renewing. For my concept of a 'canon' was of an artificial construct, imposed by an elite of literary pundits who decided what was good literature, and hence what should and should not be read: abhorrent in any society, and particularly in one which has so recently become free from the mantle of English literature and from criteria of quality determined in the metropolitan centre.

But the topic of this panel, linking canon formation with anthologies, invites another way of perceiving. Instead of the canon as a list of writers and literature determined from above or outside, the canon may be regarded as the literature which is most widely known, enjoyed, remembered; which is quoted and recalled, which is used by people to define their everyday experience and which in turn prompts them to redefine their own experience in words. Such a canon, formed by a widely-based consensus of people using a literature, is creatively operative and valid. I suggest that whatever canon of Caribbean literature now exists has resulted from the use in Caribbean schools of particular texts, and that these texts are primarily anthologies. The school use of texts: because schools are still where Caribbean literature is most widely read in Caribbean society. As Kenneth Ramchand opens his prose anthology, *West Indian Narrative* (1966, N. Ed 1980): 'The reading of literature outside school is not a general practice in the West Indies. Many people do not have enough leisure for reading much more than newspapers. Library facilities are not adequate in all districts. And not very many people can afford to buy novels or books of poems regularly.'[2] The texts are primarily anthologies: because they provide a selection of many writers' work and thus save the expense of buying many separate books, and relieve the teacher of the work of selecting and introducing them.

If, as I suggest, it is through school anthologies that indigenous, popular canon formation may take place, we must be alert to all the interests involved: those of the educational establishments – from universities and examination boards to the schools themselves; those of publishers – Caribbean and multi-national, of literature for the general reader and for schools; of critics – academic and general; of writers; and of anthologisers. These interests are closely inter-related and inter-dependent, and at the same time work as checks and balances on each other. The training of the academic critic may guide the teacher; the response of the students may influence the teacher; the experience of the teacher may restrain the anthologiser; the requirements of the examinations board may deter or stimulate the publisher. It is, I suggest, the dynamic arising from such a complexity of interests which makes canon formation through school anthologies a reality.

The earliest anthologies were confined to the literature of one of the then West Indian colonies, and grew from the nationalist movements of the 30s and 40s. By the mid-60s a few Caribbean-wide anthologies of prose fiction had been published: the Pioneer Press of Jamaica's *Caribbean Short Stories* (W. Adolphe Roberts, 1953), and Fabers' *West Indian Stories* (Andrew Salkey, 1960); of poetry, the *Kyk-over-al* No 22 *Anthology of West Indian Poetry* (A.J. Seymour, 1957). Anthologies of poems and stories were used in primary schools, in Jamaica at any rate. No selection existed for secondary schools, although by then plenty of good Caribbean prose and poetry had been published. Caribbean literature was not studied at the Universities of the West Indies and of Guyana (UWI and UG), and school teachers were not trained to teach it. The focus was on Cambridge, London, or Joint Board 'O' and 'A' level examinations and their English literature set texts. Hence the example which Merle Collins cites of her literary alienation when, as a young person in Grenada, she found herself quoting lines from Thomas Hardy – 'I leant against a coppice gate/ When frost was spectre grey'.[3] Hence writing such as this, by the secondary school students whom I taught in Jamaica:

> The country around, although it seems rather quiet from the bustle of the town, has its own beauty. There are canefields, dancing and swishing their leaves in the breeze while the sun shines happily down. There are low hills covered with evergreen shrub. The countryside is scattered here and there with houses surrounded by hedges. The countryside really looks as if the Queen of May is bestowing gifts on the countryside throughout the year, which attracts even a child's eye although he may not be able to express his feeling.[4]

The first anthologies for post-primary, early secondary school use were compiled by teachers and university lecturers, and came out from British educational publishers between 1966 and 1968. Their material was drawn from the earlier, nationally-based collections or from the 'little magazines' – *Focus*, *Bim* and *Kyk-over-Al*. Selection in these new school anthologies meant that poems and short fiction previously only read and known to a small educated elite, or the exclusive literary circles of Kingston or Georgetown, Bridgetown or Port of Spain, were read and studied by a young mass audience.

Dreams and Visions (John Figueroa, 1966)[5] was prepared and published when its editor was Professor of Education at UWI in Jamaica. Himself a poet, Figueroa had contributed to the BBC programme *Caribbean Voices*, the title of his two-part anthology; the programme's unpublished scripts formed the basis of his selection. The school focus determined which poets' work should be included in the first volume: hence his justification for representing Derek Walcott with only two poems, and for leaving out Louise Bennett and Edward Brathwaite, 'because their work is more suitable for Volume 2'.[6] Why were the direct, humorous ballads of Bennett judged unsuitable, but Evan Jones' 'Song of the Banana Man' was included? '"Praise God an' m' big right han'/ I will live an' die a banana man."' The middle class, outsider tone, viewpoint and use of 'dialect', was judged acceptable, but not the work-a-day ballad of a popular radio and theatre performer. Also in 1966 came the first collection of Caribbean prose for schools: Kenneth Ramchand's *West Indian Narrative*.[7] Ramchand, then a post-graduate research student at Edinburgh, knew from growing up in Trinidad how the generally indifferent attitudes to literature were formed at school. But in this anthology, he explained, 'literature is being presented as something to which we respond, not something which we learn'.[8] The selection confirmed and extended the 'canon' of prose writers first established by Salkey's Faber collection: Michael Anthony, E.R. Braithwaite, Jan Carew, Geoffrey Drayton, Wilson Harris, John Hearne, C.L.R. James, George Lamming, Roger Mais, Edgar Mittleholzer, V.S. Reid – and V.S. Naipaul, who had refused permission to Salkey. Ramchand also included extracts from novels by Namba Roy and Andrew Salkey, but dropped them in his 1980 new edition. In 1967 and 1968 the anthologies compiled by O.R. Dathorne, Guyanese novelist and university teacher, were published.[9] *Caribbean Verse* has been widely used in secondary schools; *Caribbean Prose*, however, seems to have been found far less useful than Ramchand's equivalent volume. In 1968, too, my anthology, *The Sun's Eye*[10] was published, for a younger age group. Its concept, and much of its content, dates from the early 60s when I taught English to the three junior forms of a Jamaican rural secondary school: a mix of prose and verse, which reflected the society and environment of my students and which they had enjoyed and responded to. The history of its publication shows up some of the current 'canon' determinants. When I offered a sample selection to the Publications Branch of the Jamaican Ministry of Education in 1961, they replied that their readers had not recommended it for publication: 'They found most of the extracts too sophisticated for pupils in the Senior School; moreover, the use of the vernacular creates a problem, as it is not the policy of the Branch to produce books containing dialect.'[11]

Then I tried Longmans, but without Ministry of Education co-publishing, they did not dare. They changed their minds when I offered it again in 1964, but still with the constraint that only in dialogue would 'dialect' be permitted. The verse and the prose were selected from similar sources but independently from what soon appeared in Figueroa's and Ramchand's anthologies. But our choice of authors, if not always of precise text, was often the same: in poetry, work by K.E. Ingram, E.M. Roach, Neville Dawes, Frank Collymore, P.M. Sherlock, A.J. Seymour, Derek Walcott; H.D. Carberry's 'Nature':

> We have neither Summer nor Winter
> Neither Autumn nor Spring.
> We have instead the days
> When the gold sun shines on the lush green canefields
> Magnificently.

and Evan Jones's 'Song of the Banana Man', in the Standard English form in which it had first appeared, in *Focus*. For prose, the same writers as Ramchand had chosen, without James, Mittelholzer and Harris; Naipaul refused to give me permission, saying that he was not interested in his work being read by young West Indians.

With these anthologies were the beginnings of 'classic' poems and prose fiction, of a 'canon' of writers, confirmed and spread: work which consciously described and reclaimed the Caribbean environment – what Edward Kamau Brathwaite has called 'the nativization of consciousness',[12] but in the traditional forms of English literature, and in predominantly Standard English. The young mass audience were the students in new Junior Secondary Schools: the first substantial post-Independence change in the education system of most of the Caribbean. For the first time, the schooling of children who failed the Common Entrance exam was taken seriously, and a new three-year non-academic curriculum was drawn up for Grades 7, 8 and 9. Because these students were not preparing for overseas exams they could study and enjoy their own literature. Cecil Gray, of the Department of Education, prepared a number of anthologies specially for this new curriculum, of which the prose *Response*[13] and the 3-book poetry *Bite In* have been extensively used.[14]

If the mid-60s anthologies were prompted by Independence and the demand for cultural decolonisation, those of the early 70s were a response to the new creative energy of the post-Independence social and cultural upheavals surrounding the Rodney affair in Jamaica (1968) and the Black Power revolt in Trinidad (1970). They were initiated and encouraged by writers and academics who had been active in the Caribbean Artists Movement (CAM) in London from 1966, and who had now returned to work in the Caribbean – Gordon Rohlehr to Trinidad and Don Wilson to Jamaica in 1967, Edward Brathwaite and Kenneth Ramchand to Jamaica in 1968. They brought with them a strong sense of regional identity, of concern for wider participation in West Indian literature at every level of society, and for the change of consciousness which such participation would bring. Don Wilson, in the Department of Education of UWI at Mona, encouraged a group of Dip. Ed. students to select West Indian poems for teaching in Jamaica's Junior Secondary Schools, and to compile the anthology *The New Ships*.[14] *Savacou*, CAM's co-operative publishing venture, brought it out in 1971, and the Ministry of Education bought and distributed it. Here again are 'Nature', 'Song of the Banana Man', and a few favourites already included in *Dreams and Visions* and *The Sun's Eye*: George Campbell's 'Litany' and K.E. Ingram's 'Sheep', A.L. Hendriks' 'A Old Jamaican Woman thinks about the Hereafter', and Dennis Scott's 'Bird'. But the range is now far wider, particularly in form and language. Louise Bennett poems in 'dialect' are included for all three three grades, and two poems by Edward Brathwaite for each of the two higher grades: work by both had been read and discussed at CAM meetings in London, where the language of Caribbean poetry was the topic of lively debate, especially following Gordon Rohlehr's landmark paper, 'Sparrow and the Language of Calypso'.[15] Edward Baugh, then Head of the English Department of UWI at Mona, in a Foreword, predicted that 'an anthology such as this one should help to foster among Jamaicans an awareness of the potential importance of poetry in human life'.[16] Kenneth Ramchand, now a lecturer in the English Department with Baugh, was working to fulfil the aim expressed in a letter to Brathwaite of January 1967, and which his experience and associations within CAM had strengthened: 'My ambition is to get back to the West Indies and try to make West Indian literature popular.'[17] Ramchand was a driving force behind the transformation of the UWI English syllabus at Mona and St Augustine, behind the teaching of West Indian literature in senior secondary schools and its study at 'O' level. Interviewed about his part in CAM he recalls: 'As graduates went out, the pressure grew. The texts were becoming available. We should not underestimate the activities that were going on at the University: the part they played in altering the consciousness in secondary school and in society as a whole and indeed in lifting the prestige of West Indian literature.'[18] With Cecil Gray, Ramchand established a course on the school teaching of West Indian poetry, from which developed their 1961 anthology, *West Indian Poetry*,[19] boldly pitched at Form 4 level. The anthology had generous representation of newly published work: by Brathwaite again, and notably by two new young writers, Anthony McNeill and Wayne Brown. Poems not in Standard English were placed in a section called, 'Dialect into Poetry': they ranged from Tom Redcam to Edward Brathwaite ('The Dust'), via Louise Bennett, A.L. Hendriks and Dennis Scott. Dialect poetry had been accepted in the canon, even if placed in a separate section.

School anthologies of the 80s have given generous space to new writing of the 70s. Their poetry has been drawn mainly from three issues of

CAM's journal, Savacou, its 'ground-breaking' anthologies: 3/4, *New Writing 1970* (1971); 9/10, *Writing Away from Home* (1972); and particularly from 14/15, *New Poets from Jamaica* (1979/80), which introduced to readers outside Jamaica work by five young women and four young men who were to become leading writers of the 80s, including Christine Craig, Pam Mordecai and Lorna Goodison; Oku Onuora and Michael Smith – much of the work in what is now generally known as 'nation language', Brathwaite's term.[20] These 1980s school anthologies were prepared, or adjusted, for the long-awaited Caribbean Examinations Council (CXC) literature B syllabus which first appeared in 1979. Since 1981, set texts have been prescribed for three-year periods and have included an anthology of poetry and a collection or anthology of short stories, with particular poems and stories specified for study, and with suggested lists of themes. In 1984 the first set texts in poetry – *Dreams and Visions* and *West Indian Poetry* – were succeeded by *Poetry Now* (Stewart Brown),[21] for two consecutive three-year periods. This anthology showed awareness of an existing canon and a conscious attempt to break into it: by excluding almost all poems written before 1964, and by giving a quarter of the space to poets of the 80s. Mervyn Morris, in his Foreword, points to how it, 'brings together writers of established reputation and some whose names are less familiar (but who have often been writing well for years)'.[22] He goes on to welcome the work of less familiar writers as ones whose poems 'seem to invite or require performance ... Oku Onuora, Malik, the late Mikey Smith'. Michael Smith's 'Roots' –

Roots

Youtman dem searchin
de crivices an corners
fi fem roots

    Lawwwwwwd
    an dem a roots
    an dem a roots

– is sandwiched between Basil McFarlane's 'Arawak Prologue' and Martin Carter's 'University of Hunger': the absence of a separate division for poems in 'nation language' indicates the new direction of the canon. Similarly, the early CXC choices of collections of short stories – *Ways of Sunlight* (Sam Selvon), *Miguel Street* (V.S. Naipaul), *Commonwealth Short Stories* (Anna Rutherford) – have been succeeded by the short fiction in an 80s anthology, *Facing the Sea: A New Anthology from the Caribbean Region,*[23] which I compiled with Nick Caistor, a Latin American literature specialist and translator. Two-thirds of the content is by writers from the English-speaking Caribbean, several of them young and relatively unknown; one-third is by writers from the French, Spanish and Dutch-speaking countries of the Caribbean, in translation. This anthology, too, grew from CAM, whose introduction to work by Aime Cesaire and Leon Damas, Alejo Carpentier and Nicolas Guillen, and whose insistence on regional consciousness, first prompted me to plan it. Longmans, by the way, proved less adventurous than the CXC Board; in 1983 they turned it down, on the grounds that it did not fit the syllabus. Heinemann were less short-sighted.

The two anthologies from which the current CXC selections of poems and short prose fiction are drawn demonstrate ways in which this school 'canon' has evolved from that of the 60s. The complete Caribbean language continuum is represented, from E.M. Roach's 'To My Mother' and V.S. Naipaul's 'His Chosen Calling' to Mikey Smith's 'Mi C-Yaan beLieVe it' and Victor Questel's prose monologue, 'On Mourning Ground'. In form, linear prose narrative is extended to more complex structures; rhythms echoing English poetry are jostled by those drawn from the beat of peoples' speech and music. Suggested themes now include 'The Supernatural', thus accommodating the magic realism of Gabriel Garcia Marquez and Carlos Fuentes' contemporary treatment of Aztec myth, and so opening the door of the 'canon' to Anglophone Caribbean writing which explores its subterranean folk culture. Indeed, the themes suggested by the CXC, perhaps more than any other single element, have ensured that the writing included in school anthologies moved on from 'Nature' and widened beyond straight narrative or realistic description of the Caribbean environment and society.

Caribbean anthologies have, over a 60-year period, constantly been re-selected and renewed. The anthologies of each decade have built on past anthologies and brought in new work. Since the 1960s anthologies have been widely used in schools. If, as I suggest, it is here that indigenous broadly-based canon formation takes place, all the interests need to be alert to overweight from any one direction. Caribbean poetry had until recently been spared an establishment, definitive anthology, a Palgrave or an Oxford Book. *The Penguin Book of Caribbean Verse* (Paula Burnett, 1986)[24] is widely welcomed for its comprehensive, judicious selection, but not for its division of poets into 'The Oral Tradition' and 'The Literary Tradition'. As Mervyn Morris puts it, 'Segregating the poets into these two classes, separate but equal, the editor has missed a signal opportunity to keep (and to show) us truly together. The organisation of her anthology encourages notions of "Them" and "Us".'[25] More such voices may be needed to guard such segregation from becoming enshrined in the canon. The latest anthology, the eagerly awaited new edition of *West Indian Poetry* (Ramchand and Gray, 1989) is also divided into two parts: not by literary tradition, but between 'popular, well-established poets', 'major landmarks in Caribbean Poetry', and 'less established poets and further material from major poets'.[26] The anthology now contains, in Part One, all ten poems on the current CXC set list, and seven from the previous three-year list: the consensus of previous anthologisers' choice, already selected by the CXC Board, re-selected by anthologisers who are or have been university teachers. May there be a danger of freezing the 'canon'?

Giving the Guyana Prize Feature Address in Georgetown, in December 1987, Gordon Rohlehr spoke of how, 'Certain aspects of our consciousness have become paralysed in ancient attitudes of crippledom... Our neo-colonial situation of simultaneous freedom and mental enchainment is one of deep and perplexing paradox.'[27] If a Caribbean canon is being formed through anthologies used in schools, then I, an Englishwoman, have represented many interests: of teacher and critic, of anthologiser and publisher. I know myself vulnerable to charges of colonialism and neo-colonialism. As a young Trinidadian woman in London says each time we meet: 'Why do people like you go on producing Caribbean anthologies, why don't more of our people have the confidence to do so?' Equally, I know the strength of other interests in this complex of canon determinants. I wish them well in keeping on with the checks and balances, in working together towards constant renewal of a canon which enables full Caribbean consciousness and creativity.

NOTES

1. James T. Livingston, ed., *Caribbean Rhythms: The Emerging English Literature of the West Indies* (Washington: Washington Square Press, 1974).

2. Kenneth Ramchand, ed., *West Indian Narrative: An Introductory Anthology* (London: Nelson, 1966; Revised Edition, 1980).

3. Merle Collins, 'The Writer and Cultural Identity', talk at the Commonwealth Institute, London, 8.5.89; also, but misquoted, in Keith Thomas, 'A Shared Teaching Experience with Merle Collins', in *Wasafiri* No 8, Spring 1988.

4. A similar example from my students' written work was quoted by Edward Kamau Brathwaite in *Contradictory Omens* (Kingston, Jamaica: Savacou Publications, 1974), p. 17.

5. John Figueroa, ed., *Caribbean Voices: An Anthology of West Indian Poetry*, Volume I, *Dreams and Visions* (London: Evans, 1966).

6. Ibid, p. xiii.

7. Ramchand, op. cit.

8. Ibid, p. vii.

9. O.R. Dathorne, ed., *Caribbean Narrative: An Anthology of West Indian Writing* (London: Heinemann 1967); O.R. Dathorne, ed., *Caribbean Verse*, (London: Heinemann, 1967).

10. Anne Walmsley, ed., *The Sun's Eye: West Indian Writing for Young Readers* (London: Longmans Green, 1968: New Edition, Harlow: Longman Caribbean, 1989).

11. Letter from Clifton R. Smith for Permanent Secretary, Ministry of Education, Jamaica, to Anne Walmsley, 30.5.61.

12. Edward Kamau Brathwaite, ed., *Savacou 14/15, New Poets from Jamaica: An Anthology*, 1979, p. 3.

13. Cecil Gray, ed., *Response: A Course in Narrative Comprehension and Composition for Caribbean Secondary Schools* (London: Nelson, 1969).

14. D.G. Wilson, ed., *The New Ships: An Anthology of West Indian Poems* (Kingston, Jamaica: Savacou Publications, 1971).
15. Gordon Rohlehr, 'Sparrow and the Language of Calypso', talk given to the Caribbean Artists Movement at the West Indian Students Centre, London, 7.4.67, reprinted in *Savacou* 2, September 1970.
16. Wilson, op. cit., p. iv.
17. Letter from Kenneth Ramchand to Edward Brathwaite, 4.1.67.
18. Kenneth Ramchand interviewed by Anne Walmsley, 29.7.86.
19. Kenneth Ramchand and Cecil Gray, ed., *West Indian Poetry: An Anthology for Schools* (Harlow: Longman Caribbean, 1971; New Edition, 1989).
20. Edward Kamau Brathwaite, *History of the Voice: The Development of Nation Language in Anglophone Caribbean Poetry* (London & Port of Spain: New Beacon, 1984).
21. Stewart Brown, ed., *Caribbean Poetry Now* (London: Hodder and Stoughton, 1984).
22. Mervyn Morris, Foreword, in Brown op. cit., p vi.
23. Anne Walmsley and Nick Caistor, ed., *Facing the Sea: A New Anthology from the Caribbean Region* (London: Heinemann, 1986).
24. Paula Burnett, ed., *The Penguin Book of Caribbean Verse* (Harmondsworth: Penguin, 1986).
25. Mervyn Morris, 'Printing the Performance: "Them" and "Us"', paper given to the XIIth Annual Conference of the German-Speaking Countries on the New Literatures in English, Giessen, 14-18 June 1989, pp. 11, 12.
26. Kenneth Ramchand & Cecil Gray, ed., *West Indian Poetry* (New Edition, (Harlow: Longman Caribbean, 1989), back cover.
27. Gordon Rohlehr, 'Trophy and Catastrophe', *Kyk-over-al* No 38, June 1988, p. 22.

NEW STRATEGIES/
TRANSFORMATIVE IMAGES

It is those who in all honesty and earnestness are looking at the horse and not the rider, who can fit neatly into no tradition except one that is in the making.
        Nayantara Sahgal, 'The Schizophrenic Imagination'

To write is to claim a text of one's own; textuality is an instrument of territorial repossession; because the other confers on us an identity that alienates us from ourselves, narrative is crucial to the discovery of our selfhood.
        Nuruddin Farah

SIMON GIKANDI

The Politics and Poetics of National Formation: Recent African Writing

The Politics of Post-colonial Narratives

A useful starting point in my consideration of the politics and poetics of recent African writing is provided by Abiola Irele, the eminent Nigerian critic, who observes, at the beginning of a recent survey of contemporary thought in French Speaking Africa, that 'there is beginning to be a redefinition of what we may call the "African problematic", and this redefinition appears to be related to the changed realities of the contemporary African situation in the post-colonial era.'[1] Three key terms in Irele's assertion will frame my discussion and will help us to understand the function and nature of recent African writing, especially its continued concern with, and appeal to, notions of national identity and relations of power and knowledge in the post-colonial state: the African situation as a problematic with inherent theoretical problems, the redefinition of the African terrain, and the assumption that the African space is indeed defined by changed political and social realities.

First of all, African writers and intellectuals are increasingly beginning to realize that Africa is not simply an entity whose nature and history can be taken for granted; rather, the African space is being re-configured as a theoretical problematic in the sense the term has been defined by Althusser and Foucault among others.[2] As a problematic, Africa is not considered to be a historical reality, a linguistic entity, or even a philosophical concept which exists in isolation from other systems of discourse; rather, there is an impulse to analyze the African terrain as part of a discursive formation which functions 'in the theoretical or ideological framework in which it is used'.[3] Instead of assuming that there is a unified African world view, African writers are beginning to pay closer attention to the discursive systems, both native and foreign, through which, to quote V.Y. Mudimbe, 'African worlds have been established as realities for knowledge.'[4] Such discursive systems, as Mudimbe argues in *The Invention of Africa*, are often the foundations of an African order of knowledge, and 'today Africans themselves read, challenge, rewrite these discourses as a way of explicating and defining their culture, history, and being'.[5]

The second important term in Irele's proposition is the strategy of re-definition inferred in any re-reading of African literature: African writers are increasingly obsessed with questions of redefining the African context and the transformation it has been undergoing since independence. If pre-vious paradigms and literary ideologies, such as Negritude and the Afri-can personality, and the narratives they generated, were predicated on the assumption that African cultures and selves were natural and holistic entities which colonialism had repressed and which it was the duty of the African writer, in the period of decolonization, to recover (if only the right linguistic and narrative tools could be developed), there is now an urgent need to question the ideological foundations on which the narratives of decolonization were constructed. In the colonial period, narration, and related acts of cultural production, were predicated on a simple ethical assumption: it was the duty of the African writer to recover the African political unconscious, a fundamental history which colonialism had re-pressed.[6] Indeed, in the nationalist period, it was taken for granted that the liberation of the nation was an important precondition for the genera-tion of an 'authentic' African narrative. Clearly, nation, national conscious-ness, and narration would walk hand in hand in African literature.

Nothing illustrates this emmis better than Frantz Fanon's influential theorizing on the relationship between the nation, national consciousness and cultural production in *The Wretched of the Earth*. For Fanon, the legit-imacy of the nation was nothing less than the enabling condition for a new post-colonial culture; as a result, it was imperative that strategies of narration – in the narratives of the nation – be geared toward asserting this legitimacy, in the process restoring the form and content which the colonizer had emptied from the natives' mentality. Because the colonial ideological machinery was driven by what Fanon saw as a perverted logic, one bent on distorting, disfiguring and destroying the oppressed people and their history, the narrative of liberation derived its authority from its capacity to realize the 'truths of the nation'.[7] The African problematic was hence defined by its manichean relationship to the very colonial culture it sought to negate.

In the first decade of independence, however, the colonizer/colonized paradigm became more complex, forcing African writers to reassess their commitment to the 'truths of the nation', leading to the rise of the so-called literature of disillusionment. The forms and ideologies of works such as Ngugi wa Thiong'o's *A Grain of Wheat*, Chinua Achebe's *A Man of the People*, Wole Soyinka's *The Interpreters*, and Ayi Kwei Armah's *The Beautyful Ones Are Not Yet Born* seemed to have been over-determined by their author's disillusionment with the ideals of the nation evoked in earlier African texts. In the texts of the 1960s, narrative strategies are propelled by the belief that African countries had entered a neo-colonial phase, one in which colonial structures and institutions continued their gigantic hold on the new states wearing the ideological masks of blackness and modernity. But as Neil Lazarus has persuasively argued, this notion of independence as a fraud was based on an ideological misunderstanding, not so much of the terms of liberation and its narrative claims, but of the possibilities of an epistemological revolution inherent in the decolonization gesture; the literature of 'disillusionment'

> remained possessed of the illusion that the era of independence marked a revolutionary conjuncture in African societies. It was this illusion that motivated the intellectual obsession with loss and failure and betrayal in these works of the 1960s. As such the prevalent way of thinking about post-colonialism, as it was articulated during that decade, can be said to have been predicated upon a preliminary overestimation of the emancipatory potential of independence.[8]

Furthermore, the literature of 'disillusionment', like the narratives of decolonization before, still suffered from the values and images generated by colonial discourse, even as it sought to evoke a world beyond colonial structures. To paraphrase Foucault's famous discussion of the relationship between madness and leprosy, colonialism had disappeared but its structures remained; thus the substitution of the theme of colonialism for that of neo-colonialism 'does not mark a break, but rather a torsion within the same anxiety'.[9] In this context, the third term in Irele's assertion – 'the changed realities of the contemporary African situation' – points to new conditions of possibility, signals ways in which recent African writing has attempted to break away from the colonial paradigm and its anxieties. For in trying to redefine the African context, and the forms which it takes in narrative and discourse, it is no longer enough to cast African culture as one long struggle with colonialism, a struggle which continues into the post-colonial period; in spite of the dominance of colonial structures and the colonial episteme in many African countries, there is a need to recognize, at least on the cultural level, that the 'paradigmatic oppositions' engendered by colonialism are no longer enough to account for the contemporary African situation.[10]

My thesis here is that a new African literature is emerging in which notions of betrayal and the failure of nationalism are seen as inadequate strategies for representing and explaining a post-colonial situation which is proving to be much more confusing than earlier theories of neocolonialism entail. Writers who still seem to believe that the post-colonial situation is simply the continuation of colonialism under the guise of independence, or that the narratives of decolonization can be projected into the post-colonial world, seem to be entrapped in an ideological and narrative cul-de-sac. Ngugi's new novel, *Matigari*, is exemplary in this regard; it is both a symptom of the problems which arise when the narrative of decolonization is evoked in a transformed post-colonial era and a commentary on the problematics of a belated national narrative.[11] The novel sustains a rhetoric which privileges the colonial paradigm and its anxieties, but it also uniquely ironizes the ideological assumption that national independence is a mask for new forms of colonialism. Thus, Matigari, the subject of the novel, is bewildered by the post-colonial scene precisely because his mode of knowledge is still imprisoned in the romance of the nation and of national independence, both notions triggered by the colonial epistemology.

If we accept the basic assumption that the desire for national independence is generated by colonial independence, then this desire and the forms it takes are still functions of the colonial episteme. What Ngugi does not allow for – hence his conception of Matigari as a heroic and allegorical character – is that the paradigms that define the nation, and hence the discourse on liberation, have changed while the hero was in the forest. Matigari, like the African writer in the nationalist period, conceived the nation as the highest stage of African consciousness; the national interest (embodied in the novel by the hero's house) was a divine right to be fought for and protected. In the post-colonial situation, however, the divinity of the nation has collapsed; the nation is not the manifestation of a common interest but a repressor of desires; class alliances are sometimes confused for, or rationalized by, ethnic configurations. In the circumstances, Matigari's search for his house is notable for the innocence that underlies it as well as its historical belatedness.[12] Matigari seems to search for truth in a world which he is not even equipped to understand; his mode of knowledge is structured in a Christian allegorical structure which pits goodness against evil, but the resulting insights are also forms of blindness. In other words, what Matigari does not understand is more important than what he purports to know. And there are many things which Matigari does not comprehend: there is intractable warfare between members of the ruling class which goes beyond the patriot/betrayer dichotomy; women now constitute a new and important centre of identity and are not simply whoring figures who offer their bodies to help the hero in the task of liberation. In short, Matigari is a prisoner of the emancipatory narrative he promotes.

Of course, the allegory of the nation is confounded by the fact that the national interest, which seemed so clear during the struggle for independence, has become paradoxical. Our new global situation demands narratives which face up to the task of representing the ambivalences of the post-colonial situation, a situation that is more ironic than we are often willing to admit: international capital continues to oppress many peoples in the so-called 'third world', but from the perspective of the governing classes in those countries, this is development; the oppressed continue to suffer under economic doctrines which are expressed through Orwellian doublespeak – 'structural adjustment', for example – but what they continue to aspire for, even as they suffer, are the values and images of the West, the juices from the source of suffering itself. For Africans, as Achebe has aptly noted, this topsy-turvy world presents new narrative challenges: 'We are in a period so different from anything else that has happened that everything that is presented to us has to be looked at twice.'[13] The relationship between the imaginary space and its historical condition has to be re-evaluated.

Before independence, African writers committed their narratives to the articulation of the nation as what Benedict Anderson would call 'the imagined community'.[14] Even when they recognized that the nation in Africa was an invented community, these writers believed that their works would harmonize national ideals and values; by realizing the realities of the nation, to borrow Fanon's term, the writer would find 'the seething pot out of which the learning of the future emerged'.[15] After independence, however, the interests of the nation became more confused. For example, by the early 1970s Achebe would see the gesture of writing as an engagement with the seething pot of the nation even when his function as an ideologue of the Biafran cause might be construed as a commitment to the breakup of the Nigerian nation. Moreover, the novelist saw his narratives as forms of articulating the African revolution 'that aims toward true independence, that moves toward the creation of modern states in place of the new colonial enclaves we have today, a revolution that is informed with African ideologies'.[16] At the same time, however, Achebe would acknowledge that a consensus no longer existed on the meaning of the nation: 'Having fought with the nationalist movement and been on the side of the politicians, I realized after independence that they and I were now on different sides, because they were not doing what we had agreed they should do. So I had to become a critic.'[17]

Of course, what has changed in the last thirty years is not merely the relationship between the writer, the politician, and the people they both claim to serve; the terms of nation-building and the construction of identities have also changed, perhaps they have become more inscrutable; but the post-colonial situation is also a context that offers great possibilities for narratives concerned with national formation. The basic question which recent African writing has had to deal with, but one which we have yet to theorize adequately, is the problematic of power and the state. For if you look at almost any literary text published recently in Africa, the character of power and how it is exercised seems paramount. In Achebe's *Anthills of the Savannah* and Soyinka's *Play of Giants* the primary drama takes place in a field defined by relations of power; Matigari's allegorical quest in Ngugi's novel is certainly confined to a field delimited by relations of production, but the resulting struggle is one which pits an individual against the materiality of the state and its instruments of power and coercion. And as Nicos Poulantzas notes in his discussion of the State and ideologies of power, 'Although the relations of production delimit the given field of the State, it has a role of its own in the formation of these same relations.'[18]

In Ngugi's text, we cannot fail to see the ways in which Matigari's primeval ideology (expressed through Gikuyu legends and Christian allegories) is pitted against ideologies elaborated and reproduced through state apparatus and the discourses of organization which the state articulates to reproduce its power. Matigari's visionary world is built around notions of natural justice and truth; in contrast, the utterances of the Minister of Truth and Justice ('I am the soul of the government. I am the soul of the nation. I am the light in the dark of the tunnel' (p. 102)) elaborate a political tactic which has become a technique of knowledge. Ngugi's text raises another question: who represents the interests of the nation, who speaks its truths? The text, of course, provides a rather simplistic answer: it insists that Matigari is the voice of the nation, he is the crystallization of the collective desires of the oppressed. This answer is, however, achieved only at the expense of repressing the reality that evokes it in the first place: Matigari may have right and justice on his side, but the interests of the nation and the national community, in all their contradictions and perversions, are ideologically manifested by the state in its master narratives.

Matigari's words may resonate with the truth, but the ideological machinery of the state determines the realities of the nation. To quote Poulantzas, again, 'Ideology does not consist merely in a system of ideas or representations: it also involves a series of *material practices*, embracing the customs and life-style of the agents and setting like cement in the totality of social (including political and economic) practices.'[19] The nation, too, is an ideological practice which is only available to us in its representations and contradictions. The paradox of national formation in post-colonial Africa, as I hope to show in my reading of Nuruddin Farah's *Maps*, is that the nation is the source of identities and, paradoxically, the entity that represses their formation.

Maps: Nation, Body, and Text

Now, the motive for narration in *Maps*, as in many other post-colonial texts, is the contemporary African writer's consciousness of his or her alienation and exile, an awareness that the nation does not naturally proffer identities, nor lead to the fulfilment of the desire to belong to a real or mythical community, but often comes between post-colonial subjects and their quest for a communal ideal, a *natio*, a space of belonging. But exile, by distancing the subject from the idealized space of the nation, also generates the desire for a compensatory national narrative – one in which the individual's longing for a unified image of the self is cast within the country's epic quest for its soul. In Farah's novel, however, Askar's quest for selfhood, which parallels Somalia's dream of unification during the Ogaden war of 1977, does not generate a linear narrative in which temporal progression takes us from a situation of alienation and dispossession (in the past) to a sense of fulfilment and identity (in the present). At the end of the novel, which is also its inaugural moment of narration, Askar is no closer to discovering the meaning of his life – and of Somalia – than he was as a child seeking the signifiers of the nation in geography books. Indeed, the various strategies he adopts to evoke his Somali identity – for example his attachment to real and imaginary maps of his nation and even his desire to fight for the liberation of the Ogaden – have only complicated notions of national identity in the text.[20]

When Askar is arrested at the end of the novel, apparently to be questioned about his relationship with Misra, the Ethiopian woman who brought him up, it is no longer clear whether there is any natural difference between a Somali and Ethiopian, although this assumed difference is the source of the conflict between the two countries; a narrative which sets out to interrogate the two entities (Ethiopia and Somalia) will end up collapsing inherited notions of cultural and natural differences. *Maps* is, of course, the story which Askar tells the secret police ostensibly to assert his Somaliness; nevertheless, the narrative, by 'going backwards and forwards in time' (p. 138), and by shifting narrative voice between the first, second and third person, problematizes previous notions of selfhood and national identity. In effect, what makes narration possible in this novel is not the quest for identity (since this condemns the narrative to a circle or maze), but the narrator's reflections on, and postivization, of his alienation, a gesture which allows him to recognize that Somalia is defined, not by a unified signifier, but by its 'split personality' (p. 120). Like other post-colonial narratives of national formation, narration is not predicated on any positive affirmation of the nation as an imagined community, but what Jean Franco, in another context, calls 'a sceptical reconstruction of past errors'; the novel makes 'visible that absence of any signified that could correspond to the nation'.[21]

Of course, Farah's narrative ideology has always been predicated on the adoption of alienation (itself a sign of absence and error) as a positive force rather than a problem to be erased or overcome. Despite Somalia's historical claims to a unified and integrating culture, Farah underscores the extent to which to be a Somali, especially under colonialism, was to be alienated from the idealized symbols of the nation. In a revealing reflection on his background in 'Why I Write', Farah asserts that the text-books used for the Somali-speaking peoples of the Horn of Africa 'were meant for *other people*': 'Not only did we feel alienated from the texts we read, but the universe which these portrayed had nothing familiar to offer to a Somali child like myself, in a Somali-speaking Ogaden.'[22] Such forms of alienation are now, of course, familiar descriptions of the colonial situation; however, Farah saw them as conditions which made writing possible because 'to live in the world of which I was part, I had to make it my own' (WW, p. 1592). Writing became a way of claiming the authority of invention; and narration a strategy of self-inscription: 'the Quran could not be mine because it was God's and no human could own it, but at least

I could make a small claim in other areas, recreating the cosmos as I knew it in the hope that I would see the world and my friends in, the way one sees a mirror's reflection in another mirror' (WW, p. 1592). To write is to claim a text of one's own; textuality is an instrument of territorial repossession; because the other confers on us an identity that alienates us from ourselves, narrative is crucial to the discovery of our selfhood. The text is the mirror in which the Somali subject will see itself reflected.

But the relationship between narratives and mirrors is a problematic one in *Maps*. At the end of the novel, the secret police will pose a simple question to Askar: 'What is your name?' (p. 246). Simple as it is, though, this question can only be answered by tracing the history of the self against the background of the Somali mythology of nationhood, retracing the errors of the nation in the post-colonial period, thus exposing what Franco calls 'the disappearance of the nation, its failure to provide systems of meaning and belief'.[23] For what defines the Somaliness of Somalia – language, culture, or biology? As a boy, Askar is troubled by many questions, but none is as dominant as the nature of his identity on both the biological and cultural level: do mirrors reflect 'the true identity of things and persons?' (p. 43); and are 'bodies tattooed with their identities' such that no nationality is interchangeable with another? (p. 42). Because Askar is obsessed with such questions, questions that point to the absence of a stable system of meanings in the Somali cultural body, his frustration is heightened by the realization that answers to issues of identity must be self-engendered: 'He was saddest that there was no one else to whom he could put questions about his own identity; there was no one to answer his nagging, "Who am I?" or "Where am I?"' (p. 44).

Narration creates a text which becomes the mirror in which the character hopes to identify himself. But there is no guarantee that the image in the mirror is authentic, for mirrors have immense powers of distortion. In his narrative mirror, Askar assumes one image only to see it wrenched out of his control and disfigured in the process. At one stage in the novel he looks at his 'newer self' and sees it as a dot in the distance, a dot 'which assumed features you could identify, becoming now a man, now a woman – or even an animal, your perceptions of the new self altering with the distance or nearness of the spot of consciousness' (p. 61). Narration is adopted as one way by which the narrator can capture an image of the self and represent its uniqueness in language. In this instance, however, the act of identifying the self through writing leads to self-alienation; the mirror vanishes in front of Askar to be replaced by a wall on which 'appeared shadows and the shadows were speaking with one another, some laughing, some listening and some holding hands or touching one another' (p. 61). So, the self is alienated through the agencies it sought to represent itself. If narration was initially posited as the solution to Askar's crisis of identity – the resolution of his initial doubts on whether he exists outside his own thoughts and ideas – it seems to have compounded the problem because he still remains 'a question to himself' even after narration is over.

There is even a prior, more elementary problem – the narrating self has no authority of representation because the narrator has no means of collectivizing the desires of the Somali nation. The ideal allegory of self – which is evident in the African epics which Askar tries to emulate – assumes a fundamental relationship between self and nation. For Askar, however, the relationship to his 'people's past history and present experience' (p. 3) is marked by misfortune and displacement just as his desire to reinvent himself is retarded by his confused origins. In both an individual and collective sense, Askar cannot derive his authority from any genealogy: 'What survived my real mother was "memory", not I. People were, in a general sense, kinder and more generous to me, because my parents had died and I was an orphan' (p. 25). Without a mother to connect him to a genealogical tradition, Askar appears to many people 'as though I had made myself' (p. 23). His state of orphanage does not become the source of a melancholy that might allow the subject to identify with a nation, but it is an important licence to invent.[24]

However, it is Askar's sense of the incompleteness that haunts the Somali nation that allows his narrative to continue in spite of the crisis of consciousness that often grips him. Consider his reflections on his impeding circumcision: the moment when the individual is supposed to enter the communitas is here represented as one of confusion about selfhood and language. When Misra mentions the day of his circumcision, we are told, Askar is filled with fear that chokes his speech. When he recovers his composure, he observes that

> 'I was back where I had begun – I was motherless, I was fatherless, I was an orphan and had to give birth to myself. Yes, I was an orphan and had to give birth to myself. Yes, I was to re-create myself in a worldly image, I thought to myself, now that the Word had deserted me, now that I couldn't depend on its keeping me company.' (p. 86)

In effect, Askar cannot substitute language for the absent mother figure: 'The Word, I said to myself, was not a womb; the Word, I convinced myself, wouldn't receive me as might a mother, a woman, a Misra' (pp. 86-87).

The conflict between the Word and the mother would also appear to be one between texts and bodies. After all, a major cause of tension in the novel, especially in regard to the source and nature of Somalia's identity, is whether 'Somalia' is a text, i.e. a map on the wall, or a body, a mother figure? When the Somali ruling class talks about the realities of Somalia and discourse about the Somali character, they take pains to emphasize the natural, or rather biological, nature of the nation. Because such notions of identity only lead to either mystification or justify repression, Farah thinks that we can only penetrate the veil of nationhood which the Barre regime has wrapped around itself by foregrounding the textuality of Somalia: 'Somalia was a badly written play.... Siad Barre was its author' (WW, p. 1597). Moreover, Farah's anxiety about his position as a writer, especially at the beginning of his career, arose from the fear that his art could not measure to Barre's text and hence could not offer an effective counter-discourse: 'You can imagine how Siad-Barre-as-subject oppressed and obsessed me. I was in awe of it, afraid that I was not up to it, that I would mess it all up for future writers dealing with same material even if from a detached historical angle' (WW, p. 1597).

How does a writer counter an idea which has become nationalized and naturalized in public discourse? Other African nations may at least accede to their arbitrary invention in the halls of European imperialism, but not Somalia which, says Farah, 'is a country peopled by a race of men and women who are decidedly united in their unmitigated arrogance and pride in being unique, the only country in Africa that qualifies to be called a nation' (WW, p. 1597). The 'promiscuity of the Somali-idea', concludes Farah, is an instrument which the Somali ruling class or regime uses to repress other discourses on the Somali character; in the words of a Somali diplomat, 'you cannot invent a nation as unique as ours. That's the truth that matters' (WW, p. 1598). Obviously, Farah will not subscribe to this 'truth'; as a result, his narrative strategies are often geared toward the deconstruction of the naturalized Somali idea. Many of the ambivalences toward the idea of nationhood which we see in *Maps* arise from the fact that Farah must simultaneously counter the dominant idea of Somali as a natural entity, but at the same time propose alternative ways of constituting national formation, since, as he told Maya Jaggi recently, the writer is 'the depository of the nation's memory'.[25]

In any case, the idea that the nation can be signified by its maps comes up for closer scrutiny in Farah's novel. The Somali nation lacks the authority of a state, since its people are spread across different countries, hence the ironic suggestion that the Somali people 'have a case in wanting to form a state of their own nation' (p. 149). One could of course argue, as many Somali nationalists have argued, that Somalia needs to redraw its maps to reinvent its nationhood. But such an act of reinvention would also threaten the mythology that gives the Somali idea its doctrinal hold – that the Somali are a homogeneous people; that they are 'homogeneous culturally speaking and speak the same language wherever they may be found' (p. 166). Does this mean that an Ethiopian who adopts the Somali culture and language can also be considered Somali? This is the problem posed by Misra in the novel: although she will not be accepted as a Somali, by all the indices used to determine a Somali, Misra is surely one. But since she will always be denied this identity because of her Ethiopian origins, Misra is the figure Farah uses to deconstruct the hegemonic doctrine of Somali national purity.

Furthermore, Misra allows Askar to recognize that given identities have an adverse effect, too, especially when they deform the self (p. 42), and that national identity is a strategy which goes beyond the cultural text and territorial claims. Indeed, an important strategy of national formation in *Maps* is the use of the human body as a third site of identity formation, a site beyond Askar's individual fantasies about Somalia as signified by maps and official doctrines of the Somali nation as a natural entity. In examining the relationship between Askar and Misra, in 'bodily' terms, the narrative questions the 'wall' that is supposed to separate Ethiopians from Somalis. This wall, it seems, has been elected at the expense of human bodies which the state finds it easy to dispense with to realize its ideals. To ally himself with 'the notion of a nationhood', Askar is momentarily forced to detach himself from 'his mother-figure, Misra' (p. 96); his desire now is to become 'a fully grown man, a man ready for a conscription into the liberation army, ready to die and kill for his mother country, ready to avenge his father' (p. 105). The ideal of manhood, which underlies nationhood is, nevertheless, perverse – its logic demands that Askar should even be ready to kill the woman who has been his mother because she is of Ethiopian origin. It is also the source of acute anxiety, an anxiety that forces Askar's body to recoil from the doctrines of manhood as he begins to 'menstruate', an act which dissolves the binary opposition between men and women (p. 105). If men can menstruate, then the biological division between the sexes is called into question; and if such 'natural' divisions can be collapsed, then the fixedness of the Ethiopian/Somali chasm cannot derive its legitimacy from the laws of nature.

In the end, Askar's body seems to reject notions of nation formation as defined by the state for three reasons: the ideals embedded in such notions can only be achieved at the expense of human bodies whose collective desires the state claims to represent; he cannot countenance his separation from the woman whom he has called mother just because she was born in another country; and because he realizes that the Somalia which Said Barre has scripted is an ideological practice which the regime uses to justify its authoritarian grip and stifling of the Somali people. When Askar makes Misra, the Ethiopian woman, the heroine of his narrative – 'Misra was the heroine of your tale now and you played only a minor supporting role' (p. 141) – he begins to acknowledge that the official idea of the homogeneous and unique Somali nation is quite arbitrary if not false. Like other recent writing from Africa, *Maps* is a narrative whose goal is to critique, rather than simply valorize, the notions of African identity inherited from a colonial past and sanctioned by independence. In the process, the modern state becomes 'a kind of illusionist which needs the past only as a lament and whose miracle is the economic miracle of dependency'.[26]

ACKNOWLEDGMENT

I thank Juandamarie Brown for providing research assistance for this article.

NOTES

1. Abiola Irele, 'Contemporary Thought in French Speaking Africa,' in Isaac James
   Mowoe & Richard Bjornson, eds., *Africa and the West: The Legacies of Empire* (West-
   port, Ct.: Greenwood Press, 1986), p. 122.
2. Louis Althusser and Etienne Balibar, *Reading Capital*, trans. Ben Brewster (London:
   NLB/Verso, 1979), pp. 25-28; Michel Foucault, *Madness and Civilization: A History
   of Insanity in the Age of Reason*, trans. Richard French (New York: Vintage, 1988),
   pp. 3-37.
3. Ben Brewster, Glossary to *Reading Capital*, p. 316.
4. V.Y. Mudimbe, *The Invention of Africa: Gnosis, Philosophy, and the Order of Knowledge*
   (Bloomington: Indiana UP, 1988), p. xi.
5. *The Invention of Africa*, p. xi.
6. Frederic Jameson, *The Political Unconscious: Narrative as a Socially Symbolic Act*
   (Ithaca, NY: Cornell UP, 1981), pp. 20-21.
7. Frantz Fanon, *The Wretched of the Earth*, trans. Constance Farrington (New York:
   Grove Press, 1968), p. 225.
8. Neil Lazarus, *Resistance in Postcolonial African Fiction* (New Haven: Yale University
   Press, 1990), p. 23.
9. *Madness and Civilization*, p. 16.
10. *The Invention of Africa*, p. 4.
11. Ngugi wa Thiong'o, *Matigari*, trans. Wangui wa Goro (Oxford: Heinemann, 1989).
    Further page references to this text are made in parenthesis after the quotation.
12. This point is made by Peter Nazareth in 'Taking Fiction Beyond the Text', *Third
    World Quarterly*, Vol. 11 (3), July 1989, p. 204.
13. Bill Moyers, 'Chinua Achebe: Nigerian Novelist', in Betty Sue Flowers, ed., *A World
    of Ideas* (New York: Doubleday, 1989), p. 343.
14. Benedict Anderson, *Imagined Communities: Reflections on the Origin and Spread of
    Nationalism* (London: Verso, 1983), pp. 14-15.
15. *The Wretched of the Earth*, p. 225.
16. 'Interview with Chinua Achebe', in Bernth Lindfors et al., eds., *Palaver: Interviews
    with Five African Writers in Texas* (Austin, TX: African and Afro-American Research
    Institute, 1972), p. 6.
17. 'Interview with Chinua Achebe', p. 8.
18. Nicos Poulantzas, *State, Power, Socialism*, trans. Patrick Camiller (London: NLB,
    1978), p. 25.
19. *State, Power, Socialism*, p. 28.
20. Nuruddin Farah, *Maps* (New York: Pantheon Books, 1986). Further page references
    to this text are made in parenthesis after the quotation. Important studies of Farah's
    novels include, D.R. Ewen, 'Nuruddin Farah', in G.D. Killam, ed., *The Writing of
    East and Central Africa* (London: Heinemann, 1984), pp. 92-212; G.H. Moore,
    'Nomads and Feminists: The Novels of Nuruddin Farah', *International Fiction Review*,
    Vol. 11 (1), Winter 1984), pp. 3-12; Juliet Okonkwo, 'Literature and Politics in
    Somalia: The Case of Nuruddin Farah', *Africa Today*, Vol. 32 (3), pp. 57-65.
21. Jean Franco, 'The Nation as Imagined Community', in H. Aram Veeser, ed., *The
    New Historicism* (New York: Routledge, 1989), p. 205.

22. Nuruddin Farah, 'Why I Write', *Third World Quarterly*, Vol. 10 (4), October 1988, p. 1591. This article is henceforth referred to as WW in the text.
23. 'The Nation as Imagined Community', p. 208.
24. The notion that melancholy is one of the ways subjects express identification with a nation was recently proposed by Homi Bhaba at a conference on 'Nationalisms and Sexualities' held at Harvard University, 16-18 June 1989.
25. Maya Jaggi, 'A Combining of Gifts: An Interview with Nuruddin Farah', *Third World Quarterly*, Vol. 11 (3), July 1989, p. 187.
26. 'The Nation as Imagined Community', p. 206.

DOROTHY JONES

Decolonizing Women's Romance

Just as the day to day realities of colonized peoples have been shaped and controlled by the impact of British and European discourses, so the pattern of most women's lives is powerfully determined by the weight of patriarchal discourse. The re-reading and rewriting of the European historical and fictional record is vital to the process of literary decolonization, and some post-colonial writers have chosen to create their own versions of imperialist texts such as *The Tempest* and *Robinson Crusoe*.[1] Women writers engaging with patriarchal discourse have adopted comparable strategies of subversion and appropriation, and those who also write from a post-colonial position usually find themselves challenging imperialist and patriarchal discourse simultaneously. This paper considers novels from Canada (Margaret Atwood's *Lady Oracle*), the Caribbean (Jean Rhys's *Wide Sargasso Sea*) and India (Namita Gokhale's *Paro*), where the writer interrogates the genre of romantic fiction within a post-colonial context. Atwood satirizes popular women's romance while demonstrating its insidious appeal. Jean Rhys reinscribes *Jane Eyre*, creating her own version of the 'mad' Mrs Rochester and delineating the colonial exploitation and racial oppression marginalised by Brontë, when it is mentioned at all. Gokhale also satirizes popular women's romance, focusing on Daphne du Maurier's *Rebecca*, as she sardonically considers the theme of female liberation in the wider context of what liberation might mean for India itself.

According to Rachel Blau du Plessis, the standard romance plot is a trope for the sex-gender system as a whole. It represents successful courtship and marriage as the rightful end of women, with death as the only alternative for those whose inability to conform signifies their sexual and social failure.[2] In the nineteenth century, when the middle-class woman as gendered subject had 'barely any realistic options in work or vocation', the romance formula determines the outcome for most women characters in fiction.[3] Either they subordinate their questing and aspiration to the demands of love, like Dorothea Brooke in her marriage to Will Ladislaw, or they are swept to their doom like Maggie Tulliver. Because of social and economic change, the romance plot no longer encodes so fully the range of possibilities now open to women, and du Plessis demonstrates how twentieth century women authors have striven to write 'beyond the ending' it imposes on their characters' lives. But, just as it is impossible for those living in a post-colonial society to recreate the cultural conditions existing prior to colonization, it is equally difficult for women to avoid the taint of patriarchal discourse, so the romance formula, because it reinforces the dominant gender discourse of our society, still retains its hold on women writers and readers. 'The romance plot separates love and quest, values sexual asymmetry, including the division of labour by gender, is based on extremes of sexual difference and evokes an aura around the couple itself.'[4]

Although serious fiction is gradually breaking away from the confines imposed by romance, our century has seen an increasing rise in the genre of popular women's romance published by firms like Harlequin and Mills and Boon. Margaret Atwood examines the narrative ideology of such romance in *Lady Oracle*, representing it as a labyrinth into which women are irresistibly drawn until they are implicated in the plot at its centre, victims of a conspiracy to deny them an independent existence. The protagonist, Joan Foster, herself a successful author of popular romances, is vulnerable to the lure of their generic conventions in her own life even while fully aware of how contrived and manipulative they are. Her career as fiction writer is a guilty secret she hides from everyone, especially her husband, Arthur, for she knows that while her novels force women ever more firmly into the restrictive and monotonous roles society tries to impose, they also offer herself and her readers escape fantasies which make those roles more endurable. But Joan is increasingly driven to transgress the boundaries within which she tries to compartmentalise her various selves until her life comes increasingly to resemble a lurid gothic romance, while the plot of her current novel is turned upside down. This narrative disruption, however, enables her to escape, at least temporarily, the marriage/death ending patriarchal discourse seeks to impose on women's lives. 'The only way out of such closure, which male texts ... offer women, is to resist the final transformation, to refuse an ending.'[5]

At one point, Joan even contemplates promoting in one of her romances the socialist and Canadian nationalist causes so dear to her political activist husband, only to realize that such alien material would shatter the book into absurdity.

> Perhaps I could write a Costume Gothic just for him, putting his message into a form that the people could understand ... at least a hundred thousand people read my books, and among them were the mothers of the nation. *Terror at Casa Loma*, I'd call it, I would get in the evils of the Family Compact, the martyrdom of Louis Riel, the horrors of colonialism, both English and American, the struggle of the workers, the Winnipeg General Strike...[6]

Lady Oracle presents romantic fiction as a form of colonialist discourse and Joan's escapes into the romantic labyrinth are linked with her attempts to escape from Canada, first to England and later to Italy. In England as a nineteen year old she hopes to discover another life for herself. Although the country appears like a message in code which she doesn't know how to decipher (p. 145), it is here she is initiated into romance writing by her first lover, an exiled Polish count who writes nurse novels for a living – 'the mushy kind that have a nurse on the cover and a doctor in the background gazing at her with interest and admiration' (p. 153). Joan derives inspiration and local colour for the costume gothics she writes from the costume room of the Victoria and Albert Museum and the stalls selling Victorian bric-a-brac in the Portobello Road. Even when back in Canada, she must continue to recreate the ambience of an English aristocratic past to allure her readers.

Although Joan Foster is doubly colonized by patriarchy and by British cultural discourse, white women in a settler society like Canada are themselves implicated in the process of colonial oppression. 'While the native woman is truly doubly oppressed or doubly colonized, by male dominance as well as by white economic and social dominance, the white settler woman can best be described as half-colonized. Although she too is oppressed by white men and patriarchal structures, she shares in the power and guilt of the colonists.'[7] This half-colonization is explored by Jean Rhys in *Wide Sargasso Sea* which presents the Creole woman, Antoinette Cosway, as child, bride and incarcerated wife. Antoinette's family, fallen on hard times since the emancipation of the slaves, are regarded as white niggers by the neighbouring whites and derided as white cockroaches by the blacks. When their mansion, Coulibri, is burnt down by former slaves, Antoinette turns to her playmate, the little black girl, Tia.

> As I ran, I thought, I will live with Tia and I will be like her. Not to leave Coulibri. Not to go. Not. When I was close I saw the jagged stone in her hand but I did not see her throw it. I did not feel it either, only something wet, running down my face. I looked at her and I saw her face crumple up as she began to cry. We stared at each other, blood on my face, tears on hers. It was as if I saw myself. Like in a looking-glass.[8]

Antoinette's alienation becomes complete when her family sells her into marriage with a wealthy young Englishman, the Mr Rochester figure. Through giving voice to a character rendered voiceless in *Jane Eyre*, Jean Rhys vindicates a colonial point of view.

> The mad wife in *Jane Eyre* has always interested me. I was convinced that Charlotte Brontë must have had something against the West Indies and I was angry about it. Otherwise why did she take a West Indian for that horrible lunatic, for that really dreadful creature? I hadn't really formulated the idea of vindicating the mad woman in the novel but when I was rediscovered I was encouraged to do so.[9]

Identity is asserted through contrasting visions of place, with England represented as insubstantial. The black woman, Christophine, refuses to believe it actually exists - 'I never see the damn place, how I know?' (p. 92) – and for Antoinette it is at first a dreamlike image and then, once she is there, a world made out of cardboard. Rochester, on the other hand, perceives the West Indies as a dream, finding it *too* substantial: 'Too much blue, too much purple, too much green. The flowers too red, the mountains too high, the hills too near' (p. 59). Although he acknowledges the place is beautiful, he cannot tolerate its mystery: 'What I see is nothing – I want what it *hides* – that is not nothing' (p. 73). In his mind, Antoinette is associated with the rich abundance and sensuality of a region he cannot comprehend, and while his hatred of her is prompted by intimations of family scandal, it arises primarily because he cannot bear her wildness, her unabashed sexuality, her otherness.

Worse still, Rochester associates Antoinette with blackness and witchcraft, qualities represented still more strongly by her maid, Christophine, a key figure in the novel. Although, from an English perspective, Christophine, who commands the magical power of obeah, is identified with forbidden knowledge and forces beyond the power of reason, her command of the invaders' language - 'She could speak good English if she wanted to, and French as well as patois' (p. 18) - enables her to present a highly rational analysis of the Antoinette/Rochester relationship as she passes judgement on each. Hers is the most powerfully subversive voice in the novel, defying patriarchal authority: 'Three children I have. One living in this world, each one a different father, but no husband. I thank my God. I keep my money. I don't give it to no worthless man' (p. 91). She also despises British law while recognizing its power: 'No more slavery! She had to laugh! "These new ones have Letter of the Law. Same thing. They got magistrate. They got fine. They got jail house and chain gang. They got tread machine to mash up peoples' feet"' (pp. 22-3). Although Rochester finally succeeds in driving Christophine away from his wife by invoking the threat of this power, she asserts she is a 'free woman' and, as Benita Parry points out, this is 'exactly how she functions in the text'.[10]

But Antoinette, ambiguously placed between colonizers and indigenes and bound legally and economically to her English husband, is not free. Eager to assert his supremacy over the people, the landscape and its mysteries, Rochester, in actions which equate precisely with the process of colonial appropriation, makes his wife a prisoner, denatured, renamed and totally under his control, after first possessing himself of her fortune. In Rachel du Plessis' words: 'a woman from a colony is a trope for the woman as a colony'.[11] Once in England, Antoinette is identified still more closely with the raging passions Rochester has sought to stifle within a rationally ordered existence. This means she is even more strongly linked with the oppressed blacks in the West Indies, becoming an agent of destruction who threatens the white man's life and property. In her dreams of burning down Thornfield Hall, she re-enacts the burning of Coulibri early in the novel and experiences a hope of reunion with her mirror image, the black girl, Tia.

But when I looked over the edge I saw the pool at Coulibri. Tia was there. She beckoned to me and when I hesitated, she laughed. I heard her say, You frightened? And I heard the man's voice, Bertha! Bertha! All this I saw and heard in a fraction of a second. And the sky so red. Someone screamed and I thought, *Why did I scream?* I called 'Tia!' and jumped and woke. (p. 155)

Wide Sargasso Sea counters *Jane Eyre* not only by presenting a colonial viewpoint but also by challenging the romance plot which so often pairs the demure and consciously virtuous heroine with a rival for the hero's affections who is usually more sophisticated, socially superior and sexually assertive. Jane Eyre is provided with two rivals, the shallow, upper-class Blanche Ingram, who is easily vanquished, and the mad, animal-like Bertha Rochester who presents a more formidable obstacle. Not only is Jane, prototype of the virtuous heroine, omitted from *Wide Sargasso Sea*, the non-conforming, sexually powerful woman whom Brontë presents as a monster is now the figure who commands our sympathy, revealed by Rhys as victim of an oppressive social system and a heartless husband. The image of woman as monster is profoundly ambivalent, as Margaret Atwood reveals in *Lady Oracle*. Monstrosity is both something men impose on women, and a form of power they may choose to assume. Joan Foster, as a teenager rebelling against her mother's and society's expectations of her as a woman, overeats until she becomes grotesquely fat, and, even after she slims down, remains conscious of her potential as a fat lady. But women who seek to conform with society's ideals of femininity and impose them on others are equally monstrous. Joan dreams of her mother applying make-up before her triple mirror: 'I suddenly realized that instead of three reflections she had three actual heads, which rose from her towelled shoulders on three separate necks' (pp. 66-7). As Joan's life grows more complicated, it is increasingly difficult for her to reward Charlotte, the virtuous heroine in the romance she is currently writing, because the supposedly wicked Lady Felicia develops into a far more interesting and sympathetic character. In romance, the virtuous heroine and her rival, the female monster, may be inseparably linked, or even interdependent.

Namita Gokhale explores this idea in her novel *Paro: Dreams of Passion* through allusions to Daphne du Maurier's *Rebecca* in which a virtuous, self-effacing heroine becomes obsessed with the upper-class, sexually predatory Rebecca, her husband's first wife whom he murdered for threatening the patriarchal order. Gokhale's narrator, Priya, is considerably more assertive than du Maurier's nameless heroine, but, like Atwood's Joan Foster, she is ensnared by the narrative ideology of romance. An avid reader of Mills and Boon, her favourite book is *Rebecca* and she is also familiar with *Jane Eyre*. The novel chronicles Priya's love-hate relationship with Paro who corresponds in some respects to Rebecca, but, unlike her fictional counterpart, remains very much alive throughout most of the narrative. Both women are rivals for B.R., Priya's boss, the romantic heart throb whose firm manufactures Sita sewing machines, promoted as 'the housewife's friend' - though the phrase really applies to B.R. himself and the romantic ideal he embodies. He seduces Priya but marries Paro and the pair become 'twin divinities' in Priya's 'private mythology'.[12]

Paro's name is an ironic allusion to Parvati, heroine of the Indian film classic *Devdas*, who nobly suppresses her love for the hero to enter into a marriage arranged by her father, remaining a paragon of wifely virtue while still providing emotional support for Devdas. But Gokhale's Paro shatters every notion of how a good Indian wife should behave: 'Paro has done it all, she's left a husband and a lover, she has a small son of ambiguous parentage. She is a conversation piece at dinner parties, and it is considered daring and chic to know her' (p. 26). When, after her divorce from B.R., Priya asks if she feels uncomfortable living off his money, Paro replies: 'Look sweetie ... *they* made the rules' (p. 32). With age (for the novel spans a period from the mid-sixties to the early eighties), Paro grows massively large – 'She wore her corpulence like expensive jewellery' (p. 125) – and her increased size carries the same significance of transgressing male-defined boundaries as it does for Joan Foster in *Lady Oracle*. Despite her attraction to Paro and all she represents, Priya is not courageous enough to defy convention openly, though her commitment to wifely virtue is very superficial. She accepts an arranged marriage with Suresh, an aspiring young lawyer, for the material prosperity and improved social position it offers. 'I realised that my only weapon in an indifferent world was Suresh, and I decided to groom him patiently until my ministrations bore dividends' (p. 24). Together, Priya and Suresh manipulate and claw their way up the social ladder till they make it into the upper reaches of Delhi society.

Gokhale savagely satirises this fashionable milieu. Although India is now free of colonial rule, this group of socialites is still profoundly colonised by Western fashions and Western culture. Paro stars as Clytemnestra in a Hindi production of the *Oresteia*, and Priya revels in her Yves St Laurent sun glasses, ikebana flower arrangements and starched linen traycloths embroidered with cross-stitch roses. She is, however, a little baffled by the catch-phrases of Western psychology. 'I didn't know what a Primal Scene was, and he explained that it was the trauma of witnessing your father and mother copulating. I told him that every Indian child living in a chawl watched it every day and didn't get so worked up, and break down and things...' (p. 128). Gokhale keeps reminding readers of the massive poverty which exists outside the charmed circle in which her characters live, while they continually make pronouncements beginning, 'The trouble with India is...' Their analyses vary - the country is a nation of middle men; the upper classes are not producing enough children; the men all want only one thing. But the novel itself suggests that the country's major problem is the corruption and decadence of its ruling class.

Gokhale also implies, however, that 'the trouble with India' may also be the limitations imposed on its women's lives. For many years, Priya refuses to reconcile herself to her unsatisfactory, stifling marriage and Paro's outrageous behaviour, which she finds so fascinating, symbolises her own inner rebellion. The diary she begins keeping, which becomes the novel we read, expresses her discontent and, significantly, it is Paro who discovers and shows it to Suresh, who then demands a separation. Priya then finds herself without economic resources, apart from the uncertain income her husband allows, and dependent on her brother and hostile sister-in-law in Bombay for a home. In the flat where she once lived with her mother, she discovers the books of her adolescence, *Jane Eyre*, and *Rebecca*. On re-reading the latter, she realises she had fallen victim to the ideology of Western romance.

> I felt betrayed, utterly betrayed. Rebecca had after all, done nothing wrong; the dazzlers in the new pulp paperbacks committed adultery almost as a rite of passage. Rebecca's only fault was that she was strong, stronger than Max! Not very profound observations, I am sure, but for me they held the blinding flash of revelation. My entire system of values was suddenly upturned. (p. 111)

But this discovery is not particularly liberating, for Priya turns next to her mother's shelf of Hindi romances where heroines have even narrower choices. After reading them she can only conclude – 'I am an Indian woman ... and for me my husband is my God' – prior to negotiating a return to Suresh. She does, however, make a couple of comically feeble attempts at suicide and has one last fling with her romantic idol B.R. before returning to a dead end existence in Delhi.

Priya's return to her husband is equated with Paro's latest scandalous escapade – her marriage to a homosexual Greek film director with a Madonna complex for whom she represents 'the universal mother'. Paro has earlier born a child who, by the end of the novel, appears a young man of some promise, whereas two women characters, Priya and Geeta, who have chosen the path of virtuous wifehood, more or less, both miscarry in the course of the narrative. But although Paro's approach to life appears more fruitful, her Greek marriage is a sterile union, for her options are narrowing and in the book's final pages she is increasingly associated with death. There is no outlet for her enormous energy within her own social sphere, and in a gesture which may have been intended merely as melodrama rather than a genuine suicide attempt, she slashes her wrists and dies. Paro's death means the end of Priya's story for, as she says in the novel's opening sentence: 'I saw myself in her', and with Paro dead, she can no longer maintain any sense of self.

Lady Oracle, *Wide Sargasso Sea* and *Paro* show how popular romance colonizes women while allowing them a certain imaginative freedom. All three novels challenge a major convention of women's romance by revers-

ing the values traditionally attached to the submissive heroine and her foil
the dangerous, sexually powerful woman. For these authors she becomes
a representative of female energy whose presence is essential if the heroine is to exist at all. Atwood and Rhys also associate this energy with the
supernatural, through comic allusions to the triple goddess in one case,
and associations with obeah magic in the other, while all three authors
assert its monstrosity in the eyes of a society constantly seeking to repress
it. Atwood's women characters internalise this repression through rather
ineffectual attempts at self-censorship. Rhys equates the suppression of
female energy with the imposition of colonial rule on an indigenous
people. Ghokale, however, shows how an indigenous society, released
from colonial rule, continues to maintain various forms of colonial
oppression, and the lack of purpose and direction she perceives among
India's ruling class is due in part to its failure to allow any scope to the
full force of female energy. Although the shadow of death lies over Joan
Foster, Antoinette Cosway and Paro, there is a suggestion that none of
them can be wholly vanquished. Joan, having staged her pretended demise to escape a life of turmoil, writes as one who has been resurrected.
Antoinette, who will perish in the fire she lights at Thornfield, is
associated in her death with the energy and rebellion of the blacks in the
West Indies. Ghokale's novel ends with an image of the cremation ground
where Paro's body burns on one of the funeral pyres, but the funeral fire
is also a symbol of regeneration and rebirth. As Sylvia Plath suggests at
the end of her poem 'Lady Lazarus', female energy continues to flare up
against those who try to suppress it.

> Herr God, Herr Lucifer
> Beware
> Beware.
>
> Out of the ash
> I rise with my red hair
> And I eat men like air.[13]

NOTES

1. Helen Tiffin discusses these issues in 'Post-Colonial Literatures and Counter-
Discourses', *Kunapipi*, Vol. IX, No. 3, 1987, pp. 17-34.
2. Rachel Blau du Plessis, *Writing Beyond the Ending* (Bloomington: Indiana U.P., 1985),
pp. 1-19.
3. Ibid., p. 14.
4. Ibid., p. 5.

5. Barbara Godard, 'Tales Within Tales: Margaret Atwood's Folk Narratives', *Canadian Literature*, no. 109, Summer 1986, p. 68.

6. Margaret Atwood, *Lady Oracle* (London: Virago, 1977), pp. 246-7. All further references are to this edition and are included in the text.

7. Robin Visel, 'A Half-Colonization: The Problem of the White Colonial Writer', *Kunapipi*, Vol. X, No. 3, 1988, p. 39.

8. Jean Rhys, *Wide Sargasso Sea* (Harmondsworth: Penguin, 1968), p. 38. All further references are to this edition and are included in the text.

9. Quoted in Elizabeth R. Baer, 'The Sisterhood of Jane Eyre and Antoinette Cosway' in *The Voyage in Fictions of Female Development*, ed. Elizabeth Abel, Marianne Hirsch and Elizabeth Langland (Hanover: U.P. of New England, 1983), p. 38.

10. Benita Parry, 'Problems in Current Theories of Colonial Discourse', *Oxford Literary Review*, Vol. 9, nos. 1-2, 1987, p. 38.

11. du Plessis, op. cit., p. 46.

12. Namita Gokhale, *Paro: Dreams of Passion* (London: Pan Books, 1985), p. 97. All further references are to this edition and are included in the text.

13. Sylvia Plath, *Collected Poems*, ed. Ted Hughes (London: Faber, 1981), pp. 246-7.

ROBIN DIZARD

Love Stories

Christina Stead places the experience of being in love at the centre of almost all of her work. The love story is her road to knowledge.[1] Writing love stories might not seem to be a very bold move, but in Stead's hands, love stories turn subversive. She maps the relationships of imperialism, social class, money and the individual person in erotic terms. Not only do her love stories attack conventions such as the sexual double standard, her stories also undermine political myths.

For Stead, the project of investigating love in order to seek knowledge is doubly a return to basics. The Western philosophical tradition running back to the Greeks considers love as one kind of knowledge.[2] Stead placed herself firmly in this tradition when she stated she thought the Australians are like the ancient Greeks, 'no compliment to either party'. The other sense in which investigating love returns to basics is that sentimental love is a major Western cliché. Its icons and gestures are common property. Having the status of second nature, it is taken for granted, and as such, expected not to tangle with serious pursuits like business, politics and the life of the mind. This intellectual prejudice, aided by sexual prudery, makes love an ideal subject for a woman writer. She can examine conventions, what everyone knows, as an insider, yet she writes down what 'nice girls' don't talk about or even know, so she is a social outlaw. In treating the stories considered unfeminine (too raw) or too feminine (trifling), she can turn the spotlight toward the social fictions about stories and sex. She can show how sexual relationships rely on fictions and fetishes, and how stories circulate and reproduce. She can show how the power to define what the story is, who is the hero and what is the plot, supports social power. Stead tells stories, and she tells the social life of stories.

Stead liked to start writing a novel, she said, by developing the characters. To her, meeting the character was like the start of a love story. 'My novels usually begin with a person. I think, ah, he'll develop, he's the one, just as in a love affair.'[3] Stead employs the sentimental convention of love at first sight as her way into her subject. Love is her topic, and loving, her mode of proceeding.

To exhibit Stead's procedure as a teller of love stories, I will examine closely some of the scenes from her third book, *The Beauties and Furies*.[4] The novel brilliantly blends the aim of social realism (show modern social relations as they are, trace the hidden links between social classes) and surrealism (interrupt the logic of conscious thought, reconcile reality and dream, honour *l'hasard objectif*).[5] The original, working title of the text was *Student Lovers*. Set in Paris, in 1934, the novel is about lovers who are new at love, apprentices, in the student phase of loving. In *The Beauties and Furies*, one character is a 'somnambulist', a sly reference to the surrealist announcement that dreaming is a form of artistic labour. I think surrealism/somnambulism informs Stead's style in this novel not as just parody, but as a method. Her characters in this novel resemble sleepwalkers, walking and dreaming, half-aware and half-oblivious of their world.

One of the oldest love conventions is that lovers stare. Sometimes they exchange stares, sometimes the stare is one-way. There is, in addition, the specialized stare which opens the adventure we call love at first sight. I have thought it appropriate to demonstrate Stead's love of stories, and her way of telling the stories of love, by analyzing selected sequences organized by intense stares. In each, a stare ignites a power struggle among competing fictions.

The Beauties and Furies begins with a woman staring out of the window of a train: 'The express flew towards Paris over the flooded March swamps. In a parlour car, the melancholy dark young woman looked out persistently.... The small dark young woman was slipping her new shoe off her swollen right foot when she saw the Italian looking at her sociably...' and she, immediately, in order to break away from his stare, begins to enact a charade (*The Beauties and Furies*, p. 1). For the man's benefit, she pretends to read her letter as if for the first time – and this shifts our stare from the first level of the story into the second, the love-letter. Reading the letter, we can guess why she is going to Paris, why she is wearing new shoes, why she avoids the 'friendly, inquisitive glance of the Italian' – the traveller is on her way to join the man who sent the letter signed 'Now and forever, Yours, Oliver Fenton'.

Of course, it is always fun to read mail addressed to other people, and this is no exception, so now our stare splits, and we readers may take in Elvira, Oliver Fenton, and the man watching Elvira. And we begin guessing. Elvira (Mrs. Paul Western, Mecklenburg Square, London) skipped part of Oliver's letter. Why? The skipped part was about going to a rally for the defense of the Scottsboro Boys. (This was a celebrated cause of the international left in the thirties, in which several blacks in Alabama were charged with rape of two whites; the American Communist Party organized the defense, the accused were acquitted, and the case established in U.S. law the right of blacks to serve on juries.) So – a reader guesses – Oliver Fenton is probably a socialist – and Elvira Western finds politics in general and left-wing causes in particular a bore. She probably thinks politics spoil a love letter. Her 'Western' name is the right label.

On looking up from the letter, Elvira encounters the Italian's stare again, and glances away, again. This time, she looks at the other travellers in the car, and so begins the montage of the voices of the British travellers.

A very old Anglican clergyman shook his wattled chin at two young officers going out to Bombay: 'Indubitably a don, pronounced them *Ahoy! Foo Gah Kaze*. I suppose to you young men I am almost prehistoric; indeed it is fifty years since Brown, my tutor, murmured them with perhaps a touch of more than donnish melancholy...' (*The Beauties and Furies*, pp. 2-3)

In this passage, Stead exposes social class conventions framed within the tentative relationship of a man and a woman when she meets his glance. *He* attempts to establish their mutual standpoint as outsiders, drawing her into regarding the English travellers as alien, to make her share an understanding with him. *She* tries to meld with the bourgeois background, and finds she is in fact already separating from it. The writer's strategy, which she builds into the montage, turns the seamy side of class relations outward, and discloses Elvira in the process of changing her mind, even as she changes countries. In her ambivalence, she tries to explain and defend 'her England' – while she is in flight away from her comfortable English home.

For a closer look at the seams in the social fictions, notice the opinion of the 'very old clergyman' that nowadays even university dons mispronounce Latin. In his remark, Stead arrays the props of empire: elite education, racism, class privilege, complacent religion. Yet the parcel seems not to have been made, but found instead, quoted from mere disregarded scraps of overheard conversations. The clergyman's ridicule of Latin pronunciation exposes racist assumptions in his creaky joke about the purport of the syllables 'Ahoy, foo-gah-keys'. To him, they suggest a drunken man on a wharf in China, but in fact the sounds are empty signifiers, so to find a 'drunken Celestial' in them, is to import a racist stereotype, and hear what is not there. Stead leaves her readers to guess he is a racist. The intended listeners, the young officers bound for Bombay, would not make these guesses – the clergyman assumes they move in the same circles as he ('remember me to Sir Charles') and that they share his disdain for 'modern shoddy'. The intercuts between received ideas plainly expose the essential myths of empire: the myth of cultural superiority, and the myth of exoticism, of eroticised native peoples ('another tongue beguiles your frontier nights') and the myth that superior intelligence is rationale behind class privilege ('I told Rudges when he comes to do the garden to mark the date [when the cuckoo returns] and, if possible, the hour, in chalk upon the coal-shed', *The Beauties and Furies*, p. 4). Not only are the quotations significant themselves, they signify in relation to each other, where one voice ceases and the next cuts in. Elvira, at a loss to complete her triad, 'charades and Horace, and...' picks up Wordsworth from the clergyman, (*The Beauties and Furies*, p. 5). Likewise, she scoops up the number 450 million from the background conversation. She uses the number to indicate English gallantry, glossing over the context of its use in a complaint that England lags behind in the arms race.

A second scene organized with a stare – in this case, the stare of the voyeur, exhibits another application of Stead's technique. Using found materials, she picks up the quoted gestures of a dancer to reveal one character imposing his vision on the others, to establish himself as their dramaturge. In this scene, the stare penetrates a window (an emblem of possibility or insight), looking inward, and true to Annibale Marpurgo's claim, the man in the window becomes transparent behind the transparent window – a human cocktail. 'It takes years, Fenton, to get the right mixture of malice, melodrama, sentimentality, ethnology, psychology: when you get it right, you shake together, toss it off, and immediately the people under your eyes become translucent: drunkenness of the human cocktail' (*The Beauties and Furies*, pp. 22-23).

In the metamorphosis, one banker watches another turn into a dancer; meanwhile, he turns into an audience. In a last arpeggio of detail, the dancer is quoting, commenting and criticizing, 'drawing in air the enormous pair of legs he has portrayed'.

The way this stare is organized, Elvira and Oliver peer into a window, and we peer in behind them. Inside, the pallid man performs for the unseen watcher with the saffron hand. Here a performance imitates a performance, meaning that the window frames another window, inside. The dancer at the centre transforms himself into herself – a representation of the very emblem of desire – shifting between the sexes, a change which makes almost every notion of categories waver at the base.

Finally, take note of the implications of seeing a faun inside a bank. Fauns we associate with grassy banks, flowery banks, but not commercial and saving banks. Normally banks and fauns belong to totally different paradigms. Can there be more to this split perspective than a pun? Possibly, the intrusion of creatures from myth into banks hints at elements of crisis in the economy. In 1934, the German currency had given way, in the U.S.A. the depression held sway, and all over Europe panicky investors wondered whether banks were safe places for their money. A faun in a bank suggests a panic, fitting sign of the times.

Stead's stories arrange ideas into deliberately clashing designs, composed of intersecting contexts. As Suzanne Kiernan points out, Stead's 'characteristic structural principle is the sequence [which] can be said to have opened when one of its terms has no logically solidary antecedent and to have closed when another of its terms has no consequence'.[6] I agree and further say that Stead's sequences contain other, potential sequences which threaten to interrupt and alter the point of view. Stead once proposed that her writing adopts Jules Romain's principle of 'creative error' and honours Ralph Fox's ideal, which is, to write about change so as to portray 'man alive'.[7] The living core of such writing is a portrait of metamorphosis. In the first two scenes metamorphosis comes about as a character enacts a charade. In the next scenes, social stereotypes supply the roles the characters try, flaunt and then use or discard.

In this third scene organized with a stare, Oliver and Elvira talk about love stories while they stare at some prostitutes. Each of them tries to control the story, and make the other, the object. They try on and parade in the forms their story could assume: 'the prodigal wife' or 'student lovers' or 'the philanderer' for instance. 'They went to the pictures that night. There was a moving picture of the well-worn prodigal wife pattern.... All middle-class novels are about the trials of three, all upper-class novels about mass fornication, all revolutionary novels about a bad man turned good by a tractor...' (*The Beauties and Furies*, p. 130). The first fiction is the sentimental tale of the prodigal's return, a fiction Elvira prefers because she can be its hero. Looking for ways to confirm herself, she finds appropriate fictions on-screen. Oliver proposes a different, competing context, namely a narrative in which he can star. He bills himself as the intellectual who sees through the trashy cinema stereotypes of human relations. Then both lovers see the male and female prostitutes. Oliver sums them up as 'exploited labour'. His remark reveals his own pomposity and the limits of his political dogma. She sees both faults and counters, 'It's all a formula.... You could exploit a woman ... turning her into a idiot with ideas about mouseholes and curtain-rods, while you wrote essays on labour-unions' (p. 130). His marxism is abstract, and her feminism is only self-pity. In the meantime, there are the prostitutes, hungry and in the streets, their misery only a pretext for a conversation which negates them, since their stories fit neither Oliver's marxist analysis nor Elvira's assumptions about conventional marriage. The lovers' fictions about their own love affair are thrown into relief by the fictions around them. Elvira enjoys the coincidence of seeing a part of her story in a film, forgetting the same conventions govern her life and Hollywood plots. Oliver thinks a good marxist could never go to a prostitute, forgetting his politics address economics, not desire. As usual, Stead gives readers no either/or dilemma, but a text in which three paradigms collide: the good marxist, the bourgeois wife, and 'mass fornication', in the secret Paris of desire.

Later in the novel, Stead brings the prostitute from the background to the foreground. The scene is another incident of love at first sight; in it, the prostitute returns Oliver's stare, with interest.

> '[G]irls kept speaking to him; the streets swarmed with them, as the air with pollen. He passed under the lamps, and his ripe youth shone out in the dirty vulgar street like the visit of an angel; his well-cut clothes, fancy tie and polished shoes were apparent too. At a doorway standing above a step, he started back. A girl was harbouring there, silk legs glistening under a short frock. Her thick, short bronze hair was brushed in curls around a beret, her milky skin was brushed with artificial colour, the moving iris of each eye glowed in the filtered light, her varnished feet tapped as she hummed. He had seen that in a glance, and was passing, when a voice came out of the doorway:

Je suis belle, o mortels! comme un rêve de pierre,
Et mon sein, ou chacun s'est meurtri tour a tour
Est fait pour inspirer au poète un amour –

She stopped murmuring this chant of beauty as he came closer. 'Have you a ren-
dezvous with someone?' he questioned. 'With everyone,' she answered, looking at
him with scorn.' (*The Beauties and Furies*, pp. 226-7)

In this layered glance, the first level makes the prostitutes part of the celebration of spring; they are just the human equivalent to the plantlife's
pollen. The next level puts Baudelaire's words in the woman's mouth, but
complicatedly, because she is quoting him, quoting her. So doing, she is
like Pygmalion's Galatea, the sculptor's dream of desire within a stone,
ventriloquist's voice issuing from a statue. Later, in her own voice, she
explains, 'Baudelaire loved us, girls like us, and in return we sometimes
learn one of his poems as a bait – a bait,' and she took a large bite of
steak, 'a bait for men' (*The Beauties and Furies*, p. 227). In this ironic image,
while the girl eats what her bait has drawn in, she explains hunting-and-
gathering to her quarry. So cocksure is she, she first boasts to her catch,
and then, persuades him to let her display him. 'She took him along her
accustomed beat to show him to her friends and sisters. In the dark of
their way sometimes soft ironic or harsh sardonic voices called. "Is he
handsome, though?" "You have picked up a novice?" "A fat one!"' (*The
Beauties and Furies*, p. 229). Thus Oliver changes from himself into a
trophy, and willingly parts from his political convictions. Making moves
apparently at random, he nevertheless runs true to type, that is, to the
philanderer. Dazzled by poetry, stunned by beauty, he acts the part in the
play the prostitutes are running, and pays the asking price.

In *The Beauties and Furies*, Stead created one of her most bizarre and
beautiful examples of love at first sight in her portrait of the relationship
of a pair of designers, Coromandel and Amelie Paindebled, mother and
daughter, dwellers in a private museum. 'The designs are not very clear,'
said Oliver.... At this moment Coromandel chose to recall his senses, wandering all over the visible world, to herself, and, foundering in a volcanic
bay, he had no time to recollect anything more than a windmill of dancing
heads looking at him from the minatory shutters of heaven' (*The Beauties
and Furies*, pp. 166-7). The maps, globes and star-charts are the antique
tools of empire, all here remade in the service of Eros ('the egg of the
compass ... displayed more clearly a minute crystal Eros at the sign of the
north' (*The Beauties and Furies*, p. 165). Everything from Coromandel's
name (from the coast of India opposite Sri Lanka) to the objects around
her, signals the lust for dominion.

Stead delights in mining clichés for their unexpected metaphysical
power. She takes 'you mean the world to me' to its ultimate, grotesque
development in her metaphysical images of Coromandel enjoying love.
Piled around Coromandel, who is as arrogant as a buccaneer, are signs of

wealth made into the signs of desire. In a paradigmatic shift, initially hinted by the narrator's remark that Coromandel 'had not bothered' to have her breasts tattooed with lines of latitude and longitude, Coromandel and the world become equivalent. When she decides Oliver should cease to be amazed, and start making love to her, they make the Pacific shake beneath the 'unparalleled blanket' of the map of the world which fell down over them because it 'had been pinned inadequately' above their couch. The clashing images of artistry and accident are deliberate disruptions of the design. By exaggerating comical incongruities which are spliced together inside clichés, Stead calls attention to the rich ambiguity latent in ordinary experiences. She searches stereotypes for contradictions, for as yet unapprehended patterns. She regards disruption and errors as opportunities for discovery, as spaces, in other words, where possibilities of still more riches open.

As in the scene of the faun in the bank, Stead lets marvels into her love scene through the agency of accident. In the characteristic scenes of *The Beauties and Furies*, textual intercuts work like a series of cinematic cuts, so that a receding series of fictions, each inside another, reverberate. In this museum scene, a chance encounter, a stare, leads to an interior where a madwoman, a designer, and a mother live.

The first layer is the museum collection of maps and star charts. Here are the records of superseded knowledge from the ages of exploration and empire. They signify one kind of received ideas. The heirlooms also signify the contest between memory traces. Oliver, though no art student, notices the centre of the design is missing: 'I suppose there is some design in the centre of all this also' (*The Beauties and Furies*, p. 165). Eventually he sees the centre reflected in Coromandel's iris. The ceiling design opens in the centre. Looking into her eye, he sees the scene he is in, reflected. A tarpaulin rolls back, and a head thrusts through, into the treasure room, and into her eye. Through her eye, he sees how Coromandel's mother sees him. The mother is both the centre and the contradiction in the design. She pokes through a hole in the centre of the ceiling decorated with emblems of the hours, so she interrupts the ideal, polished surface with her human, wrinkled face. She likewise interrupts a seduction. In the profound glance the daughter and mother share is an image of the age of discovery made personal; at a point where the division between 'I' and 'thou' is almost erased in a metaphysical image, the lover meets the lover who preceded him, namely, the mother. At the same time, the mother's stare makes lovemaking impossible, and she must be shut out. Coromandel interrupts the stare and gathers all Oliver's attention to herself, so her design triumphs.

Stead uses the surrealist technique for exposing competing paradigms, a way to splice night Paris, dream-Paris, the secret Paris of fabulous sexual adventure to the workday city of banks, business and commerce. She leaves behind the limits of socialist realism (the tractor novels) because she

depicts characters enraptured by sexual fantasies. She gives fantasy standing in the actual world. She mocks the self-indulgence of the surrealists,
whose scepticism about ruling paradigms did not extend to questioning
the taxonomy of sentimental love. Unlike the surrealists Stead understood
that sex is not a pure preserve of untrammelled natural impulses, but
thoroughly social. Unlike either surrealists or social realists Stead was ever
mindful that sex can be converted into goods that can be taken to market.
This means, sexual allure helps drive the economy. Since the marketplaces
are pervaded by sex, tracing the tangled stories of a set of lovers leads in
time to decoding the social hierarchies of dreams and commodities which
define a modern capital.

NOTES

1. 'Sexuality is related to the creative spirit – it is the motivation of creation. Something to be cherished and something that enriches literature', is what Stead remarked about the close tie linking work and love. Greeba Jamison, 'Christina Stead
   Can't Help Being Original', *Walkabout*, 36, 1970, pp. 36-37. Also, 'The beauties and
   furies referred to are surely those of SEX: the minstrel thinks a good deal about
   SEX', Christina Stead, 'Did It Sell?' *Ocean of Story*, ed. R.G. Geering (Victoria,
   Australia: Penguin, 1985), p. 523.
2. Socrates describes his wisdom, in the Platonic dialogues, as 'nothing but a knowledge of erotic things' in two places. Ann Carson, *Love the Bittersweet* (Princeton,
   1986), p. 170.
3. Graeme Kinross Smith, 'Christina Stead: A Profile', *Westerly*, March 1976, p. 74.
4. Christina Stead, *The Beauties and Furies* (New York: Appleton-Century, 1936). All
   subsequent references will be to this edition.
5. Stead was well informed about the artistic debates taking place in the thirties about
   partisanship, aesthetics and representation. Cf. her report on the Congress of
   Writers for the Defense of Culture: 'The Writers Take Sides', *The Left Review*
   (August, 1935), pp. 453-463, and Ch. 2, 'Love Story, Paris, June, 1935', *I'm Dying
   Laughing* (New York: Henry Holt and Company), 1986.
6. Suzanne Kiernan, '"Ugly by Design" : The Fiction of Christina Stead', *Modern Fiction
   Studies* 1988, Summer 34(2), p. 194.
7. 'Christina Stead', *Contemporary Authors*, ed. Kunitz and Haycraft, 1942.

VERONICA MARIE GREGG

Ideology and Autobiography in the Jean Rhys *oeuvre*

As an account of my life [memories] are misleading, because the things one does not remember are as important; perhaps they are more important.

Virginia Woolf

[A]utobiography [is] ... a work of art shaped by a writer bent on making an ideological point.

Ralph Ellison

I can't make things up. I can't invent. I have no imagination. I can't invent character. I don't think I know what character is. I just write about what happened. Not that my books are entirely my life but almost.... *Though I guess the invention is in the writing.*

Jean Rhys[1]

It is precisely this kind of apparently self-revelatory (but disingenuous) comment which has encouraged Rhys critics, preoccupied with reading her fiction as barely disguised autobiographical details of her life, to insist on the intimate connection between her female protagonists and herself. These critics read her life through her literary works and read her fiction as a statement of emotional and psychological disturbance. In order to sustain this line of enquiry into Rhys's *oeuvre*, critics and commentators have put forward the thesis of the 'composite heroine' – the view that the main characters in her first four novels are the same woman at different ages and stages of disrepair. Closely linked to this position is the other thesis of the 'internal chronology' of her fiction. According to this reading, the actual writing and publication of her novels are discontinuous with the events of her life. This means that her third novel, *Voyage in the Dark*, which deals with a young chorine who 'slipped and fell', is actually her first in terms of Rhys's life story. This biographical pillory forms the basis for much of the criticism of Jean Rhys as writer and woman.[2]

But it is possible to start an analysis of Jean Rhys's work with a radically different premise: namely, the proposition that Rhys's fiction is fiction and any attempt to view her literary enterprise as transparent will leave much of her work inaccessible. Not Jean Rhys, but Jean Rhys reading and writing, seems to be the real subject of her art. There is, I hope to show, a clear disjunction between Rhys's oft-repeated claim that she is writing about herself (and only herself) and the internal workings of the fiction itself. The key observation in Rhys's statement is that 'the invention is in the writing'. At the most basic and important level, Rhys is suggesting that she is constituted as a subject in her writing. The self that she invents in her writing is necessarily different from the person she is. The relationship between her personal history and her writing is mediated by the writing itself.

The ideology and the strategies she brings to her writing project and shape the outcome and the 'meanings' which may be read into her work. Rhys has often been considered an apolitical writer, concerned, as her critics say she is, with her personal demons and sordid personal life. However, close investigation reveals that Rhys's stance in relation to the discursive field from which she draws her art is not only oppositional but transgressive. Her provocatively entitled essay, 'The Bible is Modern', reveals a Rhysian poetics shaped by her efforts to counter the ideological presumptions of the metropolitan centres in which she lived and worked:

> God said, 'Let there be Light and there was Light.' There is something short, snappy and utterly modern about this sentence. You have only got to alter, 'God said' to 'Said God', put a stop in the middle, and you could almost call it a quotation from the newest, starkest American novel.
>
> The real English of this obviously is 'In His great wisdom the Deity commanded that the firmament be illuminated, and it was amply illuminated....'
>
> Instead of this, you get the stark, modern touch – 'Let there be Light, and there was Light.' In this marvellous book ... there are many such stories expressed in the modern manner. And, though it is obvious that the significance of this manner is entirely dependent on the intensity of feeling let us remember that we are dealing with a primitive people who express themselves in the primitive way. These people are Oriental people who have never learned to keep a stiff upper lip.
>
> So buy the Bible more modern than you know...
>
> You cannot understand it unless you understand the English social system. It is a great crime to feel intensely about anything in England, because if the average Englishman felt intensely about anything, England as it is could not exist; or, certainly, the ruling class in England could not continue to exist.
>
> Thus you get the full force of a very efficient propaganda machine turned on the average Englishman from the cradle to the grave, warning him that feeling intensely about anything is a quality of the subject peoples or that it is old-fashioned, or that it is not done, or something like that.
>
> The idea that books written in short effective sentences depending for their effectiveness on the intensity of the author, are inferior books, follows automatically, because the solidarity of the English social system is extraordinary.... But then what is difficult for us black people [sic] to understand is the ingenious way they set about making money out of 'God said let there be Light, and there was Light'.[3]

In attacking the social and historical framework which provides the discursive field for literature written in England, the land of the colonizer, Rhys is also making clear that her working aesthetic is to write books written in short, simple sentences. Her aim is to prune language of its bourgeois and imperialist accretions, to purify and liberate it for her purposes. Her political standpoint derives from her liminality within the metropolitan and 'peripheral' cultures to which she belonged. Jean D'Costa observes:

> Rhys's fiction belongs, as she did, to worlds whose mutual understanding has the feeling ... of ... things that ... couldn't fit together.... The dissonances of seemingly different worlds inform the Rhysian novel, finding coherence in her art: in order to read Rhys adequately, the reader must be alive to her use of class structures; of colonialism and the metropolis seen from within and without; of love and sex defined by money, race and gender; of exile as a human universal; and the solitary, observing, experiencing self. All of her work is charged with a sense of belonging in many wheres at once.[4]

One of Rhys's major strategies is the use of pastiche and parody. In her fiction, there is an unrelenting engagement with the literary and ideological traditions of England and Europe. Her work implicitly and explicitly, directly and indirectly, speaks to and with such inaugural texts as *Ulysses*, *The Good Soldier*, *Kubla Khan*, *A Passage to India*, *Jane Eyre*, *Wuthering Heights*, to name only a few. She criticises, admires and attacks contemporary and precursory conventions, genres and artists. The Parnassians, the Symbolists, the Impressionists, especially Modigliani and Whistler all contribute to the raw material of her art. Rhys's engagement with this world is aimed at inventing a self-exploratory and culturally re-evaluative literary project in which the central formal and narrative stance is founded on cultural criticism.[5] As woman and colonial, she challenges assumptions which commanded universal or natural status, examining these with the eye of the outcast, the object, the Other. Her work delineates a structural contradiction between her lived experiences and the ways in which she is defined by the dominant ideology. It is at this point and in this way that autobiography and ideology are interconnected, in a sense become one and the same, in Rhys's writing. As Judith Kegan Gardiner acutely observes, 'for Rhys, autobiography provides a way of testing others' perceptions about fiction and history against her own experience. She anchors the fiction in her own life not simply because she cannot see outside it, but because she must validate her rejection of prior literary views about women [and the outsider] by comparing them to her memories and experience'.[6]

'Temps Perdi', a short story written after Rhys had returned for a visit to the West Indies in the 1930s, suggests her heritage and sensibility not only through description, nostalgia and recall, but through a particular and distinctive attitude toward history and culture. The title of the story is an obvious gloss on Marcel Proust's *A la Recherche du temps perdu*. The narrating consciousness in the West Indian work displays disbelief and contempt toward a so-called historical account by an Englishman of the traditions and beliefs of the indigenous people of the West Indies. She observes that from his account of her West Indian reality, he seems to have 'a lot of imagination'. She also displays increasing suspicion toward books which inculcate the values of the dominant ideology, thereby distorting the reality of others like herself:

> Now I am almost as wary of books as I am of people. They are also capable of hurting you, pushing you into the limbo of the forgotten. They can tell lies – and vulgar, trivial lies – and when they are so many all saying the same thing they can shout you down and make you doubt, not only your memory, but your senses.[7]

The narrative concretises the 'they' to suggest specifically a response to England which is strongly antagonistic; 'It would be a very humorous idea if England was designated as the land of the dead ... as hell. In such a form, in truth, as England appeared to many a stranger' (To many a stranger..., p. 145). As a West Indian, a 'stranger' misrepresented in the metropolitan canon, the narrating consciousness is exposing the bias and partiality of the ideological framework which has constructed her otherness.

If Rhys is constantly rewriting and recasting the canonical texts of metropolitan Europe, she is also at pains to criticise the ways in which the values of that world are used to codify her West Indian reality. In a short story, 'The Insect World', written during the Second World War, but completed while Rhys was working on *Wide Sargasso Sea*, she connects her work to a little known novel about the West Indies, *Nothing So Blue* (1927). This novel was written by Elma Napier, the daughter of Sir William Gordon Cumming, who settled in Dominica, Rhys's home, during the 1930s. She was later to become the first woman to be elected to Government. Rhys's literary criticism of her novel reveals not only her insistence on the Flaubertian dictum that 'the form of thought is its very flesh' but also her increasingly sharp criticisms of the false perceptions of the West Indies.

Under Rhys's literary and cultural criticism/analysis, *Nothing So Blue* reveals certain aesthetic and moral defects which are exposed and commented upon in her short story. These can be considered her perennial themes – woman's suffering and degradation in society, the evils of class distinction and imperialism, and her condemnation of works of art which accept as normative the prevailing social order. The opening sentences of 'The Insect World' incorporate Napier's novel and thematize the form and content of the precursory text: 'Audrey began to read. Her book was called *Nothing So Blue*. It was set in the tropics. She started at the paragraph which described the habits of an insect called the jigger' (p. 79). As Audrey reads her second-hand book, the narrator observes that any book was better than life to Audrey, who lived a hard monotonous existence even though she tried very hard to fit in, to acquiesce to the dictates of society. Audrey was particularly worried that the First World War had swallowed her youth, and now, at twenty nine, she was worried that it might last forever. As she reads the book, however, Audrey is appalled at the comments about women written in by the first owner, a man. 'He had written "Women are an unspeakable abomination" with such force that the pencil had driven through the paper' (p. 80). The second-hand book in which a man had previously written a savage and deprecatory view of women is a metaphor of the sexual and spiritual colonization of the woman. The man's words are interpolated between Audrey and the book. Her reading of the book is over-determined by the social and cultural assumptions about womanhood. The destructive and dangerous complicity of social and discursive practices in controlling and containing a woman's reality is foregrounded in Rhys's story. It calls attention to 'the second hand' reality of a woman's existence. As a colonial and colonized woman, Audrey is always and already read and inscribed. The structuring principle of 'The Insect World' emphasizes that writers (even or especially women writers) who practice unresistingly within the dominant socio-cultural framework are also complicit.

The narrative of 'The Insect World' reveals that the book itself is part of the problem:

> The book was not so cheering, either. It was about damp, moist heat, birds that did not sing, flowers that had no scent. Then there was this horrible girl whom the hero simply had to make love to, though he didn't really want to, and when the lovely, cool English girl heard about it she turned him down.
>
> The natives were surly. They always seemed to be jeering behind your back. And they were stupid. They believed everything they were told, so they could be easily worked against somebody. Then they became cruel – so horribly cruel, you wouldn't believe....
>
> Finally, there were the minute crawling unseen things that got at you as you walked along harmlessly. Most horrible of all these was the jigger. (p. 81)

The *précis* of *Nothing So Blue*, which highlights its one-dimensional portrayal of 'cardboard' characters and stereotypical depiction of the 'surly natives', parodies the formal structures and ideological assumptions which shape Napier's novel. In her insightful and elegant study, 'Scratches on the Face of the Country; or, What Mr Barrow Saw in the Land of the Bushmen', Mary Louise Pratt observes:

> The portrait of manners and customs is a normalizing discourse, whose work is to codify difference, to fix the Other in a timeless present where all 'his' actions and reactions are repetitions of 'his' normal habits. Thus it textually produces the Other without an explicit anchoring either in an observing self or in a particular encounter in which the contact with the Other takes place. . . . Manners-and-customs description could serve as a paradigmatic case of the ways in which ideology normalizes, codifies, and reifies. Such reductive normalizing is sometimes seen as the primary or defining characteristic of ideology.[8]

The West Indian writer believed, like Pratt, that writers were often co-opted, whether willingly or unwillingly, into the conventional framework of colonizing and imperialist society (in particular England). For Rhys, the writers were often challenged by the need to tell their truth but bowed instead to the domination and force of the prevailing ideology. Referring to the organization of English society as a kind of ant civilization, she points to the damaging constraints which convention and politics impose on literature: 'I believe that if books were brave enough the repressive education would fail but nearly all English books and writers slavishly serve the ant civilization. Do not blame them too much for the Niagara of repression is also beating on them and breaking their heart.'[9]

Rhys's persistent criticism of the 'ant civilization' to which many writers conformed is implicit in the structural development of her story around the motifs of Napier's *Nothing So Blue*. Rhys's criticism also implies her awareness of how the insurmountable barrier of point of view shaped by culture and history can create roadblocks to understanding. Audrey understands that the writer's (of *Nothing So Blue*) perception of the tropics is shaped by the writer's own point of view, which sharply contradicts hers. She observes: 'It all depends on how people see things. If someone wanted to write a horrible book about London, couldn't he write a horrible book? I wish somebody would. I'd buy it' (p. 84). The implicit suggestion is that the native of the West Indies, considered to be a non-speaking subject, is asserting her strong disagreement with the partial and biased system which passes itself off as normative.

In order to demonstrate the implicit and unspoken politics of narrative and structure in Napier's novel, 'The Insect World' demonstrates that core assumptions can be changed if the teller of the story is changed. The description of the jiggers is what Audrey remembers most vividly in Napier's account of the tropics. As she travels in the London Underground, the people not only look like insects, but under her gaze and with the memory of the jiggers still fresh in her imagination, they metamorphose into large insects:

> She pressed her arm against her side and felt the book. That started her thinking about jiggers again. Jiggers got in under your skin when you didn't know it and laid eggs inside you. Just walking along, as you might be walking along the street to the Tube station, you caught a jigger as easily as you bought a newspaper or turned on the radio. And there you were – infected – and not knowing a thing about it. (pp. 84-85)

Like Caliban possessing Prospero's books, the Rhys short story with a deft and ironic twist turns the assumption of the metropolitan writer about the tropics on its head, even as it acknowledges the power of the text over the reader's mind. 'The Insect World' appropriates the jiggers motif, symbol of the reification of the native people of the West Indies, refuses its assumptions, and uses it as a trope to lay bare the cultural and social specifity of the novel's point of view. Rhys directly 'transforms [the] imperial codes of recognition from *within* the rhetorical stance of their own cognitive strategies'.[10] The mirror returns the gaze.

All of Rhys's work, whether wholly or partially, is concerned with reading, writing and re-writing. *Quartet*, as Judith Kegan Gardiner observes, in relation to Ford Madox Ford's *The Good Soldier* 'blazons its aesthetic tutelage and its moral independence ... and subtly exposes [Ford] as a novelist, rewriting his masterpiece ... as though from the inside out, or, more accurately, from the underside up. [*Quartet*] demonstrates Rhys' [sic] seriousness about the craft of writing and about her place in literary history.' Gardiner concludes that *Quartet*'s plot, character and imagery demonstrate Rhys's fruitful immersion in Ford's technique. Yet Rhys's vision is entirely her own.[11] *After Leaving Mr Mackenzie*, through its narrative structure and formal properties, provides an interesting index to Rhys's critical approach to her literary precursors and contemporaries in terms of their ideological framework. The preoccupation of *Mr Mackenzie* is with the literary model of the nineteenth century, realism juxtaposed with the concerns of modernism, which seeks in some measure to repudiate the aesthetics of its precursor. Rhys's attitude to these literary traditions is based on her gender and her view of herself as an outsider. In *Voyage in the Dark*, the protagonist reads Zola's *Nana* and her story represents a rewriting, a truth-telling about the lives of women who are considered to be prostitutes. As another character, Maudie observes, 'I bet you a man writing a book about a tart tells a lot of lies one way and another. Besides, all books are like that – just somebody stuffing you up' (*Voyage*, p. 10). The business of *Good Morning, Midnight* is an enquiry into the nature of language, fiction and a literary tradition, and their connection to economics and ideology. Through an examination of the aesthetics of modernist Europe, its sexual politics, class distinctions and 'silences' are laid bare. Gardiner argues that *Good Morning, Midnight* criticizes modernist pretensions just as it is a sustained critique of polarizations about sex, class and moral values that oppress women and the poor. The polarizations are reinforced by bourgeois and male domination of language and the literary tradition.[12] The protagonist, Sasha, powerfully and eloquently indicts the social system and the cultural oppression which is perpetuated through language and fiction. She also recognizes, however, that language can be both the oppressor and the liberator and that fiction does possess recuperative power if used with a clear understanding of one's place.

> I came to England between sixteen and seventeen, a very impressionable age and *Jane Eyre* was one of the books I read then.
>
> Of course Charlotte Brontë makes her own world, of course she convinces you, and that makes the poor Creole lunatic all the more dreadful. I remember being quite shocked, and when I re-read it rather annoyed. 'That's only one side – the English side' sort of thing.

(I think too that Charlotte had a 'thing' about the West Indies being rather sinister places – because in another of her books *Villette* she drowns the hero Professor Somebody [Paul Emmanuel] on the voyage to Guadeloupe, another very alien place – according to her.)

Perhaps most people had this idea then, and perhaps in a way they were right. Even now white West Indians can be a bit trying – a bit very (not only white ones) but not quite so awful surely. They have a side and a point of view.[13]

Wide Sargasso Sea is a culmination of Rhys's concern with re-writing. This novel represents a form-induced quarrel with a Victorian canonical text, *Jane Eyre*. In setting out to confront the presuppositions of the novel through a formal and ideological critique of the work, Rhys stresses that her quarrel with Brontë is over the moral imperative of technique. In Rhys's opinion, the 'cardboard' character of the mad West Indian woman in the attic is not only unfair, but technically flawed. Brontë, Rhys insists, did not work hard enough to develop a character who was true even within the fictive reality of *Jane Eyre*, despite her centrality to the text:

I've read and re-read *Jane Eyre*.... The Creole in Charlotte Brontë's novel is a lay figure – repulsive which does not matter, and not once alive which does. She's necessary to the plot, but always she shrieks, howls, laughs horribly, attacks all and sundry – *off stage*. For me ... she must be right *on stage*. She must be at least plausible with a past, the *reason* why Mr Rochester treats her so abominably and feels justified, the *reason* why he thinks she is mad and why of course she goes mad, even the *reason* why she tries to set everything on fire and eventually succeeds....

I do not see how Charlotte Brontë's madwoman could possibly convey all this. (*Letters*, pp. 156-57)

Brontë herself was unhappy with her own technical and moral portrait of Bertha, accepting that her character's humanity was not fully realised: 'It is true that profound pity ought to be the only sentiment elicited by the view of such degradation [as Bertha's], and equally true that I have not sufficiently dwelt on that feeling. I have erred by making *horror* too predominant.' The Victorian writer's recognition of the too predominant horror resembles Rhys's description of Bertha as a '"paper tiger" lunatic' (*Letters*, p. 262).

Rhys also records her own struggles to create a plausible character and text as a counter-discourse to Brontë's portrayal of the mad West Indian woman in the attic. In the canonical text, her isolation is linguistically acceptable. In the West Indian novel, the psychological and materialist world in which Antoinette lives is scrupulously rendered. Rhys observes:

So I will struggle on and try to make it as convincing as possible.

I can see it all up to a point. I mean a man *might* come to England with a crazy wife. He *might* leave her in [the] charge of a housekeeper and a nurse and dash away to Europe. She *might* be treated far more harshly than he knows and so get madder and madder. He *might* funk seeing her when he returns. But really, to give a house party in the same house – I can't believe that. But then I've never believed in Charlotte's lunatic, that's why I wrote this book and really what a *devil* it's been. (*Letters*, p. 296)

In attempting to revise the Victorian text, Rhys's *Wide Sargasso Sea* is necessarily bound by the reach of the European work. If she attacks what Gayatri Spivak terms 'the imperialist narrativization of history'[14] in *Jane Eyre*, the structural motors of Rhys's work are to some extent constructed by the English novel, through the connection of language, writing and history. Rhys wrestled with this challenge in technical, moral and ideological terms. One method of facing her problem was to try to cut loose from *Jane Eyre* in terms of time frame:

> I realise what I lose by cutting loose from Jane and Mr Rochester – only too well (Indeed can I? Names? Dates?)
> But I believe and firmly too that there was more than one Antoinette. The West Indies was rich in those days, *for* those days, and there was no 'married woman's property act'. The girls ... would soon once in kind England be *Address Unknown*. So. Gossip. So a legend. If Charlotte Brontë took her horrible Bertha from the legend I have the right to take lost Antoinette. And, how to reconcile the two and fix dates I do not know – yet. But, I will. (*Letters*, p. 237)

She did find a way to fix dates through literary allusion, as Mark McWatt observes. *Marmion*, newly published when Jane is given a copy toward the end of Victorian novel, appeared in 1808, whereas the date of the Emancipation Act is 1833. Bertha Mason was already confined to the attic of Thornfield Hall by the first decade of the nineteenth century, whereas Antoinette Cosway in *Wide Sargasso Sea* was still a child in the 1840s. In terms of *Jane Eyre* the literary references in *Wide Sargasso Sea* are equally anachronistic: 'Jeannie with the Light Brown Hair' was written by Stephen Foster, who was born in 1826; Tennyson's 'Miller's Daughter' was not well known until into the 1840s; most of Byron's poetry and all of Scott's novels (noticed by the husband on the bookshelf at Granbois) appeared after 1800.[15] Rhys finally insisted that her characters were not those of Brontë; 'I think there were several Antoinettes and Mr Rochesters. Indeed I am sure. Mine is *not* Miss Brontë's though much suggested by *Jane Eyre*.'

Rhys's discussion of the connections between her work and Brontë's is important for several reasons. Firstly, it demonstrates Rhys's preoccupation with the interrelation of aesthetic and social formations or what Pratt calls 'interlocking information orders'. She is aware of the powers and the prowess of literary discourse to normalize or treat as invisible the economic and social framework out of which it is produced. Her intention is to excavate and make visible the cultural and ideological specificity which the English novel suppresses. By insisting on a background and history for Brontë's madwoman, in particular the world of slavery and emancipation, Rhys is directing attention to the complicity of politics and text in capturing and containing the West Indian woman. By using *Jane Eyre* as a referent both within her novel and as a point of departure for multiple substitutions, Rhys, as Wilson Harris observes, disrupts the homogeneous cultural model of realism and dramatizes her repudiation of the dominant ideology which shapes literary and social history:

> Jean Rhys's significance ... lies in the ... subtly visible pressure to alter the rock-fast nineteenth century convention.... [T]he subtle, ambiguous, poignant, disruptions of homogeneous cultural model may be misunderstood or misconceived as the logic of pathos, as a psychology of pathos, whereas their significance ... is much more profound in their potential bearing on the evolution of original Caribbean or South American novel form.[16]

When Rhys repeatedly said that her aim and her desire was to 'write [Antoinette] a life', she was determined to wrest from the discursive field of the English novel a language, a set of signs which opposes, transgresses even, the assumptions of that discourse.

In recuperating language and discourse from the dominant ideological framework, Rhys's novel not only gives voice to the non-speaking subject of Brontë's work, but implicitly and explicitly interrogates the assumptions which shape the other characters in Brontë's novel, in particular, Edward Rochester. This conscious character parallelism is a mainstay of Rhys's fictional method from her earliest work. And in *Wide Sargasso Sea* it becomes a necessary and inevitable part of giving voice and meaning to the life of the madwoman in the attic.

Almost two thirds of the novel *Wide Sargasso Sea* is told by the husband. The creation of the character and the narrative viewpoint he embodies, Rhys tells us, gave her tremendous difficulties. She described it as 'moving a mountain', being 'impossibly difficult', and she says the character was making her 'very thin'. Her attitude to the personality suggested by the character is unequivocal: 'Dreadful man, but I tried to be fair and all that, and give some *reason* for his acting like he did. So *that* led me into by-ways' (*Letters*, p. 233). The question of point of view is of seminal importance in Rhys's fiction.[17] In her fiction, there is a clear distinction between the aesthetic and the perceptual point of view, the former being the more fundamentally ideological. The angle from which the object of representation – Antoinette's life – is to be seen is presented through the husband and his point of view; but his consciousness and utterances are analyzed and often corrected by the techniques with which they are developed and rendered. In the creation and development of the husband, Rhys uses 'technique as discovery'. The technical material of the work defines the quality of the character not by moral epithet or comment but by the texture of its style. Aspects of style include irony, suppression, mirroring, ellipses, and the epistolary method. In the last section, the stream-of-consciousness technique more comprehensively evaluates the character. His utterances are a polyphonic soliloquy which heralds his final retreat from the world and the word of his dissolution into the void.

In depicting the events leading to Antoinette's suicide leap, *Wide Sargasso Sea* tells the story from two main narrative viewpoints, two apparently autonomous angles of vision: that of Antoinette and that of her husband. However, the apparent symmetry and simplicity soon reveal themselves to be provocative and misleading. In her bid to 'write a life' for the mad West Indian Creole in *Jane Eyre*, Rhys is necessarily and radically questioning and overturning Rochester's story. (See in particular Chapters 26 and 27 of Brontë's novel.) The Englishman in *Wide Sargasso Sea* enters as a nameless person, and his last words before disappearing from the action of the novel state that he is nothing. He says that a little boy is sobbing in a heart-breaking manner because the child loves him and he has spurned him: 'That stupid boy followed us, the basket balanced on his head. He used the back of his hand to wipe away his tears. Who would have thought that any boy would cry like that. For nothing. Nothing...' (sic, p. 142). The husband had just said that the little boy had been crying for him. Hence when he says 'for nothing', his words assert that he is a nothing. The repetition of the word further reinforces the sense of nothingness. The elliptical dots at the end suggest his drifting away into an existential void. This is the last we see of him in the text.

His namelessness operates throughout the work as a technical device and a statement of meaning. The husband's 'character' connotes not only a person in a fiction, but a cipher, a fiction. His end as a nothing echoes the beginning of his narrative, where he appeared apparently out of nowhere and with no introduction. The formal and structural premises of *Wide Sargasso Sea* make manifest the silences and absences in *Jane Eyre*. It is imagery and technique, not authorial silence, which deconstruct the husband. The anonymous man in the West Indian novel is divested of the literary conventions which the character in *Jane Eyre* wears so heavily. Edward Rochester is a Romantic figure – dark, brooding, Byronic. In fact, since he is mainly seen from the outside, it is his overwhelming physical characteristics which most impress themselves on the reader. Names, labels, conventions, the Rhysian text suggests, can be used to conceal, distort, obfuscate. The West Indian writer has taken on to her self the task of unnaming and revealing Charlotte Brontë's Rochester. She is writing her way to the 'truth' by writing away the false images which she perceives in Brontë's writing. He has no name, no word, no cover. He is allowed in part to construct himself through his thoughts and utterances, while the assumptions of the text deromanticises, demythifies and dissects him. The Englishman, whose economic and spiritual 'power' and status rested almost entirely on the containment of the woman and the West Indian, the Other, is exposed as being empty.

Rhys's integrity as an artist combined with her subtly manipulated crafting elevates her character and her work far above a mere amendment or correction of Brontë's character. *Wide Sargasso Sea* is suggesting that Edward Rochester of *Jane Eyre*, and by extension of Victorian England and its social and aesthetic conventions, is an invention of that ethos. The novel's radical exposure of the Englishman is a critique of the nineteenth-century British novel as a domestic, cultural enterprise whose ability to portray, characterise and depict was rigidly circumscribed and socially regulated by the historical fact of the British Empire. The West Indian novel further suggests that the tradition out of which Brontë's fiction was created accepted as a law of nature imperial control of other lands, other people. Such a tradition depended for its existence on the reconstitution of others as creatures of European will. Rhys's character is left unnamed on purpose and nameless he should remain.

Rhys's essays, letters and creative writing demonstrate that fact and fiction, art and criticism are mutually constituting. Her response to Brontë's (and the English) portrayal of her world was intensely personal, viscerally felt, primarily because it contradicted her own experience, her lived reality, her history. Working outwards from what she knows – 'facts' – she seeks to understand and explore the ideological underpinnings of her experience and the ways in which it transgresses the values of the dominant economic and political system: 'the starting point of critical elaboration is the consciousness of what one really is, and is "knowing thyself" as a product of the historical process to date, which has deposited in you an infinity of traces, without leaving an inventory ... therefore it is imperative at the outset to compile such an inventory.'[18]

NOTES

1. David Plante, 'Jean Rhys: A Remembrance', *Paris Review* 76 (1979), p. 273.
2. Although there has been a trend in recent criticism to avoid the blatantly autobiographical reading of her fiction, I believe that there still remains too much emphasis on this approach to her writing.
3. 'The Bible is Modern', unpublished essay (Jean Rhys Collection, University of Tulsa, Oklahoma, n.d.).
4. Jean D'Costa, 'Jean Rhys 1890-1979', in Daryl Dance, ed., *Fifty Caribbean Writers* (New York: Greenwood Press, 1986).
5. My wording here is indebted to Rachel Blau DuPlessis, in *Writing Beyond the Ending: Narrative Strategies of Twentieth Century Women Writers* (Bloomington: Indiana University Press, 1985).
6. Judith Kegan Gardiner, *Rhys, Stead, Lessing, and the Politics of Empathy* (Bloomington: Indiana University Press, 1989), p. 22.
7. Jean Rhys, 'Temps Perdi' in *Tales of the Wide Caribbean*, selected and introduced by Kenneth Ramchand (London: Heinemann, 1986), p. 145. All further references to Jean Rhys's stories, including 'The Insect World', are from this edition and are included in the text. Other works cited by Jean Rhys: *Quartet* (1928; Harmondsworth: Penguin, 1971); *After Leaving Mr Mackenzie* (1930; Harmondsworth: Penguin, 1971); *Voyage in the Dark* (1934; Harmondsworth: Penguin, 1969); *Good Morning, Midnight* (1939; Harmondsworth: Penguin, 1969); *Wide Sargasso Sea* (1966; Harmondsworth: Penguin, 1968)

8. Mary Pratt, 'Scratches on the Face of the Country; or, What Mr Barrow Saw in the Land of the Bushmen', in *'Race', Writing and Difference* (Chicago: University of Chicago Press, 1985), pp. 139-40.
9. Jean Rhys Collection, British Library, Folio 152.
10. Stephen Slemon, 'Post-Colonial Allegory and the Transformation of History', *Journal of Commonwealth Literature*, 23 1.1 (1988), p. 164. See also Stephen Slemon, 'Reading for Resistance in the Post-Colonial Literatures' in *A Shaping of Connections: Commonwealth Literature Studies Then and Now* (Mundelstrup: Dangaroo Press, 1989) and Helen Tiffin, 'Post-Colonialism, Post-Modernism and the Rehabilitation of Post-Colonial History', *Journal of Commonwealth Literature*, 23 1.1 (1988), pp. 169-81.
11. Judith Kegan Gardiner, 'Rhys recalls Ford: *Quartet* and *The Good Soldier*', *Tulsa Studies in Women's Literature* 1.1 (1982), p. 67.
12. Judith Kegan Gardiner, 'Good Morning, Midnight, Good Night, Modernism', *Boundary 2*, 11.2 (1982), pp. 233-52.
13. *Jean Rhys: Letters 1931-1966* (London: André Deutsch, 1984), pp. 296-97. All further references are to this edition and are included in the text.
14. Gayatri Spivak, 'Three Women's Texts as Critiques of Imperialism', *Critical Inquiry* 12 (1985), pp. 243-61.
15. Mark McWatt, 'The Preoccupation with the Past in West Indian Literature', *Caribbean Quarterly* (1983), pp. 12-19.
16. Wilson Harris, 'Carnival of Psyche: Jean Rhys's *Wide Sargasso Sea*', *Kunapipi*, Vol. 2, No. 2, 1980, pp. 142-50.
17. Jean D'Costa, 'Jean Rhys 1890-1979', in Daryl Dance, ed., *Fifty Caribbean Writers* (New York: Greenwood Press, 1986).
18. Antonio Gramsci, *The Prison Notebooks: Selections*, quoted in Edward Said, *Orientalism* (New York: Random House, 1979), p. 25.

RUSSELL McDOUGALL

Stow's *Tourmaline*: A Test Town for Structural Anthropology

One of the most exciting developments in the discipline of anthropology in the late 1950s and early '60s, prior to *Tourmaline*'s publication in 1963, was the structuralism of Lévi-Strauss. While it is true that most of Lévi-Strauss's work was not translated until later, Randolph Stow's fluency in French and his dual interest in Anthropology and Linguistics (which he studied concurrently at the University of Sydney) make it unlikely that he would have remained unaware of what was then an extremely controversial proposition: namely that 'the different aspects of social life (including even art and religion) cannot only be studied by the methods of, and with the help of concepts similar to, those employed in linguistics, but also ... constitute phenomena whose inmost nature is the same as that of language'.[1] At the time that Stow entered the University of Sydney's Department of Anthropology the 'old gods' – 'Darwin, Durkheim and a dash of Kant' – were being eyed with withering scorn by all of the young anthropologists of the day: 'It had become *de rigeur*, not just to look at beliefs, or totems, or rituals; not just to classify data. It had become fashionable to set oneself a problem, apply a theory, see if it stood up against the data.'[2]

This is the background to *Tourmaline*, a novel that foregrounds its interest in language in many ways, while isolating a small community in time and space: Tourmaline, an isolated outback town forgotten by the world, 'not a ghost town. It simply lies in a coma' – a test town for structural anthropology.[3] This, at least, is one way in which the novel may be read – as a controlled experiment in cultural analysis, where the relationships between characters are not simply psychological, sexual, emotional relationships between individuals; they are also structural relationships, arranged to test the validity of cross-cultural composition. The textual self-consciousness of the fiction is related precisely to an anthropological understanding of language as the model for every aspect of cultural organisation.

In the brief space I have here I obviously cannot examine every aspect of the culture of Tourmaline – nor can I hope to give a 'reading' of the text as a whole. Instead, I will try to demonstrate the general force of what I have been saying by focusing on one exemplary social aspect of the culture of Tourmaline – its law. This means focusing initially on one character, for in the text of *Tourmaline* the Law is the narrator. This, in fact, is the narrator's name; and, although he is also a character in the story he tells, he has no other name: he is, as he tells us, simply 'the Law'.

Only by visiting the War Memorial every day does the Law manage to convince himself that he is real – 'Those names give me a name. But when I am quiet and alone ... I cannot believe in it' (p. 9). It is crucial, I think, that his doubtful existence should hinge upon the question of language – upon the *naming* of his person. In structural linguistics there is nothing of material substance in the name of an object, in the word itself. Rather, it is the structural relationship between, say, the concept of the Law as a person and our naming of that person that enables us to identify him. The nature of that relationship, as Saussure would have it, is arbitrary. Thus Stow refuses to underwrite the character of the Law by allowing him some appeal to a reality beyond the structure of language. Other names, as the Law himself says, give him his own name. His self-consciousness in this regard is consistent with his being the narrator of a text, the text and 'testament' of *Tourmaline*: for, as he describes himself, he is a 'naming ghost ... formless but forming' (p. 9). As a character, and an obviously *unreliable* narrator, he is at least permitted the futility of *attempting* to underwrite his existence by appeal to a reality beyond language; but of course he is doomed to failure. As structural linguists would have it, there is no access available to a pre-linguistic authorising reality:

> and so [I] come to the time of day when I doubt the reality of myself ... when I am quiet and alone and have turned on the wireless (as on every morning for – ah, too many years) and have spoken, and have listened, and as on every morning since these terrible things began have heard no answer ... (p. 9)

Of course, if he heard what he wants to hear, it would still be within language. But his desire alone should be sufficient for us to distrust him. How can we trust his memory, when there are no origins for his existence – 'Who gave me this name? And beside the name, what is there?' (p. 9). He tells us, too, that he 'must imagine and invent' (p. 73). It is possible, then, that he invents his own past, the history of the town, in order to give some weight, some material substance, to his existence. (Hence the epigraph taken from St John Perse, 'O gens de peu de poids dans/ la mémoire de ces lieux ...' – in T.S. Eliot's translation, 'O men of little weight/ in the memory of these lands.') If the Law has no name apart from that given him by other names then he is unable to signify at all except through relationship with other characters, who exist similarly as a function of language. As a word, he requires other words if he is to signify at all. And *as a character*, this is the source of his suffering – his dependence upon the good will of others.

It is when we read the Law as a character, within the frame of allegory, that we move from the demonstration of linguistic propositions toward their translation into structural anthropology. In other words, as a model character derived from structural linguistics and named *allegorically*, the Law *enacts* a structuralist characterisation of 'law' *per se*. Through him we see how law functions as a social phenomenon, 'whose inmost nature *is the same as that of language*' (my italics).

We learn for instance that law is self-regarding, as language is self-regulating. Nothing precedes the memory of law – nothing prior to law is admissable – and yet it is characterised by an obsessive concern with reminiscence, nostalgia, precedent. That is, law is differential – systematic but arbitrary in its selection of the meaningful event. Law's concern is less with people than with what the narrator calls 'the rights of ownership', 'property' (p. 28), 'citizenship' (p. 30). Functioning as language does, law is 'formless, but forming', self-constitutive – that is, insubstantial, structural rather than essential. All this we learn from the horse's mouth, as it were – from the Law himself – for he is nothing if not our false servant, this narrator: law, it seems, is self-serving. The narrator, the Law, is an egoist! The novel begins with the words '*I* say *we* have a bitter heritage' (p. 7, my italics). The narrator's attitude to language is particularly interesting in terms of his allegorical personification of law – 'I find there is no speech that is not soliloquy. And yet, always, I sense an audience.' If law is self-serving, it is also unreliable – inevitably inventive – although it rarely admits error and prefers self-definition: '"I am the law," I said ... I meant by it, the memory and conscience of Tourmaline' (p. 42).

In *Tourmaline*, because the town lies in a coma, the Law is derelict – 'tormented by the persistence of the living' (p. 10). Indeed, as the narrator himself states ironically: 'There is no law in Tourmaline' (p. 10). Accordingly, we witness a culture in disintegration. Take the issue of kinship, for example. Lévi-Strauss argued (from Mauss) that culture is based on a system of exchange, the underlying law of which is reciprocity. This for him was the key to understanding kinship systems, as a means of organising the exchange of women in marriage. 'The precondition of such a system was a rule banning incest.... In this sense, the incest taboo is the beginning of culture' – for it necessitates the establishment of a system of exchange as the basis for society.[4] Is there any such taboo in *Tourmaline*? Is there a system of exchange?

The hardest person to 'place' in any reading of the novel, the one whose absence flaws so many otherwise persuasive readings in my view, is Deborah. She seems so 'real', a character of realism rather than an allegorical creature of words. There is not one character in the novel who approves of her relationship with Kestrel, the publican; nor is there a system, however, against which to judge it, because the culture system has deteriorated. Deborah is of mixed race, the daughter of an Aboriginal mother named Agnes Day; but she is the foster child of Tom and Mary Spring, owners of the general store.

There were some who suggested that Deborah was the daughter of Mary's late uncle; but as there were few men in Tourmaline who might not have fathered a child on Agnes Day, no judgement was ever taken. Whatever the reason, Mary fostered Deborah, and loved her, and brought her up to be as promising a girl as had been seen in Tourmaline since Mary herself was young. And one day ... Deborah had walked across the road to the hotel, and stayed there.

Her 'marriage' (I must use the terms of Tourmaline) remained as mysterious as her paternity. But still Mary hoped, and plotted to win the girl away from Kestrel, whose imposing double bed had more and darker occupants than Deborah (indeed, Agnes Day was one of them) ... (p. 18)

In other words, there is the disturbing hint that Kestrel may now be 'married' to his own daughter. We are never told why Mary detests him, or what other husband she has in mind, although the Law idly speculates, concluding disarmingly 'who could say?' (p. 18). No judgment, legal or moral, is possible; and the Law does not allude even obliquely to the taboo of incest.

It would seem, then, that in the 'culture' of Tourmaline (if we are still entitled to call it 'culture') the 'unconscious grammar of opposition and reciprocity' that underlies the exchange system of kinship has broken down – and there are hints that the reason for this may be ironically imperialist, that the white exploitation of Aboriginal culture has had damaging effects in both directions. In *Tourmaline*, the distinction between white and fringe-dwelling black culture is largely one of the *degree* of marginalisation. The town itself has been forgotten by the rest of the world – missing, presumed dead. Be that as it may, the anthropological interest of the narrative is to see what happens to this racially mixed 'culture' (by Lévi-Strauss's definition, a non-culture) – this coma culture – when an entirely new and unknown element is introduced into it. A random element!

Enter the diviner, Michael Random. He arrives from the surrounding desert in the back of the monthly truck which comes 'from the back of the blue ranges' (p. 14). The driver (cargo 'carrier') with the locust-like voice has picked him up on the road like a disease; but the arrival of this messenger of death seems to stir the town to life, so that the diviner grows as he infects and is soon a complex symbol of ambivalent threat and hope. The townspeople turn him into a prophet; and the prophet would be king. The model for this 'progress' is again anthropological. It is the cargo cult, which, as Helen Tiffin argues,[5] provided Stow with a narrative for exploring the dangers of colonial nostalgia for the green world, the well-watered world which the residents of Tourmaline seek through the supposedly rejuvenating magic of their deathly diviner. The ambivalence of this allegorical narrative of imperialism focuses on the broadly legal question of possession: whose *property* is the diviner?

'All right. I'll have him.' [says Kestrel]
'No,' Mary said. She was quite determined.
Kestrel got up off his haunches and looked at her, grinning a little with his bitter mouth. 'Why's that, Mary?'
'We'll have him,' she said.
'You think I ought to trade you this bloke for Deborah?' (p. 17)

His cruel gibe here points to the unconscious ideological implication of Lévi-Strauss's definition of culture: that women are property. But Kestrel's parody of exchange – offering his wife for a young man, offering Mary a choice between foster daughter and surrogate son – is particularly interesting in structuralist perspective. It is in fact a deconstruction of the structuralist model of kinship, which centres habitually on women as the object of exchange.

Deborah, as we have seen, is the biological daughter of Agnes Day. It is the diviner, however, who is most recognisably the Lamb of God – it is he who is moulded by the congregation into a ritual figure in whom they invest all hope for the future. In fact, the first words spoken when the doors of the truck open to reveal its special cargo are not necessarily of pity, possibly of recognition: '"Ah, Christ," Kestrel said ... "Ah, Jesus Christ, the poor bastard"' (p. 16). Allegorically, then, it is possible to read Deborah as the daughter of a female (and Aboriginal) Christ and, simultaneously, as the daughter of the Random Christ. If it is further possible to see Kestrel as the father-figure lover of this doubling daughter of Christ, his offer to exchange her for her diviner 'father' must involve a power-play in relation to his own double, his alter-ego diviner, in order that he does not lose control of his life, lose self-possession. His repression of Deborah is then related to his fear of the Other. His is the 'sin' of cruelty. In the resurrected morality of the novel's dying fall into silence, on the final page, we learn that there is only one other sin – the complement of Kestrel's cruelty – and that is the one that the town at large has committed: 'that original sin, that began when a man first cried to another, in his matted hair: Take charge of my life, I am close to breaking' (p. 174). The two faces of imperialism are finally revealed as those of the paymaster of the wages of sin, spreading the Luciferean symbolism that has attended the false Christ diviner into a wide-angle perspective of the community that enabled him. Out of focus is Tom Spring – most noticeably, for he has disappeared from the narrative altogether: his death might be seen as enabling the dismantling of narrative, of structure, almost a ritual sacrifice in the cause of freedom and, not incidentally, art. Hence the nomenclature – 'Spring' – and the irony of his valuing silence above words. But this redemption of narrative is far from obvious and exists more in the potential of re-reading (re-vision) signposted by the ending's circling back to the beginning.

The structure of community under the Random influence is such that the falcon feeds on the lamb. Kestrel leaves town; the prophet fails; Kestrel returns, stronger, to claim power in the prophet's place. What enables this is structure – narrative and communal structure – pure and simple:

> 'So you're the diviner now,' Tom said. 'I might have seen it coming.'
> 'Someone had to take charge.'
> 'Had to?'
> 'Was bound to.'
> 'Oh, sure. He left a gap, didn't he. And the organisation was there.' (p. 171)

Structuralism underscores even the mythic manifestations of the narrative. We are given two versions of the one myth: the white myth of the coming of Christ, and the Aboriginal myth of Mongga: 'He like Mongga ... that's who he is.' The Law asks his Aboriginal informant, 'Who is Mongga?' And Charlie Yandana replies: 'Mongga come from the west ... and go through all this country. This his country, they reckon, and we Mongga's people' (p. 134). In the context of the novel as a whole, these two myths seem interchangeable. In Lévi-Strauss's terms, they are members of a 'paradigm class' of myth – and the paradigm, as I have said, is that of cargo cult belief. Stow is making a point about Christianity here, about the coming of Christ, by means of cross-cultural structuralist plotting of narrative. But the two myths do vary at one point – for Mongga is also the Creator, whereas Christ is not:

> He make a rock in one place, he make a hill in another place, or a cave, or something. Some places he make a waterhole. At last he get very tired, and he think: 'I like to die now.' So he go deep down into the ground and he never come back again; and the water come rushing out of that hole ... (p. 135)

This single difference in the two myths makes them functionally opposite, and quite possibly one could tease out the opposition in terms of the famous structuralist cultural coding of the raw and the cooked. That, however, is not my purpose – except to say that it is at this level, in terms of the opposition of Nature and Culture that is central to Lévi-Strauss's thinking, that the fiction again takes a deconstructive turn.

Michael Random arrives in the town already cooked, dehydrated and almost dead from heat exhaustion and sunstroke; and his socialisation is cast in terms of his identity as the town's diviner, which is surely in the category of the raw. At the end, too, the town – and the text – appear to unravel into cultural absence, into wordlessness, decomposition, in the direction of Nature rather than Culture. On the other hand, at the end, we are in a very literal sense back at the beginning – the narrative structure, as I have said, is circular – so that the paradigmatic opposition of Nature and Culture seems itself called into question.

It seems pertinent to conclude with the quotation from Lévi-Strauss that Derrida placed as an epigraph before his deconstructive analysis of Lévi-Struass's Nature/Culture opposition: 'It [writing] seems to favour rather the exploitation than the enlightenment of mankind.'[6] This is neither true nor false – it is both: 'What is going to be called *enslavement* can equally be called *liberation*. And it is at the moment that this oscillation is *stopped* that the discourse is frozen into a determined ideology that we would judge disturbing ...'[7] *Tourmaline* is a fiction that demonstrates precisely this point of *difference*. Its ideology, despite its discursive *appearance* of absolute structuralism, is not finally frozen. I have indicated some of its sutures – the sexual difference between Deborah and Michael Random in a system of exchange; the difference between Mongga and Christ in a homogenising system of myth classification; the radically subversive and transformative potential of Tom Spring as a creator figure. There is more. The Law may be given, as it were, to writing (it is *his* narration, his testament), but he is not granted domination; although he has some authority, both as narrator and as a policeman in a small outback town, his power or even his desire for exploitation is minimal – whereas Lévi-Strauss would have us believe that law is universally associated with literacy: 'For it is only when everyone can read that Authority can decree that "ignorance of law is no defence"' (*Of Grammatology*, p. 132). In *Tourmaline*, rather, the Law must finally learn the value of silence, of speechlessness, and so of lawlessness – although as the narrator of a looping narrative, of course, he will continue to speak.

The model for this fiction is in many ways structuralist; but its interest in the dynamics of power, and in language as it operates within the field of power, rather seems an anticipation of post-structuralism – which, as more than one speaker at this conference has already argued, is true of many post-colonial writers. Indeed, this is one of the characterisations of the post-colonial: its having politicised the strategies of deconstructive reading and translated them into differential writing strategies long before post-structuralism had been posted – even before structuralism had been prefixed.

NOTES

1. Claude Lévi-Strauss, *Structural Anthropology*, trans. Claire Jacobson and Brooke Grundfest Schoepf (1958; London: Penguin, 1972), p. 62.
2. Tigger Wise, *The Self-Made Anthropologist: A Life of A.P. Elkin* (Sydney: Allen and Unwin, 1985), p. 224.
3. Randolph Stow, *Tourmaline* (Ringwood: Penguin, 1965), p. 8. Further references are given in the text.
4. Adam Kuper, *Anthropology and Anthropologists: The Modern British School* (1973; rev. ed. London: Routledge and Kegan Paul, 1983), p. 170.
5. Helen Tiffin, 'Melanesian Cargo Cults in *Tourmaline* and *Visitants*', *Journal of Commonwealth Literature*, 16 (1981), pp. 109-125.

6. Lévi-Strauss, *Tristes Tropiques*, trans. John Russell (1955; New York: Atheneum, 1961), p. 292.
7. Jacques Derrida, *Of Grammatology*, trans. Gayatri Chakravorty Spivak (1967; Baltimore: Johns Hopkins University Press, 1976), p. 131. Further references are given in the text.

HELEN TIFFIN

Transformative Imageries

At the conclusion of Chinua Achebe's *Things Fall Apart* the District Commissioner, accompanied by an armed band of soldiers, is himself suddenly 'arrested' by the spectacle of Okonkwo's suicide, and, at that moment, 'the resolute administrator in him gave way to the student of primitive customs'.[1] This does not, however, mark any moment of insight or accommodation to a different way of seeing, but simply a change from military/ political control to textual control. Like the biologist dissecting the exotic animal he has just shot, the District Commissioner, having 'pacified' a 'native', proceeds to make him the raw material of narrative. Of course, as words like 'natives' and 'monkey tricks' indicate, the District Commissioner will simply recirculate a script already written for him by centuries of travel narrative, autobiography, fiction, drama, history in which Europe, projecting its own deepest fears and desires onto other peoples, prescripted the rest of the world. Achebe encapsulates in a nineteenth-century African moment, both the history and the perpetuation of this practice.

But Europe's textual capture of the rest of the world is not limited to the centripetal process of domesticating Otherness for its own imaginative consumption. Through all the institutional apparatus of empire, and especially education, Europe projected back on to the colonised world its own already-refracted self-portraiture, thereby defining the 'natural' configuration of relations between Europe and other peoples. *Heart of Darkness* (a text which *Things Fall Apart* deliberately engages) was taught in Nigerian universities as an example of great literature whose 'values' were 'universal'. But for all that text's surface critique of progress and the European enterprise in Africa, its narrative is inevitably and inescapably embedded in the binary opposites which underwrote and justified the imperial project – black/white, civilisation/savagery, Europe/Africa. The educational processes of empire (what Erna Brodber in *Myal*[2] refers to as 'zombification'), whether formal or informal, ensured that the colonial learned by heart that his or her subjectification was in the 'natural order of things'. Caliban is naturally corrupt, sly and rebellious, and deserves to lose the isle. Friday, as the natural inferior of Crusoe, is 'naturally' only too glad (as Crusoe reads the encounter) to become his slave. Kurtz, who took up the white man's burden, is 'naturally' corrupted by too close a contact with an African savagery imaginable by a European sensibility only as 'unimaginable'. Ella O'Grady, reciting Kipling by heart for the visiting Anglican parson in *Myal* has learned her 'lesson' well.

Take up the white man's burden
Send forth the best ye breed
Go bind your sons to exile
To serve your captive's need
To wait in heavy harness
On filtered folk and wild
Your new caught sullen peoples
Half devil and half child. (p. 6)

The complex process of 'spirit thievery', to use another of Brodber's terms, is commented on in *Myal* by Mr Dan, and a way out of these containing images of empire (internalised throughout the colonised world, and still very much in operation, albeit in apparently altered form) is posited:

My people have been separated from themselves ... by several means, one of them being the printed word and the ideas it carries. Now we have ... people who are about to see through that. And who are these people...? People who are familiar with the print and the language of the print. Our people are now beginning to see how it, and they themselves have been used against us.... Now we have people who can and are willing to correct images from the inside, destroy what should be destroyed, replace it with what it should be replaced and put us back together, give us back ourselves with which to chart our course to go where we want to go. (pp. 109-10)

In this paper I want to trace the possibilities of escape from the texts and images of Western imperialism through four works, two symptomatic of the route taken by post-colonial white settler writers (Jean Rhys and Randolph Stow), and two symptomatic of that pursued by black or indigenous writers (Keri Hulme and Erna Brodber). But I should say at the outset that this sort of division – black/white, alien/indigenous – is precisely the one these four texts set out to destabilise, and its erosion in the course of each text, points the way from imperialist imageries towards transformative ones.

Before I look briefly at these four texts, I want to stress the difficulties inherent in the post-colonial project of imaginative transformation, for these are not only historical in the terms in which I have been outlining, but persist within the whole field of literary discourse in all its contemporary manifestations.

'Otherness' as a source of interest, revivification, even celebration (and certainly academic exploitation) is pervasive in European and Euro-American post-structuralist theory. But as it is currently theorised, it remains perpetually foreclosed, its apparent avenues of newness and difference always turning out to be culs-de-sac contained by that same European archive. This foreclosure may be lamented, but while the 'Other' remains as the specular image of Europe, she poses no real threat to literary hegemony. Post-structuralist excursions into difference, still rediscovers Europe. For all its potentially useful insights, post-structuralist philosophy remains the handmaiden of repression, and if I may mix the metaphor, serves as a District Commissioner of the 1980s, his book title now changed from *The Pacification of the Primitive Tribes of the Lower Niger* to *Enjoying the Other: or Difference Domesticated*. But while Europe continues to contain and control, post-colonial writers, tackling the problem from a genuinely *other* perspective in which Europe or England is 'Other', have been moving towards transformation and escape. (It is no accident that so few Euro-American post-structuralist critics have taken an interest in texts outside their own areas of control.)

The problem of European textual containment is of course a pervasive one in all post-colonial societies, whether in those white settler societies where indigenes were, and are annihilated or marginalised; or those cultures of Africa and India, which had a foreign language, literature and the institutions of a foreign law and government imposed on them. As writers from white-settler societies came and come increasingly to identify not with their European origins but with the land they had invaded, and more recently with the peoples they had decimated and marginalised, their own status in terms of the European colonialist text, and their relationship to those they colonised – but with whom they shared a colonial status in the eyes of Europe – has become increasingly problematic.

Post-colonial writers then on both sides of the 'fence' have addressed the problem of their colonization by text and adopted as an inescapable strategy, the re-entry into Europe's written archive with a view to destabilising those ontological and epistemological codes which underwrote and powered conquest, colonisation and continuing subjectification. But they have often also employed different strategies to different (though related) ends. Black (and sometimes white) writers from various post-colonial cultures have identified with, for instance, Caliban and rewritten the terms of his relationship with Prospero, while Caribbean, Australian and Canadian writers have sought in the figure of Ariel, passage through the colonialist impasse. A number of Canadian writers have gone back to Miranda to re-script their role (and hers) in Prospero's imperial enterprise.[3]

But as George Lamming in *Water With Berries* and V.S. Naipaul in *Guerrillas* have noted, passage back through the European text may not issue in transformation. Lamming uses *The Tempest* in *Water With Berries* to demonstrate an apparently inescapable textual closure. The rebellious and potentially revolutionary acts of his three protagonists, their attempts to escape Prospero's 'book' through arson, rape and murder, simply reinscribe them within the European archive, since their actions are already pre-scripted not as potentially creative rejection of domination, but as essentialist 'native' or black stereotype. V.S. Naipaul in his elaborately intertextual *Guerrillas* tests the efficacy of Jean Rhys's counter-discursive experiment in *Wide Sargasso Sea* and comes to a similarly pessimistic conclusion: that a revolutionary passage out of European textual containment is impossible for the colonial. For Naipaul the post-colonial text can contest the mechanisms of the imperial but never attain to that 'extra-transgressive condition of genuinely revolutionary practice or figure the possibility for genuine social change'.[4]

Okonkwo of *Things Fall Apart* committed suicide because he could bear neither military capture nor impending cultural contamination. In Randolph Stow's *Visitants* and Jean Rhys's *Wide Sargasso Sea* the protagonists also commit suicide, but in these latter cases their deaths signal the withdrawal of the author/ity of Europe and its obdurately determined binaries in order to facilitate that very cultural hybridization Okonkwo feared. They die so that the suicide of white author/ity will provide space for cultural transformation. Both *Wide Sargasso Sea* and *Visitants* thematise the European capture of colonial worlds and explore possible escape routes out of this enclosure. Both texts 'write back' to those canonically interpellative English works, *The Tempest* and *Heart of Darkness*. And both attempt to invoke other codes against western epistemologies and ontologies, including Caribbean Creole and Biga Kiriwini against capital E English. Both sketch careers for their white protagonists (whose whiteness is deliberately equivocated in various ways) which appear to shift them from the positions of white coloniser, slave-owner, administrator, to 'black', to slave or colonised positions – but significantly, only in death.

In *Wide Sargasso Sea*, Antoinette undergoes, at the hands of the English male protagonist, a fate comparable to that of her black creole compatriots. Like the slaves she is bought for profit by an (almost) absentee landlord who regards her as wild, exotic, 'half-devil and half-child', a burden he has to bear after the 'honeymoon' is over and he has acquired her wealth. Like the slaves, Antoinette thus becomes the prisoner of another culture, and is incarcerated as a lunatic, her every attempt at rebellion and attaining freedom only re-confirming her pre-constituted 'lunatic' status. Her final retaliation is the classic slave one – the firing of the Great House – the moment which both simultaneously (and paradoxically) locks Rhys's text to Brontë's *Jane Eyre* and releases the Creole Bertha Mason/Antoinette Cosway from it. It also destabilises the essentialist, racist base of the slave stereotype in metaphorically linking Antoinette with her black compatriots through the commission of their 'stereotypical' revolutionary action.

This parallel and transformative imagery does not, however, equate or seek to equate Antoinette's experiences of physical brutality, capture and incarceration with those of black Caribbean slaves. Rather, it demonstrates the European construction of *both* black slaves *and* white creoles, through the imperial imageries of 'otherness', and by thus exposing the potent political implications of such characterisations as 'half-devil half-child', places that imagery under erasure.[5]

In *Visitants*, Cawdor, the 'dark Scot', is said, from the beginning, to be 'going away', out of the text, paradoxically at the same time as the testimonies of the 'other' observers recreate and replace him, cross-culturally, after his death, not in his role as Patrol Officer Cawdor, but as a man caught between his wish to identify with the Papua New Guineans and his enmeshment in the institution of their government. Like Antoinette/ Bertha, Cawdor is, however, already dead when the novel opens,[6] and it is that removal of white authority, that 'prior' absence which allows for transformative possibility. The text thus becomes an enquiry into the suicide of white authority, one which collapses the dialectically defined positions of Prospero, Ariel, and Caliban in an (ostensibly) oral account of Cawdor, one which also counters the 'shame' associated with writing, with the white man's historical and administrative record. This retrieval of Trobriand society, and its issue in an account that includes both black and white voices, both coloniser and colonised, is not predicated on a facile reconciliation or an amnesia of the colonial past and present. It is, instead, energised by the metaphorical suicide of the authority vested in Prospero; his burning of his books – by extension the pre-texts of empire – in the way in which Rhys, at the end of *Wide Sargasso Sea* 'burned' the book of *Jane Eyre*, its imperialist imageries, and the whole of that discursive field within which those imageries were taught, reproduced and given social effectivity in colonial and post-colonial worlds.

But this suicide of white authority, imaged as offering the potential for liberation of the colonised voice, does not signal a return to pre-colonial cultural purity. Though, like Keri Hulme and Erna Brodber, Rhys and Stow invoke alter/native cultural and linguistic systems against an English dominant, the purpose is a radical destabilisation of the European pre-text, not a Utopian reversal or replacement by an/other system.

The Bone People, as Graham Huggan has noted,[7] also redeploys elements of *The Tempest* to destabilise the bases of those relationships between Europe and 'others' which it served to 'naturalise', *and* those which were inherited and redeployed through time, during, for instance, the twentieth century, in the politics of High Modernism.

Equivocation of the racial backgrounds of the protagonists formed part of the basis of transformative possibility in Rhys's and Stow's novels, and *The Bone People* also opposes the fetishisation of 'original/ity'. Its principal characters represent different degrees of connection and commitment. Kerewin Holmes has quarrelled with her (racially-mixed) family and retreated to a sterile individualism, a repudiation of all communal responsibility. Joe, by contrast, is still both supported and stifled by his extended (predominantly Maori) family, though his immediate family, since his wife's death, now consists solely in his adopted pakeha son, Sim. Sim has been cast ashore, half-drowned, after a 'tempest', and the mystery of his background seems initially to provide the narrative focus and direction.

Gradually, however, the mystery of Sim's 'origin' is overshadowed and all but erased by the more immediate problem of the cryptic source of his recurrent physical beatings. The literal 'solution' of one mystery provides the allegorical solution to the other. The abuse Sim suffers at the hands of a 'bad' parent, his apparent origin in a 'tempest', his shadowy upperclass British ancestry and particularly his voicelessness are all clues to the novel's post-colonial vector. Storm, tempest and violence subtend both Sim's current condition (he both endures and perpetrates violence), and the colonial intrusion of which he is the mute and broken legacy. His silence opposes and reproaches Kerewin's detached ivory tower of art and words, until she destroys the talkative little archive, also rejecting medical treatment in favour of a meta/physic outside the comprehension of a western tradition (and therefore also outside its control) as a prelude to the tentative forming of a new kind of community/family with Joe and Sim, an 'original relation', in Emerson's phrase, 'with the universe'.

The recuperation of the Maori past is also an important prelude to the establishment of this 'relation'. Just as the building of the Maori hall at Moerangi and the reunion with her family serve to prepare Kerewin for a rather different future with Joe and Sim, so Joe's resolve to remain reclusive guardian of an uncontaminated Maori past – at the moment of its arrival in Aotearoa – is thwarted by the earthquake, and Joe is precipitated back into the difficulties of the hybridised and violent present. In *The Bone People*, as in the novels of Wilson Harris, the destructive violence of the colonial past can be transformed through the very energetics of its own violence into a creative hybridity. This transformative impulse implies, as it does in Brodber's works, the complementary processes of recuperation of erased and abused cultures and the dis/mantling of the European 'word' whose texts powered conquest and colonisation, and rendered the colonised voiceless.

In Erna Brodber's *Myal* the purgation processes of textual interpellation, the ridding of the colonised body of that which has been 'learned by heart',is imaged, as in *The Bone People*, as an internal swelling or cancer which western medicine is incapable of curing. The story of Ella O'Grady, the 'little cat choked on foreign' (p. 4) is exemplary in this regard. Like Kerewin and Joe of *The Bone People*, Ella is of mixed blood, a hybridity that is initially symbolic of a destructive colonial subjectification, but which becomes in the end, after the purgation process, facilitating and catalytic.

Ella Langley's ability to recite invites the attention of the Reverend Brassington, and subsequently his wife, Maydene. Their 'adoption' of Ella leads to her passage to the United States. In this way the break-up of the traditional family, a violent and destructive aspect of slavery, is transformed to produce a state of positive potential as in *The Bone People*. There, for the first time, she becomes conscious of her Jamaican heritage, a consciousness she lacked when she lived there because the world of English literature, the foreign text was more 'real' to her than her everyday world. Every one of us who had a colonial education knows exactly what this means. But out of a growing home-sickness now for Jamaica, she tells her new husband all about her home life in Grove Town. Selwyn Langley is keen to become a 'producer' and sees his opportunity. He steals Ella's story, makes it into a coon stage show, and triumphantly presents it to Ella on opening night for her approval. This is of course a less cryptic re-play of the Kipling poem episode, with the United States now in the role of textual imperialist. But this time Ella refuses interpellation. Horrified by the violent misrepresentation, in which construction she can now perceive her own unconscious collusion, she falls ill with an apparently incurable internal swelling. She is rescued by Maydene Brassington and taken back to Jamaica, cured eventually not by western medicine but by the ancient Afro-Jamaican skills of Mass Cyrus.

Significantly Ella's story does not end there, but returns to the institu-tional source of the original infection, the school. On her return to Jamaica, Ella becomes a schoolteacher and is almost immediately troubled by a particular text in the syllabus. She puzzles over the pernicious allegory of Mr Joe's farm where the enslaved animals at first rebel ('half devil'), and then find that they are too innocent and inept ('half child') to cope with freedom. They all return gratefully to the farm where Mr Joe orders his overseer to overlook their aborted rebellion and feed them. Ella is forced by the syllabus to teach this story, but is enraged by it. In consultation with the Reverend Simpson, however, she evolves a method of dealing with this imperialist text, which has been thrust upon her and the children she would educate. Since she can't get rid of the text (without refusing the syllabus and thus losing her place as a teacher) she will alter the way in which she teaches it, exposing the interpellative allegory for what it is; teaching *against* the lesson it is designed to inculcate by exposing its strat-egies and stereotypes. Instead of perpetuating her own people's slavery and colonisation, she turns the imperial text against the imperialist, teach-ing her class what it was designed to inculcate and the importance of their refusal of it. As the 'Myal' of the title indicates, Ella's counter-discursive teaching is a form of 'myalism', part of the processes of a 'white' magic designed to counteract the effects of a 'bad' magic or 'obeah'. Antoinette of Jean Rhys's *Wide Sargasso Sea* used the concept of 'obeah' to image her colonialist capture and interpellation by the unnamed male narrator. But unlike Ella, she had no 'other' tradition and communal strategy available to her to counteract its effects.

The story of Mr Joe, a story included in Jamaican readers of a generation or so ago, is also re-written in another way within *Myal*. Against the his-tory of Europe's writing of the other, Brodber sets an Afro-Jamaican system of intuitive oral communication. And the participants in this creat-ive cross-cultural dialogue are the 'animals' of Mr Joe's farm – Mother Hen, White Hen, Dan and so on. Only here of course they are neither rebellious devils, innocent children nor disgusting animals (Saladin Chamcha's 'transfiguration' in Rushdie's text revised). They are sophistic-ated individuals, re-making their own present through negotiation be-tween different systems and 'realities' rather than out of the obdurately determined and violent neuroses of the slave and colonial pasts. Participation in this process is not restricted to Black Jamaicans, though it occurs within the auspices of their cultural survivals. Maydene Brassington – White Hen – and her Christianity participate in a genuine dialogue, through the representation of an Afro-Jamaican oral (not written) communication. Hear Mother Hen:

> Different rhymes for different times
> Different styles for different climes
> Someday them rogues in Whitehall
> Be forced to change their tune. (p. 111)

The 'their' is significant. The repercussions of the transformative imageries pioneered by post-colonial writers and transforming their own societies will be felt eventually in that ancient and continuing Euro-American imperium.

NOTES

1. Chinua Achebe, *Things Fall Apart* (London: Heinemann Educational Books, 1977), p. 147.
2. Erna Brodber, *Myal* (London: New Beacon, 1988). All further references are to this edition and are included in the text.
3. See for example, Chantal Zabus, 'A Calibanic Tempest in Anglophone and Francophone New World Writing', *Canadian Literature* 104 (Spring 1985), pp. 35-50, and Diana Brydon, 'Re-writing *The Tempest*', *WLWE* 23.1 (1984), pp. 75-88.
4. Stephen Slemon, 'Allegory and Empire: Counter-Discourse in Post-Colonial Writing'. Unpublished Ph.D. thesis, University of Queensland, 1988. p. 392.
5. In *The Satanic Verses* Rushdie's depiction of Saladin Chamcha's transformation into 'goat' in the police van also exposes this power of the white imperial gaze to construct the illegal immigrant as other, as disgusting, as (in their terms) 'animal'.
6. Although Antoinette is not 'dead' when *Wide Sargasso Sea* opens, she has been, as it were, 'revived' by Rhys after her 'death' in Brontë's *Jane Eyre*.
7. See Graham Huggan, 'Opting out of the (Critical) Common Market: Creolisation and the Post-Colonial Text' in Stephen Slemon and Helen Tiffin, eds., *After Europe: Critical Theory and Post-Colonial Writing* (Aarhus: Dangaroo Press, 1989), pp. 27-40, and Anne Maxwell, 'Reading *The Bone People*: Toward a Literary Post-colonial Nationalist Discourse', *Antithesis* 1.1 (1987), pp. 63-86.

GARETH GRIFFITHS

Culture and Identity:
Politics and Writing in Some
Recent Post-Colonial Texts

The importance of writing in the formation of identity in post-colonial societies has long been acknowledged. George Lamming's claim for the importance of the novel in modern West Indian history and consciousness since it was able to function as 'a way of investigating and projecting the inner experience of the West Indian community' has been triumphantly vindicated by recent events, and is reinforced by the stress in modern theories of cultural formation on the intense and continuous reflexivity between cultural formation and more overtly political and social processes. For the earlier writers such as Vic Reid this relationship involved using 'fiction' to construct a wider and more comprehensive historiography of the culture of a society such as Jamaica. As he said of his novel *New Day* 'This novel rests upon a single proposition, that Jamaica has a history. This history is distinct from its various racial groups separately viewed... It follows that there is such a creature as a Jamaican, and we can only get to know him by looking at his island and following his story.' Whilst such a project liberates the writer from a narrow racial basis, and takes as its end the investigation of the distinctive, if hybridized, characteristics that are uniquely Jamaican, shaped by the specific historical and geographical conditions of this society, it remains limited by a lingering essentialism in its perception of the idea of cultural formation.

The impulse behind such early essentialist statements of cultural difference and identity is clear. They sought to establish by abrogating the universalist claims of the imperial centre a distinctive and historically specific basis for post-colonial perceptions of their own societies, and to reject and deny the imposition of Eurocentric ideas of value as well as Eurocentric discourses of place and significant chronology masquerading as objective historical narrative. In so far as they do this they are at one with other national liberationist texts, and form a vital and primary step in the task facing the post-colonial intellectual of freeing the perception of himself and his society from the burden of such discourses and their hidden ideological formations. The inevitability of this hybridising factor in the formation of West Indian texts is more easily perceived than is the case either of those societies which possessed a separate and distinctive pre-colonial culture, or those of the more ambivalently situated invader/settler cultures. But as I have argued more extensively elsewhere the same fundamental discursive conditions exist across all post-colonial societies to some degree or another, and the idea of a 'pure' essential culture is a mythic imposition on the contemporary reality of all such societies.[1]

The modern condition and identity of post-colonial societies needs to continue to oppose and dismantle the hegemonic implications of colonial and neo-colonial ideology but it must also insist that the representation of a contemporary post-colonial identity must go beyond a merely atavistic resurgence of the traditional, the function of which, as the problems faced by so many post-colonial societies in recent times have demonstrated, may be to initiate and perpetuate, through a form of symbolic domination, rigid and discriminatory divisions within that society based on racial, caste or class claims to unique authenticity. The danger implicit in such a situation is in Paul Rabinow's words to forget that 'Tradition is a moving image of the past. When a culture stops moving, when its structures of belief no longer offer a means to integrate, create and make meaningful new experiences, then a process of alienation begins. Tradition is opposed not to modernity but to alienation.'[2] It is in the light of these perceptions, and within a consciousness of the political and cultural problems they involve, that we need to move beyond the merely abrogating stage of post-colonial culture. We need to perceive that in recent work new levels of influence between and across these cultures have sprung up and between and across the colonial and neo-colonial aspects of these cultures. As a result of this wider process of cross culturation new radically appropriating claims are being made on the culture of the erstwhile imperial centre, claims which wrest the discourse of that centre from its imperial function and subvert it to a new appropriated usage in the post-colonial world. Similarly the earlier models of national identity and culture fit more and more uneasily with the complex relationships of the neo-colonial period. Texts which have emerged recently in a number of post-colonial societies fit only with difficulty into an essentialist concept of national or regional identity, and question the discourses of race, language and 'tradition' which they invoke, or at least, the simplified version of such discourses which the early post-colonial project sometimes acted to underwrite. Contemporary texts engage with subjects sometimes quite remote from the immediate issues of identity or oppositional ethnography, they frequently rework classic texts from the European canon, or seek to express in a crosscultural form the intricate and tangled relationships which can and have sprung up between post-colonial societies in the neo-colonial period. In so doing I want to argue that they constitute a more challenging representation of the problem of 'authentic' cultural expression than texts which refuse the challenge of such new forms.

In establishing a claim for the importance of these new forms I am very cognisant of Benita Parry's timely warning that the deconstructive project of recent colonialist discourse theory (especially, in her opinion, the work of Spivak, Bhabha and the later work of Abdul JanMohamed), which often seems to underpin the project of recent new textual forms in many post-colonial literatures, may function as 'alternative narratives of colonialism [to obscure] the "murderous and decisive struggle between two protagon-ists" (Fanon *The Wretched of the Earth*, 30), and discount or write out the counter-discourses which every liberation movement records'. That is to say that such discourses may serve only to establish an apolitical dimen-sion in the analysis and practice of post-colonial literatures.[3] And I am at pains to insist that whilst the appropriating stage which these texts represent may seem to be less confrontationary it in fact marks a further and indeed absolutely necessary stage in the struggle for cultural self-definition within post-colonial societies, the neglect of which means not a continuation of 'liberationist' narratives but rather an endless re-inscription of tradition as fixed and dead, a re-inscription which culturally and polit-ically may in fact serve to nurture highly regressive and oppressive re-gimes which actively resist addressing the problems of their contempor-ary, pluralist post-colonial condition and instead resort to an essentialist statement of cultural origin and identity. As indeed it has in cultures as diverse as Fiji, Sri Lanka, and Malaysia in recent times. Such regressive reversals, far from producing a liberationist and oppositional stance, serve merely to replicate the epistemology which sustained the racial, religious and linguistic oppressions of the colonial period. If post-colonial societies are not to endorse such cynical and regressive reversals they have to go beyond the simple task of opposing a local model of essentialist culture and identity to the universalist essentialist model of cultural imperialism.

A number of different strategies for addressing this problem have emerged, some more conscious than others. I have singled out some texts which represent important choices, though I cannot obviously analyse them fully in a presentation such as this; nor, in line with the instruction to panellists that papers should seek to address the general themes and issues rather than specific texts and traditions, would it be appropriate to do so. Nevertheless the first two, Malouf's *An Imaginary Life* and Stow's *Visitants*, are distinguished examples of two new forms which have emerged in recent Australian writing. To choose to examine this problem within the literature of an invader/settler culture such as Australia is to assert the continuity of this problem of the relationship between the 'tradi-tional' and the authentic beyond its inscription within a limited historical contestation between a traditional and modern cultural allegiance within any single racial or linguistic community of that culture. It insists on the continuing inscription of this problem in the contemporary relationships of groups within the pluralistic reality of contemporary post-colonial societies.

An Imaginary Life, like many other recent Australian texts, does not deal overtly with either Australia or even post-colonial societies in general. An account of the exile and death of the Roman poet, Ovid, it might seem, at first glance, to have little to do with Australian or post-colonial concerns.[4] However, both at the level of theme and treatment the text invites us to read its presentation of Ovid's world via a distinctly Australian and post-colonial perspective.

For example, the contrast of imperial centre and exiled 'fatal shore'; of linguistic dislocation when the poet of Rome's Silver Age is cast amongst the illiterate speakers of diverse barbarian tongues he cannot comprehend; of identification via a figure (the *enfant sauvage* he encounters in the woods and whom he raises and educates) with the new culture not the old (he teaches the boy the barbarian tongue, not Latin); and finally his perception that the endless and initially featureless world of the steppes is a sign of the limits of the 'changes' possible within his own cultural perception whilst being simultaneously a sign of the boundless possibilities of human signification *per se* (the child 'constructs' the reality by entering it, (or, as the text finally makes clear, by re-entering it), moving beyond the categories possible within Ovid's cultural taxonomy).

In this last instance Ovid can only perceive the child's particular category as 'super' natural, a mythic 'future' ideal state, signifiable within his own construction by the sign of the 'gods',

'I have tried to induce out of the animal in him some notion of what it is to be human. I wonder now if he hasn't already begun to discover in himself some further being. Is he, in fact, as the villagers thought (their view was always simpler than mine, and perhaps therefore nearer the truth) some foundling of the gods? Is it his own nature as a god that his body is straining towards, at this edge of his own life where any ordinary child might be about to burst into manhood, and into his perfect limits as man?' (pp. 149-50)

The text at this moment, and in the whole final section, inscribes the limitations of any present historical episteme via the particular episteme the text dramatises (in this case Roman and classical) and within which Ovid's capacity for transformation is constructed. Ovid struggles to organise perception of a world in which there is a more profound interaction between the natural and the human than that defined by the 'civilised' world of Rome and the 'barbarian' world of his exile with the Outlanders. For this more ideal world, which he couches in terms of a world where 'we shall begin to take back into ourselves the lakes, the rivers, the oceans of the earth ... [when] the spirit of things will migrate back into us' (p.96), the text turns to the language of the hunter-gatherer, to an imagery that is consonant with the Australian Aboriginal. In so doing, of course, it imports the discursive economy of its own text into the representation of the social text of contemporary Australia and the relationship in that society between its pre-colonial traditions and the society created by the invader/settlers in the last two hundred years.

He is lighter. He moves faster over the earth. He is alert to every shift of the wind and mood of the sky as it carries the weather of tomorrow and the day after towards us, to every scene of the hundred grasses and herbs, and fat little buds that spread around us their invisible particles. It is these grasses and their parasites, the worms, the grubs, the small winged grasshoppers, that provide us with nourishment.

The degree to which this world is intended to be read by the reader as a world of nature, different to, indeed unrecognisable as such, by Ovid, but certainly not a 'super' natural world, one beyond the human and the natural, as his final perception suggests, is rooted in its invocation of the pre-colonial discourse of the Aboriginal. Throughout the text, without any violent or overt imposition of the discourse of the Dreamtime, or of the habits of the hunter gatherer Aboriginals in the manner of a more overtly ethnographic text such as Bruce Chatwin's *The Songlines*, this text employs the invocation of the Aboriginal, as it does the landscape of Australia (the endless grass steppes of the final paragraphs) to anchor the text in a profoundly material perception of cultural change and human diversity. It insists, that is, on the material perception that human culture is never simply universal, nor detachable from the social and cultural formations which bring it into being, it insists that is on its fundamental corrigibility. The distancing achieved by employing the figure of the classical poet, and the geographical locations of the late Roman Empire, allows the text to resist the Romantic allure of essentialist notions of an 'innocent' and 'super' human ideal (which the boy finally represents for Ovid) as it does the transcendent implications of the claims to universal values implicit in the civilised/ barbarian distinctions of Ovid's early Latin perceptions of his new place. Neither, it insists, is adequate. The text replaces this hierarchical structure with a pluralist view of culture which the reader must construct within and against the developing but always limited perceptions of the narrator. In this sense the text can be said to be both anti-authoritarian and metahistorical. It acts to invite the reader to question its own construction and to employ his or her perception in an active construction of a sense of the limitations implicit in any historical grand narrative.

Finally, the placement of the text in a fictional historical and geographical 'location' resists the reincorporation of the alternative perception of the post-colonial world into the category of 'exotica' (the fate, for example, of the kind of 'traveller's tale' text I have represented by Chatwin's *The Songlines*). In fact it is arguably the fact that it does *not* directly present the post-colonial world which makes its representation of that world so powerful and effective.

Randolph Stow's *Visitants* also employs a perception of the difficulty of representing post-colonial culture by an essentialist view when post-colonial societies have themselves frequently functioned as colonisers in their turn, either of the Indigenous peoples such as the Australian Aboriginals or Canadian Inuits or, as in the case of Stow's text, of the peoples of Papua New Guinea, over whom Australia exercised a neo-colonial 'protectorate' in the period before and after the Second World War.

Visitants develops the Lyotardian concept of the *petit récit* in its narrative structure.[5] It creates from each character a specific and culturally determined view of an 'event' which does not exist except in so far as it exists as an amalgam of a series of 'accounts'. By setting each narrative account against and alongside all the others, it suggests the need to deconstruct all so-called objective 'historical' evidence, all the grand narratives which offer to provide a universally satisfactory totalising account. In other words it does not set one 'history' against another 'history' in a contest but suggests that each form of narrative, 'objective or scientific', 'customary' or 'super' natural (mythic) presents a distinctive and legitimate representation of experience. It mediates between the *petit* and the *grand récit* and describes the interaction of the various modalities employed by both scientific and customary accounts to construct totalities. In an important sense then it articulates the limitations of all narratives, and inscribes (the choice of the verb is specific) the culturally determined origin of all total explanations of the corrigible 'facts' of history and narrative (rendering them only in terms of their problematic status as accounts). The text openly and specifically acknowledges the privileged status of the discourse of the 'dominant' culture within the historical moment of the text's dramatic setting by italicising the objective reports' of Mister Cawdor; by constructing a foreword couched in the form of an objective denial of authorial interpretative function, a prologue which adopts the language of a court report; and by prefacing the narrative with a list of the narrators/speakers as 'Witnesses at the inquiry' held by the colonial authorities into the events they relate. In this respect it dramatises the processes of specific cultural production within which one view is privileged over another in the 'production' of histories. However it seeks simultaneously to deny by a process of juxtaposition the claims of any view, whether it be this colonial view or its suppressed counter-discourses, to be absolute or universal.

Finally, of course, Stow's project is limited by the fact that the objective account 'contains', at least within the terms of the production of the written text, such 'customary' 'oral' and 'reported' accounts as those of the PNG characters Benoni, Salibu etc. To go beyond this restriction would require a dismantling at the level of the text's confirmation of the rational as the equivalent of the linear and logical, in ways which Stow's work finally resists but which the more consciously deconstructive techniques of Wilson Harris's work undertakes more explicitly.

Both Malouf and Stow's texts though do embrace the perception, articulated most fully by the texts and critical writings of Wilson Harris, that cultural encounters in post-colonial societies inevitably involve a mutuality, in which the categories of oppressor and oppressed are bound together in what Harris terms a mutual erosion of bias. The result is a dismissal of fixed and dead categories of history, or the freezing of specific moments of the ongoing historical dialectic into new universal and ahistorical 'realities'.

It will be clear to many at this point why I have been careful to note Benita Parry's concern at the beginning of this paper of the dangers implicit here of 'depoliticising' the colonial encounter by the employment of a discourse which stresses the doubleness of the colonial encounter, but as I have said above, it is at least equally as important to avoid the reinscription of the 'native' into a fixed and dead tradition whose action in the world of politics may prove powerfully regressive and oppressive, as it is doing in many contemporary post-colonial societies at this time.

Harris's own work, though it seems to refuse a rhetoric of politics, is, oddly enough, profoundly radical as a result, insisting, as it does, very vigorously on the need to consume the biases of fixed cultural and political positions, to initiate that is an ongoing sense of dialectic and historical change. The title of his recent novel *The Infinite Rehearsal* draws attention to this very fact, insisting that linear narrative itself by constructing endless successive *petits récits* (however discrete they are) confirms the assurances of 'history' that the perception of the moment is privileged in the role it assumes of interpreter of past and future events. In place of this assurance Harris's narrator, Robin Redbreast Glass, seeks to insist that 'I KNEW EVERYTHING. I KNEW NOTHING. I WAS THE SUBJECT OF AN INFINITE REHEARSAL OF A PLAY OF THE BIRTH OF HISTORY'. The novel places the 'story' of history precisely within a narrative of linguistic and cultural construction, both literally to the extent to which it functions within and against the 'authorising' classic narrative of the Faust legend, a narrative whose authority and status it both extends and renders problematic, and, simultaneously within a continuous referencing of the shifting narratives of 'historical events'...

> THE BROW DARKENED. NIGHT WAS FALLING. BUT STILL I WAS ABLE TO DECIPHER A GHOSTLY FINGER OF INK. '1914-18. The axe falls on dynasties and privileges. Where will the unemployed go? *They march to the sound of a patriotic drum*. If you could see them as I do,
>
> > My friend, you would not tell with such high zest
> > To children ardent for some desperate glory,
> > The old Lie: *Dulce et decorum est*
> > *Pro patria mori*
>
> NIGHT FALLS BUT THE BROW FLICKERS AGAIN. '1939, the axe falls on Chamberlain's *peace in our times...*'
> I could read no further but cried in desperation, 'WHY, WHY?'[6]

Clearly the shortness of this presentation begs many questions, and the analysis of all these texts could be much more extensive. Yet I hope I have done enough to show how each text demonstrates ways in which the project of the post-colonial text is increasingly recognising that syncreticity is neither a threat to identity nor a denial of the uniqueness of post-colonial 'reality'. Instead texts which embrace the complex and syncretic nature of the post-colonial world inevitably end by questioning both a cultural politics which seeks to incorporate the post-colonial world back into some new universal and Eurocentric paradigm and that which seeks simply to reconstitute the local and traditional outside a very conscious awareness of historical change and present political realities.

NOTES

1. *The Empire Writes Back: Theory and Practice in Post-colonial Literatures* (London: Routledge, 1989).
2. Paul Rabinow, *Symbolic Domination: Cultural Form and Historical Change in Morocco* (Chicago and London: University of Chicago Press, 1975), p. 1.
3. Benita Parry, 'Problems in Current Theories of Colonial Discourse', *Oxford Literary Review*, 9, nos. 1 & 2, p. 43.
4. In this respect it resembles other recent Australian texts, such as the two novels of the young writer Martin Buzzacott, or the plays and prose writings of Louis Nowra.
5. See J.F. Lyotard, *The Post-modern Condition: A Report on Knowledge,* translated by Bennington & Massumi (Manchester: Manchester U.P., 1984).
6. Wilson Harris, *The Infinite Rehearsal* (London: Faber, 1987), pp. 8-9.

Notes on Contributors

CHRISTOPHER BALME is a lecturer at the Institute of Theatre Studies, University of Munich. Prior to that he was a lecturer in English and drama at the University of Würzburg where he introduced the first courses on Commonwealth literature. He has published on German theatre, theatre theory, and essays on Aboriginal and Maori theatre. He is currently completing a book for the Open University Press entitled *Decolonizing the Stage: Essays in Syncretic Theatre*.

ELLEKE BOEHMER is the author of *Screens Against the Sky*, a South African novel. She teaches Commonwealth literature at Leeds University.

CAROLYN COOPER teaches in the Department of English, University of the West Indies. She has published articles on Black American and Caribbean writing and on feminist literary theory.

T.J. CRIBB is Director of Studies in English at Churchill College, Cambridge, and Secretary to the appeal for funding to introduce the teaching of Commonwealth literature at Cambridge; he is editing a volume of papers on Commonwealth literature given to a staff seminar currently exploring critical approaches to the subject.

ROBIN DIZARD teaches composition at Greenfield Community College in Greenfield, Massachusetts. She is a graduate of Radcliffe College and the University of Massachusetts at Amherst. She writes on post-colonial literature and multi-ethnic literature of the United States. She is currently working on a book about Christina Stead.

PAULINE DODGSON teaches English at West London Polytechnic. She previously spent six years teaching in Zimbabwe.

SIMON GIKANDI is an Associate Professor of English language and literature at the University of Michigan, Ann Arbor. He is the author of *Writing in Limbo: Modernism and Caribbean Literature* (Cornell U.P., 1992), *Reading Chinua Achebe: Language and Ideology in Fiction* (James Currey/Heinemann, 1991), and *Reading the African Novel* (James Currey/Heinemann, 1987).

D.C.R.A. GOONETILLEKE is Professor and Chairman, Department of English, University of Kelaniya, Sri Lanka. He is the current Chairman of the Sri Lanka ACLALS. His books include *Developing Countries in British Fiction* (Macmillan, 1977), *Images of the Raj: South Asia in the Literature of Empire* (Macmillan, 1988), and *Joseph Conrad: Beyond Culture and Background* (Macmillan, 1990). He has edited anthologies of Sri Lankan literature, most recently *Penguin New Writing in Sri Lanka* (Penguin India, 1991).

VERONICA MARIE GREGG obtained her Ph.D. from the University of Kent, Canterbury. Until 1990 she taught at Spelman College. She is now Assistant Professor in English and Comparative literature at the University of Michigan, Ann Arbor. She has published articles on Jean Rhys and Caribbean and African women writers.

GARETH GRIFFITHS is Professor of English and Head of the Department of English at the University of Western Australia, Perth. He is the author of *A Double Exile: African and West Indian Writing Between Two Cultures* (1978) and (with Bill Ashcroft and Helen Tiffin) *The Empire Writes Back: Theory and Practice in Post-Colonial Literatures* (1989), as well as numerous articles on post-colonial literatures and contemporary drama. He is currently completing editing a book of essays on Australian playwright John Romeril and is writing a History of African Literature (East and West).

WILSON HARRIS, a well-known Guyanese writer, is one of the very few post-war novelists who has offered a third, genuinely original alternative to the Manichaean contemporary fictional output (mimesis vs. playful experiment) in the novels he has written over the past thirty years. He has repeatedly explored the capacity of the creative, intuitive imagination to meet the present-day crisis of civilization. His major essays are collected in *The Womb of Space, Explorations* and, recently, *The Radical Imagination* (English Department, University of Liège, 1992).

DOROTHY JONES is Associate Professor at the University of Wollongong where she teaches principally in the areas of post-colonial and women's writing, areas in which she has also published widely.

KETU H. KATRAK, born in India, now works as Associate Professor in the Department of English at the University of Massachusetts, Amherst. She is the author of *Wole Soyinka and Modern Tragedy: A Study of Dramatic Theory and Practice* (Greenwood Press, 1986). Katrak specializes in post-colonial literatures in the English language, and has published several essays in this field. She is currently working on a book about African, Indian and Caribbean women writers.

BRUCE KING is one of the pioneers in the comparative study of Commonwealth literature. He is the general editor of the Macmillan Modern Dramatists series and the author of a number of books and articles, including *The New English Literatures: Cultural Nationalism in a Changing World* and *Modern Indian Poetry in English*. He edited *Introduction to Nigerian Literature, West Indian Literature, Celebration of Black and African Writing* and *World Literature in English*. He has also published four books on seventeenth-century English literature. He has recently edited *The Commonwealth Novel Since 1960*.

VINEY KIRPAL teaches at the Department of Humanities and Social Sciences in the Indian Institute of Technology, Bombay. She has published several articles in international journals. Her books include *The Third World Novel of Expatriation* (1989) and *The New Indian Novel in English: A Study of the 1980s* (1990). Her third book, *Has the Indian Novel Been Understood?*, from which the present piece is taken, is under preparation.

KOH TAI ANN is Associate Professor of English at the National University of Singapore and has published work on Southeast Asian and Commonwealth writing. She is currently co-editing a study of the novel in Southeast Asia as well as annotating and providing a critical introduction to a bibliography of the literature in English from Malaya/Malaysia, Singapore and Brunei.

ROGER LANGEN was born in Perth-Andover, New Brunswick, Canada. He teaches at York University, Canada. His area is post-colonial literature with special interest in race and gender.

SHIRLEY GEOK-LIN LIM is Professor of Asian American Studies and English at the University of California, Santa Barbara. She received the Commonwealth Poetry Prize for *Crossing the Peninsula* in 1980 and the 1990 American Book Award for the co-edited anthology, *The Forbidden Stitch*. Her critical work has appeared in *The Journal of Commonwealth Literature, World Literature Written in English, Women's Studies, Feminist Studies, World Englishes*, and other journals. *Modern Secrets* (Dangaroo Press), her most recent collection of poems, appeared in 1989.

ISHRAT LINDBLAD was born in 1940 of Muslim parents in Lucknow. Her family moved to Pakistan upon its creation, and she herself married and settled in Sweden in 1962. Until recently she was professor at the Department of English, at the University of Stockholm. In addition to her interest in Commonwealth literature, she has published articles on the work of Shakespeare, Shaw, Beckett, John Fowles and Pamela Hansford Johnson. She is at present teaching at the University of the United Arab Emirates in Al-Ain.

CHANDANI LOKUGÉ is from Sri Lanka and is now completing her doctoral studies at Flinders University, South Australia. her first collection of stories, *Moth and Other Stories*, will be published by Dangaroo Press in 1992.

OLIVER LOVESEY has worked at Dalhousie University and the University of British Columbia, and is presently teaching at Okanagan College. He has published articles on various aspects of narrative, and is presently revising a manuscript on 19th-century fiction for monograph publication and completing an essay on the use of allegory in Ngugi's last novel.

AMIN MALAK, a graduate of the universities of Baghdad (Iraq) and Alberta (Canada), teaches Commonwealth and comparative literature at Grant MacEwan College in Edmonton, Canada. he has published articles in numerous international journals on modern fiction, post-colonial literature, and third-world discourse.

RUSSELL McDOUGALL is Senior Lecturer at the University of New England, Armidale, and editor of *South of Capricornia: Stories by Xavier Herbert 1925-34* (Oxford, 1990) and *Henry Kendall: The Muse of Australia* (1992). He is currently completing a biography of Xavier Herbert (Oxford).

GANESWAR MISHRA was educated at Utkal, Kent and London Universities, and is Professor and Head of the Department of English at Utkal University (Bhubaneswar, India). A specialist in Commonwealth literature, he has published seven books and a large number of research papers. He is an eminent creative writer in Oriya with fifteen books (both fiction and non-fiction) to his credit.

EMMANUEL S. NELSON received his undergraduate education in India and his M.A. and Ph.D. from the University of Tennessee. A specialist in Afro-American literature, he has held Visiting Assistant Professorships at Colby College (Maine) and at York College (CUNY). During 1985-86 he was a Postdoctoral Research Fellow at the University of Queensland and currently is an Assistant Professor of Afro-American and Third-World literatures at the State University College of New York at Cortland. He has published several articles on ethnic American and Aboriginal Australian literatures and is the editor of *Connections: Essays on Black Literatures*.

OYEKAN OWOMOYELA was born in Nigeria where he received his B.A. from the University of Ibadan. He later studied at the University of California at Los Angeles where he received an M.F.A. in Motion Pictures and a Ph.D. in Theatre History. He taught for some time at the University of Ibadan, and is now a Professor in the English Department of the University of Nebraska, Lincoln.

RAJEEV S. PATKE was educated at Poona (India) and Oxford (Rhodes Scholar at Oriel College; M.Phil. 1978, D.Phil. 1983). In 1985 he was Fulbright Scholar at Yale University. He is currently Senior Lecturer, National University of Singapore. Publications include *The Long Poems of Wallace Stevens: An Interpretative Study* (Cambridge U.P., 1985) and contributions to compilations on Shakespeare, on literary theory and on the poets Arthur Yap, Robert Yeo, and Gieve Patel.

VELMA POLLARD is a Senior Lecturer in language education in the Faculty of Education of the University of the West Indies, Mona, Jamaica. Her major research interests are Creole languages of the Anglophone Caribbean, the language of Caribbean literature and Caribbean women's writing. She is also involved in creative writing and has published poems and short stories in regional and international journals. Her publications include a volume of poetry, *Crown Point and Other Poems* (Peepal Tree Press); a volume of short fiction, *Considering Woman* (The Women's Press, London); and another book of poetry, *Shame Trees Don't Grow Here* (Peepal Tree Press).

DAVID RICHARDS has an M.A. and Ph.D. from Cambridge University and an M.A. from the School of Oriental and African Studies, London University. He now teaches English and Commonwealth literature at Leeds University. He has published a number of articles on post-colonial writing and on anthropology. He is currently writing a book (with Shirley Chew and Lynette Hunter) on new Commonwealth writing and a book entitled *The Masks of Difference* on the relationship of anthropological and literary representations.

ANNA RUTHERFORD is a graduate of the University of Newcastle, NSW, and since 1966 has taught at the University of Aarhus, Denmark. She was founding editor of *Commonwealth Newsletter*, later to become *Kunapipi*, and in 1986 she was elected international chairperson of ACLALS (the first woman to be elected to this post). She has published widely in the field of Commonwealth literature and is founder/director of Dangaroo Press.

NAYANTARA SAHGAL is the author of eight novels, two autobiographies, and a study of Indira Gandhi's political style. She is also a political journalist whose chief involvement outside writing is civil liberties. In 1990 she was elected Foreign Honorary Member of the American Academy of Arts and Sciences. Her novel *Rich Like Us* won the Sinclair Prize for Fiction and the Sahitya Akademi Award in India, and *Plans for Departure* was awarded the Commonwealth Writers Prize for Eurasia.

EDWARD W. SAID is Parr Professor at Columbia University. He was born in Jerusalem in 1935 and educated at Victoria College, Cairo, Mount Hermon School, Massachusetts, and at Princeton and Harvard Universities. His books include *The Question of Palestine, The World, The Text and The Critic* and *Orientalism*.

PAUL SHARRAD teaches post-colonial literatures at Wollongong University. He has published a book, *Raja Rao and Cultural Tradion*, and co-edits *New Literatures Review*.

BEHEROZE F. SHROFF is an independent film-maker who divides her time between her native India and Los Angeles where she completed her Master of Fine Arts at UCLA. She directed *Sweet Jail: The Sikhs of Yuba City*, an ethnographic documentary on the Indian/Sikh community in Northern California. She is currently involved in making documentary films in India.

CAROL SICHERMAN is Professor of English at Lehman College of the City University of New York. She published extensively on Renaissance literature before turning to Commonwealth studies. In recent years she has written on Ngugi – a bibliography and a reference work (Hans Zell) as well as an article – and has published an interview with Charles Mungoshi.

KIRPAL SINGH, who previously taught at the National University of Singapore, now teaches at the Nanyang Technological University in Singapore. He was (and still is) a prime mover for the promotion of Commonwealth literature in Singapore and for many years was on the executive committee of the Singaporean branch of ACLALS. He has also served as the Regional Chairperson of the Commonwealth Writers Prize. He has published widely in the field of Commonwealth studies, both as a writer and as a critic. He is presently writing a book, *The Writer as Visitor: Cross-cultural Perceptions in Literature*.

HELEN TIFFIN teaches at the University of Queensland, Australia. She has published numerous articles on post-colonial literatures and post-colonial literary theory. She is co-author, with Gareth Griffiths and Bill Ashcroft, of *The Empire Writes Back* (Routledge), editor, with Stephen Slemon, of *After Europe* (Dangaroo), and author, with Diana Brydon, of *Decolonizing Fictions* (Dangaroo, 1992).

KATHRIN M. WAGNER was born in Germany and until recently taught in the Department of English, University of the Witwatersrand. Her publications include work on J.M. Coetzee, Andre Brink, Nadine Gordimer, South African poetry, and Joseph Conrad; she is currently working on a book-length study of Gordimer to be published by Macmillan. She is now teaching in the United States.

ANNE WALMSLEY was born in Derbyshire; she has a B.A. in English from Durham University and an M.A. in African Studies from Sussex University. She taught for three years in Jamaica and has worked for Faber & Faber and for Longmans – in the Caribbean and Africa, for the BBC, and for *Index on Censorship*. Her two anthologies of Caribbean writing, *The Sun's Eye* (1968, new edition 1989), and, with Nick Caistor, *Facing the Sea* (1986), are widely used. Her current work is on the Caribbean Artists Movement of which Aubrey Williams was a founder member and through which they met, in 1967. She is the compiler of *Guyana Dreaming: The Art of Aubrey Williams* (Dangaroo, 1990).

NOTE TO CONTRIBUTORS

As I said in my introduction, the task of selecting the papers was difficult. I would also like to add that so too was that of editing them. As I worked away, it became obvious to me that people I had always thought of as critics were actually harbouring secret desires to be creative writers. This creative urge manifested itself in their re-writing of the texts of the authors about whom they were writing so that very often the text quoted bore little resemblance to the actual text. On occasions I was sorely tempted to place the critic's quotation against that of the author and let the readers decide who had done the better job. Then another thought occurred to me. If I had a false conception about some of the critics, it is possible that they also had one about me. Perhaps they believed that what I really wanted to be was a detective and that my secret delight was to track down inaccuracies and find dates of publication, publishers, etc. to fill in the blanks or the question marks that they, the critics, had left on their manuscripts. Please believe me, I have no ambitions to be a sleuth.

But it is not my intention to end on a negative note. I apologize for the late publication of these papers, a delay, I'm afraid, that was caused by circumstances beyond my control. I wish to thank all the contributors for their patience, understanding and kind words. I hope you enjoy the book and feel that it has been worth while waiting for.

ANNA RUTHERFORD